American Stories

A History of the United States

American Stories

A History of the United States

Volume II

H. W. BRANDS
University of Texas

T. H. BREEN
Northwestern University

R. HAL WILLIAMS
Southern Methodist University

ARIELA J. GROSS
University of Southern California

PEARSON

Longman

New York   San Francisco   Boston
London   Toronto   Sydney   Tokyo   Singapore   Madrid
Mexico City   Munich   Paris   Cape Town   Hong Kong   Montreal

Library of Congress Cataloging-in-Publication Data

American Stories / H. W. Brands, T. H. Breen, R. Hal Williams, Ariela J. Gross
    p. cm.
  Includes index.
  ISBN 978-0-321-51088-4 (single v. ed.)—ISBN 978-0-205-57269-4 (v. 1)–ISBN 978-0-205-57270-0 (v. 2)
    1. United States—History.   I. Brands, H. W.

E178.A5544 2009
973—dc22

2007041333

Credits and acknowledgments borrowed from other sources and reproduced, with permission, in this textbook appear on appropriate page within the text or on pages C-1–C-2.

Text Credits: Page 492, From *The Price* by Arthur Miller, Copyright © 1968 by Arthur Miller and Ingeborg M. Miller, Trustee. Used by permission of Viking Penguin, a division of Penguin Group (USA) Inc; p. 810, "I Have a Dream" by Martin Luther King, Jr. © 1963 by Martin Luther King, Jr., Copyright renewed © 1991 by Coretta Scott King. Reprinted by arrangement with the Heirs to the Estate of Martin Luther King, Jr., c/o Writers House as agent for the proprietor New York, NY.

Pearson Education LTD.
Pearson Education Australia PTY Limited
Pearson Education Singapore, Pte. Ltd.
Pearson Education North Asia Ltd.
Pearson Education, Canada, Ltd.
Pearson Educación de Mexico, S.A. de C.V.
Pearson Education—Japan
Pearson Education Malaysia, Pte. Ltd.

10 9 8 7 6 5 4 3 2 1

ISBN-10:   0-205-57270-7
ISBN-13:978-0-205-57270-0

BRIEF CONTENTS

DETAILED CONTENTS

CHAPTER **22**

The Progressive Era, 1895–1917   588

CHAPTER **23**

From Roosevelt to Wilson in the Age of Progressivism, 1900–1920   614

CHAPTER **24**

The Nation at War, 1901–1920   646

MAPS, FIGURES, AND TABLES

A NOTE TO MY FELLOW TEACHERS

FROM H. W. BRANDS

I've been teaching American history for almost thirty years now (I started young—really), and in that time I've noticed something that almost certainly has occurred to many of you: that our students come to our classrooms with increasingly varied backgrounds. Some students are better prepared than ever, having taken advanced placement courses and acquired a solid grounding in historical facts, interpretations, and methods. Other students arrive less well prepared. Many of these are international students; some are students for whom English is a second or third language. Some of these, and some others, simply never took American history in high school. Some, finally, just didn't do well in the history courses they did take.

Different students require different methods of teaching, including different textbooks. Students well versed in American history do best with a book that presupposes their preparation and takes them beyond it. Students for whom the subject is new or otherwise challenging are more likely to succeed with a book that is more selective in its coverage, that focuses on essential themes, and that offers features designed to facilitate the learning process. Any textbook can be intimidating, as even my best students have reminded me over the years. The hundreds of pages and thousands of facts can put anyone off. For that reason, whatever reduces the intimidation factor can help students succeed.

This is the philosophy behind *American Stories: A History of the United States*. A single purpose has motivated the creation of this book: to enhance the accessibility of American history and thereby increase students' chances of success. This goal is what brought me to the classroom, it's what keeps me there, and it's one I think I share with you. If *American Stories: A History of the United States* contributes to achieving this goal, we all—teachers and students—will be the winners.

Approach and Themes

The most frequent complaint I get from students regarding history textbooks is that the mass of information is overwhelming. There are too many facts and ideas, and it is difficult to determine what to focus on. Many students need help pulling the key concepts from the narrative. This complaint provided the starting point for *American Stories*, which differs from our *America Past and Present* in two fundamental respects.

First, we reduced the number of topics covered, retaining the essential elements of the American story while eliminating others. We surveyed over five hundred instructors from across the country to find out what topics were most commonly covered in a typical survey classroom. Every subject in the U.S.

history course was rated according to what respondents thought must be covered. Once we received the results, we culled the most commonly taught topics and selected them for inclusion in *American Stories*. Making choices wasn't easy; at times it was painful. But we considered it necessary. Some topics are simply not taught as often as others, and our job as historians is to let students know what they need to know.

Second, we added a variety of study aids. These include chapter outlines, preview questions—known as Spotlight Questions—to guide the students' reading, review questions to consolidate their learning, practice quizzes, and sample essay questions. We worked closely with specialists to create and effectively execute a pedagogical plan that fosters student understanding. (See "A Personal Welcome to Students" for examples.) Dr. Kathleen T. McWhorter, who is a professor and author with more than 40 years of experience at both two- and four-year colleges, including Niagara Community College, and specializes in developmental reading, writing, composition, and study skills, helped us figure out how to design the pages to make learning easier. Not only did she advise us on the different purposes of the text and margin (the text is where one goes to learn, whereas the margin is where one goes to reinforce with the use of pedagogy), but Kathleen also kept us in tune to the students' perspective. For example, when students get to major sections, it's important they see the heading before the question so that they can ground themselves in the text more readily.

Debby Kalk was also invaluable to us in determining the rationale behind each of the pedagogical elements. Debby is an instructional designer and author with more than 20 years of experience producing materials for educational publishers, corporate training, and public education and who speaks frequently on instructional design at workshops and conferences. She spent hours deliberating with us on the goals of each element and how to present it to students in the best way possible. Debby helped us make our questions more explicit and our connections clearer. She also ensured that we were careful to keep all pedagogy grounded in the chapters themselves. With the help of both Kathleen and Debby, *American Stories* is the first college-level U.S. history survey completely designed to meet the needs of the instructor and the student.

Beyond this, *American Stories* retains the strong narrative emphasis and chronological organization of most traditional texts. We—I and my fellow authors—have used significant incidents and episodes to reflect the dilemmas, the choices, and the decisions made by the American people as well as by their leaders. However, our story of American history goes beyond the major events that have helped shape the nation—the wars fought, the presidents elected, the legislation enacted, the treaties signed. The impact of change on human lives adds a vital dimension to our understanding of history. How did the American Revolution affect the lives of ordinary citizens? What was it like for both blacks and whites to live in a plantation society? How did the shift from an agrarian to an industrial economy affect both men and women? What impact did technology, in such forms as the automobile and computer, have on patterns of life in the twentieth century? Our narrative explores these issues.

We believe that while history rarely repeats itself, the story of the American past is relevant to the problems and dilemmas facing the nation today. As in *America Past and Present*, we have sought to stress themes and ideas that continue to shape our national culture.

Structure and Features

Every pedagogical element in *American Stories* has been carefully constructed to be accessible to students and to support a better, deeper understanding of U.S. history.

- The **Chapter Opener** establishes the foundation for the entire chapter.
  - The **Chapter Opening Image** provides a visual representation of the chapter theme.
  - The **SPOTLIGHT QUESTIONS** ❓ preview the main ideas in each major section and provide the big picture for the entire chapter. Students should keep these questions in mind as they read the entire section since they offer a framework and alert students to the major themes on which they are likely to be tested. We repeat these questions in the margin after each major section to remind students what they should be focusing on.
  - The **Chapter Outline** serves as a roadmap to the chapter.
  - The **Vignette** illustrates the theme and sets the tone for the entire chapter.
- The **Key Events** overview important events in the chapter and help students see the framework. Page references are included for easy look-up of information.
- The **Chapter Headings** and **Spotlight Questions** are linked together to remind students of the main issues in each major section.
- The ✔ **QUICK CHECK QUESTIONS** follow each subsection and enable students to check their recall of key information presented in each section. We've placed these questions at the end of each subsection so that students can test themselves. If they've read the section, get to the Quick Check Question, and are unable to answer it, it's a signal that they should go back and re-read the subsection since they've missed the main idea.
- The **Marginal Glossary** defines important key terms that are highlighted in each chapter.
- The **Study Resources** at the end of each chapter provide reinforcement and review. Students can use the tools in this section to prepare for tests.
  - The **Key Terms** are listed with page references that take students back to the place where the highlighted term is introduced.
  - The **Chapter Review** captures the main points in each major section and reinforces factual content presented in the chapter by answering the Spotlight Questions. Students can review the major ideas in the chapter so that they are well-prepared for a test. Page references are included for easy locating of information.
  - The **Making Connections** make connections between main ideas among major sections within the chapter. These questions test higher level thinking skills; students may be asked to make inferences, draw conclusions, connect events, analyze outcomes, consider alternative outcomes, identify causes and effects, make comparisons, draw contrasts, and so forth. This feature emphasizes synthesis and encourages students to draw conclusions. In this way, students are clear on how the main ideas in a chapter work together and are better prepared to take a test on the subject.
  - The **Practice Quiz** tests students on each chapter. Answers to the quiz appear upside down at the bottom of the page so students can self-evaluate. The quiz reinforces learning and identifies areas of weakness.

- The **Sample Essay Questions** provide open-ended essay questions that allow students to practice their test-taking and writing skills. This gives students opportunities to synthesize the chapter's content and to strengthen their writing skills.
- The **Visual Program** is full of rich, full-color maps and illustrations, drawing directly from the narrative. Each visual advances and expands the themes, provides elaboration and contrast, tells more of a story, and generally adds another dimension of learning. Captions invite readers to consider the historical significance of artifacts. Caption questions ask readers to make visual connections to history.

MyHistoryLab

- **MyHistoryLab Icons** can be found in the margin and identify additional material on MyHistoryLab.com, Pearson's premium Web site for U.S. history. Icons enable students to take more tests and provide a fully integrated learning environment. For more information, or to review a demo, please see www.myhistorylab.com.

A Final Word

My fellow authors and I, with the assistance of the professionals at Pearson, have devoted a great deal of effort to making a textbook of which we are all very proud. Our goal with *American Stories* is to convey our excitement for history to our students in the most accessible manner possible. We've done what we can toward this goal, but we realize that our success depends on you, the classroom instructors. Our job is to make your job easier. All of us—authors and instructors—are in this together. So keep up the good work, and thanks!

A PERSONAL WELCOME TO STUDENTS

Every autumn for many years I have taught an introductory course in American history. Over that time I've come to appreciate the value of devoting the first class session to the fundamentals of studying and learning history. Every subject—mathematics, chemistry, psychology, English, art—has its peculiarities; each reveals itself to students in particular ways. And different students have different learning styles. But the experiences of the many students I've taught have convinced me that certain general rules apply.

I always tell students that these rules aren't the Ten Commandments; they may have their own methods of studying. But I also tell them that these rules—call them helpful hints, if "rules" sounds too stuffy—have worked for a lot of students in the past, and might work for them.

Rules for Studying History

I divide the rules into two categories. The first category involves **the philosophy of history and the nature of learning**. The six rules in this category apply to any history course—American history, world history, you name it—and any textbook. Each rule starts with a broad observation about history and ends with a specific recommendation for effective study.

1. History is a *story*, not just an assortment of facts. The connections are critical. How do the events and people you are reading or hearing about relate to one another? This is what historians want to know, and what distinguishes them from chroniclers, who simply list events and leave it at that.

Therefore:

Find the story line, the plot. Identify the main characters, the turning points. How did the story—or the part of the story you are studying in a given chapter or lecture—turn out? Why did it turn out that way and not some other?

2. Dates matter, but order matters more. Students often get the idea that history is all about dates. It's not. It's about what caused what (as in a story: see Rule 1 above). Dates are useful only in that they help you remember what happened before what else. This is crucial, because the thing that came first might have caused, or at least influenced, the thing that came later.

Therefore:

Concentrate on the order of events. If you do, the dates will fall into place by themselves.

3. History takes time—to happen, and to learn. History is nothing more or less than how people deal with each other (again, it's a story). But like any richly detailed story, it can take time to absorb.

Therefore:

Spread out your studying. If you have three hours of reading to do, do it over three days for an hour a day. If you have a test coming up, give yourself two weeks to study, allocating a half hour each day. You'll learn more easily; you'll retain more. And you'll have a better chance to enjoy the story.

4. **History's stories are both spoken and written**. That's why most classes involve both lectures and readings. In the typical syllabus, readings—chapters of the text, supplementary documents and articles—are keyed to the lectures, with the readings chosen to complement the lectures, and vice versa.

Therefore:

Read the assigned materials before the corresponding lectures. It's tempting not to—to let the reading slide. But resist the temptation. Advance reading makes the lectures far more understandable—and far more enjoyable.

5. **Less is more**, at least in note-taking. Not every word in the text or other reading is equally important; not every word uttered by your instructor in a lecture has equal value. The point of notes is to distill a chapter or a lecture into a smaller, more manageable size.

Therefore:

Hit the high points. Focus on where the text and lecture overlap. Write down key phrases and words; don't write complete sentences. And if you are using a highlighter on a book, be sparing. If yellow (or pink or whatever color you prefer) starts to become the prevailing motif of your pages, you've gone too far.

6. **History is a twice-told tale**. History is both what happened and how we've remembered what happened. Think of your first exposure to a particular historical topic as history *happening*, and your second exposure as history *being remembered*. An awareness of both is necessary to making the history stick in your head.

Therefore:

Take a rest after reading a chapter or attending a lecture. **Then go back and review**. Your class notes should not be comprehensive (see Rule 5), but as you go back over them, you will remember details that will help you fill out your notes. While you are reviewing a chapter, ask yourself what your notes on the chapter mean, and why you highlighted this particular phrase or that.

To summarize, when approaching a history course:

- **Find the story line.**
- **Concentrate on the order of events.**
- **Spread out your studying.**
- **Read the assignments before the lectures.**
- **Hit the high points in taking notes.**
- **Take a rest, then review.**

Rules for Using This Book to Study History

The second category of rules applies specifically to this book. My coauthors and I have designed this text to be particularly accessible to students. Every feature has a purpose, and all are intended to make the task of learning history easier. Learning history is still a task—I'd like to say it's all fun and games, but you wouldn't believe

SPOTLIGHT QUESTIONS   OUTLINE

WHAT conflicts arose among Lincoln, Johnson, and Congress during Reconstruction?

The President versus Congress

WHAT problems did southern society face during Reconstruction?

Reconstructing Southern Society

WHAT forces brought on the end of Reconstruction?

Retreat from Reconstruction

WHO benefited and who suffered from the reconciliation of North and South?

Reunion and the New South

me, and you'd be right not to. Like anything else worthwhile, learning history requires effort. But it can be an enjoyable task, and we've configured the book to make the effort you devote to learning history as effective as possible. The following rules will help **you get the most out of this book**.

1. **Get hooked**. Each chapter tells a story and conveys a theme. The story and the theme are introduced in the opening section. We—my fellow authors and I—have written these to catch your attention and draw you into the story, and also to illustrate the central theme of the chapter. Spend five minutes reading the opener. Enjoy it—these are good stories. And write down or highlight the overall theme of the chapter.

2. **Get in the spotlight**. The **SPOTLIGHT QUESTIONS** ? come next. These ask the most important questions the chapter will answer. Highlight these questions, and fix them in your mind.

3. **Get keyed**. The KEY EVENTS are the most important things that happened during the period of the chapter. Don't memorize them, but do read them, and come back to them as you read the chapter.

4. **Give it the once-over-lightly**. At this point, flip through the rest of the chapter. Take no more than five minutes. Pay attention to the section headings. Look at the pictures and maps, and read their captions. These ask questions the text will answer. Don't worry about the answers now; just let the questions roll around in your head.

KEY EVENTS

1863 Lincoln sets forth 10 percent Reconstruction plan, *p. 420*

1864 Wade-Davis Bill passes Congress but is pocket-vetoed by Lincoln, *p. 420*

1865 Lincoln assassinated (April), *p. 420* ■ Johnson moves to reconstruct the South on his own initiative, *p. 421* ■ Congress refuses to seat representatives and senators elected from states reestablished under presidential plan (December), *p. 421*

1866 Johnson vetoes Freedmen's Bureau Bill (February), *p. 423* ■ Johnson vetoes Civil Rights Act; it passes over his veto (April), *p. 423* ■ Congress passes Fourteenth Amendment (June), *p. 424* ■ Republicans increase their congressional majority in the fall elections, *p. 424*

1867 First Reconstruction Act is passed over Johnson's veto (March), *p. 425*

1868 Johnson is impeached; he avoids conviction by one vote (February–May), *p. 426* ■ Southern blacks vote and serve in constitutional conventions, *p. 435* ■ Grant wins presidential election, *p. 435*

1869 Congress passes Fifteenth Amendment, granting African Americans the right to vote, *p. 435*

1870–1871 Congress passes Ku Klux Klan Acts to protect black voting rights in the South, *p. 437*

1872 Grant re-elected president, *p. 437*

1873 Financial panic plunges nation into depression, *p. 440*

1876–1877 Disputed presidential election resolved in favor of Republican Hayes over Democrat Tilden, *p. 438*

1877 Compromise of 1877 ends military intervention in the South and causes fall of the last Radical governments, *p. 439*

5. **Take it one step—that is, section—at a time**. Each chapter is divided into subsections. These range from two pages to five or six. The end of each subsection includes ✔ **QUICK CHECK QUESTIONS**. Use these questions to test your understanding of the section. If you have trouble answering any of the questions after you've read the subsection, go back and re-read that section. Highlight or take note of the answers as you come across them.

6. **Wrap it up**. Each chapter ends with a **Conclusion**, which recapitulates the main theme; a **Chapter Review**, which summarizes answers to the **Spotlight Questions**; and a series of questions called **Making Connections**, which ask you to think about how the sections relate to one another. This is where you consolidate what you've learned in the chapter. Don't skimp; an hour here is worth four hours of general study. A **Practice Quiz** and **Sample Essay Questions** let you test yourself—before your instructor does. If you need more help, go to www.myhistorylab.com to access more quizzes online.

To summarize, when reading each chapter:

- **Get hooked**
- **Get in the spotlight**
- **Get keyed**

- **Give it the once-over-lightly**
- **Take it one section at a time**
- **Wrap it up**

A final suggestion: Allow enough time for this course so you aren't rushed. If you give yourself time to get into the story, you'll come to enjoy it. And what you enjoy, you'll remember.

Best wishes,
H. W. Brands

ACKNOWLEDGMENTS

The authors acknowledge with special gratitude the contribution of Kathleen T. McWhorter and Debby Kalk for their work in developing a sound pedagogical plan. We are also most grateful to our consultants and reviewers whose thoughtful and constructive work contributed greatly to this edition. Their many helpful suggestions led to significant improvements in the final product.

Guy Aronoff, *California State University–Channel Islands;* Andrew Bacha, *Harrisburg Area Community College;* Frank M. Baglione, *Tallahassee Community College;* David Darryl Bibb, *University of Great Falls;* Marcia Schmidt Blaine, *Plymouth State University;* Chuck Boening, *Shelton State Community College;* Edward Bond, *Alabama A & M University;* Barbara Booth, *Santa Ana College;* Robert E. Brown, *Tunxis Community College;* J. Michael Butler, *South Georgia College;* Shvonnie R. Caffey, *Bishop State Community College;* Charles L. Cohen, *University of Wisconsin-Madison;* Andria Crosson, *University of Texas at San Antonio;* Thomas A. DeBlack, *Arkansas Tech University;* Terrence Delaney, *Three Rivers Community College;* Rick Dodgson, *Lakeland College;* Shawn Dry, *Oakland Community College;* Richard M. Filipink, *Western Illinois University;* Hal M. Friedman, *Henry Ford Community College;* Michael Gherke, *Glenville State College;* Janet Golden, *Rutgers University;* Susan Gonda, *Grossmont College;* Karen Hagan, *The Victoria College;* Gregory M. Havrilcsak, *The Universityof Michigan–Flint;* David M. Head, *John Tyler Community College;* Matthew Hiner, *Lakeland Community College;* Andrew G. Hollinger, *Tarrant County College;* Charles W. Hope, *Tarrant County College–Southeast Campus;* Wallace H. Hutcheon, *Northern Virginia Community College;* Diane B. Jackson, *Lost Angeles Trade Technical College;* Juli A. Jones, *San Diego Mesa College;*

Sandra Jowers-Barber, *University of the District of Columbia;* Mark S. Joy, *Jamestown College;* John S. Kemp, *Truckee Meadows Community College;* Melissa LaPrelle, *Collin County Community College;* William P. Leeman, *Providence College;* John Maddox, *Los Angeles Valley Community College;* Robert W. Malick, *Harrisburg Area Community College;* Evelyn DeLong Mangie, *University of South Florida;* Edwin Martini, *Western Michigan University;* Peter C. Messer, *Mississippi State University;* Mary M. McClendon, *Chipola College;* Greg Miller, *Hillsborough Community College;* Sarah E. Miller, *University of South Carolina–Salkehatchie;* Gary B. Ostrower, *Alfred University;* Chris Padgett, *American River College;* Ronnie Peacock, *Metropolitan State College of Denver;* Jeffrey J. Pilz, *North Iowa Area Community College;* Ann Marie Plane, *University of California at Santa Barbara;* Brian K. Plummer, *Azusa Pacific University;* David B. Raymond, *Northern Maine Community College;* Miriam Reumann, *The University of Rhode Island;* Tara Ross, *Onondaga Community College;* Sandra Schackel, *Boise State University;* Earl A. Shoemaker, *University of Wisconsin–Eau Claire;* Terry L. Shoptaugh, *Minnesota State University Moorhead;* David L. Snead, *Liberty University;* Jean A. Stuntz, *West Texas A&M University;* Brad Tennant, *Presentation College;* James Treu, *North Central Missouri College;* John Turner, *University of Southern Alabama;* Marcus S. Turner, *San Jacinto College Central;* Kenneth A. Watras, *Park University's College of Distance Learning;* Scott M. Williams, *Weatherford College;* Larry C. Wilson, *San Jacinto College;* and Patricia Zelman, *Tarleton State University.*

This book owes much to the many conscientious historians who reviewed previous editions of *America Past and Present* and offered valuable suggestions that led to many improvements in the text. We acknowledge with gratitude the contributions of the following:

Frank W. Abbott, *University of Houston;* Joseph L. Adams, *St. Louis Community College at Meramec;* Frank Alduino, *Anne Arundel Community College;* Kenneth G. Alfers, *Mountain View College;* Elizabeth Ansnes, *San Jose State University;* Thomas Archdeacon, *University of Wisconsin;* James Axtell, *College of William and Mary;* Kenneth R. Bain, *Northwestern University;* James Banks, *Cuyahoga Community College;* Lois W. Banner, *Hamilton College;* Samantha Barbas, *Chapman University;* Donald Scott Barton, *East Central University;* James Baumgardner, *Carson-Newman College;* David Bernstein, *California State University, Long Beach;* Chad Berry, *Maryville College;* Joseph E. Bisson, *San Joaquin Delta College;* Kent Blaser, *Wayne State College;* Eric J. Bolsterli, *University of Texas at Arlington;* James D. Border, *Berkshire Community College;* Alexander O. Boulton, *Villa Julie College;* Mary C. Brennan, *Ohio State University;* Blanche Brick, *Blinn College;* Daniel Patrick Brown, *Moorpark College;* Thomas Camfield, *Sam Houston State University;* Clayborne Carson, *Stanford University;* Cynthia Carter, *Florida Community College at Jacksonville;* Kathleen S. Carter, *High Point University;* Raphael Cassimere, Jr., *University of New Orleans;* Katherine Chavigny, *Sweet Briar College;* Francis Coan, *Central Connecticut State University;* Charles L. Cohen, *University of Wisconsin;* Jerald Combs, *San Francisco State University;* John Cooper, *University of Wisconsin;* Yvonne Sutton Cornelius, *Nashville State Community College;* Nancy F. Cott, *Yale University;* Virginia Crane, *University of Wisconsin, Oshkosh;* Edward R. Crowther, *Adams State University;* James C. Curtis, *University of Delaware;* Roger P. Davis, *University of Nebraska at Kearney;* Cole Dawson, *Warner Pacific College;* James Denham, *Florida Southern College;* Patricia Norred Derr, *Kutztown University;* Bruce J. Dierenfield, *Canisius College;* Charles Douglass, *Florida Community College at Jacksonville;* Thomas Dublin, *State University of New York at Binghamton;* Perry R. Duis, *University of Illinois at Chicago;* Richard Ellis, *State University of New York at Buffalo;* John P. Farr, *Chattanooga State Technical Community College;* Kathleen Feely, *University of Redlands;* James E. Fell, Jr.,

University of Colorado, Denver; Eric Foner, *Columbia University;* Stephen Foster, *Northern Illinois University;* William W. Freehling, *Johns Hopkins University;* Fred E. Freidel, *Bellevue Community College;* Richard Frey, *Southern Oregon State College;* Jennifer Fry, *King's College;* Gary W. Gallagher, *Pennsylvania State University;* Sara E. Gallaway, *Oxnard College;* Don R. Gerlach, *University of Akron;* August W. Giebelhaus, *Georgia Institute of Technology;* Louis S. Gomolak, *Southwest Texas State University;* Lewis L. Gould, *University of Texas;* Lawrence Grear, *Langston University;* Richard C. Haney, *University of Wisconsin, Whitewater;* George Harrison, *Jones County Junior College;* Edward F. Hass, *Wright State University;* Paul B. Hatley, *Rogers State University;* Sarah Heath, *Texas A&M University-Corpus Christi;* Tim Heinrichs, *Bellevue Community College;* Mary Ann Heiss, *Kent State University;* Kenneth E. Hendrickson, *Sam Houston State University;* Sondra Herman, *De Anza Community College;* Wallace Hettle, *University of Northern Iowa;* Anne Hickling, *San Jose City College;* James Hollingsworth, *Pasco-Hernando Community College;* Ranford Hopkins, *Moorpark College;* Brian Hosmer, *University of Delaware;* John R. Howe, *University of Minnesota;* Nathan I. Huggins, *Harvard University;* Susan Hult, *Houston Community College;* James A. Hurst, *Northwest Missouri State University;* Wallace S. Hutcheon, *Northern Virginia Community College;* Robert M. Ireland, *University of Kentucky;* Virginia G. Jelatis, *Western Illinois University;* Carol E. Jenson, *University of Wisconsin, La Crosse;* Ben Johnson, *Southern Arkansas University;* Juli A. Jones, *St. Charles County Community College;* Robert R. Jones, *University of Southwestern Louisiana;* Carol Keller, *San Antonio College;* John Kelley, *Shawnee State Community College;* Richard S. Kirkendall, *University of Washington;* I. E. Kirkpatrick, *Tyler Junior College;* Fred Koestler, *Tarleton State University;* Lawrence F. Kohl, *University of Alabama;* Elizabeth Kuebler-Wolf, *Indiana University-Purdue University Fort Wayne;* Steven Lawson, *Rutgers University;* Edward Lee, *Winthrop University;* Kathy Long, *Chattanooga State Technical Community College;* Henry Louis, *Kansas City Kansas Community College;* Warren Mackey, *Chattanooga State Technical Community College;* Thomas R. Mandeville, *Clinton Community College;* Karen Marcotte, *Palo Alto*

College; Herbert F. Margulies, *University of Hawaii;* Myron Marty, *National Endowment for the Humanities;* Robert C. McMath, Jr., *Georgia Institute of Technology;* T. Ronald Melton, *Brewton-Parker College;* James H. Merrell, *Vassar College;* Joseph C. Miller, *University of Virginia;* William G. Morris, *Midland College;* Harmon Mothershead, *Northwest Missouri State University;* Timothy Moy, *University of New Mexico;* Peter Murray, *Methodist College;* Rick Murray, *College of the Canyons;* John M. Murrin, *Princeton University;* John K. Nelson, *University of North Carolina;* Roger L. Nichols, *University of Arizona;* Elizabeth R. Osborne, *Indiana University–Purdue University at Indianapolis;* Elliot Pasternack, *Middlesex County College;* J'Nell L. Pate, *Tarrant County Junior College;* Michael Perman, *University of Illinois, Chicago;* Charles A. Pilant, *Cumberland College;* Carrie Pritchett, *Northeast Texas Community College;* Nora Ramirez, *San Antonio Community College;* Marlette Rebhorn, *Austin Community College;* Thomas S. Reid, *Valencia Community College;* Douglas W. Richmond, *University of Texas, Arlington;* Andrew W. Robertson, *Louisiana State University;* David Sandoval, *University of Southern Colorado;* Mark Schmellor, *Binghamton University;* Howard Schonberger, *University of Maine;* Ingrid Winther Scobie, *Texas Women's University;* Rebecca S. Shoemaker, *Indiana State University;* C. Edward Skeen, *University of Memphis;* Kathryn Kish Sklar, *State University of New York at Binghamton;* Allan Spetter, *Wright State University;* Ronald Spiller, *Edinboro University of Pennsylvania;* Cherry L. Spruill, *Indiana University–Purdue University at Indianapolis;* Mark J. Stegmaier, *Cameron University;* George G. Suggs, Jr., *Southeast Missouri State University;* H. Micheal Tarver, *McNeese State University;* Paul F. Taylor, *Augusta College;* Michael E. Thompson, *South Seattle Community College;* Pat Thompson, *University of Texas, San Antonio;* Stephen Tootle, *University of Northern Colorado;* George Torok, *El Paso Community College;* Clyde D. Tyson, *Niagara County Community College;* Nancy C. Unger, *San Francisco State University;* Richard Vanderpool, *Umpqua Community College;* Donna L. VanRaaphorst, *Cuyahoga Community College;* Russell Veeder, *Dickinson State University;* Daniel C. Vogt, *Jackson State University;* Sandra Wagner-Wright, *University of Hawaii at Hilo;* Forrest A. Walker, *Eastern New Mexico State University;* James P. Walsh, *Central Connecticut State University;* Ronald Walters, *Johns Hopkins University;* Stephen Warren, *Augustana College;* Stephen Webre, *Louisiana Tech University;* Marli Weiner, *University of Maine;* Frank Wetta, *Galveston Community College;* James C. Williams, *De Anza College*; James M. Woods, *Georgia Southern University;* David Yancey, *San Jose City College;* Rosemarie Zagarri, *Catholic University;* and Robert F. Zeidel, *University of Wisconsin, Stout*

The staff at Pearson continued its generous support and assistance for our efforts. We thank our Executive Editor Michael Boezi for his attention, support, and thoughtful guidance throughout this revision; Assistant Development Manager David Kear and Development Editor Stephanie Ricotta, who helped us augment and enhance the appeal of the text; and Executive Marketing Manager Sue Westmoreland, who worked zealously to convey the message and vision of the authors to the Pearson sales force and to the marketplace. Production Managers Savoula Amanatidis and Debra Wechsler, Cover Design Manager/Cover Designer Maria Lange, and the staff at Elm Street Publishing Services put the finishing touches on this new edition and deftly guided it through the many phases of production.

Finally, each author received aid and encouragement from many colleagues, friends, and family members. T. H. Breen thanks Strother Roberts for his splendid help with this edition. Hal Williams extends thanks to Carole S. Cohen, Jacqueline Bradley, and Susan Harper-Bisso for their help with revisions for this edition. Ariela Gross extends thanks to Riaz Tejani for invaluable help with this edition.

H. W. BRANDS
T. H. BREEN
R. HAL WILLIAMS
ARIELA J. GROSS

SUPPLEMENTS

For Qualified College Adopters

- **Instructor's Resource Manual** Each chapter of this resource manual contains a chapter outline, interpretive essay, anecdotes and references to biographical or primary sources, and a comprehensive summary of the text.
- **Test Bank** This supplement contains hundreds of multiple-choice, true/false, and essay questions. Multiple-choice and true/false questions are referenced by topic and text page number.
- **TestGen-EQ Computerized Testing System** This flexible, easy-to-master computerized test bank on a dual-platform CD includes all of the items in the printed test bank and allows instructors to select specific questions, edit them, and add their own items to create exams.
- **MyTest** Pearson MyTest is a powerful assessment generation program that helps instructors easily create and print quizzes and exams.
- **Instructor Resource Center (IRC) (www.pearsonhighered.com/educator)** Through the Instructor Resource Center, instructors can log into premium online products, browse and download book-specific instructor resources, and receive immediate access and instructions to installing course management content.
- **Research Navigator™ and Research Navigator Guide** Research Navigator™ is a comprehensive Web site offering EBSCO's ContentSelect Academic Journal & Abstract Database, the *New York Times* Search-by-Subject Archive, *Financial Times* Article Archive and Company Financials, and "Best of the Web" Link Library. The Research Navigator Guide provides your students with access to the Web site and includes reference material and hints about conducting online research.
- **Study Card for American History** Colorful, affordable, and packed with useful information, Longman's Study Cards make studying easier, more efficient, and more enjoyable.
- **Digital Transparency Masters** A downloadable document containing digital masters of all maps featured in the text. Available exclusively on the IRC.
- **History Digital Media Archive CD-ROM** This CD-ROM contains electronic images and interactive and static maps, along with media elements such as video. It is fully customizable and ready for classroom presentation. All images and maps are available in PowerPoint™ as well.
- **Digital Media Archive, Updated Second Edition** This encyclopedic collection contains dozens of narrated vignettes and videos as well as hundreds of photos and illustrations.
- **Video Lecture Launchers** Prepared by Mark Newman, University of Illinois at Chicago, these video lecture launchers cover key issues in American history from 1877 to the present.
- **PowerPoint Presentations** These presentations contain an average of 30 slides for each chapter, including key points and terms as well as maps, graphs, and charts.

For Students

- **Study Guide** Available in two volumes, each chapter in the study guide includes a summary; a timeline activity; map and geography questions; key terms, people, and events; and identification, multiple-choice, and critical-thinking questions.
- **American History Study Site (www.pearsonamericanhistory.com.)** Students can take advantage of this online course companion that includes practice tests, Web links, and flash cards that cover the scope of topics covered in a typical American history class.
- *Mapping American History,* **Third Edition: Student Activities** Created by Sharon Ballinger, El Paso Community College, this map workbook features exercises designed to teach students to interpret and analyze cartographic materials such as historical documents.
- *Longman American History Atlas* This atlas features carefully selected historical maps that provide comprehensive coverage for the major historical periods.
- *A Short Guide to Writing About History,* **Fifth Edition** Written by Richard Marius, late of Harvard University, and Melvin E. Page, Eastern Tennessee State University, this engaging and practical text helps students get beyond merely compiling dates and facts. Covering both brief essays and the documented resource paper, the text explores the writing and researching processes, identifies different modes of historical writing, including argument, and concludes with guidelines for improving style.

MyHistoryLab (www.myhistorylab.com)

MyHistoryLab provides students with an online package complete with the entire comprehensive electronic textbook and numerous study aids. With several hundred primary sources, many of which are assignable and link to a gradebook, pre- and post-tests that link to a gradebook and result in individualized study plans, videos and images, as well as map activities with gradable quizzes, the site offers students a unique, interactive experience that brings history to life. The comprehensive site also includes a History Bookshelf with fifty of the most commonly assigned books in history classes and a History Toolkit with tutorials and helpful links. Other features include gradable assignments and chapter review materials; a Test Bank; and Research Navigator™.

Delivered in CourseCompass™, Blackboard™, or WebCT™, as well as in a non-course-management version, MyHistoryLab is easy to use and flexible. MyHistoryLab is organized according to the table of contents of the comprehensive textbook. With the course-management version, instructors can create a further customized product by adding their own syllabus, content, and assignments, or they can use the materials as presented.

Longman Library of American Biography Series

Pocket-sized and brief, each biography in the Library of American Biography series relates the life of its subject to the broader themes and developments of the time. Series titles include: Edmund S. Morgan, *The Puritan Dilemma: The Story of John Winthrop;* Charles W. Akers, *Abigail Adams: A Revolutionary American Woman;* Harold C. Livesay, *Andrew Carnegie and the Rise of Big Business;* Jack N. Rakove, *James Madison and the Creation of the American Republic;* Sam W. Haynes, *James K. Polk and the Expansionist Impulse;* and J. William T. Youngs, *Eleanor Roosevelt: A Personal and Public Life.* New additions to the series include John L. Bullion, *Lyndon B. Johnson and the Transformation of American Politics,* John A. Moretta, *William Penn and the Quaker Legacy,* Susan Oliver, *Betty Friedan: The Personal is Political,* Joseph A. Palermo, *Robert F. Kennedy and the Death of American Idealism,* and Herbert S. Permet, *Richard M. Nixon: An American Enigma.*

Penguin-Longman Partnership

The partnership between Penguin Books and Longman Publishers offers a discount on a wide range of titles when bundled with any Pearson history survey textbook. Visit www.ablongman.com/penguin for more information.

ABOUT THE AUTHORS

H. W. BRANDS

H. W. Brands is the Dickson Allen Anderson Centennial Professor of History at the University of Texas at Austin. He is the author of numerous works of history and international affairs, including *The Devil We Knew: Americans and the Cold War* (1993), *Into the Labyrinth: The United States and the Middle East* (1994), *The Reckless Decade: America in the 1890s* (1995), *TR: The Last Romantic* (a biography of Theodore Roosevelt) (1997), *What America Owes the World: The Struggle for the Soul of Foreign Policy* (1998), *The First American: The Life and Times of Benjamin Franklin* (2000), *The Strange Death of American Liberalism* (2001), *The Age of Gold: The California Gold Rush and the New American Dream* (2002), *Woodrow Wilson* (2003), and *Andrew Jackson* (2005). His writing has received critical and popular acclaim; *The First American* was a finalist for the Pulitzer Prize and a national bestseller. He lectures frequently across North America and in Europe. His essays and reviews have appeared in the *New York Times*, the *Wall Street Journal*, the *Washington Post*, the *Los Angeles Times*, and *Atlantic Monthly*. He is a regular guest on radio and television, and has participated in several historical documentary films.

T. H. BREEN

T. H. Breen is the Director of the Center for Historical Studies and William Smith Mason Professor of American History at Northwestern University. He received his Ph.D. from Yale University in 1968. He has taught at Northwestern since 1970. Breen's major books include *The Character of the Good Ruler: A Study of Puritan Political Ideas in New England* (1974); *Puritans and Adventurers: Change and Persistence in Early America* (1980); *Tobacco Culture: The Mentality of the Great Tidewater Planters on the Eve of Revolution* (1985); and, with Stephen Innes of the University of Virginia, *"Myne Owne Ground": Race and Freedom on Virginia's Eastern Shore* (1980). His *Imagining the Past* (1989) won the 1990 Historic Preservation Book Award. His most recent book is *Marketplace of Revolution: How Consumer Politics Shaped American Independence* (2004). In addition to receiving several awards for outstanding teaching at Northwestern, Breen has been the recipient of research grants from the American Council of Learned Societies, the Guggenheim Foundation, the Institute for Advanced Study (Princeton), the National Humanities Center, and the Huntington Library. He has served as the Fowler Hamilton Fellow at Christ Church, Oxford University (1987–1988), the Pitt Professor of American History and Institutions, Cambridge University (1990–1991), the Harmsworth Professor of American History at Oxford University (2000–2001), and was a recipient of the Humboldt Prize (Germany). He is currently completing a book to be entitled *The Revolutionary Moment: American Insurgency, 1774–1776*.

R. HAL WILLIAMS

R. Hal Williams is professor of history at Southern Methodist University. He received his A.B. from Princeton University in 1963 and his Ph.D. from Yale University in 1968. His books include *The Democratic Party and California Politics, 1880–1896* (1973); *Years of Decision: American Politics in the 1890s* (1978); and *The Manhattan Project: A Documentary Introduction to the Atomic Age* (1990). A specialist in American political history, he taught at Yale University from 1968 to 1975 and came to SMU in 1975 as chair of the Department of History. From 1980 to 1988, he served as dean of Dedman College, the school of humanities and sciences, at SMU, where he is currently dean of Research and Graduate Studies. In 1980, he was a visiting professor at University College, Oxford University. Williams has received grants from the American Philosophical Society and the National Endowment for the Humanities, and he has served on the Texas Committee for the Humanities. He is currently working on a study of the presidential election of 1896 and a biography of James G. Blaine, the late-nineteenth-century speaker of the House, secretary of state, and Republican presidential candidate.

ARIELA J. GROSS

Ariela Gross is John B. and Alice R. Sharp Professor of Law and History, and Co-Director of the Center for Law, History and Culture, at the University of Southern California. She has been a visiting Professor at Tel Aviv University and the École des Hautes Études en Sciences Sociales. She is the author of *Double Character: Slavery and Mastery in the Antebellum Southern Courtroom* (2000), *What Blood Won't Tell: A History of Race on Trial in America* (2008) and numerous articles and book chapters, including "The Caucasian Cloak: Mexican Americans and the Politics of Whiteness in the Twentieth-Century Southwest" in the *Georgetown Law Journal* (2007) and "When is the Time of Slavery? The History of Slavery in Contemporary Legal and Politics Argument" in the *California Law Review* (2008). Gross has received fellowships from the American Council of Learned Societies, the Guggenheim Foundation, the National Endowment for the Humanities, and the Huntington Library. She is currently working on a study of law, history, and memory in the Americas, Europe, and Africa.

American Stories

A History of the
United States

CHAPTER 16

The Agony of Reconstruction

1863–1877

BLACK VOTING *The First Vote*, drawn by A. H. Ward for *Harper's Weekly*, November 16, 1867.

Why does the artist have each voter dressed so differently?

Robert Smalls and Black Politicians during Reconstruction

During the Reconstruction period immediately following the Civil War, African Americans struggled to become equal citizens of a democratic republic. A number of remarkable leaders won public office. Robert Smalls of South Carolina was perhaps the most famous and widely respected southern black leader of the Civil War and Reconstruction era.

Born a slave in 1839, Smalls was allowed as a young man to live and work independently, hiring his own time from a master who may have been his half brother. Smalls worked as a sailor and trained himself to be a pilot in Charleston Harbor. When the Union navy blockaded Charleston in 1862, Smalls, who was then working on a Confederate steamship called the *Planter*, saw a chance to win his freedom. At three o'clock in the morning on May 13, 1862, when the white officers of the *Planter* were ashore, he took command of the vessel and its slave crew, sailed it out of the heavily fortified harbor, and surrendered it to the Union navy. Smalls immediately became a hero to those antislavery northerners who were seeking evidence that the slaves were willing and able to serve the Union. The *Planter* was turned into a Union army transport, and Smalls was made its captain after being commissioned as an officer. During the remainder of the war, he rendered conspicuous and gallant service as captain and pilot of Union vessels off the coast of South Carolina.

Like a number of other African Americans who had fought valiantly for the Union, Smalls went on to a distinguished political career during Reconstruction, serving in the South Carolina constitutional convention, in the state legislature, and for several terms in the U.S. Congress. He was also a shrewd businessman and became the owner of extensive properties in Beaufort, South Carolina, and its vicinity. The electoral organization Smalls established was so effective that he was able to control local government and get himself elected to Congress even after the election of 1876 had placed the state under the control of white conservatives bent on depriving blacks of political power. Organized mob violence defeated him in 1878, but he bounced back to win by decision of Congress a contested congressional election in 1880. He did not leave the House of Representatives for good until 1886, when he lost another contested election that had to be decided by Congress.

In their efforts to defeat him, Smalls's white opponents frequently charged that he had a hand in the corruption that was allegedly rampant in South Carolina during Reconstruction. But careful historical investigation shows that he was, by the standards of the time, an honest and responsible public servant. In the South Carolina convention of 1868 and later in the state legislature, he was a conspicuous champion of free and compulsory public education. In Congress, he fought for the enactment and enforcement of federal civil rights laws. Not especially radical on social questions, he sometimes bent over backward to accommodate what he regarded as the legitimate interests and sensibilities of South Carolina whites. Like other middle-class black political leaders in Reconstruction-era South Carolina, he can perhaps be faulted in hindsight for not doing more to help poor blacks gain access to land of their own. But in 1875, he sponsored congressional legislation that opened for purchase at low prices the land in his own district that had been confiscated by the federal government during the war. As a result, blacks were able to buy most of this land, and they soon owned three-fourths of the land in Beaufort and its vicinity.

Robert Smalls spent the later years of his life as U.S. collector of customs for the port of Beaufort, a beneficiary of the patronage that the Republican party continued to provide for a few loyal southern blacks. But the loss of real political clout for Smalls and men like him was one of the tragic consequences of the fall of Reconstruction.

For a brief period of years, black politicians such as Robert Smalls exercised more power in the South than they would for another century. A series of political developments on the national and regional stage made Reconstruction "an unfinished revolution," promising but not delivering true equality for newly freed

ROBERT SMALLS   With the help of several black crewmen, Robert Smalls—then twenty-three years old—commandeered the *Planter*, a Confederate steamship used to transport guns and ammunition, and surrendered it to the Union vessel, *USS Onward*. Smalls provided distinguished service to the Union during the Civil War and after the war went on to become a successful politician and businessman.

What were some of the goals Robert Smalls pursued in Congress?

African Americans. A number of factors—national party politics; shifting priorities among northern Republicans; white southerners' commitment to white supremacy, which was backed by legal restrictions as well as massive extralegal violence against blacks—all combined to stifle the promise of Reconstruction.

Yet the Reconstruction era also saw major transformations in American society in the wake of the Civil War—new ways of organizing labor and family life, new institutions within and outside of the government, and new ideologies regarding the role of institutions and government in social and economic life. Many of the changes begun during Reconstruction laid the groundwork for later revolutions in American life.

The President versus Congress

The problem of how to reconstruct the Union in the wake of the South's military defeat was one of the most difficult and perplexing challenges ever faced by American policymakers. The Constitution provided no firm guidelines, for the Framers had not anticipated a division of the country into warring sections. After emancipation became a northern war aim, the problem was compounded by a new issue: How far should the federal government go to secure freedom and civil rights for four million former slaves?

The debate that evolved led to a major political crisis. Advocates of a minimal Reconstruction policy favored quick restoration of the Union with no protection for the freed slaves beyond the prohibition of slavery. Proponents of a more radical policy wanted re-admission of the southern states to be dependent on guarantees that "loyal" men would displace the Confederate elite in positions of power and that blacks would acquire basic rights of American citizenship. The White House favored the minimal approach, whereas Congress came to endorse the more radical and thoroughgoing form of Reconstruction. The resulting struggle between Congress and the chief executive was the most serious clash between two branches of government in the nation's history.

WHAT conflicts arose among Lincoln, Johnson, and Congress during Reconstruction?

Wartime Reconstruction

Tension between the president and Congress over how to reconstruct the Union began during the war. Occupied mainly with achieving victory, Lincoln never set forth a final and comprehensive plan for bringing rebellious states back into the fold.

Ten Percent Plan

Reconstruction plan proposed by President Abraham Lincoln as a quick way to readmit the former Confederate states. It called for full pardon of all southerners except Confederate leaders and readmission to the Union for any state after 10 percent of its voters in the 1860 election signed a loyalty oath and the state abolished slavery.

Radical Republicans

The Radical Republicans in Congress, headed by Thaddeus Stevens and Charles Sumner, insisted on black suffrage and federal protection of civil rights of African Americans.

Wade-Davis Bill

In 1864, Congress passed the Wade-Davis Bill to counter Lincoln's Ten Percent Plan for Reconstruction. The bill required that a majority of a former Confederate state's white male population take a loyalty oath and guarantee equality for African Americans. President Lincoln pocket-vetoed the bill.

QUICK CHECK ✔

On what matters did Lincoln and Congress disagree?

But he did take initiatives that indicated he favored a lenient and conciliatory policy toward southerners who would give up the struggle and repudiate slavery. In December 1863, he issued a Proclamation of Amnesty and Reconstruction, which offered a full pardon to all southerners (with the exception of certain classes of Confederate leaders) who would take an oath of allegiance to the Union and acknowledge the legality of emancipation. This **Ten Percent Plan** provided that once 10 percent or more of the voting population of any occupied state had taken the oath, they were authorized to set up a loyal government. By 1864, Louisiana and Arkansas, states that were wholly or partially occupied by Union troops, had established Unionist governments. Lincoln's policy was meant to shorten the war. First, he hoped to weaken the southern cause by making it easy for disillusioned or lukewarm Confederates to switch sides. Second, he hoped to further his emancipation policy by insisting that the new governments abolish slavery.

Congress was unhappy with the president's Reconstruction experiments and in 1864 refused to seat the Unionists elected to the House and Senate from Louisiana and Arkansas. A minority of congressional Republicans—the strongly antislavery **Radical Republicans**—favored protection for black rights (especially black male suffrage) as a precondition for the readmission of southern states. But a larger group of Congressional moderates opposed Lincoln's plan, not on the basis of black rights but because they did not trust the repentant Confederates who would play a major role in the new governments. Congress also believed the president was exceeding his authority by using executive powers to restore the Union. Lincoln operated on the theory that secession, being illegal, did not place the Confederate states outside the Union in a constitutional sense. Since individuals and not states had defied federal authority, the president could use his pardoning power to certify a loyal electorate, which could then function as the legitimate state government.

After refusing to recognize Lincoln's 10 percent governments, Congress passed a Reconstruction bill of its own in July 1864. Known as the **Wade-Davis Bill**, this legislation required that 50 percent of the voters take an oath of future loyalty before the restoration process could begin. Once this had occurred, those who could swear they had never willingly supported the Confederacy could vote in an election for delegates to a constitutional convention. The bill in its final form did not require black suffrage, but it did give federal courts the power to enforce emancipation. Faced with this attempt to nullify his own program, Lincoln exercised a pocket veto by refusing to sign the bill before Congress adjourned. He justified his action by announcing that he did not want to be committed to any single Reconstruction plan. The sponsors of the bill responded with an angry manifesto, and Lincoln's relations with Congress reached their low.

Congress and the president remained stalemated on the Reconstruction issue for the rest of the war. During his last months in office, however, Lincoln showed some willingness to compromise. He persisted in his efforts to obtain full recognition for the governments he had nurtured in Louisiana and Arkansas but seemed receptive to the setting of other conditions—perhaps including black suffrage—for readmission of those states in which wartime conditions had prevented execution of his plan. However, he was assassinated before he made clear his intentions, leaving historians to speculate whether his quarrel with Congress would have worsened or been resolved. Given Lincoln's past record of political flexibility, the best bet is that he would have come to terms with the majority of his party.

Andrew Johnson at the Helm

Andrew Johnson, the man suddenly made president by an assassin's bullet, attempted to put the Union back together on his own authority in 1865. But his policies eventually set him at odds with Congress and the Republican party and provoked the most serious crisis in the history of relations between the executive and legislative branches of the federal government.

Johnson's background shaped his approach to Reconstruction. Born in dire poverty in North Carolina, he migrated as a young man to eastern Tennessee, where he made his living as a tailor. Lacking formal schooling, he did not learn to read and write until adult life. Entering politics as a Jacksonian Democrat, he became known as an effective stump speaker. His railing against the planter aristocracy made him the spokesman for Tennessee's nonslaveholding whites and the most successful politician in the state. He advanced from state legislator to congressman to governor and in 1857 was elected to the U.S. Senate.

When Tennessee seceded in 1861, Johnson was the only senator from a Confederate state who remained loyal to the Union and continued to serve in Washington. But his Unionism and defense of the common people did not include antislavery sentiments. Nor was he friendly to blacks. While campaigning in Tennessee, he had objected only to the fact that slaveholding was the privilege of a wealthy minority. He revealed his attitude when he wished that "every head of family in the United States had one slave to take the drudgery and menial service off his family."

During the war, while acting as military governor of Tennessee, Johnson endorsed Lincoln's emancipation policy as a means of destroying the power of the hated planter class rather than as a recognition of black humanity. He was chosen as Lincoln's running mate in 1864 because it was thought that a pro-administration Democrat, who was a southern Unionist in the bargain, would strengthen the ticket. No one expected that this fervent white supremacist would become president. Some Radical Republicans initially welcomed Johnson's ascent to the nation's highest office. Their hopes make sense in the light of Johnson's record of fierce loyalty to the Union and his apparent agreement with the Radicals that ex-Confederates should be severely treated. Unlike Lincoln, who had spoken of "malice toward none and charity for all," Johnson seemed likely to punish southern "traitors" and prevent them from regaining political influence. Only gradually did the deep disagreement between the president and the Republican congressional majority become evident.

The Reconstruction policy that Johnson initiated on May 29, 1865, created some uneasiness among the Radicals, but most Republicans were willing to give it a chance. Johnson placed North Carolina, and eventually other states, under appointed provisional governors chosen mostly from among prominent southern politicians who had opposed the secession movement and had rendered no conspicuous service to the Confederacy. The governors were responsible for calling constitutional conventions and ensuring that only "loyal" whites were permitted to vote for delegates. Participation required taking the oath of allegiance that Lincoln had prescribed earlier. Once again, Confederate leaders and former officeholders who had participated in the rebellion were excluded. To regain their political and property rights, those in the exempted categories had to apply for individual presidential pardons. Johnson made one significant addition to the list of the excluded: all those possessing taxable property exceeding $20,000 in value. In this fashion, he sought to prevent his longtime adversaries—the

JUST LIKE SLAVERY   "Slavery Is Dead?" asks this 1866 cartoon by Thomas Nast. To the cartoonist, the Emancipation Proclamation of 1863 and the North's victory in the Civil War meant little difference to the treatment of the freed slaves in the South. Freed slaves convicted of crimes often endured the same punishments as had slaves—sale, as depicted in the left panel of the cartoon, or beatings, as shown on the right.

What is represented in the female statue poised behind this freed slave at left and right?

The Mississippi Black Code (1865)

Thirteenth, Fourteenth, and Fifteenth Amendments (1865, 1868, 1870)

Thirteenth Amendment
Ratified in 1865, this amendment to the U.S. Constitution prohibited slavery and involuntary servitude.

wealthy planters—from participating in the Reconstruction of southern state governments.

Johnson urged the convention delegates to do three things: declare the ordinances of secession illegal, repudiate the Confederate debt, and ratify the **Thirteenth Amendment** abolishing slavery. After governments had been reestablished under constitutions meeting these conditions, the president assumed that the Reconstruction process would be complete and that the ex-Confederate states could regain their full rights under the Constitution.

The results of the conventions, which were dominated by prewar Unionists and representatives of backcountry yeoman farmers, were satisfactory to the president but troubling to many congressional Republicans. Rather than quickly accepting Johnson's recommendations, delegates in several states approved them begrudgingly or with qualifications. Furthermore, all the resulting constitutions limited suffrage to whites, disappointing the large number of northerners who hoped, as

Lincoln had, that at least some African Americans—perhaps those who were educated or had served in the Union army—would be given the vote. Republican uneasiness turned to disillusionment and anger when the state legislatures elected under the new constitutions proceeded to pass **Black Codes** subjecting former slaves to a variety of special regulations and restrictions on their freedom. Especially troubling were vagrancy and apprenticeship laws that forced African Americans to work and denied them a free choice of employers. Blacks in some states were also prevented from testifying in court on the same basis as whites and were subject to a separate penal code. To Radicals, the Black Codes looked suspiciously like slavery under a new guise. More upsetting to northern public opinion in general, a number of prominent ex-Confederate leaders were elected to Congress in the fall of 1865.

Johnson himself was partly responsible for this turn of events. Despite his lifelong feud with the planter class, he was generous in granting pardons to members of the old elite who came to him, hat in hand, and asked for them. When former Confederate Vice President Alexander Stephens and other proscribed ex-rebels were elected to Congress even though they had not been pardoned, Johnson granted them special amnesty so they could serve.

The growing rift between the president and Congress came into the open in December, when the House and Senate refused to seat the recently elected southern delegation. Instead of recognizing the state governments he had called into being, Congress established a joint committee to review Reconstruction policy and set further conditions for readmission of the seceded states.

Black Codes
Laws passed by southern states immediately after the Civil War in an effort to maintain the prewar social order. The codes attempted to tie freedmen to field work and prevent them from becoming equal to white southerners.

QUICK CHECK
Why did northerners and Republicans grow uneasy and disillusioned with Johnson's approach to Reconstruction?

Congress Takes the Initiative

The struggle over how to reconstruct the Union ended with Congress doing the job of setting policy all over again. The clash between Johnson and Congress was a matter of principle and could not be reconciled. President Johnson, an heir of the Democratic states' rights tradition, wanted to restore the prewar federal system as quickly as possible and without change except that states would not have the right to legalize slavery or to secede.

Most Republicans wanted firm guarantees that the old southern ruling class would not regain regional power and national influence by devising new ways to subjugate blacks. They favored a Reconstruction policy that would give the federal government authority to limit the political role of ex-Confederates and provide some protection for black citizenship.

Republican leaders—with the exception of a few extreme Radicals such as Charles Sumner—lacked any firm conviction that blacks were inherently equal to whites. They did believe, however, that in a modern democratic state, all citizens must have the same basic rights and opportunities, regardless of natural abilities. Principle coincided easily with political expediency; southern blacks, whatever their alleged shortcomings, were likely to be loyal to the Republican party that had emancipated them and thus increase that party's political power in the South.

The disagreement between the president and Congress became irreconcilable in early 1866, when Johnson vetoed two bills that had passed with overwhelming Republican support. The first extended the life of the **Freedmen's Bureau**—a temporary agency set up to aid the former slaves by providing relief, education, legal

Freedmen's Bureau
Agency established by Congress in March 1865 to provide freedmen with shelter, food, and medical aid and to help them establish schools and find employment. The Bureau was dissolved in 1872.

help, and assistance in obtaining land or employment. The second was a civil rights bill meant to nullify the Black Codes and guarantee to freedmen "full and equal benefit of all laws and proceedings for the security of person and property as is enjoyed by white citizens."

Johnson's vetoes shocked moderate Republicans who had expected the president to accept the relatively modest measures. Johnson succeeded in blocking the Freedmen's Bureau bill, although a modified version later passed. But the Civil Rights Act won the two-thirds majority necessary to override his veto, signifying that the president was now hopelessly at odds with most of the congressmen from what was supposed to be his own party. Never before had Congress overridden a presidential veto.

Johnson soon revealed that he intended to abandon the Republicans and place himself at the head of a new conservative party uniting the small minority of Republicans who supported him with a reviving Democratic party that was rallying behind his Reconstruction policy. In preparation for the elections of 1866, Johnson helped found the National Union movement to promote his plan to readmit the southern states to the Union without further qualifications. A National Union convention meeting in Philadelphia in August 1866 called for the election to Congress of men who endorsed the presidential plan for Reconstruction.

Meanwhile, the Republican majority on Capitol Hill, fearing that Johnson would not enforce civil rights legislation or that the courts would declare such federal laws unconstitutional, passed the **Fourteenth Amendment.** This, perhaps the most important of all the constitutional amendments, gave the federal government responsibility for guaranteeing equal rights under the law to all Americans. Section 1 defined national citizenship for the first time as extending to "all persons born or naturalized in the United States." The states were prohibited from abridging the rights of

Fourteenth Amendment
Ratified in 1868, this amendment provided citizenship to ex-slaves after the Civil War and constitutionally protected equal rights under the law for all citizens. Its provisions were used by Radical Republicans to enact a congressionally controlled Reconstruction policy of the former Confederate states.

RECONSTRUCTION AMENDMENTS, 1865–1870			
Amendment	Main Provisions	Congressional Passage (2/3 majority in each house required)	Ratification Process (3/4 of all states required, including ex-Confederate states)
13	Slavery prohibited in United States	January 1865	December 1865 (27 states, including 8 southern states)
14	National citizenship; State representation in Congress reduced proportionally to number of voters disfranchised; Former Confederates denied right to hold office; Confederate debt repudiated	June 1866	Rejected by 12 southern and border states, February 1867; Radicals make readmission of southern states hinge on ratification; ratified July 1868
15	Denial of franchise because of race, color, or past servitude explicitly prohibited	February 1869	Ratification required for readmission of Virginia, Texas, Mississippi, Georgia; ratified March 1870

American citizens and could not "deprive any person of life, liberty, or property, without due process of law; nor deny to any person… equal protection of the laws." The amendment was sent to the states with the understanding that southerners would have no chance of being readmitted to Congress unless their states ratified it.

The congressional elections of 1866 served as a referendum on the Fourteenth Amendment. Johnson opposed the amendment on the grounds that it created a "centralized" government and denied states the right to manage their own affairs; he also counseled southern state legislatures to reject it, and all except Tennessee followed his advice. But the president's case for state autonomy was weakened by the publicity resulting from bloody race riots in New Orleans and Memphis. These and other reported atrocities against blacks made it clear that the existing southern state governments were failing abysmally to protect the "life, liberty, or property" of the ex-slaves.

Johnson further weakened his cause by taking the stump on behalf of candidates who supported his policies. In his notorious "swing around the circle," he toured the nation, slandering his opponents in crude language and engaging in undignified exchanges with hecklers. Enraged by southern inflexibility and the antics of a president who acted as if he were still campaigning in the backwoods of Tennessee, northern voters repudiated the administration. The Republican majority in Congress increased to a solid two-thirds in both houses, and the Radical wing of the party gained strength at the expense of moderates and conservatives.

> **QUICK CHECK** ✓
>
> What events caused Congress to take the initiative in passing the Fourteenth Amendment?

Congressional Reconstruction Plan Enacted

Congress was now in a position to implement its own plan of Reconstruction. In 1867 and 1868, it passed a series of acts that nullified the president's initiatives and reorganized the South on a new basis. Generally referred to as **Radical Reconstruction**, the measures actually represented a compromise between genuine Radicals and more moderate elements within the party.

Consistent Radicals such as Senator Charles Sumner of Massachusetts and Congressmen Thaddeus Stevens of Pennsylvania and George Julian of Indiana wanted to reshape southern society before readmitting ex-Confederates to the Union. Their program of "regeneration before Reconstruction" required an extended period of military rule, confiscation and redistribution of large landholdings among the freedmen, and federal aid for schools to educate blacks and whites for citizenship. But the majority of Republican congressmen found such a program unacceptable because it broke too sharply with American traditions of federalism and regard for property rights and might mean that decades would pass before the Union was back in working order.

The First Reconstruction Act, passed over Johnson's veto on March 2, 1867, did place the South under the rule of the army by reorganizing the region into five military districts. But military rule would last for only a short time. Subsequent acts of 1867 and 1868 opened the way for the quick readmission of any state that framed and ratified a new constitution providing for black suffrage. Ex-Confederates disqualified from holding federal office under the Fourteenth Amendment were prohibited from voting for delegates to the constitutional conventions or in the elections to ratify the conventions' work. Since blacks were allowed to participate in this process, Republicans thought they had found a way to ensure that "loyal" men would dominate the new governments. Radical Reconstruction was based on the dubious

Radical Reconstruction
The Reconstruction Acts of 1867 divided the South into five military districts. They required states to guarantee black male suffrage and to ratify the Fourteenth Amendment as a condition of their readmission to the Union.

MAP

Reconstruction

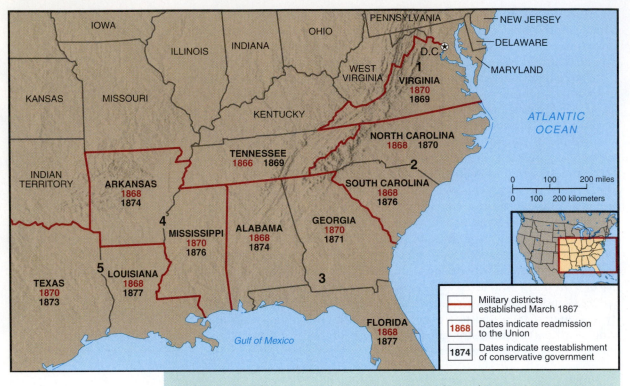

RECONSTRUCTION   During the Reconstruction era, the southern state governments passed through three phases: control by white ex-Confederates; domination by Republican legislators, both white and black; and, finally, the regain of control by conservative white Democrats.

What caused the removal of blacks from elected offices in the South?

QUICK CHECK ✓

What was "Radical Reconstruction" and how did it differ from previous plans?

assumption that once blacks had the vote, they would have the power to protect themselves against white supremacists' efforts to deny them their rights. The Reconstruction Acts thus signaled a retreat from the true Radical position that a sustained use of federal authority was needed to complete the transition from slavery to freedom and prevent the resurgence of the South's old ruling class Most Republicans were unwilling to embrace centralized government and an extended period of military rule over civilians. Yet a genuine spirit of democratic idealism did give legitimacy and fervor to the cause of black male suffrage. Enabling people who were so poor and downtrodden to have access to the ballot box was a bold and innovative application of the principle of government by the consent of the governed. The problem was finding a way to enforce equal suffrage under conditions then existing in the postwar South.

The Impeachment Crisis

The first obstacle to enforcement of congressional Reconstruction was resistance from the White House. Johnson thoroughly disapproved of the new policy and sought to thwart the will of Congress by administering the plan in his own

obstructive fashion. He immediately began to dismiss officeholders who sympathized with Radical Reconstruction, and he countermanded the orders of generals
in charge of southern military districts who were zealous in their enforcement of
the new legislation. Some Radical generals were transferred and replaced by conservative Democrats. Congress responded by passing laws designed to limit presidential
authority over Reconstruction matters. One of the measures was the Tenure of
Office Act, requiring Senate approval for the removal of cabinet officers and
other officials whose appointment had needed the consent of the Senate. Another
measure—a rider to an army appropriations bill—sought to limit Johnson's
authority to issue orders to military commanders.

Johnson objected vigorously to the restrictions on the grounds that they violated the constitutional doctrine of the separation of powers. When it became
clear that the president was resolute in fighting for his powers and using them to
resist the establishment of Radical regimes in the southern states, some congressmen began to call for his impeachment. A preliminary effort foundered in 1867,
but when Johnson tried to discharge Secretary of War Edwin Stanton—the only
Radical in the cabinet—and persisted in his efforts despite the disapproval of the
Senate, the pro-impeachment forces gained in strength.

In January 1868, Johnson ordered General Grant, who already commanded
the army, to replace Stanton as head of the War Department. But Grant had
his eye on the Republican presidential nomination
and refused to defy Congress. Johnson subsequently
appointed General Lorenzo Thomas, who agreed to
serve. Faced with this apparent violation of the Tenure
of Office Act, the House voted overwhelmingly to
impeach the president on February 24, and he was
placed on trial before the Senate.

Because seven Republican senators broke with
the party leadership and voted for acquittal, the effort
to convict Johnson and remove him from office fell
one vote short of the necessary two-thirds. This
outcome resulted in part from a skillful defense.
Attorneys for the president argued for a narrow interpretation of the constitutional provision that a president could be impeached only for "high crimes and
misdemeanors," asserting that this referred only to
indictable offenses. Responding to the charge that
Johnson had deliberately violated the Tenure of
Office Act, the defense contended that the law did not

Impeachment
Trial of
Andrew
Johnson

THE PAROQUET OF THE WH—E HO—E.

IMPEACHED Andrew Johnson's successful defense
against conviction in his impeachment case centered on his
invocation of the Constitution to defend his presidential
rights and powers. Impeached in 1868, Johnson escaped
conviction by a single vote.

**Although the impeachment failed, what message
did it send to the nation?**

apply to the removal of Stanton because he had been appointed by Lincoln, not Johnson.

The prosecution countered with a different interpretation of the Tenure of Office Act, but the core of their case was that Johnson had abused the powers of his office in an effort to sabotage the congressional Reconstruction policy. Obstructing the will of the legislative branch, they claimed, was sufficient grounds for conviction even if no crime had been committed. The Republicans who broke ranks to vote for acquittal could not endorse such a broad view of the impeachment power. They feared that removal of a president for essentially political reasons would threaten the constitutional balance of powers and open the way to legislative supremacy over the executive.

Failure to remove Johnson from office was an embarrassment to congressional Republicans, but the episode did ensure that Reconstruction in the South would proceed as the majority in Congress intended. During the trial, Johnson helped influence the verdict by pledging to enforce the Reconstruction Acts, and he held to this promise during his remaining months in office. Unable to depose the president, the Radicals had at least succeeded in neutralizing his opposition to their program.

QUICK CHECK ✓

What prompted Congress to initiate impeachment against Johnson, and what was the outcome of that action?

Reconstructing Southern Society

WHAT? problems did southern society face during Reconstruction?

Carl Schurz, *Report on the Condition of the South* (1865)

The Civil War left the South devastated, demoralized, and destitute. Slavery was dead, but what this meant for future relationships between whites and blacks was still in doubt. The overwhelming majority of southern whites wanted to keep blacks adrift between slavery and freedom—without rights, in a status resembling that of the "free Negroes" of the Old South. Blacks sought to be independent of their former masters and viewed the acquisition of land, education, and the vote as the best means of achieving this goal. The thousands of northerners who went south after the war for materialistic or humanitarian reasons hoped to extend Yankee "civilization" to what they viewed as an unenlightened and barbarous region. For most of them, this reformation required aiding the freed slaves.

The struggle of these groups to achieve their conflicting goals bred chaos, violence, and instability. This was scarcely an ideal setting for an experiment in interracial democracy, but one was attempted nonetheless. Its success depended on massive and sustained support from the federal government. To the extent that this was forthcoming, progressive reform could be achieved. When it faltered, the forces of reaction and white supremacy were unleashed.

Reorganizing Land and Labor

The Civil War scarred the southern landscape and wrecked its economy. One devastated area—central South Carolina—looked to an 1865 observer "like a broad black streak of ruin and desolation." Several major cities—including Atlanta, Columbia, and Richmond—were gutted by fire. Most factories were dismantled or destroyed, and long stretches of railroad were torn up.

Nor was there adequate investment capital available for rebuilding. The substantial wealth represented by Confederate currency and bonds had melted away, and emancipation of the slaves had divested the propertied classes of their most valuable and productive assets. According to some estimates, the South's per capita wealth in 1865 was only about half what it had been in 1860.

Recovery could not even begin until a new labor system replaced slavery. It was widely assumed in both the North and the South that southern prosperity would continue to depend on cotton and that the plantation was the most efficient unit for producing the crop. Hindering efforts to rebuild the plantation economy were lack of capital, the deep-rooted belief of southern whites that blacks would work only under compulsion, and the freedmen's resistance to labor conditions that recalled slavery.

Blacks strongly preferred to determine their own economic relationships, and for a time they had reason to hope the federal government would support their ambitions. The freed slaves were placed in a precarious position and were, in effect, fighting a two-front war. Although they were grateful for the federal aid in ending slavery, freed slaves often had ideas about freedom that contradicted the plans of their northern allies. Many ex-slaves wanted to hold on to the family-based communal work methods that they utilized during slavery. Freed slaves in areas of South Carolina, for example, attempted to maintain the family task system rather than adopting the individual piecework system pushed by northern capitalists. Many ex-slaves opposed plans to turn them into wage laborers who produced exclusively for a market. Finally, freed slaves often wanted to stay on the land their families had spent generations farming rather than move elsewhere to assume plots of land as individual farmers.

While not guaranteeing all of the freed slaves' hopes for economic self-determination, the northern military attempted to establish a new economic base for the freed men and women. General Sherman, hampered by the huge numbers of black fugitives that followed his army on its famous march, issued an order in January 1865 that set aside the islands and coastal areas of Georgia and South Carolina for exclusive black occupancy on 40-acre plots. Furthermore, the Freedmen's Bureau, as one of its many responsibilities, was given control of hundreds of thousands of acres of abandoned or confiscated land and was authorized to make 40-acre grants to black settlers for three-year periods, after which they would have the option to buy at low prices. By June 1865, forty thousand black farmers were at work on 300,000 acres of what they thought would be their own land.

But for most of them the dream of "forty acres and a mule," or some other arrangement that would give them control of their land and labor, was not to be realized. President Johnson pardoned the owners of most of the land consigned to the ex-slaves by Sherman and the Freedmen's Bureau, and proposals for an effective program of land confiscation and redistribution failed to get through Congress. Among the considerations prompting most congressmen to oppose land reform were a tenderness for property rights, fear of sapping the freedmen's initiative by giving them something they allegedly had not earned, and the desire to restore cotton production as quickly as possible to increase agricultural exports and stabilize the economy. Consequently, most blacks in physical possession of small farms failed to acquire title, and the mass of freedmen were left with little or no prospect of becoming landowners. Recalling the plight of southern blacks in 1865, an ex-slave later wrote that "they were set free without

LISTEN
Free at Last

Affidavit of ex-Slave Enoch Braston (1866)

Clinton B. Fisk, "Plain Counsels for Freedom" (1865)

Legal Form for the Restoration of Confiscated Property

Southern Skepticism of the Freedmen's Bureau (1866)

SHARECROPPING The Civil War brought emancipation to slaves, but the sharecropping system kept many of them economically bound to their employers. At the end of a year the sharecropper tenants might owe most—or all—of what they had made to their landlord. Here, a sharecropping family poses in front of their cabin. Ex-slaves often built their living quarters near woods in order to have a ready supply of fuel for heating and cooking. The cabin's chimney lists away from the house so that it can be easily pushed away from the living quarters should it catch fire. (*Source: Collection of The New-York Historical Society, negative number 50475.*)

How did sharecropping work in practice to keep many blacks from ever owning land?

A Sharecrop
Contract
(1882)

sharecropping

After the Civil War, the southern states adopted a sharecropping system as a compromise between former slaves, who wanted land of their own, and former slave owners, who needed labor. The landowners provided land, tools, and seed to a farming family, who in turn provided labor. The resulting crop was divided between them, with the farmers receiving a "share" of one-third to one-half of the crop.

a dollar, without a foot of land, and without the wherewithal to get the next meal even."

Despite their poverty and landlessness, ex-slaves were reluctant to settle down and commit themselves to wage labor for their former masters. Many took to the road, hoping to find something better. Some were still expecting grants of land, but others were simply trying to increase their bargaining power. One freedman later recalled that an important part of being free was that, "we could move around [and] change bosses." As the end of 1865 approached, many freedmen had still not signed up for the coming season; anxious planters feared that blacks were plotting to seize land by force. Within a few weeks, however, most holdouts signed for the best terms they could get.

One common form of agricultural employment in 1866 was a contract labor system. Under this system, workers committed themselves for a year in return for fixed wages, a substantial portion of which was withheld until after the harvest. Since many planters were inclined to drive hard bargains, abuse their workers, or cheat them at the end of the year, the Freedmen's Bureau assumed the role of reviewing the contracts and enforcing them. But bureau officials had differing notions of what it meant to protect African Americans from exploitation. Some stood up strongly for the rights of the freedmen; others served as allies of the planters.

Growing up alongside the contract system and eventually displacing it was an alternative capital-labor relationship—**sharecropping**. First in small groups known as "squads" and later as individual families, blacks worked a piece of land independently for a fixed share of the crop, usually one-half. Credit-starved landlords liked this arrangement because it did not require much expenditure in advance of the harvest and the tenant shared the risks of crop failure or a fall in cotton prices.

African Americans initially viewed sharecropping as a step up from wage labor in the direction of landownership. But during the 1870s, this form of tenancy evolved into a new kind of servitude. Croppers had to live on credit until their cotton was sold, and planters or merchants seized the chance to "provision" them at high prices and exorbitant rates of interest. Creditors were entitled to deduct what was owed to them out of the tenant's share of the crop, and this left most sharecroppers with no net profit at the end of the year—more often than not with a debt that had to be worked off in subsequent years.

QUICK CHECK ✓

What were the conflicting visions of the planters, the Freedmen's Bureau agents, and the freed slaves with regard to what a new labor system should look like?

Black Codes: A New Name for Slavery?

While landless African Americans in the countryside were being reduced to economic dependence, those in towns and cities found themselves living in an increasingly segregated society. The Black Codes of 1865 attempted to require separation of the races in public places and facilities; when most of the codes were overturned by federal authorities as violations of the Civil Rights Act of 1866, the same end was often achieved through private initiative and community pressure. In some cities, blacks successfully resisted being consigned to separate streetcars by appealing to the military during the period when it exercised authority or by organizing boycotts. But they found it almost impossible to gain admittance to most hotels, restaurants, and other privately owned establishments catering to whites. Although separate black, or "Jim Crow," cars were not yet the rule on railroads, African Americans were often denied first-class accommodations. After 1868, black-supported Republican governments passed civil rights acts requiring equal access to public facilities, but little effort was made to enforce the legislation.

The Black Codes had other onerous provisions meant to control African Americans and return them to quasi-slavery. Most codes even made black unemployment a crime, which meant blacks had to make long-term contracts with white employers or be arrested for vagrancy. Others limited the rights of African Americans to own property or engage in occupations other than those of servant or laborer. The codes were set aside by the actions of Congress, the military, and the Freedmen's Bureau, but vagrancy laws remained in force across the South.

Furthermore, private violence and discrimination against blacks continued on a massive scale unchecked by state authorities. Hundreds, perhaps thousands, of blacks were murdered by whites in 1865–1866, and few of the perpetrators were brought to justice. The imposition of military rule in 1867 was designed in part to protect former slaves from such violence and intimidation, but the task was beyond the capacity of the few thousand troops stationed in the South. When new constitutions were approved and states readmitted to the Union under the congressional plan in 1868, the problem became more severe. White opponents of Radical Reconstruction adopted systematic terrorism and organized mob violence to keep blacks away from the polls.

The freed slaves, in the face of opposition from both their Democratic enemies and some of their Republican allies, tried to defend themselves by organizing their own militia groups for protection and to assert their political rights. However, the militia groups were not powerful enough to overcome the growing power of the anti-Republican forces. Also, the military presence was progressively reduced, leaving the new Republican regimes to fight a losing battle against armed white supremacists.

Republican Rule in the South

Hastily organized in 1867, the southern Republican party dominated the constitution making of 1868 and the regimes that came out of it. The party was an attempted coalition of three social groups (which varied in their relative strength from state to state). One was the same class that was becoming the backbone of the Republican party in the North—businessmen with an interest in enlisting government aid for private enterprise. Many Republicans of this stripe were recent arrivals from the North—the so-called carpetbaggers—but some were scalawags, former Whig planters or merchants who were born in the South or had immigrated to the region before the war and now saw a chance to realize their dreams for commercial and industrial development.

Poor white farmers, especially those from upland areas where Unionist sentiment had been strong during the Civil War, were a second element in the original coalition. These owners of small farms expected the party to favor their interests at the expense of the wealthy landowners and to come to their aid with special legislation when—as was often the case in this period of economic upheaval—they faced the loss of their homesteads to creditors. Newly enfranchised blacks were the third group to which the Republicans appealed. Blacks formed the vast majority of the Republican rank and file in most states and were concerned mainly with education, civil rights, and landownership.

Under the best of conditions, these coalitions would have been difficult to maintain. Each group had its own distinct goals and did not fully support the aims of the other segments. White yeomen, for example, had a deeply rooted resistance to black equality. And for how long could one expect essentially conservative businessmen to support costly measures for the elevation or relief of the lower classes of either race? In some states, astute Democratic politicians exploited these divisions by appealing to disaffected white Republicans.

But during the relatively brief period when they were in power in the South—varying from one to nine years depending on the state—the Republicans chalked up some notable achievements. They established (on paper at least) the South's first adequate systems of public education, democratized state and local government, and appropriated funds for an enormous expansion of public services and responsibilities.

As important as these social and political reforms were, they took second place to the Republicans' major effort—to foster economic development and restore southern prosperity by subsidizing the construction of railroads and other internal improvements. But the policy of aiding railroads turned out to be disastrous, even though it addressed the region's real economic needs and was initially very popular. Extravagance, corruption, and routes laid out in response to local political pressure rather than on sound economic grounds made for an increasing burden of public debt and taxation.

The policy did not produce the promised payoff of efficient, cheap transportation. Subsidized railroads frequently went bankrupt, leaving the taxpayers holding the bag. When the Panic of 1873 brought many southern state governments to the verge of bankruptcy, and railroad building came to an end, it was clear the Republicans' "gospel of prosperity" through state aid to private enterprise had failed miserably. Their political opponents, many of whom had originally favored such policies, now saw an opportunity to take advantage of the situation by charging that Republicans had ruined the southern economy.

In general, the Radical regimes failed to conduct public business honestly and efficiently. Embezzlement of public funds and bribery of state lawmakers or officials were common occurrences. State debts and tax burdens rose enormously, mainly because governments had undertaken heavy new responsibilities, but partly because of waste and graft. The situation varied from state to state; ruling cliques in Louisiana and South Carolina were guilty of much wrongdoing, yet Mississippi had a relatively honest and frugal regime.

Furthermore, southern corruption was not exceptional, nor was it a special result of the extension of suffrage to uneducated African Americans, as critics of Radical Reconstruction have claimed. It was part of a national pattern during an era when private interests considered buying government favors to be a part of the cost of doing business, and many politicians expected to profit by obliging them.

Blacks bore only a limited responsibility for the dishonesty of the Radical governments. Although sixteen African Americans served in Congress—two in the Senate—between 1869 and 1880, only in South Carolina did blacks constitute a majority of even one house of the state legislature. Furthermore, no black governors were elected during Reconstruction (although Pinkney B. S. Pinchback served for a time as acting governor of Louisiana). The biggest grafters were opportunistic whites. Some of the most notorious were carpetbaggers, but others were native southerners. Businessmen offering bribes included members of the prewar gentry who were staunch opponents of Radical programs. Some black legislators went with the tide and accepted "loans" from those railroad lobbyists who would pay most for their votes, but the same men could usually be depended on to vote the will of their constituents on civil rights or educational issues.

If blacks served or supported corrupt and wasteful regimes, it was because the alternative was dire. Although the Democrats, or Conservatives as they called themselves in some states, made sporadic efforts to attract African American voters, it was clear that if they won control, they would attempt to strip blacks of their civil and political rights. But opponents of Radical Reconstruction were able to capitalize on racial prejudice and persuade many Americans that "good government" was synonymous with white supremacy.

Contrary to myth, the small number of African Americans elected to state or national office during Reconstruction demonstrated on the average more integrity and competence than their white counterparts. Most were fairly well educated, having been free Negroes or unusually privileged slaves before the war. Among the most capable were Robert Smalls (whose career was described earlier); Blanche K. Bruce of Mississippi, elected to the U.S. Senate in 1874 after rising to deserved prominence in the Republican party of his home state; Congressman Robert Brown Elliott of South Carolina, an adroit politician who was also a consistent champion of civil rights; and Congressman James T. Rapier of Alabama, who stirred Congress and the nation in 1873 with his eloquent appeals for federal aid to southern education and new laws to enforce equal rights for African Americans.

IMAGE

"From Plantation to the Senate"

QUICK CHECK

What were the three social groups that made up the southern Republican party?

Slave Narrative, "The Story of Mattie J. Jackson"

Claiming Public and Private Rights

The ways that freed slaves claimed rights for themselves were as important as party politics to the changing political culture of the Reconstruction South. Ex-slaves fought for their rights not only in negotiations with employers and in public meetings and convention halls, but also through the institutions they created, and perhaps most important, the households they formed.

Some ex-slaves used institutions formerly closed to them like the courts to assert rights they considered part of citizenship. Many ex-slaves rushed to formalize their marriages before the law, and they used their new status to fight for custody of children who had been taken from them under the apprenticeship provisions of the Black Clodes. Ex-slaves brought lawsuits against white people as well as other blacks, suing over domestic violence, child support, assault, and debt. Freed women sued their husbands for desertion and alimony in order to enlist the Freedmen's Bureau to help them claim property from men. Immediately after the war, freed people flocked to create institutions that had been denied to them under slavery: churches, fraternal and benevolent associations, political organizations, and schools. Many joined all-black denominations such as the African Methodist Episcopal church, which provided freedom from white dominance and a more congenial style of worship. Black women formed all-black chapters of organizations such as the Women's Christian Temperance Union, and

This church was founded in 1867 by Rev. John Jasper, who continued as pastor until death in 1901. Rev. R. V. Peyton served as pastor until 1924, and was succeeded by Rev. A. W. Brown, the present pastor.

BLACK CHURCHES As slaves, many blacks attended white churches and listened to sermons preached by white ministers. After the Civil War and the end of slavery, African Americans joined or founded black churches, such as the Sixth Mount Zion Baptist Church of Richmond, Virginia. This postcard of the church's history includes a photograph of its founding pastor, John Jasper.

Why do you think ex-slaves were anxious for their own churches?

FREEDMEN'S SCHOOLS   A Freedmen's school, one of the more successful endeavors supported by the Freedmen's Bureau. The bureau, working with teachers from northern abolitionist and missionary societies, founded thousands of schools for freed slaves and poor whites.

What brought the end of the Freedmen's Bureau?

created their own women's clubs to oppose lynching and work for "uplift" in the black community.

A top priority for most ex-slaves was the opportunity to educate their children; the first schools for freed people were all-black institutions established by the Freedmen's Bureau and various northern missionary societies. At the time, having been denied all education during the antebellum period, most blacks viewed separate schooling as an opportunity rather than as a form of discrimination. However, these schools were precursors to the segregated public school systems first instituted by Republican governments. Only in city schools of New Orleans and at the University of South Carolina were there serious attempts during Reconstruction to bring white and black students together in the same classrooms.

In a variety of ways, African American men and women during Reconstruction claimed freedom in the "private" realm as well as the public sphere by claiming rights to their own families and building their own institutions. They did so in the face of the vigorous efforts of their former masters as well as the new government agencies to control their private lives and shape their new identities as husbands, wives, and citizens.

QUICK CHECK

What new rights and institutions did free blacks create and use following emancipation?

Retreat from Reconstruction

WHAT
forces brought on the end of Reconstruction?

The era of Reconstruction began coming to an end almost before it got started. Although it was only a scant three years from the end of the Civil War, the impeachment crisis of 1868 represented the high point of popular interest in Reconstruction issues. That year, Ulysses S. Grant was elected president. From 1868 on, political issues other than southern Reconstruction moved to the forefront of national politics, and the plight of African Americans in the South receded in white consciousness.

Final Efforts of Reconstruction

Fifteenth Amendment
Ratified in 1870, this amendment prohibited the denial or abridgment of the right to vote by the federal government or state governments on the basis of race, color, or prior condition as a slave. It was intended to guarantee African Americans the right to vote in the South.

The Republican effort to make equal rights for blacks the law of the land culminated in the **Fifteenth Amendment**. Passed by Congress in 1869 and ratified by the states in 1870, the amendment prohibited any state from denying a male citizen the right to vote because of race, color, or previous condition of servitude. A more radical version, requiring universal manhood suffrage, was rejected partly because it departed too sharply from traditional views of federal-state relations. States therefore could still limit the suffrage by imposing literacy tests, property qualifications, or poll taxes allegedly applying to all racial groups; such devices would eventually be used to strip southern blacks of the right to vote. But the makers of the amendment did not foresee this result. They believed their action would prevent future Congresses or southern constitutional conventions from repealing or nullifying the provisions for black male suffrage included in the Reconstruction Acts. A secondary aim was to enfranchise African Americans in those northern states that still denied them the vote.

Many feminists were bitterly disappointed that the amendment did not extend the vote to women as well as freedmen. A militant wing of the women's rights movement, led by Elizabeth Cady Stanton and Susan B. Anthony, was so angered that the Constitution was being amended in a way that, in effect, made gender a qualification for voting that they campaigned against ratification of the Fifteenth Amendment. Another group of feminists led by Lucy Stone supported the amendment on the grounds that this was "the Negro's hour" and that women could afford to wait a few years for the vote. This disagreement divided the woman suffrage movement for a generation to come.

The Grant administration was charged with enforcing the amendment and protecting black men's voting rights in the reconstructed states. Since survival of the Republican regimes depended on African American support, political partisanship dictated federal action, even though the North's emotional and ideological commitment to black citizenship was waning.

1868 Democratic National Convention

The State of the South (1872)

QUICK CHECK

What did the Fifteenth Amendment stipulate, and whom did it benefit?

Hannah Irwin Describes Ku Klux Klan Ride

Albion W. Tourgee, Letter on KKK Activities

A Reign of Terror Against Blacks

Between 1868 and 1872, the main threat to southern Republican regimes came from the **Ku Klux Klan** and other secret societies bent on restoring white supremacy by intimidating blacks who sought to exercise their political rights. First organized

THE ELECTION OF 1868			
Candidate	Party	Popular Vote	Electoral Vote
Grant	Republican	3,012,833	214
Seymour	Democratic	2,703,249	80
Not voted*			23

*Unreconstructed states did not participate in the election.

Ku Klux Klan

A secret terrorist society first organized in Tennessee in 1866. The original Klan's goals were to disfranchise African Americans, stop Reconstruction, and restore the prewar social order of the South. The Ku Klux Klan re-formed after World War II to promote white supremacy in the wake of the "Second Reconstruction."

in Tennessee in 1866, the Klan spread rapidly to other states, adopting increasingly lawless and brutal tactics. A grassroots vigilante movement and not a centralized conspiracy, the Klan thrived on local initiative and gained support from whites of all social classes. Its secrecy, decentralization, popular support, and utter ruthlessness made it very difficult to suppress. As soon as blacks had been granted the right to vote, hooded "night riders" began to visit the cabins of those who were known to be active Republicans; some victims were only threatened, but others were whipped or even murdered.

Such methods were first used effectively in the presidential election of 1868. Grant lost in Louisiana and Georgia mainly because the Klan—or the Knights of the White Camellia, as the Louisiana variant was called—launched a reign of terror to prevent prospective black voters from exercising their rights. In Louisiana, political violence claimed more than a thousand lives, and in Arkansas, which Grant managed to carry, more than two hundred Republicans, including a congressman, were assassinated.

Thereafter, Klan terrorism was directed mainly at Republican state governments. Virtual insurrections broke out in Arkansas, Tennessee, North Carolina, and parts of South Carolina. Republican governors called out the state militia to fight the Klan, but only the Arkansas militia succeeded in bringing it to heel.

KU KLUX KLAN   This 1868 photograph shows typical regalia of members of the Ku Klux Klan, a secret white supremacist organization. Before elections, hooded Klansmen terrorized African Americans to discourage them from voting.

Why did the Klansmen disguise themselves in this way?

THE ELECTION OF 1872			
Candidate	Party	Popular Vote	Electoral Vote*
Grant	Republican	3,597,132	286
Greeley	Democratic and Liberal Republican	2,834,125	Greeley died before the electoral college voted.

*Out of a total of 366 electoral votes. Greeley's votes were divided among the four minor candidates.

Force acts

Congress attacked the Ku Klux Klan with three Enforcement or "Force" acts in 1870–1871. Designed to protect black voters in the South, these laws placed state elections under federal jurisdiction and imposed fines and imprisonment on those guilty of interfering with any citizen exercising his right to vote.

In Tennessee, North Carolina, and Georgia, Klan activities helped undermine Republican control, thus allowing the Democrats to come to power in all of these states by 1870.

In 1870–1871, Congress passed a series of laws to enforce the Fifteenth Amendment by providing federal protection for black suffrage and authorizing use of the army against the Klan. The **Force acts,** also known as the Ku Klux Klan acts, made interference with voting rights a federal crime and established provisions for government supervision of elections. In addition, the legislation empowered the president to call out troops and suspend the writ of habeas corpus—the legal tool individuals could use to challenge their imprisonment—to quell insurrection. In 1871–1872, thousands of suspected Klansmen were arrested by the military or U.S. marshals, and the writ was suspended in nine counties of South Carolina that had been virtually taken over by the secret order. Although most of the accused Klansmen were never brought to trial, were acquitted, or received suspended sentences, the enforcement effort was vigorous enough to put a damper on hooded terrorism and ensure relatively fair and peaceful elections in 1872.

A heavy black turnout in these elections enabled the Republicans to hold on to power in most states of the Deep South, despite efforts of the Democratic-Conservative opposition to cut into the Republican vote by taking moderate positions on racial and economic issues. This setback prompted the Democratic-Conservatives to make a significant change in their strategy and ideology. No longer did they try to take votes away from the Republicans by proclaiming support for black suffrage and government aid to business. Instead they began to appeal openly to white supremacy and to the traditional Democratic and agrarian hostility to government promotion of economic development. Consequently, they were able to bring back to the polls a portion of the white electorate, mostly small farmers.

This new and more effective electoral strategy dovetailed with a resurgence of violence meant to reduce Republican, especially black Republican, voting. The new reign of terror differed from the previously discussed Klan episode; its agents no longer wore masks but acted quite openly. They were effective because the northern public was increasingly disenchanted with federal intervention on behalf of what were widely viewed as corrupt and tottering Republican regimes. Grant used force in the South for the last time in 1874 when an overt paramilitary organization in Louisiana, known as the White League, tried to overthrow a Republican government accused of stealing an election. When another unofficial militia in Mississippi instigated a series of bloody race riots prior to the state elections of 1875, Grant refused the governor's request for federal troops. As a result, black voters were successfully intimidated—one county registered only seven Republican votes where there had been a black majority of two thousand—and Mississippi fell to the Democratic-Conservatives.

By 1876, Republicans held on to only three southern states: South Carolina, Louisiana, and Florida. Partly because of Grant's hesitant and inconsistent use of presidential power, but mainly because the northern electorate would no longer tolerate military action to sustain Republican governments and black voting rights, Radical Reconstruction was falling into total eclipse.

Reunion and the New South

The end of Radical Reconstruction in 1877 opened the way to a reconciliation of North and South. But the costs of reunion were high for less privileged groups in the South. The civil and political rights of African Americans, left unprotected, were progressively and relentlessly stripped away by white supremacist regimes. Lower-class whites saw their interests sacrificed to those of capitalists and landlords. Despite the rhetoric hailing a prosperous "New South," the region remained poor and open to exploitation by northern business interests.

WHO
benefited and who suffered from the reconciliation of North and South?

The Compromise of 1877

The election of 1876 pitted Rutherford B. Hayes of Ohio, a Republican governor untainted by the scandals of the Grant era, against Governor Samuel J. Tilden of New York, a Democratic reformer who had battled against Tammany Hall and the Tweed Ring. Honest government was apparently the electorate's highest priority. When the returns came in, Tilden had clearly won the popular vote and seemed likely to win a narrow victory in the electoral college. But the result was placed in doubt when the returns from the three southern states still controlled by the Republicans—South Carolina, Florida, and Louisiana—were contested. If Hayes were to be awarded these three states, plus one contested electoral vote in Oregon, Republican strategists realized, he would triumph in the electoral college by a single vote.

The outcome of the election remained undecided for months, plunging the nation into a major political crisis. To resolve the impasse, Congress appointed a special electoral commission of fifteen members to determine who would receive the votes of the disputed states. Originally composed of seven Democrats, seven Republicans, and an independent, the commission fell under Republican control when the independent member resigned to

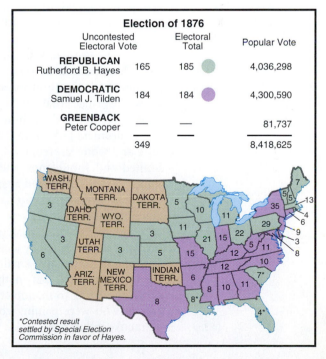

Election of 1876

	Uncontested Electoral Vote		Electoral Total	Popular Vote
REPUBLICAN Rutherford B. Hayes	165	🟢	185	4,036,298
DEMOCRATIC Samuel J. Tilden	184	🟣	184	4,300,590
GREENBACK Peter Cooper	—		—	81,737
	349			8,418,625

*Contested result settled by Special Election Commission in favor of Hayes.

Compromise of 1877

Compromise struck during the contested presidential election of 1876, in which Democrats accepted the election of Rutherford B. Hayes (Republican) in exchange for the withdrawal of federal troops from the South and the ending of Reconstruction.

QUICK CHECK ✓

Who agreed upon the Compromise of 1877, and why?

run for the Senate and a Republican was appointed to take his place. The commission split along party lines and voted eight to seven to award Hayes all of the disputed votes. But this decision still had to be ratified by both houses of Congress, and in the House there was strong Democratic opposition. To ensure Hayes's election, Republican leaders negotiated secretly with conservative southern Democrats, some of whom seemed willing to abandon the filibuster if the last troops were withdrawn and home rule restored to the South. Eventually an informal bargain was struck, which historians have dubbed the **Compromise of 1877**. What precisely was agreed to and by whom remains a matter of dispute, but one thing at least was understood by both sides: Hayes would be president and southern blacks would be abandoned to their fate. With southern Democratic acquiescence, the filibuster was broken, and Hayes took the oath of office. He immediately ordered the army not to resist a Democratic takeover of state governments in South Carolina and Louisiana. Thus fell the last of the Radical governments, and the entire South was firmly under the control of white Democrats. The trauma of the war and Reconstruction had destroyed the chances for a renewal of two-party competition among white southerners.

"Redeeming" a New South

Redeemers

A loose coalition of prewar Democrats, Confederate army veterans, and southern Whigs who took over southern state governments in the 1870s, supposedly "redeeming" them from the corruption of Reconstruction. They shared a commitment to white supremacy and laissez-faire economics.

The men who came to power after Radical Reconstruction fell in one southern state after another are usually referred to as the **Redeemers**. They had differing backgrounds and previous loyalties. Some were members of the Old South's ruling planter class who had warmly supported secession and now sought to reestablish the old order with as few changes as possible. Others, of middle-class origin or outlook, favored commercial and industrial interests over agrarian groups and called for a New South committed to diversified economic development. A third group consisted of professional politicians bending with the prevailing winds.

The Redeemers subscribed to no single coherent ideology but are perhaps best characterized as power brokers mediating among the dominant interest groups of the South in ways that served their own political advantage. In many ways, the "rings" that they established on the state and county level were analogous to the political machines developing at the same time in northern cities.

Redeemers did, however, agree on and endorse two basic principles: laissez-faire and white supremacy. Laissez-faire—the notion that government should be limited and should not intervene openly and directly in the economy—could unite planters, frustrated at seeing direct state support going to businessmen, and capitalist promoters, who had come to realize that low taxes and freedom from government regulation were even more advantageous than state subsidies. It soon became clear that the Redeemers responded only to privileged and entrenched interest groups, especially landlords, merchants, and industrialists, and offered little or nothing to tenants, small farmers, and working people. As industrialization began to gather steam in the 1880s, Democratic regimes became increasingly accommodating to manufacturing interests and hospitable to agents of northern capital who were gaining control of the South's transportation system and its extractive industries.

James T. Rapier Testimony on Sharecropping (1880)

The growing industrialization that was characteristic of the New South is evident in this photograph of a South Carolina cotton mill.

How did steam power and the abundance of cheap coal in the Appalachians affect the textile industry in the North?

White supremacy was the principal rallying cry that brought the Redeemers to power in the first place. Once in office, they found they could stay there by charging that opponents of ruling Democratic cliques were trying to divide "the white man's party" and open the way for a return to "black domination." Appeals to racism could also deflect attention from the economic grievances of groups without political clout.

The new governments were more economical than those of Reconstruction, mainly because they cut back drastically on appropriations for schools and other needed public services. But they were scarcely more honest—embezzlement of funds and bribery of officials continued to occur to an alarming extent. The Redeemer regimes of the late 1870s and 1880s badly neglected the interests of small white farmers. Whites, as well as blacks, were suffering from the notorious crop lien system, which gave local merchants who advanced credit at high rates of interest during the growing season the right to take possession of the harvested crop on terms that buried farmers deeper and deeper in debt. As a result, increasing numbers of whites lost title to their homesteads and were reduced to tenancy. When a depression of world cotton prices added to the burden of a ruinous credit system, agrarian protesters began to challenge the ruling elite, first through the Southern Farmers' Alliance of the late 1880s and then by supporting its political descendant—the Populist party of the 1890s.

QUICK CHECK

Which principles divided, and which united, the new "Redeemer" governments?

The Rise of Jim Crow

African Americans bore the greatest hardships imposed by the new order. From 1876 through the first decade of the twentieth century, southern states imposed a series of restrictions on black civil rights known as **Jim Crow laws.** While segregation and disfranchisement began as informal arrangements, they culminated in a legal regime of separation and exclusion that took firm hold in the 1890s.

The rise of Jim Crow practices in the political arena was especially bitter for southern blacks who realized that only political power could ensure other rights. The Redeemers promised, as part of the understanding that led to the end of federal intervention in 1877, that they would respect the rights of blacks as set forth in the Fourteenth and Fifteenth Amendments. Governor Wade Hampton of South Carolina was especially vocal in pledging that African Americans would not be reduced to second-class citizenship by the new regimes. But when blacks tried to vote Republican in the "redeemed" states, they encountered renewed violence and intimidation. "Bulldozing" African American voters remained common practice in state elections during the late 1870s and early 1880s; those blacks who withstood the threat of losing their jobs or being evicted from tenant farms if they voted for the party of Lincoln were visited at night and literally whipped into line. The message was clear: Vote Democratic, or vote not at all.

Furthermore, white Democrats now controlled the electoral machinery and were able to manipulate the black vote by stuffing ballot boxes, discarding unwanted votes, or reporting fraudulent totals. Some states also imposed complicated new voting requirements to discourage black participation. Full-scale disfranchisement did not occur until literacy tests and other legalized obstacles to voting were imposed in the period from 1890 to 1910, but by that time, less formal

Jim Crow laws

Laws enacted by states to segregate the population. They became widespread in the South after Reconstruction.

SUPREME COURT DECISIONS AFFECTING BLACK CIVIL RIGHTS, 1875–1900	
Case	**Effects of Court's Decisions**
Hall v. DeCuir (1878)	Struck down Louisiana law prohibiting racial discrimination by "common carriers" (railroads, steamboats, buses). Declared the law a "burden" on interstate commerce, over which states had no authority.
United States v. Harris (1882)	Declared federal laws to punish crimes such as murder and assault unconstitutional. Declared such crimes to be the sole concern of local government. Ignored the frequent racial motivation behind such crimes in the South.
Civil Rights Cases (1883)	Struck down Civil Rights Act of 1875. Declared that Congress may not legislate on civil rights unless a state passes a discriminatory law. Declared the Fourteenth Amendment silent on racial discrimination by private citizens.
Plessy v. Ferguson (1896)	Upheld Louisiana statute requiring "separate but equal" accommodations on railroads. Declared that segregation is *not* necessarily discrimination.
Williams v. Mississippi (1898)	Upheld state law requiring a literacy test to qualify for voting. Refused to find any implication of racial discrimination in the law, although it permitted illiterate whites to vote if they "understood" the Constitution. Using such laws, southern states rapidly disfranchised blacks.

and comprehensive methods had already made a mockery of the Fifteenth Amendment.

Nevertheless, blacks continued to vote freely in some localities until the 1890s; a few districts, like the one Robert Smalls represented, even elected black Republicans to Congress during the immediate post-Reconstruction period. The last of these, Representative George H. White of North Carolina, served until 1901. His farewell address eloquently conveyed the agony of southern blacks in the era of Jim Crow (strict segregation):

> These parting words are in behalf of an outraged, heart-broken, bruised, and bleeding but God-fearing people, faithful, industrious, loyal people—rising people, full of

LYNCHING Perhaps no event better expresses the cruel and barbaric nature of the racism and white supremacy that swept the South after Reconstruction than lynching. Although lynchings were not confined to the South, most occurred there, and African American men were the most frequent victims. Here two men lean out of a barn window above a black man who is about to be hanged. Others below prepare to set on fire the pile of hay at the victim's feet. Lynchings were often public events, drawing huge crowds to watch the victim's agonizing death.

What aspects of American justice do lynchings violate, and why were they so common?

potential force…. The only apology that I have to make for the earnestness with which I have spoken is that I am pleading for the life, the liberty, the future happiness, and manhood suffrage of one-eighth of the entire population of the United States.

The dark night of racism that fell on the South after Reconstruction seemed to unleash all the baser impulses of human nature. Between 1889 and 1899, an average of 187 blacks were lynched every year for alleged offenses against white supremacy. Those convicted of petty crimes against property were often little better off; many were condemned to be leased out to private contractors whose brutality rivaled that of the most sadistic slaveholders. The convict-lease system enabled entrepreneurs, such as mine owners and extractors of forest products, to rent prisoners from the state and treat them as they saw fit. Unlike slaveowners, they suffered no loss when a forced laborer died from overwork. Finally, the dignity of blacks was cruelly affronted by the wave of segregation laws passed around the turn of the century, which served to remind them constantly that they were deemed unfit to associate with whites on any basis that implied equality. To some extent, the segregation laws were a white reaction to the refusal of many blacks to submit to voluntary segregation of railroads, streetcars, and other public facilities.

QUICK CHECK ✓

What aspects of southern society did the Jim Crow laws regulate?

The North and the federal government did little or nothing to stem the tide of racial oppression in the South. A series of Supreme Court decisions between 1878 and 1898 gutted the Reconstruction amendments and the legislation passed to enforce them, leaving blacks virtually defenseless against political and social discrimination.

Conclusion: Henry McNeal Turner and the "Unfinished Revolution"

The career of Henry McNeal Turner sums up the bitter side of the black experience in the South during and after Reconstruction. Born free in South Carolina in 1834, Turner became a minister of the African Methodist Episcopal (AME) Church just before the outbreak of the Civil War. During the war, he recruited African Americans for the Union army and later served as chaplain for black troops. After the fighting was over, he went to Georgia to work for the Freedmen's Bureau but encountered racial discrimination from white Bureau officers and left government service for church work and Reconstruction politics. Elected to the 1867 Georgia constitutional convention and to the state legislature in 1868, he was one of a number of black clergymen who assumed leadership roles among the freedmen. But whites won control of the Georgia legislature and expelled all the black members. As the inhabitant of a state in which blacks never gained the degree of power that they achieved in some other parts of the South, Turner was one of the first black leaders to see the failure of Reconstruction as the betrayal of African American hopes for citizenship.

Becoming a bishop of the AME Church in 1880, Turner emerged as the late nineteenth century's leading proponent of black emigration to Africa. Because he believed that white Americans were so deeply prejudiced against blacks that they would never grant them equal rights, Turner became an early advocate of black nationalism and a total separation of the races. Emigration became a popular

BLACK LEADER   Henry McNeal Turner, who was born in freedom, became a bishop of the African Methodist Episcopal Church and was elected to the Georgia legislature.

How does Turner's career symbolize the end of Reconstruction?

movement among southern blacks, who were especially hard hit by terror and oppression just after the end of Reconstruction. Still, a majority of blacks in the nation as a whole and even in Turner's own church refused to give up on the hope of eventual equality on American soil. But Bishop Turner's anger and despair were the understandable responses of a proud man to the way that he and his fellow African Americans had been treated in the post–Civil War period.

By the late 1880s, the wounds of the Civil War were healing, and white Americans were seized by the spirit of sectional reconciliation and their common Americanism. But whites could come back together only because northerners had tacitly agreed to give southerners a free hand in their efforts to reduce blacks to a new form of servitude. The "outraged, heart-broken, bruised, and bleeding" African Americans of the South paid the heaviest price for sectional reunion.

For a list of additional titles related to this chapter's topics, please see www.pearsonamericanhistory.com.   MyHistoryLab

STUDY RESOURCES

KEY TERMS

CHAPTER REVIEW

WHAT conflicts arose among Lincoln, Johnson, and Congress during Reconstruction?

Both Lincoln and Johnson had their own notions of how Reconstruction should be governed. Lincoln's Ten Percent Plan was especially challenged by the Radical Republicans who sought more protection for black rights. Later, when Johnson hesitated to renew the Freedmen's Bureau and fight the Black Codes, Congress swiftly passed the Fourteenth Amendment hoping to ensure equal rights to all Americans. *(p. 419)*

WHAT problems did southern society face during Reconstruction?

The immediate problems facing the South were economic and physical devastation, and the mass of freed slaves to be provided for. While former slaveholders hoped to reduce ex-slaves to conditions not unlike slavery, northern Republicans wanted to reorganize southern land and labor on a northern free-labor model. Freedmen's Bureau agents emphasized that ex-slaves had to sign contracts and work for wages. The freed slaves hoped instead to own land. Sharecropping was a compromise. *(p. 428)*

WHAT forces brought on the end of Reconstruction?

Although intended to further protect civil rights, the Fifteenth Amendment allowed states to limit local suffrage through difficult voting prerequisites. Further, the Ku Klux Klan campaigned through increasingly illegal means to intimidate black voters and representation. By 1876, these tactics led to the defeat of the Republicans in most southern states and Reconstruction was nearly dead. *(p. 436)*

WHO benefited and who suffered from the reconciliation of North and South?

Reunion came at the expense of African Americans. In the Compromise of 1877, a secret deal struck between Republicans and Democrats restored autonomous government in the South to resolve the 1876 election. The North would no longer enforce unpopular civil rights, allowing the Redeemers to bring back laissez-faire economics and restore white supremacy through the Jim Crow laws. *(p. 439)*

MAKING CONNECTIONS

1. How do you think Reconstruction might have turned out differently if Lincoln had not been assassinated?
2. Why was it difficult to enforce social and cultural changes using military force?
3. What role did local, grassroots efforts play in reversing federal government policy? How did people retain that much autonomy even under a strong federal government?
4. Do you think the "Redemption" of southern government was an inevitable backlash to Reconstruction? How could things have turned out differently?

PRACTICE QUIZ

1. The _____ embodied President Lincoln's initial idea for reuniting the nation.
   a. Radical Reconstruction
   b. Ten Percent Plan
   c. 90 Percent Plan
   d. Carpetbagger Plan

2. The _____ Republicans wanted to punish the South for rebelling against the Union.
   a. Radical
   b. Conservative
   c. Moderate
   d. Copperhead

3. The controversial _____ Bill passed Congress in 1864.
   a. Wade-Davis
   b. Johnson-Sumner
   c. Sumner-Stevens
   d. Davis-Stevens

4. The _____ amendment to the U.S. Constitution abolished slavery.
   a. Eleventh
   b. Twelfth
   c. Thirteenth
   d. Fifteenth

5. The _____ restricted the rights of former slaves in the South in 1865.
   a. Insurrection Act
   b. Black Codes
   c. Radical Republicans
   d. African American church

6. The most important government agency to help ex-slaves during Reconstruction was the
   a. Freedmen's Bureau
   b. Interior Department
   c. Sanitary Commission
   d. Red Cross

7. The Fourteenth Amendment to the U.S. Constitution
   a. Made the federal government responsible for enforcing equal rights.
   b. Abolished indentured servitude.
   c. Provided the vote to black men.
   d. Ended the Civil War.

8. Former slaves acted in all of the following ways after the Civil War *except*
   a. They were reluctant to settle down for wages with former masters.
   b. Many walked around the South searching for better opportunities.
   c. Many engaged in contract labor, and later sharecropping.
   d. Most blacks kept possession of small farms obtained from whites.

9. Which of the following *does not* describe the education of ex-slaves in the South after the Civil War?
   a. One of the highest priorities of ex-slaves was education for their kids.
   b. The Freedmen's Bureau and missionary societies founded the first ex-slave schools.
   c. Most ex-slaves viewed segregated schooling as a bad idea.
   d. The federal government made minimal efforts to integrate public schools in the South.

10. What right did the Fifteenth Amendment provide for the American people?
   a. The vote for all men regardless of race or ethnicity.
   b. Free speech.
   c. Freedom of the press.
   d. Freedom from unlawful search and seizure.

QUIZ

Find more practice at
www.myhistorylab.com

SAMPLE ESSAY QUESTIONS

1. Describe how President Johnson dealt with Congress regarding Reconstruction policy.

2. Discuss the historical factors that explain why Reconstruction ended.

Answers to Practice Quiz 1. b, p. 420 **2.** a, p. 420 **3.** a, p. 420 **4.** c, p. 422 **5.** b, p. 423 **6.** a, p. 423 **7.** a, p. 424 **8.** d, p. 429 **9.** c, p. 435 **10.** a, p. 436

The West
Exploiting an Empire, 1849–1902

CHARLES M. RUSSELL *Cowboy Camp During Roundup*, ca. 1885–1887. Artist Charles Russell here documents the cowboys' activities during the annual spring roundup. Before setting off on the long trek to drive cattle to market, the cowboys had to rope and break in horses that might have gone a little wild over the winter.

Why do you think this cowboy camp had both canvas and wooden structures?

Lean Bear's Changing West

In 1863, federal Indian agents took a delegation of Cheyenne, Arapaho, Comanche, Kiowa, and Plains Apache to visit the eastern United States, hoping to impress them with the power of the white man. The visitors were, in fact, impressed. In New York City, they stared at the tall buildings and crowded streets, so different from the wide-open plains with which they were accustomed. They visited the museum of the great showman Phineas T. Barnum, who in turn put them on display; they even saw a hippopotamus.

In Washington, they met with President Abraham Lincoln. Lean Bear, a Cheyenne chief, assured Lincoln that Indians wanted peace but worried about the numbers of white people who were pouring into their country. Lincoln swore friendship, said the Indians would be better off if they began to farm, and promised he would do his best to keep the peace. But, he said, smiling at Lean Bear, "You know it is not always possible for any father to have his children do precisely as he wishes them to do."

KEY EVENTS

1849 Gold Rush to California, *p. 460*

1862 Congress passes Homestead Act encouraging western settlement, *p. 462*

1864 Colonel John Chivington leads massacre of Indians at Sand Creek, Colorado, *p. 455*

1865–1867 Sioux War against white miners and U.S. Army, *p. 455*

1866 "Long drive" of cattle touches off cattle bonanzas, *p. 464*

1867 Horace Greeley urges Easterners to "Go West, young man," *p. 450* ■ National Grange of the Patrons of Husbandry (the Grange) founded to enrich farmers' lives, *p. 471*

1867–1868 Policy of "small reservations" for Indians adopted, *p. 456*

1873 Big bonanza discovered on the Comstock Lode in Nevada, *p. 466*

1874 Joseph F. Glidden invents barbed wire, *p. 471* ■ Discovery of gold in Dakota Territory sets off Black Hills Gold Rush, *p. 456*

1876 Custer and his men defeated and killed by the Sioux at battle of the Little Bighorn (June), *p. 456*

1883 Museum expedition discovers fewer than two hundred buffalo in the West, *p. 459*

1886–1887 Severe drought and winter damage cattle and farming bonanzas, *p. 471*

1887 Congress passes Dawes Severalty Act, making Indians individual landowners, *p. 458*

1889 Oklahoma Territory opened to settlement, *p. 468*

1890 Teton Sioux massacred at battle of Wounded Knee, South Dakota (December), *p. 456*

1893 Young historian Frederick Jackson Turner analyzes closing of the frontier, *p. 472*

1902 Congress passes National Reclamation Act (the Newlands Act), *p. 463*

Lean Bear, who had children of his own, understood what Lincoln had had to say in Washington, at least in a way. Just a year later, back on his own lands, he watched as federal troops, Lincoln's "children," approached his camp. Wearing a peace medal that Lincoln had given him, Lean Bear rode slowly toward the troops to once again offer his friendship. When he was twenty yards away, they opened fire, then rode closer and fired again and again into his fallen body.

As Lean Bear had feared, in the last three decades of the nineteenth century, a flood of settlers ventured into the vast lands across the Mississippi River. Prospectors searched for "pay dirt," railroads crisscrossed the continent, eastern and foreign capitalists invested in cattle and land bonanzas, and farmers took up the promise of free western lands. In 1867, Horace Greeley, editor of the New York *Tribune,* told New York City's unemployed: "If you strike off into the broad, free West, and make yourself a farm from Uncle Sam's generous domain, you will crowd nobody, starve nobody, and neither you nor your children need evermore beg for something to do."

With the end of the Civil War, white Americans again claimed a special destiny to expand across the continent. In the process, they crushed the culture of the Native Americans and ignored the contributions of people of other races, such as the Chinese miners and laborers and the Mexican herdsmen. As millions moved west, the states of Colorado, Washington, Montana, the Dakotas, Idaho, Wyoming, and Utah were carved out of the lands across the Mississippi. At the turn of the century, only Arizona, New Mexico, and Oklahoma remained as territories.

The West became a great colonial empire, harnessed to eastern capital and tied increasingly to national and international markets. Its raw materials, sent east by wagon, train, and ship, helped fuel eastern factories. Western economies relied heavily on the federal government, which subsidized their railroads, distributed their land, and spent millions of dollars for the upkeep of soldiers and Indians.

By the 1890s, the lands west of the Mississippi had undergone substantial change. In place of buffalo and unfenced vistas, there were cities and towns, health resorts, homesteads, sheep ranches, and in the arid regions, the beginnings of the irrigated agriculture that would reshape the West in the twentieth century. Ghost towns, abandoned farms, and the scars in the earth left by miners and farmers spoke to the less favorable side of settlement. As the new century dawned, the West had become a place of conquest and exploitation, as well as a mythic land of cowboys and quick fortunes.

Beyond the Frontier

The line of white settlement had reached the edge of the Missouri timber country by 1840. Beyond lay an enormous land of rolling prairies, parched deserts, and rugged, majestic mountains. Emerging from the timber country, travelers first encountered the Great Plains—treeless, nearly flat, an endless "sea of grassy hillocks" extending from the Mississippi River to the Rocky Mountains.

Running from Alaska to central New Mexico, the Rockies presented a formidable barrier, and most travelers crossed the northern passes, emerging in the desolate basin of present-day southern Idaho and Utah. On the west, the lofty Coast Ranges—the Cascades and Sierra Nevada—held back rainfall; beyond were the temperate lands of the Pacific coast.

Few rivers cut through the Plains; those that did raged in the winter and trickled in the summer. Rainfall usually did not reach 15 inches a year, not enough to support

WHAT were the particular challenges of settling the country west of the Mississippi?

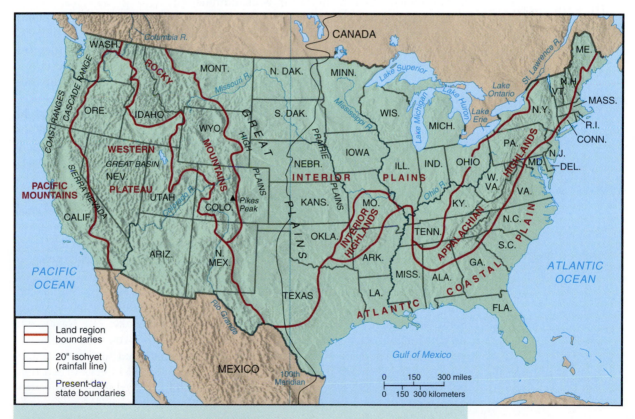

PHYSIOGRAPHIC MAP OF THE UNITED STATES   In the Great Plains and Rocky Mountains, the topography, altitudes, crops, and climate—especially the lack of rain west of the rainfall line shown here—led to changes in a mode of settlement that had been essentially uniform from the Atlantic coast through Kentucky, Ohio, and Missouri. The rectangular land surveys and quarter-section lots that were traditional before could not accommodate Great Plains conditions.

How did settlers adapt to the different conditions?

extensive agriculture. There was little lumber for homes and fences, and the tools of eastern settlement—the cast-iron plow, the boat, and the ax—were virtually useless on the tough and treeless Plains soil. "East of the Mississippi," historian Walter Prescott Webb noted, "civilization stood on three legs—land, water, and timber; west of the Mississippi not one but two of these legs were withdrawn—water and timber—and civilization was left on one leg—land."

Crushing the Native Americans

HOW

did white Americans crush the culture of the Native Americans as they moved west?

When Greeley urged New Yorkers to move West and "crowd nobody," he—like almost all white Americans—ignored the fact that large numbers of people already lived there. At the close of the Civil War, Native Americans inhabited nearly half the United States. By 1880, they had been driven onto smaller and smaller reservations and were no longer an independent people. A decade later, even their culture had crumbled under the impact of white domination.

In 1865, nearly a quarter million Native Americans lived in the western half of the country. Tribes such as the Winnebago, Menominee, Cherokee, and Chippewa were resettled there, forced out of their eastern lands by advancing white settlement. Other tribes were native to the region. In the Southwest there were the Pueblo groups, including the Hopi, Zuni, and Rio Grande Pueblos. Peaceful farmers and herders, they had built up complex traditions around a settled way of life.

More nomadic were the Camp Dwellers, the Jicarilla Apache and Navajo who roamed eastern New Mexico and western Texas. The Navajo herded sheep and produced beautiful ornamental silver, baskets, and blankets. Fierce fighters, Apache horsemen were feared by whites and fellow Indians across the southwestern Plains.

Farther west were the tribes that inhabited present-day California. Divided into many small bands, they eked out a difficult existence living on roots, grubs, berries, acorns, and small game. In the Pacific Northwest, where fish and forest animals made life easier, the Klamath, Chinook, Yurok, and Shasta tribes developed a rich civilization. They built plank houses and canoes, worked extensively in wood, and evolved a complex social and political organization.

By the 1870s, most of these tribes had been destroyed or beaten into submission. The powerful Ute, crushed in 1855, ceded most of their Utah lands to the United States and settled on a small reservation near Great Salt Lake. The Navajo and Apache fought back fiercely, but between 1865 and 1873 they too were confined to reservations. The Native Americans of California succumbed to the contagious diseases carried by whites during the Gold Rush of 1849. Miners burned their villages, and by 1880, fewer than twenty thousand Indians lived in California.

Life of the Plains Indians

In the mid-nineteenth century, nearly two-thirds of the Native Americans lived on the Great Plains. The Plains tribes included the Sioux of present-day Minnesota and the Dakotas; the Blackfoot of Idaho and Montana; the Cheyenne, Crow, and Arapaho of the central Plains; the Pawnee of western Nebraska; and the Kiowa, Apache, and Comanche of present-day Texas and New Mexico.

After the buffalo was killed, women skinned the hide, cut up the meat, and then cured the hide, as shown in the painting *Halcyon Days* by George Catlin. Women also decorated the tepees and preserved the meat by drying it in the sun.

What are the men doing in Catlin's painting?

Nomadic and warlike, the Plains Indians depended on the buffalo and horse. The modern horse, first brought by Spanish explorers in the 1500s, spread north from Mexico onto the Plains, and by the 1700s the Plains Indians' way of life had changed. The Plains tribes gave up farming almost entirely and hunted the buffalo, ranging widely over the rolling plains. The men became superb warriors and horsemen, among the best light cavalry in the world.

Migratory in culture, the Plains Indians formed tribes of several thousand people but lived in smaller bands of three to five hundred. The bands followed and lived off the buffalo. Buffalo provided food, clothing, and shelter; the Indians, unlike later white hunters, used every part of the animal. The meat was dried or "jerked" in the hot Plains air. The skins made tepees, blankets, and robes. Buffalo bones became knives; tendons were made into bowstrings; horns and hooves were boiled into glue. Buffalo "chips"—dried manure—were burned as fuel.

The Plains tribes divided labor tasks according to gender. Men hunted, traded, supervised ceremonial activities, and cleared ground for planting. They usually held the positions of authority, such as chief or medicine man. Women were responsible for child rearing and artistic activity. They also performed the camp work, grew vegetables, prepared buffalo meat and hides, and gathered berries

LISTEN

Rituals of the Maize

QUICK CHECK ✓

What characterized the life of the Plains Indians?

and roots. In most tribes, women played an important role in political, economic, and religious activities. Among the Navajo and Zuni, kinship descended from the mother's side, and Navajo women were in charge of most of the family's property. In tribes such as the Sioux, there was little difference in status. Men were respected for hunting and war, women for their artistic skills with quill and paint.

Searching for an Indian Policy

Before the Civil War, Americans used the land west of the Mississippi as "one big reservation." The government named the area "Indian Country," moved eastern tribes there with firm treaty guarantees, and in 1834 passed the Indian Intercourse Act, which prohibited any white person from entering Indian country without a license.

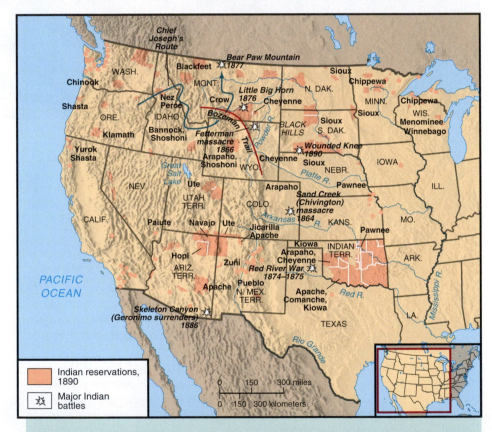

NATIVE AMERICANS IN THE WEST: MAJOR BATTLES AND RESERVATIONS   "They made us many promises, more than I remember, but they never kept but one; they promised to take our land, and they took it." So said Red Cloud of the Oglala Sioux, summarizing Native American–white relations in the 1870s.

What factors were behind the location of the major Indian reservations in the West?

The situation changed in the 1850s. Wagon trains wound their way to California and Oregon, miners pushed into western goldfields, and there was talk of a transcontinental railroad. To clear the way for settlement, the federal government in 1851 abandoned "One Big Reservation" in favor of a new policy of concentration. For the first time, it assigned definite boundaries to each tribe. The Sioux, for example, were given the Dakota country north of the Platte River, the Crow a large area near the Powder River, and the Cheyenne and Arapaho the Colorado foothills between the North Platte and Arkansas Rivers for "as long as waters run and the grass shall grow."

The concentration policy lasted only a few years. Accustomed to hunting widely for buffalo, many Native Americans refused to stay within their assigned areas. White settlers poured into Indian lands, then called on the government to protect them. Indians were pushed out of Kansas and Nebraska in the 1850s, even as white reformers fought to hold those territories open for free blacks. In 1859, gold miners moved into the Pikes Peak country, touching off warfare with the Cheyenne and Arapaho.

In 1864, tired of the fighting, the two tribes asked for peace. Certain that the war was over, Chief Black Kettle led his seven hundred followers to camp on Sand Creek in southeastern Colorado. Early on the morning of November 29, 1864, a group of Colorado militia led by Colonel John M. Chivington attacked the sleeping group. "Kill and scalp all, big and little," Chivington told his men. "Nits make lice." Black Kettle tried to stop the ambush, raising first an American flag and then a white flag. Neither worked. The Native American men, women, and children were clubbed, stabbed, and scalped.

The Chivington massacre set off angry protests in Colorado and the East. Congress appointed an investigating committee, and the government concluded a treaty with the Cheyenne and Arapaho, condemning "the gross and wanton outrages." Still, the two tribes were forced to surrender their Sand Creek reservation in exchange for lands elsewhere. The Kiowa and Comanche were also ousted from areas they had been granted "forever" only a few years before. As the Sioux chief Spotted Tail said, "Why does not the Great Father put his red children on wheels so that he can move them as he will?"

Before long, the powerful Sioux were on the warpath in the great Sioux War of 1865–1867. Once again, an invasion of gold miners touched off the war, which flared even more intensely when the federal government announced plans to connect the various mining towns by building the Bozeman Trail through the heart of the Sioux hunting grounds in Montana. Red Cloud, the Sioux chief, determined to stop the trail. In December 1866, pursued by an army column under Captain William J. Fetterman, he lured the incautious Fetterman deep into the wilderness, ambushed him, and wiped out all eighty-two soldiers in his command.

Chief Red Cloud's Speech

The Fetterman massacre, coming so soon after the Chivington massacre, sparked a public debate over the nation's Indian policy. Like the policy itself, the debate reflected differing white views of the Native Americans. In the East, some reform, humanitarian, and church groups wanted a humane peace policy, directed toward educating and "civilizing" the tribes. Many white people, in the East and West, questioned this approach, convinced that Native Americans were savages unfit for civilization. Westerners, of course, had some reason to fear Indian attacks, and the fears often fed on wild rumors of scalped settlers and besieged forts. As a result, Westerners in general favored firm control over the Native Americans, including swift punishment of any who rebelled.

Congressional Report on the Sand Creek Massacre (1867)

In 1867, the peace advocates won the debate. Halting construction on the Bozeman Trail, Congress created a Peace Commission of four civilians and three generals to end the Sioux War and eliminate permanently the causes of Indian wars. Setting out for the West, the Peace Commissioners agreed that only one policy offered a permanent solution: a policy of "small reservations" to isolate the Native Americans on distant lands, teach them to farm, and gradually "civilize" them.

The Kiowa, Comanche, Cheyenne, and Arapaho agreed to the plan in 1867, the Sioux in 1868. The policy was extended beyond the Plains, and the Ute, Shoshone, Bannock, Navajo, and Apache tribes also accepted small reservations.

QUICK CHECK ✔

How did American policy toward the Indians evolve in these years?

Final Battles on the Plains

Ghost Dances
A religious movement that arose in the late nineteenth century under the prophet Wovoka, a Paiute Indian. It involved a set of dances and rites that its followers believed would cause white men to disappear and restore lands to the Native Americans. The Ghost Dance religion was outlawed by the U.S. government, and army intervention to stop it led to the Wounded Knee Massacre.

Wounded Knee Massacre
In December 1890, troopers of the Seventh Cavalry, under orders to stop the Ghost Dance religion among the Sioux, took Chief Big Foot and his followers to a camp on Wounded Knee Creek in South Dakota. It is uncertain who fired the first shot, but violence ensued and approximately two hundred Native American men, women, and children were killed.

Few Native Americans settled peacefully into life on the new reservations. The reservation system not only changed their age-old customs; it chained them in a situation of poverty and isolation. Soon, young warriors and minor chiefs denounced the treaties and drifted back to the open countryside. In late 1868, warfare broke out again, and it took more than a decade of violence to beat the Indians into submission.

On the northern Plains, fighting resulted from the Black Hills Gold Rush of 1875. As prospectors tramped across Native American hunting grounds, the Sioux gathered to stop them. They were led by Rain-in-the-Face, the great war chief Crazy Horse, and the famous medicine man Sitting Bull. The army sent several columns of troops after the Indians, but one, under flamboyant Lieutenant Colonel George Armstrong Custer, pushed recklessly ahead, eager to claim the victory. On the morning of June 25, 1876, thinking he had a small band of Native Americans surrounded in their village on the banks of the Little Bighorn River in Montana, Custer divided his column and took 265 men toward it. Instead of finding a small band, he discovered he had stumbled on the main Sioux camp with 2500 warriors. It was the largest Native American army ever assembled in the United States.

By midafternoon it was over; Custer and his men were dead. Custer was largely responsible for the loss, but "Custer's Last Stand," set in blazing headlines across the country, set off a nationwide demand for revenge. Within a few months, the Sioux were surrounded and beaten, three thousand of them surrendering in October 1876. Sitting Bull and a few followers who had fled to Canada gave up in 1881.

The Sioux War ended the major Indian warfare in the West, but occasional outbreaks occurred for several years thereafter. In 1890, the Teton Sioux of South Dakota, bitter and starving, became restless. Many of them turned to the **Ghost Dances,** a set of dances and rites that grew from a vision of a Paiute messiah named Wovoka. Performance of the dances, Wovoka said, would bring back Native American lands and would cause the whites to disappear. All Native Americans would reunite, the earth would be covered with dust, and a new earth would come upon the old. The vanished buffalo would return in great herds.

The army intervened to stop the dancing, touching off violence that killed Sitting Bull and a number of other warriors. Frightened Native Americans fled southwest to join other Ghost Dancers under the aging chief Big Foot. Moving quickly, troops of the Seventh Cavalry, Custer's old regiment, caught up with

This pictogram by Oglala Sioux Amos Bad Heart Bull is a Native American version of the battle of the Little Bighorn, also known as Custer's Last Stand.

What was important about Custer's Last Stand?

WATCH

Sioux Ghost Dance

DOCUMENT

Accounts of the Wounded Knee Massacre

Big Foot's band and took them to the army camp on Wounded Knee Creek in South Dakota. A Native American, it is thought, fired the first shot, returned by the army's new machine guns. Firing a shell a second, they shredded tepees and people. In the infamous **Wounded Knee Massacre**, about two hundred men, women, and children were killed in the snow.

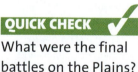

QUICK CHECK

What were the final battles on the Plains?

The End of Tribal Life

The final step in Indian policy came in the 1870s and 1880s. Some reformers had long argued against segregating the Native Americans on reservations, urging instead that the nation assimilate them individually into white culture. These "assimilationists" wanted to use education, land policy, and federal law to eradicate tribal society.

Congress began to adopt the policy in 1871 when it ended the practice of treaty making with Native American tribes. Since tribes were no longer separate nations, they lost many of their political and judicial functions, and the power of the chiefs was weakened.

DOCUMENT

Secretary of the Interior's Report on Indian Affairs

TOM TORLINO A Navajo Indian, photographed before and after his "assimilation." Torlino attended the Carlisle Indian School in Pennsylvania.

What are the differences in Tom Torlino's "before" and "after" appearance?

Dawes Severalty Act
Legislation passed by Congress that aimed at breaking up traditional Indian life by promoting individual land ownership. It divided tribal lands into small plots that were distributed among members of each tribe. Provisions were made for Indian education and eventual citizenship. The law led to corruption, exploitation, and the weakening of Native American tribal culture.

Laundry Class at Carlisle Indian School

Act of Congress, General Allotment Act (Dawes Act)

While Congress worked to break down the tribes, educators trained young Native Americans to adjust to white culture. In 1879, fifty Pawnee, Kiowa, and Cheyenne youths were brought east to the new Carlisle Indian School in Carlisle, Pennsylvania. Other Native American schools soon opened, including the Haskell Institute in Kansas and numerous day schools on the western reservations. The schools taught students to fix machines and farm; they forced young Indians to trim their long hair and made them speak English, banned the wearing of tribal paint or clothes, and forbade tribal ceremonies and dances. "Kill the Indian and save the man," said Richard H. Pratt, the army officer who founded the Carlisle School.

Land ownership was the final and most important link in the new policy. Native Americans who owned land, it was thought, would become responsible, self-reliant citizens. Deciding to give each Native American a farm, Congress in 1887 passed the **Dawes Severalty Act,** the most important legal development in Indian-white relations in more than three centuries.

Aiming to end tribal life, the Dawes Act divided tribal lands into small plots for distribution among members of the tribe. Each family head received 160 acres, single adults 80 acres, and children 40 acres. Once the land was distributed, any surplus was sold to white settlers, with the profits going to Native American schools.

Through the Dawes Act, 47 million acres of land were distributed to Native Americans and their families, but many Native Americans knew little about farming. Their tools were rudimentary, and in the culture of the Plains Indians, men had not ordinarily participated in farming. In 1934, the government returned to the idea of tribal land ownership, but by then 138 million acres of Indian land had shrunk to 48 million acres, half of which was barren.

The final blow to tribal life came not in the Dawes Act but in the virtual extermination of the buffalo, the Plains Indians' chief resource and the basis for their unique way of life. The killing began in the 1860s as the transcontinental railroads pushed west, and it stepped up as settlers found they could harm the Indians by harming the buffalo. "Kill every buffalo you can," an army officer said. "Every buffalo dead is an Indian gone." Then, in 1871, a Pennsylvania tannery discovered that buffalo hides made valuable leather. Professional hunters such as William F. "Buffalo Bill" Cody swarmed across the Plains, killing millions of the beasts.

Huge buffalo herds grazing along railroads in the West frequently blocked the path of passing trains. Passengers often killed for sport, shooting at the beasts with "no intention of using or removing the animal carcasses."

Why did the people shooting the buffalo think they were harming Native Americans?

IMAGE

Stuffed Buffalo

Between 1872 and 1874, professional hunters slaughtered three million buffalo a year. By 1883, the buffalo were almost gone. When the government set out to produce the famous "buffalo nickel," the designer had to go to the Bronx Zoo in New York City to find a buffalo.

By 1900, there were only 250,000 Native Americans in the country. (There were 600,000 within the limits of the present-day United States in 1800, and more than 5 million in 1492, when Columbus first set foot in the New World.) Most of the Indians lived on reservations. Many lived in poverty. Alcoholism and unemployment were growing problems, and Native Americans, no longer able to live off the buffalo, became wards of the state. They lost their cultural distinctiveness. Once possessors of the entire continent, they had been crowded into smaller and smaller areas, overwhelmed by the demand to become settled, literate, and English-speaking. "Except for the internment of the West Coast Japanese during World War II," said historian Roger L. Nichols, "Indian removal is the only example of large-scale government-enforced migration in American history. For the Japanese, the move was temporary; for the Indians it was not."

Even as the Native Americans lost their identity, they entered the romantic folklore of the West. Dime novels, snapped up by readers young and old, told tales of Indian fighting on the Plains. "Buffalo Bill" Cody turned it all into a profitable business. Beginning in 1883, his Wild West Show ran for more than three decades, playing to millions of viewers in the United States, Canada, and Europe. It featured Plains Indians chasing buffalo, performing a war dance, and attacking a settler's cabin. In 1885, Sitting Bull himself, victor over Custer at the battle of the Little Bighorn, performed in the show.

QUICK CHECK

What events and measures ended tribal life?

Settlement of the West

WHAT

led Americans and others to move to the West?

Between 1870 and 1900, white—and some African, Hispanic, and Asian—Americans settled the enormous total of 430 million acres west of the Mississippi; they took over more land than had been occupied by Americans in all the years before 1870.

People moved West for many reasons. Some sought adventure; others wanted to escape the drab routine of factory or city life. Many moved to California for their health. The Mormons settled Utah to escape religious persecution. Others followed the mining camps, the advancing railroads, and the farming and cattle frontier.

Whatever the specific reason, most people moved West to better their lot. On the whole, their timing was good, for as the nation's population grew, so did demand for the livestock and the agricultural, mineral, and lumber products of the expanding West. Contrary to older historical views, the West did not act as a major "safety valve," an outlet for social and economic tensions. The poor and unemployed did not have the means to move there and establish farms.

Men and Women on the Overland Trail

Gold Rush of 1849

Individual prospectors made the first gold strikes along the Sierra Nevada Mountains in 1849, touching off a mining boom that helped shape the development of the West and set the pattern for subsequent strikes in other regions.

Overland Trail

The route taken by thousands of travelers from the Mississippi Valley to the Pacific coast in the last half of the nineteenth century. It was extremely difficult, often taking six months or more to complete.

The first movement west aimed not for the nearby Plains but for California and Oregon on the continent's far shore. It started in the **Gold Rush of 1849,** and in the next three decades perhaps as many as half a million individuals made the long journey over the **Overland Trail,** a network of trails leading west. Some walked; others rode horses alone or in small groups. About half joined great caravans, numbering 150 wagons or more, that inched across the two thousand miles between the Missouri River and the Pacific coast.

More often than not, men made the decision to make the crossing, but, except for the stampedes to the mines, migration usually turned out to be a family affair. Wives were consulted, though in some cases they had little real choice. They could either go along or live alone at home. While many women regretted leaving family and friends, they agreed to the trip, sometimes as eagerly as the men. The majority of people traveled in family groups, including in-laws, grandchildren, aunts, and uncles. As one historian had said, "The quest for something new would take place in the context of the very familiar."

Individuals and wagon trains set out from various points along the Missouri River. During April, travelers gradually assembled in spring camp just across the Missouri River, waiting for the new grass to ripen into forage. They packed and repacked the wagons and elected the trains' leaders, who would set the line of march, look for water and campsites, and impose discipline. Some trains adopted detailed rules, fearing a lapse into savagery in the wild lands across the Missouri. "Every man to carry with him a Bible and other religious books, as we hope not to degenerate into a state of barbarism," one agreement said.

Setting out in early May, travelers divided the enormous route into manageable portions. The first leg of the journey followed the Platte River west to Fort Kearney in central Nebraska Territory, a distance of about three hundred miles. From a distance, the white-topped wagons seemed driven by a common force, but, in fact, internal discipline broke down almost immediately. Arguments erupted over the pace of the march, the choice of campsites, the number of guards to post, whether to rest or push on. Elected leaders quit; new ones were chosen. Every train was filled with individualists, and as the son of one train captain said, "If you think it's any snap to run a wagon train of 66 wagons with every man in the train having a different idea of what is the best thing to do, all I can say is that some day you ought to try it."

Men, women, and children had different tasks on the trail. Men concerned themselves almost entirely with hunting buffalo and antelope, guard duty, and transportation. They rose at 4 A.M. to hitch the wagons, and after breakfast began the day's march. At noon, they stopped and set the teams to graze. After the mid-day meal, the march continued until sunset. Then, while the men relaxed, the women fixed dinner and the next day's lunch, and the children kindled the fires, brought water to camp, and searched for wood or other fuel. Walking fifteen miles a day, in searing heat and mountain cold, travelers were exhausted by late afternoon.

For women, the trail was lonely, and they worked to exhaustion. Before long, some adjusted their clothing to the harsh conditions, adopting the new bloomer pants, shortening their skirts, or wearing regular "wash dresses"—so called because they had shorter hemlines that did not drag on the wet ground on washday. Other women continued to wear their long dresses, thinking bloomers "indecent." Both men and women carried firearms in case of Indian attacks, but most emigrants saw few Indians en route.

What they often did see was trash, miles of it, for the wagon trains were an early example of the impact of migration and settlement on the western environment. On the Oregon and other trails, travelers sidestepped mounds of garbage, tin cans, furniture, cooking stoves, kegs, tools, and clothing, all discarded by people who had passed through before.

The first stage of the journey was deceptively easy, and travelers usually reached Fort Kearney by late May. The second leg led another 300 miles up the Platte River to Fort Laramie on the eastern edge of Wyoming Territory. The heat of June had dried the grass, and there was no wood. Anxious to beat the early snowfalls, travelers rested a day or two at the fort, then hurried on to South Pass, 280 miles to the west, the best route through the forbidding Rockies. It was now mid-July, but the mountain nights were so cold that ice formed in the water buckets.

Beyond South Pass, some emigrants turned south to the Mormon settlements on the Great Salt Lake, but most headed 340 miles north to Fort Hall on the Snake River in Idaho. It took another three months to cover the remaining 800 miles. California-bound travelers followed the Humboldt River through the summer heat of Nevada. Well into September, they began the final arduous push: first, a 55-mile stretch of desert; then 70 difficult miles up the eastern slopes of the Sierra Nevada, laboriously hoisting wagons over massive outcrops of rock; and finally the last 100 miles down the western slopes to the welcome sight of California's Central Valley in October.

Under the best of conditions the trip took six months, sixteen hours a day, dawn to dusk, of hard, grueling labor. Walking halfway across the continent was no easy task, and it provided a never-to-be-forgotten experience for those who did it. The wagon trains, carrying the dreams of thousands of individuals, reproduced society in small focus: individualistic, hopeful, mobile, divided by age and gender roles, apprehensive, yet willing to strike out for the distant and new.

QUICK CHECK

What was life like on the Overland Trail?

Land for the Taking

As railroads pushed west in the 1870s and 1880s, locomotive trains replaced wagon trains, but the shift was gradual, and until the end of the century, emigrants often combined both modes of travel. Early railroad transportation was expensive, and the average farm family could not afford to buy tickets and ship supplies. Many Europeans traveled by rail to designated outfitting places and then proceeded West with wagons and oxen.

Traffic flowed in all directions, belying the image of a simple "westward" movement. Many people did go west, of course, but others, such as migrants from Mexico, became westerners by moving north, and Asian Americans moved eastward from the Pacific coast. Whatever their route, they all ended up in the meeting ground of cultures that formed the modern West.

Why did they come? "The motive that induced us to part with the pleasant associations and the dear friends of our childhood days," explained Phoebe Judson, an early emigrant, "was to obtain from the government of the United States a grant of land that 'Uncle Sam' had promised to give to the head of each family who settled in this new country." A popular camp song reflected the same motive:

> Come along, come along—don't be alarmed,
> Uncle Sam is rich enough to give us all a farm.

Uncle Sam owned about one billion acres of land in the 1860s, much of it mountain and desert land unsuited for agriculture. By 1900, various land laws had distributed half of it. Between 1862 and 1890, the government gave away 48 million acres to western farmers, sold about 100 million acres to private citizens and corporations, granted 128 million acres to railroad companies to tempt them to build across the unsettled West, and sold huge tracts to the states.

Homestead Act of 1862

Legislation granting 160 acres of land to anyone who paid a $10 fee and pledged to live on and cultivate the land for five years. Although there was a good deal of fraud, the act encouraged a large migration to the West. Between 1862 and 1900, nearly 600,000 families claimed homesteads under its provisions.

The **Homestead Act of 1862,** a law of great significance, gave 160 acres of land to anyone who would pay a $10 registration fee and pledge to live on it and cultivate it for five years. The offer set off a mass migration of land-hungry Europeans, dazzled by a country that gave its land away. Americans also seized on the act's provisions, and between 1862 and 1900, nearly 600,000 families claimed free homesteads under it.

Yet the Homestead Act did not work as Congress had hoped. Few farmers and laborers had the cash to move to the frontier, buy farm equipment, and wait out the year or two before the farm became self-supporting. Tailored to the timber and water conditions of the East, the act did not work as well in the semiarid West. In the fertile valleys of the Mississippi, 160 acres provided a generous farm. A farmer on the Great Plains needed either a larger farm for dry farming or a smaller one for irrigation.

Speculators made ingenious use of the land laws. Sending agents in advance of settlement, they moved along choice river bottoms or irrigable areas, accumulating large holdings to be held for high prices. In the arid West, where control of water meant control of the surrounding land, shrewd ranchers plotted their holdings accordingly. In Colorado, one cattleman, John F. Iliff, owned only 105 small parcels of land, but by placing them around the few water holes, he effectively dominated an empire stretching over 6000 square miles.

Water, in fact, became a dominant western issue, since aside from the Pacific Northwest, northern California, parts of the Rocky Mountain West, and the eastern half of the Great Plains, much of the trans-Mississippi West was arid, receiving less than 20 inches of rainfall annually. People speculated in water as if it were gold and planned great irrigation systems in Utah, eastern Colorado, and California's Central Valley to "make the desert bloom."

Irrigators received a major boost in 1902 when the **National Reclamation Act (Newlands Act)** set aside most of the proceeds from the sale of public lands in sixteen western states to finance irrigation projects in the arid states. Over the next decades, dams, canals, and irrigation systems channeled water into dry areas, creating a "hydraulic" society that was rich in crops and cities (such as Los Angeles and Phoenix), but ever thirstier and in danger of outrunning the precious water on which it all depended.

As beneficiaries of the government's policy of land grants for railway construction, the railroad companies were the West's largest landowners. Eager to have immigrants settle on the land they owned near the railroad right-of-way, and eager to boost their freight and passenger business, the companies sent agents to the East and Europe.

In all, half a billion acres of western land were given or sold to speculators and corporations. At the same time, only 600,000 homestead patents were issued, covering 80 million acres. Thus, only one acre in every nine initially went to individual pioneers, the intended beneficiaries of the nation's largesse. Two-thirds of all homestead claimants before 1890 failed in their efforts to farm their new land.

National Reclamation Act (Newlands Act)

Passed in 1902, this legislation set aside the majority of the proceeds from the sale of public land in sixteen western states to fund irrigation projects in the arid states.

By what measures did the government distribute land in the West?

The Spanish-Speaking Southwest

In the nineteenth century, almost all Spanish-speaking people in the United States lived in California, Arizona, New Mexico, Texas, and Colorado. Their numbers were small—California had only 8086 Mexican residents in 1900—but the influence of their culture and institutions was large. In some respects, the southwestern frontier was more Spanish American than Anglo-American.

Pushing northward from Mexico, the Spanish gradually established the present-day economic structure of the Southwest. They brought with them techniques of mining, stock raising, and irrigated farming. After winning independence in the 1820s, the Mexicans brought new laws and ranching methods as well as chaps and the burro. Both Spanish and Mexicans created the legal framework for distributing land and water, a precious resource in the Southwest. They gave large grants of land to communities for grazing, to individuals as rewards for service, and to the various Native American pueblos.

In Southern California, the Californios, descendants of the original colonizers, began after the 1860s to lose their once vast landholdings to drought and mortgages. As they died out, Mexican Americans continued the Spanish-Mexican influence. In 1880, one-fourth of the residents of Los Angeles County were Spanish speaking.

Throughout the Southwest, the Spanish-Mexican heritage gave a distinctive shape to society. Men headed the families and dominated economic life. Women had substantial economic rights (though few political ones), and they enjoyed a status their English American counterparts did not have. Wives kept full control of property acquired before their marriage; they also held half title to all property in a marriage, which later caused many southwestern states to pass community property laws.

In addition, the Spanish-Mexican heritage fostered a modified economic caste system, a strong Roman Catholic influence, and the primary use of the Spanish

INVITATION TO THE DANCE In this painting by Theodore Gentilz, a young woman stands in the doorway of her San Antonio home to greet the group of *caballeros* riding up on their horses and making music on the violin and guitar. The caballeros' flared trousers, known as *calzoneras*, were well suited for riding and dancing. Note the distinctive architectural style of the white building at the left where a couple is dancing.

Why did the Spanish heritage play such a large role in the American Southwest?

QUICK CHECK ✔

In what ways did the Spanish-Mexican heritage of the Southwest shape its development?

language. Continuous immigration from Mexico kept language and cultural ties strong. Spanish names and customs spread, even among Anglos. David Starr Jordan, arriving from Indiana to become the first president of Stanford University in California, bestowed Spanish names on streets, houses, and a Stanford dormitory. Spanish was the region's first or second language. Confronted by Sheriff Pat Garrett in a darkened room, New Mexico's famous outlaw Billy the Kid died asking, "Quién es? Quién es?" ("Who is it? Who is it?").

The Bonanza West

WHAT ?

were the factors behind the West as a bonanza of dreams and get-rich-quick schemes?

Between 1850 and 1900, wave after wave of newcomers swept across the trans-Mississippi West. There were riches for the taking, hidden in gold-washed streams, spread lushly over grass-covered prairies, or available in the gullible minds of greedy newcomers. The nineteenth-century West took shape in the search for mining, cattle, and land bonanzas that drew eager settlers from the East and around the world.

As with all bonanzas, the consequences in the West were uneven growth, boom-and-bust economic cycles, and wasted resources. Society seemed constantly in the making. People moved here and there, following river bottoms, gold strikes, railroad tracks, and other opportunities. "Instant cities" arose. San Francisco, Salt Lake City, and Denver were the most spectacular examples, but every cow town and mining camp witnessed similar phenomena of growth. Boston needed more than two centuries to attract one-third of a million people; San Francisco did the same in a little more than twenty years.

Many Westerners had left home to get rich quickly, and they adopted institutions that reflected that goal. In their lives, the West was an idea as well as a region, and the idea molded them as much as they molded it.

The Mining Bonanza

Mining was the first important magnet to attract people to the West. Many hoped to "strike it rich" in gold and silver, but at least half the newcomers had no intention of working in the mines. Instead, they provided food, clothing, and services to the thousands of miners.

The California Gold Rush of 1849 began the mining boom and set the pattern for subsequent strikes in other regions. Individual prospectors made the first strikes, discovering pockets of gold along streams flowing westward from the Sierra Nevada. To get the gold, they used a simple process called **placer mining**, which required little skill, technology, or capital. A placer miner needed only a shovel, a washing pan, and a good claim. As the placers gave out, a great deal of gold remained, but it was locked in quartz or buried deep in the earth. Mining became an expensive business, far beyond the reach of the average miner.

Large corporations moved in to dig the deep shafts and finance costly equipment. Quartz mining required heavy rock crushers, mercury vats to dissolve the gold,

placer mining
A form of mining that required little technology or skill, placer mining techniques included using a shovel and a washing pan to separate gold from the ore in streams and riverbeds. An early phase of the mining industry, placer mining could be performed by miners working as individuals or in small groups.

Before the California Gold Rush of 1849, San Francisco was a sleepy little Spanish-Mexican village called Yerba Buena. Gold seekers turned it into a boomtown with an international population. Here, Spanish-Mexican rancheros, white prospectors, Chinese laborers, and a top-hatted professional gambler mingle in a San Francisco saloon. (*Source: Collection of The New-York Historical Society, negative number 16212.*)

What is important about the artist's rendering of the design of the saloon?

and large retorts to recapture it. Eastern and European financiers assumed control, labor became unionized, and mining towns took on some of the characteristics of the industrial city. Individual prospectors meanwhile dashed on to the next find. Unlike other frontiers, the mining frontier moved from west to east, as the original California miners—the "yonder-siders," they were called—hurried eastward in search of the big strike.

In 1859, fresh strikes were made near Pikes Peak in Colorado and in the Carson River Valley of Nevada. News of both discoveries set off wild migrations—100,000 miners were in Pikes Peak country by June 1859. The gold there quickly played out, but the Nevada find uncovered a thick bluish black ore that was almost pure silver and gold. A quick-witted drifter named Henry T. P. Comstock talked his way into partnership in the claim, and word of the **Comstock Lode**—a fabulous mine with ore worth $3876 a ton—flashed over the mountains.

Thousands of miners climbed the Sierra Nevada that summer; but the biggest strike was yet to come. In 1873, John W. Mackay and three partners formed a company to dig deep into the mountain, and at 1167 feet they hit the Big Bonanza, a seam of gold and silver more than 54 feet wide. It was the richest discovery in the history of mining. Between 1859 and 1879, the Comstock Lode produced gold and silver worth $306 million. Most of it went to financiers and corporations. Mackay himself became the richest person in the world.

In the 1860s and 1870s, important strikes were made in Washington, Idaho, Nevada, Colorado, Montana, Arizona, and Dakota. Extremely mobile, miners flocked from strike to strike, and new camps and mining towns sprang up overnight.

The final fling came in the Black Hills rush of 1874 to 1876. The army had tried to keep miners out of the area, the heart of the Sioux hunting grounds, and even sent a scientific party under Colonel George Armstrong Custer to disprove the rumors of gold and stop the miners' invasion. Instead, Custer found gold all over the hills, and the rush was on. Miners, gamblers, desperadoes, and prostitutes flocked to Deadwood, the most lawless of all the mining camps. There, Martha Jane Canary—a crack shot who, as Calamity Jane, won fame as a scout and teamster—fell in love with "Wild Bill" Hickok. Hickok himself—a western legend who had tamed Kansas cow towns, killed an unknown number of men, and toured in Buffalo Bill's Wild West Show—died in Deadwood, shot in the back of the head. Hickok was 39 years old.

Towns such as Deadwood, in the Dakota Territory; Virginia City, Nevada; Leadville, Colorado; and Tombstone, Arizona, demonstrated a new development process in the frontier experience. The farming frontier had developed naturally in a rural setting. On the mining frontier, the germ of a city—the camp—appeared almost simultaneously with the first "strike." Periodicals, the latest fashions, theaters, schools, literary clubs, and lending libraries came quickly to the camps, providing civilized refinements not available on other frontiers. Urbanization also created the need for municipal government, sanitation, and law enforcement.

Mining camps were governed by a simple democracy. Soon after a strike, the miners in the area met to organize a mining "district" and adopted rules governing behavior in it. Rules regulated the size and boundaries of claims, established procedures for settling disputes, and set penalties for crimes. Petty criminals were banished from the district; serious offenders were hanged. In the case of a major dispute, the whole camp gathered, chose legal counsel for both sides, and heard the evidence. If all else failed, miners formed secret vigilance committees to hang a few offenders as a lesson to the rest. Early visitors to the mining country were struck by the way miners, solitary and competitive, joined together, founded a camp, and created a society.

Comstock Lode

Discovered in 1859 near Virginia City, Nevada, this ore deposit was the richest discovery in the history of mining. Named after T. P. Comstock, a drifter who talked his way into partnership in the claim, the deposit produced silver and gold worth more than $306 million between 1859 and 1879.

LISTEN

Wild Bill Hickock

DOCUMENT

John Lester, "Hydraulic Mining"

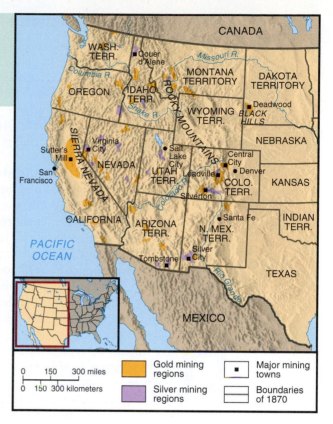

MINING REGIONS OF THE WEST   Gold and silver mines dotted the West, drawing settlers and encouraging political organization in many areas.

What were the characteristics of the mining towns?

The camps were mostly male, made up of "men who can rough it" and a few "ladies of spirit and energy." In 1870, men outnumbered women in the mining districts by more than two to one; there were few children. Prostitutes followed the camps around the West, and a "respectable" woman was an object of curiosity. Some women worked claims, but more often they took jobs as cooks, housekeepers, and seamstresses—for wages considerably higher than in the East.

In most camps, between one-quarter and one-half of the population was foreign born. The lure of gold drew large numbers of Chinese, Chileans, Peruvians, Mexicans, French, Germans, and English. Experienced miners, the Latin Americans brought valuable mining techniques. At least six thousand Mexicans joined the California rush of 1849, and by 1852, there were twenty-five thousand Chinese in California. Painstaking, the Chinese profitably worked claims others had abandoned. In the 1860s, almost one-third of the miners in the West were Chinese.

Hostility often surfaced against foreign miners, particularly the French, Latin Americans, and Chinese. Riots against Chinese laborers occurred in the 1870s and 1880s in Los Angeles, San Francisco, Seattle, Reno, and Denver. Responding to pressure, Congress passed the **Chinese Exclusion Act of 1882**, which suspended immigration of Chinese laborers for ten years. The number of Chinese in the United States fell drastically.

By the 1890s, the early mining bonanza was over. All told, the western mines contributed billions of dollars to the economy. They had helped finance the Civil War and provided needed capital for industrialization. The vast boost in silver production from the Comstock Lode changed the relative value of gold and silver, the base of American currency. Bitter disputes over the currency affected politics and led to the famous "battle of the standards" in the presidential election of 1896 (see Chapter 20).

The mining frontier populated portions of the West and sped its process of political organization. Nevada, Idaho, and Montana were granted early statehood because of mining. Merchants, editors, lawyers, and ministers moved with the advancing frontier, establishing permanent settlements. Women in the mining camps helped to foster family life and raised the moral tone by campaigning against drinking, gambling, and prostitution. But not all the effects of the mining boom were positive. The industry also left behind painful scars in the form of invaded Indian reservations, pitted hills, and lonely ghost towns.

Chinese Exclusion Act of 1882

Legislation passed in 1882 that excluded Chinese immigrant workers for ten years and denied U.S. citizenship to Chinese nationals living in the United States. It was the first U.S. exclusionary law that was aimed at a specific racial group.

 QUICK CHECK

What were the characteristics of the mining industry?

The Cattle Bonanza

"There's gold from the grass roots down," said California Joe, a guide in the gold districts of Dakota in the 1870s, "but there's more gold from the grass roots up." Ranchers began to recognize the potential of the vast grasslands of the West. The Plains were covered with buffalo or grama grass, a wiry variety with short, hard stems. Cattle thrived on it.

For twenty years after 1865, cattle ranching dominated the "open range," a vast fenceless area extending from the Texas Panhandle north into Canada. The techniques of the business came from Mexico. Long before American cowboys moved herds north, their Mexican counterparts, the *vaqueros,* developed the essential techniques of branding, roundups, and roping. The cattle themselves, the famous Texas longhorns, also came from Mexico. Spreading over the grasslands of southern Texas, the longhorns multiplied rapidly. Although their meat was coarse and stringy, they fed a nation hungry for beef at the end of the Civil War.

The problem was getting the beef to eastern markets, and Joseph G. McCoy, a livestock shipper from Illinois, solved it. Looking for a way to market Texas beef, McCoy conceived the idea of taking the cattle to railheads in Kansas. He talked first with the president of the Missouri Pacific, who ordered him out of his office, and then with the head of the Kansas Pacific, who laughed at the idea. The persistent McCoy finally signed a contract in 1867 with the Hannibal and St. Joseph Railroad. Searching for an appropriate rail junction, he settled on the sleepy Kansas town of Abilene, "a very small, dead place," he remembered, with about a dozen log huts and one nearly bankrupt saloon.

Joseph G. McCoy, Historic Sketches of the Cattle Trade

In September 1867, McCoy shipped the first train of twenty cars of longhorn cattle. By the end of the year, a thousand carloads had followed, all headed for Chicago markets. In 1870, 300,000 head of Texas cattle reached Abilene, followed the next year—the peak year—by 700,000 head. The Alamo Saloon, crowded with tired cowboys at the end of the drive, now employed seventy-five bartenders, working three 8-hour shifts.

The profits were enormous. Drivers bought cheap Texas steers for $4 a head and sold them for $30 or $40 a head at the northern railhead. The most famous trail was the Chisholm, running from southern Texas through Oklahoma Territory to Ellsworth and Abilene, Kansas, on the Kansas Pacific Railroad. Dodge City, Kansas, became the prime shipping center between 1875 and 1879.

Cowboys pushed steers northward in herds of two to three thousand. Novels and films have portrayed the cowboys as white, but at least a quarter of them were black, and possibly another quarter were Mexicans. A typical crew on the trail north might have eight men, half of them black or Mexican. Most of the trail bosses were white; they earned about $125 a month.

Perspectives on the American Cowboy

Like miners, cattlemen lived beyond the formal reach of the law and so established their own. Before each drive, Charles Goodnight drew up rules governing behavior on the trail. A cowboy who shot another was hanged on the spot. Ranchers adopted rules for cattle ownership, branding, roundups, and drives, and they formed associations to enforce them. The Wyoming Stock Growers' Association, the largest and most formidable, had four hundred members owning two million cattle; its reach extended well beyond Wyoming into Colorado, Nebraska, Montana, and the Dakotas. Throughout this vast territory, the "laws" of the association were often the law of the land.

By 1880, more than six million cattle had been driven to northern markets. But the era of the great cattle drive was ending. Farmers were planting wheat on the old

CATTLE TRAILS   Cattle raised in Texas were driven along the cattle trails to the northern railheads, and trains carried them to market.

What factors led to the location of the major cattle trails?

buffalo ranges; barbed wire, a recent invention, cut across the trails and divided up the big ranches. Mechanical improvements in slaughtering, refrigerated transportation, and cold storage modernized the industry. Ranchers bred the Texas longhorns with heavier Hereford and Angus bulls, and as the new breeds proved profitable, more and more ranches opened on the northern ranges. Stories of vast profits circulated, attracting outside capital. Large investments transformed ranching into big business, often controlled by absentee owners and subject to new problems.

By 1885, however, experienced cattle ranchers were growing alarmed. The winter of 1885 to 1886 was cold, and the following summer was one of the hottest on record. Water holes dried up; the grass turned brown. Beef prices fell.

The winter of 1886–1887 was one of the worst in western history. Temperatures dropped to 45 degrees below zero, and cattle that once would have saved themselves by drifting ahead of the storms came up against the new barbed wire fences. Herds jammed together, pawing the frozen ground or stripping bark from trees in search of food. Cattle died by the tens of thousands. In the spring of 1887, when the snows thawed, ranchers found stacks of carcasses piled up against the fences.

The melting snows did, however, produce a lush crop of grass for the survivors. The cattle business recovered, but it took different directions. Outside capital, so plentiful in the boom years, dried up. Ranchers began fencing their lands, reducing their herds, and growing hay for winter food.

The last roundup on the northern ranges took place in 1905. Ranches grew smaller, and some ranchers, at first in the scrub country of the Southwest, then on the Plains themselves, switched to raising sheep. By 1900, there were nearly thirty-eight million sheep west of the Missouri River, far more than there were cattle.

Ranchers and sheepherders fought bitterly to control the grazing lands, but they had one problem in common: the troubles ahead. Homesteaders, armed with barbed wire and new strains of wheat, were pushing onto the Plains, and the day of the open range was over.

QUICK CHECK ✓

What characterized the growth of the cattle business in these years?

The Farming Bonanza

Like miners and cattle ranchers, millions of farmers moved into the West in the decades after 1870 to seek crop bonanzas and new ways of life. Some realized their dreams; many fought just to survive.

Between 1870 and 1900, farmers cultivated more land than ever before in American history. They peopled the Plains from Dakota to Texas, pushed the Indians out of their last sanctuary in Oklahoma, and poured into the basins and foothills of the Rockies. By 1900, the western half of the nation contained almost 30 percent of the population, compared to less than 1 percent just a half century earlier.

Unlike mining, farm settlement often followed predictable patterns, taking population from states east of the settlement line and moving gradually westward. Crossing the Mississippi, farmers settled first in western Iowa, Minnesota, Nebraska, Kansas, Texas, and South Dakota. The movement slumped during the depression of the 1870s, but then a new wave of optimism carried thousands more west. Several years of above average rainfall convinced farmers that the Dakotas, western Nebraska and Kansas, and eastern Colorado were the "rain belt of the Plains." Between 1870 and 1900, the population on the Plains tripled.

In some areas, the newcomers were blacks who had fled the South, fed up with beatings and murders, crop liens, and the Black Codes that institutionalized their subordinate status. In 1879, about six thousand African Americans known as the **Exodusters** left their homes in Louisiana, Mississippi, and Texas to establish new and freer lives in Kansas, the home of John Brown and the Free-Soil campaigns of the 1850s. Once there, they farmed or worked as laborers; women worked in the fields alongside the men or cleaned houses and took in washing to make ends meet. All told, the Exodusters homesteaded 20,000 acres of land, and though they met prejudice, it was not as extreme as they had known at home.

Other African Americans moved to Oklahoma, thinking they might establish the first African American state. Whether headed for Oklahoma or Kansas, they picked up and moved in sizable groups that were based on family units; they took with them the customs they had known, and in their new homes they were able, for the first time, to have some measure of self-government.

Exodusters
A group of about six thousand African Americans who left their homes in Louisiana, Mississippi, and Texas in 1879, seeking freer lives in Kansas, where they worked as farmers or laborers.

For blacks and whites alike, farming on the Plains presented new problems. There was little surface water, and wells ranged between 50 and 500 feet deep. Well drillers charged up to $2 a foot. Taking advantage of the steady Plains winds, windmills brought the water to the surface, but they too were expensive, and until 1900, many farmers could not afford them. Lumber for homes and fences was also scarce.

Unable to afford wood, farmers often started out in dreary sod houses. Cut into 3-foot sections, the thick prairie sod was laid like brick, with space left for two windows and a door. Since glass was scarce, cloth hung over the windows; a blanket was hung from the ceiling to make two rooms. Sod houses were small, provided little light and air, and were impossible to keep clean. When it rained, water seeped through the roof. Yet a sod house cost only $2.78 to build.

Outside, the Plains environment sorely tested the men and women who moved there. In the winters, savage storms swept the open grasslands. Ice caked on the cattle until their heads were too heavy to hold up. Summertime temperatures stayed near 110 degrees for weeks at a time. Fearsome rainstorms, building in the summer's heat, beat down the young corn and wheat. The summers also brought grasshoppers, arriving without warning, flying in clouds so huge they shut out the sun. The grasshoppers ate everything in sight: crops, clothing, mosquito netting, tree bark, even plow handles. In the summer of 1874, they devastated the whole Plains from Texas to the Dakotas, eating everything "but the mortgage," as one farmer said.

Farmers adopted new techniques to meet these conditions. Most importantly, they needed cheap and effective fencing material, and in 1874, Joseph F. Glidden, a farmer from De Kalb, Illinois, provided it with the invention of barbed wire. By 1883, his factory was turning out 600 miles of barbed wire every day, and farmers were buying it faster than it could be produced. Barbed wire fences helped them to pen their own stock and keep other animals out.

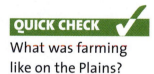

QUICK CHECK

What was farming like on the Plains?

Discontent on the Farm

Touring the farming areas in the 1860s, Oliver H. Kelley, a clerk in the Department of Agriculture, was struck by the drabness of rural life. In 1867, he founded the **National Grange of the Patrons of Husbandry,** known simply as the Grange. The Grange provided social, cultural, and educational activities for its members. Its constitution banned involvement in politics, but Grangers often ignored the rules and supported railroad regulation and other measures.

The Grange grew rapidly during the depression of the 1870s, and by 1875, it had more than 800,000 members in 20,000 local Granges. Most were in the Midwest and South. The Granges set up cooperative stores, grain elevators, warehouses, insurance companies, and farm machinery factories. Many failed, but in the meantime the organization made its mark. Picking up where the Grange left off, farm-oriented groups such as the Farmers' Alliance, with branches in both South and West, began to attract followers.

Like the cattle boom, the farming boom ended sharply after 1887. A severe drought that year cut harvests, and other droughts followed in 1889 and 1894. Thousands of new farmers were wiped out on the western Plains. Between 1888 and 1892, more than half the population of western Kansas left. Farmers grew angry and restless. They complained about declining crop prices, rising railroad rates, and heavy mortgages.

National Grange of the Patrons of Husbandry

Founded by Oliver H. Kelley in 1867, the Grange sought to relieve the drabness of farm life by providing a social, educational, and cultural outlet for its members. It also set up grain elevators, cooperative stores, warehouses, insurance companies, and farm machinery factories. Although its constitution banned political involvement, the Grange often supported railroad regulation and other measures.

Although many farmers were unhappy, the peopling of the West in those years transformed American agriculture. The states beyond the Mississippi became the garden land of the nation. California sent fruit, wine, and wheat to eastern markets. Under the Mormons, Utah flourished with irrigation. Texas beef stocked the country's tables, and vast wheat fields, stretching to the horizon, covered Minnesota, the Dakotas, Montana, and eastern Colorado. All produced more than Americans could consume. By 1890, American farmers were exporting large amounts of wheat and other crops.

Farmers became more commercial and scientific. They needed to know more and work harder. Mail-order houses and rural free delivery diminished their isolation and tied them ever closer to the national future. "This is a new age to the farmer," said a statistician in the Department of Agriculture in 1889. "He is now, more than ever before, a citizen of the world."

QUICK CHECK

Why were so many farmers unhappy in the last decades of the nineteenth century, and what did they try to do about it?

The Purposes of the Grange

The Final Fling

As the West filled in with people, pressure mounted on the president and Congress to open the last Indian territory, Oklahoma, to settlers. In March 1889, Congress acted and forced the Creek and Seminole tribes, which had been moved into Oklahoma in the 1820s, to surrender their rights to the land. With arrangements complete, President Benjamin Harrison announced the opening of the Oklahoma District as of noon, April 22, 1889.

Preparations were feverish all along the frontier. On the morning of April 22, nearly a hundred thousand people lined the Oklahoma borders. At noon, the starting flag dropped. Bugles and cannon signaled the opening of the "last" territory. Horsemen lunged forward; overloaded wagons collided and overturned. By sunset that day, settlers claimed twelve thousand homesteads, and the 1.92 million acres of the Oklahoma District were officially settled. The "Boomers" (those who waited for the signal) and "Sooners" (those who had jumped the gun) reflected the speed of western settlement. "Creation!" a character in Edna Ferber's novel *Cimarron* declared. "Hell! That took six days. This was done in one. It was History made in an hour—and I helped make it."

QUICK CHECK

Who were the "Boomers," and who were the "Sooners"?

Conclusion: The Meaning of the West

Turner, "The Significance of the Frontier in American History"

Between the Civil War and 1900, the West witnessed one of the greatest migrations in history. With the Native Americans driven into smaller and smaller areas, farms, ranches, mines, and cities took over the vast lands from the Mississippi to the Pacific. The 1890 census noted that for the first time in the country's history, "there can hardly be said to be a frontier line." Picking up the theme, Frederick Jackson Turner, a young history instructor at the University of Wisconsin, examined its importance in an influential 1893 paper, "The Significance of the Frontier in American History."

"The existence of an area of free land," Turner wrote, "its continuous recession, and the advance of American settlement westward, explain American development." It shaped customs and character; gave rise to independence, self-confidence, and individualism; and fostered invention and adaptation. Historians have substantially modified **Turner's thesis** by pointing to frontier conservatism and imitativeness, the influence of varying racial groups, and the persistence of European ideas and institutions. Most recently, they have shown that family and community loomed as large as individualism on the frontier; men, women, and children played very much the same roles as they had back home.

Rejecting Turner almost completely, a group of "new Western historians" has advanced a different and complex view of the West, and one with few heroes and heroines. Emphasizing the region's racial and ethnic diversity, these historians stress the role of women as well as men, trace struggles between economic interests instead of fights between gunslingers, and question the impact of development on the environment. White English-speaking Americans, they suggest, could be said to have conquered the West rather than settled it.

The West, in this view, was not settled by a wave of white migrants moving west across the continent (Turner's "frontier") but by a set of waves—Anglo, Mexican American, African American, Asian American, and others—moving in many directions and interacting with each other and with Native American cultures to produce the modern West. Nor did western history end in 1890 as Turner would have it. Instead, migration, development, and economic exploitation continued into the twentieth and twenty-first centuries, illustrated in the fact that the number of people who moved to the West after 1900 far exceeded those who had moved there before.

In the nineteenth, twentieth, and twenty-first centuries, there can be no doubt that the image of the frontier and the West influenced American development. Western lands attracted European, Latin American, and Asian immigrants, adding to the society's talent and diversity. The mines, forests, and farms of the West fueled the economy, sent raw materials to eastern factories, and fed the growing cities. Though defeated in warfare, the Native Americans and Mexicans influenced art, architecture, law, and western folklore. The West was the first American empire, and it had a profound impact on the American mind and imagination.

Turner's thesis

Put forth by historian Frederick Jackson Turner in his 1893 paper, "The Significance of the Frontier in American History," this thesis asserted that the existence of a frontier and its settlement had shaped American character; given rise to individualism, independence, and self-confidence; and fostered the American spirit of invention and adaptation. Later historians, especially a group of "new Western historians," modified the thesis by pointing out the environmental and other consequences of frontier settlement, the role of the federal government in peopling the arid West, and the clash of races and cultures that took place on the frontier.

For a list of additional titles related to this chapter's topics, please see www.pearsonamericanhistory.com.

MyHistoryLab

STUDY RESOURCES

KEY TERMS

CHAPTER REVIEW

WHAT were the particular challenges of settling the country west of the Mississippi?

As people began moving west of the Mississippi River, they encountered new conditions, including vast treeless plains and towering mountain ranges. Above all, they left behind the water and timber on which they had depended in the East, forcing them to devise ways to deal with the different challenges. (*p. 451*)

HOW did white Americans crush the culture of the Native Americans as they moved west?

Through the centuries before Europeans and others arrived, Native Americans had developed a complex culture suited to the various environments in which they lived. The United States government and white settlers employed a variety of methods—political, military, legal, and cultural—to oust the Indians from their lands, "civilize" them, and contain and control them. (*p. 452*)

WHAT led Americans and others to move to the West?

There were many reasons Americans moved west, including a desire to get rich, to seek religious freedom, and to improve health, among other things. The federal government helped out with generous land laws and with laws favoring irrigation in the arid West. In the Southwest a proud culture took shape around Spanish laws and customs, involving water, the rights of women, and the sale, ownership, and use of land. (*p. 460*)

WHAT were the factors behind the West as a bonanza of dreams and get-rich-quick schemes?

The West attracted hundreds of thousands of people seeking a better economic life. Many failed, of course, but many also succeeded, finding their own particular bonanzas in mining, cattle ranching, and farming. In many of these areas, western development paralleled trends in the rest of the nation: larger and larger businesses, new uses for technology, and the employment of outside capital. (*p. 464*)

MAKING CONNECTIONS

1. What kinds of conditions did settlers find as they moved into lands west of the Mississippi River, and how had the peoples who already lived there dealt with these conditions?
2. What was the nature of Indian culture on the Plains, and how did it deal with the hordes of settlers moving into the area?
3. By what methods did settlers move west and adjust to the "bonanzas" they found in the West and Southwest?
4. What were the three bonanzas that drew settlers into the West, and in what ways did they lead to the destruction of Native American culture and shape the growth of the area?

PRACTICE QUIZ

1. In 1865 approximately _____ Indians lived west of the Mississippi River.
   - **a.** 1 million
   - **b.** 750,000
   - **c.** 500,000
   - **d.** 250,000

2. The _____ Indians depended on buffalo for food, clothing, and tools.
   - **a.** Plains
   - **b.** Iroquois
   - **c.** Pueblo
   - **d.** Cherokee

3. In 1864 the _____ massacre in Colorado ignited white protests in the eastern states.
   - **a.** Ludlow
   - **b.** Sand Creek
   - **c.** Chivington
   - **d.** Wounded Knee

4. The great _____ took place between 1865 and 1867.
   - **a.** Modoc War
   - **b.** Sioux War
   - **c.** Iroquois War
   - **d.** Seminole War

5. At the Little Bighorn River in 1876, Native American warriors wiped out
   - **a.** Ulysses S. Grant
   - **b.** William Tecumseh Sherman
   - **c.** Zachary Taylor
   - **d.** George Armstrong Custer

6. Congress stopped making treaties with Native American tribes in the year
   - **a.** 1865
   - **b.** 1871
   - **c.** 1881
   - **d.** 1891

7. After 1840 many white settlers expanded west into which of the following regions?
   - **a.** Missouri
   - **b.** New Jersey
   - **c.** Georgia
   - **d.** South Carolina

8. All of the following describe the Ghost Dance in the late nineteenth century *except*
   - **a.** In 1890 the Teton Sioux turned to the Ghost Dance for spiritual salvation.
   - **b.** A Paiute messiah named Wovoka started the Ghost Dance.
   - **c.** Wovoka said that dancing would return Indian lands and make whites disappear.
   - **d.** The federal government approved of the Ghost Dances.

9. Which of the following *does not* describe the Dawes Act of 1887?
   - **a.** Native Americans knew much about farming before the act was passed.
   - **b.** The policy held that each Indian would receive a farm.
   - **c.** The Dawes Act extended the assimilation campaign.
   - **d.** Each Indian family head received 160 acres of land under the act.

10. Which of the following statements most accurately explains why the buffalo declined in the United States during the late 1800s?
    - **a.** Professional Anglo American hunters and the U.S. military wiped out buffalo herds.
    - **b.** Native Americans hunted the buffalo to extinction.
    - **c.** A major disease outbreak wiped out the buffalo population.
    - **d.** The majority of buffalo were driven to Texas by Mexican vaqueros.

Find more practice at
www.myhistorylab.com

SAMPLE ESSAY QUESTIONS

1. Evaluate federal Indian policy after the Civil War.

2. Explain how factors such as geography and climate shaped the development of the American West after the Civil War.

Answers to Practice Quiz **1.** d, p.452 **2.** a, p.453 **3.** c, p.453 **4.** b, p.455 **5.** d, p.455 **6.** b, p.457 **7.** a, p.451 **8.** d, p.456 **9.** a, p.458 **10.** a, p.459

The Industrial Society
1850–1901

THE CORLISS ENGINE A "mechanical marvel" at the Centennial Exposition, the Corliss engine was a prime example of the giantism so admired by the public. (*Source: "The Corliss Engine," The Metropolitan Museum of Art, New York, NY, U.S.A. Image copyright © The Metropolitan Museum of Art/Art Resource, NY.*)

What did the Corliss engine symbolize in the new industrial society?

A Machine Culture

In 1876, Americans celebrated their first century of independence. Survivors of a recent civil war, they observed the centenary proudly and rather self-consciously, in song and speech, and above all in a grand Centennial Exposition held in Philadelphia, Pennsylvania.

Spread over several hundred acres, the exposition occupied 180 buildings and attracted nine million visitors, about one-fifth of the country's population at the time. Significantly, it focused more on

KEY EVENTS

1859   First oil well drilled near Titusville, Pennsylvania, *p. 488*

1869   Transcontinental railroad completed at Promontory, Utah, *p. 483* ■ Knights of Labor organize, *p. 496*

1876   Alexander Graham Bell invents the telephone, *p. 490* ■ Centennial Exposition held in Philadelphia, *p. 477*

1877   Railroads cut workers' wages, leading to bloody and violent strikes, *p. 498*

1879   Thomas A. Edison invents the incandescent lamp, *p. 491*

1882   Rockefeller's Standard Oil Company becomes nation's first trust, *p. 489*

1883   Railroads introduce standard time zones, *p. 483*

1886   Samuel Gompers founds American Federation of Labor (AFL), *p. 497* ■ Labor protest erupts in violence in Haymarket Riot in Chicago, *p. 498* ■ Railroads adopt standard gauge, *p. 482*

1892   Workers strike at Homestead steel plant in Pennsylvania, *p. 499*

the present than the past. Fairgoers strolled through exhibits of life in colonial times, then hurried off to see the main attractions: machines, inventions, and products of the new industrial era. They saw linoleum, a new, easy-to-clean floor covering. For the first time, they tasted root beer, supplied by a young druggist named Charles Hires, and the exotic banana, wrapped in foil and selling for a dime. They saw their first bicycle, an awkward high-wheeled contraption with solid tires.

A Japanese pavilion generated widespread interest in the culture of Japan. There was also a women's building, the first ever in a major exposition. Inside were displayed paintings and sculpture by women artists, along with rows of textile machinery staffed by female operators.

In the entire exposition, machinery was the focus, and Machinery Hall was the most popular building. Here were the products of an ever improving civilization. Long lines of the curious waited to see the telephone, Alexander Graham Bell's new device. ("My God, it talks!" the emperor of Brazil exclaimed.) Thomas A. Edison displayed several recent inventions, while nearby, whirring machines turned out bricks, chewing tobacco, and other products. Fairgoers saw the first public display of the typewriter, Elisha Otis's new elevator, and the Westinghouse railroad air brake.

But above all, they crowded around the mighty Corliss engine, the focal point of the exposition. A giant steam engine, it dwarfed everything else in Machinery Hall, its twin vertical cylinders towering almost four stories in the air. Alone, it supplied power for the eight thousand other machines, large and small, on the exposition grounds. Poorly designed, the Corliss was soon obsolete, but for the moment it captured the nation's imagination. It symbolized swift movement toward an industrial and urban society. John Greenleaf Whittier, the aging rural poet, likened it to the snake in the Garden of Eden and refused to see it.

As Whittier feared, the United States was fast becoming an industrial society. Developments earlier in the century laid the basis, but the most spectacular advances in industrialization came during the three decades after the Civil War. At the start of the war, the country lagged well behind industrializing nations such as Great Britain, France, and Germany. By 1900, it had vaulted far into the lead, with a manufacturing output that exceeded the *combined* output of its three European rivals. Over the same years, cities grew, technology advanced, and farm production rose. Developments in manufacturing, mining, agriculture, transportation, and communications changed society.

In this change, railroads, steel, oil, and other industries, all shaped by the hands of labor, played a leading role. Many Americans eagerly welcomed the new directions. William Dean Howells, a leading novelist, visited the Centennial Exposition and stood in awe before the Corliss. Comparing it to the paintings and sculpture on display, Howells preferred the machine: "It is in these things of iron and steel," he said, "that the national genius most freely speaks."

Industrial Development

American industry owed its remarkable growth to several considerations. It fed on an abundance of natural resources: coal, iron, timber, petroleum, waterpower. An iron manufacturer likened the nation to "a gigantic bowl filled with treasure." Labor was also abundant, drawn from American farm families and the hosts of European immigrants who flocked to American mines, cities, and factories. Nearly eight million immigrants arrived in the 1870s and 1880s; another fifteen million came between 1890 and 1914—large figures for a nation whose total population in 1900 was about seventy-six million people.

The burgeoning population led to expanded markets, which new devices such as the telegraph and telephone helped to exploit. The swiftly growing urban populations devoured goods, and the railroads, spreading pell-mell across the land, linked the cities together and opened a national market. Within its boundaries, the United States had the largest free trade market in the world, while tariff barriers partially protected its producers from outside competition.

Expansive market and labor conditions buoyed the confidence of European and American investors, who provided large amounts of capital. Technological progress, so remarkable in these years, doomed some older industries (tallow, for example) but increased productivity in others, such as the kerosene industry, and created entirely new industries as well. Through inventions such as the harvester and the combine, it also helped foster a firm agricultural base, on which industrialization depended.

Eager to promote economic growth, government at all levels—federal, state, and local—gave manufacturers money, land, and other resources. Other benefits, too, flowed from the American system of government: stability, commitment to the concept of private property, and, initially at least, a reluctance to regulate industrial activity. Unlike their European counterparts, American manufacturers faced few legal or social barriers, and their main domestic rivals, the southern planters, had lost political power in the Civil War.

In this atmosphere, entrepreneurs flourished. Taking steps crucial for industrialization, they organized, managed, and assumed the financial risks of the new enterprises. Admirers called them captains of industry; foes labeled them robber barons. To some degree, they were both—creative *and* acquisitive. If sometimes they seemed larger than life, it was because they dealt in concepts, distances, and quantities often unknown to earlier generations.

Industrial growth was neither a simple nor steady nor inevitable process. It involved human decisions and brought with it large social benefits and costs. Growth varied from industry to industry and from year to year. It was concentrated in the Northeast, where in 1890, more than 85 percent of America's manufactured goods originated. The more sparsely settled West provided raw materials, while the South, although making major gains in iron, textiles, and tobacco, had to rebuild after wartime devastation.

Still, industrial development proceeded at an extraordinary pace. Between 1865 and 1914, the real gross national product—the total monetary value of all goods and services produced in a year, with prices held stable—grew at a rate of more than 4 percent a year, increasing about eightfold overall. As Robert Higgs, an economic historian, noted, "Never before had such rapid growth continued for so long."

WHAT were the factors that enabled the United States to build an industrial economy?

An Empire on Rails

HOW

?

and why did the railroad system grow?

Genuine revolutions happen rarely, but a major one occurred in the nineteenth century: a revolution in transportation and communications. When the nineteenth century began, people traveled and communicated much as they had for centuries before; when it ended, the railroad, the telegraph, the telephone, and the oceangoing steamship had wrought enormous changes.

The steamship sliced in half the time of the Atlantic crossing and introduced new regularity in the movement of goods and passengers. The telegraph, flashing messages almost instantaneously along miles of wire (400,000 miles of it in the early 1880s), transformed communications, as did the telephone a little later. But the railroad worked the largest changes of all. Along with Bessemer steel, it was the most significant technical innovation of the century.

Advantages of the Railroad

The railroad dramatically affected economic and social life. Economic growth would have occurred without it, of course; canals, inland steamboats, and the country's superb system of interior waterways already provided the outlines of an effective transportation network. But the railroad added significantly to the network and contributed advantages all its own.

Those advantages included more direct routes, greater speed, greater safety and comfort than other modes of land travel, more dependable schedules, a larger volume of traffic, and year-round service. A day's land travel on stagecoach or horseback might cover fifty miles. The railroad covered 50 miles in about an hour, 700 miles in a day. It went where canals and rivers did not go—directly to the loading platforms of great factories or across the arid West. As construction crews pushed tracks onward, vast areas of the continent opened for settlement.

Consequently, American railroads differed from European ones. In Europe, railroads were usually built between cities and towns that already existed; they carried mostly the same goods that earlier forms of transportation had. In the United States, they did that and more: They often created the very towns they then served, and they ended up carrying cattle from Texas, fruit from Florida, and other goods that had never been carried before.

Linking widely separated cities and villages, the railroad ended the relative isolation and self-sufficiency of the country's "island communities." It tied people together, brought in outside products, fostered greater interdependence, and encouraged economic specialization. The railroad made possible a national market and in so doing pointed the way toward mass production and mass consumption, two of the hallmarks of twentieth-century society. It also pointed the way toward later business development.

A railroad corporation, far-flung and complex, was a new kind of business. It stretched over thousands of miles, employed thousands of people, dealt with countless customers, and required a scale of organization and decision making unknown in earlier business. Railroad managers never met most customers or even many employees; thus arose new problems in marketing and labor relations. Year by year, railroad companies consumed large quantities of iron, steel, coal, lumber, and glass, stimulating growth and employment in numerous industries.

No wonder, then, that the railroad captured so completely the country's imagination. For nearly a hundred years—the railroad era lasted through the 1940s—children gathered at depots, paused in the fields to wave as the fast express flashed by, listened at night to far-off whistles, and wondered what lay down the tracks. They lived in a world grown smaller.

QUICK CHECK ✔

What advantages did the railroad have over earlier forms of transportation?

Building the Empire

When Lee surrendered at Appomattox in 1865, the country already had 35,000 miles of track, and much of the railroad system east of the Mississippi River was in place. Farther west, the rail network stood poised on the edge of settlement. Although southern railroads were in shambles from the war, the United States had nearly as much railroad track as the rest of the world.

After the Civil War, rail construction increased by leaps and bounds. From 35,000 miles in 1865, the network expanded to 193,000 miles in 1900—more than in all Europe, including Russia. Mileage peaked at 254,037 miles in 1916, just before the industry began its long decline into the mid-twentieth century.

To build such an empire took vast amounts of capital. American and European investors provided some of the money; government supplied the rest. The federal government loaned nearly $65 million to a half dozen western railroads and donated millions of acres of the public domain.

Almost 90 percent of the federal land grants lay in twenty states west of the Mississippi River. Federal land grants helped build 18,738 miles of track, less than

MAP

Railroads and New Transportation Systems

RAILROAD CONSTRUCTION, 1830–1920

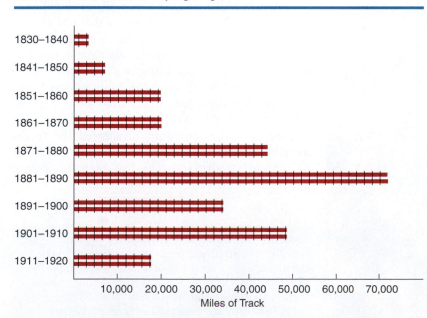

Source: U.S. Bureau of the Census, *Historical Statistics of the United States, Colonial Times to 1970,* Bicentennial Edition, Washington, D.C., 1975.

8 percent of the system. The land was frequently distant and difficult to market. Railroad companies sometimes sold it to raise cash, but more often they used it as security for bonds or loans.

Beyond doubt, the grants of cash and land promoted waste and corruption. The companies built fast and wastefully, eager to collect the subsidies that went with each mile of track. The grants also enabled railroads to build into territories that were pledged to the Indians, thus contributing to the wanton destruction of Indian life.

Yet, on balance, the grants probably worked more benefits than evils. As Congress had hoped, the grants were the lure for railroad building across the rugged, unsettled West, where it would be years before the railroads' revenues would repay their construction. Farmers, ranchers, and merchants poured into the newly opened areas, settling the country and boosting the value of government and private land nearby. The grants seemed necessary in a nation which, unlike Europe, expected private enterprise to build the railroads. In return for government aid, Congress required the railroads to carry government freight, troops, and mail at substantially reduced rates—resulting in savings to the government of almost $1 billion between 1850 and 1945. In no other cases of federal subsidies to carriers—canals, highways, and airlines—did Congress exact specific benefits in return.

QUICK CHECK

How did the railroad empire grow?

Cornelius Vanderbilt, in this cartoon of the "Modern Colossus of (Rail) Roads," is shown towering over his rail empire and pulling the strings to control its operations. In addition to the New York Central, Vanderbilt gained control of the Hudson River Railroad, the Lake Shore and Michigan Southern Railway, and the Canadian Southern Railway.

What does this cartoon suggest about Vanderbilt's power?

Linking the Nation via Trunk Lines

The early railroads may seem to have linked different regions, but in fact they did not. Built with little regard for through traffic, they were designed more to protect local interests than to tap outside markets. Many extended less than fifty miles. To avoid cooperating with other lines, they adopted conflicting schedules, built separate depots, and above all, used different gauges. Gauges, the distance between the rails, ranged from 4 feet $8\frac{1}{2}$ inches, which became the standard gauge, to 6 feet. Without special equipment, trains of one gauge could not run on tracks of another.

The Civil War showed the value of fast long-distance transportation, and after 1865, railroad managers worked to provide it. In a burst of consolidation, the large companies swallowed the small; integrated rail networks became a reality. Railroads also adopted standard schedules, signals, and equipment and finally, in 1886, the standard gauge.

In the Northeast, four great **trunk lines** took shape, all intended to link eastern seaports with the rich traffic of the Great Lakes and western rivers. Like a massive river system, trunk lines drew traffic from dozens of tributaries (feeder lines) and carried it to major markets. The Baltimore and Ohio (B & O), which reached Chicago in 1874, was one; the Erie Railroad, which ran from New York to Chicago, was another. The Erie competed bitterly with the New York Central Railroad, the third trunk line, and its owner, Cornelius Vanderbilt, a multimillionaire from the shipping business.

J. Edgar Thomson and Thomas A. Scott built the fourth trunk line, the Pennsylvania Railroad, which initially ran from Philadelphia to Pittsburgh. Restless and energetic, they dreamed of a rail empire stretching through the South and West.

In the war-damaged South, however, consolidation took longer. As Reconstruction waned, northern and European capital rebuilt and integrated the southern lines, especially during the 1880s, when rail construction in the South led the nation. By 1900, the South had five large systems linking its major cities and farming and industrial regions. Four decades after the secession crisis, these systems tied the South into a national transportation network.

Over that rail system, passengers and freight moved in relative speed, comfort, and safety. Automatic couplers (1867), air brakes (1869), refrigerator cars (1867), dining cars, heated cars, electric switches, and stronger locomotives transformed railroad service. George Pullman's lavish sleeping cars became popular.

In November 1883, the railroads even changed time. Ending the crazy quilt jumble of local times that caused scheduling difficulties, the American Railway Association divided the country into four time zones and adopted the modern system of standard time. Congress took thirty-five years longer; it adopted standard time in 1918, in the midst of World War I.

trunk lines
Four major railroad networks that emerged after the Civil War to connect the eastern seaports to the Great Lakes and western rivers. They reflected the growing integration of transportation across the country that helped spur large-scale industrialization.

QUICK CHECK

How did the railroad tie the nation together?

Rails Across the Continent

The dream of a transcontinental railroad, linking the Atlantic and Pacific Oceans, stretched back many years but had always been lost to sectional quarrels over the route. In 1862 and 1864, with the South out of the picture, Congress moved to build the first transcontinental railroad. It chartered the Union Pacific Railroad Company to build westward from Nebraska and the Central Pacific Railroad Company to build eastward from the Pacific coast.

Construction began simultaneously at Omaha and Sacramento in 1863, lagged during the war, and moved vigorously ahead after 1865. It became a race, each company vying for land, loans, and potential markets. General Grenville M. Dodge, a tough Union army veteran, served as construction chief for the Union Pacific, while Charles Crocker, a former Sacramento dry goods merchant, led the Central Pacific crews. Dodge organized an army of ten thousand workers, many of them ex-soldiers and Irish immigrants. Pushing rapidly westward, he encountered frequent attacks from Native Americans defending their lands, but he had the advantage of building over flat prairie.

Crocker faced more trying conditions in the high Sierra Nevada along California's eastern border. After several experiments, he decided that Chinese laborers worked best, and he hired six thousand of them, most brought directly from China. "I built the Central Pacific," Crocker enjoyed boasting, but the Chinese crews in fact did the awesome work. Under the most difficult conditions, they dug, blasted, and pushed their way slowly east.

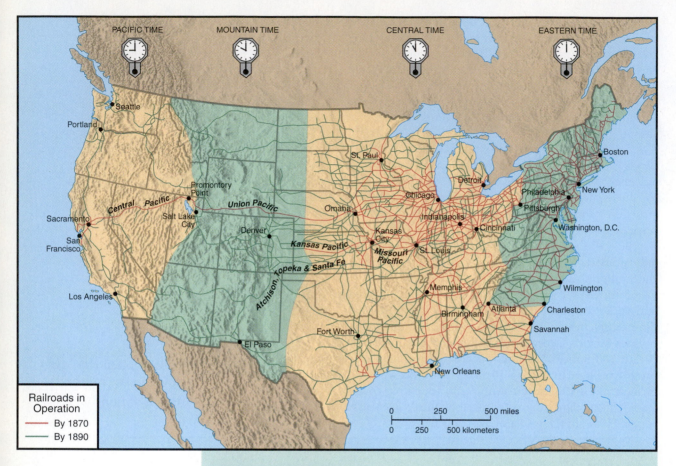

RAILROADS, 1870 AND 1890   In the last quarter of the nineteenth century, railroads expanded into Texas, the far Southwest, and the Northwest, carrying settlers, businesses, and government to the far-flung areas.

What led the railroads to divide the country into four time zones?

QUICK CHECK ✔

What characterized the building and completion of the transcontinental railroads?

On May 10, 1869, the two lines met at Promontory, Utah, near the northern tip of the Great Salt Lake. Dodge's crews had built 1086 miles of track, Crocker's 689. The Union Pacific and Central Pacific presidents hammered in a golden spike (both missed it on the first try), and the dreamed-of connection was made. The telegraph flashed the news east and west, setting off wild celebrations. A photograph was taken, but it included none of the Chinese who had worked so hard to build the road; they were all asked to step aside.

The transcontinental railroad symbolized American unity and progress. Along with the Suez Canal, completed the same year, it helped knit the world together. Three more railroads reached the coast in 1883: the Northern Pacific, running from Minnesota to Oregon; the Atchison, Topeka, and Santa Fe, connecting Kansas City and Los Angeles; and the powerful Southern Pacific, running from San Francisco and Los Angeles to New Orleans.

Problems of Growth

Overbuilding during the 1870s and 1880s caused serious problems for the railroads. Competition was severe, and managers fought desperately for traffic. They offered special rates and favors: free passes for large shippers; low rates on bulk freight, carload lots, and long hauls; and, above all, rebates—secret, privately negotiated reductions below published rates. Fierce rate wars broke out frequently, convincing managers that ruthless competition helped no one. Managers tried first to arrange pooling agreements, a way to control competition by sharing traffic, but none survived the intense pressures of competition.

Railroad owners next tried to consolidate. Through purchase, lease, and merger, they gobbled up competitors and built "self-sustaining systems" that dominated entire regions. But many of the systems, expensive and unwieldy, collapsed in the economic Panic of 1893. By mid-1894, a quarter of the railroads were bankrupt. The victims of the panic included such legendary names as the Erie, B & O, Santa Fe, Northern Pacific, and Union Pacific.

Needing money, railroads turned naturally to bankers, who finally imposed order on the industry. J. Pierpont Morgan, head of the New York investment house

J. P. Morgan

After the last spike was hammered in at Promontory, Utah, the pilots of the two locomotives exchanged champagne toasts. The chief engineers of the two lines are seen shaking hands. Conspicuously absent from the photograph are the Chinese laborers who helped build the railroad.

Why were the Chinese excluded from the photograph?

of J. P. Morgan and Company, took the lead. Massively built, with eyes so piercing they seemed like the headlights of an onrushing train, Morgan was the most powerful figure in American finance. He liked efficiency, combination, and order. He disliked "wasteful" competition.

After 1893, Morgan and a few other bankers refinanced ailing railroads, and in the process they took control of the industry. Their methods were direct: Fixed costs and debt were ruthlessly cut, new stock was issued to provide capital, rates were stabilized, rebates and competition were eliminated; and control was vested in a "voting trust" of handpicked trustees. Between 1894 and 1898, Morgan reorganized—critics said "Morganized"—the Southern Railway, the Erie, the Northern Pacific, and the B & O. By 1900, he was a dominant figure in American railroading.

As the new century began, the railroads had pioneered the patterns followed by most other industries. Seven giant systems controlled nearly two-thirds of the mileage, and they in turn answered to a few investment banking firms such as the house of Morgan. For good and ill, a national transportation network, centralized and relatively efficient, was now in place.

QUICK CHECK ✔

What problems did railroads face as they grew?

An Industrial Empire

WHAT were the main characteristics of the new steel and oil industries?

The new industrial empire was based on a number of dramatic innovations, including steel, oil, and inventions of all kinds that transformed ordinary life. In this process, steel was as important as the railroads. Harder and more durable than other kinds of iron, steel wrought changes in manufacturing, agriculture, transportation, and architecture. It permitted construction of longer bridges, taller buildings, stronger railroad track, deadlier weapons, better plows, heavier machinery, and faster ships. Made in great furnaces by strong men, it symbolized the tough, often brutal nature of industrial society. From the 1870s onward, steel output became the worldwide accepted measure of industrial progress, and nations around the globe vied for leadership.

The Bessemer process, developed in the late 1850s by Henry Bessemer in England and independently by William Kelly in the United States, made increased steel production possible. Both Bessemer and Kelly discovered that a blast of air forced through molten iron burned off carbon and other impurities, resulting in steel of a more uniform and durable quality. The discovery transformed the industry. While earlier methods produced amounts a person could lift, a Bessemer converter handled 5 tons of molten metal at a time. The mass production of steel was now possible.

Carnegie and Steel

Bessemer plants demanded extensive capital investment, abundant raw materials, and sophisticated production techniques. Using chemical and other processes, the plants required research departments, which became critical components of later American industries. Costly to build, they limited entry into the industry to the handful who could afford them.

Great steel districts arose in Pennsylvania, Ohio, and Alabama—in each case around large coal deposits that fueled the huge furnaces. Pittsburgh became the center of the industry, its giant mills employing thousands of workers. Output shot up. In 1874, the United States produced less than half the amount of pig iron produced in Great Britain. By 1890, it took the lead, and in 1900, it produced four times as much as Britain.

Like the railroads, steel companies grew larger and larger. In 1880, only nine companies could produce more than 100,000 tons a year. By the early 1890s, several companies exceeded 250,000 tons, and two—including the great Carnegie Steel Company—produced more than 1 million tons a year. As operations expanded, managers needed more complex skills. Product development, marketing, and consumer preferences became important.

Andrew Carnegie emerged as the undisputed master of the industry. Born in Scotland, he came to the United States in 1848 at the age of 12. Settling near Pittsburgh, he went to work as a bobbin boy in a cotton mill, earning $1.20 a week. He soon took a job in a telegraph office, where in 1852 his hard work and skill caught the eye of Thomas A. Scott of the Pennsylvania Railroad. Starting as Scott's personal telegrapher, Carnegie spent a total of twelve years on the Pennsylvania, a training ground for company managers. By 1859, he had become a divisional superintendent. He was 24 years old.

Soon rich from shrewd investments, Carnegie plunged into the steel industry in 1872. With his warmth and salesmanship, he attracted able partners and subordinates such as Henry Clay Frick and Charles M. Schwab, whom he drove hard and paid well. Although he had written magazine articles defending the rights of workers, Carnegie kept the wages of the laborers in his mills low and disliked unions. With the help of Frick, he crushed a violent strike at his Homestead works in 1892 (see p. 499).

In 1878, he won the steel contract for the Brooklyn Bridge. During the next decade, as city building boomed, he converted the huge Homestead works near Pittsburgh to the manufacture of structural beams and angles, which went into the New York City elevated railway, the first skyscrapers, and the Washington Monument. In 1900, Carnegie Steel alone produced more steel than Great Britain. Employing twenty thousand people, it was the largest industrial company in the world.

In 1901, Carnegie sold it. Believing that wealth brought social obligations, he wanted to devote his full time to philanthropy. He found a buyer in J. Pierpont Morgan, who in the late 1890s had put together several steel companies, including Federal Steel, Carnegie's chief rival. Carnegie Steel had blocked Morgan's well-known desire for control, and in mid-1900, when a war loomed between the two interests, Morgan decided to buy Carnegie out. In early January 1901, Morgan told Charles M. Schwab: "Go and find his price." Schwab cornered Carnegie on the golf course; Carnegie listened, and the next day he handed Schwab a note, scribbled in blunt pencil, asking almost a half billion dollars. Morgan glanced at it and said, "I accept this price."

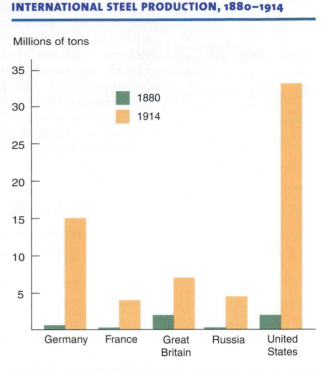

INTERNATIONAL STEEL PRODUCTION, 1880–1914

Millions of tons

Legend: 1880, 1914

Andrew Carnegie, "Wealth" (1889)

Drawing other companies into the combination, Morgan on March 3, 1901, announced the creation of the United States Steel Corporation. The new firm was capitalized at $1.4 billion, the first billion-dollar company. It absorbed more than 200 other companies, employed 168,000 people, and produced 9 million tons of iron and steel a year. It controlled three-fifths of the country's steel business. Soon there were other giants, including Bethlehem Steel, Republic Steel, and National Steel. As the nineteenth century ended, steel products—rare just thirty years before—had altered the landscape. Huge firms, investment bankers, and professional managers dominated the industry.

QUICK CHECK

What were the main characteristics of the growth of the steel industry?

Rockefeller and Oil

Petroleum worked comparable changes in the economic and social landscape, although mostly after 1900. Distilled into oil, it lubricated the machinery of the industrial age. There seemed little use for gasoline (the internal combustion engine had only just been developed). But kerosene, another major distillate, brought inexpensive illumination into almost every home. Whale oil, cottonseed oil, and even tallow candles were expensive to burn; consequently, many people went to bed at nightfall. Kerosene lamps opened the evenings to activity, altering the patterns of life.

Like other changes in these years, the oil boom happened with surprising speed. In 1859, Edwin L. Drake drilled the first oil well near Titusville in northwest Pennsylvania, and the "black gold" fever struck. Chemists soon discovered ways to transform petroleum into lubricating oil, grease, paint, wax, varnish, naphtha, and paraffin. Within a few years, there was a world market in oil.

At first, growth of the oil industry was chaotic. Early drillers and refiners produced for local markets, and since drilling wells and even erecting refineries cost little, competition flourished. Output fluctuated dramatically; prices rose and fell, with devastating effect.

A young merchant from Cleveland named John D. Rockefeller imposed order on the industry. "I had an ambition to build," he later recalled, and beginning in 1863 at the age of 24, he built the Standard Oil Company, soon to become one of the titans of corporate

John D. Rockefeller, satirized in a 1901 *Puck* cartoon, is enthroned on oil, the base of his empire; his crown is girded by other holdings.

What does this cartoon suggest about the nature of Rockfeller's empire?

business. Like Morgan, Rockefeller considered competition wasteful, small-scale enterprise inefficient, and consolidation the path of the future.

Methodically, Rockefeller absorbed or destroyed competitors in Cleveland and elsewhere. As ruthless in his methods as Carnegie, he lacked the steel master's spontaneous charm.

In the end, Rockefeller triumphed over his competitors by marketing products of high quality at the lowest unit cost. But he employed other, less savory methods as well. He threatened rivals and bribed politicians. He employed spies to harass the customers of competing refiners. Above all, he extorted railroad rebates that lowered his transportation costs and undercut competitors. By 1879, he controlled 90 percent of the country's entire oil-refining capacity.

Vertically integrated, Standard Oil owned wells, timberlands, barrel and chemical plants, refineries, warehouses, pipelines, and fleets of tankers and oil cars. Its marketing organization served as the model for the industry. Standard exported oil to Asia, Africa, and South America; its 5-gallon kerosene tin, like Coca-Cola bottles and cans of a later era, was a familiar sight in the most distant parts of the world.

To manage it all, the company developed a new plan of business organization, the **trust**, which had profound significance for American business. In 1881, Samuel C. T. Dodd, Standard's attorney, set up the Standard Oil Trust, with a board of nine trustees empowered "to hold, control, and manage" all Standard's properties. Stockholders exchanged their stock for trust certificates, on which dividends were paid. On January 2, 1882, the first of the modern trusts was born. As Dodd intended, it immediately centralized control of Standard's far-flung empire.

Competition almost disappeared; profits soared. A trust movement swept the country as industries with similar problems—whiskey, lead, and sugar, among others—followed Standard's example. The word *trust* became synonymous with monopoly, amid vehement protests from the public. *Antitrust* became a watchword for a generation of reformers from the 1880s through the era of Woodrow Wilson. But Rockefeller's purpose had been *management* of a monopoly, not monopoly itself, which he had already achieved.

Other companies organized their own trusts, including American Sugar Refining, the Northern Securities Company, and the National Biscuit Company. Merger followed merger. By 1900, 1 percent of the nation's companies controlled more than one-third of its industrial production.

In 1897, Rockefeller retired with a fortune of nearly $900 million, but for Standard Oil and petroleum in general, the most expansive period was yet to come. The great oil pools of Texas and Oklahoma had not yet been discovered. Plastics and other oil-based synthetics were several decades in the future. There were only four usable automobiles in the country, and the day of the gasoline engine, automobile, and airplane lay just ahead.

trust
A business-management device designed to centralize and make more efficient the management of diverse and far-flung business operations. It allowed stockholders to exchange their stock certificates for trust certificates, on which dividends were paid. John D. Rockefeller organized the first major trust, the Standard Oil Trust, in 1882.

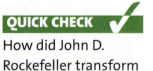

QUICK CHECK

How did John D. Rockefeller transform the oil industry?

The Business of Invention

"America has become known the world around as the home of invention," boasted the commissioner of patents in 1892. It had not always been so; until the last third of the nineteenth century, the country had imported most of its technology. Then an extraordinary group of inventors and tinkerers—"specialists in invention," Thomas A. Edison, the most famous inventor of them all, called them—began to study the world around them. Some of their inventions gave rise to new industries; a few actually changed the quality of life.

In the very act of inventing, Edison and others drew on a deeper "invention," a realization that people could mold nature to their own ends. As a result, the number of patents issued to inventors soared. During the 1850s, fewer than 2000 patents were issued each year. By the 1880s and 1890s, the figure reached more than 20,000 a year. Between 1790 and 1860, the U.S. Patent Office issued just 36,000 patents; in the decade of the 1890s alone, it issued more than 200,000.

Some of the inventions transformed communications. In 1866, Cyrus W. Field improved the transatlantic cable linking the telegraph networks of Europe and the United States. By the early 1870s, land and submarine cables ran to Brazil, Japan, and the China coast; in the next two decades, they reached Africa and spread across South America. Diplomats and business leaders could now "talk" to their counterparts in Berlin or Hong Kong. Even before the telephone, the cables quickened the pace of foreign affairs, revolutionized journalism, and allowed businesses to expand and centralize.

The typewriter (1867), stock ticker (1867), cash register (1879), calculating machine (1887), and adding machine (1888) helped business transactions. High-speed spindles, automatic looms, and electric sewing machines transformed the clothing industry, which for the first time in history turned out ready-made clothes for the masses. In 1890, the Census Bureau first used machines to sort and tabulate data on punched cards, a portent of a new era of information storage and processing.

In 1879, George Eastman patented a process for coating gelatin on photographic dry plates, which led to celluloid film and motion pictures. By 1888, he was marketing the Kodak camera, which weighed 35 ounces, took 100 exposures, and cost $25. Even though early Kodaks had to be returned to the factory, camera and all, for film developing, they revolutionized photography. Now almost anyone could snap a picture.

Other innovations changed the diet. There were new processes for flour, canned meat, vegetables, condensed milk, and even beer (from an offshoot of Louis Pasteur's discoveries about bacteria). Packaged cereals appeared on breakfast tables. Refrigerated railroad cars, ice-cooled, brought fresh fruit from Florida and California to all parts of the country. In the 1870s, Gustavus F. Swift, a Chicago meat packer, hit on the idea of using the cars to distribute meat nationwide. Setting up "disassembly" factories to butcher meat (Henry Ford later copied them for his famous "assembly" lines), he started an "era of cheap beef," as a newspaper said.

No innovation, however, rivaled the importance of the telephone and the use of electricity for light and power. The telephone was the work of Alexander Graham Bell, a shrewd and genial Scot who settled in Boston in 1871. Interested in the problems of the deaf, Bell experimented with ways to transmit speech electrically, and after several years he had developed electrified metal disks that, much like the human ear, converted sound waves to electrical impulses and back again. On March 10, 1876, he transmitted the first sentence over a telephone: "Mr. Watson, come here; I want you." Later that year, he exhibited the new device to excited crowds at the Centennial Exposition in Philadelphia.

In 1878—the year a telephone was installed in the White House—the first telephone exchange opened in New Haven, Connecticut. Fighting off competitors who challenged the patent, the young Bell Telephone Company dominated the growing industry. By 1895, there were about 310,000 phones; a decade later, there were 10 million—about one for every ten people. American Telephone and

Telegraph Company, formed by the Bell interests in 1885, became another of the vast holding companies, consolidating more than a hundred local systems.

If the telephone dissolved communication barriers as old as the human race, Thomas Alva Edison, the "Wizard of Menlo Park," invented processes and products of comparable significance. Born in 1847, Edison had little formal education, although he was an avid reader. Like Carnegie, he went into the new field of telegraphy. Tinkering in his spare time, he made several important improvements, including a telegraph capable of sending four messages over a single wire. Gathering teams of specialists to work on specific problems, Edison built the first modern research laboratory at Menlo Park, New Jersey. It may have been his most important invention.

The laboratory, Edison promised, would turn out "a minor invention every ten days and a big thing every six months or so." In 1877, it turned out a big thing, the phonograph. Those unable to afford a phone, he thought, could record their voices for replay from a central telephone station. Using tin foil wrapped around a grooved, rotating cylinder, he shouted the verses of "Mary Had a Little Lamb" and then listened in awe as the machine played them back. "I was never so taken aback in all my life," he later said. "Everybody was astonished. I was always afraid of things that worked the first time." For the first time in history, people could listen again and again to a favorite symphony or piano solo. The phonograph made human experience repeatable in a way never before possible.

Edison with Phonograph

In 1879 came an even larger triumph, the incandescent lamp. Sir Joseph William Swan, an English inventor, had already experimented with the carbon filament, but Edison's task involved more than finding a durable filament. He set out to do nothing less than change light. A trial-and-error inventor, Edison tested sixteen hundred materials before producing, late in 1879, the carbon filament he wanted. Then he had to devise a complex system of conductors, meters, and generators by which electricity could be divided and distributed to homes and businesses.

With the financial backing of J. P. Morgan, he organized the Edison Illuminating Company and built the Pearl Street power station in New York City, the testing ground of the new apparatus. On September 4, 1882, as Morgan and others watched, Edison threw a switch and lit the house of Morgan, the stock exchange, the *New York Times*, and a number of other buildings. Amazed, a *Times* reporter marveled that writing stories in the office at night "seemed almost like writing in daylight." Power stations soon opened in Boston, Philadelphia, and Chicago. By 1900, there were 2774 stations, lighting some 2 million electric lights around the country. In a nation alive with light, the habits of centuries changed. A flick of the switch lit homes and factories at any hour of the day or night.

Thomas Edison, The Success of the Electric Light

Electricity could light a lamp or illuminate a skyscraper, pull a streetcar or drive an entire railroad, run a sewing machine or power a mammoth assembly line. Transmitted easily over long distances, it freed factories and cities from location near water or coal. Electricity, in short, brought a revolution.

Taking advantage of the new devices, Frank J. Sprague, a young engineer, electrified the Richmond, Virginia, streetcar system in 1887. Other cities quickly followed. Electric-powered subway systems opened in Boston in 1897 and New York City in 1904. Overhead wires and third rails made urban transportation quieter, faster, and cleaner. Buried under pavement or strung from pole to pole, wires of every description—trolley, telephone, and power—marked the birth of the modern city.

QUICK CHECK

What were the most important inventions of the years between 1870 and 1900?

The Sellers

WHY

were the new methods of advertising so important?

The increased output of the industrial age alone was not enough to ensure huge profits. The products still had to be sold, and that gave rise to a new "science" of marketing. Some business leaders—such as Swift in meatpacking, James B. Duke in tobacco, and Rockefeller in oil—built extensive marketing organizations of their own. Others relied on retailers, merchandising techniques, and advertising, developing a host of methods to convince consumers to buy.

In 1867, businesses spent about $50 million on advertising; in 1900, they spent more than $500 million, and the figure was increasing rapidly. The rotary press (1875) churned out newspapers and introduced a new era in newspaper advertising. Bringing producer and consumer together, nationwide advertising was the final link in the national market. From roadside signs to newspaper ads, it pervaded American life.

The idea of consumption became prominent. R. H. Macy in New York, John Wanamaker in Philadelphia, and Marshall Field in Chicago turned the department store into a national institution. There people could browse (a relatively new concept) and buy. Innovations in pricing, display, and advertising helped customers develop wants they did not know they had. In 1870, Wanamaker took out the first full-page newspaper ad, and Macy, an aggressive advertiser, touted "goods suitable for the millionaire at prices in reach of the millions."

The Department Store: Another View

In similar fashion, Sears, Roebuck and Montgomery Ward sold to rural customers through mail-order catalogs—a means of selling that depended on effective transportation and a high level of customer literacy. As a traveler for a dry goods firm, Aaron Montgomery Ward had seen an unfulfilled need of people in the rural West. He started the mail-order trend in 1872, with a one-sheet price list offered from a Chicago loft. By 1884, he offered almost ten thousand items in a catalog of 240 pages.

Richard W. Sears also saw the possibilities in the mail-order business. Starting with watches and jewelry, he gradually expanded his list. In the early 1880s, he moved to Chicago and with Alvah C. Roebuck founded Sears, Roebuck and Company. Sears sold anything and everything, prospering in a business that relied on mutual faith between unseen customers and distant distributors. Sears catalogs, soon more than five hundred pages long, exploited four-color illustration and other new techniques. By the early 1900s, Sears distributed six million catalogs annually.

Advertising, brand names, chain stores, and mail-order houses brought Americans of all varieties into a national market. Even as the country grew, a certain homogeneity of goods bound it together, touching cities and farms, East and West, rich and poor. There was a common language of consumption. Americans had become a community of consumers, surrounded by goods unavailable just a few decades before, and able to purchase them. They had learned to make, want, and buy. "Because you see the main thing today is—shopping," Arthur Miller, a twentieth-century playwright, said in *The Price*:

> Years ago a person, he was unhappy, didn't know what to do with himself—he'd go to church, start a revolution—something. Today you're unhappy? Can't figure it out? What is the salvation? Go shopping.

A cutaway view of the "bee-hive" headquarters of mail-order giant Montgomery Ward & Co. of Chicago. By the time Ward moved into this building in 1899, rival retailer Sears, Roebuck & Co. was challenging Ward's mail-order business. (*Source: Courtesy of the Chicago Historical Society.*)

What were the essential features of mail-order companies?

The Wage Earners

Although entrepreneurs were important, it was the labor of millions of men and women that built the new industrial society. In their individual stories, nearly all unrecorded, lay much of the achievement, drama, and pain of these years.

In a number of respects, their lot improved during the last quarter of the nineteenth century. Real wages rose, working conditions improved, and the workers' influence in national affairs increased. Like others, workers also benefited from expanding health and educational services.

WHO were the wage earners in the new economy?

Working Men, Working Women, Working Children

Still, life for workers was not easy. Before 1900, most wage earners worked at least ten hours a day, six days a week. If skilled, they earned about 20 cents an hour; if unskilled, just half that. On average, workers earned between $400 and $500 a year. It took about $600 for a family of four to live decently. Construction workers, machinists, government employees, printers, clerical workers, and western miners made more than the average. Eastern coal miners, agricultural workers, garment workers, and unskilled factory hands made considerably less.

There were few holidays or vacations, and there was little respite from the grueling routine. Safety standards were low, and accidents were common, more common in fact than in any other industrial nation in the world at that time. On the railroads, 1 in every 26 workers was injured and 1 in every 399 was killed each year. Thousands suffered from chronic illness, unknowing victims of dust, chemicals, and other pollutants. In the early 1900s, physician Alice Hamilton established a link between jobs and disease, but meanwhile, illness weakened or struck down many a breadwinner.

Mother Jones, "The March of the Mill Children"

The breadwinner might be a woman or a child; both worked in increasing numbers. In 1870, about 15 percent of women over the age of 16 were employed for wages; in 1900, 20 percent were. Of 303 occupations listed in the 1900 census, women were represented in 296. The textile industry was their largest single employer. Between 1870 and 1900, the number of working children more than doubled. In 1900, 1 out of every 10 girls and 1 out of every 5 boys between the ages of 10 and 15 held jobs.

There were so many children in the labor force that when people spoke of child labor, they often meant boys and girls under the age of 14. Boys were paid little enough, but girls made even less. Girls, it was argued, were headed for marriage; those who worked were just doing so in order to help out their families. "We try to employ girls who are members of families," a box manufacturer said, "for we don't pay the girls a living wage in this trade."

Most working women were young and single. Many began working at 16 or 17, worked a half dozen years or so, married, and quit. In 1900, only 5 percent of all married women were employed outside the home, although African American women were an important exception. Among them, 25 percent of married women worked in 1900, usually on southern farms or as low-paid laundresses or domestic servants. As clerical work expanded, women learned new skills such as typing and stenography. Moving into formerly male occupations, they became secretaries, bookkeepers, typists, telephone operators, and clerks in the new department stores.

As demand for workers grew, women took over many of the duties formerly performed by men. Despite their performance in the workplace, however, the women were usually overseen by male supervisors.

What were conditions like for workers after 1900?

A few women—very few—became ministers, lawyers, and doctors. Arabella Mansfield, admitted to the Iowa bar in 1869, was the first woman lawyer in the country. But change was slow, and in the 1880s, some law schools still were refusing to admit women because they "had not the mentality to study law." Among women entering the professions, the overwhelming majority became nurses, schoolteachers, and librarians. In such professions, a process of "feminization" occurred: Women became a majority of the workers, a small number of men took the management roles, and most men left for other jobs, lowering the profession's status.

Massachusetts Bureau of Statistics of Labor (1884)

In most jobs, status and pay were divided unequally between men and women. Many of both sexes thought a woman's place was in the home. When employed in factories, women tended to occupy jobs that were viewed as natural extensions of household activity. They made clothes and textiles, processed food, and made cigars, tobacco, and shoes. In the women's garment industry, which employed large numbers of women, they were the sewers and finishers, doing jobs that paid less; men were the higher-paid cutters and pressers.

In general, adults earned more than children, the skilled more than the unskilled, native born more than foreign born, Protestants more than Catholics or Jews, and whites more than blacks and Asians. On average, women made a little more than half as much as men, according to contemporary estimates. In some cases, employers defended the differences—the foreign born, for example, might not speak English—but most simply reflected bias against race, creed, or gender. In the industrial society, white, native-born Protestant men—the bulk of the male population—reaped the greatest rewards.

Chinese Exclusion Act (1882)

Blacks labored on the fringes, usually in menial occupations. The last hired and first fired, they earned less than other workers at almost every level of skill. On the Pacific coast, the Chinese—and later the Japanese—lived in enclaves and suffered periodic attacks of discrimination. In 1882, Congress passed the Chinese Exclusion Act, prohibiting the immigration of Chinese workers for ten years.

QUICK CHECK

What were conditions like for working men, women, and children?

Culture of Work

Among almost all groups, industrialization shattered age-old patterns, including work habits and the culture of work, as Herbert G. Gutman, a social historian, noted. It made people adapt "older work routines to new necessities and strained those wedded to premodern patterns of labor." Adaptation was difficult and often demeaning. Virtually everyone went through it, and newcomers repeated the experiences of those who came before.

Men and women fresh from farms were not accustomed to the factory's disciplines. Now they worked indoors rather than out, paced themselves to the clock rather than the movements of the sun, and followed the needs of the market rather than the natural rhythms of the seasons. They had supervisors and hierarchies and strict rules.

As industries grew larger, work became more impersonal. Machines displaced skilled artisans, and the unskilled tended the machines for employers they never saw. Workers picked up and left their jobs with startling frequency, and factories

HOW
did wage earners organize in this period, and what demands did they make?

drew on a churning, highly mobile labor supply. Historian Stephan Thernstrom, who carefully studied the census records, found that only about half the people recorded in any census still lived in the same community ten years later. "The country had an enormous reservoir of restless and footloose men, who could be lured to new destinations when opportunity beckoned."

Thernstrom and others have also found substantial economic and social mobility. The rags-to-riches stories of Horatio Alger had always said so, and careers of men such as Andrew Carnegie—the impoverished immigrant boy who made good—seemed to confirm it. The actual record was considerably more limited. Most business leaders in the period came from well-to-do or middle-class families of old American stock. Of 360 iron and steel barons in Pittsburgh, Carnegie's own city, only 5 fit the Carnegie characteristics, and one of those was Carnegie himself. Still, if few workers became steel magnates, many workers made major progress during their lifetimes. Thernstrom discovered that a quarter of the manual laborers rose to middle-class positions, and working-class children were even more likely to move up the ladder.

The chance for advancement played a vital role in American industrial development. It gave workers hope, wedded them to the system, and tempered their response to the appeal of labor unions and working-class agitation. Very few workers rose from rags to riches, but a great many rose to better jobs and higher status.

Labor Unions

Weak throughout the nineteenth century, labor unions never included more than 2 percent of the total labor force or more than 10 percent of industrial workers. To many workers, unions seemed "foreign," radical, and out of step with the American tradition of individual advancement. Craft, ethnic, and other differences fragmented the labor force, and its extraordinary mobility made organization difficult. Employers opposed unions. "I have always had one rule," said an executive of U.S. Steel. "If a worker sticks up his head, hit it."

As the national economy emerged, however, national labor unions gradually took shape. In 1869, Uriah S. Stephens and a group of Philadelphia garment workers founded the Noble and Holy Order of the Knights of Labor, known simply as the **Knights of Labor**. A secret fraternal order, it grew slowly through the 1870s, until Terence V. Powderly, the new Grand Master Workman elected in 1879, ended the secrecy and embarked on an aggressive recruitment program. Wanting to unite all labor, the Knights welcomed everyone who "toiled," regardless of skill, creed, sex, or color. Unlike most unions, it organized women workers, and at its peak, it had 60,000 black members.

Harking back to the Jacksonians, the Knights set the "producers" against monopoly and special privilege. As members they excluded only "nonproducers"— bankers, lawyers, liquor dealers, and gamblers. Since employers were "producers," they could join; and since workers and employers had common interests, the Knights maintained that workers should not strike. The order's platform included the eight-hour day and the abolition of child labor, but more often it focused on uplifting, utopian reform. Powderly, the eloquent and idealistic leader, spun dreams of a new era of harmony and cooperation.

In March 1885, ignoring Powderly's dislike of strikes, local Knights in St. Louis, Kansas City, and other cities won a victory against Jay Gould's Missouri Pacific Railroad, and membership increased. However, in 1886, the wily Gould struck

Knights of Labor
Also known as the Noble and Holy Order of the Knights of Labor. Founded in 1869, this labor organization pursued broad-gauged reforms as much as practical issues such as wages and hours. Unlike the American Federation of Labor, the Knights of Labor welcomed all laborers regardless of race, gender, or skill.

back, crushing the Knights on the Texas and Pacific Railroad. The defeat punctured the union's growth and revealed the ineffectiveness of its national leaders. Tens of thousands of unskilled laborers, who had recently rushed to join, deserted the ranks. The Haymarket Riot turned public sympathy against unions like the Knights. By 1890, the order had shrunk to 100,000 members, and a few years later, it was virtually defunct.

Even as the Knights waxed and waned, another organization emerged that was to endure. Founded in 1886, the **American Federation of Labor (AFL)** was a loose alliance of national craft unions. It organized only skilled workers along craft lines, avoided politics, and worked for specific practical objectives. "I have my own philosophy and my own dreams," said Samuel Gompers, the founder and longtime president, "but first and foremost I want to increase the workingman's welfare year by year."

Born in a London tenement in 1850, Gompers was a child of the union movement. Settling in New York, he worked as a cigar maker, took an active hand in union activities, and experimented for a time with socialism and working-class politics. As leader of the AFL, he adopted a pragmatic approach to labor's needs. Gompers accepted capitalism and did not argue for fundamental changes in it. For labor he wanted simply a recognized place within the system and a greater share of the rewards.

Unlike Powderly, Gompers and the AFL assumed that most workers would remain workers throughout their lives. The task, then, lay in improving lives in "practical" ways: higher wages, shorter hours, and better working conditions. The AFL offered some attractive assurances to employers. As a trade union, the AFL would use the strike and boycott, but only to achieve limited gains; if treated fairly, the organization would provide a stable labor force. The AFL would not oppose monopolies and trusts, as Gompers said, "so long as we obtain fair wages."

By the 1890s, the AFL was the most important labor group in the country, and Gompers, the guiding spirit, was its president, except for one year, until his death in 1924. The AFL then included almost one-third of the country's skilled workers. By 1914, it had more than 2 million members. The great majority of workers—skilled and unskilled—remained unorganized, but Gompers and the AFL had become a significant force in national life.

The AFL either ignored or opposed women workers. Only two of its national affiliates—the Cigar Makers' Union and the Typographical Union—accepted women as members; others prohibited them outright, and Gompers himself often complained that women workers undercut the pay scales for men.

The AFL did not expressly forbid black workers from joining, but member unions used high initiation fees, technical examinations, and other means to discourage black membership. The AFL's informal exclusion practices were, all in all, a sorry record, but Gompers defended his policy toward blacks, women, and the unskilled by pointing to the dangers that unions faced. Only by restricting membership, he argued, could the union succeed.

American Federation of Labor (AFL)
Founded by Samuel Gompers in 1886, the AFL was a loose alliance of national craft unions that organized skilled workers by craft and worked for specific practical objectives such as higher wages; shorter hours, and better working conditions. The AFL avoided politics, and while it did not expressly forbid black and women workers from joining, it used exclusionary practices to keep them out.

QUICK CHECK ✔

What was the history of the Knights of Labor and the American Federation of Labor during the late nineteenth century?

Labor Unrest

Workers used various means to adjust to the factory age. To the dismay of managers and "efficiency" experts, the employees often dictated the pace and quality of their work and set the tone of the workplace. Friends and relatives of newly arrived immigrants found jobs for them, taught them how to deal with factory conditions, and humanized the workplace.

Organizing American Labor in the Late Nineteenth Century

Violence and fires associated with the great railroad strike of 1877 destroyed railyards across the country. By the end of the strike, which lasted about two weeks, $10 million of railroad property had been reduced to rubble, and more than a hundred people had died.

What does this scene suggest about the mood of railroad laborers in 1877?

Workers also formed their own institutions to deal with their jobs. Overcoming differences of race or ethnic origin, they often banded together to help each other. They joined social or fraternal organizations, and their unions offered companionship, news of job openings, and much needed insurance plans for sickness, accident, or death. Workers went to the union hall to play cards or pool, sing union songs, and hear older workers tell of past labor struggles. Unions provided food for sick members, and there were dances, picnics, and parades. Unions also helped argue for higher wages.

Many employers, however, believed in an "iron law of wages" in which supply and demand, not the welfare of their workers, dictated wages. Employers wanted a docile labor force and would often fire union members, hire scabs to replace strikers, and use a new weapon, the court injunction, to quell strikes.

The injunction, which forbade workers to interfere with their employers' business, was used to break the great Pullman Strike of 1894, and the Supreme Court upheld use of the injunction in 1895.

As employers' attitudes hardened, strikes and violence broke out. The United States had the greatest number of violent confrontations between capital and labor in the industrial world. Between 1880 and 1900, there were more than 23,000 strikes involving 6.6 million workers. The great railroad strike of 1877 paralyzed railroads from West Virginia to California, resulted in the deaths of more than a hundred workers, and required federal troops to suppress it.

The worst incident took place at Haymarket Square in Chicago, where workers had been campaigning for an eight-hour workday. In early May 1886, police, intervening in a strike at the McCormick Harvester works, shot and killed two workers. The next evening, May 4, labor leaders called a protest meeting at Haymarket Square near downtown Chicago. The meeting was peaceful, even a bit dull. About three thousand people were there; police ordered them to disperse, and someone threw a dynamite bomb that instantly killed one policeman and fatally wounded six others. Police fired into the crowd and killed four people.

The authorities never discovered who threw the bomb, but many Americans—not just business leaders—immediately demanded action against labor "radicalism."

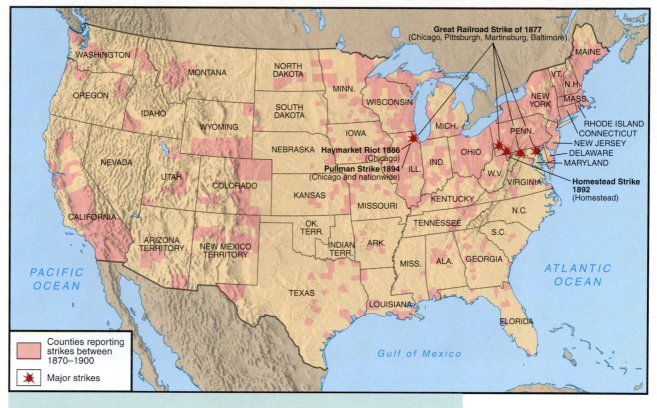

Counties reporting strikes between 1870–1900

Major strikes

Great Railroad Strike of 1877 (Chicago, Pittsburgh, Martinsburg, Baltimore)

Haymarket Riot 1886 (Chicago)

Pullman Strike 1894 (Chicago and nationwide)

Homestead Strike 1892 (Homestead)

LABOR STRIKES, 1870–1900   More than 14,000 strikes occurred in the 1880s and early 1890s, involving millions of workers.

Why were there so many strikes during these years?

Cities strengthened their police forces and armories. Chicago police rounded up eight anarchists, who were convicted of murder. Although there was no evidence of their guilt, four were hanged, one committed suicide, and three remained in jail until pardoned by the governor in 1893. Linking labor and anarchism in the public mind, the Haymarket Riot weakened the national labor movement.

Violence again broke out in the unsettled conditions of the 1890s. In 1892, Carnegie and Henry Clay Frick, Carnegie's partner and manager, cut wages nearly 20 percent at the Homestead steel plant. The Amalgamated Iron and Steel Workers, an AFL affiliate, struck, and Frick responded by locking the workers out of the plant. The workers surrounded it, and Frick, furious, hired a small private army of Pinkerton detectives to drive them off. But alert workers spotted the detectives, pinned them down with gunfire, and forced them to surrender. Three detectives and ten workers died in the battle.

A few days later, the Pennsylvania governor ordered the state militia to impose peace at Homestead. On July 23, an anarchist named Alexander Berkman, who was not one of the strikers, walked into Frick's office and shot him twice, then stabbed him several times. Incredibly, Frick survived. In late July, the Homestead works reopened under military guard, and in November the strikers gave up.

DOCUMENT

George Engel, Address by a Haymarket Anarchist

In the rioting that followed the bomb explosion in Haymarket Square in Chicago, seven police officers and five workers died and more than sixty officers were wounded, many of them by fellow police.

What was the reaction of most Americans to the violence in Haymarket Square?

QUICK CHECK ✓

What major strikes occurred between the 1870s and the 1890s?

Events like the **Homestead Strike** troubled many Americans who wondered whether industrialization, for all its benefits, might carry a heavy price in social upheaval, class tensions, and even outright warfare. Most workers did not share in the immense profits of the industrial age, and as the nineteenth century came to a close, there were some who rebelled against the inequity.

Homestead Strike

In July 1892, wage-cutting at Andrew Carnegie's Homestead steel plant in Pittsburgh provoked a violent strike in which three company-hired detectives and ten workers died. Using ruthless force and strikebreakers, the company officials effectively broke the strike and destroyed the union.

Conclusion: Industrialization's Benefits and Costs

In the half century after the Civil War, the United States became an industrial nation—the leading one, in fact, in the world. On one hand, industrialization meant "progress," growth, world power, and in some sense, fulfillment of the American promise of abundance. National wealth grew from $16 billion in 1860 to $88 billion in 1900; wealth per capita more than doubled. For the bulk of the population, the standard of living—a particularly American concept—rose.

But industrialization also meant rapid change, social instability, exploitation of labor, and growing disparity in income between rich and poor. Industry flourished, but control rested in fewer and fewer hands. Maturing quickly, the young system became a new corporate capitalism: giant businesses, interlocking in ownership, managed by a new professional class, and selling an expanding variety of goods in an increasingly controlled market. As goods spread through the society, so did a sharpened, aggressive materialism. Workers felt the strains of the shift to a new social order.

In 1902, a well-to-do New Yorker named Bessie Van Vorst decided to see what it was like to work for a living in a factory. Disguising herself in coarse woolen clothes, a shabby felt hat, a cheap piece of fur, and an old shawl and gloves, she went to Pittsburgh and got a job in a canning factory. She worked ten hours a day, six days a week, including four hours on Saturday afternoons when she and the other women, on their hands and knees, scrubbed the tables, stands, and entire factory floor. For that she earned $4.20 a week, $3 of which went for food alone.

Van Vorst was lucky—when she tired of the life, she could go back to her home in New York. The working men and women around her were not so fortunate. They stayed on the factory floor and, by dint of their labor, created the new industrial society.

For a list of additional titles related to this chapter's topics, please see
www.pearsonamericanhistory.com.   MyHistoryLab

STUDY RESOURCES

KEY TERMS

trunk lines, p. 483   Knights of Labor, p. 496   Homestead Strike, p. 500
trust, p. 489   American Federation of Labor
                            (AFL), p. 497

CHAPTER REVIEW

WHAT were the factors that enabled the United States to build an industrial economy?

The United States had somewhat unique advantages in developing its industries, including an abundance of natural resources, a plentiful supply of labor from Europe and American farms, numerous inventions, a national market, plentiful capital, favorable government policies, and a number of entrepreneurs who saw the possibilities in developing a national economy. (p. 479)

HOW and why did the railroad system grow?

Through the infusion of foreign and domestic capital, and the help of local, state, and federal government, a railroad system grew that dwarfed systems in other countries. It changed the economic, political, and social landscape, creating a nation very different from the country that had come before. (p. 480)

WHAT were the main characteristics of the new steel and oil industries?

In the late nineteenth century, an industrial empire took shape, centered around steel and oil, leading to the importance of the automobile in the new twentieth century. The result was large and more complex business organizations, greater concentrations of wealth and capital, and greater concentration of control by a relatively few individuals and companies. (p. 486)

WHY were the new methods of advertising so important?

Advertising, a relatively new industry, helped to sell the goods of the new industrial economy. Americans learned to buy goods they did not even know they wanted. When bored or troubled, they went to the store—the current mall—to shop. (p. 492)

WHO were the wage earners in the new economy?

By dint of hard work, millions of men and women built the new factory society. Their work was grueling and often dangerous. Men, women, and children did the labor, often for low wages in unsafe conditions. (p. 493)

HOW did wage earners organize in this period, and what demands did they make?

Laborers faced many challenges in the new economy, including work that followed the clock, the increasing size of the industry they worked for, machines, and wages. Various unions formed, including the American Federation of Labor, which still survives today. Labor unrest took peaceful forms of looking for better wages and safer working conditions, but also resulted from time to time in violence that disturbed other Americans. (p. 495)

MAKING CONNECTIONS

1. What were eight advantages the United States possessed that helped spur industrial development, and in what ways did these advantages lead to the growth of specific industries?
2. In what ways did the revolution in transportation and communications also spur industrial development?
3. Drawing on the conditions leading to the growth of industry, how did the huge steel and oil industries grow?
4. What role did the culture of work and advances in areas like advertising play in shaping economic growth?
5. In what ways did the hard work of men, women, and children contribute to the growth of industry?
6. How did American workers respond to the demands of industrial growth, and what did their various responses indicate about the dangerous effects of industrialization?

PRACTICE QUIZ

1. Four railroad _____ developed in the United States during the 1860s and 1870s.
   a. trunk lines
   b. labor strikes
   c. locomotive engines
   d. insurance agencies

2. The _____ collapsed many of the railroad companies formed in the 1870s.
   a. Great Railroad Strike
   b. Panic of 1893
   c. Stock Market Crash of 1929
   d. California Gold Rush

3. The _____ increased steel production beginning in the 1850s.
   a. Cotton gin
   b. Light bulb
   c. Telephone
   d. Bessemer process

4. The _____ began as a loose alliance of craft unions.
   a. Knights of Labor
   b. Socialist Party
   c. American Federation of Labor
   d. International Workers of the World

5. The _____ broke out in Pennsylvania in 1892 at a steel plant.
   a. Great Railroad Strike
   b. Longshoremen's Strike
   c. Homestead Strike
   d. McCormick Strike

6. In the late 1800s, only two major labor unions accepted the membership of
   a. Women
   b. African Americans
   c. European immigrants
   d. White native-born men

7. One of the most important oil tycoons of the early 1900s was
   a. Theodore Roosevelt
   b. John D. Rockefeller
   c. Samuel Dodd
   d. Woodrow Wilson

8. Which of the following *does not* describe the Haymarket bombing of 1886?
   a. Police shot two striking workers at the McCormick plant in Chicago.
   b. The next evening, labor leaders called a protest meeting at Haymarket Square, Chicago.
   c. A large crowd of thirty thousand people attended the meeting.
   d. Someone threw a dynamite bomb, killing a policeman.

9. Which of the following were business inventions created in the late 1800s?
   a. The stock ticker
   b. The cash register
   c. Calculating machine
   d. All of the above are correct.

10. All of the following describe the experiences of ethnic minority workers in U.S. industry *except*
    a. Blacks had to take menial jobs.
    b. In 1862 Congress passed the Chinese Exclusion Act.
    c. Blacks earned less than other workers at almost every skill level.
    d. The Chinese lived in enclaves on the Pacific Coast and suffered violence.

Find more practice at
www.myhistorylab.com

SAMPLE ESSAY QUESTIONS

1. Discuss how workers responded to the rise of industrialization during the late 1800s.

2. Evaluate the impact of the railroad industry upon American society in the late 1800s.

Answers to Practice Quiz 1. a, *p. 483* **2.** b, *p. 485* **3.** d, *p. 486* **4.** c, *p. 497* **5.** c, *p. 500* **6.** a, *p. 496* **7.** b, *p. 488* **8.** c, *p. 498* **9.** d, *p. 490* **10.** b, *p. 498*

Toward an Urban Society

1877–1900

During the second half of the nineteenth century, cities of the Midwest drew people and businesses to America's heartland. Milwaukee, shown here in a photograph by William Henry Jackson, was a major center of German immigration.

What does the architecture here suggest about the late nineteenth century?

The Overcrowded City

One day around 1900, Harriet Vittum, a settlement house worker in Chicago, went to the aid of a young Polish girl who lived in a nearby slum. The girl, aged 15, had discovered she was pregnant and had taken poison. An ambulance was on the way, and Vittum, told of the poisoning, rushed over to do what she could.

Quickly, she raced up the three flights of stairs to the floor where the girl and her family lived. Pushing open the door, she found the father, several male boarders, and two or three small boys asleep on the kitchen floor. In the next room, the mother was on the floor among several women boarders and one or two small children. Glancing out the window, Vittum saw the wall of another building so close she could reach out and touch it.

There was a third room; in it lay the 15-year-old girl, along with two more small children who were asleep. Looking at the scene, Vittum thought about the girl's life in the crowded tenement. Should she try to save her? Vittum asked herself. Should she even try to bring the girl back "to the misery and hopelessness of the life she was living in that awful place"?

The young girl died, and in later years, Vittum often told her story. It was easy to see why. The girl's life in the slum, the children on the floor, the need to take in boarders to make ends meet, the way the mother and father collapsed at the end of a workday that began long before sunup—all reflected the experiences of millions of people living in the nation's cities.

Vittum and people like her were attempting to respond to the overwhelming challenges of the nation's burgeoning cities. People poured into cities in the last part of the nineteenth century, lured by glitter and excitement, by friends and relatives who were

KEY EVENTS

1862   Morrill Land Grant gives land to states for establishment of colleges, *p. 521*

1869   Rutgers and Princeton play in nation's first intercollegiate football game, *p. 517*

1873   Nation's first kindergarten opens in St. Louis, Missouri, *p. 521*

1874   Women's Christian Temperance Union formed to crusade against evils of liquor, *p. 516*

1879   Henry George analyzes problems of urbanizing America in *Progress and Poverty*, *p. 525*

1881   Booker T. Washington opens Tuskegee Institute in Alabama, *p. 522*

1883   Metropolitan Opera opens in New York, *p. 517*

1887   Edward Bellamy promotes idea of socialist utopia in *Looking Backward, 2000–1887*, *p. 525*

1889   Jane Addams opens Hull House in Chicago, *p. 526*

1890   National Woman Suffrage Association and the American Woman Suffrage Association, both formed in 1869, merge to consolidate the woman suffrage movement, *p. 519*

1894   Immigration Restriction League formed to limit immigration from southern and eastern Europe, *p. 510*

1896   Supreme Court decision in *Plessy v. Ferguson* establishes constitutionality of "separate but equal" facilities, *p. 520*

already there, and, above all, by the greater opportunities for jobs and higher wages. Between 1860 and 1910, the rural population of the United States almost doubled; the number of people living in cities increased sevenfold. Little of the increase came from natural growth, since urban families had high rates of infant mortality, a declining fertility rate, and a high death rate from injury and disease. Many of the newcomers came from rural America, and many more came from Europe, Latin America, and Asia. In one of the most significant migrations in American history, thousands of African Americans began in the 1880s to move from the rural South to northern cities. By 1900, there were large black communities in New York, Baltimore, Chicago, Washington, D.C., and other cities. Yet to come was the even greater black migration during World War I.

Two major forces reshaped American society between 1870 and 1920. One was industrialization; the other was urbanization, the headlong rush of people from their rural roots into the modern urban environment. In these years, cities grew upward and outward, attracting millions of newcomers and influencing politics, education, entertainment, and family life. By 1920, they had become the center of American economic, social, and cultural life.

The Lure of the City

WHAT factors led to the growth of cities in the United States between 1880 and 1900?

Between 1870 and 1900, the city—like the factory—became a symbol of a new America. Drawn from farms, small towns, and foreign lands, newcomers swelled the population of older cities and created new ones almost overnight. At the beginning of the Civil War, only one-sixth of the American people lived in cities of eight thousand people or more. By 1900, one-third did; by 1920, one-half.

This dramatic increase brought growth of an explosive sort. Thousands of years of history had produced only a handful of cities with more than a half million in population. In 1900, the United States had six such cities, including three—New York, Chicago, and Philadelphia—with populations greater than one million.

Skyscrapers and Suburbs

Like so many things in these years, the city was transformed by a revolution in technology. Beginning in the 1880s, the age of steel and glass produced the skyscraper; the streetcar produced the suburbs and new residential patterns.

On the eve of the change, American cities were a crowded jumble of small buildings. Church steeples stood out on the skyline, clearly visible above the roofs of factories and office buildings. Buildings were usually made of masonry, and since the massive walls had to support their own weight, they could be no taller than a dozen or so stories. Steel frames and girders ended that limitation and allowed buildings to soar higher and higher. "Curtain walls," which concealed the steel framework, were no longer load bearing; they were pierced by many windows that let in fresh air and light.

To a group of talented Chicago architects, the new trends served as a springboard for innovative forms. The leaders of the movement were John Root and Louis H. Sullivan, both of whom were attracted by the chance to rebuild Chicago after the great fire of 1871. Noting that the fire had fed on fancy exterior ornamentation, Root developed a plain, stripped-down style, bold in mass and form—the keynotes of modern architecture. He had another important insight, too. In an age of business, Root thought, the office tower, more than a church or a government building, symbolized the society, and he designed office buildings that carried out, as he said, "the ideas of modern business life: simplicity, stability, breadth, dignity."

Sullivan had studied at the Massachusetts Institute of Technology (MIT) and in Paris before settling in Chicago. In 1886, at the age of 30, he began work on the Chicago Auditorium, one of the last great masonry buildings. "Then came the flash of imagination which saw the single thing," he later said. "The trick was turned; and there swiftly came into being something new under the sun." Sullivan's skyscrapers, that "flash of imagination," changed the urban skyline.

Electric elevators, first used in 1871, carried passengers upward in the new skyscrapers. During the same years, streetcars, another innovation, carried the people outward to expanded boundaries that transformed urban life.

Cities were no longer largely "walking cities," confined to a radius of two or three miles, the distance an individual might walk. Streetcar systems extended the radius and changed the urban map. Cable lines, electric surface lines, and elevated rapid transit brought shoppers and workers into central business districts and sped them home again. Offering a modest five-cent fare with a free transfer, the mass transit systems fostered commuting, and widely separated business and residential districts sprang up. The middle class moved farther and farther out to the leafy greenness of the suburbs.

As the middle class moved out of the cities, the immigrants and working class poured in. They took over the older brownstones, row houses, and workers' cottages, turning them into the slums of the central city. In the cities of the past, classes and occupations had been thrown together; without streetcars and subways, there was no other choice. The streetcar city, sprawling and specialized, became a more fragmented and stratified society with middle-class residential rings surrounding a business and working-class core.

QUICK CHECK ✓

How did cities change between the 1870s and 1900?

Tenements and the Problems of Overcrowding

In the shadow of the skyscrapers, grimy rows of tenements filled the central city, crowding people into cramped apartments. In the late 1870s, architect James E. Ware won a competition for tenement design with the "dumbbell tenement."

YARD

PARLOR
11' 4" x 13' 0"

LIVING ROOM

LIVING ROOM
9' 0" x 10' 0"

BED ROOM

BED RM
7' 8" x 8' 4"

BED RM
7' 8" x 10' 6"

HALL

W.C.

W.C.

BED RM
7' 8" x 8' 4"

BED RM
7' 8" x 10' 6"

BED RM
7' 8" x 8' 4"

BED RM
7' 8" x 8' 4"

BED RM.
9' 0" x 10' 0"

LIVING ROOM

LIVING ROOM
11' 4" x 13' 0"

PARLOR

This 1879 dumbbell floor plan was meant to provide four apartments to a floor. However, a whole family might live in each room. Crowded, unsanitary conditions contributed to the spread of tuberculosis, the chief cause of death in the United States until 1909.

Why would fires spread so quickly in dumbbell tenements?

Rising seven or eight stories in height, the dumbbell tenement packed about 30 four-room apartments on a lot only 25 by 100 feet. Between four and sixteen families lived on a floor; two toilets in the hall of each floor served their needs. Narrowed at the middle, the tenement resembled a giant dumbbell in shape.

In 1890, nearly half the dwellings in New York City were tenements. That year, more than 1.4 million people lived on Manhattan Island, one of whose wards had a population density of 334,000 people per square mile. Many people lived in alleys and basements so dark they could not be photographed until flashlight photography was invented in 1887. Exploring the city, William Dean Howells, the prominent author, inhaled "the stenches of the neglected street… [and] the yet fouler and dreadfuller poverty smell which breathes from the open doorways."

Howells smelled more than poverty. In the 1870s and 1880s, cities stank. One problem was horse manure, hundreds of tons of it a day in every city. Another was the privy, "a single one of which," said a leading authority on public health, "may render life in a whole neighborhood almost unendurable in the summer."

Baltimore smelled "like a billion polecats," recalled H. L. Mencken, who grew up there. Said one New York City resident, "The stench is something terrible." Another wrote that "the stink is enough to knock you down." In 1880, the Chicago *Times* said that a "solid stink" pervaded the city. "No other word expresses it so well as stink. A stench means something finite. Stink reaches the infinite and becomes sublime in the magnitude of odiousness."

Cities dumped their wastes into the nearest body of water, then drew drinking water from the same site. Many built modern purified waterworks but could not keep pace with spiraling growth. In 1900, fewer than one in ten city dwellers drank filtered water. Factories, the pride of the era, polluted the urban air.

Crime was another growing problem. The nation's homicide rate nearly tripled in the 1880s, much of the increase coming in the cities. Slum youths formed street gangs with names such as the Hayes Valley Gang in San Francisco and the Baxter Street Dudes, the Daybreak Boys, and the Alley Gang in New York. After remaining constant for many decades, the suicide rate rose steadily between 1870 and 1900, according to a study of Philadelphia. Alcoholism also rose, especially among men, though recent studies have shown that for working-class men, the urban saloon was as much a gathering spot as it was a place to drink. Nonetheless, a 1905 survey of Chicago counted as many saloons as grocery stores, meat markets, and dry goods stores combined.

QUICK CHECK ✓

What were the main challenges of life in the overcrowded city?

DOCUMENT

Charles Loring Brace, "The Life of the Street Rats" (1872)

Strangers in a New Land

While some of the new city dwellers came from farms and small towns, many more came from abroad. Most came from Europe, where unemployment, food shortages, and increasing threats of war sent millions fleeing across the Atlantic to make a fresh start. Often they knew someone already in the United States, a friend or relative who had written them about prospects for jobs and freer lives in a new land.

The kitchen of a tenement apartment was often a multipurpose room. Here the tenement dwellers prepared and ate their meals; the room might also serve as a workroom, and it might be used as sleeping quarters for one or more members of the family. (*Source: © The Museum of the City of New York, The Byron Collection*).

What was life like for the child in this photograph?

All told, the immigration figures were staggering. Between 1877 and 1890, more than 6.3 million people entered the United States. In one year alone, 1882, almost 789,000 people came. By 1890, about 15 percent of the population, 9 million people, were foreign born.

Most newcomers were job seekers. Nearly two-thirds were males, and the majority were between the ages of 15 and 40. Most were unskilled laborers. Most settled on the eastern seaboard. In 1901, the Industrial Relocation Office was established to relieve overcrowding in the eastern cities; opening Galveston, Texas, as a port of entry, it attracted many Russian Jews to Texas and the Southwest. But most immigrants preferred the shorter, more familiar journey to New York. Entering through Ellis Island in New York harbor, as four in every ten immigrants did, most tended to crowd into northern and eastern cities, settling in areas where others of their nationality or religion lived.

Cities had increasingly large foreign-born populations. In 1900, four-fifths of Chicago's population was foreign born or of foreign-born parentage, two-thirds of Boston's, and one-half of Philadelphia's. New York City, where most immigrants arrived and many stayed, had more Italians than lived in Naples, more Germans than lived in Hamburg, and twice as many Irish as lived in Dublin. Four out of five New York City residents in 1890 were of foreign birth or foreign parentage.

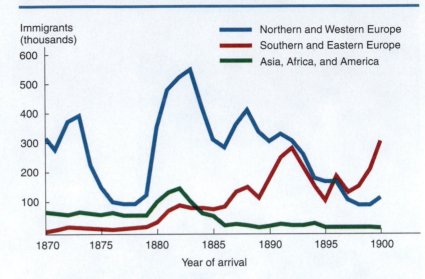

IMMIGRATION TO THE UNITED STATES, 1870–1900

Note: For purposes of classification, "Northern and Western Europe" includes Great Britain, Ireland, Scandinavia, the Netherlands, Belgium, Luxembourg, Switzerland, France, and Germany. "Southern and Eastern Europe" includes Poland, Austria-Hungary, Russia and the Baltic States, Romania, Bulgaria, European Turkey, Italy, Spain, Portugal, and Greece. "Asia, Africa, and America" includes Asian Turkey, China, Japan, India, Canada, the Caribbean, Latin America, and all of Africa.

Source: U.S. Bureau of the Census, *Historical Statistics of the United States, Colonial Times to 1970,* Bicentennial Edition, Washington, D.C., 1975.

new immigrants
Starting in the 1880s, immigration into the United States began to shift from northern and western Europe, its source for most of the nation's history, to southern and eastern Europe. These new immigrants tended to be poor, non-Protestant, and unskilled; they tended to stay in close-knit communities and retain their language, customs, and religions. Between 1880 and 1910, approximately 8.4 million of these so-called new immigrants came to the United States.

Secret Oath of the American Protective Association (1893)

QUICK CHECK ✔

What drew the river of immigrants to the United States?

Beginning in the 1880s, the sources of immigration shifted dramatically away from northern and western Europe, the chief source of immigration for more than two centuries. More and more immigrants came from southern and eastern Europe: Italy, Greece, Austria-Hungary, Poland, and Russia. Between 1880 and 1910, approximately 8.4 million people came from these lands. The **new immigrants** tended to be Catholics or Jews rather than Protestants. Like their predecessors, most were unskilled rather than skilled, and they often spoke "strange" languages. Most were poor and uneducated; sticking together in close-knit communities, they clung to their native customs, languages, and religions.

More than any previous group, the so-called new immigrants troubled the mainstream society. Could they be assimilated? Did they share "American" values? Such questions preoccupied groups like the American Protective Association, a midwestern anti-Catholic organization that expanded in the 1890s and worked to limit or end immigration.

Anti-Catholicism and anti-Semitism flared up again, as they had in the 1850s. The Immigration Restriction League, founded in 1894, demanded a literacy test for immigrants from southern and eastern Europe. Congress passed such a law in 1896, but President Cleveland vetoed it as violating the country's traditions.

Immigrants and the City

Industrial capitalism—the world of factories and foremen and grimy machines—tested the immigrants and placed an enormous strain on their families. Many immigrants came from peasant societies where life proceeded according to outdoor

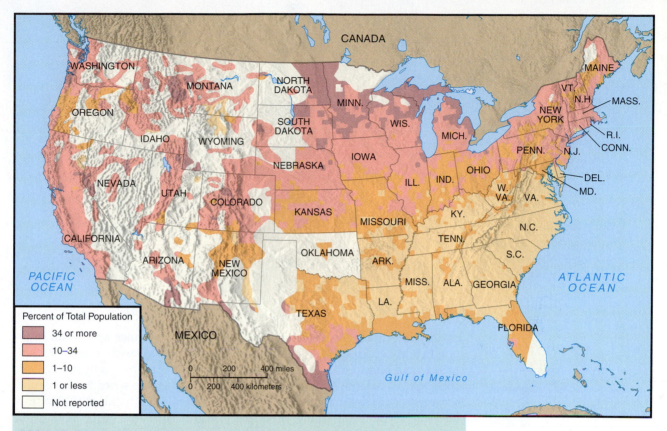

FOREIGN-BORN POPULATION, 1890   Immigrants tended to settle in regions where jobs were relatively plentiful or conditions were similar to those they had left in their homelands. Cities of the northeast, Midwest, and West offered job opportunities, while land available for cultivation drew immigrant farmers to the plains and prairies of the nation's midsection.

What drew so many immigrants to the band of states from Maine to Iowa?

routine and age-old tradition. In their new city homes, they found both new freedoms and new confinements, a different language, and a novel set of customs and expectations. Historians have only recently begun to discover the remarkable ways in which they learned to adjust.

Like native-born families, most immigrant families were nuclear in structure—they consisted of two parents and their children. Though variations occurred from group to group, men and women occupied roles similar to those in native families: Men were wage earners, and women were housekeepers and mothers. However, immigrants tended to marry at a later age than natives, and they tended to have more children, a fact that worried nativists opposed to immigration.

Immigrants shaped the city as much as it shaped them. Most of them tried to retain their traditional culture for themselves and their children while at the same time adapting to life in their new country. To do this, they spoke their native language, practiced their religious faith, read their own newspapers, and established special parochial or other schools. They observed traditional holidays and formed a myriad of social organizations to maintain ties among members of the group.

Immigrant associations—there were many of them in every city—offered fellowship in a strange land. They helped newcomers find jobs and homes; they

In a *Puck* cartoon titled "Looking Backward," the shadows of their immigrant origins loom over the rich and powerful who wanted to deny the "new" immigrants from central and southern Europe admission to America. The caption on the cartoon reads, "They would close to the newcomer the bridge that carried them and their fathers over."

What led the rich men in this cartoon to forget so quickly their own immigrant origins?

Letter to the
*Jewish Daily
Forward*

provided important services such as unemployment insurance and health insurance. In a Massachusetts textile town, the Irish Benevolent Society said, "We visit our sick, and bury our dead." Some groups were no larger than a neighborhood; others spread nationwide. In 1914, the Deutsch-Amerikanischer Nationalbund, the largest of the associations, had more than two million members in dozens of cities and towns. Many women belonged to and participated in the work of the immigrant associations; in addition, there were groups exclusively for women, such as the Polish Women's Alliance, the Jednota Ceskyck Dam (Society of Czech Women), and the National Council of Jewish Women.

Every major city had dozens of foreign language newspapers, with circulations large and small. The first newspaper published in the Lithuanian language appeared in the United States, not in Lithuania. Eagerly read, the papers not only carried news of events in the homeland but also reported on local ethnic leaders, told readers how to vote and become citizens, and gave practical tips on adjusting to life in the United States.

The church and the school were the most important institutions in every immigrant community. Eastern European Jews established synagogues and religious schools wherever they settled; they taught the Hebrew language and raised their children in a heritage they did not want to leave behind. Among such groups as the Irish and the Poles, the Roman Catholic church provided spiritual and educational guidance. In the parish schools, Polish priests and nuns taught Polish American children about Polish as well as American culture in the Polish language.

Church, school, and fraternal societies shaped the way in which immigrants adjusted to life in America. By preserving language, religion, and heritage, they also shaped the country itself.

In what specific ways did immigrants respond to the American city?

The Tweed Ring

Closely connected with explosive urban growth was the emergence of the powerful city political machine. As cities grew, lines of responsibility in city governments became hopelessly confused, increasing the opportunity for corruption and greed.

Burgeoning populations required streets, buildings, and public services; immigrants needed even more services. In this situation, political party machines played an important role.

The machines traded services for votes. Loosely knit, they were headed by a strong, influential leader—the "boss"—who tied together a network of ward and precinct captains, each of whom looked after his local constituents. In New York, "Honest" John Kelly, Richard Croker, and Charles F. Murphy led Tammany Hall, the famous Democratic party organization that dominated city politics from the 1850s to the 1930s. Other bosses included "Hinky Dink" Kenna and "Bathhouse John" Coughlin in Chicago, James McManes in Philadelphia, and Christopher A. Buckley—the notorious "Blind Boss," who used an exceptional memory for voices to make up for failing eyesight—in San Francisco.

Tammany Hall

William M. Tweed, head of the famed Tweed Ring in New York, provided the model for them all. Nearly six feet tall, weighing almost three hundred pounds, Tweed rose through the ranks of Tammany Hall. He served in turn as city alderman, member of Congress, and New York State assemblyman. A man of culture and warmth, he moved easily between the rough back alleys of New York and the parlors and clubs of the city's elite. Behind the scenes, he headed a ring that plundered New York for tens of millions of dollars.

The role of the political bosses can be overemphasized. Power structures in the turn-of-the-century city were complex, involving a host of people and institutions. Banks, real estate investors, insurance companies, architects, and engineers, among others, played roles in governing the city. Viewed in retrospect, many city governments were remarkably successful. With populations that in some cases doubled every decade, city governments provided water and sewer lines, built parks and playgrounds, and paved streets. When it was over, Boston had the world's largest public library and New York City had the Brooklyn Bridge and Central Park, two of the finest achievements in city planning and architecture of any era. By the 1890s, New York also had 660 miles of water lines, 464 miles of sewers, and 1800 miles of paved streets, far more than comparable cities in Europe.

Why did voters keep the bosses in power? The answers are complex, but two reasons were skillful political organization and the fact that immigrants and others made up the bosses' constituency. Most immigrants had little experience with democratic government and proved easy prey for well-oiled machines. For the most part, however, the bosses stayed in power because they paid attention to the needs of the least privileged city voters. They offered valued services in an era when neither government nor business lent a hand.

If an immigrant, tired and bewildered after the long crossing, came looking for a job, bosses like Tweed or Buckley found him one in city offices or local businesses. If a family's breadwinner died or was injured, the bosses donated food and clothing and saw to it that the family made it through the crisis.

Most bosses became wealthy; they were not Robin Hoods who took from the rich to give to the poor. They took for themselves as well. Reformers occasionally ousted them. Tweed fell from power in 1872, "Blind Boss" Buckley in 1891, Croker in 1894. But the reformers rarely stayed in power long. Drawn mainly from the middle and upper classes, they had little understanding of the needs of the poor.

"What tells in holdin' your grip on your district," Tammany's George Washington Plunkitt once said, "is to go right down among the poor families and help them in the different ways they need help…. It's philanthropy, but it's politics, too—mighty good politics…. The poor are the most grateful people in the world."

QUICK CHECK

What role did politicians play in American cities?

Social and Cultural Change, 1877–1900

HOW did the growth of American cities affect social, cultural, and political life?

The rise of cities and industry between 1877 and the 1890s affected all aspects of American life. Customs changed; family ties loosened. Factories turned out consumer goods, and the newly invented cash register rang up record sales. Public and private educational systems burgeoned, illiteracy declined, life expectancy increased. While many people worked harder and harder just to survive, others found they had a greater amount of leisure time. The roles of women and children changed in a number of ways, and the family took on functions it had not had before. Thanks to advancing technology, news flashed quickly across the oceans, and for the first time in history, people read of the day's events in distant lands when they opened their daily newspapers.

The population continued to grow as well. In 1877, the country had 47 million people. In 1900, it had nearly 76 million. Nine-tenths of the population was white; just under one-tenth was black. There were 66,000 American Indians, 108,000 Chinese, and 148 Japanese. The bulk of the white population, most of whom were Protestant, came from the so-called Anglo-Saxon countries of northern Europe. WASPs—white Anglo-Saxon Protestants—were the dominant members of American society.

Though the rush to the cities was about to begin, most people of 1877 still lived on farms or in small towns. Their lives revolved around the farm, the church, and the general store. In 1880, nearly 75 percent of the population lived in communities of fewer than 2500 people. In 1900, in the midst of city growth, 60 percent still did. The average family in 1880 had three children, dramatically fewer than at the beginning of the century, and life expectancy was about 43 years. By 1900, it had risen to 47 years, a result of improved health care. For blacks and other minorities, who often lived in unsanitary rural areas, life expectancy was substantially lower: 33 years.

Meals tended to be heavy, and so did people. Even breakfast had several courses and could include steak, eggs, fish, potatoes, toast, and coffee. Food prices were low. Families ate fresh homegrown produce in the summer and "put up" their fruits and vegetables for the long winters. Toward the end of the century, eating habits changed. New packaged breakfast cereals became popular; fresh fruit and vegetables came in on fast trains from Florida and California, and commercially canned food became safer and cheaper. The newfangled icebox, cooled by blocks of ice, kept food fresher and added new treats such as ice cream.

Medical science was in the midst of a major revolution. Louis Pasteur's recent discovery that germs cause infection and disease created the new science of microbiology and led the way to the development of vaccines and other preventive measures. But tuberculosis, typhoid, diphtheria, and pneumonia—all now curable— were still the leading causes of death. Infant mortality declined between 1877 and 1900, but the decline was gradual; a great drop did not come until after 1920.

There were few hospitals and no hospital insurance. Most patients stayed at home, although medical practice, especially surgery, expanded rapidly. Once brutal and dangerous, surgery in these years became relatively safe and painless. Anesthetics—ether and chloroform—eliminated pain, and antiseptic practices helped prevent postoperative infections. Antiseptic practices at childbirth also cut down on puerperal fever, an infection that for centuries had killed many women and newborn infants. The new science of psychology began to explore the mind, hitherto uncharted. William James, a leading American psychologist and philosopher,

Victorian fashion ideals for women emphasized elaborate, confining dress styles with a tiny waistline and full skirts that reached to the floor. Throughout the 1890s, as women began to participate in some of the new sports or go to work in factories, stores, or business offices, styles gradually became less restrictive. This 1900 cover of *Ladies' Home Journal* shows women wearing tailored jackets and simple pleated skirts hemmed above the ankle playing golf with men.

In the late nineteenth century, how did a new craze for bicycling affect women's fashion?

MARCH   1900   TEN CENTS
THE LADIES' HOME JOURNAL

THE CURTIS PUBLISHING COMPANY, PHILADELPHIA

laid the foundations of modern behavioral psychology, which stressed the importance of the environment on human development.

Manners and Mores

The code of Victorian morality, its name derived from the British queen who reigned throughout the period, set the tone for the era. The code prescribed strict standards of dress, manners, and sexual behavior. It was both obeyed and disobeyed, and it reflected the tensions of a generation that was undergoing a change in moral standards.

In 1877, children were to be seen and not heard. They spoke when spoken to, listened rather than chattered—or at least that was the rule. Older boys and girls were often chaperoned, although they could always find moments alone. They played post office and spin the bottle; they puffed cigarettes behind the barn. Journalist William Allen White recalled the high jinks of his boyhood. He and his friends smeared their naked bodies with mud and leaped out in full view of passengers on passing trains. Counterbalancing such youthful exuberance was strong pride in virtue and self-control. "Thank heaven I am absolutely pure," Theodore Roosevelt, the future president, wrote in 1880 after proposing to Alice Lee. "I can tell Alice everything I have ever done."

Gentlemen of the middle class dressed in heavy black suits, derby hats, and white shirts with paper collars. Women wore tight corsets, long dark dresses, and black shoes reaching well above the ankles. As with so many things, styles changed dramatically toward the end of the century, spurred in part by new sporting fads such as golf, tennis, and bicycling, which required looser clothing. By the 1890s, a middle-class woman wore a tailored suit or a dark skirt and a blouse, called a shirtwaist, modeled after men's shirts. Her skirts still draped about the ankles, but more and more she removed or loosened the corset, the dread device that squeezed skin and internal organs into fashionable 18-inch waistlines.

Religious and patriotic values were strong. A center of community life, the church often set the tenor for family and social relationships. In the 1880s, eight out of ten church members were Protestants; most of the rest were Roman Catholics.

Mugwumps

Drawing their members mainly from among the educated and upper class, these reformers crusaded for lower tariffs, limited federal government, and civil service reform to end political corruption. They were best known for their role in helping to elect Grover Cleveland to the presidency in 1884.

With slavery abolished, reformers turned their attention to new moral and political issues. One group, known as the **Mugwumps,** worked to end corruption in politics. Other zealous reformers campaigned for prohibition of the sale of intoxicating liquors, hoping to end the social evils that stemmed from drunkenness. In 1874, women who advocated total abstinence from alcoholic beverages formed the **Women's Christian Temperance Union (WCTU).** Their leader, Frances E. Willard, served as president of the group from 1879 until her death in 1898. By then, the WCTU had 500,000 members.

QUICK CHECK

What was the nature of Victorian morality?

Leisure and Entertainment

In the 1870s, people tended to rise early. They first washed from the pitcher and bowl in the bedroom. After dressing and eating, they went off to work and school. Without large refrigerators, housewives marketed almost daily. In the evening, families gathered in the "second parlor" or living room, where the children did their lessons, played games, sang around the piano, and listened to that day's verse from the Bible.

As early as 1866, Currier and Ives described baseball as the "American National Game." Although we can recognize some similarities between the game portrayed here and the modern game of baseball, there are also some notable differences. For example, the players depicted in the lithograph do not wear any protective gear: The batter wears no batting helmet, the catcher has no face mask or chest protector, and none of the players appear to wear a baseball glove.

What does the landscape of this baseball park say about the popularity of the game?

Popular games included cards, dominoes, backgammon, chess, and checkers. Many homes had a packet of "author cards" that required knowledge of books, authors, and noted quotations. The latest fad was the stereopticon or "magic lantern," which brought three-dimensional life to art, history, and nature. Like author cards and other games, it was instructional as well as entertaining.

Sentimental ballads such as "Silver Threads Among the Gold" (1873) remained the most popular musical form, but the insistent syncopated rhythms of ragtime were being heard, reflecting the influence of the new urban culture. By the time the strains of Scott Joplin's "Maple Leaf Rag" (1899) popularized ragtime, critics complained that "a wave of vulgar, filthy and suggestive music has inundated the land." Classical music flourished. The New England Conservatory (1867), the Cincinnati College of Music (1878), and the Metropolitan Opera (1883) were new sources of civic pride; New York, Boston, and Chicago launched first-rate symphony orchestras between 1878 and 1891.

Fairs, horse races, balloon ascensions, bicycle tournaments, and football and baseball contests attracted avid fans. The years between 1870 and 1900 saw the rise of organized spectator sports, a trend reflecting both the rise of the city and the new uses of leisure. Baseball's first professional team, the Cincinnati Red Stockings, appeared in 1869, and baseball soon became the preeminent national sport. Fans sang songs about it ("Take Me Out to the Ballgame"), wrote poems about it ("Casey at the Bat"), and made up riddles about it ("What has eighteen feet and catches flies?"). Modern rules were adopted. Umpires were designated to call balls and strikes; catchers wore masks and chest protectors and moved closer to the plate instead of staying back to catch the ball on the bounce. Fielders had to catch the ball on the fly rather than on one bounce in their caps. By 1890, professional baseball teams were drawing crowds of sixty thousand daily. In 1901, the American League was organized, and two years later the Boston Red Sox beat the Pittsburgh Pirates in the first modern World Series.

In 1869, Princeton and Rutgers played the first intercollegiate football game. Soon, other schools picked up the sport, and by the early 1890s, crowds of fifty thousand or more attended the most popular contests. Basketball, invented in 1891, gained a large following.

As gas and electric lights brightened the night, and streetcars crisscrossed city streets, leisure habits changed. Delighted with the new technology, people took advantage of an increasing variety of things to do. They stayed home less often. New York City's first electric sign—"Manhattan Beach Swept by Ocean Breezes"— appeared in 1881, and people went out at night filling the streets on their way to the theater, vaudeville shows, and dance halls or just out for an evening stroll.

Women's Christian Temperance Union (WCTU)

Founded by Frances E. Willard, this organization campaigned to end drunkenness and the social ills that accompanied it. The largest women's organization in the country, by 1898 it had 10,000 branches and 500,000 members. The WCTU illustrated the large role women played in politics and reform long before they won the right to vote.

LISTEN

"Silver Threads Among the Gold"

IMAGE

Cincinnati Red Stockings Baseball Club, ca. 1869

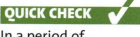

QUICK CHECK ✔

In a period of increasing leisure, what did people do in their free time?

Changes in Family Life

Under the impact of industrialization and urbanization, family relationships were changing. On the farm, parents and children worked more or less together, and the family was a producing unit. In factories and offices, family members rarely worked together. In working-class families, mothers, fathers, and children separated at dawn and returned, ready for sleep, at dark.

Working-class families of the late nineteenth century, like the family of the young Polish girl that Harriet Vittum saw, often lived in complex household units—taking in relatives and boarders to pay the rent. As many as one-third of all households contained people who were not members of the immediate family.

Although driven apart by the daily routine, family ties among the working class tended to remain strong, cemented by the need to join forces in order to survive in the industrial economy.

The middle-class wife and children, however, became increasingly isolated from the world of work. Turning inward, the middle-class family became more self-contained. Older children spent more time in adolescence, and periods of formal schooling were lengthier. Families took in fewer apprentices and boarders. By the end of the century, most middle-class offspring continued to live with their parents into their late teens and their twenties, a larger proportion than today.

Fewer middle-class wives participated directly in their husbands' work. As a result, they and their children occupied what contemporaries called a "separate sphere of domesticity," set apart from the masculine sphere of income-producing work. The family home became a "walled garden," a place to retreat from the crass materialism of the outside world. Middle-class fathers began to move their families out of the city to the suburbs, commuting to work on the new streetcars and leaving wives and children at home and school.

The middle-class family had once functioned in part to transmit a craft or skill, arrange marriages, and offer care for dependent kin. Now, as these functions declined, the family took on new emotional and ideological responsibilities. In a society that worried about the weakening hold of other institutions, the family became more and more important as a means of social control.

Magazines such as the *Ladies' Home Journal*, which started in 1889, glorified motherhood and the home, but its articles and ads featured women as homebound, child-oriented consumers. While society's leaders spoke fondly of the value of homemaking, the status of housewives declined under the factory system, which emphasized money rewards and devalued household labor.

Underlying all these changes was one of the modern world's most important trends, a major decline in fertility rates that lasted from 1800 to 1939. Though blacks, immigrants, and rural dwellers continued to have more children than white native-born city dwellers, the trend affected all classes and races; among white women, the birthrate fell from seven in 1800 to just over four in 1880 to about three in 1900. People everywhere tended to marry later and have fewer children.

Since contraceptive devices were not yet widely used, the decline reflected abstinence and a conscious decision to postpone or limit families. Some women decided to devote greater attention to a smaller number of children, others to pursue their own careers. There was a marked increase in the number of young unmarried women working for wages or attending school, an increase in the number of women delaying marriage or not marrying at all, and a gradual decline in rates of illegitimacy and premarital pregnancy.

In large part, the decline in fertility stemmed from people's responses to the social and economic forces around them, the rise of cities and industry. In a host of individual decisions, they decided to have fewer children, and the result reshaped some of the fundamental attitudes and institutions of American society.

QUICK CHECK

How did the process of urbanization affect the family?

Changing Views: A Growing Assertiveness Among Women

In and out of the family, there was growing recognition of self-sufficient working women, employed in factory, telephone exchange, or business office, who were entering the workforce in increasing numbers. Most were single and worked out of necessity rather than choice.

Many regarded this "new woman" as a corruption of the ideal vision of the American woman, in which man worshiped "a diviner self than his own," innocent, helpless, and good. Women were to be better than the world around them. They were brought up, said Ida Tarbell, a leading political reformer, "as if wrongdoing were impossible to them."

Views changed, albeit slowly. One important change occurred in the legal codes pertaining to women, particularly in the common law doctrine of *femme couverte*. Under that doctrine, wives were chattel of their husbands; they could not legally control their own earnings, property, or children unless they had drawn up a specific contract before marriage. By 1890, many states had substantially revised the doctrine to allow wives control of their earnings and inherited property. In cases of divorce, the new laws also recognized women's rights to custody or joint custody of their children. Although divorce was still far from being socially acceptable, divorce rates more than doubled during the last third of the century. By 1905, one in twelve marriages was ending in divorce.

In the 1870s and 1880s, a growing number of women were asserting their own humanness. They fought for the vote, lobbied for equal pay, and sought self-fulfillment. The new interest in psychology and medicine strengthened their causes. Charlotte Perkins Gilman, author of *Women and Economics* (1898), joined other women in questioning the ideal of womanly "innocence," which, she argued, actually meant ignorance. In medical and popular literature, menstruation, sexual intercourse, and childbirth were becoming viewed as natural functions instead of taboo topics. For example, Edward Bliss Foote's *Plain Home Talk of Love, Marriage, and Parentage*, a best-seller that went through many editions between the 1880s and 1900, challenged Victorian notions that sexual intercourse was unhealthy and intended solely to produce children.

Women espoused causes with new fervor. Susan B. Anthony, a veteran of many reform campaigns, tried to vote in the 1872 presidential election and was fined $100, which she refused to pay. In 1890, she helped form the **National American Woman Suffrage Association** to work for the enfranchisement of women.

Women Working in a Factory

National American Woman Suffrage Association
Founded by Susan B. Anthony in 1890, this organization worked to secure women the right to vote. While some suffragists urged militant action, this group stressed careful organization and peaceful lobbying. By 1920 it had nearly two million members.

QUICK CHECK ✓

In what ways did women respond to life in the urban-industrial society?

Educating the Masses

Continuing a trend that stretched back a hundred years, childhood was becoming an even more distinct time of life. There was still only a vague concept of adolescence—the special nature of the teenage years—but the role of children was changing. Less and less were children perceived as "little adults," valued for the additional financial gain they might bring into the family. Now children were to grow and learn and be nurtured rather than rushed into adulthood.

As a result, schooling became more important, and American children came closer than ever before to universal education. By 1900, thirty-one states and territories (out of fifty-one) had enacted laws making school attendance compulsory, though most required attendance only until the age of 14. In 1870, there were only 160 public high schools; in 1900, there were 6000. Illiteracy declined from 20 percent to just over 10 percent of the population. Still, even as late as 1900, the average adult had only five years of schooling.

Educators saw the school as the primary means to train people for life and work in an industrializing society. Hence teachers focused on basic skills—reading and mathematics—and on values—obedience and attentiveness to the clock.

Schools, regarded primarily as training grounds for a life of work, stressed conformity and deportment—feet on the floor, hands folded and resting atop the desk. The teacher was drillmaster and disciplinarian as well as instructor.

What was it like to be a student in one of these classrooms?

Most schools had a highly structured curriculum, built around discipline and routine. In 1892, Joseph Rice, a pediatrician, toured twelve hundred classrooms in thirty-six cities. In a typical classroom, he reported, the atmosphere was "damp and chilly," the teacher strict. "The unkindly spirit of the teacher is strikingly apparent; the pupils being completely subjugated to her will, are silent and motionless." One teacher asked her pupils, "How can you learn anything with your knees and toes out of order?"

School began early; boys attended all day, but girls often stayed home after lunch, since it was thought they needed less in the way of learning. Many children dropped out of school, and not just to earn money. Helen Todd, a factory inspector in Chicago, found a group of young girls working in a hot, stuffy attic. When she asked why they were not in school, Tillie Isakowsky, who was 14, said, "School! School is de fiercest t'ing youse kin come up against. Factories ain't no cinch, but schools is worst." Curious, Todd asked 500 children whether they would go to school or work in a factory if their families did not need the money—412 preferred the factory.

The South lagged far behind in education. The average family size was about twice as large as in the North, and a greater proportion of the population lived in isolated rural areas. State and local authorities mandated fewer weeks in the average school year, and many southern states refused to adopt compulsory education laws. Most important, southerners insisted on maintaining separate school systems to segregate the races. North Carolina and Alabama mandated segregated schools in 1876, South Carolina and Louisiana in 1877, Mississippi in 1878, and Virginia in 1882. A series of Supreme Court decisions in the 1880s and 1890s upheld the concept of segregation. In the *Civil Rights Cases* (1883), the Court ruled that the Fourteenth Amendment barred state governments from discriminating on account of race but did not prevent private individuals or organizations from doing so. *Plessy v. Ferguson* (1896) established the doctrine of "separate but equal" and upheld a Louisiana law requiring different railroad cars for whites and blacks. The Court applied the doctrine directly to schools in *Cumming v. County Board of*

Civil Rights Cases
A group of cases in 1883 in which the Supreme Court ruled that the Fourteenth Amendment barred state governments from discriminating on the basis of race but did not prevent private individuals or organizations from doing so. The ruling dealt a major blow to the Republican party's earlier efforts to provide protection for African Americans.

Education (1899), which approved the creation of separate schools for whites, even if there were no comparable schools for blacks. Supported by the U.S. Supreme Court decision in **Plessy v. Ferguson,** segregated schooling added a devastating financial burden to education in the South.

Southern school laws often implied that the schools would be "separate but equal," and they were often separate but rarely equal. Black schools were usually dilapidated, and black teachers were paid considerably less than white teachers. In 1890, only 35 percent of black children attended school in the South; 55 percent of white children did. That year nearly two-thirds of the country's black population was illiterate.

Educational techniques changed after the 1870s. Educators paid more attention to early elementary education, a trend that placed young children in school and helped the growing number of mothers who worked outside the home. The kindergarten movement, started in St. Louis in 1873, spread across the country. In kindergartens, 4- to 6-year-old children learned by playing, not by keeping their knees and toes in order. For older children, social reformers advocated "practical" courses in manual training and homemaking.

Opinion of the Supreme Court for *Plessy v. Ferguson* (1896)

QUICK CHECK ✔

In what ways did ideas about education change during these years?

Higher Education

Nearly 150 new colleges and universities opened in the twenty years between 1880 and 1900. The Morrill Land Grant Act of 1862 gave large grants of land to the states for the establishment of colleges to teach "agriculture and the mechanic arts." The act fostered 69 "land-grant" institutions, including the great state universities of Wisconsin, California, Minnesota, and Illinois.

Private philanthropy, born of the large fortunes of the industrial age, also spurred growth in higher education. Leland Stanford gave $24 million to endow Stanford University on his California ranch, and John D. Rockefeller, founder of the Standard Oil Company, gave $34 million to found the University of Chicago. Other industrialists established Cornell (1865), Vanderbilt (1873), and Tulane (1884).

As colleges expanded, their function changed and their curriculum broadened. No longer did they exist primarily to train young men for the ministry. They moved away from the classical curriculum of rhetoric, mathematics, Latin, and Greek toward "reality and practicality," as President David Starr Jordan of Stanford University said. The Massachusetts Institute of Technology (MIT), founded in 1861, focused on science and engineering.

Women still had to fight for educational opportunities. Some formed study clubs, an important movement that spread rapidly between 1870 and 1900. Club members read Virgil and Chaucer, studied history and architecture, and discussed women's rights.

Clubs sprang up almost everywhere there were women: in Caribou, Maine; Tyler, Texas; and Leadville, Colorado—as well as San Francisco, New York, and Boston. Although they were usually small, study clubs sparked a greater interest in education among women and their daughters and contributed to a rapid rise in the number of women entering college in the early 1900s.

Before the Civil War, only three private colleges admitted women to study with men. After the war, educational opportunities increased for women. A number of women's colleges opened, including Vassar (1865), Wellesley (1875), Smith (1875),

The Morrill Act (1862)

Plessy v. Ferguson

A Supreme Court case in 1896 that established the doctrine of "separate but equal" and upheld a Louisiana law requiring that blacks and whites occupy separate rail cars. The Court applied it to schools in *Cumming v. County Board of Education* (1899). The doctrine was finally overturned in 1954, in *Brown v. Board of Education of Topeka*.

A physics lecture at the University of Michigan in the late 1880s or early 1890s. The land-grant university admitted women, but seating in the lecture hall was segregated by gender—although not by race. Notice that both whites and African Americans are seated in the back rows of the men's section.

What is different about this lecture hall from classrooms today?

Bryn Mawr (1885), Barnard (1889), and Radcliffe (1893). The land-grant colleges of the Midwest, open to women from the outset, spurred a nationwide trend toward coeducation, although some physicians, such as Harvard Medical School's Dr. Edward H. Clarke in his popular *Sex in Education* (1873), continued to argue that the strain of learning made women sterile. By 1900, women made up about 40 percent of college students, and four out of five colleges admitted them.

Fewer opportunities existed for African Americans and other minorities. Jane Stanford encouraged the Chinese who had worked on her husband's Central Pacific Railroad to apply to Stanford University, but her policy was unusual. Most colleges did not accept minority students, and only a few applied. W. E. B. Du Bois, the brilliant African American sociologist and civil rights leader, attended Harvard in the late 1880s but found the society of Harvard Yard closed against him. Disdained and disdainful, he "asked no fellowship of my fellow students." Chosen as one of the commencement speakers, Du Bois picked as his topic "Jefferson Davis," treating it, said an onlooker, with "an almost contemptuous fairness."

Black students turned to black colleges such as the Hampton Normal and Industrial Institute in Virginia and the Tuskegee Institute in Alabama. These colleges were often supported by whites who favored manual training for blacks. Booker T. Washington, an ex-slave, put into practice his educational ideas at Tuskegee, which opened in 1881. Washington began Tuskegee with limited funds, four run-down buildings, and only thirty students; by 1900, it was a model industrial and agricultural school. Spread over forty-six buildings, it offered instruction in thirty trades to fourteen hundred students.

Washington stressed patience, manual training, and hard work. "The wisest among my race understand," he said in a widely acclaimed speech at the Atlanta Exposition in 1895, "that the agitation of questions of social equality is the extremest folly." Blacks should focus on economic gains; they should go to school, learn skills, and work their way up the ladder. "No race," he said at Atlanta, "can prosper till it learns that there is as much dignity in tilling a field as in writing a poem. It is at the bottom of life we must begin, and not at the top." Southern whites should help out because they would then have "the most patient, faithful, law-abiding, and unresentful people that the world has seen."

IMAGE

American History Students at Tuskegee Institute

Booker T. Washington, who served as the first president of Tuskegee Institute, advocated work efficiency and practical skills as keys to advancement for African Americans. Students like these at Tuskegee studied academic subjects and received training in trades and professions.

Why would this class, as the blackboard says, focus on "Soil Analyses"?

Outlined most forcefully in Washington's speech in Atlanta, the philosophy became known as the Atlanta Compromise, and many whites and some blacks welcomed it. Acknowledging white domination, it called for slow progress through self-improvement, not through lawsuits or agitation. Rather than fighting for equal rights, blacks should acquire property and show they were worthy of their rights. But Washington did believe in black equality. Often secretive in his methods, he worked behind the scenes to organize black voters and lobby against harmful laws. In his own way, he bespoke a racial pride that contributed to the rise of black nationalism in the twentieth century.

Du Bois wanted a more aggressive strategy. Born in Massachusetts in 1868, the son of poor parents, he studied at Fisk University in Tennessee and the University of Berlin before he went to Harvard. Unable to find a teaching job in a white college, he took a low-paying research position at the University of Pennsylvania. He had no office but did not need one. Du Bois used the new discipline of sociology, which emphasized factual observation in the field, to study the condition of blacks.

Notebook in hand, he set out to examine crime in Philadelphia's black seventh ward. He interviewed five thousand people, mapped and classified neighborhoods, and produced *The Philadelphia Negro* (1898). The first study of the effect of urban life on blacks, it cited a wealth of statistics, all suggesting that crime in the ward stemmed not from inborn degeneracy but from the environment in which blacks lived. Change the environment, and people would change, too; education was a good way to go about it.

In *The Souls of Black Folk* (1903), Du Bois openly attacked Booker T. Washington and the philosophy of the Atlanta Compromise. He urged African Americans to aspire to professional careers, to fight for the restoration of their civil rights, and, wherever possible, to get a college education. Calling for integrated schools with equal opportunity for all, Du Bois urged blacks to educate their "talented tenth," a highly trained intellectual elite, to lead them.

Du Bois was not alone in promoting careers in the professions. Throughout higher education there was increased emphasis on professional training, particularly in medicine, dentistry, and law. Enrollments swelled, even as standards of admission tightened. The number of medical schools in the country rose from 75 in 1870 to 160 in 1900, and the number of medical students—including more and more women—almost tripled. Schools of nursing grew from only 15 in 1880 to 432 in 1900. Doctors, lawyers, and others became part of a growing middle class that shaped the concerns of the Progressive Era of the early twentieth century.

Although less than 5 percent of the college-age population attended college during the 1877–1890 period, the new trends had great impact. A generation of men and women encountered new ideas that changed their views of themselves and society. Courses never before offered, such as Philosophy II at Harvard, "The Ethics of Social Reform," which students called "drainage, drunkenness, and divorce," heightened interest in social problems and the need for reform. Some graduating students burned with a desire to cure society's ills. "My life began… at Johns Hopkins University," Frederic C. Howe, an influential reformer, recalled. "I came alive, I felt a sense of responsibility to the world, I wanted to change things."

QUICK CHECK ✔

What were the trends in higher education between the 1870s and 1900?

The Stirrings of Reform

HOW did life in the growing city lead to ideas of reform?

social Darwinism
Adapted by English social philosopher Herbert Spencer from Charles Darwin's theory of evolution, this theory held that the "laws" of evolution applied to human life, that change or reform therefore took centuries, and that the "fittest" would succeed in business and social relationships. It promoted the ideas of competition and individualism, saw as futile any intervention of government into human affairs, and was used by influential members of the economic and social elite to oppose reform.

When Henry George, one of the era's leading reformers, asked a friend what could be done about the problem of political corruption in American cities, his friend replied: "Nothing! You and I can do nothing at all…. We can only wait for evolution. Perhaps in four or five thousand years evolution may have carried men beyond this state of things."

This stress on the slow pace of change reflected the doctrine of **social Darwinism,** a doctrine that argued against the usefulness of reform, and was based on the writings of English social philosopher Herbert Spencer. In several influential books, Spencer took the evolutionary theories of Charles Darwin and applied Darwinian principles of natural selection to society, combining biology and sociology in a theory of "social selection" that tried to explain human progress. Like animals, society evolved, slowly, by adapting to the environment. The "survival of the fittest"—a term that Spencer, not Darwin, invented—preserved the strong and weeded out the weak.

Social Darwinism had a number of influential followers in the United States, including William Graham Sumner, a professor of political and social science at Yale University. One of the country's best known academic figures, Sumner was forceful and eloquent. In writings such as *What Social Classes Owe to Each Other* (1883) and "The Absurd Effort to Make the World Over" (1894), he argued that government action on behalf of the poor or weak interfered with evolution and sapped the species. Reform tampered with the laws of nature.

The influence of social Darwinism on American thinking has been exaggerated, but in the powerful hands of Sumner and others it did influence some journalists, ministers, and policymakers. Between 1877 and the 1890s, however, it came under increasing attack. In fields such as religion, economics, politics, literature, and law, thoughtful people raised questions about established conditions and suggested the need for reform.

Progress and Poverty

Read and reread, passed from hand to hand, Henry George's nationwide best-seller *Progress and Poverty* (1879) led the way to a more critical appraisal of American society in the 1880s and beyond. The book jolted traditional thought.

Disturbed by the depression of the 1870s and labor upheavals such as the great railroad strikes of 1877, George saw modern society—rich, complex, with material goods hitherto unknown—as sadly flawed. "The wealthy class," he wrote, "is becoming more wealthy; but the poorer class is becoming more dependent. The gulf between the employed and the employer is growing wider; social contrasts are becoming sharper…"

George proposed a simple solution. Land, he thought, formed the basis of wealth, and a few people could grow wealthy just because the price of their land rose. Since the rise in price did not result from any effort on their part, it represented an "unearned increment," which, George argued, should be taxed for the good of society. A "single tax" on the increment, replacing all other taxes, would help equalize wealth and raise revenue to aid the poor. "Single-tax" clubs sprang up around the country, but George's solution, simplistic and unappealing, had much less impact than his analysis of the problem itself. He raised questions a generation of readers set out to answer.

William Graham Sumner, from *What Social Classes Owe to Each Other*

QUICK CHECK ✓

What was Henry George's solution to economic inequity in the late nineteenth century?

New Currents in Social Thought

George's emphasis on deprivation in the environment excited a young country lawyer in Ashtabula, Ohio—Clarence Darrow. Unlike the social Darwinists, Darrow was sure that criminals were made and not born. They grew out of "the unjust condition of human life." In the mid-1880s, he left for Chicago and a forty-year career working to convince people that poverty lay at the root of crime. "There is no such thing as crime as the word is generally understood," he told a group of startled prisoners in the Cook County jail. "If every man, woman and child in the world had a chance to make a decent, fair, honest living there would be no jails and no lawyers and no courts."

Edward Bellamy, from *Looking Backward*

Edward Bellamy also dreamed of a cooperative society in which poverty, greed, and crime no longer existed. A lawyer from western Massachusetts, Bellamy published *Looking Backward, 2000–1887*, in 1887 and became a national reform figure virtually overnight. The novel's protagonist, Julian West, falls asleep in 1887 and awakes in the year 2000. Wide-eyed, he finds himself in a socialist utopia: The government owns the means of production, and citizens share the material rewards. Cooperation, rather than competition, is the watchword.

The world of *Looking Backward* had limits; it was regimented, paternalistic, and filled with the gadgets and material concerns of Bellamy's own day. But it had a dramatic effect on many readers. The book sold at the rate of ten thousand copies a week, and its followers formed Nationalist Clubs to work for its objectives. By 1890, there were such clubs in twenty-seven states, all calling for the nationalization of public utilities and a wider distribution of wealth.

Despite these ideas, some Protestant sects stressed individual salvation and a better life in the next world, not in this one. Poverty was evidence of sinfulness; the poor had only themselves to blame. "God has intended the great to be great and the little to be little," said Henry Ward Beecher, the country's best known pastor. Wealth and destitution, suburbs and slums—all formed part of God's plan.

Challenging those traditional doctrines, a number of churches in the 1880s began establishing missions in the city slums. Living among the poor and homeless, the urban missionaries grew impatient with religious doctrines that endorsed the status quo.

Many of the new trends were reflected in an emerging religious philosophy known as the **Social Gospel.** As the name suggests, the Social Gospel focused on society as well as individuals, on improving living conditions as well as saving souls. Sermons in Social Gospel churches called on church members to fulfill their social obligations, and adults met before and after the regular service to discuss social and economic problems. Children were excused from sermons, organized into age groups, and encouraged to make the church a center for social as well as religious activity. Soon churches included dining halls, gymnasiums, and even theaters.

QUICK CHECK ✔
What new ideas did Henry George and others offer, and what effect did those ideas have?

Social Gospel
Preached by a number of urban Protestant ministers, the Social Gospel focused as much on improving the conditions of life on earth as on saving souls for the hereafter. Its adherents worked for child-labor laws and measures to alleviate poverty.

settlement houses
Located in poor districts of major cities, these were community centers that tried to soften the impact of urban life for immigrants and other families. Often run by young, educated women, they provided social services and a political voice for their neighborhoods. Chicago's Hull House, founded by Jane Addams in 1889, became the most famous of the settlement houses.

The Settlement Houses

Like Tweed and Plunkitt, a growing number of social reformers living in the urban slums appreciated the dependency of the poor; unlike them, they wanted to eradicate the conditions that underlay it. To do so, they formed **settlement houses** in the slums and went to live in them to experience the problems they were trying to solve.

Youthful, idealistic, and mostly middle class, these social workers took as their model Toynbee Hall, founded in 1884 in the slums of East London to provide community services. Stanton Coit, a moody and poetic graduate of Amherst College, was the first American to borrow the settlement house idea; in 1886, he opened the Neighborhood Guild on the Lower East Side of New York. The idea spread swiftly. By 1900, there were more than a hundred settlements in the country; five years later, there were more than two hundred, and by 1910, more than four hundred.

The settlements included Jane Addams's famous Hull House in Chicago (1889), Robert A. Woods's South End House in Boston (1892), and Lillian Wald's Henry Street Settlement in New York (1893). The reformers wanted to bridge the socioeconomic gap between rich and poor and to bring education, culture, and hope to the slums. They sought to create in the heart of the city the values and sense of community of small-town America.

Many of the settlement workers were women, some of them college graduates, who found that society had little use for their talents and energy. Jane Addams, a graduate of Rockford College in Illinois, opened Hull House on South Halsted Street in the heart of the Chicago slums. Twenty-nine years old, endowed with a forceful and winning personality, she intended "to share the lives of the poor" and humanize the industrial city. "American ideals," she said, "crumbled under the overpowering poverty of the overcrowded city."

Occupying an old, rundown house, Hull House stressed education, offering classes in elementary English and Shakespeare, lectures on ethics and the history of art, and courses in cooking, sewing, and manual skills. A pragmatist, Addams believed in investigating a problem and then doing something to solve it. Noting the lack of medical care in the area, she established an infant welfare clinic and free medical dispensary. Because the tenements lacked bathtubs, she installed showers in the basement of the house and built a bathhouse for the neighbors. Because there was no local library, she opened a reading room. Gradually, Hull House expanded to occupy a dozen buildings sprawling over more than a city block.

OPENING OF

HULL=HOUSE
PLAY GROUND

Polk Street, Near Halsted

Saturday, May 1st, 1897,
AT 3 O'CLOCK, P. M.

"The air is warm, the skies are clear,
Birds and blossoms all are here,
Come old and young with spirits gay,
To welcome back the charming May."

MUSIC BY THE BRASS BAND

...Kindergarten Games---May Pole Dance...

ALL KINDS OF RACES

Jane Addams founded Chicago's Hull House in 1889. The settlement house provided recreational and day-care facilities; offered extension classes in academic, vocational, and artistic subjects; and, above all, sought to bring hope to poverty-stricken slum dwellers.

What does this poster say about activities and attitudes at Hull House in Chicago?

Like settlement workers in other cities, Addams and her colleagues studied the immigrants in nearby tenements. Laboriously, they identified the background of every family in a one-third-square-mile area around Hull House. Finding people of eighteen different nationalities, they taught them American history and the English language, yet Addams also encouraged them—through folk festivals and art—to preserve their own heritage.

The settlement house movement had its limits, though. Hull House, one of the best, attracted two thousand visitors a week, still just a fraction of the seventy thousand people who lived within six blocks. Immigrants sometimes resented the middle-class "strangers" who told them how to live. Dressed always in a brown suit and dark stockings, Harriet Vittum, the head resident of Chicago's Northwestern University Settlement (who told the story of the suicide victim at the beginning of this chapter), was known in the neighborhood as "the police lady in brown." She once stopped a dance because it was too wild, and then watched in disgust as the

QUICK CHECK ✓

What were the
causes and
characteristics of the
numerous settlement
houses formed in
these years?

boys responded by "making vulgar sounds with their lips." Though her attempts to help were sincere, in private Vittum called the people she was trying to help "ignorant foreigners, who live in an atmosphere of low morals… surrounded by anarchy and crime."

Although Addams tried to offer a few programs for blacks, most white reformers did not, and after 1900, a number of black reformers opened their own settlements. Like the whites, they offered employment information, medical care, and recreational facilities, along with concerts, lectures, and other educational events. White and black, the settlement workers made important contributions to urban life.

A Crisis in Social Welfare

The depression of 1893 jarred the young settlement workers, many of whom had just begun their work. In cities and towns across the country, traditional methods of helping the needy foundered in the crisis. Churches, Charity Organization Societies, and Community Chests did what they could, but their resources were limited, and they functioned on traditional lines. Many of them still tried to change rather than aid individual families, and people were often reluctant to call on them for help.

Gradually, a new class of professional social workers arose to fill the need. Unlike the church and charity volunteers, these social workers wanted not only to feed the poor but to study their condition and alleviate it. Revealingly, they called themselves "case workers" and daily collected data on the income, housing, jobs, health, and habits of the poor. Prowling tenement districts, they gathered information about the number of rooms, number of occupants, ventilation, and sanitation of the buildings, putting together a fund of useful data.

Studies of the poor popped up everywhere. W. E. B. Du Bois did his pioneering study of urban blacks; Lillian Pettengill took a job as a domestic servant to see "the ups and downs of this particular dog-life from the dog's end of the chain." Others became street beggars, miners, lumberjacks, and factory laborers.

QUICK CHECK ✓

What effect did the
panic and depression
of the 1890s have on
social thought?

William T. Stead, a prominent British editor, visited the Chicago World's Fair in 1893 and stayed to examine the city. He roamed the flophouses and tenements and dropped in at Hull House to drink hot chocolate and talk over conditions with Jane Addams. Later he wrote an influential book, *If Christ Came to Chicago* (1894), and in a series of mass meetings during 1893, he called for a civic revival. In response, Chicagoans formed the Civic Federation, a group of forty leaders who aimed to make Chicago "the best governed, the healthiest city in this country." Setting up task forces for philanthropy, moral improvement, and legislation, the new group helped spawn the National Civic Federation (1900), a nationwide organization devoted to reform of urban life.

Conclusion: The Pluralistic Society

"The United States was born in the country and moved to the city," historian Richard Hofstadter said. Much of that movement occurred during the nineteenth century when the United States was the most rapidly urbanizing nation in the Western world. American cities bustled with energy; they absorbed millions of migrants who came from Europe and other distant and not-so-distant parts of the world. That migration, and the urban growth that accompanied it, reshaped American politics and culture.

By 1920, the census showed that, for the first time, most Americans lived in cities. By then, too, almost half the population was descended from people who had arrived after the American Revolution. As European, African, and Asian cultures met in the American city, a culturally pluralistic society emerged. Dozens of nationalities produced a culture whose members considered themselves Polish Americans, African Americans, and Irish Americans. The melting pot sometimes softened distinctions between the various groups, but it only partially blended them into a unified society.

"Ah, Vera," said a character in Israel Zangwill's popular play *The Melting Pot* (1908), "what is the glory of Rome and Jerusalem where all nations and races come to worship and look back, compared with the glory of America, where all races and nations come to labour and look forward!" Critics scorned the play as "romantic claptrap," and indeed it was. But the metaphor of the melting pot clearly depicted a new national image. In the decades after the 1870s a jumble of ethnic and racial groups struggled for a place in society.

That society, it is clear, experienced a crisis between 1870 and 1900. Together, the growth of cities and the rise of industrial capitalism brought jarring change, the exploitation of labor, ethnic and racial tensions, poverty—and, for a few, wealth beyond the imagination. At Homestead, Pullman, and a host of other places, there was open warfare between capital and labor. As reformers struggled to mediate the situation, they turned more and more to state and federal government to look after human welfare, a tendency the Supreme Court stoutly resisted. In the midst of the crisis, the depression of the 1890s struck, adding to the turmoil and straining American institutions. Tracing the changes wrought by waves of urbanization and industrialization, Henry George described the country as "the House of Have and the House of Want," almost a paraphrase of Lincoln's earlier metaphor of the "house divided." The question was, could this house, unlike that one, stand?

For a list of additional titles related to this chapter's topics, please see
www.pearsonamericanhistory.com.   MyHistoryLab

STUDY RESOURCES

KEY TERMS

new immigrants, p. 510

Mugwumps, p. 516

Women's Christian
Temperance Union (WCTU),
p. 517

National American Woman
Suffrage Association, p. 519

Civil Rights Cases, p. 520

Plessy v. Ferguson, p. 521

social Darwinism, p. 524

Social Gospel, p. 526

settlement houses, p. 526

CHAPTER REVIEW

WHAT factors led to the growth of cities in the United States between 1880 and 1900❓

American cities grew by leaps and bounds in the two decades after 1880. Among the reasons for the growth were the needs of an industrializing society; technological change in the form of electricity, elevators, steel beams, and other advances; and the arrival of millions of immigrants. Politically, city bosses responded to the needs of immigrants and other urban voters, keeping themselves in power. *(p. 506)*

HOW did the growth of American cities affect social, cultural, and political life❓

The rapid growth of cities spawned important changes in the way Americans thought and acted. Cities opened up large new areas of entertainment, employment, and behavior. They reshaped the family, brought women more and more into the workforce, and led to a greater emphasis on education. *(p. 514)*

HOW did life in the growing city lead to ideas of reform❓

Urban life, which forced many people close together, made visible the problems of life to a degree people had rarely experienced. The city could not hide the contrasts between rich and poor, the dirtiness and dangers of factory life, and the woeful lot of millions of immigrants. Reformers emerged to argue for change. Some of them, like Jane Addams, opened settlement houses in the heart of the city, where they lived among the poor. *(p. 524)*

MAKING CONNECTIONS

1. What were the main economic, social, and political characteristics of the new urban society?
2. In what ways did the social and cultural changes of urban society affect fundamental outlooks on the family, the role of women, and education, and lead to demands for reform?
3. How did reform-minded critics try to meet the challenges of urban growth?

PRACTICE QUIZ

1. Jews and _____ from southern and eastern Europe entered the United States in great numbers beginning in the late 1800s.
   a. Muslims
   b. Catholics
   c. Mormons
   d. Spiritualists

2. The _____ worked to reform corruption in city and state politics.
   a. Democrats
   b. Tweed Ring
   c. Mugwumps
   d. Catholic Church

3. The musician _____ made ragtime music popular during the late 1800s.
   a. Frances Willard
   b. Scott Joplin
   c. Harriet Vittum
   d. Edward Foote

4. The _____ became the nation's first professional baseball team.
   a. Brooklyn Dodgers
   b. Chicago White Sox
   c. Cincinnati Red Stockings
   d. Boston Red Sox

5. The first college _____ game in the United States took place in 1869.
   a. Football
   b. Soccer
   c. Baseball
   d. Basketball

6. The famous political machine known as Tammany Hall operated in the city of
   a. New York
   b. Chicago
   c. Baltimore
   d. Philadelphia

7. In 1890 Susan B. Anthony helped to form the
   a. Declaration of Sentiments
   b. Progressive Party
   c. Populist Party
   d. National American Woman Suffrage Association

8. All of the following describe the development of education in the United States during the late 1800s *except*
   a. Schooling became more important as the concept of childhood became more recognized.
   b. Illiteracy declined to just 30 percent of the population by 1900.
   c. A movement towards universal education escalated over time.
   d. By 1900 many states had passed compulsory education laws.

9. Which of the following *does not* describe the development of education in the South after the Civil War?
   a. The South fell behind the North in educational advancement.
   b. Southern families were twice as large as northern families, making it difficult to expand education in the South.
   c. Southern families were more urban, making it difficult to expand education into crowded southern cities.
   d. Many southern states refused to adopt compulsory education laws.

10. All of the following describe higher educational opportunities for ethnic minorities in the United States during the late 1800s *except*
    a. Most colleges did not accept minority students.
    b. Minority students did not apply in large numbers to white schools.
    c. Black students eventually turned to all-black colleges for higher education.
    d. Segregation and exclusion of ethnic minorities in schools ended in 1896.

Find more practice at www.myhistorylab.com

SAMPLE ESSAY QUESTIONS

1. Discuss why the city became an attractive place to the American people during the late 1800s.

2. Define the new immigrants and explain how they adjusted to changing conditions in the U.S. during the late 1800s.

Answers to Practice Quiz 1. b, p. 510 2. c, p. 516 3. b, p. 517 4. c, p. 517 5. a, p. 517 6. a, p. 513 7. d, p. 519 8. b, p. 519 9. c, p. 520 10. d, p. 522

Political Realignments

1876–1901

SPOTLIGHT QUESTIONS

This campaign card from the 1896 presidential election predicts that Republican candidate William McKinley's protariff, protectionist policy will lead to prosperity and thriving industrialism while Democratic candidate William Jennings Bryan's free trade and free silver policies will lead to economic ruin.

According to this campaign card, what were the differences in 1896 between the Republican and Democratic parties?

Hardship and Heartache

In June 1894, Susan Orcutt, a young farm woman from western Kansas, sat down to write the governor of her state a letter. She was desperate. The nation was in the midst of a devastating economic depression, and, like thousands of other people, she had no money and nothing to eat. "I take my Pen In hand to let you know that we are Starving to death," she wrote. Hail had ruined the Orcutts' crops, and none of the household could find work. "My Husband went away to find work and came home last night and told me that we would have to Starve. [H]e has bin in ten countys and did not Get no work.... I havent had nothing to Eat today and It is three oclock[.]"

As bad as conditions were on the farms, they were no better in the cities. "There are thousands of homeless and starving men in the streets," reported a journalist in Chicago in the winter of 1893. "I have seen more misery in this last week than I ever saw in my life before." Charity societies and churches tried to help, but they could not handle the huge numbers of people who were in need. The records of the Massachusetts state medical examiner told a grim story:

> K.R., 29   Suicide by drowning
> Boston   October 2, 1896
> Out of work and despondent for a long while. Body found floating in the Charles [River].

> F.S., 29   Suicide by arsenic
> Boston   January 1, 1896
> Much depressed for several weeks. Loss of employment. At 7:50 A.M. Jan. 1, she called her father and told him she had taken poison and wished to die.

> L.M., 38   Hanging suicide
> E. Boston   October 15, 1895
> Had been out of work for several weeks and was very despondent. Wife went to market at about 11 A.M. and upon returning at about 12 P.M. found him hanging from bedroom door.... Slipped noose about his neck and [fell] forward upon it.

> R.N., 23   Suicide by bullet wound of brain
> Boston   June 22, 1896
> Out of work. Mentally depressed. About 3 P.M. June 21 shot himself in right temple.... Left a letter explaining that he killed himself to save others the trouble of caring for him.

Lasting until 1897, the depression was the decisive event of the decade. At its height, three million people were unemployed—fully 20 percent of the workforce. The human costs were enormous, even among the well-to-do. "They were for me years of simple Hell," shattering "my whole scheme of life," said Charles Francis Adams, Jr., the descendant of two American presidents. "I was sixty-three years old and a tired man when at last the effects of the 1893 convulsion wore themselves out."

Like the Great Depression of the 1930s that gave rise to the New Deal, the depression of the 1890s had profound and lasting effects. Bringing to a head many of the tensions that had been building in the society, it increased rural hostility toward the cities, brought about a bitter fight over the currency, and changed people's thinking about government, unemployment, and reform. There were outbreaks of warfare between capital and labor; farmers demanded a fairer share of economic and social benefits; the new immigrants came under fresh attack. The depression of the 1890s changed the course of American history, as did another event of that decade: the war with Spain in 1898.

Under the cruel impact of the depression, ideas changed in many areas, including a stronger impulse toward reform, a larger role for the presidency, and a call for help from many farmers and laborers. One of the most important of these areas was politics. A realignment of the American political system, which had been developing since the end of Reconstruction, finally reached its fruition in the 1890s, establishing new patterns that gave rise to the Progressive Era and lasted well into the twentieth and twenty-first centuries.

Politics of Stalemate

Politics was a major fascination of the late nineteenth century. Political campaigns were events that involved the whole community, even though in most states men were the only ones who could vote. During the weeks leading up to an election, there were rallies, parades, picnics, and torchlight processions. In the six presidential elections from 1876 to 1896, an average of almost 79 percent of the electorate voted, a higher percentage than voted before or after.

White males made up the bulk of the electorate; until after the turn of the century, women could vote in national elections only in Wyoming, Utah, Idaho, and Colorado. The National Woman Suffrage Association early sued for the vote, but in 1875, the Supreme Court (*Minor* v. *Happersett*) upheld the power of the states to deny this right to women. On several occasions, Congress refused to pass a constitutional amendment for woman suffrage, and between 1870 and 1910, nearly a dozen states defeated referenda to grant women the vote.

Black men were another group kept from the polls. In 1877, Georgia adopted the poll tax to make voters pay an annual tax for the right to vote. The technique, aimed at impoverished blacks, was quickly copied across the South.

In 1890, Mississippi required voters to be able to read and interpret the federal Constitution to the satisfaction of registration officials, all of them white. Such literacy tests, which the Supreme Court upheld in the case of *Williams* v. *Mississippi* (1898), excluded poor white voters as well as blacks. In 1898, Louisiana avoided the problem by adopting the famous "grandfather clause," which used a literacy test to disqualify black voters but permitted men who had failed the test to vote anyway if their fathers and grandfathers had voted before 1867—a time, of course, when no blacks could vote. The number of black voters decreased dramatically. In 1896, there were 130,334 registered black voters in Louisiana; in 1904, there were 1342.

WHAT caused the stalemate between Republicans and Democrats that lasted until the mid-1890s?

Woodhull Reading Suffrage Proposal, 1871

The Party Deadlock

The 1870s and 1880s were still dominated by the Civil War generation, the unusual group of people who rose to power in the turbulent 1850s. In both the North and South, they had ruled longer than most generations, with a consciousness that the war experience had set them apart. Five of the six presidents elected between 1865 and 1900 had served in the war, as had many civic, business, and religious leaders. In 1890, well over one million veterans of the Union army were still alive, and Confederate veterans numbered in the hundreds of thousands.

A toy scale pitting the presidential candidates of 1888 (Harrison and Cleveland) against each other invites participation in determining the election outcome. More than a plaything, this scale symbolizes the high level of voter participation during the late nineteenth century when elections hung in balance until the last vote was counted.

Why did so many people vote in the late nineteenth century?

Party loyalties—rooted in Civil War traditions, ethnic and religious differences, and perhaps class distinctions—were remarkably strong. Voters clung to their old parties, shifts were infrequent, and there were relatively few "independent" voters. Although linked to the defeated Confederacy, the Democrats revived quickly after the war. They rested on a less sectional base than the Republicans. Identification with civil rights and military rule cut Republican strength in the South, but the Democratic party's principles of states' rights, decentralization, and limited government won supporters everywhere.

While Democrats wanted to keep government local and small, the Republicans pursued policies for the nation as a whole, in which government was an instrument to promote moral progress and material wealth. The Republicans passed the Homestead Act (1862), granted subsidies to the transcontinental railroads, and pushed other measures to encourage economic growth. They enacted legislation and constitutional amendments to protect civil rights. They advocated a high protective tariff as a tool of economic policy, to keep out foreign products while "infant industries" grew.

In national elections, sixteen states, mostly in New England and the North, consistently voted Republican; fourteen states, mostly in the South, consistently voted Democratic. Elections, therefore, depended on a handful of "doubtful" states, which could swing elections either way. These states—New York, New Jersey, Connecticut, Ohio, Indiana, and Illinois—received special attention at election time. Politicians lavished money and time on them; presidential candidates usually came from them. From 1868 to 1912, eight of the nine Republican presidential candidates and six of the seven Democratic candidates came from the "doubtful" states, especially New York and Ohio.

The two parties were evenly matched, and elections were closely fought. In three of the five presidential elections from 1876 to 1892, the victor won by less than 1 percent of the vote; in 1876 and 1888, the losing candidates actually had more popular votes than the winners but lost in the electoral college. Only twice during these years did one party control both the presidency and the two houses of Congress—the Republicans in 1888 and the Democrats in 1892.

QUICK CHECK ✓

What were the characteristics of politics in the 1870s, 1880s, and 1890s?

Reestablishing Presidential Power

Andrew Johnson's impeachment, the scandals of the Grant administrations, and the controversy surrounding the 1876 election weakened the presidency. During the last two decades of the nineteenth century, presidents fought to reassert their

THE ELECTION OF 1880			
Candidate	Party	Popular Vote	Electoral Vote
Garfield	Republican	4,454,416	214
Hancock	Democrat	4,444,952	155
Weaver	Greenback	308,578	0

authority, and by 1900, under William McKinley, they had succeeded to a remarkable degree. The late 1890s, in fact, marked the birth of the modern powerful presidency.

Rutherford B. Hayes entered the White House with his title clouded by the disputed election of 1876, but soon he began to reassert the authority of the presidency. Hayes worked for reform in the civil service, placed well-known reformers in high offices, and, ordering the last troops out of South Carolina and Louisiana, ended military Reconstruction. Committed to the gold standard—the only basis, Hayes thought, of a sound currency—in 1878 he vetoed a bill that called for the partial coinage of silver, but Congress passed this **Bland-Allison Silver Purchase Act**, a law requiring some coinage of silver, over his veto.

James A. Garfield, a Union army hero and long-time member of Congress, succeeded Hayes. Winning by a handful of votes in 1880, he took office energetically, determined to unite the Republican party (which had been split by personality differences and disagreement over policy toward the tariff and the South), lower the tariff to cut taxes, and assert American economic and strategic interests in Latin America. Garfield had looked forward to the presidency, yet within a few weeks he said to friends, "My God! What is there in this place that a man should ever want to get into it?"

Office seekers, hordes of them, caused Garfield's anguish. Each one wanted a government job, and each one thought nothing of cornering the president on every occasion. Garfield planned to leave Washington on July 2, 1881, for a vacation in New England. Walking toward his train, he was shot in the back by Charles J. Guiteau, a deranged lawyer and disappointed office seeker. Suffering through the summer, Garfield died on September 19, 1881, and Vice President Chester A. Arthur—an ally of Roscoe Conkling, a powerful senator from New York—became president.

Arthur was a better president than many had expected. He worked to lower the tariff, and in 1883, with his backing, Congress passed the **Pendleton Act** to reform the civil service. In part a reaction to Garfield's assassination, the act created a bipartisan Civil Service Commission to administer competitive examinations and appoint officeholders on the basis of merit. It laid the basis for the later expansion of the civil service.

Bland-Allison Silver Purchase Act

A compromise between groups favoring the coinage of silver and those opposed to it, calling for the partial coinage of silver.

Pendleton Act

Passed by Congress in 1883 with the backing of President Chester A. Arthur, this act sought to lessen the involvement of politicians in the running of the government.

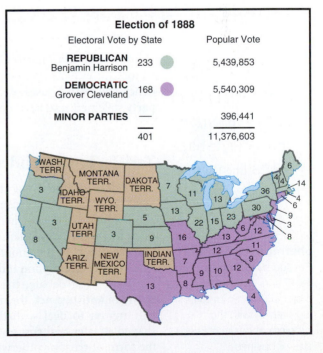

Election of 1888

	Electoral Vote by State		Popular Vote
REPUBLICAN Benjamin Harrison	233		5,439,853
DEMOCRATIC Grover Cleveland	168		5,540,309
MINOR PARTIES	—		396,441
	401		11,376,603

Pendleton Civil Service Act (1883)

Keep the Ball Rolling, 1888

THE ELECTION OF 1884			
Candidate	**Party**	**Popular Vote**	**Electoral Vote**
Cleveland	Democrat	4,874,986	219
Blaine	Republican	4,851,981	182
Butler	Greenback	175,370	0
St. John	Prohibition	150,369	0

QUICK CHECK ✔

How did each of the presidents from Rutherford B. Hayes to Benjamin Harrison work to regain the powers of his office, diminished during the impeachment of President Andrew Johnson?

In the election of 1884, Grover Cleveland, the Democratic governor of New York, won a narrow victory. The first Democratic president since 1861, Cleveland reflected the Democratic party's desire to curtail federal activities. Cleveland vetoed more than two-thirds of the bills presented to him, more than all his predecessors combined.

Late in 1887, he devoted his annual message to an attack on the tariff, "the vicious, inequitable, and illogical source of unnecessary taxation," and committed himself and the Democratic party to lowering the tariff. The Republicans accused him of undermining American industries, and in 1888, they nominated for the presidency Benjamin Harrison, a defender of the tariff. Cleveland garnered ninety thousand more popular votes than Harrison but won the electoral votes of only two northern states and the South. Harrison won the rest of the North, most of the "doubtful" states, and the election.

Republicans in Power: The Billion-Dollar Congress

WHAT ?

was the Republican party's vision, and how did it shape the "Billion-Dollar Congress"?

Despite Harrison's narrow margin, the election of 1888 was the most sweeping victory for either party in almost twenty years; it gave the Republicans the presidency and both houses of Congress. The Republicans, it seemed, had broken the party stalemate and become the majority party in the country.

Tariffs, Trusts, and Silver

As if a dam had burst, law after law poured out of the Republican Congress during 1890. The Republicans passed the McKinley Tariff Act, which raised tariff duties about 4 percent, higher than ever before. A Dependent Pensions Act granted pensions to Union army veterans and their widows and children. The pensions were modest—$6 to $12 a month—but the number of pensioners doubled by 1893, when nearly one million individuals received about $160 million in pensions.

Sherman Antitrust Act
Passed by Congress in 1890, this act was the first major U.S. attempt to deal legislatively with the problem of the increasing size of business.

With little debate, the Republicans and Democrats joined in passing the **Sherman Antitrust Act,** the first federal attempt to regulate big business. As the initial attempt to deal with the problem of trusts and industrial growth, the act shaped all later antitrust policy. It declared illegal "every contract, combination in the form of trust or otherwise, or conspiracy, in restraint of trade or commerce."

In this 1886 cartoon illustrating the silver standard versus gold standard controversy, Uncle Sam bicycles to national bankruptcy on an enormous silverite dollar.

In light of this cartoon, why did so many people in the late nineteenth century favor the coinage of silver?

Experimental in nature, the act's terms were often vague and left precise interpretation to later experience and the courts.

One of the most important laws Congress passed, the Sherman Antitrust Act made the United States virtually the only industrial nation to regulate business combinations. It tried to harness big business without harming it. Many members of Congress did not expect the new law to have much effect on businesses, and for a decade, in fact, it did not. The Justice Department rarely filed suit under it, and in the first judicial interpretation of the law, the Supreme Court severely crippled it. Though the E. C. Knight Co. controlled 98 percent of all sugar refining in the country, the Court drew a sharp distinction between commerce and manufacturing, holding that the company, as a manufacturer, was not subject to the law. But judicial interpretations changed after the turn of the century, and the Sherman Antitrust Act gained fresh power.

Another measure, the **Sherman Silver Purchase Act,** tried to end the troublesome problem presented by silver. As one of the two most commonly used precious metals, silver had once played a large role in currencies around the world, but by the mid-1800s, it had slipped into disuse. With the discovery of the great bonanza mines in Nevada, American silver production quadrupled between 1870 and 1890, glutting the world market, lowering the price of silver, and persuading many European nations to demonetize silver in favor of the scarcer metal, gold.

Support for silver coinage was especially strong in the South and West, where people thought it might inflate the currency, raise wages and crop prices, and challenge the power of the gold-oriented Northeast. Eager to avert the free coinage of silver, which would require the coinage of all silver presented at the U.S. mints, President Harrison and other Republican leaders pressed for a compromise that took shape in the Sherman Silver Purchase Act of 1890.

The act directed the Treasury to purchase 4.5 million ounces of silver a month and to issue legal tender in the form of Treasury notes in payment for it. The act was a compromise; it satisfied both sides. Opponents of silver were pleased that it did not include free coinage. Silverites, on the other hand, were delighted that the monthly purchases would buy up most of the country's silver production. The Treasury notes, moreover, could be cashed for either gold or silver at the bank, a gesture toward a true bimetallic system based on silver and gold.

Sherman Silver Purchase Act

An act that attempted to resolve the controversy over silver coinage.

QUICK CHECK

What were the three most important measures of the "Billion-Dollar Congress?"

The 1890 Elections

The Republican Congress of 1890 was one of the most important Congresses in American history. It passed a record number of significant laws that helped shape later policy and asserted the authority of the federal government to a degree the country would not then accept. Sensing the public reaction, the Democrats labeled it the "Billion-Dollar Congress" for spending that much in appropriations and grants.

"This is a billion-dollar country," Speaker of the House Thomas B. Reed replied, but the voters disagreed. The 1890 elections crushed the Republicans, who lost an extraordinary seventy-eight seats in the House. Political veterans went down to defeat, and new leaders vaulted into sudden prominence. Nebraska elected a Democratic governor for the first time in its history. The state of Iowa, once so staunchly Republican that a local leader had predicted that "Iowa will go Democratic when Hell goes Methodist," went Democratic in 1890.

QUICK CHECK ✓

Why were the 1890 elections among the most important midterm elections in American history?

The Rise of the Populist Movement

WHAT factors led to the formation and growth of the Farmers' Alliance and People's party?

The elections of 1890 drew attention to a fast-growing movement among farmers that soon came to be known far and wide as populism. During the summer of 1890, wagonloads of farm families in the South and West converged on campgrounds and picnic areas to socialize and discuss common problems. They came by the thousands, weary of drought, mortgages, and low crop prices. At the campgrounds, they picnicked, talked, and listened to recruiters from an organization called the **National Farmers' Alliance and Industrial Union,** which promised unified action to solve agricultural problems.

Farmers were joining the Alliance at the rate of 1000 a week; the Kansas Alliance alone claimed 130,000 members in 1890. The summer of 1890 became "that wonderful picnicking, speech-making Alliance summer," a time of fellowship and spirit long remembered by farmers.

National Farmers' Alliance and Industrial Union

One of the largest reform movements in American history, the Farmers' Alliance sought to organize farmers in the South and West to fight for reforms that would improve their lot, including measures to overcome low crop prices, burdensome mortgages, and high railroad rates. The Alliance ultimately organized a political party, the People's (Populist) party.

The Farm Problem

Farm discontent was a worldwide phenomenon between 1870 and 1900. With the new means of transportation and communication, farmers everywhere were caught up in a complex international market they neither controlled nor entirely understood.

American farmers complained bitterly about declining prices for their products, rising railroad rates for shipping them, and burdensome mortgages. Some of their grievances were valid. Farm profits were certainly low; agriculture in general tends to produce low profits because of the ease of entry into the industry. Despite the fact that farmers received less for their crops, their purchasing power actually increased.

In addition, the farmers' second grievance—rising railroad rates—was not entirely justified. Railroad rates actually fell during these years, benefiting shippers of all products. Farm mortgages, the farmers' third grievance, were common because many farmers mortgaged their property to expand their holdings or buy new farm machinery. While certainly burdensome, most mortgages did not bring hardship. They were often short, with a term of four years or less, after which farmers could renegotiate at new rates, and the new machinery the farmers bought enabled them to triple their output and increase their income.

Some farmers did have valid grievances, though many understandably tended to exaggerate them. More important, many farmers were sure their condition had declined, and this perception—as bitterly real as any actual fact—sparked a growing anger. Equally upsetting, everyone in the 1870s and 1880s seemed excited about factories, not farms. A literature of disillusionment emerged, which described the drabness of farm life.

What was the situation of farmers between 1870 and 1900?

The Fast-Growing Farmers' Alliance

Originally a social organization for farmers, the Grange lost many of its members as it turned more and more toward politics in the late 1870s. In its place, a multitude of farm societies sprang into existence. By the end of the 1880s, they had formed into two major organizations: the National Farmers' Alliance, located on the Plains west of the Mississippi and known as the Northwestern Alliance, and the Farmers' Alliance and Industrial Union, based in the South and known as the Southern Alliance.

Rapidly expanding, the Southern Alliance absorbed other agricultural societies. Its agents spread across the South, where farmers were fed up with crop liens, depleted lands, and sharecropping. In 1890, the Southern Alliance claimed more than a million members. It welcomed to membership the farmers' "natural friends"—country doctors, schoolteachers, preachers, and mechanics. It excluded lawyers, bankers, cotton merchants, and warehouse operators.

An effective organization, the Southern Alliance published a newspaper and distributed Alliance material to hundreds of local newspapers, and in five years it

Proceedings of Grange Session (1879)

The Alliance movement grew quickly in the late 1800s among discontented farmers. This photograph shows Southern Alliance members meeting at the cabin that was the site of their first formal meeting in 1877 in Lampasas County, Texas. The cabin was later uprooted and exhibited at the World's Columbian Exposition in Chicago in 1893.

Why did farmers join the Farmers' Alliance?

Farmer's
Delight
Tobacco Ad,
1889

Mary E.
Lease, *The
Populist
Crusader*
(1892)

Ocala Demands

Adapted by the Farmers' Alliance at an 1890 meeting in Ocala, Florida, these demands became the organization's main platform. They called for the creation of a sub-treasury system to allow farmers to store their crops until they could get the best price, the free coinage of silver, an end to protective tariffs and national banks, a federal income tax, the direct election of senators by voters, and tighter regulation of railroads.

sent lecturers to forty-three states and territories where they spoke to two million farm families. It was "the most massive organizing drive by any citizen institution of nineteenth-century America."

Loosely affiliated with the Southern Alliance, a separate Colored Farmers' National Alliance and Cooperative Union enlisted black farmers in the South. Claiming more than 1 million members, it probably had closer to 250,000, but even that figure was sizable in an era when "uppity" blacks faced not merely defeat, but death. In 1891, black cotton pickers struck for higher wages near Memphis, Tennessee. Led by Ben Patterson, a 30-year-old picker, they walked off several plantations, but a posse hunted them down and, following violence on both sides, lynched fifteen strikers, including Patterson. The abortive strike ended the Colored Farmers' Alliance.

On the Plains, the Northwestern Alliance, a smaller organization, was formed in 1880. Its objectives were similar to those of the Southern Alliance, but it disagreed with the southerners' emphasis on secrecy, centralized control, and separate organizations for blacks. In 1889, the Southern Alliance changed its name to the National Farmers' Alliance and Industrial Union and persuaded the three strongest state alliances on the Plains—those in North Dakota, South Dakota, and Kansas—to join. Thereafter, the renamed organization dominated the Alliance movement.

The Alliance mainly sponsored social and economic programs, but it turned early to politics. In the West, its leaders rejected both the Republicans and Democrats and organized their own party; in June 1890, Kansas Alliance members formed the first major People's party. The Southern Alliance resisted the idea of a new party for fear it might divide the white vote, thus undercutting white supremacy. The southerners instead followed leaders such as Benjamin F. Tillman of South Carolina, who wanted to capture control of the dominant Democratic party.

Thomas E. Watson and Leonidas L. Polk, two politically minded southerners, reflected the high quality of Alliance leadership. Georgia-born, Watson was a talented orator and organizer; he urged Georgia farmers, black and white, to unite against their oppressors. The president of the National Farmers' Alliance, Polk believed in scientific farming and cooperative action. In Kansas, Mary E. Lease helped head a movement remarkably open to female leadership. A captivating speaker, she made 160 speeches during the summer of 1890, calling on farmers to rise against Wall Street and the industrial East.

Meeting in Ocala, Florida, in 1890, the Alliance adopted the **Ocala Demands,** the platform the organization pushed as long as it existed. First and foremost, the demands called for the creation of a "sub-treasury system," which would allow farmers to store their crops in government warehouses. In return, they could claim Treasury notes for up to 80 percent of the local market value of the crop, a loan to be repaid when the crops were sold. Farmers could thus hold their crops for the best price. The Ocala Demands also urged the free coinage of silver, an end to protective tariffs and national banks, a federal income tax, the direct election of senators by voters instead of state legislatures, and tighter regulation of railroad companies.

Populist Mary E. Lease advised farmers to "raise less corn and more hell." She also said, "If one man has not enough to eat three times a day and another man has $25 million, that last man has something that belongs to the first." (*Source: The Kansas State Historical Society, Topeka, Kansas.*)

Why did the People's party welcome so many women into positions of leadership?

The Alliance strategy worked well in the elections of 1890. In Kansas, the Alliance-related People's party, organized just a few months before, elected four congressmen and a U.S. senator. Across the South, the Alliance won victories based on the "Alliance yardstick," a demand that Democratic party candidates pledge support for Alliance measures. Alliance leaders claimed thirty-eight Alliance supporters elected to Congress, with at least a dozen more pledged to Alliance principles.

QUICK CHECK ✓

What brought farmers to join the Farmers' Alliance?

The People's Party

After the 1890 elections, Northern Alliance leaders urged the formation of a national third party to promote reform, although the southerners remained reluctant, still hopeful of capturing control of the Democratic party. Plans for a new party were discussed at Alliance conventions in 1891 and the following year. In July 1892, a convention in Omaha, Nebraska, formed the new **People's (or Populist) party.** Southern Alliance leaders joined in, convinced now that there was no reason to cooperate with the Democrats who exploited Alliance popularity but failed to adopt its reforms.

In the South, some Populists had worked to unite black and white farmers. "They are in the ditch just like we are," a white Texas Populist said. Blacks and whites served on Populist election committees; they spoke from the same platforms, and they ran on the same tickets. Populist sheriffs called blacks for jury duty, an unheard-of practice in the close-of-the-century South.

Many of the delegates at the Omaha convention had planned to nominate Leonidas L. Polk for president, but he died suddenly in June, and the convention turned instead to James B. Weaver of Iowa, a former congressman, Union army general, and third-party candidate for president in 1880.

Weaver waged an active campaign but with mixed results. He won 1,027,329 votes, the first third-party presidential candidate ever to attract more than a million, and a total of twenty-two electoral votes, a measure of agrarian unrest. The Populists elected governors in Kansas and North Dakota, ten congressmen, five senators, and about fifteen hundred members of state legislatures.

Despite the Populists' victories, the election brought disappointment. Southern Democrats used intimidation, fraud, and manipulation to hold down Populist votes. Weaver was held to less than a quarter of the vote in every southern state except Alabama. In most of the country, he lost heavily in urban areas, with the exception of some mining towns in the Far West. He also failed to win over most farmers.

In the election of 1892, many voters switched parties, but they tended to realign with the Democrats rather than the Populists, whose platform on silver and other issues had relatively little appeal among city dwellers or factory workers. Although the Populists did run candidates in the next three presidential elections, they had reached their peak in 1892. That year, Farmers' Alliance membership

People's (or Populist) party

This political party was organized in 1892 by farm, labor, and reform leaders, mainly from the Farmers' Alliance. It offered a broad-based reform platform reflecting the Ocala Demands.

DOCUMENT

The People's Party Platform (1892)

Election of 1892

	Electoral Vote by State		Popular Vote
DEMOCRATIC* Grover Cleveland	277	●	5,556,918
REPUBLICAN Benjamin Harrison	145	●	5,176,108
PEOPLE'S (POPULIST) James B. Weaver	22	●	1,027,329
MINOR PARTIES	—		264,133
	444		12,024,488

*Electors classed as Democratic were in many states elected on joint Democratic and People's party tickets.

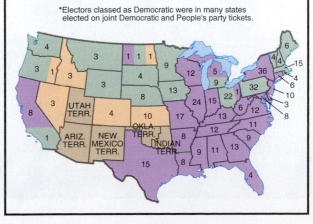

dropped for the second year in a row, and the organization, which was once the breeding ground of the People's party, was broken.

While it lived, the Alliance was one of the most powerful protest movements in American history. Catalyzing the feelings of hundreds of thousands of farmers, it attempted to solve specific economic problems while at the same time advancing a larger vision of harmony and community, in which people who cared about each other were rewarded for what they produced.

QUICK CHECK

What happened to the People's party?

The Crisis of the Depression

WHAT were the main political and labor effects of the panic and depression of the 1890s?

It was economic crisis, however, not harmony and community, that dominated the last decade of the century. Responding to the heady forces of industrialization, the American economy had expanded too rapidly in the 1870s and 1880s. Railroads had overbuilt, gambling on future growth. Companies had grown beyond their markets; farms and businesses had borrowed heavily for expansion.

The Panic of 1893

The mood changed early in 1893. In mid-February, panic suddenly hit the New York stock market. In one day, investors dumped one million shares of a leading company, the Philadelphia and Reading Railroad, and it went bankrupt. Business investment dropped sharply in the railroad and construction industries, touching off the worst economic downturn to that point in the country's history.

Frightened, people hurriedly sold stocks and other assets to buy gold. The overwhelming demand depleted the gold reserve of the U.S. Treasury. Eroding almost daily, in March 1893, the Treasury's reserve slumped toward the $100 million mark, an amount that stood for the government's commitment to maintain the gold standard. On April 22, for the first time since the 1870s, the reserve fell below $100 million.

Customers line up in front of the Farmers and Mechanics Bank in Minneapolis, Minnesota, in May 1893 to try to withdraw their savings. Many banks had loaned out most of their deposits and kept only a small portion of cash in reserve. When they could not meet depositors' demands for cash withdrawals, banks closed their doors.

Why was virtually everyone in this photograph male?

The news shattered business confidence—the stock market broke. On Wednesday, May 3, railroad and industrial stocks plummeted, and the next day, several major firms went bankrupt. When the market opened on Friday, crowds filled its galleries, anticipating a panic. Within minutes, leading stocks plunged to record lows, and there was pandemonium on the floor and in the streets outside.

Afterward, banks cut back on loans. Unable to get capital, businesses failed at an average rate of two dozen a day during the month of May. On July 26, the Erie Railroad, one of the leading names in railroading history, failed. August 1893 was the worst month. Across the country, factories and mines shut down. On August 15, the Northern Pacific Railroad went bankrupt; the Union Pacific and the Santa Fe soon followed. Some economists estimated unemployment at 2 million people, or nearly 15 percent of the labor force.

The year 1894 was even worse. The gross national product dropped again, and by midyear the number of unemployed stood at 3 million. One out of every five workers was unemployed. In the summer, a heat wave and drought struck the farm belt west of the Mississippi River, creating conditions unmatched until the devastating Dust Bowl of the 1930s. Corn withered in the fields. In the South, the price of cotton fell below five cents a pound, far under the break-even point.

People became restless and angry. As one newspaper said in 1896: "On every corner stands a man whose fortune in these dull times has made him an ugly critic of everything and everybody." There was even talk of revolution and bloodshed.

> **QUICK CHECK** ✓
>
> What were the effects of the panic and depression after 1893?

The Pullman Strike

The great **Pullman strike**—one of the largest strikes in the country's history—began when the employees of the Pullman Palace Car Company struck to protest wage cuts and layoffs. On June 26, 1894, the American Railway Union (ARU) under Eugene V. Debs joined the strike by refusing to handle trains that carried Pullman sleeping cars.

Within hours, the strike paralyzed the western half of the nation. Grain and livestock could not reach markets. Factories shut down for lack of coal. The strike extended into twenty-seven states and territories, tying up the economy and renewing talk of class warfare. In Washington, President Grover Cleveland, who had been re-elected to the presidency in 1892, decided to break the strike on the grounds that it obstructed delivery of the mail.

On July 2, he secured a court injunction against the ARU, and he ordered troops to Chicago, the center of the strike. When they arrived on the morning of Independence Day, the city was peaceful. Before long, however, violence broke out, and mobs, composed mostly of nonstrikers, overturned freight cars, looted, and burned. Restoring order, the army occupied railroad yards in Illinois, California, and other places. By late July, the strike was over; Debs was jailed for violating the injunction.

The Pullman strike had far-reaching consequences for the development of the labor movement. Working people resented Cleveland's actions in the strike, particularly as it became apparent that he sided with the railroads. Upholding Debs's sentence in *In re Debs* (1895), the Supreme Court endorsed the use of the injunction in labor disputes, thus giving business and government an effective antilabor weapon that hindered union growth in the 1890s.

Pullman strike
Beginning in May 1894, this strike of employees at the Pullman Palace Car Company near Chicago was one of the largest strikes in American history. Workers struck to protest wage cuts, high rents for company housing, and layoffs; the American Railway Union, led by Eugene V. Debs, joined the strike in June.

> **QUICK CHECK**
>
> What were the three most important causes and events of the Pullman strike?

A Beleaguered President

Building on the Democratic party's sweeping triumph in the midterm elections of 1890, Grover Cleveland decisively defeated the Populist candidate, James B. Weaver, and the incumbent president, Benjamin Harrison, in 1892. He won by nearly 400,000 votes, a large margin by the standards of the era, and the Democrats increased their strength in the cities and among working-class voters. For the first time since the 1850s, they controlled the White House and both branches of Congress.

The Democrats, it now seemed, had broken the party stalemate, but unfortunately for Cleveland, the Panic of 1893 struck almost as he took office. He was sure that he knew its cause. The Sherman Silver Purchase Act of 1890, he believed, had damaged business confidence, drained the Treasury's gold reserve, and caused the panic. The solution to the depression was equally simple: Repeal the act.

In June 1893, Cleveland summoned Congress into special session. India had just closed its mints to silver, and Mexico was now the only country in the world with free silver coinage. The silverites were on the defensive, although they pleaded for a compromise. Rejecting the pleas, Cleveland pushed the repeal bill through Congress, and on November 1, 1893, he signed it into law. Always sure of himself, he had staked everything on a single measure—a winning strategy if he succeeded, a devastating one if he did not.

Repeal of the Sherman Silver Purchase Act was probably a necessary action. It responded to the realities of international finance, reduced the flight of gold out of the country, and, over the long run, boosted business confidence. Unfortunately, it contracted the currency at a time when inflation might have helped. It did not bring economic revival. The stock market remained listless, businesses continued to close, unemployment spread, and farm prices dropped. "We are hourly expecting the arrival of the benevolent man who is to pay ten cents a pound for cotton," a Virginia newspaper said.

The repeal battle of 1893, discrediting the conservative Cleveland Democrats who had dominated the party since the 1860s, reshaped the politics of the country. It confined the Democratic party largely to the South, helped the Republicans become the majority party in 1894, and strengthened the position of the silver Democrats in their bid for the presidency in 1896. It also focused national attention on the silver issue and thus intensified the silver sentiment Cleveland had intended to dampen. In the end, repeal did not even solve the Treasury's gold problem. By January 1894, the reserve had fallen to $65 million. A year later, it fell to $44.5 million.

Still another blow to the morale of the Democrats came in 1894, when they tried to fulfill their long-standing promise to reduce the tariff. Despite all their efforts, the Wilson-Gorman Tariff Act, passed by Congress in August 1894, contained only modest reductions in duties. It also imposed a small income tax, a provision the Supreme Court overturned in 1895 (*Pollock* v. *Farmer's Loan and Trust Co.*). Very few Democrats, including Cleveland, were pleased with the measure, and the president let it become law without his signature.

QUICK CHECK ✔

How did President Grover Cleveland respond to the difficult events of the 1890s?

Breaking the Party Deadlock

The Democrats were buried in the elections of 1894. Suffering the greatest defeat in congressional history, they lost 113 House seats, while the Republicans gained 117. In twenty-four states, not a single Democrat was elected to Congress. Only one Democrat (Boston's John F. Fitzgerald, the grandfather of President

John F. Kennedy) came from all of New England. The Democrats even lost some of the "solid South," and in the Midwest, a crucial battleground of the 1890s, the party was virtually destroyed.

Wooing labor and the unemployed, the Populists made striking inroads in parts of the South and West, yet their progress was far from enough. In a year in which thousands of voters switched parties, the People's party elected only four senators and four congressmen. Southern Democrats again used fraud and violence to keep the Populists' totals down. In the Midwest, the Populists won double the number of votes they had received in 1892, yet still attracted less than 7 percent of the vote. Across the country, the discontented tended to vote for the Republicans, not the Populists, a discouraging sign for the Populist party.

For millions of people, Grover Cleveland became a scapegoat for the country's economic ills. Fearing attack, he placed new police barracks on the White House grounds. The Democratic party split, and southern and western Democrats deserted him in droves.

The elections of 1894 marked the end of the party deadlock that had existed since the 1870s. The Democrats lost, the Populists gained somewhat, and the Republicans became the majority party in the country. In the midst of the depression, the Republican doctrines of activism and national authority, which voters had repudiated in the elections of 1890, became more attractive. This was a development of great significance, because as Americans became more accepting of the use of government power to regulate the economy and safeguard individual welfare, the way lay open to the reforms of the Progressive Era, the New Deal, and beyond.

QUICK CHECK ✔

What was the outcome and significance of the midterm elections of 1894?

Changing Attitudes

The depression, brutal and far-reaching, did more than shift political alignments. Across the country, it undermined traditional views and caused people to rethink older ideas about government, the economy, and society. As men and women concluded that established ideas had failed to deal with the depression, they looked for new ones.

In prosperous times, Americans had thought of unemployment as the result of personal failure, affecting primarily the lazy and immoral. In the midst of depression, such views were harder to maintain, since everyone knew people who were both worthy and unemployed.

People debated issues they had long taken for granted. New and reinvigorated local institutions—discussion clubs, women's clubs, reform societies, university extension centers, church groups, farmers' societies—gave people a place to discuss alternatives to the existing order. Pressures for reform increased, and demand grew for government intervention to help the poor and unemployed.

WHAT changes in outlook did the panic and depression of the 1890s bring about?

Women and Children in the Labor Force

Women and children had been entering the labor force for years, and the depression accelerated the trend. As husbands and fathers lost their jobs, more and more women and children went to work. Even as late as 1901, well after the depression

Tiny children peddling newspapers and women domestics serving the rich—their meager earnings were desperately needed.

What do the young boy's clothes say about his life?

had ended, a study of working-class families showed that more than half the principal breadwinners were out of work. So many women and children worked that in 1905 there was a popular song titled "Everybody Works But Father."

During the 1890s, the number of working women rose from 4 million to 5.3 million. Trying to make ends meet, they took in boarders and found jobs as laundresses, cleaners, or domestics. Where possible, they worked in offices and factories. Far more black urban women than white worked to supplement their husbands' meager earnings. Men still dominated business offices, but during the 1890s, more and more employers noted the relative cheapness of female labor. Women telegraph and telephone operators nearly tripled in number during the decade. Women worked as clerks in the new five-and-tens and department stores, and as nurses; in 1900, a half million were teachers. They increasingly entered office work as stenographers and typists.

The depression also caused an increasing number of children to work. During the 1890s, the number of children employed in southern textile mills jumped more than 160 percent, and boys and girls under 16 years of age made up nearly one-third of the labor force of the mills. Youngsters of 8 and 9 years worked twelve hours a day for pitiful wages. In most cases, however, children worked not in factories but in farming and city street trades such as peddling and shoe shining.

Concerned about child labor, middle-class women in 1896 formed the League for the Protection of the Family, which called for compulsory education to get children out of factories and into classrooms. The Mothers Congress of 1896 gave rise to the National Congress of Parents and Teachers, the spawning ground of thousands of local Parent-Teacher Associations. The National Council of Women and the General Federation of Women's Clubs took up similar issues. By the end of the 1890s, the Federation had 150,000 members who worked for various civic reforms in the fields of child welfare, education, and sanitation.

QUICK CHECK ✔

In what ways did the depression of the 1890s affect women and children?

Changing Themes in Literature

The depression also gave point to a growing movement in literature toward realism and naturalism. In the years after the Civil War, literature often reflected the mood of romanticism—sentimental and unrealistic.

The novels of Horatio Alger, which provided simple lessons about how to get ahead in business and life, continued to attract large numbers of readers. They told of poor youngsters who made their way to the top through hard work, thrift, honesty, and luck. Louisa May Alcott's *Little Women* (1868–1869) related the daily lives of four girls in a New England family, and Anna Sewell's *Black Beauty* (1877) charmed readers with the story of an abused horse that found a happy home.

After the 1870s, however, a number of talented authors began to reject romanticism and escapism, turning instead to realism. Determined to portray life as it was, they studied local dialects, wrote regional stories, and emphasized the "true" relationships between people. In doing so, they reflected broader trends in the society, such as industrialism; evolutionary theory, which emphasized the effect of the environment on humans; and the new philosophy of pragmatism, which stressed the relativity of values.

Regionalist authors such as Joel Chandler Harris and George Washington Cable depicted life in the South. Hamlin Garland described the grimness of life on the Great Plains, and Sarah Orne Jewett wrote about everyday life in rural New England. Another regionalist, Bret Harte, achieved fame with stories that

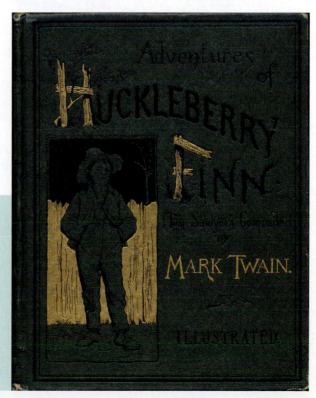

Mark Twain's novel *Adventures of Huckleberry Finn*, published in the United States in 1885, was both popular and controversial. Banned by some public libraries shortly after its publication because of Twain's use of dialect and narration from the point of view of an unschooled boy in conflict with conventional society—both shocking by the cultural and literary standards of the day—the novel is still widely read today, and is still considered controversial by some for its portrayal of race relations in the antebellum South. (*Source: University of Virginia Library, Special Collections Department.*)

In what ways did Mark Twain influence American literature?

A scene from Stephen Crane's novel *Maggie: A Girl of the Streets.* Crane's tale painted a grim picture of life in the tenements of New York City's Bowery as it chronicled the story of slum child Maggie Johnson, victimized and trapped in her squalid, violent world.

In this illustration, what are the main features that depict life in the city?

portrayed the local color of the California mining camps, particularly in his popular tale "The Outcasts of Poker Flat."

Harte was joined by a more talented writer, Mark Twain, who became the country's most outstanding realist author. Growing up along the Mississippi River in Hannibal County, Missouri, the young Samuel Langhorne Clemens observed life around him with a humorous and skeptical eye. Adopting a pen name from the river term "mark twain" (two fathoms), he wrote a number of important works that drew on his own experiences, including *The Adventures of Tom Sawyer* (1876) and *The Adventures of Huckleberry Finn* (1884). In these books, Twain used dialect and common speech instead of literary language, touching off a major change in American prose style.

Other writers, the naturalists, became impatient even with realism. Pushing Darwinian theory to its limits, they wrote of a world in which a cruel and merciless environment determined human fate. Often focusing on economic hardship, naturalist writers studied the poor, the lower classes, and the criminal mind; they brought to their writing the social worker's passion for direct and honest experience.

Stephen Crane spent a night in a seven-cent lodging house on the Bowery and in "An Experiment in Misery" captured the smells and sounds of the poor. Crane depicted the carnage of war in *The Red Badge of Courage* (1895) and the impact of poverty in *Maggie: A Girl of the Streets* (1893). Jack London, another naturalist author, traced the power of nature over civilized society in novels such as *The Sea Wolf* (1904) and *The Call of the Wild* (1903), his classic tale of a sled dog that preferred the difficult life of the wilderness to the world of human beings.

Theodore Dreiser, the foremost naturalist writer, grimly portrayed a dark world in which human beings were tossed about by forces beyond their understanding or control. In his great novel *Sister Carrie* (1901), he followed a young farm girl who took an exhausting job in a Chicago shoe factory.

Like other naturalists, Dreiser focused on environment and character. He thought writers should tell the truth about human affairs, not fabricate romance, and *Sister Carrie*, he said, was "not intended as a piece of literary craftsmanship, but was a picture of conditions."

QUICK CHECK ✔

What were some of the major changes in literature during these years?

The Presidential Election of 1896

The election of 1896 was known as the "battle of the standards" because it focused primarily on the gold and silver standards of money. As an election, it was exciting and decisive. New voting patterns replaced old, a new majority party confirmed its control of the country, and national policy shifted to suit new realities.

WHAT were the issues and importance of the presidential election of 1896?

The Mystique of Silver

Sentiment for free silver coinage grew swiftly after 1894, dominating the South and West, appearing even in the farming regions of New York and New England. Prosilver literature flooded the country. Pamphlets issued by the millions argued silver's virtues.

People wanted quick solutions to the economic crisis. During 1896, unemployment shot up and farm income and prices fell to the lowest point in the decade. "I can remember back as far as 1858," an Iowa hardware dealer said in February 1896, "and I have never seen such hard times as these are." People in favor of silver offered a solution, simple but compelling: the free and independent coinage of silver at the ratio of 16 ounces of silver to every ounce of gold. Free coinage meant that the U.S. mints would coin all the silver offered to them. Independent coinage meant that the country would coin silver regardless of the policies of other nations, nearly all of which were on the gold standard.

It is difficult now to understand the kind of faith the silverites placed in silver as a cure for the depression. But faith it was, and of a sort that some observers compared to religious fervor. Underlying it all was a belief in a quantity theory of money: The silverites believed the amount of money in circulation determined the level of activity in the economy. If money was short, that meant there was a limit on economic activity and ultimately a depression. If the government coined silver as well as gold, that meant more money in circulation, more business for everyone, and thus prosperity. Farm prices would rise; laborers would go back to work.

By 1896, silver was also a symbol. It had moral and patriotic dimensions—by going to a silver standard, the United States could assert its independence in the world—and it stood for a wide range of popular grievances. For many, it reflected rural values rather than urban ones, suggested a shift of power away from the Northeast, and spoke for the downtrodden instead of the well-to-do.

Silver was more than just a political or economic issue. It was a social movement, one of the largest in American history, but its life span turned out to be brief. As a mass phenomenon, it flourished between 1894 and 1896, then succumbed to electoral defeat, the return of prosperity, and the onset of fresh concerns. But in its time, the silver movement bespoke a national mood and won millions of followers.

QUICK CHECK ✓
Why did so many people believe in silver?

The Republicans and Gold

Scenting victory over the discredited Democrats, numerous Republicans fought for the party's presidential nomination, including a Republican favorite, William McKinley of Ohio.

Able, calm, and affable, McKinley had served in the Union army during the Civil War. In 1876, he won a seat in Congress, where he became the chief sponsor of the tariff act named for him. In the months before the 1896 national convention, Marcus A. Hanna, his campaign manager and trusted friend, built a powerful national organization that featured McKinley as "the advance agent of prosperity," an alluring slogan in a country beset with depression. When the convention met in June, McKinley had the nomination in hand, and he backed a platform that favored the gold standard against the free coinage of silver.

Republicans favoring silver proposed a prosilver platform, but the convention overwhelmingly defeated it. Twenty-three silverite Republicans, far fewer than prosilver forces had hoped, marched out of the convention hall. The remaining delegates waved handkerchiefs and flags and shouted "Good-bye" and "Put them out." Hanna stood on a chair screaming "Go! Go! Go!" William Jennings Bryan, who was there as a special correspondent for a Nebraska newspaper, climbed on a desk to get a better view.

The Democrats and Silver

Silver, meanwhile, had captured large segments of the Democratic party in the South and West. Despite President Cleveland's opposition, more than twenty Democratic state platforms came out for free silver in 1894. Power in the party shifted to the South, where it remained for decades. The party's base narrowed; its outlook increasingly reflected southern views on silver, race, and other issues. In effect, the Democrats became a sectional—no longer a national—party.

The anti-Cleveland Democrats had their issue, but they lacked a leader. Out in Nebraska, William Jennings Bryan, a young former congressman, saw the opportunity to take on that role. He was barely 36 years old and had relatively little political experience. But he had spent months wooing support, and he was a captivating public speaker—tall, slender, and handsome, with a resounding voice that, in an era without microphones, projected easily into every corner of an auditorium.

From the outset of the 1896 Democratic convention, the silver Democrats were in charge, and they put together a platform that stunned the Cleveland wing of the party. It demanded the free coinage of silver, attacked Cleveland's actions in the Pullman strike, and censured his sales of gold bonds. On July 9, as delegates debated the platform, Bryan's moment came. Striding to the stage, he stood for an instant, a hand raised for silence, waiting for the applause to die down. He would not contend with the previous speakers, he began, for "this is not a contest between persons. The humblest citizen in all the land, when clad in the armor of a righteous cause, is stronger than all the hosts of error. I come to speak to you in defense of a cause as holy as the cause of liberty—the cause of humanity."

The delegates were captivated. Like a trained choir, they rose, cheered each point, and sat back to listen for more. Easterners, Bryan said, liked to praise businessmen but forgot that plain people—laborers, miners, and farmers—were businessmen, too. Shouts rang through the hall, and delegates pounded on chairs. Savoring each cheer, Bryan defended silver. Then came the famous closing: "Having behind us the producing masses of this nation and the world… we will

William Jennings Bryan, "Cross of Gold" Speech (1896)

The religious symbolism in Bryan's "Cross of Gold" speech is satirized in this cartoon, but his stirring rhetoric captivated his audience and won him the Democratic presidential nomination for the election of 1896.

On what grounds does this cartoon attack Bryan?

answer their demand for a gold standard by saying to them: 'You shall not press down upon the brow of labor this crown of thorns, you shall not crucify mankind upon a cross of gold.'"

Bryan moved his fingers down his temples, suggesting blood trickling from his wounds. He ended with his arms outstretched as on a cross. Letting the silence hang, he dropped his arms, stepped back, then started to his seat. Suddenly, there was pandemonium. Delegates shouted and cheered. When the tumult subsided, they adopted the anti-Cleveland platform, and the next day, Bryan won the presidential nomination.

QUICK CHECK ✓

What won William Jennings Bryan the Democratic nomination in 1896?

Campaign and Election

The Democratic convention presented the Populists with a dilemma. The People's party had staked everything on the assumption that neither major party would endorse silver. Now it faced a painful choice: Nominate an independent ticket and

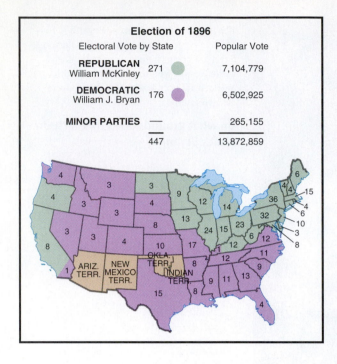

Election of 1896

Electoral Vote by State		Popular Vote
REPUBLICAN William McKinley	271 🟢	7,104,779
DEMOCRATIC William J. Bryan	176 🟣	6,502,925
MINOR PARTIES	—	265,155
	447	13,872,859

MAP

Farmers and the Election of 1896

QUICK CHECK ✓

What were the most important results of the 1896 election?

risk splitting the silverite forces, or nominate Bryan and give up its separate identity as a party.

The choice was unpleasant, and it shattered the People's party. Meeting late in July, the party's national convention nominated Bryan, but rather than accept the Democratic candidate for vice president, it named Tom Watson instead. The Populists' endorsement probably hurt Bryan as much as it helped. It won him relatively few votes, since many Populists would have voted for him anyway. It also identified him as a Populist, which he was not, allowing the Republicans to accuse him of heading a ragtag army of malcontents. The squabble over Watson seemed to prove that the Democratic-Populist alliance could never stay together long enough to govern.

In August 1896, Bryan set off on a campaign that became an American legend. Much of the conservative Democratic eastern press had deserted him, and he took his campaign directly to the voters, the first presidential candidate in history to do so in a systematic way. By his own count, Bryan traveled 18,009 miles, visited 27 states, and spoke 600 times to a total of some 3 million people. He built skillfully on a new "merchandising" style of campaign in which he worked to educate and persuade voters.

Bryan summoned voters to an older America: a land where farms were as important as factories, where the virtues of rural and religious life outweighed the doubtful lure of the city, where common people still ruled, and opportunity existed for all. He drew on the Jeffersonian tradition of rural virtue, distrust of central authority, and abiding faith in the powers of human reason.

Urged to take the stump against Bryan, McKinley replied, "I might just as well put up a trapeze on my front lawn and compete with some professional athlete as go out speaking against Bryan." The Republican candidate let voters come to him. Railroads brought them by the thousands into McKinley's hometown of Canton, Ohio, and he spoke to them from his front porch. Through use of the press, he reached fully as many people as Bryan's more strenuous effort. Appealing to labor, immigrants, well-to-do farmers, businessmen, and the middle class, McKinley defended economic nationalism and the advancing urban-industrial society.

On election day, voter turnout was extraordinarily high, a measure of the intense interest. By nightfall, the outcome was clear: McKinley won 50 percent of the vote to Bryan's 46 percent. He won the Northeast and Midwest and carried four border states. In the cities, McKinley crushed Bryan.

The election struck down the Populists, whose totals sagged nearly everywhere. Many Populist proposals were later adopted under different leadership. The graduated income tax, crop loans to farmers, the secret ballot, and direct election of U.S. senators all were early Populist ideas. But the People's party never could win over a majority of the voters, and failing that, it vanished after 1896.

The McKinley Administration

The election of 1896 cemented the voter realignment of 1894 and initiated a generation of Republican rule. For more than three decades after 1896, with only a brief Democratic resurgence under Woodrow Wilson, the Republicans remained the country's majority party.

McKinley took office in 1897 under favorable circumstances. To everyone's relief, the economy had begun to revive. The stock market rose, factories once again churned out goods, and farmers prospered. Farm prices climbed sharply during 1897 on bumper crops of wheat, cotton, and corn. Discoveries of gold in Australia and Alaska—together with the development of a new cyanide process for extracting gold from ore—enlarged the world's gold supply, decreased its price, and inflated the currency as the silverites had hoped. For the first time since 1890, the 1897 Treasury statements showed a comfortable gold reserve.

McKinley and the Republicans basked in the glow. They became the party of progress and prosperity, an image that helped them win victories until another depression hit in the 1930s. McKinley's popularity soared. An activist president, he set the policies of the administration. Conscious of the limits of power, he maintained close ties with Congress and worked hard to educate the public on national choices and priorities. McKinley struck new relations with the press and traveled far more than previous presidents. In some ways, he began the modern presidency.

Shortly after taking office, he summoned Congress into special session to revise the tariff. In July 1897, the Dingley Tariff passed the House and Senate. It raised average tariff duties to a record level, and as the final burst of nineteenth-century protectionism, it caused trouble for the Republican party. By the end of the 1890s, consumers, critics, and the Republicans themselves were wondering if the tariff had outlived its usefulness in the maturing American economy.

From the 1860s to the 1890s, the Republicans had built their party on a pledge to *promote* economic growth through the use of state and national power. By 1900, with the industrial system firmly in place, the focus had shifted. The need to *regulate,* to control the effects of industrialism, became a central public concern of the new century. McKinley prodded the Republicans to meet that shift, but he died before his plans matured.

McKinley toyed with the idea of lowering the tariff, but one obstacle always stood in the way: The government needed revenue, and tariff duties were one of the few taxes the public would support. The Spanish-American War of 1898 persuaded people to accept greater federal power and, with it, new forms of taxation. In 1899, McKinley spoke of lowering tariff barriers in a world that technology had made smaller. "God and man have linked the nations together," he said in his last speech at Buffalo, New York, in 1901. "Isolation is no longer possible or desirable."

In 1898 and 1899, the McKinley administration focused on the war with Spain, the peace treaty that followed, and the dawning realization that the war had thrust the United States into a position of world power. In March 1900, Congress passed the **Gold Standard Act,** which declared gold the standard of currency and ended the silver controversy that had dominated the 1890s.

The presidential campaign of 1900 was a replay of the McKinley-Bryan fight of 1896. McKinley's running mate was Theodore Roosevelt, hero of the Spanish-American War and former governor of New York, who was nominated for vice

WHAT did McKinley accomplish that placed the results of the 1896 election on a solid basis?

Gold Standard Act
Passed by Congress in 1900, this law declared gold the nation's standard of currency, meaning that all currency in circulation had to be redeemable in gold. The United States remained on the gold standard until 1933.

Gold triumphs over silver in this *Puck* cartoon referring to the Gold Standard Act of 1900.

What led to the triumph of gold between 1896 and 1900?

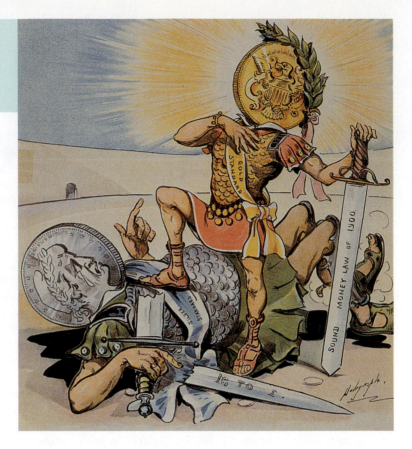

president to capitalize on his popularity and, his enemies hoped, to sidetrack his political career into oblivion. Bryan stressed the issues of imperialism and the trusts; McKinley stressed his record at home and abroad. The result in 1900 was a landslide.

On September 6, 1901, a few months after his second inauguration, McKinley stood in a receiving line at the Pan-American Exposition in Buffalo. Leon Czolgosz, a 28-year-old unemployed laborer and anarchist, moved through the line and, reaching the president, shot him. Surgeons probed the wound but could find nothing. A recent discovery called the X ray was on display at the exposition, but it was not used. On September 14, McKinley died, and Vice President Theodore Roosevelt became president. A new century had begun.

THE ELECTION OF 1900			
Candidate	**Party**	**Popular Vote**	**Electoral Vote**
McKinley	Republican	7,207,923	292
Bryan	Democrat	6,358,133	155
Woolley	Prohibition	209,004	0
Debs	Socialist	94,768	0

Conclusion: A Decade's Dramatic Changes

As the funeral train carried McKinley's body back to Ohio, Mark Hanna, McKinley's old friend and ally, sat slumped in his parlor car. "I told William McKinley it was a mistake to nominate that wild man at Philadelphia," he mourned. "I asked him if he realized what would happen if he should die. Now look, that damned cowboy is president of the United States!"

Hanna's world had changed, and so had the nation's—not so much because "that damned cowboy" was suddenly president, but because events of the 1890s had had powerful effects. In the course of that decade, political patterns shifted, the presidency acquired fresh power, and massive unrest prompted social change. The war with Spain brought a new empire and worldwide responsibilities. Economic hardship posed questions of the most difficult sort about industrialization, urbanization, and the quality of American life. Worried, people embraced new ideas and causes. Reform movements begun in the 1890s flowered in the Progressive Era after 1900.

Technology continued to alter the way Americans lived. In 1896, Henry Ford produced a two-cylinder, four-horsepower car, the first of the famous line that bore his name. In 1899, the first automobile salesroom opened in New York, and some innovative thinkers were already imagining a network of service stations to keep the new cars running. At Kitty Hawk, North Carolina, Wilbur and Orville Wright, two bicycle manufacturers, neared the birth of powered flight.

The realignments that reached their peak in the 1890s seem distant, yet they are not. Important decisions in those years shaped nearly everything that came after them. In character and influence, the 1890s were as much a part of the twentieth century as of the nineteenth and continue to have repercussions into the twenty-first century.

For a list of additional titles related to this chapter's topics, please see www.pearsonamericanhistory.com.

MyHistoryLab

STUDY RESOURCES

KEY TERMS

Bland-Allison Silver Purchase Act, p. 537

Pendleton Act, p. 537

Sherman Antitrust Act, p. 538

Sherman Silver Purchase Act, p. 539

National Farmers' Alliance and Industrial Union, p. 540

Ocala Demands, p. 542

People's (or Populist) party, p. 543

Pullman strike, p. 545

Gold Standard Act, p. 555

CHAPTER REVIEW

WHAT caused the stalemate between Republicans and Democrats that lasted until the mid-1890s?

For more than two decades after the end of Reconstruction, American politics remained the politics of stalemate, in which the Democrats and Republicans fought tenaciously for votes and focused on a handful of "doubtful" states. In general, Democrats dominated the South, and Republicans controlled crucial sections of the North. Presidents in the period worked successfully to re-establish the authority of their office. (p. 535)

WHAT was the Republican party's vision, and how did it shape the "Billion-Dollar Congress"?

Victorious in 1888, in control of both the presidency and Congress, Republicans set out to enact their policies. They succeeded to a remarkable degree, only to discover that voters were not yet ready for their form of activism. The congressional elections of 1890, one of the most important midterm elections in American history, restored the Democrats to power. (p. 538)

WHAT factors led to the formation and growth of the Farmers' Alliance and People's party?

On the farms in the late 1880s and early 1890s, a remarkable movement took shape, as farmers in the South and West joined the Farmers' Alliance, and later the People's party. The People's party sought various reforms but failed, as voters turned to the Democrats in the crucial presidential election of 1892. (p. 540)

WHAT were the main political and labor effects of the panic and depression of the 1890s?

The panic and depression of the 1890s led to changes in politics and labor. Affecting rich and poor alike, the depression encouraged people to rethink their views on the causes of poverty and unemployment. It discredited President Cleveland and crushed the Democrats in the midterm elections of 1894, giving the Republican party a long-term lease on power. (p. 544)

WHAT changes in outlook did the panic and depression of the 1890s bring about?

The depression led people to reconsider the roles of the government, the economy, and society. They had once thought that people lost their jobs because of their own failings; now they knew that economic forces were at fault. People joined organizations like women's clubs, church groups, and farm societies to discuss cures for the situation. Women and children worked in increasing numbers. Realism and naturalism played a larger role in American literature. (p. 547)

WHAT were the issues and importance of the presidential election of 1896?

The presidential election of 1896 brought to a head the fight between supporters of silver or gold, established the Republicans as the nation's majority party, and shaped the nation's politics until 1932. (p. 551)

WHAT did McKinley accomplish that placed the results of the 1896 election on a solid basis?

The McKinley administration profited from economic recovery from the depression of the 1890s. It also had the advantage of its own achievements, which included enactment of the gold standard, passage of a new tariff, and the war with Spain. The Republicans faced another challenge: how to *regulate* big business instead of simply promoting it. (p. 555)

MAKING CONNECTIONS

1. What effect did the rise of the People's party have on American politics?

2. How did the depression give rise to conditions that made the election of 1896 important?

3. How would events have been different if William Jennings Bryan and the Democrats won the election of 1896?

4. What did McKinley and the Republican party demonstrate about the changes in popular attitudes since 1890?

PRACTICE QUIZ

1. Approximately _____ percent of Americans became unemployed during the 1890s.
- **a.** 25
- **b.** 20
- **c.** 15
- **d.** 10

2. The Supreme Court in _____ upheld state laws against female voting.
- **a.** *Minor v. Happersett*
- **b.** *Roe v. Wade*
- **c.** *Williams v. Mississippi*
- **d.** *Plessy v. Ferguson*

3. The _____ passed Congress over President Hayes' veto.
- **a.** Interstate Commerce Act
- **b.** Bland-Allison Silver Purchase Act
- **c.** Sherman Antitrust Act
- **d.** Pendleton Act

4. The _____ Demands were adopted by the Farmers' Alliance in 1890.
- **a.** Oklahoma
- **b.** Florida
- **c.** Ocala
- **d.** Kansas

5. The _____ strike paralyzed the nation.
- **a.** Homestead
- **b.** Pullman
- **c.** Ludlow
- **d.** Railroad

6. The number of children in _____ increased by 160 percent during the late 1800s.
- **a.** Northern factories
- **b.** Southern plantations
- **c.** Western mines
- **d.** Southern textile mills

7. In 1868 Louisa May Alcott wrote the novel
- **a.** *Little Women*
- **b.** *Uncle Tom's Cabin*
- **c.** *The Woman's Bible*
- **d.** *Black Beauty*

8. Which of the following *does not* describe the life and work of Mark Twain?
- **a.** He grew up along the Mississippi River.
- **b.** His real name was Horatio Alger.
- **c.** He observed life around him with a comical and skeptical eye.
- **d.** He wrote *The Adventures of Huckleberry Finn*.

9. Novels considered to be part of the naturalist and realist tradition in the late 1800s include
- **a.** Stephen Crane's *The Red Badge of Courage*
- **b.** Mark Twain's *The Adventures of Tom Sawyer*
- **c.** Jack London's *The Sea Wolf*
- **d.** All of the above answers are accurate.

10. All describe the election of 1900 *except*
- **a.** McKinley's running mate was Roosevelt.
- **b.** McKinley ran against the Democratic challenger, Bryan.
- **c.** McKinley stressed his record at home and abroad.
- **d.** McKinley lost in a landslide.

Find more practice at www.myhistorylab.com

SAMPLE ESSAY QUESTIONS

1. Define the Populist Movement and explain its impact upon American society.

2. Summarize the contributions of American writers to U.S. cultural change in the late 1800s.

Toward Empire

1865–1902

NEW STEEL NAVY
Return of the Conquerors by Edward Moran celebrates the triumphant return of America's Great White Fleet. The fleet of 16 white-hulled battleships and supporting craft set off in December 1907 on a 14-month, round-the-world cruise as a dramatic show of America's naval strength.

According to this painting, what are the main features of American naval power?

Roosevelt and the Rough Riders

Many Americans regretted the start of the war with Spain that began in April 1898, but many others welcomed it. Many highly respected people believed that nations must fight every now and then to prove their power and test the national spirit.

Theodore Roosevelt, 39 years old in 1898, was one of them. Nations needed to fight in order to survive, he thought. For months, Roosevelt argued strenuously for war with Spain for three reasons: first, on grounds of freeing Cuba and expelling Spain from the hemisphere; second, because of "the benefit done to our people by giving them something to think of which isn't material gain"; and third, because the army and navy needed the practice.

In April 1898, Roosevelt was serving in the important post of assistant secretary of the navy. When war broke out, he quickly resigned to join the army, rejecting the advice of the secretary of the navy, who warned he would only "ride a horse and brush mosquitoes from his neck in the Florida sands." The secretary was wrong—dead wrong—and later had the grace to admit it. "Roosevelt was right," he said. "His going into the Army led straight to the Presidency."

Joining a friend, Roosevelt chose to enlist his own regiment, and after a few telephone calls to friends, and telegrams to the governors of Arizona, New Mexico, and Oklahoma asking for "good shots and good riders," he had more than enough men. The First United States Volunteer Cavalry, an intriguing mixture of Ivy League athletes and western frontiersmen, was born.

Known as the Rough Riders, it included men from the Harvard, Yale, and Princeton clubs of New York City, the Somerset Club of Boston, and New York's exclusive Knickerbocker Club. Former college athletes—football players, tennis players,

KEY EVENTS

and track stars—enlisted. Woodbury Kane, a wealthy yachtsman, signed up and promptly volunteered for kitchen duty.

Other volunteers came from the West—natural soldiers, Roosevelt called them, "tall and sinewy, with resolute, weather-beaten faces, and eyes that looked a man straight in the face without flinching." Among the cowboys, hunters, and prospectors, there were Bucky O'Neill, a legendary Arizona sheriff and Indian fighter; a half dozen other sheriffs and Texas Rangers; a large number of Indians; a famous broncobuster; and an ex-marshal of Dodge City, Kansas.

Eager for war, the men trained hard, played harder, and rarely passed up a chance for an intellectual discussion— if Roosevelt's memoir of the war is to be believed. Once, he overhead Bucky O'Neill and a Princeton graduate "discussing Aryan word roots together, and then sliding off into a review of the novels of Balzac, and a discussion as to how far Balzac could be said to be the founder of the modern realistic school of fiction." In such a camp, discipline was lax, and enlisted men got on easily with the officers.

DRESSED FOR WAR Colonel Theodore Roosevelt poses in his custom-designed uniform. With surgeon Leonard Wood, Roosevelt organized the First U.S. Volunteer Cavalry— the Rough Riders—for service in the Spanish-American War.

What are the important details in this photograph of Theodore Roosevelt in uniform?

The troops howled with joy when orders came to join the invasion army for Cuba. They set sail on June 14, 1898, and Lieutenant Colonel Roosevelt, who had performed a war dance for the troops the night before, caught their mood: "We knew not whither we were bound, nor what we were to do; but we believed that the nearing future held for us many chances of death and hardship, of honor and renown. If we failed, we would share the fate of all who fail; but we were sure that we would win, that we should score the first great triumph in a mighty world-movement."

That "world-movement," Roosevelt was sure, would establish the United States as a world power, whose commerce and influence would extend around the globe, particularly in Latin America and Asia. As he hoped, the nation in the 1890s underwent dramatic expansion, building on the foreign policy approaches of administrations from Lincoln to William McKinley. Policymakers fostered business interests abroad, strengthened the navy, and extended American influence into Latin America and the Pacific. Differences over Cuba resulted in a war with Spain that brought new colonies and colonial subjects, establishing for the first time an American overseas empire.

Roosevelt's
Rough Riders

America Looks Outward

The overseas expansion of the 1890s differed in several important respects from earlier expansionist moves of the United States. From its beginning, the American republic had been expanding. After the first landings in Jamestown and Plymouth, settlers pushed westward: into the trans-Appalachian region, the Louisiana Territory, Florida, Texas, California, Arizona, and New Mexico. Most of these lands were contiguous with existing territories of the United States, and most were intended for settlement, usually agricultural.

The expansion of the 1890s was different. It sought to gain island possessions, the bulk of them already thickly populated. The new territories were intended less for settlement than for use as naval bases, trading outposts, or commercial centers on major trade routes. More often than not, they were viewed as colonies, not as states-in-the-making.

Historian Samuel F. Bemis described the overseas expansion of the 1890s as "the great aberration," a time when the country adopted expansionist policies that did not fit with prior experience. Other historians, pointing to expansionist tendencies in thought and foreign policy that surfaced during the last half of the nineteenth century, have found a developing pattern that led naturally to the overseas adventures of the 1890s. In the view of Walter LaFeber, "the United States did not set out on an expansionist path in the late 1890s in a sudden, spur-of-the-moment fashion. The overseas empire that Americans controlled in 1900 was not a break in their history, but a natural culmination."

WHAT caused Americans to look outward in the last half of the nineteenth century?

Catching the Spirit of Empire

Throughout history, most people have tended to focus on domestic concerns, and Americans in the years following the Civil War were no exception. Among other things, they focused on Reconstruction, the movement westward, and simply making a living. Throughout the nineteenth century, Americans enjoyed "free security"

isolationism

A belief that the United States should stay out of entanglements with other nations. Isolationism was widespread after the Spanish-American War in the late 1890s and influenced later U.S. foreign policy.

QUICK CHECK ✓

Why did Americans for a long time resist involvement in events abroad?

without fully appreciating it. Sheltered by two oceans and the British navy, they could enunciate bold policies such as the Monroe Doctrine, which instructed European nations to stay out of the affairs of the Western Hemisphere, while remaining virtually impregnable to foreign attack.

In those circumstances a sense of **isolationism** spread, fostering a desire to stay out of foreign entanglements. Some people even urged abolition of the foreign service, considering it an unnecessary expenditure, a dangerous profession that might lead to involvement in the struggles of the world's great powers.

In the 1870s and after, however, Americans began to take an increasing interest in events abroad. There was a growing sense of internationalism, which stemmed in part from the telegraphs, telephones, and undersea cables that kept people better informed about political and economic developments in distant lands. Many Americans continued to be interested in expansion of the country's borders; relatively few were interested in **imperialism.** Expansion meant the kind of growth that had brought California and Oregon into the American system. Imperialism meant the imposition of control over other peoples through annexation, military conquest, or economic domination.

imperialism

The policy of extending a nation's power through military conquest, economic domination, or annexation.

Albert Beveridge, "The March of the Flag" (1898)

Theodore Roosevelt, "The Strenuous Life" (1900)

Josiah Strong, from *Our Country*

Reasons for Expansion

Several developments in these years combined to shift attention outward across the seas. The end of the frontier, announced officially in the census report of 1890, sparked fears about diminishing opportunities at home. Further growth, it seemed to some, must take place abroad. Factories and farms multiplied, producing more goods than the domestic market could consume. Both farmers and industrialists looked for new overseas markets, and the growing volume of exports—including more and more manufactured goods—changed the nature of American trade relations with the world. In 1898, the United States exported more than it imported, beginning a trend that lasted through the 1960s.

To some extent, Americans were also caught up in a worldwide scramble for empire. In the last third of the century, Great Britain, France, and Germany divided up Africa and looked covetously at Asia. The idea of imperialistic expansion was in the air, and the great powers measured their greatness by the colonies they acquired.

Intellectual currents that supported expansion drew on Charles Darwin's theories of evolution. Adherents pointed, for example, to *The Origin of Species,* which mentioned in its subtitle *The Preservation of Favoured Races in the Struggle for Life.* Applied to human and social development, biological concepts seemed to call for the triumph of the fit and the elimination of the unfit. "In this world," said Theodore Roosevelt, who thought of himself as one of the fit, "the nation that has trained itself to a career of unwarlike and isolated ease is bound, in the end, to go down before other nations which have not lost the manly and adventurous qualities."

John Fiske, a popular writer and lecturer, argued for Anglo-Saxon racial superiority, a result of the process of natural selection. The English and Americans, Fiske said, would occupy every land on the globe that was not already "civilized," bringing the advances of commerce and democratic institutions.

The career of Josiah Strong, a Congregational minister and fervent expansionist, suggested the strength of the developing ideas. A champion of overseas missionary work, Strong traveled extensively through the West for the Home

Missionary Society, and in 1885, drawing on his experiences, he published a book titled *Our Country: Its Possible Future and Its Present Crisis*. An immediate best-seller, the book called on foreign missions to civilize the world under the Anglo-Saxon races. Strong became a national celebrity.

Our Country argued for expanding American trade and dominion. Trade was important, it said, because the desire for material things was one of the hallmarks of civilized people. So was the Christian religion, and by exporting both trade and religion, Americans could civilize and Christianize "inferior" races around the world. As Anglo-Saxons, they were members of a God-favored race destined to lead the world.

Taken together, these developments in social, political, and economic thought prepared Americans for a larger role in the world. The change was gradual, and there was never a day when people awoke with a sudden realization of their interests overseas. But change there was, and by the 1890s, Americans were ready to reach out into the world in a more determined and deliberate fashion than ever before. For almost the first time, they felt the need for a foreign "policy."

QUICK CHECK ✓

What were some of the factors that led Americans in the late nineteenth century to become more willing to get involved in events abroad?

Foreign Policy Approaches, 1867–1900

Rarely consistent, American foreign policy in the last half of the nineteenth century took different approaches to different areas of the world. In relation to Europe, seat of the dominant world powers, policymakers promoted trade and tried to avoid diplomatic entanglements. In North and South America, they based policy on the Monroe Doctrine, a recurrent dream of annexing Canada or Mexico, a hope for extensive trade, and Pan-American unity against the nations of the Old World. In the Pacific, they coveted Hawaii and other outposts on the sea-lanes to China.

Secretary of State William Henry Seward, who served from 1861 to 1869, aggressively pushed an expansive foreign policy. "Give me… fifty, forty, thirty more years of life," he told a Boston audience in 1867, "and I will give you possession of the American continent and control of the world." Seward, it turned out, had only five more years of life, but he developed a vision of an American empire stretching south into Latin America and west to the shores of Asia. His vision included Canada and Mexico; islands in the Caribbean as strategic bases to protect a canal across the isthmus; and Hawaii and other islands as stepping-stones to Asia, which Seward and many others considered a virtually bottomless outlet for farm and manufactured goods.

In 1867, he concluded a treaty with Russia for the purchase of Alaska (which was promptly labeled "Seward's Folly") partly to sandwich western Canada between American territory and lead to its annexation. As the American empire spread, Seward thought, Mexico City would become its capital.

James G. Blaine served briefly as secretary of state under President James Garfield and laid extensive plans to establish closer commercial relations with Latin America. Blaine's successor, Frederick T. Frelinghuysen, changed Blaine's approach but not his strategy. Like Blaine, Frelinghuysen wanted to find Caribbean markets for American goods; he negotiated separate reciprocity treaties with Mexico, Cuba and Puerto Rico, the British West Indies, Santo Domingo, and Colombia. Using these treaties, Frelinghuysen hoped not only to obtain markets for American goods but to bind these countries to American interests.

When Blaine returned to the State Department in 1889 under President Benjamin Harrison, he moved again to expand markets in Latin America. Drawing on earlier ideas, he envisaged a hemispheric system of peaceful intercourse, arbitration of disputes, and expanded trade. He also wanted to annex Hawaii.

Harrison and Blaine toyed with naval acquisitions in the Caribbean and elsewhere, but in general they focused on Pan-Americanism and tariff reciprocity. Blaine presided over the first Inter-American Conference in Washington on October 2, 1889, where delegates from nineteen American nations negotiated several agreements to promote trade and created the International Bureau of the American Republics, later renamed the Pan-American Union, for the exchange of general information, including political, scientific, and cultural knowledge. The conference, a major step in hemispheric relations, led to later meetings promoting trade and other agreements.

Grover Cleveland, Harrison's successor, also pursued an aggressive policy toward Latin America. In 1895, he brought the United States precariously close to war with Great Britain over a boundary dispute between Venezuela and British Guiana. Cleveland sympathized with Venezuela, and he and Secretary of State Richard Olney urged Britain to arbitrate the dispute. When Britain failed to act, Olney drafted a stiff diplomatic note affirming the Monroe Doctrine and denying European nations the right to meddle in Western Hemisphere affairs.

Four months passed before Lord Salisbury, the British foreign secretary, replied. Rejecting Olney's arguments, he sent two letters, the first bluntly repudiating the Monroe Doctrine as international law. The second letter, carefully reasoned and sometimes sarcastic, rejected Olney's arguments for the Venezuelan boundary. Enraged, Cleveland defended the Monroe Doctrine, and he asked Congress for authority to appoint a commission to decide the boundary and enforce its decision.

Preoccupied with larger diplomatic problems in Africa and Europe, Britain changed its position. In November 1896, the two countries signed a treaty of arbitration, under which Great Britain and Venezuela divided the disputed territory. Though Cleveland's approach was clumsy—throughout the crisis, for example, he rarely consulted Venezuela—the Venezuelan incident demonstrated a growing determination to exert American power in the Western Hemisphere. Cleveland and Olney had persuaded Great Britain to recognize the United States's dominance, and they had increased American influence in Latin America. The Monroe Doctrine assumed new importance. In averting war, an era of Anglo-American friendship was begun.

QUICK CHECK ✔

What were the main characteristics of American foreign policy between 1867 and 1900?

The Lure of Hawaii

The islands of Hawaii offered a tempting way station to Asian markets. In the early 1800s, they were already called the "Crossroads of the Pacific," and trading ships of many nations stopped there. In 1820, the first American missionaries arrived to convert the islanders to Christianity. Like missionaries elsewhere, they advertised Hawaii's economic and other benefits and attracted new settlers. Their children later came to dominate Hawaiian political and economic life and played an important role in annexation.

After the Civil War, the United States tightened its connections with the islands. The reciprocity treaty of 1875 allowed Hawaiian sugar to enter the United States

THE LAST HAWAIIAN QUEEN   The first step toward American annexation of Hawaii came in 1893 when Queen Liliuokalani was removed from the throne. Hawaii was annexed to the United States as a possession in 1898 and became a U.S. territory in 1900. This photograph from ca. 1898 shows the former queen with guests and members of her household at Washington Place, her residence from 1896 until her death in 1917.

Why were so many people eager to annex Hawaii in the late nineteenth century?

free of duty and bound the Hawaiian monarchy to make no territorial or economic concessions to other powers. The treaty increased Hawaiian economic dependence on the United States; its political clauses effectively made Hawaii an American protectorate. In 1887, a new treaty reaffirmed these arrangements and granted the United States exclusive use of Pearl Harbor, a magnificent harbor that had early caught the eye of naval strategists.

Following the 1875 treaty, white Hawaiians became more and more influential in the islands' political life. The McKinley Tariff Act of 1890 ended the special status given Hawaiian sugar and at the same time awarded American producers a bounty of two cents a pound. Hawaiian sugar production dropped dramatically, unemployment rose, and property values fell. The following year, the weak King Kalakaua died, bringing to power a strong-willed nationalist, Queen

RUSSIA

Alaska

CHINA

CANADA

JAPAN

UNITED STATES

Hawaiian Islands

PACIFIC OCEAN

Equator

AUSTRALIA

Samoan Islands

Major shipping routes

HAWAIIAN ISLANDS The Hawaiian Islands provided the United States with both a convenient stopping point on the way to Asian markets and a strategic naval station in the Pacific.

Why did American policymakers want an outpost on the way to Asia?

Liliuokalani. Resentful of white minority rule, she decreed a new constitution that gave greater power to native Hawaiians.

Unhappy, the American residents revolted in early 1893 and called on the United States for help. John L. Stevens, the American minister in Honolulu, sent 150 marines ashore from the cruiser *Boston*, and within three days, the bloodless revolution was over. Queen Liliuokalani surrendered "to the superior force of the United States," and the victorious rebels set up a provisional government. On February 14, 1893, Harrison's secretary of state, John W. Foster, and delegates of the new government signed a treaty annexing Hawaii to the United States.

But only two weeks remained in Harrison's term, and the Senate refused to ratify the agreement. Five days after taking office, Cleveland withdrew the treaty; he then sent a representative to investigate the cause of the rebellion. The investigation revealed that the Americans' role in it had been improper, and Cleveland decided to restore the queen to her throne. He made the demand, but the provisional government in Hawaii politely refused and instead established the Republic of Hawaii, which the embarrassed Cleveland, unable to do otherwise, recognized.

The debate over Hawaiian annexation, continuing through the 1890s, foreshadowed the later debate over the treaty to end the Spanish-American War. People in favor of annexation pointed to Hawaii's strategic location, argued that Japan or other powers might seize the islands if the United States did not, and suggested that Americans had a responsibility to civilize and Christianize the native Hawaiians. Opponents warned that annexation might lead to a colonial army and colonial problems, the inclusion of a "mongrel" population in the United States, and rule over an area not destined for statehood.

Annexation came swiftly in July 1898 in the midst of excitement over victories in the Spanish-American War. The year before, President William McKinley had sent a treaty of annexation to the Senate, but opposition quickly arose, and the treaty stalled.

In 1898, annexationists redoubled arguments about Hawaii's commercial and military importance. McKinley and congressional leaders switched strategies to seek a joint resolution, rather than a treaty, for annexation. A joint resolution required only a majority of both houses, while a treaty needed a two-thirds vote in the Senate. Bolstered by the new strategy, the annexation measure moved quickly through Congress, and McKinley signed it on July 7, 1898. His signature, giving the United States a naval and commercial base in the mid-Pacific, realized a goal held by policymakers since the 1860s.

IMAGE

Iolani Palace, Hawaii

QUICK CHECK ✔

For what three reasons were the Hawaiian Islands important to American policymakers?

The New Navy

Large navies were vital in the scramble for colonies, and in the 1870s the United States had almost no naval power. One of the most powerful fleets in the world during the Civil War, the American navy had fallen into rapid decline. By 1880, there were fewer than two thousand vessels, only forty-eight of which could fire a gun. Ships rotted, and many officers left the service.

Conditions changed during the 1880s. A group of rising young officers, steeped in a new naval philosophy, argued for an expanded navy equipped with fast, aggressive fleets capable of fighting battles across the seas. Big-navy proponents pointed to the growing fleets of Great Britain, France, and Germany, arguing that the United States needed greater fleet strength to protect its economic and other interests in the Caribbean and Pacific.

In 1883, Congress authorized construction of four steel ships, marking the beginning of the new navy. Between 1885 and 1889, Congress budgeted funds for thirty additional ships. The initial building program focused on lightly armored

A SINKING SHIP This 1881 cartoon depicted "our top heavy navy," a decrepit vessel sinking with idle officers.

What does this cartoon say about the American navy in the 1880s?

fast cruisers for raiding enemy merchant ships and protecting American shores, but after 1890, the program shifted to the construction of a seagoing offensive battleship navy capable of challenging the strongest fleets of Europe.

Alfred Thayer Mahan, *The Interest of America in Sea Power*

Alfred Thayer Mahan and Benjamin F. Tracy were two of the main forces behind the new navy. Austere and scholarly, Mahan was the era's most influential naval strategist. After graduating from the Naval Academy in 1859, he devoted a lifetime to studying the influence of sea power in history; for more than two decades, he headed the Newport Naval War College, where officers imbibed the latest in strategic thinking. A clear, logical writer, Mahan summarized his beliefs in several major books, including *The Influence of Sea Power upon History, 1660–1783* (1890), and *The Interest of America in Sea Power* (1897).

Mahan's reasoning was simple and, to that generation, persuasive. Industrialism, he argued, produced vast surpluses of agricultural and manufactured goods, for which markets must be found. Markets involved distant ports; reaching them required a large merchant marine and a powerful navy to protect it. Navies, in turn, needed coaling stations and repair yards. Coaling stations meant colonies, and colonies became strategic bases, the foundation of a nation's wealth and power. The bases might serve as markets themselves, but they were more important as stepping-stones to other objectives, such as the markets of Latin America and Asia.

Mahan called attention to the worldwide race for power, a race, he warned, the United States could not afford to lose. To compete in the struggle, Mahan argued, the United States must expand. It needed strategic bases, a powerful oceangoing navy, a canal across the isthmus to link the East Coast with the Pacific, and Hawaii as a way station on the route to Asia.

Mahan influenced a generation of policymakers in the United States and Europe; one of them, Benjamin F. Tracy, became Harrison's secretary of the navy in 1889. Tracy organized the Bureau of Construction and Repair to design and build new ships, established the Naval Reserve in 1891, and ordered construction of the first American submarine in 1893. He also adopted the first heavy rapid-fire guns, smokeless powder, torpedoes, and heavy armor. Above all, Tracy joined with big-navy advocates in Congress to push for a far-ranging battleship fleet capable of attacking distant enemies. He wanted two fleets of battleships, eight ships in the Pacific and twelve in the Atlantic. He got four first-class battleships.

QUICK CHECK

What led the United States to build a new steel navy?

In 1889, when Tracy entered office, the United States ranked twelfth among world navies; in 1893, when he left, it ranked seventh and was climbing rapidly. "The sea," he predicted in 1891, "will be the future seat of empires. And we shall rule it as certainly as the sun doth rise." By the end of the decade, the navy had seventeen steel battleships, six armored cruisers, and many smaller craft. It ranked third in the world.

War with Spain

WHAT were the causes and results of the war with Spain?

The war with Spain in 1898 built a mood of national confidence, altered older, more insular patterns of thought, and reshaped the way Americans saw themselves and the world. Its outcome pleased some people but troubled others, who raised questions about war itself, colonies, and subject peoples. The war left a lingering strain of isolationism and antiwar feeling that affected later policy. It also left an American empire, small by European standards, but quite new to the American experience by virtue of its overseas location. When the war ended, American possessions stretched into the Caribbean and deep into the Pacific. American influence went further still, and the United States was recognized as a "world power."

The Spanish-American War established the United States as a dominant force for the twentieth century. It brought America colonies and millions of colonial subjects; it brought the responsibilities of governing an empire and protecting it. For better or worse, it involved the country in other nations' arguments and affairs. The war strengthened the office of the presidency, swept the nation together in a tide of emotion, and confirmed the long-standing belief in the superiority of the New World over the Old. When it was over, Americans looked outward as never before, touched, they were sure, with a special destiny.

A War for Principle

By the 1890s, Cuba and the nearby island of Puerto Rico comprised nearly all that remained of Spain's once vast empire in the New World. Several times, Cuban insurgents had rebelled against Spanish rule, including a decade-long rebellion from 1868 to 1878 (the Ten Years' War) that failed to settle the conflict. The depression of 1893 damaged the Cuban economy, and the Wilson-Gorman Tariff of 1894 prostrated it. Duties on sugar, Cuba's lifeblood, were raised 40 percent. With the island's sugar market in ruins, discontent with Spanish rule heightened, and in late February 1895, revolt again broke out.

Recognizing the importance of the nearby United States, Cuban insurgents established a junta in New York City to raise money, buy weapons, and wage a propaganda war to sway American public opinion. Conditions in Cuba were grim.

In January 1896, Spain sent a new commander to Cuba, General Valeriano Weyler y Nicolau. Relentless and brutal, Weyler gave the rebels ten days to lay down their arms. He then put into effect a "reconcentration" policy designed to move the native population into camps and destroy the rebellion's popular base. Herded into fortified areas, Cubans died by the thousands, victims of unsanitary conditions, overcrowding, and disease.

There was a wave of sympathy for the insurgents, stimulated by the newspapers, but so-called **yellow journalism,** sensationalist reporting practiced mainly by a handful of newspapers in New York City that were eager to increase sales, did not cause the war. The conflict stemmed from larger disputes in policies and perceptions between Spain and the United States. Grover Cleveland, under whose administration the rebellion began, preferred Spanish rule to the kind of turmoil that might invite foreign intervention. Opposed to the annexation of Cuba, he issued a proclamation of neutrality and tried to restrain public opinion.

Taking office in March 1897, President McKinley also urged neutrality but leaned slightly toward the insurgents. He immediately sent a trusted aide on a fact-finding mission to Cuba; the aide reported in mid-1897 that Weyler's policy had wrapped Cuba "in the stillness of death and the silence of desolation." The report in hand, McKinley offered to mediate the struggle, but, concerned over the suffering, he protested against Spain's "uncivilized and inhuman" conduct. The United States, he made clear, did not contest Spain's right to fight the rebellion but insisted it be done within humane limits.

Late in 1897, a change in government in Madrid brought a temporary lull in the crisis. The new government recalled Weyler and agreed to offer the Cubans

MAP

Activities of the United States in the Caribbean, 1898–1930s

yellow journalism

In order to sell newspapers to the public before and during the Spanish-American War, publishers William Randolph Hearst and Joseph Pulitzer engaged in blatant sensationalization of the news, which became known as "yellow journalism." Although it did not cause the war with Spain, it helped turn U.S. public opinion against Spain's actions in Cuba.

some form of autonomy. It also declared an amnesty for political prisoners and released Americans from Cuban jails. The new initiatives pleased McKinley, though he again warned Spain that it must find a humane end to the rebellion. Then, in January 1898, Spanish army officers led riots in Havana against the new autonomy policy, shaking the president's confidence in Madrid's control over conditions in Cuba.

McKinley ordered the battleship *Maine* to Havana to demonstrate strength and protect American citizens if necessary. On February 9, 1898, the *New York Journal*, a leader of the yellow press, published a letter stolen from Enrique Dupuy de Lôme, the Spanish ambassador in Washington. In the letter, which was private correspondence to a friend, de Lôme called McKinley "weak," "a would-be politician," and "a bidder for the admiration of the crowd." Many Americans were angered by the insult; McKinley himself was more worried about other sections of the letter that revealed Spanish insincerity in the negotiations. De Lôme immediately resigned and went home, but the damage was done.

Maine
Explosion,
1898

A few days later, at 9:40 in the evening of February 15, an explosion tore through the hull of the *Maine*, riding at anchor in Havana harbor. The ship, a trim symbol of the new steel navy, sank quickly; 266 lives were lost. McKinley cautioned patience and promised an immediate investigation. Crowds gathered quietly on Capitol Hill and outside the White House, mourning the lost men. Soon there was a new slogan: "Remember the *Maine* and to Hell with Spain!"

Burial of the
Maine
Victims

The most recent study of the *Maine* incident blames the sinking on an accidental internal explosion, caused perhaps by spontaneous combustion in poorly ventilated coal bunkers. In 1898, Americans blamed it on Spain. Spaniards were hanged in effigy in many communities. Roosevelt, William Jennings Bryan, and others urged war, but McKinley delayed, hopeful that Spain might yet agree to an armistice and perhaps Cuban independence.

In early March 1898, wanting to be ready for war if it came, McKinley asked Congress for $50 million in emergency defense appropriations, a request Congress promptly approved. The unanimous vote stunned Spain; allowing the president a latitude that was highly unusual for the era, it appropriated the money "for the National defense and for each and every purpose connected therewith to be expended at the discretion of the President." In late March, the report of the investigating board blamed the sinking of the *Maine* on an external (and thus presumably Spanish) explosion. Pressures for war increased.

On March 27, McKinley cabled Spain his final terms. He asked Spain to declare an armistice, end the reconcentration policy, and—implicitly—move toward Cuban independence. When the Spanish answer came, it conceded some things, but not, in McKinley's judgment, the important ones. Spain offered a suspension of hostilities (but not an armistice) and left the Spanish commander in Cuba to set the length and terms of the suspension. It also revoked the reconcentration policy. But the Spanish response made no mention of a true armistice, McKinley's offer to mediate, or Cuba's independence.

Teller Amendment
In this amendment, sponsored by Senator Henry M. Teller of Colorado, the United States pledged that it did not intend to annex Cuba and that it would recognize Cuban independence from Spain after the Spanish-American War.

Reluctantly McKinley prepared his war message, and Congress heard it on April 11, 1898. On April 19, Congress passed a joint resolution declaring Cuba independent and authorizing the president to use the army and navy to expel the Spanish from it. The **Teller Amendment,** offered by Colorado senator Henry M. Teller, pledged that the United States had no intention of annexing the island.

On April 21, Spain severed diplomatic relations. The following day, McKinley proclaimed a blockade of Cuba and called for 125,000 volunteers. On Monday,

April 25, Congress passed a declaration of war. Late that afternoon, McKinley signed it.

Some historians have suggested that in leading the country toward war, McKinley was weak and indecisive, a victim of war hysteria in the Congress and the country; others have called him a wily manipulator for war and imperial gains. In truth, he was neither. Throughout the Spanish crisis, McKinley pursued a moderate middle course that sought to end the suffering in Cuba, promote Cuba's independence, and allow Spain time to adjust to the loss of the remnant of empire. He also wanted peace, as did Spain, but in the end, the conflicting national interests of the two countries brought them to war.

QUICK CHECK ✓

What were the three main causes of the war with Spain in 1898?

The Spanish-American War

Ten weeks after the declaration of war, the fighting was over. For Americans, they were ten glorious, dizzying weeks, with victories to fill every headline and slogans to suit every taste. No war can be a happy occasion for those who fight it, but the Spanish-American War came closer than most. Declared in April, it ended in August. Relatively few Americans died, and the quick victory seemed to verify burgeoning American power, though Sherwood Anderson, the author, suggested that fighting a weakened Spain was "like robbing an old gypsy woman in a vacant lot at night after a fair." John Hay, soon to be McKinley's secretary of state, called it "a splendid little war."

At the outset, the United States was militarily unprepared. The regular army consisted of only 28,000 officers and men, most of them more experienced in quelling Indian uprisings than fighting large-scale battles.

When McKinley called for 125,000 volunteers, as many as 1 million young Americans responded. Ohio alone had 100,000 volunteers. Keeping the regular army units intact, War Department officials enlisted the volunteers in National Guard units that were then integrated into the national army. Men clamored to join. William Jennings Bryan, a pacifist by temperament, took command of a regiment of Nebraska volunteers; Roosevelt chafed to get to the front. The secretary of war feared "there is going to be more trouble to satisfy those who are not going than to find those who are willing to go."

In an army inundated with men, problems of equipment and supply quickly appeared. The regulars had the new 30-caliber Krag-Jorgensen rifles, but National Guard units carried Civil War Springfield rifles that used old black-powder cartridges. The cartridges gave off a puff of smoke when fired, neatly marking the troops' position. Spanish troops were better equipped; they had modern Mausers with smokeless powder, which they used to devastating effect. Food was also a problem, as was sickness. Tropical disease felled many soldiers. Scores took ill after landing in Cuba and the Philippines, and it was not uncommon for half a regiment to be unable to answer the bugle call.

Americans then believed that "a foreign war should be fought by the hometown military unit acting as an extension of their community." Soldiers identified with their hometowns, dressed in the local fashion, and thought of themselves as members of a town unit in a national army. The poet Carl Sandburg, 20 years old in 1898, rushed to join the army and called his unit a "living part" of his hometown of Galesburg, Illinois. And the citizens of Galesburg, for their part, took a special interest in Sandburg's unit, in a fashion repeated in countless towns across the country.

Not surprisingly, then, National Guard units mirrored the social patterns of their communities. Since everyone knew each other, there was an easygoing familiarity, tempered by the deference that went with hometown wealth, occupation, education, and length of residence. Enlisted men resented officers who grabbed too much authority, and they expected officers and men to call each other by their first names. Sandburg knew most of the privates in his unit, had worked for his corporal, and had gone to school with the first lieutenant.

Each community thought of the hometown unit as its own unit, an extension of itself. In later wars, the government censored news and dominated press relations; there was little censorship in the war with Spain, and the freshest news arrived in the latest letter home. Small-town newspapers printed news of the men and townswomen knit special red or white bellybands of stitched flannel, thought to ward off tropical fevers. Towns sent food, clothing, and occasionally even local doctors to the front.

QUICK CHECK ✓

What was the nature of this "splendid little war," as McKinley's Secretary of State described it?

African American Soldiers in the War

When the invasion force sailed for Cuba, nearly one-fourth of it was African American. In 1898, the regular army included four regiments of African American soldiers, the Twenty-fourth and Twenty-fifth Infantry and the Ninth and Tenth Cavalry. Black regiments had served with distinction in campaigns against the Indians in the West. Most African American troops in fact were posted in the West; no eastern community would accept them. A troop of the Ninth Cavalry was stationed in Virginia in 1891, but whites protested and the troop was ordered back to the West.

When the war broke out, the War Department called for five black volunteer regiments. The army needed men, and military authorities were sure that black men had a natural immunity to the climate and diseases of the tropics. But most state governors refused to accept black volunteers. African American leaders protested the discrimination. The McKinley administration intervened, and in the end, the volunteer army included more than ten thousand black troops.

Orders quickly went out to the four black regular army regiments in the West to move to camps in the South to prepare for the invasion of Cuba. Crowds and cheers followed the troop trains across the Plains, but as they crossed into Kentucky and Tennessee, the cheering stopped. Welcoming crowds were kept away from the trains, and the troops were hustled onward. Station restaurants refused to serve them; all waiting rooms were segregated.

Many soldiers were not prepared to put up with the treatment. Those stationed near Chickamauga Park, Tennessee, shot "at some whites who insulted them" and forcibly desegregated the railroad cars on the line into Chattanooga. Troops training near Macon, Georgia, refused to ride in the segregated "trailers" attached to the trolleys, and fights broke out.

More than four thousand black troops training near Tampa and Lakeland, Florida, found segregated saloons, cafes, and drugstores. "Here the Negro is not allowed to purchase over the same counter in some stores as the white man purchases over," Chaplain George W. Prioleau charged. "Why sir, the Negro of

THE BATTLE OF SAN JUAN HILL   *Charge of the 24th and 25th Colored Infantry and Rescue of the Rough Riders at San Juan Hill, July 2, 1898,* colored lithograph by Kurz and Allison, 1899 (above). The Twenty-fourth and Twenty-fifth Colored Infantry regiments served with exceptional gallantry in the Spanish-American War. Charles Young (left), an 1889 graduate of West Point, was the only African American officer in the army during the Spanish-American War except for a few chaplains.

What was the effect of the Spanish-American War on African Americans?

this country is a freeman and yet a slave. Talk about fighting and freeing poor Cuba and of Spain's brutality; of Cuba's murdered thousands, and starving reconcentradoes. Is America any better than Spain?"

When the invasion force sailed a few days later, segregation continued on some of the troopships. Blacks were assigned to the lowest decks, or whites and blacks were placed on different sides of the ship. But the confusion of war often ended the problem, if only temporarily. Blacks took command as white officers died, and Spanish troops soon came to fear the "smoked Yankees," as they called them. Black soldiers played a major role in the Cuban campaign and probably staved off defeat for the Rough Riders at San Juan Hill. In Cuba, they won twenty-six Certificates of Merit and five Congressional Medals of Honor.

QUICK CHECK

What role did African American troops play in the Spanish-American War?

The Course of the War

MAP

The Spanish-American War

Mahan's Naval War College had begun studying strategy for a war with Spain in 1895. By 1898, it had a detailed plan for operations in the Caribbean and Pacific. Naval strategy was simple: Destroy the Spanish fleet, damage Spain's merchant marine, and harry the colonies or the coast of Spain. Planners were excited; two steam-powered armored fleets had yet to meet in battle anywhere in the world. The army's task was more difficult. It had to defend the United States, invade Cuba and probably Puerto Rico, and undertake possible action in far-flung places such as the Philippines or Spain.

Even before war was declared, the secretary of war arranged joint planning between the army and navy. Military intelligence was plentiful, and planners knew the numbers and locations of the Spanish troops. Earlier they had rejected a proposal to send an officer in disguise to map Cuban harbors; such things, they said, were simply not done in peacetime. Still, the War Department's new Military Information Division, a sign of the increasing professionalization of the army, had detailed diagrams of Spanish fortifications in Havana and other points. On the afternoon of April 20, 1898, McKinley summoned the strategists to the White House; to the dismay of those who wanted a more aggressive policy, they decided on the limited strategy of blockading Cuba, sending arms to the insurgents, and annoying the Spanish with small thrusts by the army.

SPANISH-AMERICAN WAR: PACIFIC THEATER

Commodore Dewey, promoted to admiral immediately after the naval victory at Manila Bay, was the first hero of the war.

What were the major effects of Dewey's victory?

SPANISH-AMERICAN WAR: CARIBBEAN THEATER
President McKinley set up a "war room" in the White House, following the action on giant war maps with red and white marking pins.

What were the main features of the American campaign in Cuba?

Victories soon changed the strategy. In case of war, long-standing naval plans had called for a holding action against the Spanish base in the Philippines. On May 1, 1898, with the war barely a week old, Commodore George Dewey, commander of the Asiatic Squadron located at Hong Kong, crushed the Spanish fleet in Manila Bay. Suddenly, Manila and the Philippines lay within American grasp. At home, Dewey portraits, songs, and poems blossomed everywhere, and his calm order to the flagship's captain—"You may fire when ready, Gridley"—hung on every tongue. Dewey had two modern cruisers, a gunboat, and a Civil War paddle steamer. He sank eight Spanish warships. Dewey had no troops to attack the Spanish army in Manila, but the War Department, stunned by the speed and size of the victory, quickly raised an expeditionary force. On August 13, 1898, the troops accepted the surrender of Manila, and with it, the Philippines.

McKinley and his aides were worried about Admiral Pascual Cervera's main Spanish fleet, thought to be headed across the Atlantic for an attack on Florida. On May 13, the navy found Cervera's ships near Martinique in the Caribbean but then lost them again. A few days later, Cervera slipped secretly into the harbor of Santiago de Cuba, a city on the island's southern coast. But a spy in the Havana telegraph office alerted the Americans, and on May 28, a superior American force under Admiral William T. Sampson bottled Cervera up.

In early June, a small force of Marines seized Guantánamo Bay, the great harbor on the south of the island. They established depots for the navy to refuel and pinned down Spanish troops in the area. On June 14, an invasion force of about seventeen thousand men set sail from Tampa. Seven days later, they landed at Daiquiri on Cuba's southeastern coast. All was confusion, but the Spanish offered no resistance. Helped by Cuban insurgents, the Americans immediately pushed west toward Santiago, which they hoped to surround and capture. At first, the advance through the lush tropical countryside was peaceful.

The first battle broke out at Las Guasimas, a crossroads on the Santiago road. After a sharp fight, the Spanish fell back. On July 1, the Rough Riders, troops from the four black regiments, and the other regulars reached the strong fortifications at El Caney and San Juan Hill. Black soldiers of the Twenty-fifth Infantry charged the El Caney blockhouses, surprising the Spanish defenders with Comanche yells.

For the better part of a day, the defenders fought stubbornly and held back the army's elite corps. In the confusion of battle, Roosevelt rallied an assortment of infantry and cavalry to take Kettle Hill, adjacent to San Juan Hill.

They charged directly into the Spanish guns, Roosevelt at their head, mounted on a horse, a blue polka-dot handkerchief floating from the brim of his sombrero. "I waved my hat and we went up the hill with a rush," he recalled in his autobiography. Actually, it was not quite so easy. Losses were heavy; eighty-nine Rough Riders were killed or wounded in the attack. Dense foliage concealed the enemy and smokeless powder gave no clue to their position. At nightfall, the surviving Spanish defenders withdrew, and the Americans prepared for the counterattack.

American troops now occupied the ridges overlooking Santiago. They were weakened by sickness, a fact unknown to the Spanish, who decided the city was lost. The Spanish command in Havana ordered Cervera to run for the open sea, although he knew the attempt to escape was hopeless. On the morning of July 3, Cervera's squadron steamed down the bay and out through the harbor's narrow channel, but the waiting American fleet closed in, and in a few hours every Spanish vessel was destroyed. Two weeks later, Santiago surrendered.

Soon thereafter, army troops, meeting little resistance, occupied Puerto Rico. Cervera had commanded Spain's only battle fleet, and when it sank, Spain was helpless against attacks on the colonies or even its own shores. The war was over. Lasting 113 days, it took relatively few lives, most of them the result of accident, yellow fever, malaria, and typhoid in Cuba. Of the 5500 Americans who died in the war, only 379 were killed in battle. The navy lost one man in the battle at Santiago Bay, and only one to heatstroke in the stunning victory in Manila Bay.

QUICK CHECK ✔

What were the main events of the war itself?

Acquisition of Empire

WHAT?

were the various viewpoints about the acquisition of empire after the war with Spain?

Late in the afternoon of August 12, 1898, representatives of Spain and the United States met in McKinley's White House office to sign the preliminary instrument of peace. Secretary of State William R. Day beckoned a presidential aide over to a large globe, remarking, "Let's see what we get by this."

What the United States got was an expansion of its territory and an even larger expansion of its responsibilities. According to the preliminary agreement, Spain granted independence to Cuba, ceded Puerto Rico and the Pacific island of Guam to the United States, and allowed Americans to occupy Manila until the two countries reached final agreement on the Philippines. To McKinley, the Philippines were the problem. Puerto Rico was close to the mainland, and it appealed even to many of the opponents of expansion. Guam was small and unknown; it escaped attention. The Philippines, on the other hand, were huge, sprawling, and thousands of miles from America.

McKinley weighed a number of alternatives for the Philippines, but he liked none of them. He believed he could not give the islands back to Spain; public opinion would not allow it. He might turn them over to another nation, but then they would fall, as he later said, "a golden apple of discord, among the rival powers." Germany, Japan, Great Britain, and Russia had all expressed interest in acquiring them. Germany even sent a large fleet to Manila and laid plans to take the Philippines if the United States let them go.

Rejecting those alternatives, McKinley considered independence for the islands but was soon talked out of it. People who had been there, reflecting the era's racism, told him the Filipinos were not ready for independence. He thought of establishing an American protectorate but discarded the idea, convinced it would bring American responsibilities without full American control. Sifting the alternatives, McKinley decided there was only one practical policy: Annex the Philippines, with an eye to future independence after a period of tutelage.

At first hesitant, American opinion was swinging to the same conclusion. Religious and missionary organizations appealed to McKinley to hold on to the Philippines in order to "Christianize" them. Some merchants and industrialists saw them as the key to the China market and the wealth of Asia. Many Americans simply regarded them as the legitimate fruits of war. In October 1898, representatives of the United States and Spain met in Paris to discuss a peace treaty. Spain agreed to recognize Cuba's independence, assume the Cuban debt, and cede Puerto Rico and Guam to the United States.

Acting on instructions from McKinley, the American representatives demanded the cession of the Philippines. "Grave as are the responsibilities and unforeseen as are the difficulties which are before us, the President can see but one plain path of duty—the acceptance of the archipelago," the instructions said. In return, the United States offered a payment of $20 million. Spain resisted but had little choice, and on December 10, 1898, the American and Spanish representatives signed the **Treaty of Paris**.

American Empire, 1900

Treaty of Paris
Signed by the United States and Spain in December 1898, this treaty ended the Spanish-American War. Under its terms, Spain recognized Cuba's independence and assumed the Cuban debt; it also ceded Puerto Rico and Guam to the United States. At the insistence of the U.S. representatives, Spain also ceded the Philippines. The Senate ratified the treaty on February 6, 1899.

The Treaty of Paris Debate

Submitted to the Senate for ratification, the treaty set off a storm of debate throughout the country. Industrialist Andrew Carnegie, reformer Jane Addams, labor leader Samuel Gompers, Mark Twain, and a host of others argued forcefully against annexing the Philippines. Annexation of the Philippines, the anti-imperialists protested over and over again, violated the very principles of independence and self-determination on which the United States was founded.

Some labor leaders feared the importation of cheap labor from new Pacific colonies. Gompers warned about the "half-breeds and semi-barbaric people" who might undercut wages and the union movement. Other anti-imperialists argued against assimilation of different races, "Spanish-Americans," as one said, "with all the mixture of Indian and negro blood, and Malays and other unspeakable Asiatics, by the tens of millions!" Such racial views were also common among those favoring expansion, and the anti-imperialists usually focused on different arguments. If the United States established a tyranny abroad, they were sure, there would soon be tyranny at home.

William Jennings Bryan scoffed at the argument that colonies were good for trade, pointing out, "It is not necessary to own people to trade with them." Many

Civilization Begins at Home, 1898

Carl Schurz, Platform of the American Anti-Imperialist League

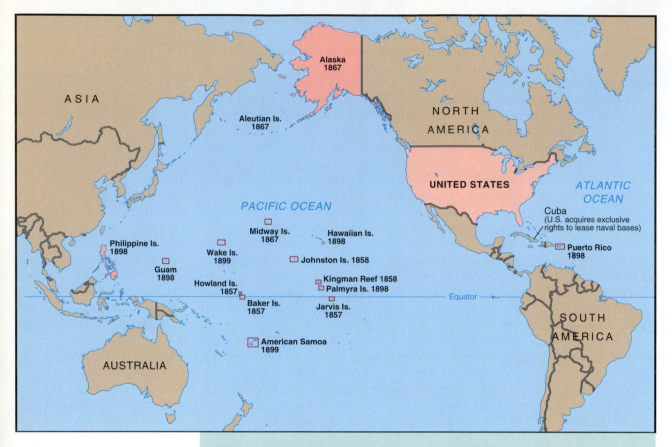

AMERICAN EMPIRE, 1900 With the Treaty of Paris, the United States gained an expanded colonial empire stretching from the Caribbean to the far Pacific. It embraced Puerto Rico, Alaska, Hawaii, part of Samoa, Guam, the Philippines, and a chain of Pacific islands. The dates on the map refer to the date of U.S. acquisition.

How did the United States' acquisitions in the Treaty of Paris differ from earlier acquisitions of territory?

Anti-Imperialist League

This organization was formed in November 1898 to fight against the Treaty of Paris, which ended the Spanish-American War. Members opposed the acquisition of overseas colonies by the United States, believing it would subvert American ideals and institutions. Membership centered in New England; the cause was less popular in the South and West.

others thought there was no way to reconcile the country's republican ideals with the practice of keeping people under heel abroad. To Booker T. Washington, the country had more important things to think about at home, including its treatment of Indians and blacks. Carnegie was so upset that he offered to buy Filipino independence with a personal check for $20 million.

In November 1898, opponents of expansion formed the **Anti-Imperialist League** to fight against the peace treaty. Membership centered in New England; the cause was less popular in the West and South. It enlisted more Democrats than Republicans, though never a majority of either. The anti-imperialists were weakened by the fact that they lacked a coherent program. Some favored keeping naval bases in the conquered areas. Some wanted Hawaii and Puerto Rico but not the Philippines. Others wanted nothing at all to do with any colonies. Most simply wished that Dewey had sailed away after beating the Spanish at Manila Bay.

The treaty debate in the Senate lasted a month. Pressing hard for ratification, McKinley earlier toured the South to rally support and consulted closely with senators. Though opposed to taking the Philippines, Bryan supported ratification in order to end the war; his support influenced some Democratic votes. Still, on the final weekend before the vote, the treaty was two votes short. That Saturday night, news reached Washington that fighting had broken out between American troops and Filipino insurgents who demanded immediate independence. The news increased pressure to ratify the treaty, which the Senate did on February 6, 1899, with two votes to spare. An amendment promising independence as soon as the Filipinos established a stable government lost by one vote. The United States had a colonial empire.

QUICK CHECK ✓

What were the main arguments on each side in the debate over the treaty that ended the war?

Guerrilla Warfare in the Philippines

Historians rarely write of the **Philippine-American War,** a guerilla war between American troops and the newly freed Filipinos, but it was an important event in American history. The war with Spain was over a few months after it began, but war with the Filipinos lasted more than three years. Four times as many American soldiers fought in the Philippines as in Cuba. For the first time, Americans fought men of a different color in an Asian guerrilla war. The Philippine-American War of 1898–1902 took a heavy toll: 4300 American lives and untold thousands of Filipino lives (estimates range from 50,000 to 200,000).

Emilio Aguinaldo, the Filipino leader, was 29 years old in 1898. An early organizer of the anti-Spanish resistance, he had gone into exile in Hong Kong, from where he welcomed the outbreak of the Spanish-American War. Certain the United States would grant independence, he worked for an American victory. Filipino insurgents helped guide Dewey into Manila Bay, and Dewey himself sent a ship to Hong Kong to bring back Aguinaldo to lead a native uprising against the Spanish. On June 12, 1898, the insurgents proclaimed their independence.

Cooperating with the Americans, they drove the Spanish out of many areas of the islands. In the liberated regions, Aguinaldo established local governments with appointed provincial governors. He waited impatiently for American recognition, but McKinley and others had concluded that the Filipinos were not ready. Soon, warfare broke out between the Filipinos and Americans over the question of Filipino independence.

By late 1899, the American army had defeated and dispersed the organized Filipino army, but claims of victory proved premature. Aguinaldo and his advisers shifted to guerrilla tactics, striking suddenly and then melting into the jungle or friendly native villages. In many areas, the Americans ruled the day, the guerrillas the night. There were terrible atrocities on both sides. The Americans found themselves using brutal, Weyler-like tactics. After any attack on an American patrol, the Americans burned all the houses in the nearest district. They tortured people and executed prisoners. They established protected "zones" and herded Filipinos into them. Seizing or destroying all food outside the zones, they starved many guerrillas into submission.

Bryan tried to turn the election of 1900 into a debate over imperialism, but the attempt failed. For one thing, he himself refused to give up the silver issue,

DOCUMENT

William McKinley, "Decision on the Philippines"

Philippine-American War

A war fought from 1899 to 1902 to quell Filipino resistance to U.S. control of the Philippine Islands. Although often forgotten, it lasted longer than the Spanish-American War and resulted in more casualties. Filipino guerrilla soldiers finally gave up when their leader, Emilio Aguinaldo, was captured.

IMAGE

U.S. Soldiers in the Philippines, 1899

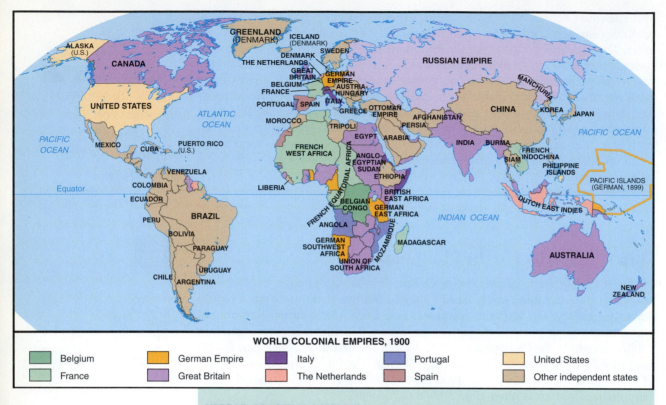

WORLD COLONIAL EMPIRES, 1900

Belgium | German Empire | Italy | Portugal | United States
France | Great Britain | The Netherlands | Spain | Other independent states

WORLD COLONIAL EMPIRES, 1900 Events of the nineteenth century increased European hegemony over the world. By 1900, most independent African nations had disappeared and the major European nations had divided the continent among themselves. In the East, the European powers and Japan took advantage of China's internal weakness to gain both trading ports and economic concessions.

Why were the policymakers in Europe and the United States so eager to acquire overseas territory in the nineteenth century?

which cost him some support among anti-imperialists in the Northeast who were for gold. McKinley, moreover, was able to take advantage of the surging economy, and he could defend expansion as an accomplished fact. Riding a wave of patriotism and prosperity, McKinley won the election handily—by an even larger margin than he had in 1896.

In 1900, McKinley sent a special Philippine Commission to the islands under William Howard Taft, a prominent Ohio judge. Directed to establish a civil government, the commission organized municipal administrations and, in stages, created a government for the Philippines. In March 1901, five American soldiers tricked their way into Aguinaldo's camp deep in the mountains and took him prisoner. Back in Manila, he signed a proclamation urging his people to end the fighting. Some guerrillas held out for another year, but to no avail. On July 4, 1901, authority was transferred from the army to Taft, who was named civilian governor of the islands, and his civilian commission. McKinley reaffirmed his purpose to grant the Filipinos self-government as soon as they were deemed ready for it.

Given broad powers, the Taft Commission introduced many changes. New schools provided education and vocational training for Filipinos of all social classes. The Americans built roads and bridges, reformed the judiciary, restructured the tax system, and introduced sanitation and vaccination programs. They established local governments built on Filipino traditions and hierarchies. Taft encouraged Filipino participation in government. During the following decades, other measures broadened Filipino rights. Independence finally came on July 4, 1946, nearly fifty years after Aguinaldo proclaimed it.

QUICK CHECK ✓

What were the causes and consequences of the Philippine-American War?

The Open Door

Poised in the Philippines, the United States had become an Asian power on the doorstep of China. Weakened by years of warfare, China in 1898 and 1899 was unable to resist foreign influence. Japan, England, France, Germany, and Russia eyed it covetously, dividing parts of the country into "spheres of influence." They forced China to grant "concessions" that allowed them exclusive rights to develop particular areas and threatened American hopes for extensive trade with the country.

McKinley first outlined a new China policy in September 1898 when he said that Americans sought more trade, "but we seek no advantages in the Orient which are not common to all. Asking only the open door for ourselves, we are ready to accord the open door to others." In September 1899, Secretary of State

U.S. POLICY IN ASIA   In this 1899 cartoon, "Putting His Foot Down" from *Puck*, the nations of Europe are getting ready to cut up China to expand their spheres of influence, but Uncle Sam stands firm on American commitments to preserve China's sovereignty.

What is important about the way various nations are depicted in this 1899 cartoon?

Open Door policy
Established in a series of notes by Secretary of State John Hay in 1900, this policy established free trade between the United States and China and attempted to enlist major European and Asian nations in recognizing the territorial integrity of China. It marked a departure from the American tradition of isolationism and signaled the country's growing involvement in the world.

John Hay addressed identical diplomatic notes to England, Germany, and Russia, and later to France, Japan, and Italy, asking them to join the United States in establishing the **Open Door policy.** This policy urged three agreements: Nations possessing a sphere of influence would respect the rights and privileges of other nations in that sphere; the Chinese government would continue to collect tariff duties in all spheres; and nations would not discriminate against other nations in levying port dues and railroad rates within their respective spheres of influence.

Under the Open Door policy, the United States would retain many commercial advantages it might lose if China was partitioned into spheres of influence. McKinley and Hay also attempted to preserve for the Chinese some semblance of national authority. Great Britain most nearly accepted the principle of the Open Door. Russia declined to approve it, and the other powers, sending evasive replies, stated they would agree only if all the other nations did. Hay turned the situation to American advantage by boldly announcing in March 1900 that all the powers had accepted the Open Door policy.

The policy's first test came just three months later with the outbreak of the Boxer Rebellion in Peking (now Beijing). In June 1900, a secret, intensely nationalistic Chinese society called the Boxers tried to oust all foreigners from their country. Overrunning Peking, they drove foreigners into their legations and penned them up for nearly two months. In the end, the United States joined Britain, Germany, and other powers in sending troops to lift the siege.

Fearing that the rebellion gave some nations, especially Germany and Russia, an excuse to expand their spheres of influence, Hay took quick action to emphasize American policy. In July, he sent off another round of Open Door notes affirming U.S. commitment to equal commercial opportunity and respect for China's independence. While the first Open Door notes had implied recognition of China's continued independence, the second notes explicitly stated the need to preserve it. Together, the two notes comprised the Open Door policy, which became a central element in American policy in the Far East.

To some degree, the policy tried to help China, but it also led to further American meddling in the affairs of another country. Moreover, by committing itself to a policy that Americans were not prepared to defend militarily, the McKinley administration left the opportunity for later controversy with Japan and other expansion-minded powers in the Pacific.

QUICK CHECK ✓

What was the "open door" policy toward China?

Conclusion: Outcome of the War with Spain

The war with Spain over, Roosevelt and the Rough Riders sailed for home in mid-August 1898. They sauntered through the streets of New York, the heroes of the city. A few weeks later, Roosevelt bade them farewell. They presented him with a reproduction of Frederick Remington's famed bronze *The Bronco-Buster,* and, close to tears, he told them, "I am proud of this regiment beyond measure." Roosevelt was soon governor of New York and on his way to the White House.

Other soldiers were also glad to be home, although they were sometimes resentful of the reception they found. "The war is over now," said Winslow Hobson, a black trooper from the Ninth Ohio, "and Roosevelt... and others (white of course) have all there is to be gotten out of it." Bravery in Cuba and the Philippines won some recognition for black soldiers, but the war itself set back the cause of civil rights. It spurred talk about "inferior" races, at home and abroad, and united whites in the North and South. "The Negro might as well know it now as later," a black editor said, "the closer the North and South get together by this war, the harder he will have to fight to maintain a footing." A fresh outburst of segregation and lynching occurred during the decade after the war.

McKinley and the Republican party soared to new heights of popularity. Firmly established, the Republican majority dominated politics until 1932. Scandals arose about the food provided for the troops and the conduct of the War Department, but there was none of the sharp sense of deception and betrayal that was to mark the years after World War I. In a little more than a century, the United States had grown from thirteen states stretched along a thin Atlantic coastline into a world power that reached from the Caribbean to the Pacific. As Seward and others had hoped, the nation now dominated its own hemisphere, dealt with European powers on more equal terms, and was a major power in Asia.

For a list of additional titles related to this chapter's topics, please see
www.pearsonamericanhistory.com. MyHistoryLab

STUDY RESOURCES

KEY TERMS

isolationism, p. 564
imperialism, p. 564
yellow journalism, p. 571
Teller Amendment, p. 572

Treaty of Paris, p. 579
Anti-Imperialist League,
  p. 580

Philippine-American War,
  p. 581
Open Door policy, p. 584

CHAPTER REVIEW

WHAT caused Americans to look outward in the last half of the nineteenth century❓

In the late nineteenth century, Americans increasingly looked overseas, influenced in part by the example of other nations and confidence in what their country could offer other peoples, including Christianity, commerce, and American values. Policymakers were sure that the nation needed a navy, colonial outposts, foreign markets, and a new foreign policy. *(p. 563)*

WHAT were the causes and results of the war with Spain❓

In 1898 the United States fought a war with Spain, which resulted in a quick victory and enormous changes for American society, including a larger military, an increased role for the federal government in American life, the acquisition of colonies, and increased power for the office of the presidency. *(p. 570)*

WHAT were the various viewpoints about the acquisition of empire after the war with Spain❓

In the peace treaty ending the war with Spain, the United States acquired a new empire, including Puerto Rico, Guam, and the Philippines. For the first time, the United States owned territories overseas, which it did not intend to grant statehood to. That fact, together with historical, racial, and other arguments, caused an angry discussion between those in favor and those opposing the new colonies. Adding to the debate was the outbreak of warfare between American troops and Filipino insurgents in the Philippines. *(p. 578)*

MAKING CONNECTIONS

1. What were the key developments in leading the United States to look abroad between the 1870s and the 1890s, and how did these developments ultimately lead to the war with Spain in 1898?

2. Why did the important causes and events of the Spanish-American War lead to the crucial decision to acquire an overseas empire?

3. What were the most important effects of the end of the war and the acquisition of empire?

PRACTICE QUIZ

1. The concept of _____ explains the U.S. response to foreign governments during the 1860s and 1870s.
   - **a.** Expansion
   - **b.** Isolation
   - **c.** Imperialism
   - **d.** Invasion

2. The first American _____ arrived in Hawaii in 1820.
   - **a.** Settler
   - **b.** Politician
   - **c.** Government agent
   - **d.** Missionary

3. The treaty of _____ allowed duty-free Hawaiian sugar to enter the United States.
   - **a.** 1895
   - **b.** 1885
   - **c.** 1875
   - **d.** 1865

4. _____ wrote the influential book, *The Interest of America in Sea Power*.
   - **a.** Theodore Roosevelt
   - **b.** Alfred Mahan
   - **c.** Benjamin Tracy
   - **d.** Woodrow Wilson

5. The United States declared war with Spain after the sinking of the battleship
   - **a.** *Maine*
   - **b.** *California*
   - **c.** *Independence*
   - **d.** *Georgia*

6. In 1883, Congress embarked on creating a new
   - **a.** Navy
   - **b.** Army
   - **c.** Air force
   - **d.** Marine Corps

7. Charles Darwin wrote the influential book,
   - **a.** *Our Country*
   - **b.** *Sister Carrie*
   - **c.** *The Call of the Wild*
   - **d.** *The Origin of Species*

8. All of the following describe the experiences of black soldiers in the Spanish-American war *except*
   - **a.** In 1898 four regiments of black troops existed in the U.S. army.
   - **b.** Most state governors welcomed black volunteers.
   - **c.** U.S. military authorities thought black troops were immune to tropical diseases.
   - **d.** African American troops suffered discrimination in the military.

9. All of the following describe Americans' views of the importance of the Philippines in 1898 *except*
   - **a.** Missionary organizations wanted to Christianize the Filipino people.
   - **b.** Merchants viewed the Philippines as a gateway to the Chinese market.
   - **c.** Many Americans regarded the Philippines as the fruits of war.
   - **d.** Most Americans favored independence of the Philippines.

10. All of the following describe the Philippine-American War *except*
    - **a.** Historians constantly write about this conflict.
    - **b.** The war began a few months after war with Spain concluded.
    - **c.** The war lasted three years.
    - **d.** The war included jungle fighting, guerrilla warfare, and human atrocities.

Find more practice at www.myhistorylab.com

SAMPLE ESSAY QUESTIONS

1. Explain the short- and long-term reasons why the United States declared war on Spain in 1898.

2. Evaluate the problems experienced by the United States in managing its first overseas empire.

The Progressive Era
1895–1917

LIFE IN THE NEW CITY

Hester Street (1905), a New York street scene by George Benjamin Luks. Luks was one of a group of artists associated with the Ashcan School, so named because of the artists' preference for painting the realities of modern urban life, including its streets and slums, backyards and bars. (*Source: George Benjamin Luks, American, 1867–1933. "Hester Street" 1905. Oil on canvas. 66.3 × 91.8 (26 1/8 × 36 1/8). Brooklyn Museum of Art. Dick S. Ramsay Fund. 40.339.*)

In this painting, what are the main characteristics of life in New York City in the early 1900s?

Muckrakers Call for Reform

In 1902, Samuel S. McClure, the shrewd owner of *McClure's Magazine*, sensed something astir in the country that his reporters were not covering. Like *Life, Munsey's*, the *Ladies' Home Journal*, and *Cosmopolitan*, *McClure's* was reaching more and more people—more than a quarter million readers a month. Americans were snapping up the new popular magazines filled with eye-catching illustrations and up-to-date fiction. Advances in photoengraving during the 1890s dramatically reduced the cost of illustrations; at the same time, income from advertisements rose sharply. By the turn of the century, some magazines earned as much as $60,000 an issue from advertising alone, and publishers could price them as low as 10 cents a copy.

McClure was always chasing new ideas and readers, and in 1902, certain that something was happening in the public mood, he told one of his editors, 36-year-old Lincoln Steffens, a former Wall Street reporter, to find out what it was. "Get out of here, travel, go—somewhere," he said to Steffens. "Buy a railroad ticket, get on a train,

KEY EVENTS

1898   Mergers and consolidations begin to sweep the business world, leading to fear of trusts, *p. 593*

1903   Ford Motor Company formed, *p. 592*
■ W. E. B. Du Bois calls for justice and equality for African Americans in *The Souls of Black Folk*, *p. 600*
■ Women's Trade Union League (WTUL) formed to organize women workers, *p. 605*

1905   Industrial Workers of the World (IWW) established, *p. 605* ■ African American leaders inaugurate the Niagara Movement, advocating integration and equal opportunity for African Americans, *p. 600*

1909   Shirtwaist workers in New York City strike in the Uprising of the 20,000, *p. 605* ■ Campaign by Rockefeller Sanitary Commission wipes out hookworm disease, *p. 597*

1910   NAACP founded, *p. 600* ■ Strike at Hart, Schaffner and Marx leads to pioneering collective bargaining agreement, *p. 605* ■ National Collegiate Athletic Association (NCAA) formed, *p. 609*

1911   Fire at the Triangle Shirtwaist Company kills 146 people, *p. 595* ■ Frederick Winslow Taylor publishes *The Principles of Scientific Management*, *p. 595*

1912   Harriet Monroe begins publishing magazine *Poetry*, *p. 611* ■ IWW leads strikes in Massachusetts and New Jersey, *p. 606*

1913   Ford introduces the moving assembly line in Highland Park, Michigan, plant, *p. 593* ■ Mother's Day becomes national holiday, *p. 598*

1915   D. W. Griffith produces the first movie spectacular, *Birth of a Nation*, *p. 609* ■ T. S. Eliot publishes "The Love Song of J. Alfred Prufrock," *p. 611*

1916   New York zoning law sets the pattern for zoning laws across the nation, *p. 608*

1917   Congress passes law requiring literacy test for all immigrants, *p. 604*

and there, where it lands you, there you will learn to edit a magazine."

Steffens traveled west. In St. Louis, he came across a young district attorney named Joseph W. Folk, who had found a trail of corruption linking politics and some of the city's respected business leaders. Eager for help, Folk did not mind naming names to the visiting editor from New York. "It is good business men that are corrupting our bad politicians," he stressed again and again. "It is the leading citizens that are battening on our city." Steffens's story, "Tweed Days in St. Louis," appeared in the October 1902 issue of *McClure's*.

The November *McClure's* carried the first installment of Ida Tarbell's scathing "History of the Standard Oil Company," and in January 1903, Steffens was back with "The Shame of Minneapolis," another tale of corrupt partnership between business and politics. McClure had what he wanted, and in the January issue he printed an editorial, "Concerning Three Articles in This Number of *McClure's*, and a Coincidence That May Set Us Thinking." Steffens on Minneapolis, Tarbell on Standard Oil, and an article on abuses in labor unions—all, McClure said, on different topics but actually on the same theme: corruption in American life. "Capitalists, workingmen, politicians, citizens—all breaking the law, or letting it be broken."

Readers were enthralled, and articles and books by other **muckrakers**—Theodore Roosevelt coined the term in 1906 to describe the writers who made a practice of exposing the corruption of public and prominent figures—spread swiftly. *Collier's* had articles on questionable stock market practices, patent medicines, and the beef trust. Novelist Upton Sinclair tackled the meatpackers in *The Jungle* (1906). In 1904, Steffens collected his *McClure's* articles in *The Shame of the Cities,* with an introduction expressing confidence that reform was possible, "that our shamelessness is superficial, that beneath it lies a pride which, being real, may save us yet."

Muckraking flourished from 1903 to 1909, and while it did, good writers and bad investigated almost every corner of American life: government, labor unions, big business, Wall Street, health care, the food industry, child labor, women's rights, prostitution, ghetto living, and life insurance.

The muckrakers were a journalistic voice of a larger movement in American society. Called **progressivism,** it lasted from the mid-1890s through World War I.

Like muckraking itself, progressivism reflected worry about the state of society, the effects of industrialization and urbanization, social disorder, political corruption, and a host of other issues. With concerns so large, progressivism often had a sense of crisis and urgency, although it was rooted in a spirit of hopefulness and confidence in human progress. For varying reasons, thousands of people became concerned about their society, and, separately and together, they set out to cure some of the ills they saw around them. The efforts of the so-called progressives changed the nation and gave the era its name.

The Changing Face of Industrialism

As the new century turned, conditions in America were better than just a few years before. Farms and factories were once again prosperous; in 1901, for the first time in years, the economy reached full capacity. Farm prices rose almost 50 percent between 1900 and 1910. Unemployment dropped. "In the United States of today," a Boston newspaper said in 1904, "everyone is middle class. The resort to force, the wild talk of the nineties are over. Everyone is busily, happily getting ahead."

Everyone, of course, was not middle class, nor was everyone getting ahead. "Wild talk" persisted. Many of the problems that had angered people in the 1890s continued into the new century, and millions of Americans still suffered from poverty and disease. Racism sat even more heavily on African Americans in both South and North, and there was increasing hostility against immigrants from southern and eastern Europe and from Mexico and Asia. Yet economic conditions were better for many people, and as a result, prosperity became one of the keys to understanding the era and the nature of progressive reform.

HOW did industrialism change in the years after 1900?

muckrakers
Unflattering term coined by Theodore Roosevelt to describe the writers who made a practice of exposing the wrongdoings of public figures. Muckraking flourished from 1903 to 1909 in magazines such as *McClure's* and *Collier's*, exposing social and political problems and sparking reform.

progressivism
Movement for social change between the late 1890s and World War I. Its origins lay in a fear of big business and corrupt government and a desire to improve the lives of countless Americans. Progressives set out to cure the social ills brought about by industrialization and urbanization, social disorder, and political corruption.

The start of the new century was another key as well, for it influenced people to take a fresh look at themselves and their times. Excited about beginning the twentieth century, people believed technology and enterprise would shape a better life. Savoring the word *new,* they talked of the new poetry, new cinema, new history, new democracy, new woman, new art, new immigration, new morality, and new city. Presidents Theodore Roosevelt and Woodrow Wilson called their political programs the New Nationalism and the New Freedom.

The word *mass* also cropped up frequently. Victors in the recent war with Spain, Americans took pride in teeming cities, burgeoning corporations, and other marks of the mass society. They enjoyed the fruits of mass production, read mass circulation newspapers and magazines, and took mass transit from the growing spiral of suburbs into the central cities.

Behind mass production lay significant changes in the nation's industrial system. Businesses grew at a rapid rate. They were large in the three decades after the Civil War, but in the years between 1895 and 1915, industries became mammoth, employing thousands of workers and equipped with assembly lines to turn out huge quantities of the company's product. Inevitably, changes in management attitudes, business organization, and worker roles influenced the entire society. Inevitably, too, the growth of giant businesses gave rise to a widespread fear of "trusts" and a desire among many progressive reformers to break them up or regulate them.

The Innovative Model T

In the movement toward large-scale business and mass production, the automobile industry was one of those that led the way. In 1895, there were only four cars on the nation's roads; in 1917, there were nearly five million, and the automobile had already helped work a small revolution in industrial methods and social mores.

In 1903, Henry Ford and a small group of associates formed the Ford Motor Company, the firm that transformed the business. That year, Ford sold the first Ford car. The price was high, and in 1905, Ford raised prices still higher. Sales

RISE OF MASS PRODUCTION   Henry Ford built his first car in 1896, then produced a number of improved models, each designated by a letter of the alphabet. Shown here are Henry Ford and a friend in a 1905 Model N, Ford's best-selling model before the Model T debuted in 1908. The "Tin Lizzie" was Ford's "motorcar for the multitudes," affordably priced so that every family could own one. The automobile wrought vast changes in American life and in the American landscape as it spawned the development of paved roads, traffic lights, and numerous auto-related businesses.

Why did the automobile have such a great effect?

plummeted. In 1907, he lowered the price; sales and revenues rose. Ford learned an important lesson of the modern economy: A smaller unit profit on a large number of sales meant enormous revenues. Early in 1908, he introduced the Model T, a four-cylinder, 20-horsepower "Tin Lizzie," costing $850, and available only in black. Eleven thousand were sold the first year.

"I am going to democratize the automobile," Ford proclaimed. "When I'm through everybody will be able to afford one, and about everyone will have one." The key was mass production, and after many experiments, Ford copied the techniques of meatpackers who moved animal carcasses along overhead trolleys from station to station. Adapting the process to automobile assembly, Ford in 1913 set up moving assembly lines in his plant in Highland Park, Michigan, that dramatically reduced the time and cost of producing cars. Emphasizing continuous movement, he strove for a nonstop flow from raw material to finished product. In 1914, he sold 248,000 Model T cars.

That year, Ford workers assembled a car in 93 minutes, one-tenth the time it had taken just eight months before. On a single day in 1925, Ford set a record by turning out 9109 Model Ts, a new car for every 10 seconds of the workday.

QUICK CHECK ✓

How did Henry Ford revolutionize the automobile industry?

The Burgeoning Trusts

As businesses like Ford's grew, capital and organization became increasingly important, and the result was the formation of a growing number of trusts. Standard Oil started the trend in 1882, but the greatest momentum came two decades later. Between 1898 and 1903, a series of mergers and consolidations swept the economy. Many smaller firms disappeared, swallowed up in giant corporations. By 1904, large-scale combinations of one form or another controlled nearly two-fifths of the capital in manufacturing in the country.

The result was not monopoly but oligopoly—control of a commodity or service by a small number of large, powerful companies. Six great financial groups dominated the railroad industry; a handful of holding companies controlled utilities and steel. Rockefeller's Standard Oil owned about 85 percent of the oil business. After 1898, financiers and industrialists formed the Amalgamated Copper Company, Consolidated Tobacco, U.S. Rubber, and a host of others. By 1909, just 1 percent of the industrial firms were producing nearly half of all manufactured goods.

Though the trend has been overstated, finance capitalists such as J. P. Morgan tended to replace the industrial capitalists of an earlier era. Able to finance the mergers and reorganizations, investment bankers played a greater and greater role in the economy. A multibillion-dollar financial house, J. P. Morgan and

BUSINESS CONSOLIDATIONS (MERGERS), 1895–1905

THE RISING OF THE USURPERS.

And the sinking of the liberties of the people.

FEAR OF TRUSTS As early as 1886, cartoonist Thomas Nast attacked trusts. Here the people's welfare is sinking as the Statue of Liberty is defaced.

What did Nast mean by the title of his cartoon, "THE RISING OF THE USURPERS"?

Company operated a network of control that ran from New York City to every industrial and financial center in the nation. Like other investment firms, it held directorships in many corporations, creating "interlocking directorates" that allowed it to control many businesses.

Massive business growth set off a decade-long debate over what government should do about the trusts. Some critics who believed that the giant companies were responsible for stifling individual opportunity and raising prices wanted to break them up into small competitive units. Others argued that large-scale business was a mark of the times, and that it produced more goods and better lives.

The debate over the trusts was one of the issues that shaped the Progressive Era, but it was never a simple contest between high-minded reformers and greedy business titans. Some progressives favored big business; others wanted it broken up. Business leaders themselves were divided in their viewpoints, and some welcomed reform-led assaults on giant competitors. As a rule, both progressives and business leaders drew on similar visions of the country: complex, expansive, hopeful, managerially minded, and oriented toward results and efficiency. They both believed in private property and the importance of economic progress. In fact, in working for reform, the progressives often drew on the managerial methods of a business world they sought to regulate.

QUICK CHECK ✓

What factors led to the rapid growth of trusts?

Managing the Machines

Mass production changed the direction of American industry. Size, system, organization, and marketing became increasingly important. Management focused on speed and product, not on workers. Assembly-line technology changed tasks and, to some extent, values. The goal was no longer to make a unique product that would be better than the one before. "The way to make automobiles," Ford said as early as 1903, "is to make one automobile like another automobile, to make them all alike, to make them come through the factory just alike."

In a development that rivaled assembly lines in importance, businesses established industrial research laboratories where scientists and engineers developed new products. General Electric founded the first one in 1900, housed in a barn. It soon attracted experts who designed improvements in light bulbs, invented the cathode-ray tube, worked on early radio, and even tinkered with atomic theory. Du Pont opened its labs in 1911, Eastman Kodak in 1912, and Standard Oil in 1919. As the source of new ideas and technology, the labs altered life in the twentieth and twenty-first centuries.

Through all this, business became large-scale, mechanized, and managed. While many shops still employed fewer than a dozen workers, the proportion of such shops shrank. By 1920, close to one-half of all industrial workers toiled in factories employing more than 250 people. More than one-third worked in factories that were part of multiplant companies.

Industries that processed materials—iron and steel, paper, cement, and chemicals—were increasingly automated and operated continuously. Workers in those industries could not fall behind. Foremen still managed the laborers on the factory floor, but more and more, the rules came down from a central office where trained professional managers supervised production flow. Systematic record keeping, cost accounting, and inventory and production controls became widespread. Workers lost control of the work pace. "If you need to turn out a little more," a manager at Swift and Company said, "you speed up the conveyor a little and the men speed up to keep pace."

Folkways of the workplace—workers passing job-related knowledge to each other, performing their tasks with little supervision, setting their own pace, and in effect running the shop—began to give way to "scientific" labor management. More than anyone else, Frederick Winslow Taylor, an inventive mechanical engineer, strove to extract maximum efficiency from each worker. "In the past," he believed, "the man has been first; in the future the system must be first."

In his book *The Principles of Scientific Management* (1911), Taylor proposed two major reforms. First, management must take responsibility for job-related knowledge and classify it into "rules, laws, and formulae." Second, management should control the workplace "through *enforced* standardization of methods, *enforced* adoption of the best implements and working conditions, and *enforced* cooperation." Although few factories wholly adopted Taylor's principles, he had great influence, and the doctrines of scientific management spread through American industry.

Workers caught up in the changing industrial system experienced the benefits of efficiency and productivity; in some industries, they earned more. But they suffered important losses as well. Performing repetitive tasks, they seemed part of the machinery, moving to the pace and needs of their mechanical pacesetters. Bored, they might easily lose pride of workmanship, though many workers, it is clear, did not. Efficiency engineers experimented with tools and methods, a process many workers found unsettling.

Jobs became not only monotonous but dangerous. As machines and assembly lines sped up, boredom or miscalculation could bring disaster. In March 1911, a fire at the Triangle Shirtwaist Company in New York focused nationwide attention on unsafe working conditions. When the fire started, five hundred men and women, mostly Italians and Jews from eastern Europe, were just finishing their workday. Firefighters arrived within minutes, but they were already too late. Terrified seamstresses raced to the exits to try to escape the flames, but most exit doors were closed, locked by the company to prevent theft and shut out union organizers. Many died in the stampede down the narrow stairways or the single fire escape. Still others, trapped on the building's top stories far above the reach of the fire department's ladders, jumped to their deaths on the street below. One hundred forty-six people died.

A few days later, eighty thousand people marched silently in the rain in a funeral procession up Fifth Avenue. A quarter million people watched. At a mass meeting held to protest factory working conditions, Rose Schneiderman, a dynamic 29-year-old

Frederick Winslow Taylor, Scientific Management (1911)

TRAGEDY AT THE TRIANGLE COMPANY   Fire nets were of no avail to the workers at the Triangle Shirtwaist Company who jumped from the upper stories to escape the flames. Speaking to a mass meeting after the fire, labor organizer Rose Schneiderman inveighed against a system that treated human beings as expendable commodities.

What were the effects of the Triangle fire?

QUICK CHECK ✓

What methods emerged to help manage the workers and machinery on the factory floor?

organizer for the Women's Trade Union League, told New York City's civic and religious leaders that they had not done enough, they had not cared. "We have tried you good people of the public and we have found you wanting…. Every week I must learn of the untimely death of one of my sister workers. Every year thousands of us are maimed. The life of men and women is so cheap and property is so sacred."

The outcry impelled New York's governor to appoint a State Factory Investigating Commission that recommended laws to shorten the workweek and improve safety in factories and stores.

Society's Masses

HOW ?

were women, children, immigrants, and African Americans affected by mass production?

Spreading consumer goods through society, mass production not only improved people's lives but sometimes cost lives, too. Tending the machines, as Rose Schneiderman pointed out, took hard, painful labor, often under dangerous conditions. As businesses expanded, they required more and more people, and the labor force increased tremendously to keep up with the demand for workers in the factories, mines, and forests. Women, African Americans, Asian Americans, and Mexican Americans played larger and larger roles. Immigration soared. Between 1901 and 1910, nearly 8.8 million immigrants entered the United States; between 1911 and 1920, another 5.7 million came.

For many of these people, life was harsh, spent in crowded slums and long hours on the job. Fortunately, the massive unemployment of the 1890s was over, and in many skilled trades, such as cigar making, there was plenty of work to go around. Though the economic recovery helped nearly everyone, the less skilled continued to be the less fortunate. Migrant workers, lumberjacks, ore shovelers, and others struggled to find jobs that paid decently.

Under such circumstances, many people fought to make a living, and many, too, fought to improve their lot. Their efforts, along with the efforts of the reform-minded people who came to their aid, became another important hallmark of the Progressive Era.

Better Times on the Farm

While people continued to flee the farms—by 1920, fewer than one-third of all Americans lived on farms, and fewer than one-half lived in rural areas—farmers themselves prospered, the beneficiaries of greater production and expanding urban markets. Rural free delivery, begun in 1896, helped diminish the farmers' sense of isolation and changed farm life. The delivery of mail to the farm door opened that door to a wider world; it exposed farmers to urban thinking, national advertising, and political events. In 1911, more than one billion newspapers and magazines were delivered over RFD routes.

Rural Free Delivery Mail

Parcel post (1913) permitted the sending of packages through the U.S. mail. Mail-order houses flourished; rural merchants suffered. Within a year, 300 million packages were being mailed annually. While telephones and electricity did not reach most rural areas for decades, better roads, mail-order catalogs, and other innovations knit farmers into the larger society. Early in the new century, Mary E. Lease—who in her Populist days had urged Kansas farmers to raise less corn and more hell—moved to Brooklyn.

Farmers still had problems. Land prices rose with crop prices, and farm tenancy increased, especially in the South. Tenancy grew from one-quarter of all farms in 1880 to more than one-third in 1910. Many southern tenant farmers were African Americans, and they suffered from farm-bred diseases. In one of the reforms of the Progressive Era, in 1909, the Rockefeller Sanitary Commission, acting on recent scientific discoveries, began a sanitation campaign that eventually wiped out the hookworm disease.

In the arid West, irrigation transformed the land as the federal government and private landholders joined to import water from mountain watersheds. The dry lands bloomed, and so did a rural class structure that sharply separated owners from workers. Under the Newlands Act of 1902, the secretary of the interior formed the U.S. Reclamation Service, which gathered a staff of thousands of engineers and technicians, "the largest bureaucracy ever assembled in irrigation history."

Dams and canals channeled water into places such as California's Imperial Valley, and as the water streamed in, cotton, cantaloupes, oranges, tomatoes, lettuce, and a host of other crops streamed out to national markets. By 1920, Idaho, Montana, Utah, Wyoming, Colorado, and Oregon had extensive irrigation systems, all drawing on scarce water supplies; California, the foremost importer of water, had 4.2 million acres under irrigation, many of them picked by migrant workers from Mexico, China, and Japan.

QUICK CHECK

Why did conditions on the farm improve after 1900?

Women and Children at Work

Women worked in larger and larger numbers. In 1900, more than five million worked—one-fifth of all adult women—and among those aged 14 to 24, the employment rate was almost one-third. Of those employed, single women outnumbered married women by seven to one, yet more than one-third of married women worked. Most women held service jobs. Only a small number held higher-paying jobs as professionals or managers.

In the 1890s, women made up more than one-quarter of medical school graduates. Using a variety of techniques, men gradually squeezed them out, and by the 1920s, only about 5 percent of the graduates were women. Few women taught in colleges and universities, and those who did were expected to resign if they married.

More women than men graduated from high school, and with professions like medicine and science largely closed to them, they often turned to the new "business schools" that offered training in stenography, typing, and bookkeeping. In 1920, more than one-quarter of all employed women held clerical jobs. Many others taught school.

Black women had always worked, and in far larger numbers than their white counterparts. The reason was usually economic; an African American man or woman alone could rarely earn enough to support a family. Unlike many white women, black women tended to remain in the labor force after marriage or the start of a family. They also had less opportunity for job advancement, and in 1920, between one-third and one-half of all African American women who were working were restricted to personal and domestic service jobs.

Critics charged that women's employment endangered the home, threatened their reproductive functions, and even, as one man said, stripped them of "that modest demeanor that lends a charm to their kind." Adding to these fears, the birthrate continued to drop between 1900 and 1920, and the divorce rate soared, in part because working-class men took advantage of the newer moral freedom and deserted their families in growing numbers. By 1916, there was one divorce for every nine marriages as compared to one for twenty-one in 1880.

Many children also worked. In 1900, about three million children—nearly 20 percent of those between the ages of 5 and 15—held full-time or almost full-time jobs. Twenty-five thousand boys under 16 worked in mining; twenty thousand children under 12, mainly girls, worked in southern cotton mills. Gradually, as public indignation grew, the use of child labor shrank.

Determined to do something about the situation, the Women's Trade Union League lobbied the federal Bureau of Labor to investigate the conditions under which women and children worked. Begun in 1907, the investigation took four years and produced nineteen volumes of data, some of it shocking, all of it factual. In 1911, spurred by the data, the Children's Bureau was formed within the U.S. Bureau of Labor, with Grace Abbott, a social worker, at its head.

Numerous middle-class women became involved in the fight for reform, while many others, reflecting the ongoing changes in the family, took increasing pride in homemaking and motherhood. Mother's Day, the national holiday, was formally established in 1913. Women who preferred smaller numbers of children turned increasingly to birth control, which became a more acceptable practice. Margaret Sanger, a nurse and outspoken social reformer, led a campaign to give physicians broad discretion in prescribing contraceptives.

John Spargo, from *The Bitter Cry of the Children* (1906)

QUICK CHECK ✔

In what conditions did women and children work in the early twentieth century?

LAD FELL TO DEATH IN BIG COAL CHUTE

Dennis McKee Dead and Arthur Allbecker Had Leg Burned In the Lee Mines.

Falling into a chute at the Chauncey colliery of the George S. Lee Coal Company at Avondale, this afternoon, Dennis McKee, aged 12, of West Nanticoke, was smothered to death and Arthur Allbecker, aged 15, had both of his legs burned and injured. Dr. Biel, of Plymouth, was summoned and dressed the burns of the injured boy.

He was removed to his home at Avondale.

Both boys were employed as breaker boys, and going too close to the chutes fell in. Fellow workmen rushed to their assistance and soon had them out of the chutes. When taken out McKee was found to be dead. His remains were removed to his home at West Nanticoke. Allbecker will recover.

CHILD LABOR Breaker boys, who picked out pieces of slate from the coal as it rushed past, often became bent-backed and suffered respiratory diseases such as bronchitis and tuberculosis after years of working fourteen hours a day in the coal mines. Accidents—and deaths—were common in the mines.

Why did these young boys work?

The Niagara Movement and the NAACP

At the turn of the century, eight of every ten African Americans still lived in rural areas, mainly in the South. Most were poor sharecroppers. Jim Crow laws segregated many schools, railroad cars, hotels, and hospitals. Poll taxes and other devices disfranchised blacks and many poor whites. Violence was common; from 1900 to 1914, white mobs murdered more than a thousand black people.

Many African Americans labored on the cotton farms and in the railroad camps, sawmills, and mines of the South under conditions of peonage. Peons traded their lives and labor for food and shelter. Often illiterate, they were forced to sign contracts allowing the planter "to use such force as he or his agents may deem necessary to require me to remain on his farm and perform good and satisfactory services." Armed guards patrolled the camps and whipped those trying to escape.

Few blacks belonged to labor unions, and blacks almost always earned less than whites in the same job. In Atlanta, white electricians earned $5.00 a day, blacks $3.50. Black songs such as "I've Got a White Man Workin' for Me" (1901)

Ida B. Wells-Barnett, False Accusations, from *A Red Record*

W. E. B. Du Bois, "Of Mr. Booker T. Washington and Others" (1903)

Niagara Movement

A movement, led by W.E.B. Du Bois, that focused on equal rights and the education of African American youth. Rejecting the gradualist approach of Booker T. Washington, members kept alive a program of militant action and claimed for African Americans all rights afforded to other Americans. It spawned later civil rights movements.

voiced more hope than reality. The illiteracy rate among African Americans dropped from 45 percent in 1900 to 30 percent in 1910, but nowhere were they given equal school facilities, teachers' salaries, or educational materials. In 1910, scarcely eight thousand African American youths were attending high schools in all the states of the Southeast.

African American leaders grew increasingly impatient with this kind of treatment, and in 1905 a group of them, led by sociologist W. E. B. Du Bois, met near Niagara Falls, New York (they met on the Canadian side of the Falls, since no hotel on the American side would take them). There they pledged action in the matters of voting, equal access to economic opportunity, integration, and equality before the law. Rejecting Booker T. Washington's gradualist approach, the **Niagara Movement** claimed for African Americans "every single right that belongs to a freeborn American, political, civil and social; and until we get these rights we will never cease to protest."

The Niagara Movement focused on equal rights and the education of African American youth, of whom it said, "They have a right to know, to think, to aspire." Keeping alive a program of militant action, it spawned later civil rights movements. Du Bois was its inspiration. In *The Souls of Black Folk* (1903) and other works, he called eloquently for justice and equality.

Still, race riots broke out in Atlanta, Georgia, in 1906 and in Springfield, Illinois, in 1908, the latter the home of Abraham Lincoln. Unlike the riots of the 1960s, white mobs invaded black neighborhoods, burning, looting, and killing. They lynched two blacks—one 84 years old—in Springfield.

Outrage was voiced by William E. Walling, a wealthy southerner and settlement house worker; Mary Ovington, a white anthropology student; and Oswald Garrison Villard, grandson of the famous abolitionist William Lloyd Garrison. Along with other reformers, white and black (among them Jane Addams and John Dewey), they issued a call for the conference that organized the **National Association for the Advancement of Colored People (NAACP),** which swiftly became the most important civil rights organization in the country. Created in 1909, within five years the NAACP grew to fifty branches and more than six thousand members. Walling headed it, and Du Bois, the only African American among the top officers, directed publicity and edited *The Crisis*, the voice of the organization.

THE FIGHT FOR CIVIL RIGHTS Cover of the first issue of *The Crisis*. Founded in 1910 by the NAACP and edited by W. E. B. Du Bois, the monthly periodical served as the voice of the organization in its crusade for civil rights.

What did W. E. B. Du Bois see as "the crisis"?

Joined by the National Urban League, which was created in 1911, the NAACP pressured employers, labor unions, and the government on behalf of African Americans. It had some victories. In 1918, in the midst of World War I, the NAACP and the National Urban League persuaded the federal government to form a special Bureau of Negro Economics within the Labor Department to look after the interests of African American wage earners.

Despite these gains, African Americans continued to experience disfranchisement, poor job opportunities, and segregation. As Booker T. Washington said in 1913, "I have never seen the colored people so discouraged and so bitter as they are at the present time."

QUICK CHECK ✔

What were the main causes for the formation of the Niagara Movement and the NAACP in the early twentieth century?

Immigrants in the Labor Force

While women and African Americans worked in growing numbers, much of the huge increase in the labor force in these years came from outside the country, particularly from Europe and Mexico. Between 1901 and 1920, the extraordinarily high total of 14.5 million immigrants entered the country, more than in any previous twenty-year period. Continuing the trend begun in the 1880s, many came from southern and eastern Europe. Still called the "new" immigrants, they met hostility from "older" immigrants of northern European stock who questioned their values, religion (often Catholic or Jewish), traditions, and appearance.

Immigrant patterns often departed from traditional stereotypes. Immigrants, for example, moved both to and from their homelands. Fifty percent or more of the members of some groups returned home, although the proportion varied. Jews and Czechs often brought their families to resettle in America; Serbs and Poles tended to come singly, intent on earning enough money to make a fresh start at home. Some migrants—Italian men, in particular—virtually commuted, returning home every slack season. These temporary migrants became known as **birds of passage.** The outbreak of World War I interrupted the practice and trapped thousands of Italians and others who had planned to return to Europe.

Older residents lumped the newcomers together, ignoring geographic, religious, and other differences. Preserving important regional distinctions, Italians tended to settle as Calabreses, Venetians, Abruzzis, and Sicilians. Old-stock Americans viewed them all simply as Italians. Henry Ford and other employers tried to erase the differences through English classes and deliberate "Americanization"

IMMIGRATION TO THE UNITED STATES, 1900–1920 (BY AREA OF ORIGIN)

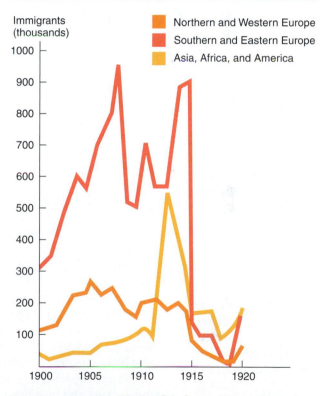

Immigrants (thousands)

- ■ Northern and Western Europe
- ■ Southern and Eastern Europe
- ■ Asia, Africa, and America

Note: For purposes of classification, "Northern and Western Europe" includes Great Britain, Ireland, Scandinavia, the Netherlands, Belgium, Luxembourg, Switzerland, France, and Germany. "Southern and Eastern Europe" includes Poland, Austria-Hungary, Russia and the Baltic States, Romania, Bulgaria, European Turkey, Italy, Spain, Portugal, and Greece. "Asia, Africa, and America" includes Asian Turkey, China, Japan, India, Canada, the Caribbean, Latin America, and all of Africa.

Source: U.S. Bureau of the Census, *Historical Statistics of the United States, Colonial Times to 1970,* Bicentennial Edition, Washington, D.C., 1975.

MEXICAN IMMIGRATION TO THE UNITED STATES, 1900–1920

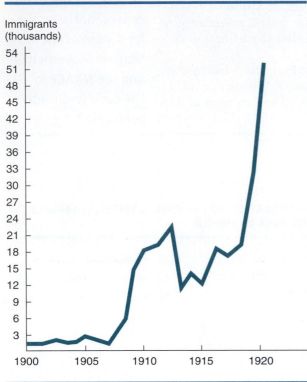

Immigrants
(thousands)

x-axis: 1900, 1905, 1910, 1915, 1920

National Association for the Advancement of Colored People (NAACP)

Created in 1909, this organization quickly became one of the most important civil rights organizations in the country. The NAACP pressured employers, labor unions, and the government on behalf of African Americans.

National
Negro
Committee
Platform
(1909)

programs. The Ford Motor Company ran a school where immigrant employees were first taught to say, "I am a good American." At the graduation ceremony, the pupils acted out a gigantic pantomime in which, clad in their old-country dress, they filed into a large "melting pot." When they emerged, they were wearing identical American-made clothes, and each was waving a little American flag.

Labor groups soon learned to counter these techniques. The Women's Trade Union League (WTUL) urged workers to ignore business-sponsored English lessons because they did not "tell the girl worker the things she really wants to know. They do not suggest that $5 a week is not a living wage. They tell her to be respectful to her employer."

In another significant development at the beginning of the twentieth century, Mexicans for the first time immigrated in large numbers, especially after a revolution in Mexico in 1910 forced many to flee across the northern border into Texas, New Mexico, Arizona, and California. Their exact numbers were unknown. American officials did not count border crossings until 1907, and even then, many migrants avoided the official immigration stations. Almost all came from the Mexican lower class, eager to escape peonage and violence in their native land. Labor agents called *coyotes*—usually in the employ of large corporations or working for ranchers—recruited Mexican workers.

Between 1900 and 1910, the Mexican population of Texas and New Mexico nearly doubled; in Arizona, it more than doubled; in California, it quadrupled. In all four states, it doubled again between 1910 and 1920. After the turn of the century, almost 10 percent of the total population of Mexico moved to the American Southwest.

In time, these Mexican Americans and their children transformed the Southwest. They built most of the early highways in Texas, New Mexico, and Arizona; dug the irrigation ditches that watered crops throughout the area; laid railroad track; and picked the cotton and vegetables that clothed and fed millions of Americans. Many lived in shacks and shanties along the railroad tracks, isolated in a separate Spanish-speaking world. Like other immigrant groups, they also formed enclaves in the cities; these *barrios* became cultural islands of family life, foods, church, and festivals.

Fewer people immigrated from China in these years, deterred in part by anti-Chinese laws and hostility. Like many other immigrants, most Chinese who came did not intend to remain. Wanting to make money and return home, they mined, farmed, and worked as common laborers. In their willingness to work hard for low wages, their desire to preserve clan and family associations from China, and their maintenance of strong ties with their home villages, Chinese Americans resembled other immigrant groups, but they differed in two important respects. As late as 1920, men outnumbered women by ten to one in the Chinese American population, and with a male median age of 42, their communities were generally dominated by the elderly.

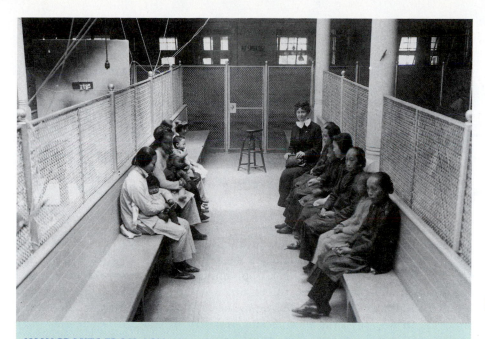

IMMIGRANTS FROM ASIA   Japanese immigrants wait with a Methodist deaconess in the administration building of the immigration station at Angel Island, near San Francisco. Quota systems and exclusionary laws severely limited Asian immigration, while other laws placed restrictions on the immigrants, curtailing their right to own or even rent agricultural land. Some Asian immigrants, after months of detention at Angel Island, were refused permission to enter the United States and were forced to return to their homelands. (*Source: Courtesy of the California Historical Society, FN-18240.*)

Why have historians tended to ignore the immigration station near San Francisco, while focusing on Ellis Island, the immigration station in New York City's harbor?

birds of passage
Temporary migrants who came to the United States to work and save money and then returned home to their native countries during the slack season. World War I interrupted the practice, trapping thousands of migrant workers in the United States.

The Chinese American population differed in another respect as well. Unlike other immigrant groups, whose numbers tended to grow, the number of Chinese Americans shrank in these years—from about 125,000 in the early 1880s to just over 60,000 in 1920. After 1910, the U.S. government set up a special immigration facility at Angel Island in San Francisco Bay, but unlike European immigrants who landed at Ellis Island in New York and were quickly sent on, Chinese immigrants were kept for weeks and months, examined and reexamined, before being allowed to cross the narrow band of water to San Francisco.

Many Japanese also arrived at Angel Island, and though at first fewer in numbers than the Chinese, they developed communities along the Pacific coast, where they settled mainly on farms. The number of Japanese Americans grew. In 1907, the heaviest year of immigration from Japan, nearly 31,000 Japanese entered the United States; by 1920, there were 111,000 Japanese in the country, nearly three-quarters of them in California.

As the newcomers arrived from Asia, Europe, and Mexico, nativist sentiment, which had criticized earlier waves of immigrants, intensified. Old-stock Americans sneered at their dress and language. Racial theories emphasized the superiority of northern Europeans, and the new "science" of eugenics suggested the need to control

Mary Antin, from *The Promised Land* (1912)

Lee Chew, "Life of a Chinese Immigrant" (1903)

QUICK CHECK ✓

In what ways did immigrants adjust, or not adjust, to their new society?

the population growth of "inferior" peoples. Hostility toward Catholics and Jews was common but touched other groups as well.

In 1902, Congress enacted a law prohibiting immigration from China. Statutes requiring literacy tests designed to curtail immigration from southern and eastern Europe were vetoed by William Howard Taft in 1913 and by Woodrow Wilson in 1915 and 1917. In 1917, such a measure passed despite Wilson's veto. Other measures tried to limit immigration from Mexico and Japan.

Conflict in the Workplace

WHAT conditions brought about the large number of strikes in the period?

Assembly lines, speedups, long hours, and low pay produced a dramatic increase in American industrial output (and profits) after 1900; they also gave rise to numerous strikes and other kinds of labor unrest. Sometimes strikes took place through the action of unions; sometimes workers just decided they had had enough and walked off the job. Whatever the cause, strikes were frequent. In one industry, in one city—the meatpacking industry in Chicago—there were 251 strikes in 1903 alone.

Strikes and absenteeism increased after 1910; labor productivity dropped 10 percent between 1915 and 1918, the first such decline in memory. In many industries, labor turnover became a serious problem; workers changed jobs in droves. Union membership grew. In 1900, only about a million workers—less than 4 percent of the workforce—belonged to unions. By 1920, five million workers belonged, increasing the unionized portion of the workforce to about 13 percent.

As tensions grew between capital and labor, some people in the middle class became fearful that, unless something was done to improve the workers' situation, there might be violence or even revolution. This fear motivated some of the labor-oriented reforms of the Progressive Era. While some reform supporters genuinely wanted to improve labor's lot, others embraced reform because they were afraid of something else.

LABOR UNION MEMBERSHIP, 1897–1920

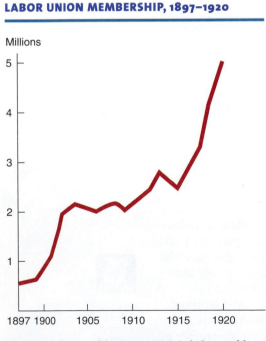

Millions

Source: U.S. Bureau of the Census, *Statistical Abstract of the United States: 1982–1983*, 103rd ed., Washington, D.C., 1982.

Organizing Labor

Samuel Gompers's American Federation of Labor, by far the largest union organization, remained devoted to the interests of skilled craftspeople. While it aimed partly at better wages and working conditions, it also sought to limit entry into the crafts and protect worker prerogatives. Within limits, the AFL found acceptance among giant business corporations eager for conservative policies and labor stability.

Of the 8 million female workers in 1910, only 125,000 belonged to unions. Gompers continued to resist organizing them, saying they were too emotional and, as union organizers, "had a way of making serious mistakes." Margaret Dreier Robins, an organizer of proven skill, scoffed at that. "These men died twenty years ago and are just walking around dead!" she protested.

Robins helped found the **Women's Trade Union League** in 1903. The WTUL led the effort to organize women into trade unions, to lobby for legislation protecting female workers, and to educate the public on the problems and needs of working women. It took in all working women who would join, regardless of skill (although not, at first, African American women), and it won crucial financial support from well-to-do women such as Anne Morgan, daughter of the feared financier J. P. Morgan. Robins's close friend Jane Addams belonged, as did Mary McDowell, the "Angel of the Stockyards," who worked with slaughterhouse workers in Chicago; Julia Lathrop, who tried to improve the lot of wage-earning children; and Dr. Alice Hamilton, a pioneer in American research on the causes of industrial disease.

The WTUL never had many members—a few thousand at most—but its influence extended far beyond its membership. In 1909, it supported the "Uprising of the 20,000," a strike of shirtwaist workers in New York City. When female employees of the Triangle Shirtwaist Company tried to form a union, the company fired them, and they walked out; 20,000 men and women in 500 other shops followed. Strike meetings were conducted in three languages—English, Yiddish, and Italian—and before being forced to go back to work, the strikers won a shorter workweek and a few other gains. Sadly, the Triangle women lost out on another important demand—for unlocked shop doors and safe fire escapes. Their loss proved lethal in the famous Triangle Shirtwaist Company fire of 1911.

The WTUL also backed a strike in 1910 against Hart, Schaffner and Marx, Chicago's largest manufacturer of men's clothing. One day, Annie Shapiro, the 18-year-old daughter of Russian immigrants, was told her wages were being cut from $7 a week to $6.20. That was a large cut, and along with sixteen other young women, Shapiro refused to accept it and walked out. "We had to be recognized as people," she said later. Soon other women walked out, and the revolt spread.

In a matter of days, some forty thousand garment workers were on strike, about half of them women. Manufacturers hurried to negotiate, and the result was the important Hart, Schaffner agreement, which created an arbitration committee composed of management and labor to handle grievances and settle disputes. The first successful experiment in collective bargaining, the Hart, Schaffner agreement became the model for the kind of agreements that govern industrial relations today.

Another union, the **Industrial Workers of the World (IWW),** attracted by far the greatest attention (and the most fears) in these years. Unlike the WTUL, it welcomed everyone regardless of gender or race. Unlike the AFL, it tried to organize the unskilled and foreign-born laborers who worked in the mass production industries. Founded in Chicago in 1905, it aimed to unite the American working class into a mammoth union to promote labor's interests. Its motto—"An injury to one is an injury to all"—stressed labor solidarity, as had the earlier Knights of Labor. But unlike the Knights, the IWW, or Wobblies as they were often known, urged social revolution.

"It is our purpose to overthrow the capitalist system by forcible means if necessary," William D. "Big Bill" Haywood, one of its founders, said; and he went on in his speeches to say he knew of nothing a worker could do that "will bring as much anguish to the boss as a little sabotage in the right place." IWW leaders included Mary Harris ("Mother") Jones, a famous veteran of battles in the Illinois coalfields; Elizabeth Gurley Flynn, a fiery young radical who joined as a teenager;

DOCUMENT

Samuel Gompers, The American Labor Movement (1914)

Women's Trade Union League (WTUL)

Founded in 1903, this group worked to organize women into trade unions. It also lobbied for laws to safeguard female workers and backed several successful strikes, especially in the garment industry. It accepted all women who worked, regardless of skill, and while it never attracted many members, its leaders were influential enough to give the union considerable power.

Industrial Workers of the World (IWW)

Founded in 1905, this radical union, also known as the Wobblies, aimed to unite the American working class into one union to promote labor's interests. It worked to organize unskilled and foreign-born laborers, advocated social revolution, and led several major strikes. Stressing solidarity, the IWW took as its slogan, "An injury to one is an injury to all."

IMAGE

The IWW Is Coming

A RADICAL UNION
Holding signs and banners that proudly display their union allegiance, including a sign with the slogan, "An injury to one is an injury to all," women of the Industrial Workers of the World participate in a strike at the Oliver Iron and Steel Company in Pittsburgh, Pennsylvania, in 1913. The Clayton Act, passed by Congress in 1914, legalized picketing and other union activity.

What factors lay behind the rapid growth of unions in the early 1900s?

and Haywood himself, the strapping one-eyed founder of the Western Federation of Miners.

The IWW led a number of major strikes. Strikes in Lawrence, Massachusetts (1912) and Paterson, New Jersey (1912) attracted national attention: in Lawrence, when the strikers sent their children, ill-clad and hungry, out of the city to stay with sympathetic families; in Paterson, when they rented New York's Madison Square Garden for a massive labor pageant. IWW leaders welcomed the revolutionary tumult sweeping Russia and other countries. In the United States, they thought, a series of local strikes would bring about capitalist repression, then a general strike, and eventually a workers' commonwealth.

The IWW fell short of these objectives, but during its lifetime—from 1905 to the mid-1920s—it made major gains among immigrant workers in the Northeast, migrant farm laborers on the Plains, and loggers and miners in the South and Far West. In factories like Ford's, it recruited workers resentful of the speedups on the assembly lines. Although IWW membership probably amounted to no more than 100,000 at any one time, workers came and left so often that its total membership may have reached as high as 1 million.

Concerned about labor unrest, some business leaders used violence and police action to keep workers in line, but others turned to the new fields of applied psychology and personnel management. A school of industrial psychology emerged. As had Taylor, industrial psychologists studied workers' routines, and, further, they showed that output was also affected by job satisfaction. As a result, some businesses established industrial relations departments, hired public relations firms to improve their corporate image, and linked productivity to job safety and worker happiness.

To please employees, companies printed newsletters and organized softball teams; they awarded prizes and celebrated retirements. Ford created a "sociology department" staffed by 150 experts who showed workers how to budget their incomes and care for their health. They even taught them how to shop for meat.

On January 5, 1914, Ford took another significant step. He announced the five-dollar day, "the greatest revolution," he said, "in the matter of rewards for workers ever known to the industrial world." With a stroke, he doubled the wage rate for common labor, reduced the working day from nine hours to eight, and established a personnel department to place workers in appropriate jobs. The next day, ten thousand applicants stood outside the gates.

As a result, Ford had the pick of the labor force. Turnover declined; absenteeism, previously as much as one-tenth of all Ford workers every day, fell to 0.3 percent. Output increased; the IWW at Ford collapsed. The plan increased wages, but it also gave the company greater control over a more stable labor force. Workers had to meet a behavior code in order to qualify for the five-dollar day. At first scornful of the "utopian" plan, business leaders across the country soon copied it, and on January 2, 1919, Ford announced the six-dollar day.

QUICK CHECK

How did labor organize to protect its interests, and how did some businesses, like Ford, respond?

A New Urban Culture

For many Americans, the quality of life improved significantly between 1900 and 1920. Jobs were relatively plentiful, and, in a development of great importance, more and more people were entering the professions as doctors, lawyers, teachers, and engineers. With comfortable incomes, a growing middle class could take advantage of new lifestyles, inventions, and forms of entertainment. Mass production could not have worked without mass consumption, and Americans in these years increasingly became a nation of consumers.

WHAT

happened to art and culture in these years so filled with change?

Production and Consumption

In 1900, business firms spent about $95 million on advertising; twenty years later, they spent more than $500 million. Ads and billboards touted cigarettes, cars, perfumes, and cosmetics. Advertising agencies boomed. Using new sampling techniques, they developed modern concepts of market testing and research. Sampling customer preferences affected business indirectly as well, making it more responsive to public opinion on social and political issues.

Mass production swept the clothing industry and dressed more Americans better than any people ever before. Using lessons learned in making uniforms during the Civil War, manufacturers for the first time developed standard clothing and shoe sizes that fit most bodies. Clothing prices dropped; the availability of inexpensive "off-the-rack" clothes lessened distinctions between rich and poor. By 1900, nine of every ten men and boys wore the new "ready-to-wear" clothes.

In 1900, people employed in manufacturing earned on average $418 a year. Two decades later, they earned $1342 a year, though inflation took much of the increase. While the middle class expanded, the rich also grew richer. In 1920, the new income tax showed the first accurate tabulation of income, and it confirmed what many had suspected all along. Five percent of the population received almost one-fourth of all income.

QUICK CHECK

What were some of the characteristics of mass production?

Living and Dying in an Urban Nation

In 1920, the median age of the population was only 25. (It is now 35.) Immigration accounted for part of the population's youthfulness, since most immigrants were young. Thanks to medical advances and better living conditions, the death rate dropped in the early years of the century; the average life span increased. Between 1900 and 1920, life expectancy rose from 49 to 56 years for white women and from 47 to 54 years for white men. It rose from 33 to 45 years for blacks and other racial minorities.

Despite the increase in life expectancy, infant mortality remained high; nearly 10 percent of white babies and 20 percent of minority babies died in the first year of life. In comparison to today, fewer babies on average survived to adolescence, and fewer people survived beyond middle age. In 1900, the death rate among people between 45 and 65 was more than twice the modern rate. As a result, there were relatively fewer older people—in 1900, only 4 percent of the population was older than 65 compared to nearly 13 percent today. Fewer children than today knew their grandparents. Still, improvements in health care helped people live longer, and as a result, the incidence of cancer and heart disease increased.

Cities grew, and by any earlier standards, they grew on a colossal scale. Downtowns became a central hive of skyscrapers, department stores, warehouses, and hotels. Strips of factories radiated from the center. As street railways spread, cities took on a systematic pattern of socioeconomic segregation, usually in rings. The innermost ring filled with immigrants, circled by a belt of working-class housing. The remaining rings marked areas of rising affluence outward toward wealthy suburbs, which themselves formed around shopping strips and grid patterns of streets that restricted social interaction.

The giants were New York, Chicago, and Philadelphia, industrial cities that turned out every kind of product from textiles to structural steel. Smaller cities such as Rochester, or Cleveland, Ohio, specialized in manufacturing a specific line of goods or processing regional products for the national market. Railroads instead of highways tied things together; in 1916, the rail network, the largest in the world, reached its peak—254,000 miles of track that carried more than three-fourths of all intercity freight tonnage.

Step by step, cities adopted their twentieth-century forms. Between 1909 and 1915, Los Angeles, a city of 300,000 people, passed a series of ordinances that gave rise to modern urban zoning. For the first time, the ordinances divided a city into three districts of specified use: a residential area, an industrial area, and an area open to residence and a limited list of industries. Other cities followed. Combining several features, the New York zoning law of 1916 became the model for the nation; within a decade, 591 cities copied it.

Zoning ordered city development, keeping skyscrapers out of factory districts, factories out of the suburbs. It also had powerful social repercussions. In the South, zoning became a tool to extend racial segregation; in northern cities, it acted against ethnic minorities. Jews in New York, Italians in Boston, Poles in Detroit, African Americans in Chicago—zoning laws held them all at arm's length. Like other migrants, African Americans often preferred to settle together, but zoning also helped put them there. By 1920, ten districts in Chicago were more than three-quarters black. In Los Angeles, Cleveland, Detroit, and Washington, D.C., most blacks lived in only two or three wards.

QUICK CHECK

What were some of the characteristics of the new urban culture?

Popular Pastimes

Thanks to changing work rules and mechanization, many Americans enjoyed more leisure time. The average workweek for manufacturing laborers fell from 60 hours in 1890 to 51 in 1920. By the early 1900s, white-collar workers might spend only 8 to 10 hours a day at work and a half day on weekends. Greater leisure time gave more people more opportunity for play and people flocked to places of entertainment. Baseball entrenched itself as the national pastime. Automobiles and streetcars carried growing numbers of fans to ballparks; attendance at major league games doubled between 1903 and 1920. Football also drew fans, although critics attacked the sport's violence and the use of "tramp athletes," nonstudents whom colleges paid to play. In 1905, the worst year, 18 players were killed and 150 seriously injured.

Luna Park at Coney Island

Alarmed, President Theodore Roosevelt—who had once said, "I am the father of three boys [and] if I thought any one of them would weigh a possible broken bone against the glory of being chosen to play on Harvard's football team I would disinherit him"—called a White House conference to clean up college sports. The conference founded the Intercollegiate Athletic Association, which in 1910 became the National Collegiate Athletic Association (NCAA).

Movie theaters opened everywhere. By 1910, there were 10,000 of them, drawing a weekly audience of 10 million people. Admission was usually 5 cents, and movies stressing laughter and pathos appealed to a mass market. In 1915, D. W. Griffith, a talented and creative director—as well as a racist—produced the first movie spectacular: *Birth of a Nation*. Griffith adopted new film techniques, including close-ups, fade-outs, and artistic camera angles.

Phonographs brought ready-made entertainment into the home. By 1901, phonograph and record companies included the Victor Talking Machine Company, the Edison Speaking Machine Company, and Columbia Records. Ornate mahogany Victrolas became standard fixtures in middle-class parlors. Early records were usually of vaudeville skits; orchestral recordings began in 1906. In 1919, 2.25 million phonographs were produced; two years later, more than 100 million records were sold.

As record sales grew, families sang less and listened more. Music became a business. In 1909, Congress enacted a copyright law that provided a two-cent royalty on each piece of music on phonograph records or piano rolls. The royalty, small as it was, offered welcome income to composers and publishers, and in 1914, composer Victor Herbert and others formed the American Society of Composers, Authors, and Publishers (ASCAP) to protect musical rights and royalties.

Vaudeville, increasingly popular after 1900, reached maturity around 1915. Drawing on the immigrant experience, it voiced the variety of city life and included skits, songs, comics, acrobats, and magicians. Dances and jokes showed an earthiness new to mass audiences. By 1914, stage runways extended into the crowd; women performers had bared their legs and were beginning to show glimpses of the midriff.

In songs like "St. Louis Blues" (1914), W. C. Handy took the black southern folk music of the blues to northern cities. Gertrude "Ma" Rainey, the daughter of minstrels, sang in black vaudeville for nearly thirty-five years. Performing in Chattanooga, Tennessee, about 1910, she came across a 12-year-old orphan, Bessie Smith, who became the "Empress of the Blues." Smith's voice was huge and sweeping. Recording for the Race division of Columbia Records, she made more than eighty records that together sold nearly ten million copies.

QUICK CHECK ✔

How did people use their new leisure time?

Another musical innovation came north from New Orleans. Charles (Buddy) Bolden, a cornetist; Ferdinand "Jelly Roll" Morton, a pianist; and a youngster named Louis Armstrong played an improvisational music that had no formal name. Reaching Chicago, it became "jas," then "jass," and finally "jazz." Jazz jumped, and jazz musicians relied on feeling and mood.

Experimentation in the Arts

Ashcan School
This school of early twentieth-century realist painters took as their subjects the slums and streets of the nation's cities and the lives of ordinary urban dwellers. They often celebrated life in the city but also advocated political and social reform.

"There is a state of unrest all over the world in art as in all other things," the director of New York's Metropolitan Museum said in 1908. "It is the same in literature, as in music, in painting, and in sculpture."

Isadora Duncan and Ruth St. Denis transformed the dance. Departing from traditional ballet steps, both women stressed improvisation, emotion, and the human form. The lofts and apartments of New York's Greenwich Village attracted artists, writers, and poets interested in experimentation and change. To these artists, the city was the focus of national life and the sign of a new culture. Robert Henri and the realist painters known to their critics as the **Ashcan School**—relished the city's excitement. They wanted, a friend said, "to paint truth and to paint it with strength and fearlessness and individuality."

To the realists, a painting carried into the future the look of life as it happened. Their paintings depicted street scenes, colorful crowds, and slum children

THE EXCITEMENT OF THE CITY George Bellows, *Cliff Dwellers* (1913). Bellows's work served as a commentary on contemporary urban life. (*Source: George Bellows, "Cliff Dwellers." Oil on canvas, 40³/₁₆" × 42¹/₁₆" (102.07 × 106.82 cm). Los Angeles County Museum of Art. Los Angeles County Fund. Photography © 2007 Museum.*)

What were the essential features in Bellows's depiction of the city?

swimming in the river. In paintings such as the *Cliff Dwellers*, George W. Bellows captured the color and excitement of the tenements; John Sloan, one of Henri's most talented students, painted the vitality of ordinary people and familiar scenes.

In 1913, a show at the New York Armory presented sixteen hundred modernist paintings, prints, and sculptures. The work of Picasso, Cézanne, Matisse, Brancusi, Van Gogh, and Gauguin dazed and dazzled American observers. Critics attacked the show as worthless and depraved; a Chicago official wanted it banned from the city because the "idea that people can gaze at this sort of thing without [it] hurting them is all bosh."

The postimpressionists changed the direction of twentieth-century art and influenced adventuresome American painters. John Marin, Max Weber, Georgia O'Keeffe, Arthur Dove, and other modernists experimented in ways foreign to Henri's realists. Defiantly avant-garde, they shook off convention and experimented with new forms. Using bold colors and abstract patterns, they worked to capture the energy of urban life.

There was also an extraordinary outburst of poetry. In 1912, Harriet Monroe started the magazine *Poetry* in Chicago, the hotbed of the new poetry; Ezra Pound and Vachel Lindsay, both daring experimenters with ideas and verse, published in the first issue. T. S. Eliot published the classic "Love Song of J. Alfred Prufrock" in *Poetry* in 1915. Others experimenting with new techniques in poetry included Robert Frost (*North of Boston,* 1914), Edgar Lee Masters (*Spoon River Anthology,* 1915), and Carl Sandburg (*Chicago Poems,* 1916). Sandburg's poem "Chicago" celebrated the vitality of the city.

QUICK CHECK

What were some of the important changes in the arts in the period?

Conclusion: A Ferment of Discovery and Reform

Manners and morals change slowly, and many Americans overlooked the importance of the first two decades of the twentieth century. Yet sweeping change was under way; anyone who doubted it could visit a gallery, see a film, listen to music, or read one of the new literary magazines. Garrets and galleries were filled with a breathtaking sense of change. "There was life in all these new things," Marsden Hartley, a modernist painter, recalled. "There was excitement, there was healthy revolt, investigation, discovery, and an utterly new world out of it all."

The ferment of progressivism in city, state, and nation reshaped the country. In a burst of reform, people built playgrounds, restructured taxes, regulated business, won the vote for women, shortened working hours, altered political systems, opened kindergartens, and improved factory safety. They tried to fulfill the national promise of dignity and liberty.

Marsden Hartley, it turned out, had voiced a mood that went well beyond painters and poets. Across society, people in many walks of life were experiencing a similar sense of excitement and discovery. Racism, repression, and labor conflict were present, to be sure, but there was also talk of hope, progress, and change. In politics, science, journalism, education, and a host of other fields, people believed for a time that they could make a difference, and in trying to do so, they became part of the progressive generation.

For a list of additional titles related to this chapter's topics, please see
www.pearsonamericanhistory.com.   MyHistoryLab

STUDY RESOURCES

KEY TERMS

muckrakers, p. 590

progressivism, p. 590

Niagara Movement, p. 600

National Association for the
Advancement of Colored
People (NAACP), p. 600

birds of passage, p. 601

Women's Trade Union League
(WTUL), p. 605

Industrial Workers of the
World (IWW), p. 605

Ashcan School, p. 610

CHAPTER REVIEW

HOW did industrialism change in the years after 1900?

As prosperity returned after the late 1890s, the American industrial system underwent important changes. Mass production, spurred by the spread of the moving assembly line, turned out more and more products for American and foreign consumers. New management methods arose to organize workers on the factory floor. Jobs became both routine and at the same time more dangerous. Trusts grew. *(p. 591)*

HOW were women, children, immigrants, and African Americans affected by mass production?

While life improved for many people in the post-1900 industrial society, many others faced challenges: women and children in the workforce, and laborers in their efforts to organize. Between 1901 and 1920, some 14.8 million immigrants, an extraordinary number, entered the country and began the difficult process of adjusting to life in their new home. All of these people faced difficult challenges due to low wages, dangerous working conditions, and the steady demands of the factory system. *(p. 596)*

WHAT conditions brought about the large number of strikes in the period?

Low wages, sped-up assembly lines, and dangerous conditions in the workplace brought about numerous attempts to organize workers for their own defense. The Women's Trade Union League had many successes. The International Workers of the World, a radical union, wanted to place workers in control. In the end, Samuel Gompers and the American Federation of Labor won the allegiance of the greatest number of workers. *(p. 604)*

WHAT happened to art and culture in these years so filled with change?

In the dozen years after 1900, American culture changed in important ways. Cities grew on a major scale, taking on their modern form. Suburbs flourished. Sports became increasingly popular, reflecting people's increased leisure time. Experimentation occurred in literature, poetry, painting, and the arts. *(p. 607)*

MAKING CONNECTIONS

1. How did the changing nature of industrialism after the 1890s influence the beginnings of a Progressive Era?

2. In what specific ways did workers, African Americans, and immigrants respond to the changing nature of industrial society and in the process help bring about the Progressive Era?

3. How did workers organize to try to improve their lot in the cities and factories of the advancing industrial society?

4. How did changes in popular culture mold attitudes in the new Progressive Era?

PRACTICE QUIZ

1. The manufacturer _____ became a pioneer in the automobile industry.
   - **a.** Henry Ford
   - **b.** Frederick Taylor
   - **c.** Mary Lease
   - **d.** Jim Crow

2. The _____ Movement rejected the racial accommodation of Booker Washington.
   - **a.** Harlem
   - **b.** Renaissance
   - **c.** Niagara
   - **d.** Resistance

3. Approximately _____ million immigrants entered the country between 1901 and 1920.
   - **a.** 36
   - **b.** 30
   - **c.** 25
   - **d.** 14

4. The _____ League evolved into one of the most important unions of the era.
   - **a.** Women's Trade Union
   - **b.** Women's Immigrant
   - **c.** Women Working for America
   - **d.** Women's Progressive Alliance

5. Writers who made a practice of exposing corruption in the late 1800s were known as
   - **a.** Prohibitionists
   - **b.** Muckrakers
   - **c.** Evolutionists
   - **d.** Romantics

6. All people regardless of race, gender, or ethnicity were welcome in the
   - **a.** Knights of Labor
   - **b.** American Federation of Labor
   - **c.** Socialist Party
   - **d.** Industrial Workers of the World

7. In 1920, the median age of the population was *only*
   - **a.** 35
   - **b.** 30
   - **c.** 25
   - **d.** 18

8. All of the following describe the Chinese American experience in the United States *except*
   - **a.** The number of Chinese immigrants shrank since 1882.
   - **b.** An equal number of Chinese men and women lived in the United States.
   - **c.** United States officials detained Chinese longer than European immigrants.
   - **d.** Most Chinese did not intend to remain in the United States.

9. Which of the following *does not* describe the Japanese American experience?
   - **a.** Lesser numbers of Japanese than Chinese immigrants arrived during the 1800s.
   - **b.** The Japanese established communities along the Pacific Coast.
   - **c.** The number of Japanese immigrants grew over time in the early 1900s.
   - **d.** By 1920 over 200,000 Japanese lived in California alone.

10. Which of the following *does not* describe the early record industry?
    - **a.** Families listened less and sang more as records became more prominent.
    - **b.** Phonographs became standard in American homes after 1901.
    - **c.** Early records presented vaudeville skits.
    - **d.** Orchestral records began in 1906.

Find more practice at
www.myhistorylab.com

SAMPLE ESSAY QUESTIONS

1. Describe the new urban culture of the early 1900s.

2. Discuss the key factors behind workplace conflicts during the early 1900s.

From Roosevelt to Wilson in the Age of Progressivism

1900–1920

TR'S ENORMOUS ENERGY Theodore Roosevelt leading his Rough Riders at the storming of San Juan Hill, Cuba on July 1, 1898.

What were Roosevelt's main achievements as president?

The Republicans Split

On a sunny spring morning in 1909, Theodore Roosevelt, wearing the greatcoat of a colonel of the Rough Riders, left New York for a safari in Africa. An ex-president at the age of 50, he had turned over the White House to his chosen successor, William Howard Taft, and was now off for "the joy of wandering through lonely lands, the joy of hunting the mighty and terrible lords" of Africa, "where death broods in the dark and silent depths."

KEY EVENTS

Some of Roosevelt's enemies hoped he would not return. "I trust some lion will do its duty," Wall Street magnate J. P. Morgan said. Always prepared, Roosevelt took nine extra pairs of eyeglasses, and, just in case, several expert hunters accompanied him. When the nearsighted Roosevelt took aim, three others aimed at the same moment. "Mr. Roosevelt had a fairly good idea of the general direction," the safari leader said, "but we couldn't take chances with the life of a former president."

It was all good fun, and afterward Roosevelt set off on a tour of Europe. He attended the funeral of the king of England with the crowned heads of Europe, dined with the king and queen of Italy—an experience he likened to "a Jewish wedding on the East Side of New York"—and happily spent five hours reviewing troops of the German empire. Less happily, he followed events back home where, in the judgment of many friends, Taft was not working out as president. Gifford Pinchot, Roosevelt's close companion in the conservation movement, came to Italy to complain personally about Taft, and at almost every stop there were letters waiting for him from other disappointed Republicans.

For his part, Taft was puzzled by it all. Honest and warm-hearted, he had intended to continue Roosevelt's policies, even writing Roosevelt that he would "see to it that your judgment in selecting me as your successor and bringing about that succession shall be vindicated." But events turned out differently. The conservative and progressive wings of the Republican party split, and Taft often sided with the conservatives. Among progressive Republicans, Taft's troubles stirred talk of a Roosevelt "back from Elba" movement, akin to Napoleon's return from exile.

Thousands gathered to greet Roosevelt on his return from Europe. He sailed into New York harbor on June 18, 1910, to the sound of naval guns and loud cheers. In characteristic fashion, he had helped make the arrangements: "If there is to be a great crowd, do arrange it so that the whole crowd has a chance to see me and that there is as little disappointment as possible." Greeting Pinchot, one of Taft's leading opponents, with a hearty "Hello, Gifford," Roosevelt slipped away to his home in Oyster Bay, New York, where other friends awaited him.

He carried with him a touching letter from Taft, received just before he left Europe. "I have had a hard time—I do not know that I have had harder luck than other Presidents, but I do know that thus far I have succeeded far less than have others. I have been conscientiously trying to carry out your policies but my method of doing so has not worked smoothly." Taft invited Teddy to spend a night or two at the White House, but Roosevelt declined, saying that ex-presidents should not visit Washington. Relations between the two friends cooled.

A year later, there was no longer thought of friendship, only a desperate fight between Taft and Roosevelt for the Republican presidential nomination. Taft won the nomination, but, angry and ambitious, Roosevelt bolted and helped form a new party, the **Progressive (or "Bull Moose") party,** to unseat Taft and capture the White House. With Taft, Roosevelt, Woodrow Wilson (the Democratic party's candidate), and Socialist party candidate Eugene V. Debs all in the race, the election of 1912 became one of the most exciting in American history.

It was also one of the most important. People were worried about the social and economic effects of urban-industrial growth. The election of 1912 provided a forum for those worries, and, to a degree unusual in American politics, it pitted deeply opposed candidates against one another and outlined differing views of the nation's future. In the spirited battle between Roosevelt and Wilson, it also brought to the forefront some of the currents of progressive reform.

Those currents built on a number of important developments, including the rise of a new professional class, reform movements designed to cure problems in the cities and states, and the activist, achievement-oriented administrations of Roosevelt and Wilson. Together they produced the age of progressivism.

Progressive (or "Bull Moose") party

This political party was formed by Theodore Roosevelt in an attempt to advance progressive ideas and unseat President William Howard Taft in the election of 1912. After Taft won the Republican party's nomination, Roosevelt ran on the Progressive party ticket.

The Spirit of Progressivism

In one way or another, progressivism touched all aspects of society. Politically, it fostered a reform movement that sought cures for the problems of city, state, and nation. Intellectually, it drew on the expertise of the new social sciences and reflected a shift from older absolutes such as religion to newer schools of thought that emphasized relativism and the role of the environment in human development. Culturally, it inspired fresh modes of expression in dance, film, painting, literature, and architecture. Touching individuals in different ways, progressivism became a set of attitudes as well as a definable movement.

Though broad and diverse, progressivism as a whole had a half dozen characteristics that gave it definition. First, the progressives acted out of concern about

WHAT were the six major characteristics of progressivism?

Herbert Croly, from *Progressive Democracy* (1914)

the effects of industrialization and the conditions of industrial life. While their viewpoints varied, they did not, as a rule, set out to harm big business, but instead sought to humanize and regulate it.

In pursuing these objectives, the progressives displayed a second characteristic: a fundamental optimism about human nature, the possibilities of progress, and the capacity of people to recognize problems and take action to solve them. Progressives believed they could "investigate, educate, and legislate"—learn about a problem, inform people about it, and, with the help of an informed public, find and enforce a solution.

Third, more than many earlier reformers, the progressives were willing to intervene in people's lives, confident that it was their right to do so. They knew best, some of them thought, and as a result, there was an element of coercion in a number of their ideas. Fourth, while progressives preferred if possible to use voluntary means to achieve reform, they tended to turn more and more to the authority of the state and government at all levels in order to put into effect the reforms they wanted.

As a fifth characteristic, many progressives drew on a combination of evangelical Protestantism (which gave them the desire—and, they thought, the duty—to purge the world of sins such as prostitution and drunkenness) and the natural and social sciences (whose theories made them confident that they could understand and control the environment in which people lived). Progressives tended to view the environment as a key to reform, thinking—in the way some economists, sociologists, and other social scientists were suggesting—that if they could change the environment, they could change the individual.

Finally, progressivism was distinctive because it touched virtually the whole nation. Not everyone, of course, was a progressive, and there were many who opposed or ignored the ideas of the movement. There were also those who were untouched by progressive reforms and those whom the movement overlooked. But in one way or another, a remarkable number of people were caught up in it, giving progressivism a national reach and a mass base.

That was one of the features, in fact, that set it off from populism, which had grown mostly in the rural South and West. Progressivism drew support from across society. "The thing that constantly amazed me," said William Allen White, a leading progressive journalist, "was how many people were with us." Progressivism appealed to the expanding middle class, prosperous farmers, and skilled laborers; it also attracted significant support in the business community.

The progressives believed in progress and disliked waste. No single issue or concern united them all. Some progressives wanted to clean up city governments, others to clean up city streets. Some wanted to purify politics or control corporate abuses, others to eradicate poverty or prostitution. Some demanded social justice in the form of women's rights, child labor laws, temperance, and factory safety. They were Democrats, Republicans, Socialists, and independents.

Andrew Carnegie, *Wealth and Its Uses* (1907)

Progressives believed in a better world and in the ability of people to achieve it. They paid to people, as a friend said of social reformer Florence Kelley, "the high compliment of believing that, once they knew the truth, they would act upon it." Progress depended on knowledge. The progressives stressed individual morality and collective action, the scientific method, and the value of expert opinion. Like contemporary business leaders, they valued system, planning, management, and predictability. They wanted not only reform but efficiency.

The Rise of the Professions

Progressivism fed on an organizational impulse that encouraged people to join forces, share information, and solve problems. Between 1890 and 1920, a host of national societies and associations took shape—nearly four hundred of them in just three decades. Groups such as the National Child Labor Committee, which lobbied for legislation to regulate the employment and working conditions of children, were formed to attack specific issues. Other groups reflected one of the most significant developments in American society at the turn of the century—the rise of the professions.

Growing rapidly in these years, the professions—law, medicine, religion, business, teaching, and social work—were the source of much of the leadership of the progressive movement. The professions attracted young, educated men and women, who in turn were part of a larger trend: a dramatic increase in the number of individuals working in administrative and professional jobs. In businesses, these people were managers, architects, technicians, and accountants. In city governments, they were experts in everything from education to sanitation. They organized and ran the urban-industrial society.

These professionals formed part of a new middle class whose members did not derive their status from birth or inherited wealth, as had many members of the older middle class. Instead, they moved ahead through education and personal accomplishment and worked to become doctors, lawyers, ministers, and teachers. Proud of their skills, they were ambitious and self-confident, and they thought of themselves as experts who could use their knowledge for the benefit of society.

As a way of asserting their status, they formed professional societies to look after their interests and govern entry into their professions. Just a few years before, for example, a doctor had become a doctor simply by stocking up on patent medicines and hanging out a sign. Now doctors began to insist they were part of a medical profession, and they wanted to set educational requirements and minimum standards for practice. In 1901, they reorganized the American Medical Association (AMA) and made it into a modern national professional society.

Other groups and professions showed the same pattern. Lawyers formed bar associations, created examining boards, and lobbied for regulations restricting entry into the profession. Teachers organized the National Education Association (1905) and pressed for teacher certification and compulsory education laws. Social workers formed the National Federation of Settlements (1911); business leaders created the National Association of Manufacturers (1895) and the U.S. Chamber of Commerce (1912); and farmers joined the National Farm Bureau Federation to spread information about farming and to try to improve their lot.

QUICK CHECK ✓
What were the causes and results of the rise of the professions?

The Social-Justice Movement

Progressivism began in the cities during the 1890s. It first took form around settlement workers and others interested in freeing individuals from the crushing impact of cities and factories.

Ministers, intellectuals, social workers, and lawyers joined in a **social-justice movement** that focused national attention on the need for tenement house laws, more stringent child labor legislation, and better working conditions for women. They brought pressure on municipal agencies for more and better parks, playgrounds, day nurseries, schools, and community services. Blending private and public action, settlement leaders turned increasingly to government aid.

Social-justice reformers were more interested in social cures than individual charity. Unlike earlier reformers, they saw problems as endless and interrelated; individuals became part of a city's larger patterns. With that insight, social-service casework shifted from a focus on an individual's well-being to a scientific analysis of neighborhoods, occupations, and classes.

Social-justice reformers, banding together to work for change, formed the National Conference of Charities and Corrections, which in 1915 became the National Conference of Social Work. Controlled by social workers, the conference reflected the growing professionalization of reform. Through it, social workers discovered each other's efforts, shared methodology, and tried to establish themselves as a separate field within the social sciences. Once content with informal training sessions in a settlement house living room, they now founded complete professional schools at Chicago, Harvard, and other universities. After 1909, they had their own professional magazine, the *Survey,* and instead of piecemeal reforms, they aimed at a comprehensive program of minimum wages, maximum hours, workers' compensation, and widows' pensions.

QUICK CHECK ✔

What were the aims of the social-justice movement?

social-justice movement

During the 1890s and after, this important movement attracted followers who sought to free people from the often devastating impact of urban life. It focused on the need for tenement house laws, more stringent child labor regulations, and better working conditions for women. Social-justice reformers also brought pressure on municipal agencies for better community services and facilities.

Report of the Vice Commission (1915)

The Purity Crusade

Working in city neighborhoods, social-justice reformers were often struck by the degree to which alcohol affected the lives of the people they were trying to help. Workers drank away their wages; some men spent more time at the saloon than at home. Drunkenness caused violence, and it angered employers who did not want intoxicated workers on the job. In countless ways, alcohol wasted human resources, the reformers believed, and along with business leaders, ministers, and others, they launched a crusade to remove the evils of drink from American life.

At the head of the crusade was the Women's Christian Temperance Union (WCTU), which had continued to grow since it was founded in the 1870s. By 1911, the WCTU had nearly a quarter of a million members; it was the largest organization of women in American history to that time. In 1893, it was joined by the Anti-Saloon League, and together the groups pressed to abolish alcohol and the places where it was consumed. By 1916, they had succeeded in nineteen states, but as drinking continued elsewhere, they pushed for a nationwide law. In the midst of the moral fervor of World War I, they succeeded, and the Eighteenth Amendment to the Constitution, prohibiting the manufacture, sale, and transportation of intoxicating liquors, took effect in January 1920.

The amendment encountered troubles later in the 1920s as the social atmosphere changed, but at the time it passed, progressives thought Prohibition was a major step toward eliminating social instability and moral wrong. In a similar fashion, some progressive reformers also worked to get rid of prostitution, convinced that poverty and ignorance drove women to the trade. By 1915,

PROGRESSIVISM IN ACTION   An Infant Welfare Society nurse treats the baby of an immigrant family in Chicago. A host of medical discoveries and improvements in the quality of medical education fostered an interest in public health work among the social-justice reformers.

What do the details in this photograph say about the life of this family?

QUICK CHECK ✓

What motivated people who opposed alcohol, and which measures did they achieve?

nearly every state had banned brothels, and in 1910, Congress passed the Mann Act, which prohibited the interstate transportation of women for immoral purposes. Like the campaign against liquor, the campaign against prostitution reflected the era's desire to purify and elevate, often through the instrument of government action.

Woman Suffrage, Women's Rights

Women played a large role in the social-justice movement. Feminists were particularly active, especially in the political sphere, between 1890 and 1914—feminists were more active then, in fact, than at any other time until the 1960s. Some working-class women pushed for higher wages and better working conditions. College-educated women—five thousand a year graduated after 1900—took up careers in the professions, from which some of them supported reform. From 1890 to 1910, the work of a number of national women's organizations, including the National

National American Woman Suffrage Association, Mother's Day Letter

Jane Addams, "Ballots Necessary for Women" (1906)

National American Woman Suffrage Association

Founded by Susan B. Anthony in 1890, this organization worked to secure women the right to vote. While some suffragists urged militant action, it stressed careful organization and peaceful lobbying. By 1920 it had nearly two million members.

Council of Jewish Women, the National Congress of Mothers, and the Women's Trade Union League, furthered the aims of the progressive movement.

Excluded from most of these organizations, African American women formed their own groups. The National Association of Colored Women was founded in 1895, fourteen years before the better known male-oriented National Association for the Advancement of Colored People (NAACP). Aimed at social welfare, the women's organization was the first African American social-service agency in the country.

From 200,000 members in 1900, the General Federation of Women's Clubs grew to more than 1 million by 1912. The clubs met, as they had before, for coffee and literary conversation, but they also began to look closely at conditions around them.

Forming an Industrial Section and a Committee on Legislation for Women and Children, the federation supported reforms to safeguard child and women workers, improve schools, ensure pure food, and beautify the community. Reluctant at first, the federation finally lent support in 1914 to woman suffrage, a cause that dated back to the first women's rights convention in Seneca Falls, New York, in 1848. Divided over tactics since the Civil War, the suffrage movement suffered from disunity, male opposition, indecision over whether to seek action at the state or at the national level, resistance from the Catholic Church, and opposition from liquor interests, who linked the cause to Prohibition.

Because politics was an avenue for reform, growing numbers of women activists became involved in the suffrage movement. After years of disagreement, the two major suffrage organizations, the National Woman Suffrage Association and the American Woman Suffrage Association, merged in 1890 to form the National American Woman Suffrage Association. The merger opened a new phase of the suffrage movement, characterized by unity and a tightly controlled national organization.

In 1900, Carrie Chapman Catt, a superb organizer, became president of the **National American Woman Suffrage Association,** which had been founded by Susan B. Anthony in 1890 to get women the vote. By 1920 it had nearly two million members. Catt and Anna Howard Shaw, who became the association's head in 1904, believed in organization and peaceful lobbying to win the vote. Alice Paul and Lucy Burns, founders of the Congressional Union, were more militant; they interrupted public meetings, focused on Congress rather than the states, and in 1917 picketed the White House.

Significantly, Catt, Paul, and others made a major change in the argument for woman suffrage. When the campaign began in the nineteenth century,

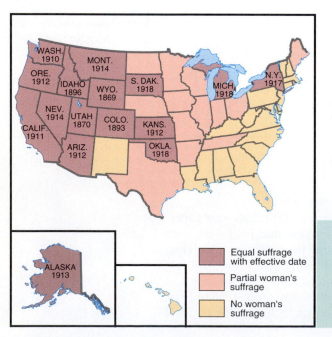

WASH. 1910
ORE. 1912
IDAHO 1896
MONT. 1914
NEV. 1914
UTAH 1870
WYO. 1869
S. DAK. 1918
COLO. 1893
CALIF. 1911
ARIZ. 1912
KANS. 1912
OKLA. 1918
MICH. 1918
N.Y. 1917

ALASKA 1913

■ Equal suffrage with effective date
■ Partial woman's suffrage
■ No woman's suffrage

WOMAN SUFFRAGE BEFORE 1920 State-by-state gains in woman suffrage were limited to the Far West and were agonizingly slow in the early years of the twentieth century.

Why did woman suffrage first take place in the West before 1920?

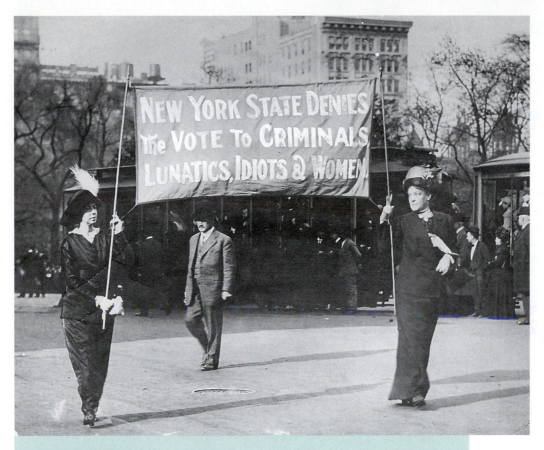

VOTES FOR WOMEN   Woman suffrage was a key element in the social-justice movement. Without the right to vote, women working actively for reform had little real power to influence elected officials to support their endeavors.

What were women's main arguments for their right to vote?

suffragists had claimed the vote as a natural right, owed to women as much as men. Now, they stressed a pragmatic argument: Since women were more sensitive to moral issues than men, they would use their votes to help create a better society. They would support temperance, clean government, laws to protect workers, and other reforms. This argument attracted many progressives who believed the women's vote would purify politics. In 1918, the House passed a constitutional amendment stating simply that the right to vote shall not be denied "on account of sex." The Senate and enough states followed, and, after three generations of suffragist efforts, the Nineteenth Amendment took effect in 1920.

QUICK CHECK
How did women go about getting the vote?

A Ferment of Ideas: Challenging the Status Quo

A dramatic shift in ideas became one of the most important forces behind progressive reform. Most of the ideas focused on the role of the environment in shaping human behavior. Progressive reformers accepted society's growing complexity, called for factual treatment of piecemeal problems, allowed room for new theories, and, above all, rejected age-encrusted divine or natural "laws" in favor of thoughts and actions that worked.

A new doctrine called **pragmatism,** based on dealing with things practically to see if if they worked, emerged in this ferment of ideas. It came from William James, a brilliant Harvard psychologist who became the key figure in American thought from the 1890s to World War I. A warm, tolerant person, James was impatient with theories that regarded truth as abstract. Truth, he believed, should work for the individual, and it worked best not in abstraction, but in action.

People, James thought, not only were shaped by their environment; they shaped it. In *Pragmatism* (1907), he praised "tough-minded" individuals who could live effectively in a world with no easy answers. The tough-minded accepted change; they knew how to pick manageable problems, gather facts, discard ideas that did not work, and act on those that did. Ideas that worked became truth.

The most influential educator of the Progressive Era, John Dewey, applied pragmatism to educational reform. A friend and disciple of William James, he argued that thought evolves in relation to the environment and that education is directly related to experience. In 1896, Dewey founded a separate School of Pedagogy at the University of Chicago, with a laboratory in which educational theory based on the newer philosophical and psychological studies could be tested and practiced.

Dewey introduced an educational revolution that stressed children's needs and capabilities. He opposed memorization, rote learning, and dogmatic, authoritarian teaching methods; he emphasized personal growth, free inquiry, and creativity.

Rejecting the older view of the law as universal and unchanging, lawyers and legal theorists instead viewed it as a reflection of the environment—an instrument for social change. Law reflected the environment that shaped it. A movement grew among judges for "sociological jurisprudence" that related the law to social reform.

In Denver, Colorado, after Judge Ben Lindsey sentenced a boy to reform school for stealing coal, the boy's mother rushed forward and, grief-stricken, beat her head against the wall. Lindsey investigated the case and found that the father was a smelting worker dying of lead poisoning; the family needed coal for heat. From such experiences, Lindsey concluded that children were not born with a genetic tendency to crime; they were made good or bad by the environment in which they grew. Lindsey "sentenced" youthful offenders to education and good care. He worked for playgrounds, slum clearance, public baths, and technical schools. Known as the "Kids' Judge," he attracted visitors from as far away as Japan, who wanted to study and copy his methods.

Socialism, a reformist political philosophy, grew dramatically before World War I. Eugene V. Debs, president of the American Railway Union, in 1896 formed the Social Democratic party. Gentle and reflective, not at all the popular image of the wild-eyed radical, Debs was thrust into prominence by the Pullman strike. In 1901, he organized the Socialist party of America. Neither Debs nor the party ever developed a cohesive platform, nor was Debs an effective organizer. But he was eloquent, passionate, and visionary.

Although torn by factions, the Socialist party doubled in membership between 1904 and 1908, then tripled in the four years after that. Running for president, Debs garnered 100,000 votes in 1900; 400,000 in 1904; and 900,000 in 1912, the party's peak year.

pragmatism

A doctrine that emerged in the early twentieth century, built largely on the ideas of Harvard psychologist and philosopher William James. Pragmatists were impatient with theories that held truth to be abstract; they believed that truth should work for the individual. They also believed that people were not only shaped by their environment but also helped to shape it. Ideas that worked, according to pragmatists, became truth.

QUICK CHECK ✔

In what ways did ideas change in the years after 1900 and open up new avenues to reform?

Reform in the Cities and States

Progressive reformers realized government could be a crucial agent in accomplishing their goals. They wanted to curb the influence of "special interests" and, through such measures of political reform as the direct primary and the direct election of senators, make government follow the public will. Once it did, they welcomed government action at whatever level was appropriate.

As a result of this thinking, the use of federal power increased, as did the power and prestige of the presidency. Progressives not only lobbied for government-sponsored reform but also worked actively in their home neighborhoods, cities, and states; much of the significant change occurred in local settings, outside the national limelight. Most important, the progressives believed in the ability of experts to solve problems. At every level—local, state, and federal—thousands of commissions and agencies took form. Staffed by trained experts, they oversaw a multitude of matters ranging from railroad rates to public health.

WHAT methods did progressive reformers use to attack problems in the cities and states?

Interest Groups and the Decline of Popular Politics

Placing government in the hands of experts was one way to get it out of the hands of politicians and political parties. The direct primary, which allowed voters rather than parties to choose candidates for office, was another way. These initiatives and others like them were part of a fundamental change in the way Americans viewed their political system.

As one sign of the change, fewer and fewer people were going to the polls. Voter turnout dropped dramatically after 1900, when the intense partisanship of the decades after the Civil War gave way to media-oriented political campaigns based largely on the personalities of the candidates. From 1876 to 1900, the average turnout in presidential elections was 77 percent. From 1900 to 1916, it was 65 percent, and in the 1920s, it dropped to 52 percent, close to the average today. Turnout was lowest among young people, immigrants, the poor, and, ironically, the newly enfranchised women.

There were numerous causes for the falloff, but among the most important was the fact that people had found another way to achieve some of the objectives they had once assigned to political parties. They had found the "interest group," a means of action that assumed importance in this era and became a major feature of politics ever after. Professional societies, trade associations, labor organizations, farm lobbies, and scores of other interest groups worked outside the party system to pressure government for things their members wanted. Social workers, women's clubs, reform groups, and others learned to apply pressure in similar ways, and the result was much significant legislation of the Progressive Era.

QUICK CHECK ✓

What brought about the dramatic drop in voter turnout in these years?

Reform in the Cities

During the early years of the twentieth century, urban reform movements, many of them born in the depression of the 1890s, spread across the nation. In 1894, the National Municipal League was organized, and it became the forum for debate over civic reform, changes in the tax laws, and municipal ownership of public

VOTER PARTICIPATION IN PRESIDENTIAL ELECTIONS, 1876–1920

Percentage

utilities. Within a few years, nearly every city had a variety of clubs and organizations directed at improving the quality of city life.

In the 1880s, reformers would call an evening conference, pass resolutions, and then go home; after 1900, they formed associations, adopted long-range policies, and hired a staff to achieve them. In the mid-1890s, only Chicago had an urban reform league with a full-time paid executive; within a decade, there were such leagues in every major city.

In city after city, reformers reordered municipal government. Tightening controls on corporate activities, they broadened the scope of utility regulation and restricted city franchises. They updated tax assessments, often skewed in favor of corporations, and tried to clean up the electoral machinery. Devoted to efficiency, they developed a trained civil service to oversee planning and operations. The generation of the 1880s also had believed in civil service, but the goal then was mostly negative: to get spoilsmen out and "good" people in. Now the goal was efficiency and, above all, results.

In constructing their model governments, urban reformers often turned to recent advances in business management and organization. They stressed continuity and expertise, a system in which professional experts staffed a government overseen by elected officials. At the top, the elected leader surveyed the breadth of city, state, or national affairs and defined directions. Below, a corps of experts—trained in the various disciplines of the new society—funneled the definition into specific scientifically based policies.

Reformers created a growing number of regulatory commissions and municipal departments. They hired engineers to oversee utility and water systems, physicians and nurses to improve municipal health, and city planners to oversee park and highway development.

QUICK CHECK ✓

What methods did reformers use to improve life in their cities?

Action in the States

Reformers soon discovered, however, that many problems lay beyond a city's boundaries, and they turned for action to the state governments. From the 1890s to 1920, reformers worked to stiffen state laws regulating the labor of women and children, to create and strengthen commissions to regulate railroads and utilities, to impose corporate and inheritance taxes, to improve mental and penal institutions, and to allocate more funds for state universities, which were viewed as the training ground for the experts and educated citizenry needed for the new society.

To regulate business, virtually every state created regulatory commissions empowered to examine corporate books and hold public hearings. Building on earlier experience, state commissions after 1900 were given new power to initiate actions, rather than await complaints, and in some cases to set maximum prices and rates. Dictating company practices, they pioneered regulatory methods later adopted in federal legislation of 1906 and 1910.

Historians have long praised the regulation movement, but the commissions did not always act wisely or even in the public interest. Elective commissions often produced commissioners who had little knowledge of corporate affairs. In addition, to win election, some promised specific rates or reforms, obligations that might bias the commission's investigative functions. Appointive commissions sometimes fared better, but they too had to oversee extraordinarily complex businesses such as the railroads.

To the progressives, commissions offered a way to end the corrupt alliance between business and politics. There was another way, too, and that was to "democratize" government by reducing the power of politicians and increasing the influence of the electorate. To do that, progressives backed three measures to make officeholders responsive to popular will: the initiative, which allowed voters to propose new laws; the refrendum, which allowed them to accept or reject a law at the ballot box; and the recall, which gave them a way to remove an elected official from office.

Oregon adopted the initiative and referendum in 1902; by 1912, twelve states had them. That year Congress added the Seventeenth Amendment to the Constitution to provide for the direct election of U.S. senators. By 1916, all but three states had direct primaries, which allowed the people, rather than nominating conventions, to choose candidates for office.

Robert M. La Follette of Wisconsin became the most famous reform governor. He won the office in 1901 and in the following six years put together the

LAFOLLETTE, A POPULAR PROGRESSIVE   The most famous of the reform leaders in the states was Wisconsin's Robert M. "Fighting Bob" La Follette. He was unanimously nominated for governor in 1900 and won the election with the largest plurality of votes ever received by a candidate for that office. He is shown here on his special campaign train during a stop at La Valle, Wisconsin, in October 1900.

What were La Follette's main accomplishments?

"Wisconsin Idea," one of the most important reform programs in the history of state government. He established an industrial commission, the first in the country, to regulate factory safety and sanitation. He improved education, workers' compensation, public utility controls, and resource conservation. He lowered railroad rates and raised railroad taxes. Under La Follette's prodding, Wisconsin became the first state to adopt a direct primary for all political nominations. It also became the first to adopt a state income tax. Theodore Roosevelt called La Follette's Wisconsin "the laboratory of democracy," and the Wisconsin Idea soon spread to many other states.

After 1905, the progressives looked more and more to Washington. For one thing, Teddy Roosevelt was there, with his zest for publicity and his alluring grin. But progressives also had a growing sense that many concerns—corporations and conservation, factory safety and child labor—crossed state lines. Federal action seemed desirable; specific reforms fit into a larger plan perhaps best seen from the nation's center. Within a few years, La Follette and Hiram Johnson became senators, and while reform went on back home, the focus of progressivism shifted to Washington.

QUICK CHECK

How did the states respond to the new industrial society?

The Republican Roosevelt

HOW would you describe the personality and programs of Theodore Roosevelt?

When President William McKinley died of gunshot wounds in September 1901, Vice President Theodore Roosevelt succeeded him in the White House. The new president initially vowed to carry on McKinley's policies. He continued some, developed others of his own, and in the end brought to them all the particular exuberance of his own personality.

At age 42, Roosevelt was then the youngest president in American history. In contrast to the dignified McKinley, he was open, aggressive, and high-spirited. At his desk by 8:30 every morning, he worked through the day, usually with visitors for breakfast, lunch, and dinner. Politicians, labor leaders, industrialists, poets, artists, and writers paraded through the White House.

If McKinley cut down on presidential isolation, Roosevelt virtually ended it. The presidency, he thought, was the "bully pulpit," a forum of ideas and leadership for the nation. The president was "a steward of the people bound actively and affirmatively to do all he could for the people." Self-confident, Roosevelt enlisted talented associates, including Elihu Root, secretary of war and later secretary of state; William Howard Taft, secretary of war; Gifford Pinchot, the nation's chief forester and leading conservationist; and Oliver Wendell Holmes, Jr., whom he named to the Supreme Court.

In 1901, Roosevelt invited Booker T. Washington, the prominent African American educator, to dinner at the White House. Many southerners protested— "a crime equal to treason," a newspaper said—and they protested again when Roosevelt appointed several African Americans to important federal offices in South Carolina and Mississippi. At first, Roosevelt considered building a biracial "black-and-tan" southern Republican party, thinking it would foster racial progress and his own renomination in 1904.

But Roosevelt soon retreated. In some areas of the South, he supported "lily-white" Republican organizations, and his policies often reflected his own belief in African American inferiority. He said nothing when a race riot broke out in Atlanta in 1906, although twelve persons died. He joined others in blaming African American soldiers stationed near Brownsville, Texas, after a night of violence there in August 1906. Acting quickly and on little evidence, he discharged "without honor" three companies of African American troops. Six of the soldiers who were discharged held the Congressional Medal of Honor.

Busting the Trusts

"There is a widespread conviction in the minds of the American people that the great corporations known as trusts are in certain of their features and tendencies hurtful to the general welfare," Roosevelt reported to Congress in 1901. Like most people, however, the president wavered on the trusts. Large-scale production and industrial growth, he believed, were natural and beneficial; they needed only to be controlled. Still he distrusted the trusts' impact on local enterprise and individual opportunity. Distinguishing between "good" and "bad" trusts, he pledged to protect the former while controlling the latter.

In 1903, Roosevelt asked Congress to create a Department of Commerce and Labor, with a Bureau of Corporations empowered to investigate corporations engaged in interstate commerce. Congress balked; Roosevelt called in reporters and, in an off-the-record interview, charged that John D. Rockefeller had organized the opposition to the measure. The press spread the word, and in the outcry that followed, the proposal passed easily in a matter of weeks. Roosevelt was delighted. With the new Bureau of Corporations publicizing its findings, he thought, the glare of publicity would eliminate most corporate abuses.

Roosevelt also undertook direct legal action. On February 18, 1902, he instructed the Justice Department to bring suit against the Northern Securities Company for violation of the Sherman Antitrust Act. It was a shrewd move. A mammoth holding company, Northern Securities controlled the massive rail networks of the Northern Pacific, Great Northern, and Chicago, Burlington & Quincy railroads.

TRUST-BUSTER A cartoon illustrating Theodore Roosevelt's promise to break up only those "bad trusts" that were hurtful to the general welfare. Despite his reputation as a "trustbuster," Roosevelt dissolved relatively few trusts.

What does this cartoon suggest about Roosevelt's views of the powers of his office?

In 1904, the Supreme Court, in a 5 to 4 decision, upheld the suit against Northern Securities and ordered the company dissolved. Roosevelt was jubilant, and he followed up the victory with several other antitrust suits. In 1902, he had moved against the beef trust, an action applauded by western farmers and urban consumers alike. After a lull, he initiated suits in 1906 and 1907 against the American Tobacco Company, the Du Pont Corporation, the New Haven Railroad, and Standard Oil.

But Roosevelt's policies were not always clear, nor his actions always consistent. He asked for (and received) business support in his bid for reelection in 1904. Large donations came in from industrial leaders, and J. P. Morgan himself later testified that he gave $150,000 to Roosevelt's campaign. In 1907, acting in part to avert a threatened financial panic, the president permitted Morgan's U.S. Steel to absorb the Tennessee Coal and Iron Company, an important competitor.

Roosevelt, in truth, was not a trustbuster, although he was frequently called that. William Howard Taft, his successor in the White House, initiated forty-three antitrust indictments in four years—nearly twice as many as the twenty-five Roosevelt initiated in the seven years of his presidency. Instead, Roosevelt used antitrust threats to keep businesses within bounds. Regulation, he believed, was a better way to control large-scale enterprise.

QUICK CHECK ✓

What were Theodore Roosevelt's views on the trusts?

"Square Deal" in the Coalfields

TR as "Jack the Giant Killer"—*Puck* Cartoon

A few months after announcing the Northern Securities suit, Roosevelt intervened in a major labor dispute involving the anthracite coal miners of northeastern Pennsylvania. Led by John Mitchell, a moderate labor leader, the United Mine Workers demanded wage increases, an eight-hour workday, and company recognition of the union. The coal companies refused, and in May 1902, 140,000 miners walked off the job. The mines closed.

As the months passed and the strike continued, coal prices rose. With winter coming on, schools, hospitals, and factories ran short of coal. Public opinion turned against the companies. Morgan and other industrial leaders privately urged them to settle, but the companies refused.

Roosevelt was furious. Complaining of the companies' arrogance, he invited both sides in the dispute to an October 1902 conference at the White House. There, Mitchell took a moderate tone and offered to submit the issues to arbitration, but the companies again refused to budge. Roosevelt ordered the army to prepare to seize the mines and then leaked word of his intent to Wall Street leaders.

Alarmed, Morgan and others again urged settlement of the dispute, and at last the companies retreated. They agreed to accept the recommendations of an independent commission the president would appoint. In late October, the strikers returned to work, and in March 1903, the commission awarded them a 10 percent wage increase and a cut in working hours. It recommended, however, against union recognition. The coal companies, in turn, were encouraged to raise prices to offset the wage increase.

More and more, Roosevelt saw the federal government as an honest and impartial "broker" between powerful elements in society. Rather than leaning toward labor, he pursued a middle way to curb corporate and labor abuses, abolish privilege, and enlarge individual opportunity. Conservative by temperament, he sometimes backed reforms in part to head off more radical measures.

During the 1904 campaign, Roosevelt called his actions in the coal miners' strike a "square deal" for both labor and capital, a term that stuck to his administration. Roosevelt was not the first president to take a stand for labor, but he was the first to bring opposing sides in a labor dispute to the White House to settle it. He was the first to threaten to seize a major industry and he was the first to appoint an arbitration commission whose decision both sides agreed to accept.

QUICK CHECK ✓

In what ways did Theodore Roosevelt enlarge presidential power by intervening in the 1902 coal strike?

Roosevelt Progressivism at Its Height

In the election of 1904, the popular Roosevelt soundly drubbed his Democratic opponent, Alton B. Parker of New York, and the Socialist party candidate, Eugene V. Debs of Indiana. Roosevelt attracted a large campaign chest and won votes everywhere. In a landslide victory, he received 57 percent of the vote to Parker's 38 percent, and on election night, he savored the public's confidence. Overjoyed, he pledged that "under no circumstances will I be a candidate for or accept another nomination," a statement he later regretted.

WHAT ?

were the major measures of Theodore Roosevelt's term from 1905 to 1909?

Regulating the Railroads

Following his election, Roosevelt in late 1904 laid out a reform program that included railroad regulation, employers' liability for federal employees, greater federal control over corporations, and laws regulating child labor, factory inspection, and slum clearance in the District of Columbia. He turned first to railroad regulation. In the Midwest and Far West, the issue was a popular one, and reform governors like La Follette in Wisconsin urged federal action. Roosevelt maneuvered cannily. As the legislative battle opened, he released figures showing that Standard Oil had reaped $750,000 a year from railroad rebates. He also skillfully traded congressional support for a strong railroad measure in return for his promise to postpone a reduction of the tariff, a stratagem that came back to plague President Taft.

Hepburn Act

A law that strengthened the rate-making power of the Interstate Commerce Commission, again reflecting the era's desire to control the power of the railroads. It increased the ICC's membership from five to seven, empowered it to fix reasonable railroad rates, and broadened its jurisdiction. It also made ICC rulings binding pending court appeals.

THE ELECTION OF 1904			
Candidate	**Party**	**Popular Vote**	**Electoral Vote**
T. Roosevelt	Republican	7,623,486	336
Parker	Democrat	5,077,911	140
Debs	Socialist	402,400	0
Swallow	Prohibition	258,596	0

Triumph came with passage of the **Hepburn Act** of 1906. A significant achievement, the act strengthened the rate-making power of the Interstate Commerce Commission. It increased membership on the ICC from five to seven, empowered it to fix reasonable maximum railroad rates, and broadened its jurisdiction to include oil pipeline, express, and sleeping car companies. ICC orders were binding, pending any court appeals, thus placing the burden of proof of injustice on the companies. Delighted, Roosevelt viewed the Hepburn Act as a major step in his plan for continuous expert federal control over industry.

Cleaning Up Food and Drugs

Upton Sinclair, from *The Jungle* (1906)

Soon Roosevelt was dealing with two other important bills, these aimed at regulating the food and drug industries. Muckraking articles had touched frequently on filthy conditions in meatpacking houses, but Upton Sinclair's *The Jungle* (1906) set off a storm of indignation. Ironically, Sinclair had set out to write a novel about the packinghouse workers, the "wage slaves of the Beef Trust," hoping to do for wage slavery what Harriet Beecher Stowe had done for chattel slavery. But readers largely ignored his story of the workers and seized instead on the graphic descriptions of the things that went into their meat.

Sinclair was disappointed at the reaction. "I aimed at the public's heart," he later said, "and by accident I hit it in the stomach." He had, indeed. After reading *The Jungle*, Roosevelt ordered an investigation. The result, he said, was "hideous," and he threatened to publish the entire "sickening report" if Congress did not act. Meat sales plummeted in the United States and Europe. Demand for reform grew. Alarmed, the meat packers themselves supported a reform law, which they hoped would be just strong enough to still the clamor. The Meat Inspection Act of 1906, stronger than the packers wanted, set rules for sanitary meatpacking and government inspection of meat products.

A second measure, the Pure Food and Drug Act, passed more easily. Samuel Hopkins Adams, a muckraker, exposed the dangers of patent medicines in several sensational articles in *Collier's*. Patent medicines,

TAINTED FOOD A poster for the movie version of Upton Sinclair's *The Jungle* promises a "wonderful story of the beef packing industry." The conditions that Sinclair described in the book brought to public attention the scandals of the meatpacking industry knowingly selling diseased meat and the filthy, disease-ridden, dangerous conditions in which the workers toiled for their subsistence wages.

What were the effects of Sinclair's novel, *The Jungle*?

Adams pointed out, contained mostly alcohol, drugs, and "undiluted fraud." Dr. Harvey W. Wiley, the chief chemist in the Department of Agriculture, led a "poison squad" of young assistants who experimented with the medicines. With evidence in hand, Wiley pushed for regulation; Roosevelt and the recently reorganized American Medical Association joined the fight, and the act passed on June 30, 1906. Requiring manufacturers to list certain ingredients on the label, it represented a pioneering effort to ban the manufacture and sale of adulterated, misbranded, or unsanitary food or drugs.

QUICK CHECK ✓

What laws regulated the food and drug industries?

Conserving the Land

An expert on birds, Roosevelt loved nature and the wilderness, and some of his most enduring accomplishments came in the field of **conservation,** an effort to preserve nature. Working closely with Gifford Pinchot, chief of the Forest Service, he established the first comprehensive national conservation policy. To Roosevelt, conservation meant the wise use of natural resources, not locking them away, so those who thought the wilderness should be preserved rather than developed generally opposed his policies.

When Roosevelt took office in 1901, there were 45 million acres in government preserves. In 1908, there were almost 195 million. As 1908 approached, Roosevelt became increasingly strident in his demand for sweeping reforms. He attacked "malefactors of great wealth," urged greater federal regulatory powers,

conservation

As president, Theodore Roosevelt made this principle one of his administration's top goals. Conservation in his view aimed at protecting the nation's natural resources, but called for the wise use of them rather than locking them away. Roosevelt's policies were opposed by those who favored preservation of the wilderness over its development.

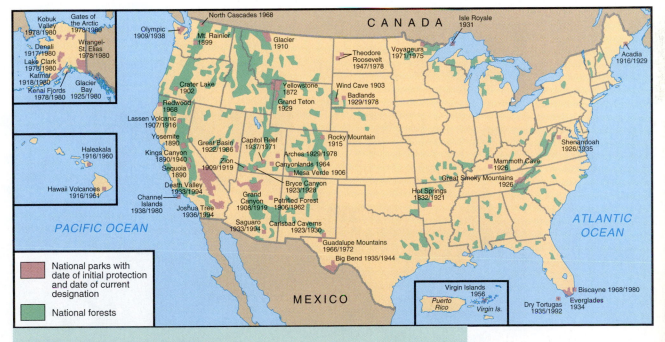

National parks with date of initial protection and date of current designation

National forests

NATIONAL PARKS AND FORESTS   During the presidency of Theodore Roosevelt, who considered conservation his most important domestic achievement, millions of acres of land were set aside for national parks and forests.

How did Roosevelt define "conservation"?

criticized the conservatism of the federal courts, and called for laws protecting factory workers. Many business leaders blamed him for a severe financial panic in the autumn of 1907, and conservatives in Congress stiffened their opposition. Divisions between Republican conservatives and progressives grew.

Immensely popular, Roosevelt prepared in 1908 to turn over the White House to William Howard Taft, his close friend and colleague. As expected, Taft soundly defeated the Democratic standard-bearer William Jennings Bryan, who was making his third try for the presidency. The Republicans retained control of Congress. Taft prepared to move into the White House, ready and willing to carry on the Roosevelt legacy.

QUICK CHECK

What did Theodore Roosevelt accomplish with regard to the environment?

The Ordeal of William Howard Taft

WHAT made the presidency of William Howard Taft so difficult for him?

Taking office in 1909, Taft felt "just a bit like a fish out of water." The son of a distinguished Ohio family and a graduate of Yale Law School, he became an Ohio judge, solicitor general of the United States, and a judge of the federal circuit court. In 1900, McKinley asked him to head the Philippine Commission, charged with the difficult and challenging task of forming a civil government in the Philippines. Later Taft was named the first governor general of the Philippines. In 1904, Roosevelt appointed him secretary of war. In all these positions, Taft made his mark as a skillful administrator. He worked quietly behind the scenes, avoided

THE TROUBLES OF TAFT A 1910 *Puck* cartoon shows Taft snarled in the intricacies of office as his disappointed mentor looks on.

According to this cartoon, what were the various challenges facing Taft?

THE ELECTION OF 1908			
Candidate	Party	Popular Vote	Electoral Vote
Taft	Republican	7,678,908	321
Bryan	Democrat	6,409,104	162
Debs	Socialist	402,820	0
Chafin	Prohibition	252,821	0

controversy, and shared none of Roosevelt's zest for politics. A good-natured man, Taft had personal charm and infectious humor. He fled from fights rather than seeking them out, and he disliked political maneuvering, preferring instead quiet solitude. "I don't like politics," he said. "I don't like the limelight."

Weighing close to 300 pounds, Taft enjoyed conversation, golf and bridge, good food, and plenty of rest. Compared to the hardworking Roosevelt and Wilson, he was lazy. He was also honest, kindly, and amiable, and in his own way he knew how to get things done.

Taft's years as president were not happy. As it turned out, he presided over a Republican party torn with tensions that Roosevelt had either brushed aside or concealed. The tariff, business regulation, and other issues split conservatives and progressives, and Taft often wavered or sided with the conservatives. Taft revered the past and distrusted change; although an ardent supporter of Roosevelt, he never had Roosevelt's faith in the ability of government to impose reform and alter individual behavior. He named five corporation attorneys to his cabinet, leaned more to business than to labor, and spoke of a desire to "clean out the unions."

At that time and later, Taft's reputation suffered by comparison to the flair of Roosevelt and the moral majesty of Woodrow Wilson. Taft was an honest and sincere president, who—sometimes firm, sometimes befuddled—faced a series of important and troublesome problems during his term of office.

Party Insurgency

Taft started his term with an attempt to curb the powerful Republican speaker of the House, Joseph "Uncle Joe" Cannon of Illinois. Using the powers of his position, Cannon had been setting House procedures, appointing committees, and virtually dictating legislation. Straightforward and crusty, he often opposed reform. In March 1909, thirty Republican congressmen joined Taft's effort to curb Cannon's power, and the president sensed success. But Cannon retaliated and, threatening to block all tariff bills, forced a compromise. Taft stopped the anti-Cannon campaign in return for Cannon's pledge to help with tariff cuts.

Republicans were divided over the tariff, and there was a growing party insurgency against high rates. The House quickly passed a bill providing for lower rates, but in the Senate, protectionists raised them. Senate leader Nelson W. Aldrich of Rhode Island introduced a revised bill that added more than eight hundred amendments to the rates approved in the House.

Angry, La Follette and other Republicans attacked the bill as the child of special interests. In speeches on the Senate floor they called themselves "progressives," invoked Roosevelt's name, and urged Taft to defeat the high-tariff proposal. Caught between protectionists and progressives, Taft wavered, then tried to compromise. In the end, he backed Aldrich. The Payne-Aldrich Act, passed in November 1909, called for higher rates than the original House bill, though it lowered them from the Dingley Tariff of 1897. An unpopular law, Payne-Aldrich helped discredit Taft and revealed the tensions in the Republican party.

Republican progressives and conservatives drifted apart. Thin-skinned, Taft resented the persistent pinpricks of the progressives who criticized him for virtually everything he did. He tried to find middle ground but leaned more and more toward the conservatives. During a nationwide speaking tour in the autumn of 1909, he praised Aldrich, scolded the low-tariff insurgents, and called the Payne-Aldrich Act "the best bill that the Republican party ever passed."

By early 1910, progressive Republicans in Congress no longer looked to Taft for leadership. As before, they challenged Cannon's power, and Taft wavered. In an outcome embarrassing to the president, the progressives won, managing to curtail Cannon's authority to dictate committee assignments and schedule debate. In progressive circles there was growing talk of a Roosevelt return to the White House.

QUICK CHECK ✓

What were the motives of the Republicans in Congress who opposed William Howard Taft?

The Ballinger-Pinchot Affair

The conservation issue dealt another blow to relations between Roosevelt and President Taft. In 1909, Richard A. Ballinger, Taft's secretary of the interior, offered for sale a million acres of public land that Pinchot, who had stayed on as Taft's chief forester, had withdrawn from sale. Pinchot, fearing that Ballinger would hurt conservation programs, protested and, seizing on a report that Ballinger had helped sell valuable Alaskan coal lands to a syndicate that included J. P. Morgan, asked Taft to intervene. After investigating, Taft supported Ballinger on every count, although he asked Pinchot to remain in office.

Pinchot refused to drop the matter. Behind the scenes, he provided material for two anti-Ballinger magazine articles, and he wrote a critical public letter that Senator Dolliver of Iowa read to the Senate. Taft had had enough. He fired the insubordinate Pinchot, an action which, though appropriate, again lost support for Taft. Newspapers followed the controversy for months, and muckrakers assailed the administration's "surrender" to Morgan and other "despoilers of the national heritage."

The Ballinger-Pinchot controversy obscured Taft's important contributions to conservation. He won from Congress the power to remove lands from sale, and he used it to conserve more land than Roosevelt did. Still, the controversy tarred Taft, and it upset his old friend Roosevelt.

QUICK CHECK ✓

What was the Ballinger-Pinchot controversy?

Taft Alienates the Progressives

Interested in railroad regulation, Taft backed a bill in 1910 to empower the ICC to fix maximum railroad rates. Progressive Republicans favored that plan but attacked Taft's suggestion of a special Commerce Court to hear appeals from ICC decisions because most judges were traditionally conservative in outlook and usually rejected attempts to regulate railroad rates. They also thought the railroads had been consulted too closely in drawing up the bill. Democratic and Republican progressives tried to amend the bill to strengthen it; Taft made support of it a test of party loyalty.

The Mann-Elkins Act of 1910 gave something to everyone. It gave the ICC power to set rates, stiffened long- and short-haul regulations, and placed telephone and telegraph companies under ICC jurisdiction. These provisions delighted progressives. The act also created a Commerce Court, pleasing conservatives. In a trade-off, conservative Republican Senate leaders pledged their support for a statehood bill for Arizona and New Mexico, which were both predicted to be Democratic. In return, enough Democratic senators promised to vote for the Commerce Court provision to pass the bill. While pleased with the act, Taft and the Republican party lost further ground. In votes on key provisions of the Mann-Elkins Act, Taft raised the issue of party regularity, and progressive Republicans defied him.

Taft attempted to defeat the progressive Republicans in the 1910 elections. He helped form antiprogressive organizations, and he campaigned against progressive Republican candidates for the Senate. Progressive Republicans retaliated by organizing a nationwide network of anti-Taft Progressive Republican Clubs.

The 1910 election results were a major setback for Taft and the Republicans—especially conservative Republicans. A key issue in the election, the high cost of living, gave an edge to the progressive wings in both major parties, lending support to their attack on the tariff and the trusts. In party primaries, progressive Republicans overwhelmed most Taft candidates, and in the general election, they tended to fare better than the conservatives, which increased progressive influence in the Republican party.

For Republicans of all persuasions, however, it was a difficult election. The Democrats swept the urban-industrial states from New York to Illinois. New York, New Jersey, Indiana, and even Taft's Ohio elected Democratic governors. For the first time since 1894, Republicans lost control of both the House and the Senate. Disappointed, Taft called it "not only a landslide, but a tidal wave and holocaust all rolled into one general cataclysm."

Despite the defeat, Taft pushed through several important measures before his term ended. With the help of the new Democratic House, he backed laws to regulate safety in mines and on railroads, create a Children's Bureau in the federal government, establish employers' liability for all work done on government contracts, and mandate an eight-hour workday for government workers.

In 1909, Congress initiated a constitutional amendment authorizing an income tax, which, along with woman suffrage, was one of the most significant legislative measures of the twentieth century. The Sixteenth Amendment took effect early in 1913. A few months later, an important progressive goal was realized when the direct election of senators was ratified as the Seventeenth Amendment to the Constitution.

An ardent supporter of competition, Taft relentlessly pressed a campaign against trusts. The Sherman Antitrust Act, he said in 1911, "is a good law that ought to be enforced, and I propose to enforce it." That year, the Supreme Court in cases against Standard Oil and American Tobacco established the "rule of reason," which allowed the Court to determine whether a business presented "reasonable" restraint on trade. Taft thought the decisions gave the Court too much discretion, and he pushed ahead with the antitrust effort.

In October 1911, he sued U.S. Steel for its acquisition of the Tennessee Coal and Iron Company in 1907. Roosevelt had approved the acquisition (see p. 630), and the suit seemed designed to impugn his action. Enraged, he attacked Taft, and Taft, for once, fought back. He accused Roosevelt of undermining the conservative tradition in the country and began working to undercut the influence of the progressive Republicans. Increasingly now, Roosevelt listened to anti-Taft Republicans who urged him to run for president in 1912. In February 1912, he announced, "My hat is in the ring."

QUICK CHECK

How did Taft lose the support of Republican progressives?

New Nationalism
Roosevelt's program called for a national approach to the country's affairs and a strong president to deal with them.

New Freedom
Wilson's program in his campaign for the presidency in 1912, the New Freedom emphasized business competition and small government.

Theodore Roosevelt, "The New Nationalism" (1910)

Theodore Roosevelt 1912 Campaign Speeches

Differing Philosophies in the Election of 1912

Delighted Democrats looked on as Taft and Roosevelt fought for the Republican nomination. As the incumbent president, Taft controlled the party machinery, and when the Republican convention met in June 1912, he took the nomination. In early July, the Democrats met in Baltimore and, confident of victory for the first time in two decades, struggled through forty-six ballots before finally nominating Woodrow Wilson, the reform-minded governor of New Jersey.

A month later, some of the anti-Taft and progressive Republicans—now calling themselves the Progressive party—whooped it up in Chicago. Naming Roosevelt for president at its convention, the Progressive party—soon known as the Bull Moose party—set the stage for the first important three-cornered presidential contest since 1860.

Taft was out of the running before the campaign even began. "I think I might as well give up so far as being a candidate is concerned," he said in July. "There are so many people in the country who don't like me." Taft stayed at home and made no speeches before the election. Roosevelt campaigned strenuously, even completing one speech after being shot in the chest by an anti-third-term fanatic. "I have a message to deliver," he said, "and will deliver it as long as there is life in my body."

Roosevelt's message involved a program he called the **New Nationalism**. An important phase in the shaping of twentieth-century American political thought, it demanded a national approach to the country's affairs and a strong president to deal with them. The New Nationalism called for efficiency in government and society. It exalted the executive and the expert; urged social-justice reforms to protect workers, women, and children; and accepted "good" trusts. The New Nationalism encouraged large concentrations of labor and capital, serving the nation's interests under a forceful federal executive.

For the first time in the history of a major political party, the Progressive campaign enlisted women in its organization. Jane Addams, the well-known settlement worker, seconded Roosevelt's nomination at Chicago, and she and other women played a leading role in his campaign. Some labor leaders, who saw potential for union growth, and some business leaders, who saw relief from destructive competition and labor strife, supported the new party.

THE BULL MOOSE CAMPAIGN "I'm feeling like a bull moose!" declared Teddy Roosevelt while campaigning in 1912 as a Progressive and inadvertently renaming the new political party. The patch depicts a strong, independent animal, much like Roosevelt himself. In 1904, Roosevelt had won re-election by promising to give Americans a "square deal."

What did Roosevelt stand for in the election of 1912?

Wilson, in contrast, set forth a program called the **New Freedom** that emphasized business competition and small government. A states' rights Democrat, he wanted to rein in federal authority, using it only to sweep away special privilege, release individual energies, and restore competition. Drawing on the thinking of Louis D. Brandeis, the brilliant shaper of reform-minded law, he echoed the Progressive party's social-justice objectives, while continuing to attack Roosevelt's planned state. For Wilson, the vital issue was not a planned economy but a free one. "The history of liberty is the history of the limitation of governmental power," he said in October 1912. "If America is not to have free enterprise, then she can have freedom of no sort whatever."

In the New Nationalism and New Freedom, the election of 1912 offered competing philosophies of government. Both Roosevelt and Wilson saw the central problem of the American nation as economic growth and its effect on individuals and society. Both focused on the government's relation to business, both believed in bureaucratic reform, and both wanted to use government to protect the ordinary citizen. But Roosevelt welcomed federal power, national planning, and business growth; Wilson distrusted them all.

On election day, Wilson won 6.3 million votes to 4.1 million for Roosevelt (who had recovered quickly from his wound) and 900,000 for Eugene V. Debs, the Socialist party candidate. Taft, the incumbent president, finished third with 3.5 million votes; he carried only Vermont and Utah for 8 electoral votes. The Democrats also won outright control of both houses.

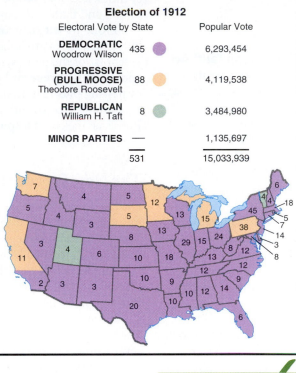

Election of 1912		
	Electoral Vote by State	Popular Vote
DEMOCRATIC Woodrow Wilson	435	6,293,454
PROGRESSIVE (BULL MOOSE) Theodore Roosevelt	88	4,119,538
REPUBLICAN William H. Taft	8	3,484,980
MINOR PARTIES	—	1,135,697
	531	15,033,939

QUICK CHECK ✓

What were the two opposing philosophies in the presidential election of 1912?

Woodrow Wilson's New Freedom

If under Roosevelt social reform took on the excitement of a circus, "under Wilson it acquired the dedication of a sunrise service." Born in Virginia in 1856 and raised in the South, Wilson was the son of a Presbyterian minister. As a young man, he wanted a career in public service, and he trained himself carefully in history and oratory. A moralist, he reached judgments easily. Once reached, almost nothing shook them. Opponents called him stubborn and smug.

From 1890 to 1902 he served as professor of jurisprudence and political economy at Princeton. In 1902, he became president of the university. Eight years later, he was governor of New Jersey, where he led a campaign to reform election procedures, abolish corrupt practices, and strengthen railroad regulation.

Wilson's rise was rapid, and he knew relatively little about national issues and personalities. But he learned fast, and in some ways the lack of experience served him well. He had few political debts to repay, and he brought fresh perspectives to older issues. Ideas intrigued Wilson; details bored him. Although he was outgoing

WHAT? were the central principles of Woodrow Wilson's New Freedom?

at times, he could also be cold and aloof, and aides soon learned that he preferred loyalty and flattery to candid criticism.

Prone to self-righteousness, Wilson often turned differences of opinion into bitter personal quarrels. Like Roosevelt, he believed in strong presidential leadership. A scholar of the party system, he cooperated closely with Democrats in Congress, and his legislative record placed him among the most effective presidents in terms of passing bills that he supported. Forbidding in individual conversation, Wilson could move crowds with graceful oratory. Unlike Taft, and to a greater degree than Roosevelt, he could inspire.

The New Freedom in Action

On the day of his inauguration, Wilson called Congress into special session to lower the tariff. When the session opened on April 8, 1913, Wilson himself was there, the first president since John Adams in 1801 to appear personally before Congress. In forceful language, he urged Congress to reduce tariff rates.

As the bill moved through Congress, Wilson showed exceptional skill. He worked closely with congressional leaders, and when lobbyists threatened the bill in the Senate, he appealed for popular support. The result was a triumph for Wilson and the Democratic party. The **Underwood Tariff Act** passed in 1913. It lowered tariff rates about 15 percent and removed duties from sugar, wool, and several other consumer goods.

To make up for lost revenue, the act also levied a modest graduated income tax, authorized under the just ratified Sixteenth Amendment. Marking a significant shift in the American tax structure, it imposed a 1 percent tax on individuals and corporations earning more than $4000 annually and an additional 1 percent tax on incomes more than $20,000. Above all, the act reflected a new unity within the Democratic party, which had worked together to pass a difficult tariff law.

Encouraged by his success, Wilson decided to keep Congress in session through the hot Washington summer. Now he focused on banking reform, and the result in December 1913 was the **Federal Reserve Act,** the most important domestic law of his administration.

Meant to provide the United States with a sound yet flexible currency, the act established the country's first

Underwood Tariff Act

An early accomplishment of the Wilson administration, this law reduced the tariff rates of the Payne-Aldrich law of 1909 by about 15 percent. It also levied a graduated income tax to make up for lost revenue.

Federal Reserve Act

This act created a central banking system, consisting of twelve regional banks governed by the Federal Reserve Board. It was an attempt to provide the United States with a sound yet flexible currency.

Woodrow Wilson, from *The New Freedom* (1913)

A NEW DEMOCRATIC PARTY By appearing personally before Congress, President Wilson broke the precedent established by Thomas Jefferson of submitting messages to Congress in writing. Appealing for popular support in his plea for tariff reform, Wilson denounced the tariff lobbyists for seeking "to overcome the interests of the public for their private profit."

Why was it important that Wilson himself appeared before Congress?

efficient banking system since Andrew Jackson killed the second Bank of the United States in 1832. It created twelve regional banks, each to serve the banks of its district. The regional banks answered to a Federal Reserve Board, appointed by the president, which governed the nationwide system.

A compromise law, the act blended public and private control of the banking system. Private bankers owned the federal reserve banks but answered to the presidentially appointed Federal Reserve Board. The reserve banks were authorized to issue currency, and through the discount rate—the interest rate at which they loaned money to member banks—they could raise or lower the amount of money in circulation. Monetary affairs no longer depended solely on the price of gold. Within a year, nearly half the nation's banking resources were in the Federal Reserve System.

The **Clayton Antitrust Act** (1914) completed Wilson's initial legislative program. It prohibited unfair trade practices. It forbade pricing policies that created monopoly, and it made corporate officers personally responsible for antitrust violations. Delighting Samuel Gompers and the labor movement, the act declared that unions were not conspiracies in restraint of trade, outlawed the use of injunctions in labor disputes unless necessary to protect property, and approved lawful strikes and picketing.

In November 1914, Wilson proudly announced the completion of his New Freedom program. Tariff, banking, and antitrust laws promised a brighter future, he said, and it was now "a time of healing because a time of just dealing." Many progressives were aghast. That Wilson could think society's ills were so easily cured, the *New Republic* said, "casts suspicion either upon his own sincerity or upon his grasp of the realities of modern social and industrial life."

QUICK CHECK

What characterized Woodrow Wilson's New Freedom program?

Wilson Moves Toward the New Nationalism

Distracted by the start of war in Europe, Wilson gave less attention to domestic issues for more than a year. When he returned to concern with reform, he adopted more and more of Roosevelt's New Nationalism and blended it with the New Freedom to set it off from his earlier policies.

One of Wilson's problems was the Congress. To his dismay, the Republicans gained substantially in the 1914 elections. Reducing the Democratic majority in the House, they swept key industrial and farm states. At the same time, a recession struck the economy, which had been hurt by the outbreak of the European war in August 1914. Some business leaders blamed the tariff and other New Freedom laws.

Preoccupied with such problems, Wilson blocked significant action in Congress through most of 1915. He refused to support a bill providing minimum wages for women workers, sidetracked a child labor bill on the ground that it was unconstitutional, and opposed a bill to establish long-term credits for farmers. He also refused to endorse woman suffrage, arguing that the right to vote was a state matter, not a federal one.

Wilson's record on race disappointed African Americans and many progressives. He had appealed to African American voters during the 1912 election, and a number of African American leaders campaigned for him. Soon after the inauguration, Oswald Garrison Villard, a leader of the NAACP, proposed a National Race Commission to study the problem of race relations. Initially sympathetic, Wilson rejected the idea because he feared he might lose southern Democratic votes in Congress. A Virginian himself, he appointed many southerners to high office, and for the first time since the Civil War, southern views on race dominated the nation's capital.

Clayton Antitrust Act
An attempt to improve the Sherman Antitrust Act of 1890, this law outlawed interlocking directorates (companies in which the same people served as directors), forbade policies that created monopolies, and made corporate officers responsible for antitrust violations. Benefiting labor, it declared that unions were not conspiracies in restraint of trade and outlawed the use of injunctions in labor disputes unless they were necessary to protect property.

At one of Wilson's first cabinet meetings, the postmaster general proposed the segregation of all African Americans in the federal service. No one dissented, including Wilson. Several government bureaus promptly began to segregate workers in offices, shops, rest rooms, and restaurants. Employees who objected were fired. African American leaders protested, and they were joined by progressive leaders and clergymen. Surprised at the protest, Wilson backed quietly away from the policy, although he continued to insist that segregation benefited African Americans.

As the year 1916 began, Wilson made a dramatic switch in focus and again pushed for substantial reforms. The result was a virtual river of reform laws, which was significant because it began the second, more national-minded phase of the New Freedom. With scarcely a glance over his shoulder, Wilson embraced important portions of Roosevelt's New Nationalism campaign.

In part, he was motivated by the approaching presidential election. A minority president, Wilson owed his victory in 1912 to the split in the Republican party, now almost healed. Roosevelt was moving back into Republican ranks, and there were issues connected with the war in Europe that he might use against Wilson. Moreover, many progressives were voicing disappointment with Wilson's limited reforms and his failure to support more advanced reform legislation on matters such as farm credits, child labor, and woman suffrage.

To his advantage, though, Wilson was already popular within the labor movement. Going beyond Roosevelt's policies, which had sought a balance between business and labor, he defended union recognition and collective bargaining. In 1913, he appointed William B. Wilson, a respected leader of the United Mine Workers, as the first head of the Labor Department, and he strengthened the department's Division of Conciliation.

WATCH

Charles E. Hughes 1916 Presidential Campaign Speech

In August 1916, a threatened railroad strike again revealed Wilson's sympathies with labor. Like Roosevelt, he invited the two sides to the White House, where he urged the railroad companies to grant an eight-hour day and labor leaders to abandon the demand for overtime pay. Labor leaders accepted the proposal; railroad leaders did not. "I pray God to forgive you, I never can," Wilson said as he left the room. Soon he signed the Adamson Act (1916) that imposed the eight-hour day on interstate railways and established a federal commission to study the railroad problem. Ending the threat of a strike, the act marked a milestone in the expansion of the federal government's authority to regulate industry.

In September, Wilson signed the Tariff Commission Act creating an expert commission to recommend tariff rates. The same month, the Revenue Act of 1916 boosted income taxes and furthered tax reform. Four thousand members of the National American Woman Suffrage Association cheered when Wilson finally came out in support of woman suffrage. Two weeks later he endorsed the eight-hour day for all the nation's workers.

The 1916 presidential election was close, but Wilson won it on the issues of peace and progressivism. By the end of 1916, he and the Democratic party had enacted most of the important parts of Roosevelt's Progressive party platform of 1912. To do it, Wilson abandoned portions of the New Freedom and accepted much of the New Nationalism, including greater federal power and commissions governing trade and tariffs. In mixing the two programs, he blended some of the competing doctrines of the Progressive Era, established the primacy of the federal government, and foreshadowed the pragmatic outlook of Franklin D. Roosevelt's New Deal of the 1930s.

QUICK CHECK ✓

In what five ways did Wilson move more closely to Theodore Roosevelt's ideas of New Nationalism?

Conclusion: The Fruits of Progressivism

The election of 1916 showed how deeply progressivism had reached into American society. "We have in four years," Wilson said that fall, "come very near to carrying out the platform of the Progressive party as well as our own; for we are also progressives."

In retrospect, however, 1916 also marked the beginning of progressivism's decline. At most, the years of progressive reform lasted from the 1890s to 1921, and in large measure they were compressed into a single decade between 1906 and American entry into World War I in 1917. Many problems the progressives addressed but did not solve; and some important ones, such as race, they did not even tackle. Yet their regulatory commissions, direct primaries, city improvements, and child labor laws marked an era of important and measured reform.

The institution of the presidency expanded. From the White House radiated executive departments that guided a host of activities. Independent commissions, operating within flexible laws, supplemented executive authority.

These developments owed a great deal to both Roosevelt and Wilson. To manage a complex society, Roosevelt developed a simple formula: expert advice; growth-minded policies; a balancing of business, labor, and other interests; the use of publicity to gather support; and stern but often permissive oversight of the economy. Roosevelt strengthened the executive office, and he called on the newer group of professional, educated, public-minded citizens to help him. "I believe in a strong executive," he said; "I believe in power."

At first, Wilson had different ideas, wanting to dismantle much of Roosevelt's governing apparatus. But driven by outside forces and changes in his own thinking, Wilson soon moved in directions similar to those Roosevelt had championed. Starting out to disperse power, he eventually consolidated it.

Through such movements, government at all levels accepted responsibility for the welfare of various elements in the social order. A reform-minded and bureaucratic society took shape, in which men and women, labor and capital, political parties and social classes competed for shares in the expansive framework of twentieth-century life. But there were limits to reform. As both Roosevelt and Wilson found, the new government agencies, understaffed and underfinanced, depended on the responsiveness of those they sought to regulate.

Soon there was a far darker cloud on the horizon. The spirit of progressivism rested on a belief in human potential, peace, and progress. After Napoleon's defeat in 1815, a century of peace began in western Europe, and as the decades passed, war seemed a dying institution. "It looks as though this were going to be the age of treaties rather than the age of wars," an American said in 1912, "the century of reason rather than the century of force." It was not to be. Two years later, the most devastating of wars broke out in Europe, and in 1917, Americans were fighting on the battlefields of France.

For a list of additional titles related to this chapter's topics, please see
www.pearsonamericanhistory.com.   MyHistoryLab

STUDY RESOURCES

23 KEY TERMS

CHAPTER REVIEW

WHAT were the six major characteristics of progressivism?

Starting in the 1890s and continuing into the 1920s, progressivism swept across the country. It sought cures for social and economic problems and was defined by six major characteristics: (1) a desire by progressives not to harm big business but to humanize and regulate it; (2) an optimism about human nature; (3) a willingness to intervene in people's lives; (4) a tendency to turn more to the authority of the state and the government; (5) a belief in the environment as a key to reform; and (6) a widespread, nationwide base. *(p. 617)*

WHAT methods did progressive reformers use to attack problems in the cities and states?

Progressive reformers turned increasingly to the government to carry out their measures. At the same time, ironically, fewer and fewer people tended to vote. Reformers focused largely on life in the cities, which had exploded in size. Robert M. LaFollette, governor of and later United States senator from Wisconsin, personified the movement. His focus was on improving factory safety, regulating the railroads, and adopting political reforms. *(p. 625)*

HOW would you describe the personality and programs of Theodore Roosevelt?

Having promised to continue the policies of William McKinley, Theodore Roosevelt brought the force of his own personality to the White House. He attacked some trusts and, through the courts, broke up a railroad holding company. His intervention in the coal strike of 1902 reflected his active, energetic personality and represented a major advance in presidential power. *(p. 628)*

WHAT were the major measures of Theodore Roosevelt's term from 1905 to 1909?

Winning easy re-election in 1904, Roosevelt turned to several favorite reform issues. He persuaded Congress to improve railroad regulation, backed pure food and drug laws, and enlarged national parks. In all these actions, he reflected the values of the progressive generation: a reliance on experts, a faith in the power of government to initiate reform, and a desire to tame the power of big business. *(p. 631)*

WHAT made the presidency of William Howard Taft so difficult for him?

Taft suffered in comparison to his old boss, who had left him a variety of difficult problems to solve, including the tariff. The election of 1912 pitted Taft's Republicans against Woodrow Wilson's Democrats and Theodore Roosevelt's Progressive party. Roosevelt campaigned on a program he called the New Nationalism and Wilson on the New Freedom political philosophies that shaped the years ahead. *(p. 634)*

WHAT were the central principles of Woodrow Wilson's New Freedom?

Victorious in the 1912 election, Wilson set out to put into effect the central principles of his New Freedom program, including tariff reform, an antitrust law, and the Federal Reserve Act, a measure that still guides our economy today. Soon, however, Wilson found greater and greater value in Roosevelt's New Nationalism, which had emphasized government intervention and the adoption of measures to protect women, labor, and other groups. *(p. 639)*

MAKING CONNECTIONS

1. How might American history have changed if the Progressive Era had not occurred?
2. How did the major measures of Roosevelt's second term continue the progressive approaches of his first term?
3. How did the differences of opinion during the Progressive Era affect the Taft administration?
4. How did the Wilson administration draw on the characteristics of the Progressive Era?

PRACTICE QUIZ

1. _____ fostered a reform movement of national problems during the early 1900s.
   a. Fascism
   b. Nepotism
   c. Progressivism
   d. Racism

2. In 1900 _____ became president of the National American Woman Suffrage Association.
   a. Susan B. Anthony
   b. Alice Paul
   c. Lucy Burns
   d. Carrie Chapman Catt

3. The concept of _____ held that people and the environment shape one another.
   a. Pragmatism
   b. Socialism
   c. Communism
   d. Sensationalism

4. The _____ party in the United States doubled in membership between 1904 and 1908.
   a. Democratic
   b. Socialist
   c. Republican
   d. Populist

5. Vice President _____ took over when President McKinley was shot in 1901.
   a. Theodore Roosevelt
   b. Robert La Follette
   c. Woodrow Wilson
   d. William Howard Taft

6. Which of the following *does not* relate to Theodore Roosevelt's actions regarding the trusts?
   a. Roosevelt took legal actions against the trusts.
   b. Roosevelt was a true trust-buster according to contemporary historians.
   c. Roosevelt used the media to pressure the trusts.
   d. Roosevelt used Congress to regulate the trusts.

7. What did the United Mine Workers demand from coal companies in 1902?
   a. Wage increases

   b. An eight-hour day
   c. Company recognition of the union
   d. All of the above answers are accurate.

8. The Hepburn Act did all of the following *except*
   a. It strengthened the rate-making power of the Interstate Commerce Commission.
   b. It placed the burden of proof of injustice on the government.
   c. It increased membership on the ICC from five to seven.
   d. It empowered the ICC to fix reasonable maximum railroad rates.

9. How did Taft alienate the Progressives?
   a. Taft worked against Progressives who wanted to strengthen the Mann-Elkins Bill.
   b. Taft made support of the Mann-Elkins Bill a major test of party loyalty.
   c. Taft formed anti-progressive organizations to defeat the Republicans in the 1910 elections.
   d. All of the above answers are accurate.

10. Which of the following *most* accurately explains the content of Roosevelt's New Nationalism?
    a. It accepted good trusts.
    b. It demanded a state approach to the nation's affairs.
    c. It advocated for a weak executive authority to guide national affairs.
    d. It called for a reduction in the use of the expert to reform national problems.

Find more practice at
www.myhistorylab.com

SAMPLE ESSAY QUESTIONS

1. Explain why the Progressive movement arose in the late 1800s.
2. Evaluate the suffrage strategies of American women during the Progressive Era.

Answers to Practice Quiz 1. c, p. 617 **2.** d, p. 622 **3.** a, p. 622 **4.** b, p. 624 **5.** a, p. 624 **6.** b, p. 628 **7.** d, p. 630
8. b, p. 631 **9.** d, p. 637 **10.** a, p. 638

LET'S KEEP THE GLOW IN OLD GLORY
AND THE FREE IN FREEDOM TOO

Lyric by
Wilbur D. Nesbit
Music by
Robert Speroy

Frank K. Root & Co.

RALLYING FOR WAR
Sheet music cover for "Let's Keep the Glow in Old Glory," an unofficial but nonetheless popular bit of propaganda during the World War I era.

What does the cover say about America's role in the war?

The Sinking of the *Lusitania*

On the morning of May 1, 1915, the German government took out the following important advertisement in the *New York World* as a warning to Americans and other voyagers setting sail for England:

NOTICE—
Travellers intending to embark on the Atlantic voyage are reminded that a state of war exists between Germany and her allies and Great Britain and her allies; that the zone of war includes the waters adjacent to the British Isles; that, in accordance with formal notice given by the Imperial German Government, vessels flying the flag of Great Britain, or of any of her allies, are liable to destruction in those waters and that travelers sailing in the war zone on ships of Great Britain or her allies do so at their own risk.

At 12:30 that afternoon, the British steamship *Lusitania* set sail from New York to Liverpool. Secretly, it carried a load of ammunition as well as passengers.

KEY EVENTS

The steamer was two hours late in leaving, but it held several speed records and could easily make up the time. The passenger list of 1257 was the largest since the outbreak of war in Europe in 1914. It took six days for it to reach the coast of Ireland. German U-boats were known to patrol the dangerous waters. When the war began, Great Britain imposed a naval blockade of Germany. In return, Germany in February 1915 declared the area around the British Isles a war zone; all enemy vessels, armed or unarmed, were at risk. Germany had only a handful of U-boats, but the submarines were a new and frightening weapon. On behalf of the United States, President Woodrow Wilson protested the German action, and on February 10, he warned Germany of its "strict accountability" for any American losses resulting from U-boat attacks.

Off Ireland, the passengers lounged on the deck of the *Lusitania*. As if it were peacetime, the ship sailed straight ahead, with no zigzag maneuvers to throw off pursuit. But the submarine U-20 was there, and its commander, seeing a large ship, fired a single torpedo. Seconds after it hit, a boiler exploded and blew a hole in the *Lusitania's* side. The ship listed immediately, hindering the launching of lifeboats, and in eighteen minutes it sank. Nearly 1200 people died, including 128 Americans. As the ship's bow lifted and went under, the U-20 commander for the first time read the name: *Lusitania*.

The sinking, the worst since the *Titanic* went down with 1500 people in 1912, horrified Americans. Theodore Roosevelt called it "an act of piracy" and demanded war. Most Americans, however, wanted to stay out of war; like Wilson, they hoped negotiations could solve the problem. "There is such a thing," Wilson said a few days after the sinking, "as a man being too proud to fight. There is such a thing as a nation being so right that it does not need to convince others by force."

In a series of diplomatic notes, Wilson demanded a change in German policy. The first *Lusitania* note (May 13, 1915) called on Germany to abandon unrestricted submarine warfare, disavow the sinking, and compensate for lost American lives. Germany sent an evasive reply, and Wilson drafted a second *Lusitania* note (June 9) insisting on specific pledges. Fearful the demand would lead to war, Secretary of State William Jennings Bryan resigned rather than sign the note. Wilson sent it anyway and followed with a third note (July 21)—almost an ultimatum— warning Germany that the United States would view similar sinkings as "deliberately unfriendly."

A FATEFUL TORPEDO   With the sinking of the *Lusitania*, the American people learned firsthand of the horrors of total war. President Wilson's decision to protest the incident through diplomacy kept the United States out of the war—but only temporarily.

How does the sinking of the *Lusitania* foreshadow later American entry into the war?

Unbeknownst to Wilson, Germany had already ordered U-boat commanders not to sink passenger liners without warning. In August 1915, a U-boat mistakenly torpedoed the British liner *Arabic*, killing two Americans. Wilson protested, and Germany, eager to keep the United States out of the war, backed down. The *Arabic* pledge (September 1) promised that U-boats would stop and warn liners, unless they tried to resist or escape. Germany also apologized for American deaths on the *Arabic*, and for the rest of 1915, U-boats hunted freighters, not passenger liners.

Although Wilson's diplomacy had achieved his immediate goal, the *Lusitania* and *Arabic* crises contained the elements that led to war. Trade and travel tied the world together, and Americans no longer hid behind safe ocean barriers. New weapons, such as the submarine, strained old rules of international law. But while Americans sifted the conflicting claims of Great Britain and Germany, they hoped for peace. A generation of progressives, inspired with confidence in human progress, did not easily accept war.

Wilson also hated war, but he found himself caught up in a worldwide crisis that demanded the best in American will and diplomacy. In the end, diplomacy failed, and in April 1917, the United States entered a war that changed the nation's history. Building on several major trends in American foreign policy since the 1890s, the years around World War I firmly established the United States as a world power, confirmed the country's dominance in Latin America, and ended with a war with Germany and her allies that had far-reaching results.

A New World Power

WHAT were the main events that showed the United States was becoming a world power?

As they had in the late nineteenth century, Americans after 1900 continued to pay relatively little attention to foreign affairs. Newspapers and magazines ran stories every day about events abroad, but people paid closer attention to what was going on at home.

For Americans at the time, foreign policy was something to be left to the president in office, an attitude the presidents themselves favored. Foreign affairs became an arena in which they could exert a free hand largely unchallenged by Congress or the courts, and Roosevelt, Taft, and Wilson all took advantage of the opportunity to do so.

The foreign policy they pursued from 1901 to 1920 was aggressive and nationalistic. During these years, the United States intervened in Europe, the Far East, and Latin America. It dominated the Caribbean.

In 1898, the United States left the peace table possessing the Philippines, Puerto Rico, and Guam. Holding distant possessions required a colonial policy; it also required a change in foreign policy, reflecting an outward approach. From the Caribbean to the Pacific, policymakers paid attention to issues and countries they had earlier ignored. Like other nations in these years, the United States built a large navy, protected its colonial empire, and became increasingly involved in economic ventures abroad.

Building the Panama Canal

Convinced the United States should take a more active international role, Theodore Roosevelt spent his presidency preparing the nation for world power. Working with Secretary of War Elihu Root, he modernized the army, using lessons learned from the war with Spain. Roosevelt and Root established the Army War College, imposed stiff tests for the promotion of officers, and in 1903 created a general staff to oversee military planning and mobilization. Determined to end dependence on the British fleet, Roosevelt doubled the strength of the navy during his term in office.

Stretching his authority to the limits, Roosevelt took steps to consolidate the country's new position in the Caribbean and Central America. European powers, which had long resisted American initiatives there, now accepted American supremacy. Preoccupied with problems in Europe and Africa, Great Britain agreed to U.S. plans for an Isthmian canal in Central America and withdrew much of its military force from the area.

Roosevelt wanted a canal to link the Atlantic and Pacific oceans across the isthmus connecting North and South America. Secretary of State John Hay negotiated with Britain the Hay-Pauncefote Treaty of 1901 that permitted the United States to construct and control an isthmian canal, providing it would be free and open to ships of all nations.

THE PANAMA CANAL ZONE Construction of the canal began in 1904, and despite landslides, steamy weather, and yellow fever, work was completed in 1914.

Why was Roosevelt so eager to build the Panama Canal?

Delighted, Roosevelt began selecting the route. One route, fifty miles long, wandered through the rough, swampy terrain of the Panama region of Colombia. A French company had recently tried and failed to dig a canal there. To the northwest, another route ran through mountainous Nicaragua. Although two hundred miles in length, it followed natural waterways, a factor that would make construction easier.

An Isthmian Canal Commission investigated both routes in 1899 and recommended the shorter route through Panama. Roosevelt backed the idea, and he authorized Hay to negotiate an agreement with the Colombian chargé d'affaires, Thomas Herrán. The Hay-Herrán Convention (1903) gave the United States a 99-year lease, with option for renewal, on a canal zone 6 miles in width. In exchange, the United States agreed to pay Colombia a onetime fee of $10 million and an annual rental of $250,000.

To Roosevelt's dismay, the Colombian Senate rejected the treaty, in part because it infringed on Colombian sovereignty. The Colombians also wanted more money. Calling them "jack rabbits" and "contemptible little creatures," Roosevelt considered seizing Panama, then hinted he would welcome a Panamanian revolt from Colombia. In November 1903, the Panamanians took the hint, and Roosevelt moved quickly to support them. Sending the cruiser *Nashville* to prevent Colombian troops from putting down the revolt, he promptly recognized the new Republic of Panama.

Two weeks later, the **Hay-Bunau-Varilla Treaty** with Panama granted the United States control of a canal zone 10 miles wide across the Isthmus of Panama. In return, the United States guaranteed the independence of Panama and agreed to pay the same fees offered Colombia. On August 15, 1914, the first ocean steamer sailed through the completed canal, which had cost $375 million to build.

Roosevelt took great pride in the canal, calling it "by far the most important action in foreign affairs." Defending his methods, he said in 1911, "If I had followed traditional conservative methods, I would have submitted a dignified state paper of 200 pages to Congress and the debate on it would have been going on yet; but I took the Canal Zone and let Congress debate; and while the debate goes on the Canal does also."

From 1903 to 1920, the United States intervened often in Latin America to protect the canal, promote regional stability, and exclude foreign influence. One problem worrying American policymakers was the scale of Latin American debts to European powers. Many countries in the Western Hemisphere owed money to European governments and banks, and often these nations were poor, prone to revolution, and unable to pay. The situation invited European intervention. In 1902,

Hay-Bunau-Varilla Treaty

This 1903 treaty granted the United States control over a canal zone 10 miles wide across the Isthmus of Panama. In return, the United States guaranteed the independence of Panama and agreed to pay Panama a onetime fee of $10 million and an annual rental of $250,000.

Building the Panama Canal

Roosevelt Corollary
A corollary to the Monroe Doctrine, which asserted that the United States would intervene in Latin American affairs if the countries themselves could not keep their affairs in order.

QUICK CHECK ✓

What did Theodore Roosevelt do to build the Panama Canal?

Venezuela defaulted on debts; England, Germany, and Italy sent Venezuela an ultimatum and blockaded its ports. American pressure forced a settlement of the issue, but the general problem remained.

Roosevelt was concerned about it, and in 1904, when the Dominican Republic defaulted on its debts, he was ready with a major announcement. Known as the **Roosevelt Corollary** of the Monroe Doctrine, the policy warned Latin American nations to keep their affairs in order or face American intervention.

Applying the new policy immediately, Roosevelt in 1905 took charge of the Dominican Republic's revenue system. American officials collected customs and saw to the payment of debt. Within two years, Roosevely also established protectorates in Cuba and Panama. In 1912, the U.S. Senate added the Lodge Corollary which warned foreign corporations not to purchase harbors and other sites of military significance in Latin America. Continued by Taft, Wilson, and other presidents, the Roosevelt Corollary guided American policy in Latin America until the 1930s, when Franklin D. Roosevelt's Good Neighbor policy replaced it.

Ventures in the Far East

The Open Door policy toward China and possession of the Philippine Islands shaped American actions in the Far East. Congress refused to arm the Philippines, and the islands were vulnerable to the growing power of Japan. Roosevelt wanted to balance Russian and Japanese power, and he was not unhappy at first when war broke out between them in 1904. As Japan won victory after victory, however, Roosevelt grew worried. Acting on a request from Japan, he offered to mediate the conflict, and both Russia and Japan accepted: Russia because it was losing, and Japan because it was financially drained.

TR'S BIG STICK A cartoon from *Judge* titled "The World's Constable." The Roosevelt Corollary claimed the right of the United States to exercise "an international police power," enforced by what many referred to as a "big stick" diplomacy.

How did the various figures in this cartoon portray the cartoonist's views of the world?

In August 1905, Roosevelt convened a peace conference at Portsmouth, New Hampshire. The conference ended the war, but Japan emerged as the dominant force in the Far East. Adjusting policy, Roosevelt sent Secretary of War Taft to Tokyo to negotiate the Taft-Katsura Agreement (1905), which recognized Japan's dominance over Korea in return for its promise not to invade the Philippines. Giving Japan a free hand in Korea violated the Open Door policy, but Roosevelt argued that he had little choice.

To show Japan his determination, Roosevelt sent sixteen battleships of the new American fleet around the world, including a stop in Tokyo in October 1908. European naval experts felt certain Japan would attack the fleet, but the Japanese welcomed it. For the moment, Japanese-American relations improved, and in 1908 the two nations, in an exchange of diplomatic notes, reached the comprehensive Root-Takahira Agreement in which they promised to maintain the status quo in the Pacific, uphold the Open Door, and support Chinese independence.

QUICK CHECK ✓

What were Theodore Roosevelt's policies toward China and Japan?

Taft and Dollar Diplomacy

In foreign as well as domestic affairs, President Taft tried to continue Roosevelt's policies. For secretary of state he chose Philander C. Knox, Roosevelt's attorney general, and together they pursued a policy of **"dollar diplomacy"** to promote American financial and business interests abroad. The policy had profit-seeking motives, but it also aimed to substitute economic ties for military alliances.

Intent, like Roosevelt, on supremacy in the Caribbean, Taft worked to replace European loans with American ones, thereby reducing the danger of outside meddling. In the Far East, Knox worked closely with Willard Straight, an agent of American bankers, who argued that dollar diplomacy was the financial arm of the Open Door. Straight had close ties to Edward H. Harriman, the railroad magnate, who wanted to build railroads in Manchuria in northern China. Knox tried to organize an international syndicate to loan China money to purchase the Manchurian railroads, and so he approached England, Japan, and Russia. In January 1910, all three turned him down.

The outcome was a blow to American policy and prestige in Asia. Russia and Japan found reasons to cooperate with each other and staked out spheres of influence in violation of the Open Door. Japan resented Taft's initiatives in Manchuria, and China's distrust of the United States deepened. Instead of cultivating friendship, as Roosevelt had envisioned, Taft had started an intense rivalry with Japan for commercial advantage in China.

QUICK CHECK ✓

What was the essential idea behind Taft's "dollar diplomacy"?

Foreign Policy Under Wilson

When he took office in 1913, Woodrow Wilson knew little about foreign policy. During the 1912 campaign he mentioned foreign policy only when it affected domestic concerns. "It would be the irony of fate if my administration had to deal chiefly with foreign affairs," he said to a friend before becoming president. And so it was. During his two terms, Wilson faced crisis after crisis in foreign affairs, including the outbreak of World War I.

WHAT did Woodrow Wilson mean by "moral diplomacy"?

"dollar diplomacy"
This policy, adopted by President William Howard Taft and Secretary of State Philander C. Knox, sought to promote U.S. financial and business interests abroad. It aimed to replace military alliances with economic ties, with the idea of increasing American influence and securing lasting peace. Under this policy, Taft worked in Latin America to replace European loans with American ones, assumed the debts of countries such as Honduras to fend off foreign bondholders, and helped Nicaragua secure a large loan in exchange for U.S. control of its national bank.

The idealistic Wilson believed in a principled, ethical world in which militarism, colonialism, and war were brought under control. He stressed moral purposes over material interests and said during one crisis, "The force of America is the force of moral principle." Rejecting the policy of dollar diplomacy, Wilson initially chose a course of **moral diplomacy,** designed to bring right to the world, preserve peace, and extend to other peoples the blessings of democracy.

Troubles Across the Border

William Jennings Bryan, whom Wilson appointed as secretary of state, was also an amateur in foreign relations. He was a fervent pacifist, and like Wilson, he believed in the American duty to "help" less favored nations.

Wilson and Bryan promised a dramatic new approach in Latin America, concerned not with the "pursuit of material interest" but with "human rights" and "national integrity." Yet in the end, Wilson, distracted by other problems and impatient with the results of his idealistic approach, continued the Roosevelt-Taft policies. He defended the Monroe Doctrine, gave unspoken support to the Roosevelt Corollary, and intervened in Latin America more than had either Roosevelt or Taft.

moral diplomacy
Policy adopted by President Woodrow Wilson that rejected the approach of "dollar diplomacy." Rather than focusing mainly on economic ties with other nations, Wilson's policy was designed to bring right principles to the world, preserve peace, and extend to other peoples the blessings of democracy. Wilson, however, often ended up pursuing policies much like those followed by Roosevelt and Taft.

Wilson's moral diplomacy encountered one of its greatest challenges across the border in Mexico. Porfirio Díaz, president of Mexico for thirty-seven years, was overthrown in 1911, and a liberal reformer, Francisco I. Madero, followed Díaz as president in 1911. But Madero could not keep order in the troubled country, and opponents of his reforms undermined him. With support from wealthy landowners, the army, and the Catholic Church, General Victoriano Huerta ousted Madero in 1913, threw him in jail, and arranged his murder. Most European nations immediately recognized Huerta, but Wilson, calling him a "butcher," refused to do so. Instead, he announced a new policy toward revolutionary regimes in Latin America. To win American recognition, they must not only exercise power but reflect "a just government based upon law, not upon arbitrary or irregular force."

On that basis, Wilson withheld recognition from Huerta and maneuvered to oust him. Early in 1914, he stationed naval units off Mexico's ports to cut off arms shipments to the Huerta regime. The action produced trouble. On April 9, 1914, several American sailors, who had gone ashore in Tampico to purchase supplies, were arrested. They were promptly released, but the American admiral demanded an apology and a 21-gun salute to the American flag. Huerta agreed—if the Americans also saluted the Mexican flag.

Wilson asked Congress for authority to use military force if needed; then, just as Congress acted, he learned that a German ship was landing arms at Veracruz on Mexico's eastern coast. With Wilson's approval, American warships shelled the harbor, and marines went ashore. Against heavy resistance, they took the city. Outraged, Mexicans of all factions denounced the invasion, and for a time the two countries hovered on the edge of war.

Retreating hastily, Wilson explained that he desired only to help Mexico. Argentina, Brazil, and Chile came to his aid with an offer to mediate the dispute, and tensions eased. In July 1914, weakened by an armed rebellion, Huerta resigned. Wilson recognized the new government, headed by Venustiano Carranza,

UNITED STATES

1 Columbus, New Mexico

2

3 **Parral**

MEXICO

Tampico 4

Veracruz
5

1. Villa's raid, March 9, 1916
2. Pershing's expedition, 1916–1917
3. Skirmish with Carranza's troops, April 12, 1916
4. American sailors arrested, April 1914
5. Seized by U.S. Navy, April 1914
6. U.S. occupation, 1912–1919, 1924–1925
7. U.S. occupation, 1912–1925, 1927–1933
8. Leased, 1903
9. Leased, 1903–1912
10. U.S. occupation, 1898–1902, 1906–1909, 1912 and 1917
11. U.S. naval base leased, 1903
12. U.S. occupation, 1915–1934
13. U.S. occupation, 1916–1924
14. Purchased from Denmark, 1917

U.S. protectorates
U.S. military expeditions
CANAL ZONE U.S. possessions labeled in red

0   250   500 miles
0   250   500 kilometers

Gulf of Mexico

BAHAMAS (Br.)

Bahía Honda   Havana
9   10
CUBA
11 **Guantánamo Bay**
HAITI
12
JAMAICA (Br.)

13
DOMINICAN REPUBLIC

VIRGIN ISLANDS (Br.)

PUERTO RICO

14 **VIRGIN ISLANDS**

Caribbean Sea

BRITISH HONDURAS
GUATEMALA
HONDURAS
6
EL SALVADOR   NICARAGUA
7

Proposed canal

COSTA RICA   PANAMA

CANAL ZONE
8

Panama Canal

VENEZUELA

COLOMBIA

ACTIVITIES OF THE UNITED STATES IN THE CARIBBEAN, 1898–1930   During the first three decades of the twentieth century, the United States policed the Caribbean, claiming the right to take action when it judged Latin American countries were doing a bad job of running their affairs.

Why was the United States so active in the Caribbean in the early twentieth century?

an associate of Madero. Early in 1916, Francisco ("Pancho") Villa, one of Carranza's generals, revolted. Hoping to goad the United States into an action against the government of Mexico that would help him seize power, he raided border towns, injuring American civilians.

Stationing militia along the border, Wilson ordered General John J. Pershing on a punitive expedition to seize Villa in Mexico. Pershing led six thousand troops deep into Mexican territory. At first, Carranza agreed to the drive, but as the Americans pushed farther and farther into his country, he changed his mind. As the wily Villa eluded Pershing, Carranza protested bitterly, and Wilson, worried about events in Europe, ordered Pershing home.

Wilson's policy had laudable goals; he wanted to help the Mexicans achieve political and agrarian reform. But his motives and methods were condescending. Wilson tried to impose gradual progressive reform on a society sharply divided along class and other lines. With little forethought, he interfered in the affairs of another country, and in doing so he revealed the themes—moralism, combined with pragmatic self-interest and a desire for peace—that also shaped his policies in Europe.

QUICK CHECK ✓

How and why did Wilson get involved in Mexico and how did his involvement reflect his "moral diplomacy"?

Toward War

WHAT

were the reasons behind and dangers of Wilson's neutrality policy?

In May 1914, Colonel Edward M. House, Wilson's close friend and adviser, sailed to Europe on a fact-finding mission. Tensions there were rising. "The situation is extraordinary," he reported to Wilson. "There is too much hatred, too many jealousies."

In Germany, the ambitious Kaiser Wilhelm II coveted a world empire to match those of Britain and France. Germany had military treaties with Turkey and Austria-Hungary, a sprawling central European country of many nationalities. Linked in another alliance, England, France, and Russia agreed to aid each other in case of attack.

On June 28, 1914, a Bosnian assassin linked to Serbia murdered Archduke Franz Ferdinand, heir to the Austro-Hungarian throne. Within weeks, Germany, Turkey, and Austria-Hungary (the Central Powers) were at war with England, France, and Russia (the Allied Powers). Americans were shocked at the events. Wilson immediately proclaimed neutrality and asked Americans to remain "impartial in thought as well as in action."

The war, he said, was one "with which we have nothing to do, whose causes cannot touch us." In private, Wilson was stunned. A man who loved peace, he had long admired the British parliamentary system, and he respected the leaders of the British Liberal party, who supported social programs akin to his own. "Everything I love most in the world," he said, "is at stake."

The Neutrality Policy

In general, Americans accepted neutrality. They saw no need to enter the conflict, especially after the Allies in September 1914 halted the first German drive toward Paris. America resisted involvement in other countries' problems, with the notable exception of Latin America, and had a tradition of freedom from foreign entanglements.

Many of the nation's large number of progressives saw additional reasons to resist. They thought war violated the very spirit of progressive reform. Why demand safer factories in which people could work and then kill them by the millions in war? To many progressives, moreover, England represented international finance, an institution they detested. Germany, on the other hand, had pioneered some of their favorite social reforms. Above all, progressives were sure that war would end reform. It consumed money and attention; it inflamed emotions.

As a result, Jane Addams, Florence Kelley, and other progressives fought to keep the United States out of war. In late 1915, they formed the American Union Against Militarism, to throw, they said, "a monkey wrench into the machinery" of war. In 1915, Addams helped organize the League to Limit Armament, and shortly thereafter, Addams and Carrie Chapman Catt formed the Woman's Peace Party to organize women against the war.

The war's outbreak also tugged at the emotions of millions of Americans. At the deepest level, a majority in the country, bound by common language and institutions, sympathized with the Allies and blamed Germany for the war. Like Wilson, many Americans admired English literature, customs, and law; they remembered Lafayette and the times when France had helped the United States in its early years. Germany, on the other hand, seemed arrogant and militaristic. When the war began, it invaded Belgium to strike at France and violated a treaty which the German chancellor called "just a scrap of paper."

Both sides sought to sway American opinion, and fierce propaganda campaigns flourished. German propaganda tended to stress strength and will; Allied propaganda called on historical ties and took advantage of German atrocities, both real and alleged. In the end, the propaganda probably made little difference. Ties of heritage and the course of the war, not propaganda, decided the American position. At the outset, no matter which side they cheered for, Americans of all persuasions preferred simply to remain at peace.

QUICK CHECK
What were the factors behind Wilson's neutrality policy?

Freedom of the Seas

The demands of trade tested American neutrality and confronted Wilson with difficult choices. Under international law, neutral countries were permitted to trade in nonmilitary goods with all belligerent countries. But Great Britain controlled the seas, and it intended to cut off shipments of war materials to the Central Powers.

As soon as war broke out, Britain blockaded German ports and limited the goods Americans could sell to Germany. American ships had to carry cargoes to neutral ports from which, after examination, they could be carried to Germany. As time passed, Britain stepped up the economic sanctions by forbidding the shipment to Germany of all foodstuffs and most raw materials, seizing and censoring mail, and "blacklisting" American firms that dealt directly with the Central Powers.

Again and again, Wilson protested against such infringements on neutral rights. Sometimes Britain complied, sometimes not, and Wilson often grew angry. But needing American support and supplies, Britain pursued a careful strategy to disrupt German-American trade without disrupting Anglo-American relations. When necessary, it also promised to reimburse American businesses after the war's end.

Other than the German U-boats, there were no constraints on trade with the Allies, and a flood of Allied war orders fueled the American economy. To finance the purchases, the Allies turned to American bankers for loans. By 1917, loans to Allied governments exceeded $2 billion; loans to Germany came to only $27 million.

In a development that influenced Wilson's policy, the war produced the greatest economic boom in the nation's history. Loans and trade drew the United States ever closer to the Allied cause. And even though Wilson often protested English maritime policy, the protests involved American goods and money, whereas Germany's submarine policy threatened American lives.

QUICK CHECK
In what ways did the demands of trade test American neutrality?

The U-Boat Threat

A relatively new weapon, the *Unterseeboot*, or submarine, strained the guidelines of international law. Traditional law required a submarine to surface, warn the target to stop, send a boarding party to check papers and cargo, then allow time for passengers and crew to board lifeboats before sinking the vessel. Flimsy and slow, submarines could ill afford to surface while the prey radioed for help.

When Germany announced the submarine campaign in February 1915, Wilson protested sharply, calling the sinking of merchant ships without checking

THE U-BOAT   A new and terrifying weapon of the war was the German U-boat, which attacked silently and without warning.

Why was the U-boat such a threat to peace?

cargo "a wanton act." The Germans promised not to sink American ships—an agreement that lasted until 1917—and thereafter the issue became the right of Americans to sail on the ships of belligerent nations. In March, an American citizen aboard the British liner *Falaba* perished when the ship was torpedoed off the Irish coast. Bryan urged Wilson to forbid Americans to travel in the war zones, but the president, determined to stand by the principles of international law, refused.

Wilson reacted more harshly in May and August of 1915 when U-boats sank the *Lusitania* and the *Arabic*. He demanded that the Germans protect passenger vessels and pay for American losses. At odds with Wilson's understanding of neutrality, Bryan resigned as secretary of state and was replaced by Robert Lansing, a lawyer and counselor in the State Department. Lansing brought a very different spirit to the job. He favored the Allies and believed that democracy was threatened in a world dominated by Germany. He urged strong stands against German violations of American neutrality.

Adolf K. G. E. von Spiegel, U-boat 202 (1919)

In February 1916, Germany declared unrestricted submarine warfare against all armed ships. Lansing protested and told Germany it would be held strictly accountable for American losses. A month later, a U-boat torpedoed the unarmed French channel steamer *Sussex* without warning, injuring several Americans. Arguing that the sinking violated the *Arabic* pledge, Lansing urged Wilson to break relations with Germany. Wilson rejected the advice, but on April 18 he sent an ultimatum to Germany, stating that unless the Germans immediately called off attacks on cargo and passenger ships, the United States would sever relations.

The kaiser, convinced he did not yet have enough submarines to risk war, yielded. In the *Sussex* pledge of May 4, 1916, he agreed to Wilson's demands and promised to shoot on sight only ships of the enemy's navy.

The *Sussex* pledge marked the beginning of a short period of friendly relations between Germany and the United States. The agreement applied not only to passenger liners but to all merchant ships, belligerent or not. There was one problem: Wilson had taken such a strong position that if Germany renewed submarine warfare on merchant shipping, war was likely. Most Americans, however, viewed the agreement as a diplomatic stroke for peace by Wilson, and the issues of peace and preparedness dominated the presidential election of 1916.

> **QUICK CHECK** ✔
>
> How did German submarines threaten to involve the United States in the war?

The Election of 1916

The "preparedness" issue pitted antiwar groups against those who wanted to prepare for war. Bellicose as always, Teddy Roosevelt led the preparedness campaign. He called Wilson "yellow" for not pressing Germany harder, but Wilson defended the military's state of readiness and refused to be stampeded.

Wilson's position was attacked from both sides as preparedness advocates charged cowardice, while pacifists denounced any attempt at military readiness. The difficulty of his situation, plus the growing U-boat crisis, soon changed Wilson's mind. In mid-1915, he asked the War Department to increase military planning, and later that year, approved large increases in the army and navy, a move that upset many peace-minded progressives.

For their standard-bearer in the presidential election of 1916, the Republicans nominated Charles Evans Hughes, a moderate justice of the Supreme Court. Hughes seemed to have all the qualifications for victory. A former reform governor of New York, he could lure back the Roosevelt progressives while at the same time appealing to the Republican conservatives. To woo the Roosevelt wing, Hughes called for a tougher line against Germany, thus allowing the Democrats to label him the "war" candidate. Even so, Roosevelt and others considered Hughes a "bearded iceberg," a dull campaigner who wavered on important issues.

The Democrats renominated Wilson in a convention marked by spontaneous demonstrations for peace. Picking up the theme, Wilson said in October, "I am not expecting this country to get into war." The

PRESSURES FOR WAR   Roosevelt's campaign for war preparedness became a personal attack on Wilson, whom he called a coward and a weakling. According to this cartoon titled "White House or Bust," Roosevelt had the election of 1916 in mind as well as military preparedness.

Why was Roosevelt eager for the United States to enter the war?

campaign slogan "He kept us out of war" was repeated again and again, and just before the election, the Democrats took full-page ads in leading newspapers:

> You Are Working—Not Fighting!
> Alive and Happy—Not Cannon Fodder!
> Wilson and Peace with Honor?
> or
> Hughes with Roosevelt and War?

On election night, Hughes had swept most of the East, and Wilson retired at 10 P.M. thinking he had lost. During the night, the results came in from California, New Mexico, and North Dakota; all supported Wilson—California by a mere 3773 votes. Holding the Democratic South, he carried key states in the Midwest and West and took large portions of the labor and progressive vote. Women—who were then allowed to vote in presidential elections in twelve states—also voted heavily for Wilson.

QUICK CHECK ✓

What were the two key issues and the main results of the 1916 presidential election?

The Final Months of Peace

Just before election day, Great Britain further limited neutral trade, and there were reports from Germany of a renewal of unrestricted submarine warfare. Fresh from his victory, Wilson redoubled his efforts for peace. Aware that time was running out, he hoped to start negotiations to end the bloodshed and create a peaceful postwar world.

In December 1916, he sent messages to both sides asking them to state their war aims. Should they do so, he pledged the "whole force" of the United States to end the war. The Allies refused, although they promised privately to negotiate if the German terms were reasonable. The Germans replied evasively and in January 1917 revealed their real objectives. Close to forcing Russia out of the war, Germany sensed victory and wanted territory in eastern Europe, Africa, Belgium, and France.

On January 22, in an eloquent speech before the Senate, Wilson called for a "peace without victory." Outlining his own ambitious aims, he urged respect for all nations, freedom of the seas, arms limitations, and a League of Nations to keep the peace. "Only a peace between equals can last, only a peace the very principle of which is equality and a common participation in a common benefit." The speech made a great impression on many Europeans, but it was too late. The Germans had decided a few weeks before to unleash the submarines and gamble on a quick end to the war. Even as Wilson spoke, U-boats were in the Atlantic west of Ireland, preparing to attack.

On January 31, the German ambassador in Washington informed Lansing that beginning February 1, U-boats would sink on sight all ships—passenger or merchant, neutral or belligerent, armed or unarmed—in the waters around England and France. Staking everything on a last effort, the Germans calculated that if they could sink 600,000

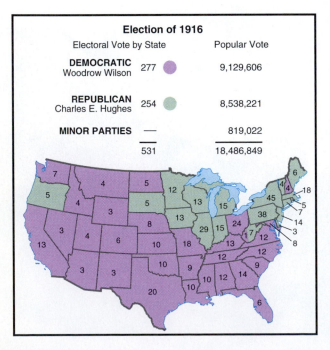

Election of 1916

	Electoral Vote by State	Popular Vote
DEMOCRATIC Woodrow Wilson	277 ●	9,129,606
REPUBLICAN Charles E. Hughes	254 ●	8,538,221
MINOR PARTIES	—	819,022
	531	18,486,849

tons of shipping a month, they could defeat England in six months. As he had pledged in 1916, Wilson broke off relations with Germany, although he still hoped for peace.

On February 25, the British government privately gave Wilson a telegram intercepted from Arthur Zimmermann, the German foreign minister, to the German ambassador in Mexico. A day later, Wilson asked Congress for authority to arm merchant ships to deter U-boat attacks. When La Follette and a handful of others threatened to filibuster, Wilson divulged the contents of the Zimmermann telegram. It proposed an alliance with Mexico in case of war with the United States, offering financial support and recovery of Mexico's "lost territory" in New Mexico, Texas, and Arizona.

Spurred by a wave of public indignation toward the Germans, the House passed Wilson's measure, but La Follette and others still blocked action in the Senate. On March 9, 1917, Wilson ordered merchant ships armed on his own authority. Three days later, he announced the arming, and on March 13, the navy instructed all vessels to fire on submarines. Between March 12 and March 21, U-boats sank five American ships, and Wilson decided to wait no longer.

He called Congress into special session and at 8:30 in the evening on April 2, 1917, asked for a declaration of war. Pacifists in Congress continued to hold out, and for four days they managed to postpone action. Finally, on April 6, the declaration of war passed, with fifty members of the House and six senators voting against it. Even then, the country was divided over entry into the war.

The Zimmermann Telegram (1917)

President Wilson's War Message to Congress (1917)

United States Declaration of War (1917)

QUICK CHECK ✔

How did the United States finally get involved in the war?

Over There

With a burst of patriotism, the United States entered a war its new allies were in danger of losing. That same month, the Germans sank 881,000 tons of Allied shipping, the highest amount for any one month during the war. There were mutinies in the French army; a costly British drive in Flanders stalled. In November, the Bolsheviks seized power in Russia, and, led by V. I. Lenin, they soon signed a separate peace treaty with Germany, freeing German troops to fight in the West. German and Austrian forces routed the Italian army on the southern flank, and the Allies braced for a spring 1918 offensive.

WHAT effect did the United States' entry into World War I have on the war?

Mobilization

The United States was not prepared for war. Some Americans hoped the declaration of war itself might daunt the Germans; there were those who thought that naval escorts of Allied shipping would be enough. Others hoped money and arms supplied to the Allies would be sufficient to produce victory without sending troops.

Bypassing older generals, Wilson named John J. ("Black Jack") Pershing, leader of the Mexican campaign, to head the American Expeditionary Force (AEF). Pershing inherited an army unready for war. In April 1917, it had 200,000 officers and men, equipped with 300,000 old rifles, 1500 machine guns, 55 out-of-date airplanes, and 2 field radio sets. Its most recent battle experience had been chasing Pancho Villa around northern Mexico. It had not caught him.

World War I

"Over There"

EUROPEAN ALLIANCES AND BATTLEFRONTS, 1914–1917 Allied forces suffered early defeats on the eastern front (Tannenberg) and in the Dardanelles (Gallipoli). In 1917, the Allies were routed on the southern flank (Caporetto); the western front then became the critical theater of the war.

What did the Germans hope to accomplish on the western front?

African American Recruiting Poster

How did the United States mobilize for war?

Although some in Congress preferred a voluntary army of the kind that had fought in the Spanish-American War, Wilson turned to conscription, which he believed was both efficient and democratic. In May 1917, Congress passed the **Selective Service Act,** providing for the registration of all men between the ages of 21 and 30 (later changed to 18 and 45). Early in June, 9.5 million men registered for the draft. By the end of the war, the act had registered 24.2 million men, about 2.8 million of whom were inducted into the army.

The draft included black men as well as white, and four African American regiments were among the first sent into action. Despite their contributions, however, no black soldiers were allowed to march in the victory celebrations that eventually took place in Paris.

War in the Trenches

World War I may have been the most terrible war of all time, more terrible even than World War II and its vast devastation. After the early offensives, the European armies dug themselves into trenches only hundreds of yards apart in places. Artillery, poison gas, hand grenades, and a new weapon—rapid-fire machine guns—kept them pinned down.

Trench Warfare

Even in moments of respite, the mud, rats, cold, fear, and disease took a heavy toll. Deafening bombardments shook the earth, and there was a high incidence of shell shock. From time to time, troops went "over the top" of the trenches in an effort to break through the enemy's lines, but the costs were enormous. The German offensive at Verdun in 1916 killed 600,000 men; the British lost 20,000 on the first day of an offensive on the Somme.

The first American soldiers reached France in June 1917. By March of the following year, 300,000 Americans were there, and by war's end, 2 million men had crossed the Atlantic.

As expected, on March 21, 1918, the Germans launched a massive assault in western Europe. Troops from the Russian front added to the force, and by May they had driven Allied forces back to the Marne River, just 50 miles from Paris. There, the Americans saw their first action. The American forces blocked the Germans at the town of Château-Thierry and four weeks later forced them out of Belleau Wood, a crucial stronghold. On July 15, the Germans threw everything into a last drive for Paris, but they were halted at the Marne, and in three days of battle they were finished. "On the 18th," the German chancellor said, "even the

Selective Service Act
This 1917 law provided for the registration of all American men between the ages of 21 and 30 for a military draft. By the end of World War I, 24.2 million men had registered; 2.8 million had been inducted into the army. The age limits were later changed to 18 and 45.

THE FACE OF BATTLE In *The Victorious Retreat Back to the Rhine* (1918), American illustrator and painter Frank Schoonover captures the intensity of aerial bombardment supporting the gathering momentum of Allied ground forces to drive back the Germans in the final stages of the war.

What does this painting say about the nature of World War I and its differences with the Spanish-American War?

Eugene Kennedy, A "Doughboy" Describes the Fighting Front (1918)

QUICK CHECK ✔

Why might World War I have been the most terrible war of all time?

most optimistic among us knew that all was lost. The history of the world was played out in three days."

With the German drive stalled, the Allies counterattacked along the entire front. On September 12, 1918, a half million Americans and a smaller contingent of French drove the Germans from the St. Mihiel salient, 12 miles south of Verdun. Two weeks later, 896,000 American soldiers attacked between the Meuse River and the Argonne Forest. Focusing their efforts on a main railroad supply line for the German army in the West, American troops broke through in early November, cut the line, and drove the Germans back along the whole front.

The German high command knew that the war was lost. On October 6, 1918, Germany appealed to Wilson for an armistice, and by the end of the month, Turkey, Bulgaria, and Austria-Hungary were out of the war. At 4 A.M. on November 11, Germany signed the armistice. The American force lost 48,909 dead and 230,000 wounded; losses to disease brought the total of dead to more than 112,000.

The American contribution, although small in comparison to the enormous costs to European nations, was vital. Fresh, enthusiastic American troops raised Allied morale; they helped turn the tide at a crucial point in the war.

Over Here

Victory at the front depended on economic and emotional mobilization at home. Consolidating federal authority, Wilson moved quickly in 1917 and 1918 to organize war production and distribution. An idealist who knew how to sway public opinion, he also recognized the need to enlist American emotions. To him, the war for people's minds, the "conquest of their convictions," was as vital as events on the battlefield.

The Conquest of Convictions

A week after war was declared, Wilson formed the **Committee on Public Information (CPI)** to mobilize support for the war, and asked George Creel, an outspoken progressive journalist, to head it. Creel hired progressives such as Ida Tarbell and Ray Stannard Baker and recruited thousands of people in the arts, advertising, and film industries to publicize the war. He worked out a system of voluntary censorship with the press, plastered walls with colorful posters, and issued more than 75 million pamphlets.

Helped along by the propaganda campaign, anti-German sentiment spread rapidly. Many schools stopped offering instruction in the German language—California's state education board called it a language "of autocracy, brutality, and hatred." Sauerkraut became "liberty cabbage"; saloonkeepers removed pretzels from the bar. Orchestral works by Bach, Beethoven, and Brahms vanished from some symphonic programs.

Rather than curbing the anti-German sentiment, Wilson encouraged it. "Woe be to the man or group of men that seeks to stand in our way," he told peace advocates soon after the war began. At his request, Congress passed

WHAT programs and changes did World War I bring at home?

Committee on Public Information (CPI) Created in 1917 by President Wilson and headed by progressive journalist George Creel, this organization rallied support for American involvement in World War I through art, advertising, and film. Creel worked out a system of voluntary censorship with the press and distributed colorful posters and pamphlets. The CPI's Division of Industrial Relations rallied labor to help the war effort.

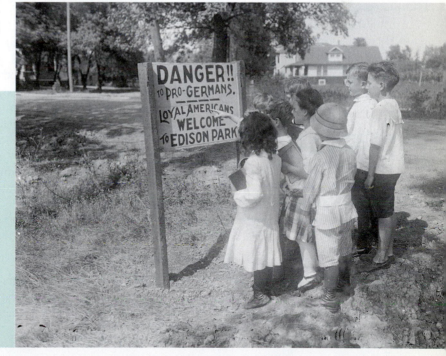

WARTIME HATRED Anti-German sentiment spread in America during World War I, escalating dramatically after the United States entered the war in April 1917. A wave of verbal and physical attacks on German Americans was accompanied by a campaign to repress German culture. In this photograph from 1917, a group of children stand in front of an anti-German sign posted in the Edison Park community of Chicago, Illinois. As the sign suggests, some Americans questioned the loyalty of their German American neighbors.

In what ways did Americans express their anti-German sentiment during World War I?

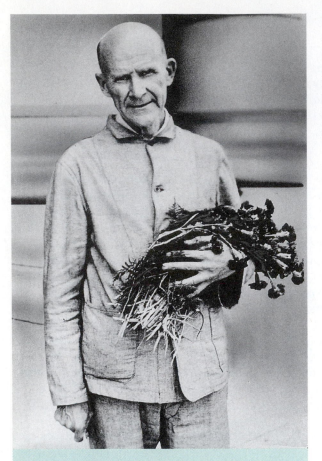

OPPOSITION TO THE WAR Eugene V. Debs, serving time in an Atlanta penitentiary for speaking out against the war, is shown here after receiving word of his nomination for the presidency. Debs campaigned in 1920 from behind bars.

Why did the Socialist party achieve the popularity it did early in the twentieth century?

QUICK CHECK ✔

What measures did Wilson pass to sway American opinions?

the **Espionage Act** of 1917, which imposed sentences of up to twenty years in prison for persons found guilty of aiding the enemy, obstructing recruitment of soldiers, or encouraging disloyalty. It allowed the postmaster general to remove from the mails materials that incited treason or insurrection. The Trading-with-the-Enemy Act of 1917 authorized the government to censor the foreign language press.

In 1918, Congress passed the **Sedition Act,** imposing harsh penalties on anyone using "disloyal, profane, scurrilous, or abusive language" about the government, flag, or armed forces uniforms. In all, more than fifteen hundred persons were arrested under the new laws.

The sedition laws clearly went beyond any clear or present danger. There were, to be sure, German spies in the country, Germans who wanted to encourage strikes in American arms factories. Moreover, the U.S. government and other national leaders were painfully aware of how divided Americans had been about entering the war. They set out to promote unity—by force, if necessary—in order to convince Germany that the nation was united behind the war.

But none of these matters warranted a nationwide program of repression. Conservatives took advantage of wartime feelings to try to stamp out American socialists, who in fact were vulnerable because, unlike their European counterparts, they continued to oppose the war even after their country had entered it. Using the sedition laws, conservatives harried the Socialist party and another favorite target, the Industrial Workers of the World.

Wilson's postmaster general banned from the mails more than a dozen socialist publications, including the *Appeal to Reason*, which went to more than half a million people weekly. In 1918, Eugene V. Debs, the Socialist party leader, delivered a speech denouncing capitalism and the war. He was convicted for violation of the Espionage Act and spent the war in a penitentiary in Atlanta. Nominated as the Socialist party candidate in the presidential election of 1920, Debs—prisoner 9653—won nearly a million votes, but the Socialist movement never fully recovered from the repression of the war.

Joseph Buffington, "Friendly Words to the Foreign Born" (1917)

Newton D. Baker, Treatment of German-Americans (1918)

A Bureaucratic War

Quick, effective action was needed to win the war. To meet the need, Wilson and Congress set up an array of new federal agencies, nearly five thousand in all. Staffed largely by businessmen, the agencies drew on funds and powers they had never had before.

By the time the war was over, it had cost $32 billion in direct war expense—in an era when the entire federal budget rarely exceeded $1 billion. To raise the money, the administration sold about $23 billion in "Liberty Bonds," and, using the new Sixteenth Amendment, boosted taxes on corporations and personal incomes.

At first, Wilson tried to organize the wartime economy along decentralized lines, almost in the fashion of his early New Freedom thinking. But that proved unworkable, and he moved instead to a series of highly centralized planning boards, each with broad authority over a specific area of the economy. There were boards to control virtually every aspect of transportation, agriculture, and manufacturing. Though only a few of them were as effective as Wilson had hoped, they did coordinate the war effort to some degree.

The **War Industries Board (WIB),** one of the most powerful of the new agencies, oversaw the production of all American factories. Headed by millionaire Bernard M. Baruch, a Wall Street broker and speculator, it determined priorities, allocated raw materials, and fixed prices. It told manufacturers what they could and could not make. The WIB set the output of steel and regulated the number of stops on elevators. Working closely with business, Baruch for a time acted as the dictator of the American economy.

Herbert Hoover, the hero of a campaign to feed starving Belgians, headed a new **Food Administration**, and he set out with customary energy to supply food to the armies overseas. Appealing to the "spirit of self-sacrifice," Hoover convinced people to save food by observing "meatless" and "wheatless" days. He fixed prices to boost production, bought and distributed wheat, and encouraged people to plant "victory gardens" behind homes, churches, and schools.

At another new agency, the Fuel Administration, Harry A. Garfield, the president of Williams College, introduced daylight saving time, rationed coal and oil, and imposed gasless days when motorists could not drive. A fourth agency, the Railroad Administration, dictated rail traffic over nearly 400,000 miles of track—standardizing rates, limiting passenger travel, and speeding arms shipments. The War Shipping Board coordinated shipping, the Emergency Fleet Corporation supervised shipbuilding, and the War Trade Board oversaw foreign trade.

As never before, the government intervened in American life. Businessmen flocked to Washington to run the new agencies, and the partnership between government and business grew closer. As government expanded, business expanded as well, responding to wartime contracts. Industries such as steel, aluminum, and cigarettes boomed, and corporate profits increased threefold between 1914 and 1919.

THE WAR AT HOME   The U.S. Food Administration urged immigrants and newcomers to America to make sacrifices in the cause of freedom.

In what ways did this poster portray the nation and its people?

QUICK CHECK ✓

What were the main bureaucratic measures that shaped American war policy in World War I?

Labor in the War

The war also brought organized labor into the partnership with government, although the results were more limited than in the business-government alliance. Samuel Gompers, president of the AFL, served on Wilson's Council of National

Espionage Act (1917)

WOMEN AT WORK Housewives did not leave home for the factory en masse in 1917 as they later did during World War II, but many women already employed outside the home found new, well-paying opportunities in jobs previously held by men.

What effects did factory work have on women during these years?

Abrams v. *United States*

Eugene V. Debs, Critique of World War I (1918)

Espionage Act

This law, passed after the United States entered World War I, imposed sentences of up to twenty years on anyone found guilty of aiding the enemy, obstructing recruitment of soldiers, or encouraging disloyalty. It allowed the postmaster general to remove from the mail any materials that incited treason or insurrection.

Defense, an advisory group formed to unify business, labor, and government. Gompers hoped to trade labor peace for labor advances, and he formed a War Committee on Labor to enlist workers' support for the war. With the blessing of the Wilson administration, membership in the AFL and other unions grew from about 2.7 million in 1916 to more than 4 million in 1919.

Hoping to encourage production and avoid strikes, Wilson adopted many of the objectives of the social-justice reformers. He supported an eight-hour day in war-related industries and improved wages and working conditions. In May 1918, he named Felix Frankfurter, a brilliant young law professor, to head a new War Labor Board (WLB). The agency standardized wages and hours, and it protected the right of labor to organize and bargain collectively.

The WLB also ordered that women be paid equal wages for equal work in war industries. In 1914, the flow of European immigrants suddenly stopped because of the war, and in 1917, the draft began to take large numbers of American men. The result was a labor shortage, filled by women, African Americans, and Mexican Americans. One million women worked in war industries. Some of them took jobs previously held by men, but for the most part, they moved from one set of "women's jobs" into another.

Still, there were some new opportunities and in some cases higher pay. In food, airplane, and electrical plants, women made up one-fifth or more of the

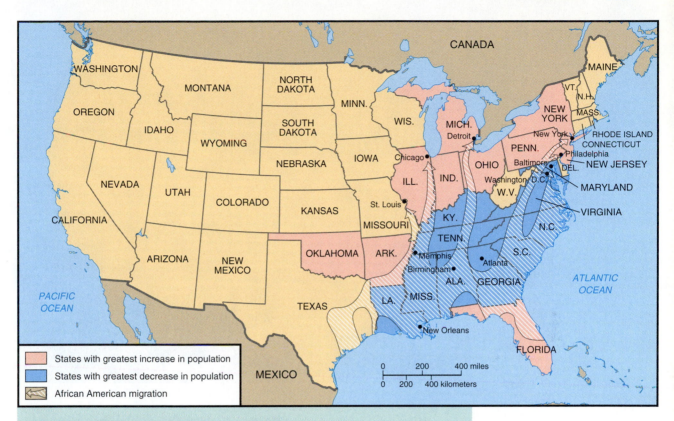

States with greatest increase in population

States with greatest decrease in population

African American migration

AFRICAN AMERICAN MIGRATION NORTHWARD, 1910–1920   The massive migration of African Americans from the South to the North during World War I changed the dynamics of race relations in the United States.

What impact did the mass migration of African Americans during World War I have on both the South and the North?

workforce. As their wages increased, so did their expectations; some became more militant, and conflict grew between them and male co-workers.

Looking for more people to fill wartime jobs, corporations found another major source among southern blacks. Beginning in 1916, northern labor agents traveled across the South, promising jobs, high wages, and free transportation. Soon the word spread, and the movement northward became a flood. Between 1916 and 1918, more than 450,000 African Americans left the Old South for the booming industrial cities of St. Louis, Chicago, Detroit, and Cleveland. In the decade before 1920, Detroit's black population grew by more than 600 percent, Cleveland's by more than 300 percent, and Chicago's by 150 percent.

Most of the newcomers were young, unmarried, and skilled or semiskilled. The men found jobs in factories, railroad yards, steel mills, packinghouses, and coal mines; black women worked in textile factories, department stores, and restaurants. In their new homes, African Americans found greater racial freedom but also different living conditions. If the South was often hostile, the North could be impersonal and lonely. Accustomed to the pace of the farm—ruled by the seasons and the sun—those blacks who were able to enter the industrial sector now worked for hourly wages in mass production industries, where time clocks and line supervisors dictated the daily routine.

"Buy War Bonds" Poster

African American Women Workers, WWI

Sedition Act

A wartime law that imposed harsh penalties on anyone using "disloyal, profane, scurrilous, or abusive language" about the U.S. government, flag, or armed forces.

HEROES OF THE WAR
The 369th infantry regiment returning from the war on the *Stockholm* in February 1919. They were awarded the Croix de Guerre for bravery in the Meuse-Argonne.

What lessons did African Americans draw from their role in World War I?

F. J. Grimke, Address to African American Soldiers (1919)

War Industries Board (WIB)

An example of the many boards and commissions created during World War I, this government agency oversaw the production of all American factories. It determined priorities, allocated raw materials, and fixed prices; it told manufacturers what they could and could not produce.

Food Administration

A wartime government agency that encouraged Americans to save food in order to supply the armies overseas. It fixed prices to boost production, asked people to observe "meatless" and "wheatless" days to conserve food, and promoted the planting of "victory gardens" behind homes, schools, and churches.

Racial tensions increased, resulting in part from growing competition for housing and jobs. In mid-1917, a race war in East St. Louis, Illinois, killed nine whites and about forty blacks. Later, there were race riots in Chicago, New York City, Omaha, and other cities. Lynch mobs killed forty-eight blacks in 1917, sixty-three in 1918, and seventy-eight in 1919. Ten of the victims in 1919 were war veterans, several still in uniform.

Blacks were more and more inclined to fight back. Two hundred thousand blacks served in France—forty-two thousand as combat troops. Returning home, they expected better treatment. "I'm glad I went," a black veteran said. "I done my part and I'm going to fight right here till Uncle Sam does his."

"Lift Ev'ry Voice and Sing," composed in 1900, became known as the "Negro National Anthem." Parents bought black dolls for their children, and W. E. B. Du Bois spoke of a "New Negro," proud and more militant: "We return. We return from fighting. We return fighting."

Eager for cheap labor, farmers and ranchers in the Southwest persuaded the federal government to relax immigration restrictions, and between 1917 and 1920, more than 100,000 Mexicans migrated into Texas, Arizona, New Mexico, and California. The Mexican American population grew from 385,000 in 1910 to 740,000 in 1920. Tens of thousands of Mexican Americans moved to Chicago, St. Louis, Omaha, and other northern cities to take wartime jobs. Often scorned and insecure, they created urban barrios similar to the Chinatowns and Little Italys around them.

Like most wars, World War I affected patterns at home as much as abroad. Business profits grew, factories expanded, and industries turned out huge amounts of war goods. Government authority swelled, and people came to expect different things of their government. Labor made some gains, as did women and blacks. Society assimilated some of the shifts, but social and economic tensions grew, and when the war ended, they spilled over in the strikes and violence of the Red Scare that followed.

The United States emerged from the war the strongest economic power in the world. In 1914, it was a debtor nation, and American citizens owed foreign investors about $3 billion. Five years later, the United States had become a creditor nation. Foreign governments owed more than $10 billion, and foreign citizens owed American investors nearly $3 billion. The war marked a shift in economic power rarely equaled in history.

QUICK CHECK ✓

What were four effects the war had on labor?

The Treaty of Versailles

Long before the fighting ended, Wilson began to formulate plans for the peace. Like many others, he was disconcerted when the new Bolshevik government in Russia began revealing the terms of secret agreements among Britain, France, and czarist Russia to divide up Germany's colonies. To try to place the war on a higher plane, he appeared before Congress on January 8, 1918, and outlined terms for a far-reaching, nonpunitive settlement. Wilson's **Fourteen Points** were generous and far-sighted, but they failed to satisfy wartime emotions that sought vindication.

England and France distrusted Wilsonian idealism as the basis for peace. They wanted Germany disarmed and crippled; they wanted its colonies; and they were skeptical of the principle of self-determination. As the end of the war neared, the Allies, who had in fact made secret commitments with one another, balked at making the Fourteen Points the basis of peace. When Wilson threatened to negotiate a separate treaty with Germany, however, they accepted.

Wilson had won an important victory, but difficulties lay ahead. As Georges Clemenceau, the 78-year-old French premier, said, "God gave us the Ten Commandments, and we broke them. Wilson gives us the Fourteen Points. We shall see."

A Peace at Paris

Unfortunately, Wilson made a grave error just before the peace conference began. He appealed to voters to elect a Democratic Congress in the November 1918 elections, saying that any other result would be "interpreted on the other side of the water as a repudiation of my leadership." Many Republicans were furious, especially those who had supported the Fourteen Points; Wilson's problems deepened when the Democrats went on to lose both the House and Senate.

Two weeks after the elections, Wilson announced he would attend the peace conference. This was a dramatic break from tradition, and his personal involvement drew attacks from Republicans. They renewed criticism when he named the rest of the delegation: Secretary of State Lansing; Colonel House; General Tasker H. Bliss, a military expert; and Henry White, a career diplomat. Wilson named no member of the Senate, and the only Republican in the group was White.

In selecting the delegation, Wilson passed over Henry Cabot Lodge, the powerful Republican senator from Massachusetts who opposed the Fourteen Points and would soon head the Senate Foreign Relations Committee. He also decided not to appoint Elihu Root or ex-President Taft, both of them enthusiastic

WHAT

? mistakes did Wilson make in negotiating the Treaty of Versailles?

Fourteen Points
In January 1918, President Wilson presented these terms for a far-reaching, nonpunitive settlement of World War I. He called, among other things, for removal of barriers to trade, open peace accords, reduction of armaments, and the establishment of a League of Nations. While generous and optimistic, the Points did not satisfy wartime hunger for revenge, and thus were largely rejected by European nations.

DOCUMENT

President Wilson's Fourteen Points

WOODROW WILSON'S FOURTEEN POINTS, 1918: SUCCESS AND FAILURE IN IMPLEMENTATION

1. Open covenants of peace openly arrived at	Not fulfilled
2. Absolute freedom of navigation on the seas in peace and war	Not fulfilled
3. Removal of all economic barriers to the equality of trade among nations	Not fulfilled
4. Reduction of armaments to the level needed only for domestic safety	Not fulfilled
5. Impartial adjustments of colonial claims	Not fulfilled
6. Evacuation of all Russian territory; Russia to be welcomed into the society of free nations	Not fulfilled
7. Evacuation and restoration of Belgium	Fulfilled
8. Evacuation and restoration of all French lands; return of Alsace-Lorraine to France	Fulfilled
9. Readjustment of Italy's frontiers along lines of Italian nationality	Compromised
10. Self-determination for the former subjects of the Austro-Hungarian Empire	Compromised
11. Evacuation of Rumania, Serbia, and Montenegro; free access to the sea for Serbia	Compromised
12. Self-determination for the former subjects of the Ottoman Empire; secure sovereignty for Turkish portion	Compromised
13. Establishment of an independent Poland, with free and secure access to the sea	Fulfilled
14. Establishment of a League of Nations affording mutual guarantees of independence and territorial integrity	Not fulfilled

Sources: Data from G. M. Gathorne-Hardy, *The Fourteen Points and the Treaty of Versailles* (Oxford Pamphlets on World Affairs, no. 6, 1939), pp. 8–34; Thomas G. Paterson et al., *American Foreign Policy: A History Since 1900*, 2nd ed., vol. 2, pp. 282–293.

internationalists. Never good at accepting criticism or delegating authority, Wilson wanted a delegation he could control—an advantage at the peace table but not in any battle over the treaty at home.

Upon his arrival, Wilson received a tumultuous welcome in England, France, and Italy. Never before had such crowds acclaimed a democratic political figure. In Paris, two million people lined the Champs-Elysees, threw flowers at him, and shouted, "Wilson le Juste [the just]" as his carriage drove by. Overwhelmed, Wilson was sure that the people of Europe shared his goals and would force their leaders to accept his peace. He was wrong. Like their leaders, many people on the Allied side hated Germany and wanted victory unmistakably reflected in the peace.

THE TREATY OF VERSAILLES Sir William Orpen, *The Signing of Peace in the Hall of Mirrors, Versailles, 28th of May 1919.* Although the United States played a major role in drafting the treaty, the Senate never ratified the document. Instead, the United States made a separate peace with Germany in 1921.

Why did the United States Senate refuse to approve the treaty of peace ending World War I?

Opening in January 1919, the Peace Conference at Paris continued until May. Although twenty-seven nations were represented, the "Big Four" dominated it: Wilson; Clemenceau of France, tired and stubborn, determined to end the German threat forever; David Lloyd George, the crafty British prime minister who had pledged to squeeze Germany "until the pips squeak"; and the Italian prime minister, Vittorio Orlando. A clever negotiator, Wilson traded various "small" concessions for his major goals—national self-determination, a reduction in tensions, and a League of Nations to enforce the peace.

Wilson had to surrender some important principles. Departing from the Fourteen Points by violating the principle of self-determination, the treaty created two new independent nations—Poland and Czechoslovakia—with large German-speaking populations. It divided up the German colonies in Asia and Africa. Instead of a peace without victory, it made Germany accept responsibility for the war and demanded enormous reparations—which eventually totaled $33 billion. It made no mention of disarmament, free trade, or freedom of the seas. Instead of an open covenant openly arrived at, the treaty was drafted behind closed doors.

But Wilson deflected some of the most extreme Allied demands, and he won his coveted Point 14, a League of Nations, designed "to achieve international peace and security." The League included a general assembly; a smaller council composed of the United States, Great Britain, France, Italy, Japan, and four nations to be elected by the assembly; and a court of international justice. League members pledged to submit to arbitration every dispute threatening peace and to enjoin military and economic sanctions against nations resorting to war. Article X, for Wilson the heart of the League, obliged members to look out for one another's independence and territorial integrity.

The draft treaty in hand, Wilson returned home in February 1919 to discuss it with Congress and the people. Most Americans, the polls showed, favored the League; thirty-three governors endorsed it. But over dinner with the Senate and House Foreign Relations Committees, Wilson learned of the strength of congressional opposition to it. On March 3, Senator Lodge produced a "round robin" signed by thirty-seven senators declaring they would not vote for the treaty without amendment. Should the numbers hold, Lodge had enough votes to defeat it.

Returning to Paris, Wilson attacked his critics, while he worked privately for changes to improve the chances of Senate approval. In return for major concessions, the Allies amended the League draft treaty, agreeing that domestic affairs remained outside League jurisdiction (exempting the Monroe Doctrine) and allowing nations to withdraw after two years' notice. On June 28, 1919, they signed the treaty in the Hall of Mirrors at Versailles, and Wilson started home for his most difficult fight.

New and reconstituted nations

EUROPE AFTER THE TREATY OF VERSAILLES, 1919

The treaty changed the map of Europe, creating a number of new and reconstituted nations. (Note the boundary changes from the map on p. 662.)

How did the treaty as shown in this map sow the seeds for World War II?

QUICK CHECK

What were the main considerations in the negotiations over the peace treaty to end the war?

Rejection in the Senate

There were ninety-six senators in 1919, forty-nine of them Republicans. Fourteen Republicans, led by William E. Borah of Idaho, were the "irreconcilables" who opposed the League on any grounds. Frank B. Kellogg of Minnesota led a group of twelve "mild reservationists" who accepted the treaty but wanted to insert several reservations that would not greatly weaken it. Finally, there were the Lodge-led "strong reservationists," twenty-three of them in all, who wanted major changes that the Allies would have to approve.

With only four Democratic senators opposed to the treaty, the Democrats and Republicans willing to compromise had enough votes to ratify it, once a few reservations were inserted. Bidding for time to allow public opposition to grow, Lodge scheduled lengthy hearings and spent two weeks reading the 268-page treaty aloud. Democratic leaders urged Wilson to appeal to the Republican "mild reservationists," but he refused: "Anyone who opposes me in that I'll crush!"

Fed up with Lodge's tactics, Wilson set out in early September to take the case directly to the people. Crossing the Midwest, his speeches aroused little emotion, but on the Pacific Coast he won ovations, which heartened him. On his way back to Washington, he stopped in Pueblo, Colorado, where he delivered one of the most eloquent speeches of his career. People wept as he talked of Americans who died in battle and the hope that they would never fight again in foreign lands. That night Wilson felt ill, returned to Washington, and on October 2, Mrs. Wilson found him lying unconscious on the floor of the White House, the victim of a stroke that paralyzed his left side.

After the stroke, Wilson could not work more than an hour or two at a time. No one was allowed to see him except family members, his secretary, and his physician. For more than seven months, he did not meet with the cabinet. Focusing his remaining energy on the fight over the treaty, Wilson lost touch with other issues, and critics charged that his wife, Edith Bolling Wilson, ran the government.

On November 6, 1919, while Wilson convalesced, Lodge finally reported the treaty out of committee, along with "Fourteen Reservations," one for each of Wilson's points. The most important reservation stipulated that implementation of Article X, Wilson's key article, required the action of Congress before any American intervention abroad.

On November 19, the treaty—with the Lodge reservations—failed, 39 to 55. Following Wilson's instructions, the Democrats voted against it. A motion to approve without the reservations lost 38 to 53, with only one Republican voting in favor. The defeat brought pleas for compromise, but neither Wilson nor Lodge would back down. When the treaty with reservations again came up for vote on March 19, 1920, Wilson ordered the Democrats to hold firm against it. Although twenty-one of them defied him,

DISAGREEMENT OVER THE TREATY Humanity is the accuser, the U.S. Senate is the assassin, and the Treaty of Versailles is the victim in this commentary on the Senate's rejection of the treaty. Isolationists, who wanted to keep the United States out of European affairs, opposed the treaty because it included the Covenant for the League of Nations.

What effects, both near-term and long-term, did the rejection of the treaty have on the United States?

THE ELECTION OF 1920			
Candidate	Party	Popular Vote	Electoral Vote
Harding	Republican	16,152,200	404
Cox	Democrat	9,147,353	127
Debs	Socialist	917,799	0

enough obeyed his orders to defeat it, 49 to 35, seven votes short of the necessary two-thirds majority.

To Wilson, walking now with the help of a cane, one chance remained: the presidential election of 1920. For a time, he thought of running for a third term himself, but his party shunted him aside. The Democrats nominated Governor James M. Cox of Ohio, along with the young and popular Franklin D. Roosevelt, assistant secretary of the navy, for vice president. Wilson called for "a great and solemn referendum" on the treaty. The Democratic platform endorsed the treaty but agreed to accept reservations that clarified the American role in the League.

On the Republican side, Senator Warren G. Harding of Ohio, who had nominated Taft in 1912, won the presidential nomination. Harding waffled on the treaty, but that issue made little difference. Voters wanted a change. Harding won in a landslide, taking 61 percent of the vote and beating Cox by seven million votes. Without a peace treaty, the United States remained technically at war, and it was not until July 1921, almost three years after the last shot was fired, that Congress passed a joint resolution ending the war.

DOCUMENT

Henry Cabot Lodge's Objections to Treaty of Versailles (1919)

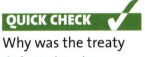

QUICK CHECK ✔

Why was the treaty defeated in the Senate?

Conclusion: Postwar Disillusionment

After 1919, there was disillusionment. World War I was feared before it started, popular while it lasted, and hated when it ended. To a whole generation that followed, it appeared futile, killing without cause, sacrificing without benefit. Books, plays, and movies showed it as waste, horror, and death.

The war and its aftermath damaged the humanitarian, progressive spirit of the early years of the century. It killed "something precious and perhaps irretrievable in the hearts of thinking men and women." Progressivism survived well into the 1920s and the New Deal, but it no longer had the old conviction and broad popular support. Bruising fights over the war and the League drained people's energy and enthusiasm.

Confined to bed, Woodrow Wilson died in Washington in 1924, three years after Harding, the new president, promised "not heroics but healing; not nostrums but normalcy; not revolution but restoration." Nonetheless, the "war to end all wars" and the spirit of Woodrow Wilson left an indelible imprint on the country.

For a list of additional titles related to this chapter's topics, please see
www.pearsonamericanhistory.com.

MyHistoryLab

STUDY RESOURCES

KEY TERMS

Hay-Bunau-Varilla Treaty, p. 651

Roosevelt Corollary, p. 652

"dollar diplomacy," p. 653

moral diplomacy, p. 654

Selective Service Act, p. 662

Committee on Public Information (CPI), p. 665

Espionage Act, p. 666

Sedition Act, p. 666

War Industries Board (WIB), p. 667

Food Administration, p. 667

Fourteen Points, p. 671

CHAPTER REVIEW

WHAT were the main events that showed the United States was becoming a world power❓

After winning the Spanish-American War, American presidents began to exert more and more influence in the world. Roosevelt took extraordinary steps to build the Panama Canal. He enlarged the country's role in the Western hemisphere and tried to deal with the growing power of Japan. Taft adopted a different approach to foreign affairs, focusing on protecting American economic interests abroad. *(p. 650)*

WHAT did Woodrow Wilson mean by "moral diplomacy"❓

Taking office, Woodrow Wilson hoped to focus on events at home but soon found himself involved in crisis after crisis abroad. He first tried some new approaches that he called "moral diplomacy," asking the United States and other countries to treat each other in a moral manner, especially in Europe and Mexico. In Mexico, he had praiseworthy aims but misjudged events and divisions in the country. *(p. 653)*

WHAT were the reasons behind and dangers of Wilson's neutrality policy❓

Wilson, like many Americans, was saddened by the outbreak of war in Europe in 1914. He immediately established a policy of neutrality, which was difficult to maintain. Neutrality, he hoped, would favor neither side and keep the United States out of war. Progressives were especially divided, knowing that war would distract attention from reform. Submarine warfare offered new threats, which Wilson tried to control but could not. On April 6, 1917, the United States joined the war. *(p. 656)*

WHAT effect did the United States' entry into World War I have on the war❓

The United States entered the war at a crucial time for Great Britain and her allies. The war brought about important changes, including the "draft," which enlarged government authority and became the method for enlisting soldiers through the Vietnam War. Entry into the war gave the United States a stake in the peace treaty that ended the war. *(p. 661)*

WHAT programs and changes did World War I bring at home❓

American participation in World War I drew on many of the techniques of progressive reformers, including using people with expertise and exploiting bureaucracy. The War Industries Board oversaw the production of all American factories; the Food Administration Board looked after food for the armies overseas. The government played a larger role in American life than ever before. *(p. 665)*

WHAT mistakes did Wilson make in negotiating the Treaty of Versailles❓

Wilson tried to come to grips with the end of the war by creating the Fourteen Points, measures that sought to reduce armaments, lower trade barriers, offer self-determination to colonial subjects, and provide for a League of Nations to prevent further wars. He was forced to compromise when negotiating at Versailles and ran into opposition in the Senate. Despite urgings from Democrats, he refused to compromise on issues such as the League of Nations, and he lost ratification of the peace treaty. *(p. 671)*

MAKING CONNECTIONS

1. What role did the United States' becoming a world power play in shaping the foreign policy of Roosevelt and Wilson?
2. What events and influences led the United States toward entry into World War I?
3. What were the main events of America's involvement in the war in Europe, and how did these events affect the treaty ending the war?
4. How might Wilson have handled the Versailles treaty negotiations differently?

PRACTICE QUIZ

1. The sinking of the _____ in 1915 helped to bring the United States into World War I.
   a. *Titanic*   b. *Lusitania*
   c. *Britannia*   d. *Maine*

2. The _____ Canal helped to launch the United States into superpower status.
   a. Suez   b. Erie
   c. Panama   d. New Orleans

3. The _____ Policy toward China shaped American actions in the Far East.
   a. Closed Door   b. Open Window
   c. Closed Window   d. Open Door

4. The _____ telegram involved German and Mexican intrigue against the United States.
   a. Zimmermann   b. Unterseeboot
   c. Sussex   d. Heinz

5. In the 1916 presidential election, the Republican party nominated
   a. Roosevelt   b. Hughes
   c. Taft   d. Wilson

6. In May 1917, Congress passed the
   a. Selective Service Act   b. War Buildup Act
   c. Anti-Submarine Act   d. Anti-German Act

7. All of the following describe functions of the Committee on Public Information *except*
   a. It relied on people in the arts, advertising, and film industries to publicize the war.
   b. It developed a voluntary system of press censorship.

   c. It issued more than 75 million pamphlets.
   d. It did not contribute to anti-German sentiment in the United States.

8. Why did Congress pass the Espionage Act?
   a. President Wilson asked Congress to pass the act to curb disloyalty.
   b. The Supreme Court insisted that Congress pass the act to suppress dissent.
   c. Foreign governments pressured Congress to pass the act.
   d. Unions wanted Congress to pass the act to suppress anti-union sentiment.

9. Which of the following *does not* explain President Woodrow Wilson's response to Mexico?
   a. Wilson refused to recognize the Huerta regime.
   b. Wilson asked Congress for a declaration of war against Mexico in 1914.
   c. Wilson moved to oust the Huerta regime in 1914.
   d. Wilson dispatched naval units to halt arms shipments to Huerta.

10. What happened to Socialist party leader Eugene Debs between 1918 and 1920?
    a. He flew airplanes for the U.S. government.
    b. He traveled to Germany to speak to the kaiser.
    c. He was in prison for dissenting against the war.
    d. He remained a hostage of the Huerta regime.

Find more practice at
www.myhistorylab.com

SAMPLE ESSAY QUESTIONS

1. Compare the foreign policy approach of President Roosevelt and President Taft.
2. Explain how World War I influenced American society.

Answers to Practice Quiz **1.** b, *p. 649* **2.** c, *p. 650* **3.** d, *p. 652* **4.** a, *p. 661* **5.** b, *p. 659* **6.** a, *p. 662* **7.** d, *p. 665* **8.** a, *p. 665* **9.** b, *p. 654* **10.** c, *p. 666*

Transition to Modern America

1919–1928

Howard Thain's painting, *The Great White Way— Times Square*, captures the bright lights and excitement of New York's entertainment center in the "Roaring Twenties." (*Source: "The Great White Way—Times Square," by Howard Thain, 1925, oil on canvas, 30 × 36 inches/ Collection of the New-York Historical Society [accession number 1963.150].*)

How does this scene capture the excitement of New York in the 1920s?

Wheels for the Millions

The moving assembly line that Henry Ford opened at Highland Park, Michigan, in 1913 for the manufacture of the Model T marked only the first step toward full mass production and the beginning of America's worldwide industrial supremacy. A year later, Ford began buying large plots of land along the Rouge River southeast of Detroit. He already had a vision of a vast industrial tract where machines, moving through a sequence of carefully arranged manufacturing operations, would transform raw materials into finished cars, trucks, and tractors. The key would be control over the flow of goods at each step along the way—from lake steamers and railroad cars bringing in the coal and iron ore, to overhead conveyor belts and huge turning tables carrying the moving parts past the stationary workers on the assembly line. "Everything must move," Ford commanded, and by the mid-1920s at River Rouge, as the plant became known, it did.

Ford began fulfilling his industrial dream in 1919 when he built a blast furnace and foundry to make engine blocks for both the Model T and his tractors. By 1924, more than forty thousand workers were turning out nearly all the metal parts used in making Ford vehicles. One tractor factory was so efficient that it took just over twenty-eight hours to convert raw ore into a new farm implement.

KEY EVENTS

Visitors from all over the world came to marvel at River Rouge. Some were disturbed by the jumble of machines (by 1926, there were forty-three thousand in operation) and the apparent congestion on the plant floor, but industrial experts recognized that the arrangement led to incredible productivity because "the work moves and the men stand still." A trained engineer summed it up best when he wrote that a visitor to the plant "sees each unit as a carefully designed gear which meshes with other gears and operates in synchronism with them, the whole forming one huge, perfectly-timed, smoothly-operating industrial machine of almost unbelievable efficiency."

In May 1927, after producing more than fifteen million Model Ts, Ford closed the assembly line at Highland Park. For the next six months, his engineers worked on designing a more compact and efficient assembly line at River Rouge for the Model A, which went into production in November. By then, River Rouge had more than justified Ford's vision. "Ford had brought together everything at a single site and on a scale no one else had ever attempted," concluded historian Geoffrey Perrett. "The Rouge plant became to a generation of engineers far more than a factory. It was a monument."

Mass production, born in Highland Park in 1913 and perfected at River Rouge in the 1920s, became the hallmark of American industry. Other carmakers copied Ford's methods, and soon his emphasis on the flow of parts moving past stationary workers became the standard in nearly every American factory. The moving assembly line—with its emphasis on uniformity, speed, precision, and coordination—took away the last vestiges of craftsmanship and turned workers into near robots. It led to amazing efficiency that produced both high profits for manufacturers and low prices for buyers. By the mid-1920s, the cost of the Model T had dropped from $950 to $290.

Most important, mass production contributed to a consumer goods revolution. American factories turned out a flood of automobiles, electrical appliances, and other items that made life easier and more pleasant for most Americans. The result was the creation of a distinctively

On the assembly line at Ford's River Rouge plant, workers performed repetitive tasks on the car chassis that moved by at a rate of 6 feet per minute. (*Source: From the Collections of Henry Ford Museum & Greenfield Village.*)

How did this increase efficiency?

modern America, one marked by the material abundance that has characterized American society ever since.

But the abundance came at a price. The 1920s have been portrayed as a decade of escape and frivolity, and for many Americans they were just that. But those years also were an era of transition: a time when the old America of traditional rural values gave way to a new America of sometimes unsettling urban values. The transition was often wrenching, and many Americans clung desperately to the old ways. Modernity finally won, but not without a struggle.

The Second Industrial Revolution

The first Industrial Revolution in the late nineteenth century had catapulted the United States into the forefront among the world's richest and most highly developed nations. With the advent of the new consumer goods industries, the American people by the 1920s enjoyed the highest standard of living of any nation on earth. After a brief postwar depression, 1922 saw the beginning of a great boom that peaked in 1927 and lasted until 1929. In this brief period, American industrial output nearly doubled, and the gross national product rose by 40 percent. Most of this explosive growth took place in industries producing consumer goods—automobiles, appliances, furniture, and clothing. Equally important, the national per capita income increased by 30 percent to $681 in 1929. American workers became the highest paid in history. Combined with the expansion of installment credit programs that allowed customers to buy now and pay later, this income growth allowed a purchasing spree like nothing the nation had ever experienced.

The key to the new affluence lay in technology. The moving assembly line pioneered by Ford became a standard feature in nearly all American plants. Electric motors replaced steam engines as the basic source of energy in factories; by 1929, 70 percent of all industrial power came from electricity. Efficiency experts broke down the industrial process into minute parts, using time and motion studies, and then showed managers and workers how to maximize the output of their labor. Production per worker-hour increased an amazing 75 percent over the decade; in 1929, a workforce no larger than that of 1919 was producing almost twice as many goods.

WHAT was new about the American economy in the 1920s?

Ford Weekly Purchase Plan, 1925

The Automobile Industry

The nature of the consumer goods revolution can best be seen in the automobile industry, which became the nation's largest in the 1920s. Rapid growth was its hallmark. In 1920, there were ten million cars in the nation; by the end of the decade, twenty-six million were on the road. Production jumped from fewer than two million units a year to more than five million by 1929.

The automobile boom, at its peak from 1922 to 1927, depended on the apparently insatiable appetite of the American people for cars. But as the decade continued, the market became saturated as more and more of those who could afford the new luxury had become car owners. Marketing became as crucial as production.

Automobile makers began to rely heavily on advertising and annual model changes, seeking to make customers dissatisfied with their old vehicles and eager to order new ones. Despite these efforts, sales slumped in 1927 when Ford stopped making the Model T, picked up again the next year with the new Model A, but began to slide again in 1929. The new industry revealed a basic weakness in the consumer goods economy; once people had bought an item with a long life, they would be out of the market for a few years. The consumer revolution also bypassed much of rural America, where farmers struggled against falling prices.

Amid the urban affluence, few noticed the underlying problems. Instead, contemporary observers focused on the stimulating effect the automobile had on the rest of the economy. The mass production of cars required huge quantities of steel; entire new rolling mills had to be built to supply sheet steel for car bodies. Rubber factories boomed with the demand for tires, and paint and glass suppliers had more business than ever before. The auto changed the pattern of city life, leading to a suburban explosion. Real estate developers, no longer dependent on streetcars and railway lines, could now build houses in ever wider concentric circles around the central cities.

The automobile had a profound effect on all aspects of American life in the 1920s. Filling stations appeared on the main streets, replacing the smithies and stables of the past. In Kansas City, Jess D. Nichols built the first shopping center, Country Club Plaza, and thus set an example quickly followed by other suburban developers.

Even in smaller communities, the car ruled. In Muncie, Indiana, site of a famous sociological survey in the 1920s, one elder replied when asked what was taking place, "I can tell you what's happening in just four letters: A-U-T-O!" A nation that had always revered symbols of movement, from the *Mayflower* to the covered wagon, now had a new icon to worship.

QUICK CHECK

How did the auto industry drive the rest of the economy?

Patterns of Economic Growth

Automobiles were the most conspicuous of the consumer products that flourished in the 1920s, but certainly not the only ones. The electrical industry grew almost as quickly. Central power stations, where massive steam generators converted coal into electricity, brought current into the homes of city and town dwellers. Two-thirds of all American families enjoyed electricity by the end of the decade, and they spent vast sums on washing machines, vacuum cleaners, refrigerators, and ranges. The new appliances eased the burdens of housework and ushered in an age of leisure.

Radio broadcasting and motion picture production also boomed in the 1920s. The early success of KDKA in Pittsburgh stimulated the growth of more than eight hundred independent radio stations, and by 1929, NBC had formed the first successful radio network. Five nights a week, *Amos 'n' Andy,* a comic serial featuring two "blackface" vaudevillians, held the attention of millions of Americans. The film industry thrived in Hollywood, reaching its maturity in the mid-1920s when in every large city there were huge theaters seating as many as four thousand people. With the advent of the "talkies" by 1929, average weekly movie attendance climbed to nearly 100 million.

Other industries prospered as well. Production of light metals such as aluminum and magnesium grew into a major business. Chemical engineering came of age with the invention of synthetics, ranging from rayon for clothing to cellophane for packaging. Americans found a whole new spectrum of products to buy—cigarette lighters, wristwatches, heat-resistant glass cooking dishes, and rayon stockings, to name just a few.

The most distinctive feature of the new consumer-oriented economy was the emphasis on marketing. Advertising earnings rose from $1.3 billion in 1915 to $3.4 billion in 1926. Skillful practitioners such as Edward Bernays and Bruce Barton sought to control public taste and consumer spending by identifying the good life with the possession of the latest product of American industry, whether it be a car, a refrigerator, or a brand of cigarettes. Chain stores advanced rapidly at the expense of small retail shops. A&P dominated the retail food industry, growing from 400 stores in 1912 to 15,500 by 1932. Woolworth's "five-and-tens" spread almost as rapidly, while such drugstore chains as Rexall and Liggetts—both owned by one huge holding company—opened outlets in nearly every town and city in the land.

Advertisements from 1925 and 1927

Uniformity and standardization, the characteristics of mass production, now prevailed. The farmer in Kansas bought the same kind of car, the same groceries, and the same pills as the factory worker in Pennsylvania. Sectional differences in dress, food, and furniture began to disappear. Even the regional accents that distinguished Americans in different parts of the country were threatened with extinction by the advent of radio and films, which promoted a standard national dialect devoid of any local flavor.

Despite all of these changes, the New Era, as business leaders labeled the decade, was not as prosperous as it first appeared. The revolution in consumer goods disguised the decline of many traditional industries in the 1920s. Hardest hit of all was agriculture. By 1921, farm exports had fallen by more than $2 billion. In addition, during the decade, factory wages rose only a modest 11 percent; in 1929, nearly half of all American families had an income of less than $1500. Organized labor proved unable to advance the interests of the workers in the 1920s; the result was a decline in union membership. In fact, middle- and upper-class Americans were the only groups who thrived in the 1920s. The rewards of this second Industrial Revolution went to the managers—the engineers, bankers, and executives—who directed the new industrial economy. All of these factors contributed to economic instability. The boom of the 1920s would end in a great crash.

QUICK CHECK ✓

What other industries contributed to the boom of the 1920s?

City Life in the Roaring Twenties

The city replaced the countryside as the focal point of American life in the 1920s. The 1920 census revealed that for the first time, slightly more than half of the population lived in cities (defined broadly to include all places of more than 2500 people). During the decade, the metropolitan areas grew rapidly as both whites and blacks from rural areas came seeking jobs in the new consumer industries. Between 1920 and 1930, cities with populations of 250,000 or more had added some eight million people to their ranks. New York City grew by nearly 25 percent, while Detroit more than doubled its population during the decade.

In the cities, life was different. The old community ties of home, church, and school were absent, but there were important gains to replace them—new ideas,

HOW
?
did life in the cities change after World War I?

new creativity, new perspectives. Some city dwellers became lost and lonely without the old institutions; others thrived in the urban environment.

Women and the Family

The urban culture of the 1920s witnessed important changes in the American family. This vital institution began to break down under the impact of economic and social change. A new freedom for women and children seemed to be emerging in its wake.

Although World War I accelerated the process by which women left the home for work, the postwar decade witnessed a return to the slower pace of the prewar years. During the 1920s there was no permanent gain in the number of working women. Two million more women were employed in 1930 than in 1920, but this represented an increase of only 1 percent. Most women workers, moreover, had low-paying jobs, ranging from stenographers to maids. The number of women doctors actually decreased, and even though women earned nearly one-third of all graduate degrees, only 4 percent of full professors were female. For the most part, the professions were reserved for men, with women relegated to such fields as teaching and nursing.

Women had won the right to vote in 1920, but the Nineteenth Amendment proved to have less impact than its proponents had hoped. Adoption of the amendment robbed women of a unifying cause, and the exercise of the franchise itself did little to change prevailing sex roles. Men remained the principal breadwinners in the family; women cooked, cleaned, and reared the children. "The creation and fulfillment of a successful home," a *Ladies Home Journal* writer advised women, "is a bit of craftsmanship that compares favorably with building a beautiful cathedral."

The feminist movement, however, still showed signs of vitality in the 1920s. Social feminists pushing for humanitarian reform won enactment of the Sheppard-Towner Act of 1921, which provided for federal aid to establish state programs for maternal and infant health care. Although the failure to enact the child labor amendment in 1925 marked the beginning of a decline in humanitarian reform, for the rest of the decade, women's groups continued to work for good-government measures, for the inclusion of women on juries, and for consumer legislation.

Other women looked beyond politics to express themselves. In the larger cities, some quickly adopted what critic H. L. Mencken called the flapper image, portrayed most strikingly by artist John Held, Jr. Cutting their hair short, raising their skirts above the knee, and binding their breasts, "flappers" set out to compete on equal terms with men on the golf course and in the speakeasy. Young women delighted in shocking their elders—they rouged their cheeks and danced the Charleston. Women smoked cigarettes and drank alcohol in public more freely than before. The flappers assaulted the traditional double standard in sex, demanding that equality with men should include sexual fulfillment before and during marriage. New and more liberal laws led to a sharp rise in the divorce rate; by 1928, there were 166 divorces for every 1000 marriages, compared to only 81 in 1900.

The family changed in other ways as well. The size of the average family became smaller as easier access to effective birth control methods enabled couples to limit the number of their offspring. More and more married women took jobs outside the home, bringing in an income and gaining a measure of independence

Margaret Sanger, from "Happiness in Marriage" (1926)

After passage of the Nineteenth Amendment, activist Alice Paul and the National Woman's Party continued to fight for women's equality. Here, fifty NWP members visit the White House to request President Harding's support for equal rights legislation.

How were their efforts received?

DOCUMENT

John F. Carter, "These Wild Young People by One of Them"

(although their rate of pay was always lower than that for men). Young people, who had once joined the labor force when they entered their teens, now discovered adolescence as a stage of life. A high school education was no longer uncommon, and college attendance increased.

Prolonged adolescence led to new strains on the family in the form of youthful revolt. Freed of the traditional burden of earning a living at an early age, youths in the 1920s went on a great spree. Heavy drinking, casual sexual encounters, and a constant search for excitement became the hallmarks of the upper-class youth immortalized by F. Scott Fitzgerald. "I have been kissed by dozens of men," one of his characters commented. "I suppose I'll kiss dozens more." The theme of rebellion against parental authority, which ran through all aspects of the 1920s, was at the heart of the youth movement.

QUICK CHECK ✓

How did women's lives change during the 1920s?

Popular Culture in the Jazz Age

Excitement ran high in the cities as both crime waves and highly publicized sports events flourished. Prohibition ushered in such distinctive features of the decade as speakeasies, bootleggers, and bathtub gin. Crime rose sharply as middle- and

IMAGE

Charles Lindbergh and *Spirit of St. Louis*

Clara Bow, "It" Girl, Film Still (1927)

Harlem Renaissance
An African American cultural, literary, and artistic movement centered in Harlem, an area in New York City, in the 1920s. Harlem, the largest black community in the world outside of Africa, was considered the cultural capital of African Americans.

upper-class Americans willingly broke the law to gain access to alcoholic beverages. City streets became the scene of violent shootouts between rival bootleggers; by 1929, Chicago had witnessed more than five hundred gangland murders. Underworld czars controlled illicit empires; Al Capone's empire produced revenue of $60 million a year.

Sports became a national mania in the 1920s as people found more leisure time. Golf boomed, with some two million men and women playing on nearly five thousand courses across the country. Spectator sports attracted even more attention. Boxing drew huge crowds to see fighters such as Jack Dempsey and Gene Tunney. Baseball attendance soared. More than twenty million fans attended games in 1927, the year Babe Ruth became a national idol by hitting sixty home runs. On college campuses, football became more popular than ever. Universities vied with each other in building massive stadiums, seating upward of seventy thousand people.

The arts also flourished in the 1920s. Authors Ernest Hemingway, F. Scott Fitzgerald, John Dos Passos, and Sinclair Lewis chronicled the experience of the post-World War I generation. In New York City, the **Harlem Renaissance**—an outpouring of African American literature, theater, visual arts, and music, especially jazz—made Manhattan seem the most exciting place on earth.

In what Frederick Lewis Allen called "the ballyhoo years," the popular yearning for release led people to seek vicarious thrills in all kinds of ways—applauding Charles Lindbergh's solo flight across the Atlantic, cheering Gertrude Ederle's swim across the English Channel, and flocking to such bizarre events as six-day bicycle races, dance marathons, and flagpole sittings. It was a time of pure pleasure-seeking, when people sought to escape from the increasingly drab world of the assembly line by worshiping heroic individuals.

Sex became another popular topic in the 1920s as Victorian standards began to crumble. Sophisticated city dwellers seemed to be intent on exploring a new freedom in sexual expression. Plays and novels focused on adultery, and the new urban tabloids—led by the *New York Daily News*—delighted in telling their readers about love nests and kept women. The popular songs of the decade, such as "Hot Lips" and "Burning Kisses," were less romantic and more explicit than those of years before. Hollywood exploited the obsession with sex by producing movies with such provocative titles as *Up in Mabel's Room*,

Several new dances were introduced on the dance floors of ballrooms and clubs in the 1920s jazz era. One of the most popular new dances was the Charleston—a dance associated with the rebellious image of the "flapper." Here, two daring flappers dance the Charleston on the roof of Chicago's Hotel Sherman in 1926.

What else was daring about the flappers?

A Shocking Night, and *Women and Lovers.* Theda Bara and Clara Bow, the "vamp" and the "It" girl, set the model for feminine seductiveness while Rudolph Valentino became the heartthrob of millions of American women. Young people embraced the new permissiveness joyfully, with the automobile giving couples an easy way to escape parental supervision.

QUICK CHECK ✓

What did people do with their spare time during the decade?

The Conservative Counterattack

The shift of population from the countryside to the city led to heightened social tensions in the 1920s. Intent on preserving traditional social values, rural Americans saw in the city all that was evil in contemporary life. Saloons, whore-houses, little Italys and little Polands, communist cells, free love, and atheism—all were identified with the city. Accordingly, the countryside struck back at the newly dominant urban areas, aiming to restore the primacy of the Anglo-Saxon and pre-dominantly Protestant culture they revered. This counterattack won considerable support in the cities from those who were recently uprooted from their rural backgrounds.

Other factors contributed to the intensity of the counterattack. The war had unleashed a nationalistic spirit that craved unity and conformity. In a nation where one-third of the people were foreign born, the attack on immigrants and the call for 100 percent Americanism took on a frightening zeal. When the war was over, groups such as the American Legion tried to root out "un-American" behavior and insisted on cultural as well as political conformity. The prewar progressive reform spirit added to the social tension. Stripped of much of its former idealism, progressivism focused on such social problems as drinking and illiteracy to justify repressive measures such as prohibition and immigration restriction. The result was tragic. Amid the emergence of a new urban culture, the movements that aimed at preserving the values of an earlier America succeeded only in complicating life in an already difficult period of cultural transition.

HOW did conservatives resist the changes of the decade?

The Fear of Radicalism

The first and most intense outbreak of national alarm, an anti-radical hysteria known as the **Red Scare,** came in 1919. The heightened nationalism of World War I, aimed at achieving unity at the expense of ethnic diversity, found a new target in communism. The Russian Revolution and the triumph of Marxism frightened many Americans. A growing turn to communism among American radicals (espe-cially the foreign born) accelerated these fears. Although the numbers involved were tiny—at most there were sixty thousand communists in the United States in 1919—they were highly visible. Located in the cities, their influence appeared to be magnified with the outbreak of widespread labor unrest.

A general strike in Seattle, a police strike in Boston, and a violent strike in the iron and steel industry thoroughly alarmed the American people in the spring and summer of 1919. A series of bombings led to panic. First the mayor of strike-bound Seattle received a small brown package containing a homemade bomb;

Red Scare

A wave of anticommunist, antiforeign, and antilabor hysteria that swept over America at the end of World War I. It resulted in the deportation of many alien residents and the violation of the civil liberties of many of its victims.

The explosion in Wall Street on September 16, 1920 left thirty-three dead and nearly two hundred wounded. Attorney General Palmer saw the blast as the work of a communist conspiracy, but relatively few Americans subscribed to his view.

Did subsequent developments support Palmer or the skeptical public?

A. Mitchell Palmer on the Menace of Communism (1920)

then an alert New York postal employee detected sixteen bombs addressed to a variety of famous citizens (including John D. Rockefeller); and finally, on June 2, a bomb shattered the front of Attorney General A. Mitchell Palmer's home. Although the man who delivered it was blown to pieces, authorities quickly identified him as an Italian anarchist from Philadelphia.

In the ensuing public outcry, Attorney General Palmer led the attack on the alien threat. A Quaker and a progressive, Palmer abandoned his earlier liberalism to launch a massive roundup of foreign-born radicals. In a series of raids that began on November 7, federal agents seized suspected anarchists and communists and held them for deportation with no regard for due process of law. In December, 249 aliens—including such well-known radical leaders as Emma Goldman and Alexander Berkman—were sent to Russia aboard the *Buford*, dubbed the "Soviet Ark" by the press. Nearly all were innocent of the charges against them. A month later, Palmer rounded up nearly four thousand suspected communists in a single evening. Federal agents broke into homes, meeting halls, and union offices without search warrants. Many native-born Americans were caught in the dragnet and spent several days in jail before being released; aliens rounded up were deported without hearings or trials.

Ben Shahn's work *The Passion of Sacco and Vanzetti* (1931–1932) depicts the members of the committee who investigated the trial and confirmed its fairness. (*Source:* The Passion of Sacco and Vanzetti *[1931–1932] by Ben Shahn, from* Sacco and Vanzetti *series of 23 paintings. Tempera, 84 1/2 × 48 inches. From the collection of Whitney Museum of American Art. Gift of Edith and Milton Lowenthal. © Estate of Ben Shahn/Licensed by VAGA, New York, NY.)*

Do you think the artist agrees with the verdict?

For a time, it seemed that the Red Scare reflected the prevailing views of the American people. Instead of condemning their government's action, citizens voiced their approval and even urged more drastic steps. One patriot said his solution to the alien problem was simple: "S.O.S.—ship or shoot." General Leonard Wood, the former army chief of staff, favored placing Bolsheviks on "ships of stone with sails of lead," while evangelist Billy Sunday preferred to take "these ornery, wild-eyed Socialists" and "stand them up before a firing squad and save space on our ships." Inflamed by public statements like these, a group of legionnaires in Centralia, Washington, dragged a radical from the town jail, castrated him, and hanged him from a railway bridge. The coroner's report blandly stated that the victim "jumped off with a rope around his neck and then shot himself full of holes."

The very extremism of the Red Scare led to its rapid demise. In early 1920, courageous government officials from the Department of Labor insisted on due process and full hearings before anyone else was deported. Prominent public leaders began to speak out against the acts of terror. Charles Evans Hughes, the defeated GOP candidate in 1916, offered to defend six socialists expelled from the New York legislature; Ohio Senator Warren G. Harding, the embodiment of middle-class values, expressed his opinion that "too much has been said about bolshevism in America." Finally, Palmer himself, with evident presidential ambition, went too far. In April 1920, he warned of a vast revolution to occur on May 1; the entire New York City police force, some eleven thousand strong, was placed on duty to prepare for imminent disaster. When no bombings or violence took place on May Day, the public began to react against Palmer's hysteria. Despite a violent explosion on Wall Street in September that killed thirty-three people, the Red Scare died out by the end of 1920. Palmer passed into obscurity, the tiny Communist party became torn with factionalism, and the American people tried hard to forget their loss of balance.

Yet the Red Scare exerted a continuing influence on American society in the 1920s. The foreign born lived in the uneasy realization that they were viewed with hostility and suspicion. Two Italian aliens in Massachusetts, Nicola Sacco and Bartolomeo Vanzetti, were arrested in May 1920 for a payroll robbery and murder. They faced a prosecutor and jury who condemned them more for their ideas than for any evidence of criminal conduct and a judge who referred to them as "those anarchist bastards." Despite a worldwide effort that became the chief liberal cause of the 1920s, the courts rejected all appeals. Sacco, a shoemaker, and Vanzetti, a fish peddler, died in the electric chair on August 23, 1927. Their fate symbolized the bigotry and intolerance that lasted through the 1920s and made that decade one of the least attractive in American history.

DOCUMENT

Court
Statements
from Sacco
and Vanzetti

QUICK CHECK

What was the
"Red Scare"?

Prohibition

In December 1917, Congress passed the Eighteenth Amendment, prohibiting the manufacture and sale of alcoholic beverages, and then sent the amendment to the states for ratification. A little over a year later, in January 1919, Nebraska was the necessary thirty-sixth state to ratify, and **prohibition** became the law of the land.

Effective January 16, 1920, the Volstead Act, which implemented prohibition, banned most commercial production and distribution of beverages containing more than one-half of 1 percent of alcohol by volume. (Exceptions were made for medicinal and religious uses of wine and spirits. Production for one's own private use was also allowed.) Prohibition was the result of both a rural effort of the Anti-Saloon League, backed by Methodist and Baptist clergymen, and the urban progressive concern over the social disease of drunkenness, especially among industrial workers. The moral issue had already led to the enactment of prohibition laws in twenty-six states by 1920; the real tragedy would occur in the effort to extend this "noble experiment" to the growing cities, where it was deeply resented by ethnic groups such as the Germans and the Irish and was almost totally disregarded by the well-to-do and the sophisticated.

Prohibition did in fact lead to a decline in drinking. Americans consumed much less alcohol in the 1920s than in the prewar years. Rural areas became totally dry, and in the cities, the consumption of alcoholic beverages dropped sharply among the lower classes, who could not afford the high prices for bootleg liquor. Among the middle class and the wealthy, however, drinking became fashionable. Bootleggers supplied whiskey, which quickly replaced lighter spirits such as wine and beer. The alcohol was either smuggled from abroad (a $40 million a year business by 1924) or illicitly manufactured in America. Exotic products such as Jackass Brandy, Soda Pop Moon, and Yack Yack Bourbon were common—and all could be fatal. Despite the risk of illness or death from extraordinarily high alcohol content or poorly controlled distillation, Americans consumed some 150 million quarts of liquor a year in the 1920s. Bootleggers took in nearly $2 billion annually, about 2 percent of the gross national product.

Urban resistance to prohibition finally led to its repeal in 1933. But in the intervening years, it damaged American society by breeding a profound disrespect for the law. The flamboyant excesses of bootleggers were only the more obvious evils spawned by prohibition. In city after city, police openly tolerated the traffic in liquor, and judges and prosecutors agreed to let bootleggers pay merely token fines, creating almost a system of licenses. Prohibition satisfied the countryside's desire for vindication, yet rural and urban America alike suffered from this overzealous attempt to legislate morals.

prohibition
The ban of the manufacture, sale, and transportation of alcoholic beverages in the United States. The Eighteenth Amendment, adopted in 1919, established prohibition. It was repealed by the Twenty-First Amendment in 1933. While prohibition was in effect, it reduced national consumption of alcohol, but it was inconsistently enforced and was often evaded, especially in the cities.

Prohibition
Raid, ca. 1928

Prohibition Is
a Failure

QUICK CHECK
How effective was prohibition?

The Ku Klux Klan

The most ominous expression of protest against the new urban culture was the rebirth of the Ku Klux Klan. On Thanksgiving night in 1915, on Stone Mountain in Georgia, Colonel William J. Simmons and thirty-four followers founded the modern Klan. Only "native born, white, gentile Americans" were permitted to join "the Invisible Empire, Knights of the Ku Klux Klan." Membership grew slowly during World War I, but after 1920, fueled by postwar fears and shrewd promotional techniques, the Klan mushroomed. In villages, towns, and small cities across the nation, Anglo-Saxon Protestant men flocked into the newly formed chapters, seeking to relieve their anxiety over a changing society by embracing the Klan's unusual rituals and by demonstrating their hatred against blacks, aliens, Jews, and Catholics.

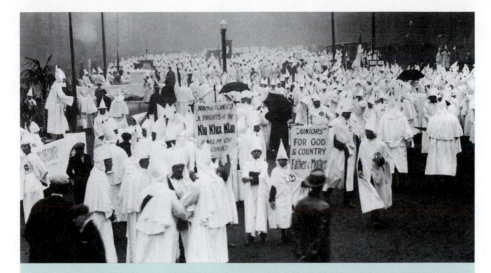

A 1925 Ku Klux Klan demonstration in Cincinnati, Ohio, attended by nearly thirty thousand robed members and marked by the induction of eight thousand young boys in the Junior Order. The original Klan, formed during the Reconstruction era to terrorize former slaves, disbanded in 1869. The Klan that formed in 1915 declined after the mid-1920s but did not officially disband until 1944.

How did the revival of the Klan reflect the mood of the 1920s?

The Klan of the 1920s, unlike the night riders of the post–Civil War era, was not just antiblack; the threat to American culture, as Klansmen perceived it, also came from aliens—Italians and Russians, Jews and Catholics. They attributed much of the tension and conflict in society to the prewar flood of immigrants, foreigners who spoke different languages, worshiped in strange churches, and lived in distant, threatening cities. The Klansmen struck back by coming together and enforcing their own values. They punished blacks who did not know their place, women who practiced the new morality, and aliens who refused to conform. Beating, flogging, burning with acid—even murder—were condoned. They also tried more peaceful methods of coercion, formulating codes of behavior and seeking communitywide support.

The Klan entered politics, at first hesitantly, then with growing confidence. The KKK gained control of the legislatures in Texas, Oklahoma, Oregon, and Indiana; in 1924, it blocked a resolution of censure at the Democratic national convention. With an estimated five million members by the mid-1920s, the Klan seemed to be fully established.

Its appeal lay in the sanctuary it offered to insecure and anxious people. Protestant to the core, the members found in the local Klavern a reassurance missing in their churches. The poor and ignorant became enchanted with the titles, ranging from Imperial Wizard to Grand Dragon, and gloried in the ritual that centered around the letter *K*: Each Klan had its own "Klalendar," held its weekly "Klonklave" in the local "Klavern," and followed the rules set forth in the Kloran. Members found a sense of identity in the group activities, whether they were peaceful picnics, ominous parades in white robes, or fiery cross burnings at night.

Although it was a men's organization, the Klan did not neglect the family. There was a Women's Order, a Junior Order for boys, and a Tri-K Klub for girls. Members had to be born in America, but foreign-born Protestants were allowed to

"Creed of
Klanswomen"
(1924)

join a special Krusaders affiliate. Only blacks, Catholics, Jews, and prostitutes were beyond redemption to these lonely and anxious men who came together to chant:

> United we stick
> Divided we're stuck.
> The better we stick
> The better we Klux!

The Klan fell even more quickly than it rose. Its more violent activities—which included kidnapping, lynching, setting fire to synagogues and Catholic churches, and, in one case, murdering a priest—began to offend the nation's conscience. Misuse of funds and sexual scandals among Klan leaders, notably in Indiana, repelled many of the rank and file; effective counterattacks by traditional politicians ousted the KKK from control in Texas and Oklahoma. Membership declined sharply after 1925; by the end of the decade, the Klan had virtually disappeared. But its spirit lived on, testimony to the recurring demons of nativism and hatred that have surfaced periodically throughout the American experience.

QUICK CHECK ✔

What groups did the Ku Klux Klan persecute during the 1920s?

Immigration Restriction

nativism

Hostility to things foreign.

The **nativism,** or hostility to things foreign, that permeated the Klan found its most successful outlet in the immigration legislation of the 1920s. The sharp increase in immigration in the late nineteenth century had led to a broad-based movement, spearheaded by organized labor and by New England aristocrats such as Henry Cabot Lodge, to restrict the flow of people from Europe. In 1917, over Wilson's veto, Congress enacted a literacy test that reduced the number of immigrants allowed into the country. The war caused a much more drastic decline—from an average of 1 million a year between 1900 and 1914 to only 110,000 in 1918.

1924
Immigration
Law

After the armistice, however, rumors began to spread of an impending flood of people seeking to escape war-ravaged Europe. Kenneth Roberts, a popular historical novelist, warned that all Europe was on the move, with only the limits of available steamship space likely to stem the flow. Worried congressmen spoke of a "barbarian horde" and a "foreign tide" that would inundate the United States with "dangerous and deadly enemies of the country." Even though the actual number of immigrants, 810,000 in 1920 (fewer than the prewar yearly average), did not match these projections, Congress in 1921 passed an emergency immigration act. The new quota system restricted immigration from Europe to 3 percent of the number of nationals from each country living in the United States in 1910.

The 1921 act failed to satisfy the nativists. The quotas still permitted more than 500,000 Europeans to come to the United States in 1923, nearly half of them from southern and eastern Europe. The declining percentage of Nordic immigrants alarmed writers such as Madison Grant, who warned the American people that the Anglo-Saxon stock that had founded the nation was about to be overwhelmed by lesser breeds with inferior genes. "These immigrants adopt the language of the native American, they wear his clothes and are beginning to take his women, but they seldom adopt his religion or understand his ideals," Grant wrote.

National Origins Quota Act

This 1924 law established a quota system to regulate the influx of immigrants to America. The system reduced immigration from southern and eastern Europe and barred immigration from Asia.

Psychologists, relying on primitive IQ tests used by the army in World War I, confirmed this judgment. One senator claimed that all the nation's ills were due to an "intermingled and mongrelized people" as he demanded that racial purity replace the older reliance on the melting pot. In 1924, Congress adopted the **National Origins Quota Act,** which limited immigration from Europe to 150,000 a year; allocated most of the available slots to immigrants from Great Britain, Ireland, Germany, and Scandinavia; and banned all Asian immigrants. The measure passed Congress with overwhelming rural support.

The new restrictive legislation marked the most enduring achievement of the rural counterattack. Unlike the Red Scare, prohibition, and the Klan, the quota system would survive until the 1960s, enforcing a racist bias that excluded Asians and limited the immigration of Italians, Greeks, and Poles to a few thousand a year while permitting a steady stream of Irish, English, and Scandinavian immigrants. Large corporations, no longer dependent on armies of unskilled immigrant workers, did not object to the 1924 law; the machine had replaced the immigrant on the assembly line. Yet even here the victory was not complete. A growing tide of Mexican laborers, exempt from the quota act, flowed northward across the Rio Grande to fill the continuing need for unskilled workers on the farms and in the service trades. The Mexican immigrants, as many as 100,000 a year, marked the strengthening of an element in the national ethnic mosaic that would grow in size and influence until it became a major force in modern American society.

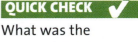

QUICK CHECK

What was the National Origins Quota Act?

The Fundamentalist Challenge

Another significant—and longest-lasting—challenge to the new urban culture was rooted in the traditional religious beliefs of millions of Americans who felt alienated from city life, from science, and from much of what modernization entailed. Sometimes this challenge was direct, as when Christian fundamentalists campaigned against the teaching of evolution in the public schools. Their success in Tennessee touched off a court battle, the **Scopes trial,** that drew the attention of the entire country to the small town of Dayton in the summer of 1925, when a high-school biology teacher was prosecuted for teaching evolution. The trial court convicted John Scopes, affirming the fundamentalist view, but the spectacle drew the derision of many Americans who saw nothing at all threatening about Darwin's theory.

Other aspects of the fundamentalist challenge were more subtle but no less important in countering the modernizing trend. As middle- and upper-class Americans drifted into a genteel Christianity that stressed good works and respectability, the Baptist and Methodist churches continued to hold on to the old faith. In addition, aggressive fundamentalist sects such as the Churches of Christ, the Pentecostals, and Jehovah's Witnesses grew rapidly. While church membership increased from 41.9 million in 1916 to 54.5 million in 1926, the number of churches actually declined during the decade. More and more rural dwellers drove their cars into town instead of going to the local crossroads chapel.

Many of those who came to the city in the 1920s brought their religious beliefs with them and found new outlets for their traditional ideas. Thus evangelist Aimee Semple McPherson enjoyed amazing success in Los Angeles with her Church of the Four-Square Gospel, building the Angelus Temple to seat more than 5000 worshipers. And in Fort Worth, the Reverend J. Frank Norris erected a 6000-seat sanctuary for the First Baptist Church, bathing it in spotlights so it could be seen for thirty miles across the North Texas prairie.

Far from dying out, as divinity professor Thomas G. Oden noted, biblical fundamentalism retained "remarkable grassroots strength among the organization men and the industrialized mass society of the 20th century." The rural counterattack, while challenged by the city, did enable some older American values to survive in the midst of the new mass production culture.

Scopes trial

Also called the "monkey trial," the 1924 Scopes trial was a contest between modern liberalism and religious fundamentalism. John T. Scopes was on trial for teaching Darwinian evolution in defiance of a Tennessee state law. He was found guilty and fined $100. On appeal, Scopes's conviction was set aside on a technicality.

QUICK CHECK

How did the Scopes trial reflect the strength of conservative religious thought?

Republican Politics

HOW
did the politics of the 1920s reflect changes in the economy and in American society?

The tensions between the city and the countryside also shaped the course of politics in the 1920s. On the whole, it was a Republican decade. The GOP ("Grand Old Party") controlled the White House from 1921 to 1933 and had majorities in both houses of Congress from 1919 to 1931. The Republicans used their return to power after World War I to halt further reform legislation and to establish a friendly relationship between government and business.

Executive Orders and Senate Resolutions on Teapot Dome

Teapot Dome scandal
A 1924 scandal in which Secretary of the Interior Albert Fall was convicted of accepting bribes in exchange for leasing government-owned oil lands in Wyoming (Teapot Dome) and California (Elk Hills) to private oil businessmen.

Harding, Coolidge, and Hoover

The Republicans regained the White House in 1920 with the election of Warren G. Harding of Ohio. A dark-horse contender, Harding won the GOP nomination when the convention deadlocked and he became the compromise choice. Handsome and dignified, Harding reflected both the virtues and blemishes of small-town America. Originally a newspaper publisher in Marion, he had made many friends and few enemies throughout his career as a legislator, lieutenant governor, and finally, after 1914, U.S. senator. Conventional in outlook, Harding was a genial man who lacked the capacity to govern and who, as president, broadly delegated power.

He made some good cabinet choices, notably Charles Evans Hughes as secretary of state and Herbert C. Hoover as secretary of commerce, but two corrupt officials—Attorney General Harry Daugherty and Secretary of the Interior Albert Fall—sabotaged his administration. Daugherty became involved in a series of questionable deals that led ultimately to his forced resignation; Fall was the chief figure in the **Teapot Dome scandal.** Two oil promoters gave Fall nearly $400,000 in loans and bribes; in return, he helped them secure leases on naval oil reserves in Elk Hills, California, and Teapot Dome, Wyoming. The scandal came to light after Harding's death from a heart attack in 1923. Fall eventually served a year in jail, and the reputation of the Harding administration never recovered.

Vice President Calvin Coolidge assumed the presidency upon Harding's death, and his honesty and integrity quickly reassured the nation. Coolidge, born in Vermont of old Yankee stock, had first gained national attention in 1919 as governor of Massachusetts when he had dealt firmly with a Boston police strike by declaring, "There is no right to strike against the public safety by anybody, anywhere, any time." A reserved, reticent man, Coolidge became famous for his epigrams, which contemporaries mistook for wisdom. "The business of America is business," he proclaimed. "The man who builds a factory builds a temple; the man who works there worships there." Consistent with this philosophy, he believed his duty was simply to preside benignly, not govern the nation. "Four-fifths of all our troubles in this life would disappear," he said, "if we would just sit down and be still." Calvin Coolidge, one observer noted, "aspired to become the least President the country ever had; he attained his desire." Satisfied with the prosperity of the mid-1920s, the people responded favorably. Coolidge was elected to a full term by a wide margin in 1924.

When Coolidge announced in 1927 that he did not "choose to run," Herbert Hoover became the Republican choice to succeed him. By far the ablest GOP leader of the decade, Hoover epitomized the American myth of the self-made man. Orphaned as a boy, he had worked his way through Stanford University and had gained both wealth and fame as a mining engineer. During World War I, he had displayed admirable administrative skills in directing Wilson's food program at home and relief activities abroad. Sober, intelligent, and immensely hardworking, Hoover embodied the nation's faith in individualism and free enterprise.

As secretary of commerce under Harding and Coolidge, he had sought cooperation between government and business. He used his office to assist American manufacturers and exporters in expanding their overseas trade, and he strongly supported a trade association movement to encourage cooperation rather than cutthroat competition among smaller American companies. He did not view business and government as antagonists. Instead, he saw them as partners, working together to achieve efficiency and affluence for all Americans. His optimistic view of the future led him to declare in his speech accepting the Republican presidential nomination in 1928 that "we in America today are nearer to the final triumph over poverty than ever before in the history of any land."

QUICK CHECK

Who were the Republican presidents of the 1920s?

A New Kind of Conservatism

During the 1920 campaign, Warren Harding urged a return to "not heroism, but healing, not nostrums, but normalcy." Misreading his speechwriter's "normality," he coined a new word that became the theme for the Republican administrations of the 1920s. Aware that the public was tired of zealous reform-minded presidents such as Teddy Roosevelt and Woodrow Wilson, Harding and his successors sought a return to traditional Republican policies. In some areas they were successful, but in others the Republican leaders were forced to adjust to the new realities of a mass production society. The result was a mixture of traditional and innovative measures that was neither wholly reactionary nor entirely progressive.

The most obvious attempt to go back to the Republicanism of William McKinley came in tariff and tax policy. Fearful of a flood of postwar European imports, Congress passed an emergency tariff act in 1921 and followed it a year later with the protectionist Fordney-McCumber Tariff Act. The net effect was to raise the basic rates substantially over the moderate Underwood Tariff schedules of the Wilson period.

Secretary of the Treasury Andrew Mellon, a wealthy Pittsburgh banker and industrialist, worked hard to achieve a similar return to normalcy in taxation. Condemning the high wartime tax rates on businesses and wealthy individuals, Mellon pressed for repealing an excess profits tax on corporations and slashing personal rates on the very rich. Using the new budget system adopted by Congress in 1921, he reduced government spending from its World War I peak of $18 billion to just over $3 billion by 1925, thereby creating a slight surplus. Congress responded in 1926 by cutting the highest income tax bracket to a modest 20 percent.

The revenue acts of the 1920s greatly reduced the burden of taxation; by the end of the decade, the government was collecting one-third less than it had in 1921, and the number of people paying income taxes dropped from more than 6.5 million to 4 million. Yet the greatest relief went to the wealthy. The public was shocked to learn in the 1930s that J. P. Morgan, Jr., and his nineteen partners had paid no income tax at all during the depths of the Great Depression.

The growing crisis in American farming during the decade forced the Republican administrations to seek new solutions. The end of the European war led to a sharp decline in farm prices and a return to the problem of overproduction.

In this 1925 political cartoon, Clifford Berryman depicts Calvin Coolidge and Andrew Mellon in a car racing downhill to tax reductions. The wealthy benefited most from Mellon's tax reduction policies, paying as much as one-third less in 1926 than they had paid in 1921.

Do you think Berryman agreed with the tax cuts?

Southern and western lawmakers formed a farm bloc in Congress to press for special legislation for American agriculture. The farm bloc supported the higher tariffs, which included protection for constituents' crops, and helped secure passage of legislation to create federal supervision over stockyards, packinghouses, and grain trading.

This special-interest legislation failed to get at the root of overproduction, however. Farmers then supported more controversial measures designed to raise domestic crop prices by having the government sell the surplus overseas at low world prices. Coolidge vetoed the legislation on grounds that it involved unwarranted government interference in the economy.

Yet the government's role in the economy increased rather than lessened in the 1920s. Republicans widened the scope of federal activity and nearly doubled the ranks of government employees. Herbert Hoover led the way in the Commerce Department, establishing new bureaus to help make American industry more efficient in housing, transportation, and mining. Under his leadership, the government encouraged corporations to develop welfare programs that undercut trade unions, and he tried to minimize labor disturbances by devising new federal machinery to mediate disputes. Instead of going back to the laissez-faire tradition of the nineteenth century, the Republican administrations of the 1920s were pioneering a close relationship between government and private business.

QUICK CHECK

What was new about the Republican approach to government?

The Election of 1928

A Heavy Load for Al, 1928

To challenge Hoover in 1928, the Democrats selected Al Smith of New York. Born on the Lower East Side of Manhattan of mixed Irish-German ancestry, Smith was the prototype of the urban Democrat. He was Catholic; he was associated with a big-city machine; he was a "wet" who wanted to end prohibition. Starting out in the Fulton Fish Market as a boy, he had joined Tammany Hall (the Democratic party in New York City) and gradually climbed the political ladder, rising from subpoena server to state legislator to governor, a post he held with distinction for nearly a decade. But as the embodiment of the big-city East, Smith had to struggle to gain the support of the West and South. His lack of education, poor grammar, and distinctive New York accent all hurt him, as did his eastern provincialism. When reporters asked him about his appeal in the states west of the Mississippi, he replied, "What states are west of the Mississippi?"

The choice facing the American voter in 1928 seemed unusually clear-cut. Herbert Hoover was a Protestant, a dry, and an old-stock American, who stood for efficiency and individualism; Smith was a Catholic, a wet, and a descendant of immigrants, who was closely associated with big-city politics. Just as Smith appealed to new voters in the cities, so Hoover won the support of many old-line Democrats who feared the city, Tammany Hall, and the pope.

Yet beneath the surface, as Allan J. Lichtman points out, there were "striking similarities between Smith and Hoover." Both were self-made men who embodied the American belief in freedom of opportunity and upward mobility. Neither advocated any significant degree of economic change nor any redistribution of national wealth or power. Though religion proved to be the most important issue in the minds of the voters, hurting Smith far more than prohibition or his identification with the city, the Democratic candidate's failure to spotlight the growing cracks in prosperity or to offer alternative economic policies ensured his defeat.

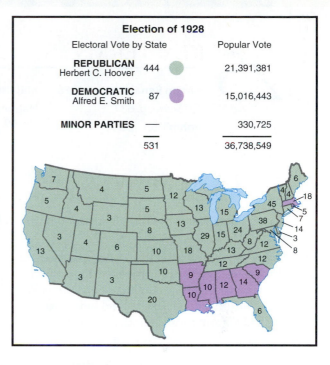

Election of 1928

Electoral Vote by State		Popular Vote
REPUBLICAN Herbert C. Hoover	444	21,391,381
DEMOCRATIC Alfred E. Smith	87	15,016,443
MINOR PARTIES	—	330,725
	531	36,738,549

The 1928 election was a dubious victory for the Republicans. Hoover won easily, defeating Smith by more than six million votes and carrying such traditionally Democratic states as Oklahoma, Texas, and Florida. But Smith succeeded for the first time in winning a majority of votes for the Democrats in the nation's twelve largest cities. A new Democratic electorate was emerging, consisting of Catholics and Jews, Irish and Italians, Poles and Greeks. Now the task was to unite the traditional Democrats of the South and West with the urban voters of the Northeast and Midwest.

QUICK CHECK ✓

How did the election of 1928 summarize the divisions of the period?

Conclusion: The Old and the New

The election-night celebrations at Hoover campaign headquarters were muted by prohibition and by the president-elect's natural reserve. Had Hoover known what lay just ahead for the country, and for his presidency, no doubt the party would have been even more somber.

During the 1920s, America struggled to enter the modern era. The economics of mass production and the politics of urbanization drove the country forward, but the persistent appeal of individualism and rural-based values held it back. Americans achieved greater prosperity than ever before, but the prosperity was unevenly distributed. Further, as the outbursts of nativism, ethnic and racial bigotry, and intolerance revealed, prosperity hardly guaranteed generosity or unity. Nor, for that matter, did it guarantee continued prosperity, even for those who benefited initially. As much as America changed during the 1920s, in one crucial respect the country remained as before. The American economy, for all its remarkable productive capacity, was astonishingly fragile. This was the lesson Hoover was soon to learn.

WATCH

Prosperity of the 1920s and the Great Depression

MHL

MyHistoryLab

For a list of additional titles related to this chapter's topics, please see
www.pearsonamericanhistory.com.

STUDY RESOURCES

KEY TERMS

Harlem Renaissance, p. 686

Red Scare, p. 687

prohibition, p. 690

nativism, p. 692

National Origins Quota Act, p. 692

Scopes trial, p. 693

Teapot Dome scandal, p. 694

CHAPTER REVIEW

WHAT was new about the American economy in the 1920s?

The American economy in the 1920s underwent a second industrial revolution. Powered by electricity and featuring the mass production of automobiles and other consumer goods, the second industrial revolution lifted the American standard of living to new heights. *(p. 681)*

HOW did life in the cities change after World War I?

During the 1920s the focus of American life shifted to the cities, which for the first time contained a majority of the American population. Women found new opportunities to express themselves, and sports, music, literature, and the arts flourished as never before. *(p. 683)*

HOW did conservatives resist the changes of the decade?

The dramatic changes of the 1920s alarmed many conservatives, who tried to resist by various methods.

The police and the courts cracked down on radicals; prohibition outlawed liquor; the Ku Klux Klan attacked immigrants and racial minorities; Congress drastically restricted immigration; and fundamentalist Christians decried the changing code of morality and the teaching of evolution in the schools. *(p. 687)*

HOW did the politics of the 1920s reflect changes in the economy and in American society?

The 1920s were a decade of Republican politics. Presidents Harding, Coolidge, and Hoover promoted measures that favored business and the wealthy classes. In the election of 1928, voters had a clear choice between Hoover, the candidate of the countryside and conservatism, and Al Smith, the candidate of the cities and change, and they chose Hoover in a landslide. *(p. 694)*

MAKING CONNECTIONS

1. How did the automobile increase the independence of young people during the 1920s?
2. Why did the new opportunities for women upset conservatives?
3. What did the Red Scare and the desire for immigration reform have in common?
4. How did the presidential election of 1928 reflect the anxieties of the postwar era?

PRACTICE QUIZ

1. The _____ industry symbolized the nature of the consumer goods revolution during the 1920s.
   - **a.** War
   - **b.** Automobile
   - **c.** Airplane
   - **d.** Television

2. The _____ replaced the countryside as the focal point of American life in the 1920s.
   - **a.** City
   - **b.** University
   - **c.** Speakeasy
   - **d.** Church

3. The _____ image of the 1920s was popularized by H.L. Mencken.
   - **a.** Gangster
   - **b.** Doughboy
   - **c.** Flapper
   - **d.** Evangelist

4. The _____ Renaissance was an outpouring of African American artistic expression during the decade.
   - **a.** Socialist
   - **b.** Detroit
   - **c.** Chicago
   - **d.** Harlem

5. How did conservatives respond to cultural change during the 1920s?
   - **a.** They fully embraced the turn towards a more urban and leisurely lifestyle.
   - **b.** They launched an attack against the new values in American society.
   - **c.** They fled the new changes by immigrating to Canada and Mexico.
   - **d.** They abandoned their core Protestant principles.

6. All of the following relate how women workers fared during the 1920s *except*
   - **a.** The number of women doctors increased.
   - **b.** The 1920s saw a deceleration of women working outside of the home.
   - **c.** No permanent gain in the number of working women took place.
   - **d.** Most women workers still had low paying jobs.

7. All of the following describe the electricity industry during the 1920s *except*
   - **a.** The industry grew rapidly.
   - **b.** Electricity reached two-thirds of American homes by the end of the 1920s.
   - **c.** Electricity powered the new appliances increasingly bought by Americans.
   - **d.** The industry helped to increase the burden of housework.

8. Which of the following sports increased in national importance during the 1920s?
   - **a.** Boxing
   - **b.** Golf
   - **c.** Baseball
   - **d.** All of the above answers are accurate.

9. All of the following contributed to panic among the American public during the summer of 1919 *except*
   - **a.** A general strike in Seattle.
   - **b.** A police strike in Boston.
   - **c.** The Haymarket Square bombing.
   - **d.** A violent strike in the iron and steel industry.

10. Attorney General A. Mitchell Palmer responded to violent events during 1919 in all of the following ways *except*
    - **a.** He ordered federal troops to keep Native Americans on reservations.
    - **b.** He launched a series of raids against anarchists.
    - **c.** He rounded up four thousand communists in a single evening.
    - **d.** He helped to arrest and deport Emma Goldman and other well-known dissenters.

Find more practice at
www.myhistorylab.com

SAMPLE ESSAY QUESTIONS

1. Evaluate the influence of the second Industrial Revolution on American society.

2. Explain the rise of prohibition, and describe how it impacted American society.

Answers to Practice Quiz 1. b, p. 681 **2.** a, p. 683 **3.** c, p. 684 **4.** d, p. 686 **5.** b, p. 687 **6.** a, p. 684 **7.** d, p. 682 **8.** d, p. 686 **9.** c, p. 687 **10.** a, p. 688

Maynard Dixon, *Okie Camp*, 1935. With the encouragement of the second of his three wives, the depression-era documentary photographer Dorothea Lange, Dixon turned his art to social criticism, making his paintings commentaries on victims of the Great Depression.

What mood do his pictures convey?

The Struggle Against Despair

Oscar Heline never forgot the terrible waste of the Great Depression. "Grain was being burned," he told interviewer Studs Terkel. "It was cheaper than coal." Heline lived in Iowa, in the heart of the farm belt. "A county just east of here, they burned corn in their courthouse all winter…. You couldn't hardly buy groceries for corn." Farmers, desperate for higher prices, resorted to destruction. As Heline recalled, "People were determined to withhold produce from the market—livestock, cream, butter, eggs, what not. If they would dump the produce, they would force the market to a higher level. The farmers would man the highways, and cream cans were emptied in ditches and eggs dumped out. They burned the trestle bridge, so the trains wouldn't be able to haul grain."

Film critic Pauline Kael recounted a different memory of the 1930s. Kael, a college student in California during the Great Depression, was struck by the number of students who were missing fathers. "They had wandered off in disgrace because they couldn't support their families. Other fathers had killed themselves, so the family could have the insurance. Families had totally broken down." Kael and many of her classmates struggled to stay in school. "There were kids who didn't have a place to sleep, huddling under bridges on the campus. I had a scholarship, but there were times when I didn't have any food. The meals were often three candy bars."

Howard Worthington resorted to trickery after losing his job in Chicago. One Easter Sunday during the depression, when his son was four years old, Worthington couldn't afford enough eggs for a proper egg hunt. So he devised a plan. "I hid a couple in the piano and all around. Tommy got his little Easter basket, and as he would find the eggs, I'd steal 'em out of the basket and re-hide them…. He hunted Easter eggs for three hours and he never knew the difference."

No American who lived through the Great Depression ever forgot the experience. As the stories of Heline, Kael, and Worthington show, the individual memories were of hard times, but also of determination, adaptation, and survival.

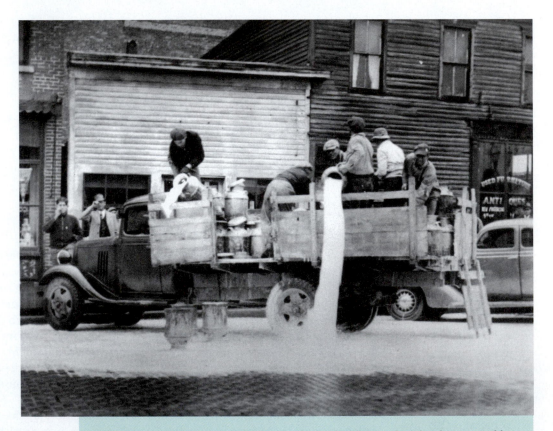

During the Great Depression, market prices for produce were so low that farmers could scarcely afford to harvest their crops. Many resorted to destroying produce in an attempt to limit supplies and force prices higher, such as these striking dairy farmers in Illinois dumping cans of milk into the street.

Did their efforts succeed?

The depression decade had an equally profound effect on American institutions. To cope with the problems of poverty and dislocation, Americans looked to government as never before, and in doing so transformed American politics and public life. The agent of the transformation—the man America turned to in its moment of trial—was Franklin D. Roosevelt. His answer to the country's demands for action was an ambitious program of relief and reform called the **New Deal.**

The Great Depression

The depression of the 1930s came as a shock to Americans who had grown used to the prosperity of the 1920s. The consumer revolution of that earlier decade had fostered a general confidence that the American way of life would continue to improve. But following the collapse of the stock market in late 1929, factories closed, machines fell silent, and millions of Americans walked the streets looking for jobs that didn't exist.

The Great Crash

The consumer goods revolution contained the seeds of its own demise. The productive capacity of the automobile and appliance industries grew faster than the effective demand. Each year after 1924, the rate of increase in the sale of cars and refrigerators and ranges slowed, a natural consequence as more and more people already owned these durable goods. Production began to falter, and in 1927, the nation underwent a mild recession. The sale of durable goods declined, and construction of houses and buildings fell slightly.

Even so, individuals with ready cash invested heavily in the stock market. The market had advanced in spurts during the 1920s; the value of all stocks listed on the New York Stock Exchange rose from $27 billion in 1925 to $67 billion in early 1929. The strongest surge began in the spring of 1928, when investors ignored the declining production figures in the belief they could make a killing in the market. People bet their savings on speculative stocks. Corporations used their large cash reserves to supply money to brokers who in turn loaned money to investors on margin; in 1929, for example, the Standard Oil Company of New Jersey loaned out $69 million a day in this fashion.

Investors could now play the market on credit, buying stock listed at $100 a share with $10 down and $90 on margin, the broker's loan for the balance. If the stock advanced to $150, the investor could sell and reap a gain of 500 percent on the $10 investment. And in the bull market climate of the 1920s, everyone was sure the market would go up.

By 1929, it seemed the whole nation was engaged in speculation. In city after city, brokers opened branch offices, each complete with a stock ticker and a huge board covered with the latest Wall Street quotations. People crowded into the customers' rooms in the offices, filling the seats and greeting the latest advances of their favorite stocks with shouts of approval. So great was the public's interest in the stock market that newspapers carried the stock averages on their front pages.

In reality, though, more people were spectators than speculators; fewer than three million Americans owned stocks in 1929, and only about a half million were

WHAT

were the causes and effects of the Great Depression?

The Great Depression

New Deal

In accepting the nomination of the Democratic party in 1932, Franklin Delano Roosevelt promised a "new deal" for the American people. After his election, the label was applied to his program of legislation passed to combat the Great Depression. The New Deal included measures aimed at relief, reform, and recovery. They achieved some relief and considerable reform but little recovery.

U.S. UNEMPLOYMENT, 1929–1942

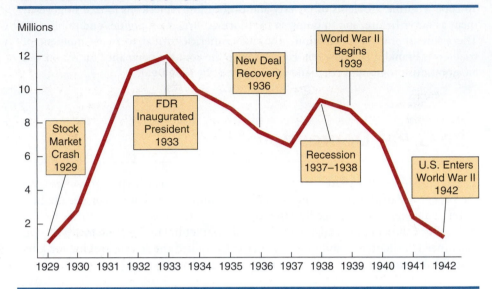

active buyers and sellers. But the bull market became a national obsession, assuring everyone that the economy was healthy and preventing any serious analysis of its underlying flaws. When the market soared to more than $80 billion in total value by mid-summer, the *Wall Street Journal* discounted any possibility of a decline, proclaiming, "The outlook for the fall months seems brighter than at any time."

And then things changed, almost overnight. On October 24—later known as Black Thursday—the rise in stock prices faltered, and when it did investors nervously began to sell. Such leading stocks as RCA and Westinghouse plunged, losing nearly half their value in a single day. Speculators panicked as their creditors demanded new collateral, and the panic caused prices to plummet still further. Within weeks the gains of the previous two years had vanished.

The great crash of the stock market soon spilled over into the larger economy. Banks and other financial institutions suffered heavy losses in the market and were forced to curtail lending for consumer purchases. As consumers came up short, factories cut back production, laying off some workers and reducing hours for others. The layoffs and cutbacks lowered purchasing power even further, so fewer people bought cars and appliances. More factory layoffs resulted, and some plants closed entirely, leading to the availability of even less money for the purchase of consumer goods.

This downward economic spiral continued for four years. By 1932, unemployment had swelled to 25 percent of the workforce. Steel production was down to 12 percent of capacity, and the vast assembly lines in Detroit produced only a trickle of cars each day. The gross national product fell to 67 percent of the 1929 level. The bright promise of mass production had ended in a nightmare.

The basic explanation for the Great Depression lies in the fact that U.S. factories produced more goods than the American people could consume. The problem was not that the market for such products was fully saturated. In 1929, there were still millions of Americans who did not own cars or radios or refrigerators. But many of them could not afford the new products. There were other contributing causes—unstable economic conditions in Europe, the agricultural decline since 1919, corporate mismanagement, and excessive speculation—but it all came down to the fact that people did not have enough money to buy the consumer products coming off the assembly lines.

QUICK CHECK ✓

What caused the Great Crash?

The Effect of the Depression

It is difficult to measure the human cost of the Great Depression. The material hardships were bad enough. Men and women lived in lean-tos made of scrap wood and metal, and families went without meat and fresh vegetables for months, existing on a diet of soup and beans. The psychological burden was even greater: Americans suffered through year after year of grinding poverty with no letup in sight. The unemployed stood in line for hours waiting for relief checks; veterans sold apples or pencils on street corners, their manhood—once prized so highly by the nation—now in question. People left the city for the countryside but found no salvation on the farm. Crops rotted in the fields because prices were too low to make harvesting worthwhile; sheriffs fended off angry crowds as banks foreclosed long-overdue mortgages on once prosperous farms.

Seattle, WA, Shantytown

Few escaped the suffering. African Americans who had left the poverty of the rural South for factory jobs in the North were among the first to be laid off. Mexican

The Great Depression devastated millions who lost their jobs and often then the means to provide food and shelter for themselves and their families. Overwhelmed local and private charities could not keep up with the demands for assistance, and many looked to the federal government. Breadlines stretched as far as the eye could see.

How do you suppose the people in the lines felt about their situation?

African American Family on the Road

immigrants, who had flowed in to replace European immigrants, met with competition from angry citizens now willing to do stoop labor in the fields and work as track layers on the railroads. Immigration officials used technicalities to halt the flow across the Rio Grande and even to reverse it; nearly a half million Mexicans were deported in the 1930s, including families with children born in the United States.

The poor—black, brown, and white—survived because they knew better than most Americans how to exist in poverty. They stayed in bed in cold weather, both to keep warm and to avoid unnecessary burning up of calories; they patched their shoes with pieces of rubber from discarded tires, heated only the kitchens of their homes, and ate scraps of food that others would reject.

The middle class, which had always lived with high expectations, was hit hard. Professionals and white-collar workers refused to ask for charity even while their families went without food; one New York dentist and his wife committed suicide and left a note saying, "We want to get out of the way before we are forced to accept relief money." People who fell behind in their mortgage payments lost their homes and then faced eviction when they could not pay the rent. Health care declined. Middle-class people stopped going to doctors and dentists regularly, unable to make the required cash payment in advance for services rendered.

Even the well-to-do were affected, giving up many of their former luxuries and weighed down with guilt as they watched former friends and business associates join the ranks of the impoverished. "My father lost everything in the depression" became an all-too-familiar refrain among young people who dropped out of college.

Many Americans sought escape in movement. Men, boys, and some women rode the rails in search of jobs, hopping freights to move south in the winter or west in the summer. On the Missouri Pacific alone, the number of vagrants increased from just over 13,000 in 1929 to nearly 200,000 in 1931. One town in the Southwest hired special police to keep vagrants from leaving the boxcars. Those who became tramps had to keep on the move, but they did find a sense of community in the hobo jungles that sprang up along the major railroad routes. Here the unfortunate could find a place to eat and sleep, and people with whom to share their misery. Louis Banks, a black veteran, told interviewer Studs Terkel what these informal camps were like:

QUICK CHECK

How did the Great Depression affect individual lives?

> Black and white, it didn't make any difference who you were, 'cause everybody was poor. All friendly, sleep in a jungle. We used to take a big pot and cook food, cabbage, meat and beans all together. We all set together, we made a tent. Twenty-five or thirty would be out on the side of the rail, white and colored: They didn't have no mothers or sisters, they didn't have no home, they were dirty, they had overalls on, they didn't have no food, they didn't have anything.

Fighting the Depression

HOW did Franklin Roosevelt fight the Depression?

The Great Depression presented an enormous challenge for American political leadership. The inability of the Republicans to overcome the economic catastrophe provided the Democrats with the chance to regain power. Although they failed to achieve full recovery before the outbreak of World War II, the Democrats did succeed in alleviating some of the suffering and establishing political dominance.

The Emergence of Roosevelt

The Great Depression took Herbert Hoover by surprise. At first the Republican president relied on the natural working of the economy to restore prosperity. When this failed, he called for voluntary cooperation among businesses to maintain wages and employment. To relieve the suffering of those thrown out of work, he looked to local governments and private charities. Eventually, and reluctantly, Hoover agreed to federal assistance to business, but by then the depression had grown to overwhelming proportions. His mishandling of the **Bonus Army,** a group of jobless World War I veterans who traveled to Washington seeking federal help, and who were forcibly dispersed by General Douglas MacArthur and troops of the regular army, made Hoover the most unpopular man in America by 1932.

His successor as president was Franklin D. Roosevelt. Born into the old Dutch aristocracy of New York, FDR was a distant cousin of the Republican Teddy. He grew up with all the advantages of wealth: private tutors, his own sailboat and pony, frequent trips to Europe, and education at Groton and Harvard. His strong-willed mother smoothed all the obstacles in the path of her only child and gave him a priceless sense of inner security. After graduation from Harvard, he briefly attended law school but left to plunge into politics. He served in the New York legislature and then went to Washington as assistant secretary of the navy under Wilson, a post he filled capably during World War I. Defeated as the Democratic vice presidential candidate in 1920, Roosevelt had just begun a banking career when he suffered an attack of polio in the summer of 1921. Refusing to give in, he fought back bravely, and though he never again walked unaided, he re-entered politics in the mid-1920s and was elected governor of New York in 1928.

Roosevelt's dominant trait was his ability to persuade and motivate other people. He possessed a marvelous voice, deep and rich; a winning smile; and a buoyant confidence he could easily transmit to others. Some believed he was too vain and superficial as a young man, but his bout with polio gave him both an understanding of human suffering and a broad political appeal as a man who had faced heavy odds and overcome them. He understood the give-and-take of politics, knew how to use flattery to win over doubters, and was especially effective in exploiting the media, whether in bantering with newspaper reporters or reaching out to the American people on the radio. Although his mind was quick and agile, he had little patience with philosophical nuances; he dealt with perceptions of issues, not their deeper substance, and he displayed a flexibility toward political principles that often dismayed even his warmest admirers.

Roosevelt took advantage of the opportunity offered by the Great Depression. With the Republicans discredited, he cultivated the two wings of the divided Democrats, appealing to both the traditionalists from the South and West and the new

Bonus Army

In June 1932, a group of twenty thousand World War I veterans marched on Washington, D.C., to demand immediate payment of their bonuses voted by Congress in 1924. Congress rejected their demands, and President Hoover, fearing that their ranks were infested with criminals and radicals, had the Bonus Army forcibly removed from their encampment. It was a public relations disaster for Hoover.

Children with "Hoover's Poor Farm" Sign

Bonus Expeditionary Force March on Washington

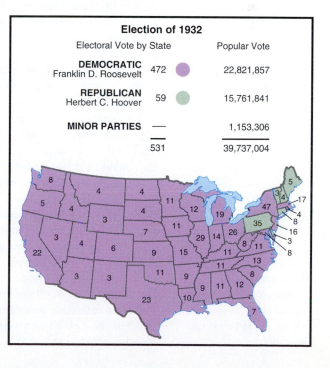

Election of 1932

	Electoral Vote by State		Popular Vote
DEMOCRATIC Franklin D. Roosevelt	472		22,821,857
REPUBLICAN Herbert C. Hoover	59		15,761,841
MINOR PARTIES	—		1,153,306
	531		39,737,004

QUICK CHECK ✓

How did Franklin Roosevelt's background prepare him to deal with the Great Depression?

urban elements in the North. After winning the party's nomination in 1932, he broke with tradition by flying to Chicago and accepting in person, telling the cheering delegates, "I pledge you—I pledge myself to a new deal for the American people."

In the fall, he defeated Herbert Hoover in a landslide for the Democrats. Roosevelt tallied 472 electoral votes as he swept the South and West and carried nearly all the large industrial states as well. Farmers and workers, Protestants and Catholics, immigrants and native born rallied behind the new leader who promised to restore prosperity.

IMAGE

Burning Bonus Army Shacks, 1932

DOCUMENT

Franklin D. Roosevelt, Speech at San Francisco, 1932

WATCH

FDR's Inauguration

DOCUMENT

Franklin D. Roosevelt, Radio Address (1933)

fireside chats

A series of radio addresses by Roosevelt from 1933–1944, in which the president spoke to the American people about such issues as the banking crisis, social security, and World War II.

Tennessee Valley Authority (TVA)

A New Deal effort at regional planning created by Congress in 1933, this agency built dams and power plants on the Tennessee River and its tributaries. Its programs for flood control, soil conservation, and reforestation helped raise the standard of living for millions in the Tennessee River valley.

The Hundred Days

When Franklin Roosevelt took the oath of office on March 4, 1933, the nation's economy was on the brink of collapse. Unemployment stood at nearly thirteen million, one-fourth of the labor force; banks were closed in thirty-eight states. On inauguration morning, the governors of New York and Illinois closed the banks in the nation's two largest cities, thus bringing the country's financial transactions to a halt. Speaking from the steps of the Capitol, FDR declared boldly, "First of all, let me assert my firm belief that the only thing we have to fear is fear itself—nameless, unreasoning, unjustified terror." Then he announced he would call Congress into special session and request "broad executive power to wage a war against the emergency, as great as the power that would be given to me if we were in fact invaded by a foreign foe."

Within the next ten days, Roosevelt won his first great New Deal victory by saving the nation's banks. On March 5, he issued a decree closing the banks and called Congress back into session. His aides drafted new banking legislation and presented it to Congress on March 9; a few hours later, both houses passed it, and FDR signed the new legislation that evening. The measure provided for government supervision and aid to the banks. Strong ones would be reopened with federal support, weak ones closed, and those in difficulty bolstered by government loans.

On March 12, FDR addressed the nation by radio in the first of his **fireside chats.** In conversational tones, he told the public what he had done. Some banks would begin to reopen the next day, with the government standing behind them. Other banks, once they became solvent, would open later, and the American people could safely put their money back into these institutions. The next day, March 13, the nation's largest and strongest banks opened their doors; at the end of the day, customers had deposited more cash than they withdrew. The crisis was over; gradually, other banks opened, and the runs and failures ceased.

"Capitalism was saved in eight days," boasted one of Roosevelt's advisers. Most surprising was the conservative nature of FDR's action. Instead of nationalizing the banks, he had simply thrown the government's resources behind them and preserved private ownership. Though some other New Deal measures would be more radical, Roosevelt set a tone in the banking crisis. He was out to reform and restore the American economic system, not change it drastically. He drew on the progressive tradition and his experience with World War I mobilization to fashion a moderate program of government action.

For the next three months, until it adjourned in June, Congress responded to a series of presidential initiatives. During these "Hundred Days," Roosevelt sent

THE TENNESSEE VALLEY AUTHORITY   The Tennessee Valley Authority (TVA) served a seven-state region in the Southeast.

What were the TVA's three major objectives?

fifteen major requests to Congress and received back fifteen pieces of legislation. A few created agencies that have become a part of American life. The **Tennessee Valley Authority (TVA)** was one of the most ambitious of Roosevelt's New Deal measures. This innovative effort at regional planning resulted in the building of a series of dams in seven states to control floods, ease navigation, and produce electricity. The **Civilian Conservation Corps (CCC)** put jobless young men from cities to work in the forests planting trees, fighting fires, and building roads and trails. Though not part of the Hundred Days, the final commitment to the idea of work relief came in 1935 when Roosevelt established the **Works Progress Administration (WPA)** to spend nearly $5 billion authorized by Congress for emergency relief. The WPA put the unemployed on the federal payroll so they could earn enough to meet their basic needs and help stimulate the stagnant economy.

Other New Deal agencies were temporary in nature, designed to meet the specific economic problems of the depression. None were completely successful; the depression would continue for another six years, immune even to Roosevelt's magic. But psychologically, the nation turned the corner in the spring of 1933. Under FDR, the government seemed to be responding to the economic crisis, enabling people for the first time since 1929 to look to the future with hope.

MAP
The Tennessee Valley Authority

DOCUMENT
An Attack on New Deal Farm Policies, 1936

QUICK CHECK ✓

What were the principal accomplishments of the Hundred Days?

Steps toward Recovery

Two major New Deal programs launched during the Hundred Days were aimed at industrial and agricultural recovery. The first was the **National Recovery Administration (NRA),** FDR's attempt to achieve economic advance through planning and cooperation among government, business, and labor. In the midst of the depression, business owners were intent on stabilizing production and raising prices for their goods. Labor leaders were equally determined to spread work through maximum hours and to put a floor under workers' income with minimum wages.

The NRA hoped to achieve both goals by permitting companies in each major industry to cooperate in writing codes of fair competition that would set realistic limits on production, allocate percentages to individual producers, and set firm guidelines for prices. Section 7a of the enabling act mandated protection for labor in all the codes by establishing maximum hours, minimum wages, and the guarantee of collective bargaining by unions. No company could be compelled to join, but the New Deal sought complete participation by appealing to patriotism. Each firm that took part could display a blue eagle and stamp the symbol on its

Civilian Conservation Corps (CCC)
One of the most popular New Deal programs, the CCC was created by Congress to provide young men between ages 18 and 25 with government jobs in reforestation and other conservation projects. It eventually employed over 300,000.

Works Progress Administration (WPA)
New Deal agency created to provide work relief for the unemployed.

The National Recovery Administration blue eagle signaled a firm's participation in the National Recovery Act. Roosevelt's innovative program met with considerable resistance, and signs modeled on this original example attempted to make participation patriotic and respectable.

Would you have been persuaded?

products. With energetic Hugh Johnson in charge, the NRA quickly enrolled the nation's leading companies and unions. By the summer of 1933, more than five hundred industries had adopted codes that covered 2.5 million workers.

The NRA quickly bogged down in a huge bureaucratic morass. The codes proved to be too detailed to enforce easily. Written by the largest companies, the rules favored big business at the expense of smaller competitors. Labor quickly became disenchanted with Section 7a. The minimum wages were often near starvation level, while business avoided the requirement for collective bargaining by creating company unions that did not represent the real needs of workers. After a brief upsurge in the spring of 1933, industrial production began to sag as disillusionment with the NRA grew. By 1934, more and more business owners were complaining about the new agency, calling it the "National Run Around." When the Supreme Court finally invalidated the NRA in 1935 on constitutional grounds, few mourned its demise. The idea of trying to overcome the depression by relying on voluntary cooperation between competing businesses and labor leaders had collapsed in the face of individual self-interest and greed.

The New Deal's attempt at farm recovery fared better. Henry A. Wallace, FDR's secretary of agriculture, came up with an answer to the farmers' old dilemma of overproduction. The government would act as a clearinghouse for producers of major crops, arranging for them to set production limits for wheat, cotton, corn, and other leading crops. The **Agricultural Adjustment Administration (AAA),** created by Congress in May 1933, would allocate acreage among individual farmers, encouraging them to take land out of production by paying them subsidies (raised by a tax on food processors). Unfortunately, Wallace preferred not to wait until the 1934 planting season to implement this program, and so farmers were paid in 1933 to plow under crops they had already planted and to kill livestock they were raising. Faced with the problem of hunger in the midst of plenty, the New Deal seemed to respond by destroying the plenty.

The AAA program worked better in 1934 and 1935 as land removed from production led to smaller harvests and rising farm prices. Farm income rose for the first time since World War I, increasing from $2 billion in 1933 to $5 billion by 1935. Severe weather, especially Dust Bowl conditions on the Great Plains, contributed to the crop-limitation program, but most of the gain in farm income came from the subsidy payments themselves rather than from higher market prices. Though the Supreme Court in 1936 ruled the AAA unconstitutional, Congress quickly reenacted its essential features in acceptable form.

National Recovery Administration (NRA)

A keystone of the early New Deal, this federal agency was created in 1933 to promote economic recovery and revive industry during the Great Depression. It permitted manufacturers to establish industrywide codes of "fair business practices," setting prices and production levels. It also provided for minimum wages and maximum working hours for labor and guaranteed labor the right to organize and bargain collectively (Section 7a). The Supreme Court declared it unconstitutional in 1935.

THE DUST BOWL Drought and soil erosion brought on by overfarming turned the agricultural land of the Great Plains into a giant dust bowl during the 1930s. Dust storms forced many farmers to abandon their land.

Where did they go?

Areas of Wind Erosion 1935–1940

■ Severe
■ Most Severe

On the whole, large farmers benefited most from the New Deal's agricultural program. Possessing the capital to buy machinery and fertilizer, they were able to farm more efficiently than before on fewer acres of land. Small farmers, tenants, and sharecroppers did not fare as well, receiving very little of the government payments and often being driven off the land as owners took the acreage previously cultivated by tenants and sharecroppers out of production. Some three million people left the land in the 1930s, crowding into the cities where they swelled the relief rolls. In the long run, the New Deal reforms improved the efficiency of American agriculture, but at a real human cost.

QUICK CHECK ✓

How did the New Deal try to promote recovery of industry and agriculture?

Reforming American Life

During his first two years in office, FDR had concentrated on fighting the Great Depression by shoring up the sagging American economy. Only a few new agencies, notably TVA, sought to make permanent changes in national life. Roosevelt was developing a "broker-state" concept of government, responding to pressures from organized elements such as corporations, labor unions, and farm groups while ignoring the needs and wants of the dispossessed who had no clear political voice. The early New Deal tried to assist bankers and industrialists, large farmers, and members of the labor unions, but it did little to help the elderly and the poor.

The continuing depression and high unemployment began to create pressure for more sweeping changes. Roosevelt faced the choice of either providing more radical programs, ones designed to end historical inequities in American life, or deferring to others who put forth solutions to the nation's ills.

HOW did the New Deal reform American life?

EXHIBITION

THE STATE MUSEUM
HARRISBURG PENNSYLVANIA
DEC.17TH THROUGH JAN.13TH
PAINTINGS PRINTS SCULPTURE

FEDERAL ART PROJECT
WORKS PROGRESS ADMINISTRATION

Federal work relief programs helped millions maintain their self-respect. Workers in the CCC (top, left) received $30 a month for planting trees and building parks and trails. As indicated on the map, the PWA hired workers to build schools, dig irrigation ditches, construct sewage treatment plants, and erect bridges across the country. Artists and writers found work in the WPA (top, right).

Who paid for all this?

Challenges to FDR

The signs of discontent were visible everywhere by 1935. In the upper Midwest, progressives and agrarian radicals, led by Minnesota governor Floyd Olson, were calling for government action to raise farm and labor income. "I am a radical in the sense that I want a definite change in the system," Olson declared. "I am not satisfied with patching." Upton Sinclair, the muckraking novelist, nearly won the governorship of California in 1934 running on the slogan "End poverty in California," while in the East a violent strike in the textile industry shut down plants in twenty states. The most serious challenge to Roosevelt's leadership, however, came from three demagogues who captured national attention in the mid-1930s.

The first was Father Charles Coughlin, a Roman Catholic priest from Detroit, who had originally supported FDR. Speaking to a rapt nationwide radio audience in his rich, melodious voice, Coughlin appealed to the discontented with a strange mixture of crank monetary schemes and anti-Semitism. He broke with the New Deal in late 1934, denouncing it as the "Pagan Deal," and founded his own National Union for Social Justice. Increasingly vitriolic, he called for monetary inflation and the nationalization of the banking system in his weekly radio sermons to an audience of more than thirty million.

A more benign but equally influential figure appeared in California. Francis Townsend, a 67-year-old physician, came forward in 1934 with a scheme to assist the elderly, who were suffering greatly during the depression. The Townsend Plan proposed giving everyone over the age of 60 a monthly pension of $200 with the proviso that it must be spent within thirty days. Although designed less as an old-age pension plan than as a way to stimulate the economy, the proposal understandably had its greatest appeal among the elderly. They embraced it as a holy cause, joining Townsend Clubs across the country. Despite the criticism from economists that the plan would transfer more than half the national income to less than 10 percent of the population, more than ten million people signed petitions endorsing the Townsend Plan, and few politicians dared oppose it.

The third new voice of protest was that of Huey Long, the flamboyant senator from Louisiana. Like Coughlin, an original supporter of the New Deal, Long turned against FDR and by 1935 had become a major political threat to the president. A shrewd, ruthless, yet witty man, Long had a remarkable ability to mock those in power. The Kingfish (a nickname he borrowed from *Amos 'n' Andy*) announced a nationwide "Share the Wealth" movement in 1934. He spoke grandly of taking from the rich to make "every man a king," guaranteeing each American a home worth $5000 and an annual income of $2500. To finance the plan, Long advocated seizing all fortunes of more than $5 million and levying a tax of 100 percent on incomes greater than $1 million. By 1935, Long claimed to have founded twenty-seven thousand Share the Wealth clubs and had a mailing list of more than seven million people, including workers, farmers, college professors, and even bank presidents. Threatening to run as a third-party candidate in 1936, Long generated fear among Democratic leaders that he might attract three to four million votes, possibly enough to swing the election to the Republicans. Although an assassin killed Huey Long in Louisiana in late 1935, his popularity showed the need for the New Deal to do more to help those still in distress.

Agricultural Adjustment Administration (AAA)

Created by Congress in 1933 as part of the New Deal, this agency attempted to restrict agricultural production by paying farmers subsidies to take land out of production. The object was to raise farm prices, and it did, but the act did nothing for tenant farmers and sharecroppers. The Supreme Court declared it unconstitutional in 1936.

President Roosevelt Focuses on America's Youth

Huey Long, "Share Our Wealth" (1935)

QUICK CHECK

Who were Charles Coughlin, Francis Townsend, and Huey Long, and what did they want?

Social Security

When the new Congress met in January 1935, Roosevelt was ready to support a series of reform measures designed to take the edge off national dissent. The recent elections had increased Democratic congressional strength significantly, with the Republicans losing thirteen seats in the House and retaining less than one-third of the Senate. Many of the Democrats were to the left of Roosevelt, favoring increased spending and more sweeping federal programs. "Boys—this is our hour," exulted Harry Hopkins. "We've got to get everything we want... now or never." Congress quickly appropriated $4.8 billion for the Works Progress Administration (WPA), a federal program to provide jobs for the unemployed, and was prepared to enact virtually any proposal that Roosevelt offered.

The most significant reform enacted in 1935, and also the most important reform of the entire New Deal, was the **Social Security Act**, which provided pensions to the elderly and income and support to the disabled and unemployed. The Townsend movement had reminded Americans that the United States, alone among modern industrial nations, had never developed a welfare system to aid the aged, the disabled, and the unemployed. A cabinet committee began studying the problem in 1934, and President Roosevelt sent its recommendations to Congress the following January.

The proposed legislation had three major parts. First, it provided for old-age pensions financed equally by a tax on employers and workers. In addition, it gave states federal matching funds to provide modest pensions for the destitute elderly. Second, it set up a system of unemployment compensation on a federal-state basis, with employers paying a payroll tax and with each state setting benefit levels and administering the program locally. Finally, it provided for direct federal grants to the states, on a matching basis, for welfare payments to the blind, handicapped, needy elderly, and dependent children.

Although there was criticism from conservatives who mourned the passing of traditional American reliance on self-help and individualism, the chief objections came from those who argued that the administration's measure did not go far enough. Democratic leaders, however, defeated efforts to incorporate Townsend's proposal for $200 monthly pensions and increases in unemployment benefits. Congress then passed the Social Security Act by overwhelming margins.

Critics began to point out its shortcomings, as they have ever since. The old-age pensions were paltry. Designed to begin in 1942, they ranged from $10 to $85 a month. Not everyone was covered; many of those who most needed protection in their old age, such as farmers and domestic servants, were not included. And all participants, regardless of income or economic status, paid in at the same rate, with no

Despite the administration's boosterism, many believed that Social Security could not fulfill its promises.

Why were they skeptical?

supplement from the general revenue. The trust fund also took out of circulation money that was desperately needed to stimulate the economy in the 1930s.

Other portions of the act were equally open to question. The cumbersome unemployment system offered no aid to those currently out of work, only to people who would lose their jobs in the future, and the benefits (depending on the state) ranged from barely adequate to substandard. The outright grants to the handicapped and dependent children were minute in terms of the need; in New York City, for example, a blind person received only $5 a week in 1937.

The conservative nature of the legislation reflected Roosevelt's own fiscal orthodoxy, but even more it was a product of his political realism. Despite the severity of the depression, he realized that establishing a system of federal welfare went against deeply rooted American convictions. He insisted on a tax on participants to give those involved in the pension plan a vested interest in Social Security. He wanted them to feel they had earned their pensions and that in the future no one would dare take them away. "With those taxes in there," he explained privately, "no damned politician can ever scrap my social security program." Above all, FDR had succeeded in establishing the principle of government responsibility for the aged, the handicapped, and the unemployed. Whatever the defects of the legislation, Social Security stood as a landmark of the New Deal, creating a system to provide for the welfare of individuals in a complex industrial society.

Frances Perkins and the Social Security Act (1935, 1960)

QUICK CHECK ✓

What motivated the Social Security Act, and what did it accomplish?

The Impact of the New Deal

The New Deal had a broad influence on the quality of life in the United States in the 1930s. Government programs reached into areas hitherto untouched. Many of them brought about long-overdue improvements, but others failed to make any significant dent in historic inequities. The most important advances came with the dramatic growth of labor unions; the conditions for working women and minorities in non-unionized industries showed no comparable advance.

WHAT
was the lasting impact of the New Deal?

The Rise of Organized Labor

Trade unions were weak at the onset of the Great Depression, with a membership of fewer than three million workers. Most were in the American Federation of Labor (AFL), composed of craft unions that served the needs of skilled workers. The nation's basic industries, such as steel and automobiles, were unorganized; the great mass of unskilled workers thus fared poorly in terms of wages and working conditions. Section 7a of the NRA had led to some growth in AFL ranks, but the union's conservative leaders, eager to cooperate with business, failed to take full advantage of the opportunity to organize the mass production industries.

John L. Lewis, head of the United Mine Workers, took the lead in forming the Committee on Industrial Organization (CIO) in 1935. The son of a Welsh coal miner, Lewis was a dynamic and ruthless man. He had led the mine workers since 1919 and was determined to spread the benefits of unions throughout industry. Lewis first battled with the leadership of the AFL, and then—after being expelled—he renamed his group the Congress of Industrial Organizations and

Wagner Act

The 1935 Wagner Act, formally known as the National Labor Relations Act, created the National Labor Relations Board to supervise union elections and designate winning unions as official bargaining agents. The board could also issue cease-and-desist orders to employers who dealt unfairly with their workers.

Evicted Black Sharecroppers —Arthur Rothstein Photo

QUICK CHECK ✔

How did the New Deal benefit organized labor?

announced that he would use the **Wagner Act,** a 1935 law that provided federal support to union efforts to organize workers, to extend collective bargaining to the nation's auto and steel industries.

Within five years, Lewis had scored a remarkable series of victories. Some came easily. The big steel companies, led by U.S. Steel, surrendered without a fight in 1937; management realized that federal support put the unions in a strong position. There was greater resistance in the automobile industry. When General Motors, the first target, resisted, the newly created United Automobile Workers (UAW) developed an effective strike technique. In late December 1936, GM workers in Flint, Michigan, simply sat down in the factory, refusing to leave until the company recognized their union, and threatening to destroy the valuable tools and machines if they were removed forcibly. When the Michigan governor refused to call out the national guard to break the strike, General Motors conceded defeat and signed a contract with the UAW. Chrysler quickly followed suit, but Henry Ford refused to give in and fought the UAW, hiring strikebreakers and beating up organizers. In 1941, however, Ford finally recognized the UAW. Smaller steel companies, led by Republic Steel, engaged in even more violent resistance; in one incident in 1937, police shot ten strikers. The companies eventually reached a settlement with the steelworkers' union in 1941.

By the end of the 1930s, the CIO had some five million members, slightly more than the AFL. The successes were remarkable—in addition to the automaking and steel unions, organizers of the CIO and the AFL had been successful in the textile, rubber, electrical, and metal industries. For the first time, unskilled as well as skilled workers were unionized. Women and African Americans benefited from the creation of the CIO, not because the union followed enlightened policies, but simply because they made up a substantial proportion of the unskilled workforce that the CIO organized.

Yet despite these impressive gains, only 28 percent of all Americans (excluding farmworkers) belonged to unions by 1940. Millions in the restaurant, retail, and service trades remained unorganized, working long hours for very low wages. Employer resistance and traditional hostility to unions blocked further progress, as did the aloof attitude of President Roosevelt, who commented to labor and management, "A plague on both your houses," during the steel strike. The Wagner Act had helped open the way, but labor leaders such as Lewis, Philip Murray of the Steel Workers Organizing Committee, and Walter Reuther of the United Automobile Workers deserved most of the credit for union achievements.

The New Deal Record on Help to Minorities

The Roosevelt administration's attempts to aid the downtrodden were least effective with African Americans and other racial minorities. The Great Depression had hit blacks with special force. Sharecroppers and tenant farmers had seen the price of cotton drop from 18 to 6 cents a pound, far below the level to sustain a family on the land. In the cities, the saying "Last hired, First fired" proved all too true; by 1933, more than 50 percent of urban blacks were unemployed. Hard times sharpened racial prejudice. "No jobs for niggers until every white man has a job" became a rallying cry for many whites in Atlanta.

The New Deal helped African Americans survive the depression, but it never tried to confront squarely the racial injustice built into the federal relief programs.

With the statue of Abraham Lincoln as a backdrop, African American contralto Marian Anderson sang on the steps of the Lincoln Memorial in a concert given April 9, 1939.

Why did she have to sing outdoors?

Although the programs served blacks as well as whites, in the South the weekly payments blacks received were much smaller. In the early days, NRA codes permitted lower wage scales for blacks, while the AAA led to the eviction of thousands of Negro tenants and sharecroppers. African American leaders referred to the NRA as standing for "Negro Robbed Again" and dismissed the AAA as "a continuation of the same old raw deal." Nor did later reform measures help very much. Neither the minimum wage nor Social Security covered those working as farmers or domestic servants, categories that comprised 65 percent of all African American workers. Thus an NAACP official commented that Social Security "looks like a sieve with the holes just large enough for the majority of Negroes to fall through."

Despite this bleak record, African Americans rallied behind Roosevelt's leadership, abandoning their historic ties to the Republican party. In 1936, more than 75 percent of those African Americans who voted supported FDR. In part, this switch came in response to Roosevelt's appointment of a number of prominent African Americans to high-ranking government positions, such as William H. Hastie in the Interior Department and Mary McLeod Bethune (founder and president of Bethune-Cookman College) in the National Youth Administration. Eleanor Roosevelt spoke out eloquently throughout the decade against racial discrimination, most notably in 1939 when the Daughters of the American Revolution refused to let African American contralto Marian Anderson sing in Constitution Hall. The first lady and Interior Secretary Harold Ickes arranged for the singer to perform at the Lincoln Memorial, where 75,000 people gathered to hear her on Easter Sunday.

Perhaps the most influential factor in the African Americans' political switch was the color-blind policy of Harry Hopkins. He had more than one million blacks working for the WPA by 1939, many of them in teaching and artistic positions as well as in construction jobs. Overall, the New Deal provided assistance to 40 percent of the nation's blacks during the depression. Uneven as his record was, Roosevelt had still done more to aid this oppressed minority than any previous president since Lincoln. One African American newspaper commented that while "relief and WPA are not ideal, they are better than the Hoover bread lines and they'll have to do until the real thing comes along."

The New Deal did far less for Mexican Americans. Engaged primarily in agricultural labor, these people found their wages in California fields dropping from 35 to 14 cents an hour by 1933. The pool of unemployed migrant labor expanded rapidly with Dust Bowl conditions in the Great Plains and the subsequent flight of

Mexican Workers and Their Cars

"Okies" and "Arkies" to the cotton fields of Arizona and the truck farms of California. The Roosevelt administration cut off any further influx from Mexico by barring entry of any immigrant "likely to become a public charge"; local authorities rounded up migrants and shipped them back to Mexico to reduce the welfare rolls.

The New Deal relief program did aid many thousands of Mexican Americans in the Southwest in the 1930s, although migrant workers had difficulty meeting state requirements. The WPA hired Mexican Americans for a variety of construction and cultural programs, but after 1937 such employment was denied to aliens. Overall, the pattern was one of great economic hardship and relatively little federal assistance for Mexican Americans.

Native Americans, after decades of neglect, fared slightly better under the New Deal. Roosevelt appointed John Collier, a social worker who championed Indian rights, to serve as commissioner of Indian affairs. In 1934, Congress passed the Indian Reorganization Act, a reform measure designed to stress tribal unity and autonomy instead of attempting (as previous policy had done) to transform Indians into self-sufficient farmers by granting them small plots of land. Collier employed more Native Americans in the Indian Bureau, supported educational programs on the reservations, and encouraged tribes to produce native handiwork such as blankets and jewelry. Despite modest gains, however, the nation's Indians—who numbered about a third of a million—remained the most impoverished citizens in America.

QUICK CHECK ✓

What did the New Deal accomplish, and not accomplish, for minorities?

The New Deal's End

HOW
and why did the New Deal end?

The New Deal reached its high point in 1936, when Roosevelt was overwhelmingly re-elected and the Democratic party strengthened its hold on Congress. This political triumph was deceptive. In the next two years, Roosevelt met with a series of defeats in Congress. Yet despite the setbacks, he remained a popular political leader who had restored American self-confidence as he strove to meet the challenges of the Great Depression.

The Supreme Court Fight

Father Charles E. Coughlin, "A Third Party" (1936)

Roosevelt's resounding re-election victory went to his head. In 1937, he attempted to overcome the one obstacle remaining in his path—the Supreme Court. During his first term, the Court had ruled several New Deal programs unconstitutional, most notably the NRA and the AAA. Only three of the nine justices were sympathetic to the need for emergency measures in the midst of the depression. Two others were unpredictable, sometimes approving New Deal measures and sometimes opposing them. Four justices were bent on using the Constitution to block Roosevelt's proposals. All were elderly men, and one, Willis Van Devanter, had planned to retire in 1932 but remained on the Court because he believed Roosevelt to be "unfitted and unsafe for the Presidency."

When Congress convened in 1937, the president offered a startling proposal to overcome the Court's threat to the New Deal. Instead of seeking a constitutional amendment either to limit the Court's power or to clarify the constitutional issues, FDR chose an oblique attack. Declaring the Court was falling behind schedule because of the age of its members, he asked Congress to appoint a new justice for each member of the Court over the age of 70, up to a maximum of six.

Although this **"court-packing" scheme,** as critics quickly dubbed it, was perfectly legal, it outraged not only conservatives but liberals as well, who realized it could set a dangerous precedent for the future. Republicans wisely kept silent, letting prominent Democrats such as Senator Burton Wheeler of Montana lead the fight against Roosevelt's plan. Despite all-out pressure from the White House, resistance in the Senate blocked early action on the proposal.

The Court defended itself well. Chief Justice Charles Evans Hughes testified tellingly to the Senate Judiciary Committee, pointing out that in fact the Court was up to date and not behind schedule as Roosevelt charged. The Court then surprised observers with a series of rulings approving such controversial New Deal measures as the Wagner Act and Social Security. In the midst of the struggle, Justice Van Devanter resigned, enabling FDR to make his first appointment to the

"court-packing" scheme

Concerned that the conservative Supreme Court might declare all his New Deal programs unconstitutional, President Franklin Delano Roosevelt asked Congress to allow him to appoint additional justices to the Court. Both Congress and the public rejected this "court-packing" scheme, and it was defeated.

Courtesy, D. R. Fitzpatrick. *St. Louis Post-Dispatch*, June 28, 1935

FDR's battle with the Supreme Court provoked both sympathy and contempt among political cartoonists of the day. In the cartoon on the right, the NRA blue eagle lies dead, nailed to the wall by the Supreme Court. The cartoon on the left, titled "Do We Want a Ventriloquist Act in the Supreme Court?" satirizes FDR's "court-packing" scheme.

How do cartoons differ from written commentary?

QUICK CHECK ✓

What prompted Roosevelt to try to "pack" the Supreme Court, and how did the effort turn out?

Court since taking office in 1933. Believing he had proved his point, the president allowed his court-packing plan to die in the Senate.

During the next few years, four more vacancies occurred, and Roosevelt was able to appoint such distinguished jurists as Hugo Black, William O. Douglas, and Felix Frankfurter to the Supreme Court. Yet the price was high. The Court fight had badly weakened the president's relations with Congress, opening deep rifts with members of his own party. Many senators and representatives who had voted reluctantly for Roosevelt's measures during the depths of the Great Depression now felt free to oppose any further New Deal reforms.

The New Deal in Decline

The legislative record during Roosevelt's second term was meager. Aside from laws on minimum wages and maximum hours, Congress did not extend the New Deal into any new areas. Attempts to institute national health insurance met with stubborn resistance, as did efforts by civil rights advocates to pass antilynching legislation. Disturbed by the growing congressional resistance, Roosevelt set out in the spring of 1938 to defeat a number of conservative Democratic congressmen and senators, primarily in the South. His targets gleefully charged the president with interference in local politics; only one of the men he sought to defeat lost in the primaries. The failure of this attempted purge further undermined Roosevelt's strained relations with Congress.

The worst blow came in the economic sector. The slow but steady improvement in the economy suddenly gave way to a sharp recession in the late summer of 1937. In the following ten months, industrial production fell by one-third, and nearly four million workers lost their jobs. Critics of the New Deal quickly labeled the downturn "the Roosevelt recession," and business executives claimed that it reflected a lack of confidence in FDR's leadership.

The criticism was overblown but not without basis. In an effort to reduce expanding budget deficits, Roosevelt had cut back sharply on WPA and other government programs after the election. Federal contributions to consumer purchasing power fell from $4.1 billion in 1936 to less than $1 billion in 1937. For several months, Roosevelt refused to heed calls from economists to restore heavy government spending. Finally, in April 1938, Roosevelt asked Congress for a $3.75 billion relief appropriation, and the economy began to revive. But FDR's premature attempt to balance the budget had meant two more years of hard times and had marred his reputation as the energetic foe of the depression.

The political result of the attempted purge and the recession was a strong Republican upsurge in the elections of 1938. The GOP won an impressive 81 seats in the House and 8 more in the Senate, as well as 13 governorships. The party many thought dead suddenly had new life. The Democrats still held a sizable majority in Congress, but their margin in the House was particularly deceptive. There were 262 Democratic representatives to 169 Republicans, but 93 southern Democrats held the balance of power. More and more often after 1938, anti–New Deal southerners voted with Republican conservatives to block social and economic reform measures. Thus not only was the New Deal over by the end of 1938, but a new bipartisan conservative coalition that would prevail for a quarter century had formed in Congress.

QUICK CHECK ✓

How did the New Deal end?

Conclusion: The New Deal and American Life

The New Deal lasted a brief five years, and most of its measures came in two legislative bursts in the spring of 1933 and the summer of 1935. Yet its impact on American life was enduring. Nearly every aspect of economic, social, and political development in the decades that followed bore the imprint of Roosevelt's leadership.

The least impressive achievement of the New Deal came in the economic realm. Whatever credit Roosevelt is given for relieving human suffering in the depths of the Great Depression must be balanced against his failure to restore prosperity in the 1930s. The moderate nature of his programs, especially the unwieldy NRA, led to slow and halting industrial recovery. Although much of the improvement that was made came as a result of government spending, FDR never embraced the concept of planned deficits, striving instead for a balanced budget. As a result, the nation had barely reached the 1929 level of production a decade later, and there were still nearly ten million men and women unemployed.

Equally important, Roosevelt refused to make any sweeping changes in the American economic system. Aside from the TVA, there were no broad experiments in regional planning and no attempt to alter free enterprise beyond imposing some limited forms of government regulation. The New Deal did nothing to alter the basic distribution of wealth and power in the nation. The outcome was the preservation of the traditional capitalist system with a thin overlay of federal control.

More significant change occurred in American society. With the adoption of Social Security, the government acknowledged for the first time its responsibility to provide for the welfare of those unable to care for themselves in an industrial society. The Wagner Act helped stimulate the growth of labor unions to balance corporate power, and the minimum wage law provided a much needed floor for many workers.

Yet the New Deal tended to help only the more vocal and organized groups, such as union members and commercial farmers. Those without effective voices or political clout—African Americans, Mexican Americans, women, sharecroppers, restaurant and laundry workers—received little help from the New Deal. For all the appealing rhetoric about the "forgotten man," Roosevelt did little more than Hoover in responding to the long-term needs of the dispossessed.

The most lasting impact of the Roosevelt leadership came in politics. Taking advantage of the emerging power of ethnic voters and capitalizing on the frustration growing out of the depression, FDR proved to be a genius at forging a new coalition. Overcoming the friction between rural and urban Democrats that had prolonged Republican supremacy in the 1920s, he attracted new groups to the Democratic party, principally African Americans and organized labor. His political success led to a major realignment that lasted long after he left the scene.

His political achievement also revealed the true nature of Roosevelt's success. He was a brilliant politician who recognized the essence of leadership in a democracy—appealing directly to the people and giving them a sense of purpose. He succeeded in infusing them with the same indomitable courage and jaunty optimism that had marked his own battle with polio. Thus, despite his limitations as a reformer, Roosevelt proved to be the leader the American people needed in the 1930s—a president who provided the psychological lift that helped them endure and survive the Great Depression.

For a list of additional titles related to this chapter's topics, please see www.pearsonamericanhistory.com. MyHistoryLab

STUDY RESOURCES

KEY TERMS

New Deal, p. 703
Bonus Army, p. 707
fireside chats, p. 708
Tennessee Valley Authority (TVA), p. 709

Civilian Conservation Corps (CCC), p. 709
Works Progress Administration (WPA), p. 709
National Recovery Administration (NRA), p. 709

Agricultural Adjustment Administration (AAA), p. 710
Social Security Act, p. 714
Wagner Act, p. 716
"court-packing" scheme, p. 719

CHAPTER REVIEW

WHAT were the causes and effects of the Great Depression?

The Great Depression resulted from the imbalances in the American economy that developed during the 1920s. Wealth was unequally distributed, depriving millions of the purchasing power necessary to keep America's factories and farms operating at full capacity. The depression threw millions out of work, out of their homes, onto the highways, and into despair. (p. 703)

HOW did Franklin Roosevelt fight the Depression?

Franklin Roosevelt led the fight against the depression by persuading Congress to pass a series of relief, recovery, and reform measures known collectively as the New Deal. Begun during the Hundred Days, the New Deal reorganized American industry, assisted American agriculture, and put Americans to work conserving and restoring the nation's resources. (p. 706)

HOW did the New Deal reform American life?

In responses to the challenges of Charles Coughlin, Francis Townsend, and Huey Long, Roosevelt persuaded

Congress to approve sweeping measures to reform American life. Chief among these was the Social Security Act, which established a system of old-age and disability pensions designed to alleviate poverty among the elderly and those unable to work. (p. 711)

WHAT was the lasting impact of the New Deal?

The New Deal encouraged the emergence of organized labor as a major force in American economic life. It modestly improved the lot of African Americans, although it failed to tackle the racial prejudice that was at the heart of much black poverty. It did little for Mexican Americans and other Latinos, and only a bit more for Native Americans. (p. 715)

HOW and why did the New Deal end?

After a high point in 1936, the New Deal declined as a result of Roosevelt's overreaching in the court-packing effort, growing resistance among conservatives of both parties, and a sharp recession in 1937 that reminded the country that for all the New Deal's accomplishments, it hadn't ended the Great Depression. (p. 718)

MAKING CONNECTIONS

1. Could the Great Depression have been averted? What steps might the government have taken to prevent it?
2. Why did Americans respond so positively to Franklin Roosevelt?
3. How was the popularity of Francis Townsend and Huey Long like the popularity of Roosevelt? How was it different?
4. Why did minorities not fully share the benefits of New Deal reforms?
5. Why was Roosevelt's "court-packing" scheme so unpopular?

PRACTICE QUIZ

1. The _____ was President Roosevelt's relief and reform program of the 1930s.
   - **a.** Square Deal
   - **b.** New Freedom
   - **c.** New Deal
   - **d.** Fair Deal

2. The _____ of 1929 helped propel the nation into the Great Depression.
   - **a.** Great Crash
   - **b.** Great Escape
   - **c.** Great Earthquake
   - **d.** Great Affair

3. The _____ suffered attack by government troops in Washington D.C. in 1932.
   - **a.** Japanese army
   - **b.** Bonus Army
   - **c.** Ku Klux Klan
   - **d.** Women's Trade Union League

4. The _____ describes the initial period of FDR's presidency when new policies began the process of relief and reform.
   - **a.** Hundred Hours
   - **b.** Hundred Minutes
   - **c.** Hundred Days
   - **d.** Hundred Weeks

5. The _____ became one of FDR's most ambitious New Deal measures.
   - **a.** Tennessee Valley Authority
   - **b.** Brooklyn Bridge construction
   - **c.** Clearing of Yellowstone National Park
   - **d.** None of the above answers are accurate.

6. President Roosevelt calmed the nation during regular radio sessions called
   - **a.** Muckraker moments
   - **b.** Moments of Encouragement
   - **c.** At home with Franklin
   - **d.** Fireside chats

7. All of the following are impacts of the Great Depression on the American people *except*
   - **a.** Americans left the city for the countryside and found relief on farms.
   - **b.** Americans suffered an increase of poverty and homelessness.
   - **c.** Americans experienced a high rate of unemployment.
   - **d.** Americans suffered psychological depression.

8. Which of the following *most* accurately describes the Agricultural Adjustment Act of 1933?
   - **a.** It allocated land to groups of farmers organized in large collectives.
   - **b.** It discouraged farmers from taking land out of production.
   - **c.** It reduced crop acreages and helped raise crop prices.
   - **d.** It became immediately successful.

9. Which of the following individuals presented a major political challenge to FDR?
   - **a.** Father Charles Coughlin
   - **b.** Huey Long
   - **c.** Francis Townsend
   - **d.** All of the above answers are accurate.

10. Which of the following was *not* a major part of the Social Security Act?
    - **a.** Immediate pensions for the elderly.
    - **b.** Old-age pensions financed by a tax on employers and workers.
    - **c.** A system of unemployment compensation on a federal-state basis.
    - **d.** Direct federal grants to the states for welfare payments.

QUIZ

Find more practice at
www.myhistorylab.com

SAMPLE ESSAY QUESTIONS

1. Explain how the New Deal reversed the economic decline of the United States.

2. Discuss how workers responded to the Depression and New Deal.

Answers to Practice Quiz **1.** c, p. 703 **2.** a, p. 703 **3.** b, p. 707 **4.** c, p. 708 **5.** a, p. 708 **6.** d, p. 709 **7.** a, p. 705 **8.** c, p. 710 **9.** d, p. 713 **10.** a, p. 714

America and the World

1921–1945

W.F. Draper

SPOTLIGHT QUESTIONS

WHAT was isolationism, and why was it so appealing to Americans in the 1920s and 1930s❓

HOW did the United States go from neutrality in the 1930s to war in 1941❓

HOW did America and its allies halt the advances of Germany and Japan❓

WHAT changes occurred in American domestic life during World War II❓

HOW did the war end, and what were its consequences❓

The Landing at Saipan by William Draper, who painted combat scenes he witnessed while serving in the U. S. Navy. The global conflict of World War II involved every major power in the world as it was fought on land, at sea, and in the air.

How well does this painting convey the reality of the Pacific war?

A Pact Without Power

On August 27, 1928, U.S. Secretary of State Frank B. Kellogg, French Foreign Minister Aristide Briand, and representatives of twelve other nations met in Paris to sign a treaty outlawing war. Several hundred spectators crowded into the ornate clock room of the Quai d'Orsay to watch the historic ceremony. Six huge klieg lights illuminated the scene so photographers could record the moment for a world eager for peace. Briand opened the ceremony with a speech in which he declared, "Peace is proclaimed," and then Kellogg signed the document with a foot-long gold pen given to him by the citizens of Le Havre as a token of Franco-American friendship. In the United States, a senator called the **Kellogg-Briand Pact** "the most telling action ever taken in human history to abolish war."

KEY EVENTS

1928 Kellogg-Briand Pact outlaws war (August), *p. 725*

1936 Hitler's troops reoccupy Rhineland, *p. 727*

1937 FDR signs permanent Neutrality Act (May), *p. 729*

1938 Munich Conference appeases Hitler (September), *p. 730*

1939 Germany invades Poland; World War II begins, *p. 731*

1941 Japan attacks Pearl Harbor; United States enters World War II, *p. 736*

1942 U.S. defeats Japanese at battle of Midway (June), *p. 740* ▪ Allies land in North Africa (November), *p. 739*

1943 Soviets smash Nazis at Stalingrad, *p. 739*

1944 Allies land on Normandy beachheads, *p. 746*

1945 Big Three meet at Yalta (February), *p. 747* ▪ FDR dies; Harry Truman becomes president (April), *p. 749* ▪ Germany surrenders unconditionally (May), *p. 749* ▪ United States drops atomic bombs on Hiroshima and Nagasaki; Japan surrenders (August), *p. 750*

Kellogg-Briand Pact

Also called the Pact of Paris, this 1928 agreement was the brainchild of U.S. Secretary of State Frank B. Kellogg and French premier Aristide Briand. It pledged its signatories, eventually including nearly all nations, to shun war as an instrument of policy. Derided as an "international kiss," it had little effect on the actual conduct of world affairs.

In reality, the Pact of Paris was the result of a determined American effort to avoid involvement in the European alliance system. In June 1927, Briand had sent a message to the American people inviting the United States to join with France in signing a treaty to outlaw war between the two nations. The invitation struck a sympathetic response, especially among pacifists who had advocated the outlawing of war throughout the 1920s, but the State Department feared correctly that Briand's true intention was to establish a close tie between France and the United States. The French had already created a network of alliances with the smaller countries of eastern Europe; an antiwar treaty with the United States would at least ensure American sympathy, if not involvement, in case of another European war. Kellogg delayed several months and then outmaneuvered Briand by proposing the pledge against war not be confined just to France and the United States, but instead be extended to all nations. An unhappy Briand, who had wanted a bilateral treaty with the United States, had no choice but to agree, and so the diplomatic charade finally culminated in the elaborate signing ceremony in Paris.

Eventually the signers of the Kellogg-Briand Pact included nearly every nation in the world, but the effect was negligible. All promised to renounce war as an instrument of national policy, except of course, as the British made clear in a reservation, in matters of self-defense. Enforcement of the treaty relied solely on the moral force of world opinion. The Pact of Paris was, as one senator shrewdly commented, only "an international kiss."

Unfortunately, the Kellogg-Briand Pact was symbolic of American foreign policy in the years immediately following World War I. Instead of asserting the role of world leadership its resources and power commanded, the United States retreated from involvement with other nations. America went its own way, extending trade and economic dominance but refusing to take the lead in maintaining world order. This retreat from responsibility seemed unimportant in the 1920s when exhaustion from World War I ensured relative peace and tranquility. But in the 1930s, when threats to world order arose in Europe and Asia, the American people retreated even deeper, searching for an isolationist policy that would spare them the agony of another great war.

There was no place to hide in the modern world. The Nazi onslaught in Europe and the Japanese expansion in Asia finally convinced America to reverse its isolationist stance and become involved in World War II in late 1941, at a time when the chances for an Allied victory seemed most remote. With incredible swiftness, the nation mobilized its military and industrial strength. American armies were soon fighting on three continents, the U.S. Navy controlled the world's oceans, and the nation's factories were sending a vast stream of war supplies to more than twenty Allied countries.

Secretary of State Frank Kellogg signs the Kellogg-Briand Treaty renouncing war. A grand document, the treaty included no method to enforce its provisions.

Why not?

When the Allied victory came in 1945, the United States was by far the most powerful nation in the world. But the end of the war, rather than bringing them peace, began a new era of tension and rivalry. This time the United States could not retreat from responsibility. World War II was a coming of age for American foreign policy.

Isolationism

American disillusionment with international affairs became evident soon after World War I. The Senate's rejection of the Treaty of Versailles left the United States outside the League of Nations, where it remained for the life of that ill-fated organization. American financial connections to Europe persisted, and even grew during the 1920s, but the United States kept its distance politically. The retreat from an active world policy in the 1920s turned into a headlong flight back to isolationism in the 1930s. Two factors were responsible. First, the depression made foreign policy seem remote and unimportant to most Americans. As unemployment increased and the economic crisis intensified after 1929, many people grew apathetic about events abroad. Second, the danger of war abroad, when it did finally penetrate the American consciousness, served only to strengthen the desire to escape involvement.

Three powerful and discontented nations were on the march in the 1930s—Germany, Italy, and Japan. In Germany, Adolf Hitler came to power in 1933 as the head of a National Socialist, or Nazi, movement. A shrewd and charismatic leader, Hitler capitalized on both domestic discontent and bitterness over World War I. Blaming the Jews for all of Germany's ills and asserting the supremacy of the "Aryan" race of blond, blue-eyed Germans, he quickly imposed a totalitarian dictatorship in which the Nazi party ruled and the *Führer* was supreme. At first, his foreign policy seemed harmless, but as he consolidated his power, the ultimate threat to world peace became clearer. Hitler took Germany out of the League of Nations, reoccupied the Rhineland, and formally denounced the Treaty of Versailles. His boasts of uniting all Germans into a Greater Third Reich that would last a thousand years filled his European opponents with terror, blocking any effective challenge to his regime.

In Italy, another dictator, Benito Mussolini, had come to power in 1922. Emboldened by Hitler's success, he embarked on an aggressive foreign policy in 1935.

WHAT was isolationism, and why was it so appealing to Americans in the 1920s and 1930s?

IMAGE

Nazi Book Bonfire, 1933

Hitler and
Mussolini
in Munich,
1940

Axis Powers

During World War II, the
alliance between Italy,
Germany, and Japan was
known as the "Rome-
Berlin-Tokyo axis," and the
three members were called
the Axis Powers. They
fought against the Allied
Powers, led by the United
States, Britain, and the
Soviet Union.

His invasion of the independent African nation of Ethiopia led its emperor, Haile Selassie, to call on the League of Nations for support. With England and France far more concerned about Hitler, the League's halfhearted measures utterly failed to halt Mussolini's conquest. "Fifty-two nations had combined to resist aggression," commented historian A. J. P. Taylor; "all they accomplished was that Haile Selassie lost all his country instead of only half." Collective security had failed its most important test.

Japan formed the third element in the threat to world peace. Militarists began to dominate the government in Tokyo by the mid-1930s, using tactics of fear and even assassination against their liberal opponents. By 1936, Japan had left the League of Nations. A year later, its armies began an invasion of China that marked the beginning of the Pacific phase of World War II.

The resurgence of militarism in Germany, Italy, and Japan undermined the Versailles settlement and threatened to destroy the existing balance of power. England and France in Europe proved as powerless as China in Asia to stop the tide of aggression. In 1937, the three totalitarian nations signed an anti-Comintern pact completing a Berlin-Rome-Tokyo axis. The alliance of the **Axis Powers** ostensibly was aimed at the Soviet Union, but in fact it threatened the entire world. Only a determined American response could unite the other nations against the Axis threat. Unfortunately, the United States deliberately abstained from assuming this role of leadership until it was nearly too late.

The Lure of Pacifism and Neutrality

The growing danger of war abroad led to a rising American desire for peace and noninvolvement. Memories of World War I contributed heavily. Erich Maria Remarque's novel *All Quiet on the Western Front,* as well as the movie based on it, reminded people of the brutality of war. Historians began to treat the Great War as a mistake, criticizing Wilson for failing to preserve American neutrality and claiming the clever British had duped the United States into entering the war. Walter Millis advanced this thesis in *America's Road to War, 1914–1917,* published in 1935. It was hailed as a vivid description of the process by which "a peace-loving democracy, muddled but excited, misinformed and whipped to a frenzy, embarked upon its greatest foreign war."

American youth made clear their determination not to repeat the mistakes of their elders. Pacifism

Millions of Germans idolized Adolf Hitler, portrayed in this captured German painting as a white knight. After the painting came into American hands, a GI slashed Hitler's face to indicate his displeasure with the mystique of the Führer.

Why did Germans look up to Hitler?

The pacifism that swept college campuses in the 1930s touched students at the University of Chicago. The university undergraduates shown here hold placards bearing antiwar slogans as they wait to join a parade as part of a nationwide demonstration against war.

What historical memories prompted the protest?

swept across college campuses. A Brown University poll indicated 72 percent of the students opposed military service in wartime. At Princeton, undergraduates formed the Veterans of Future Wars, a parody on veterans' groups, to demand a bonus of $1000 apiece before they marched off to a foreign war. In April 1934, students and professors alike walked out of class to attend massive antiwar rallies, which became an annual rite of spring in the 1930s. Demonstrators carried signs reading "Abolish the R.O.T.C." and "Build Schools—Not Battleships," and pacifist orators urged students to sign a pledge not to support their country "in any war it might conduct."

The pacifist movement found a scapegoat in the munitions industry. The publication of several books exposing the unsavory business tactics of large arms dealers such as Krupp in Germany and Vickers in Britain led to a demand to curb these "merchants of death." Senator Gerald Nye of North Dakota headed a special Senate committee that spent two years investigating American munitions dealers. The committee revealed the enormous profits firms such as Du Pont reaped from World War I, but Nye went further, charging that bankers and munitions makers were responsible for American intervention in 1917. No proof was forthcoming, but the public—prepared to believe the worst of businessmen during the Great Depression—accepted the "merchants of death" thesis.

The Nye Committee's revelations culminated in neutrality legislation. In 1935, Senator Nye and another Senate colleague introduced measures to ban arms sales and loans to belligerents and to prevent Americans from traveling on belligerent ships. By outlawing the activities that led to World War I, they hoped, the United States could avoid involvement in the new conflict. This "never again" philosophy proved irresistible. In August 1935, Congress passed the first of three **neutrality acts,** laws designed to keep the United States out of war. The 1935 law banned the sale of arms to nations at war and warned American citizens not to sail on belligerent ships. In 1936, a second act added a ban on loans, and in 1937, a third neutrality act made these prohibitions permanent and required, on a two-year trial basis, that all trade other than munitions be conducted on a cash-and-carry basis.

neutrality acts
Reacting to their disillusionment with World War I and absorbed in the domestic crisis of the Great Depression, Americans backed Congress's three neutrality acts in the 1930s. The 1935 and 1936 acts forbade selling munitions or lending money to belligerents in a war. The 1937 act required that all remaining trade be conducted on a cash-and-carry basis.

QUICK CHECK

What was the purpose of the neutrality acts?

War in Europe

The neutrality legislation played directly into the hands of Adolf Hitler. Bent on the conquest of Europe, he could now proceed without worrying about American interference. In March 1938, he seized Austria in a bloodless coup. Six months later, he was demanding the Sudetenland, a province of Czechoslovakia with a large German population. When the British and French leaders agreed to meet with Hitler at Munich, FDR voiced his approval. Roosevelt carefully kept the United States aloof from the decision to surrender the Sudetenland in the hopes of appeasing Hitler's demand for land. At the same time, the president gave his tacit approval of the policy of appeasement by telling the British prime minister that he shared his "hope and belief that there exists today the greatest opportunity in years for the establishment of a new order based on justice and on law."

Six months after the meeting at Munich, Hitler violated his promises by seizing nearly all of Czechoslovakia. In the United States, Roosevelt permitted the State Department to press for neutrality revision. The administration proposal to repeal the arms embargo and place *all* trade with belligerents, including munitions,

World War II
in Europe

Hitler sent his armies into Poland with tremendous force and firepower, devastating the country. Here German troops observe as the German *Luftwaffe* bombs Warsaw in September 1939, destroying the city and forcing its inhabitants to surrender.

How did Americans react to the outbreak of war?

on a cash-and-carry basis soon met stubborn resistance from isolationists. They argued that cash-and-carry would favor England and France, who controlled the sea. The House rejected the measure by a narrow margin, and the Senate's Foreign Relations Committee voted 12 to 11 to postpone any action on neutrality revision.

In July 1939, Roosevelt finally abandoned his aloof position and met with Senate leaders to plead for reconsideration. Warnings of the imminence of war in Europe by both the president and the secretary of state failed to impress the isolationists. Senator William Borah, who had led the fight against the League of Nations in 1919, responded that he believed the chances for war in Europe were remote. After canvassing the senators present, Vice President John Nance Garner bluntly told FDR that the neutrality revision was dead. "You haven't got the votes," Garner commented, "and that's all there is to it."

On September 1, 1939, Hitler began World War II by invading Poland. England and France responded two days later by declaring war, although there was no way they could prevent the German conquest of Poland. Russia had played a key role, refusing Western overtures for a common front against Germany and finally signing a nonaggression treaty with Hitler in late August. The Nazi-Soviet Pact enabled Germany to avoid a two-front war; the Russians were rewarded with a generous slice of eastern Poland.

President Roosevelt reacted to the outbreak of war by proclaiming American neutrality, but the successful aggression by Nazi Germany brought into question the isolationist assumption that American well-being did not depend on the European balance of power. Strategic as well as ideological considerations began to undermine the earlier belief that the United States could safely pursue a policy of neutrality and noninvolvement. The long retreat from responsibility was about to end as Americans came to realize that their own democracy and security were at stake in the European war.

QUICK CHECK ✓

What was the American response to the outbreak of war in Europe?

The Road to War

For two years, the United States tried to remain at peace while war raged in Europe and Asia. In contrast to the climate of the country while Wilson attempted to be impartial during most of World War I, the American people displayed an overwhelming sympathy for the Allies and total distaste for Germany and Japan. Roosevelt made no secret of his preference for an Allied victory, but a fear of isolationist criticism compelled him to move slowly, and often deviously, in adopting a policy of aid for England and France.

HOW ?

did the United States go from neutrality in the 1930s to war in 1941?

From Neutrality to Undeclared War

Two weeks after the outbreak of war in Europe, Roosevelt called Congress into special session to revise the neutrality legislation. He wanted to repeal the arms embargo in order to supply weapons to England and France, but he refused to state this aim openly. Instead he asked Congress to replace the arms embargo with cash-and-carry regulations. Belligerents would be able to purchase war supplies in the United States, but they would have to pay cash and transport the goods in their own ships. Public opinion strongly supported the president, and Congress passed the revised neutrality policy by heavy margins in early November 1939.

A series of dramatic German victories had a profound impact on American opinion. Quiet during the winter of 1939–1940, the Germans struck with lightning speed and devastating effect in the spring. In April, they seized Denmark and Norway, and on May 10, 1940, they unleashed the *blitzkrieg* (lightning war) on the western front. Using tanks, armored columns, and dive-bombers in close coordination, the German army overran the Netherlands, Belgium, and Luxembourg en route to France. It split the British and French forces, driving the British off the Continent at Dunkirk. In June, France fell to Hitler's war machine.

Americans were stunned. Hitler had taken only six weeks to achieve what Germany had failed to do in four years of fighting in World War I. Suddenly they realized they did have a stake in the outcome; if England fell, Hitler might well gain control of the British navy. The Atlantic would no longer be a barrier; instead, it would be a highway for German penetration of the New World.

Roosevelt responded by invoking a policy of all-out aid to the Allies, short of war. In a speech at Charlottesville, Virginia, in June (just after Italy entered the war by invading France), he denounced Germany and Italy as representing "the gods of force and hate" and vowed, "The whole of our sympathies lies with those nations that are giving their life blood in combat against these forces." It was too late to help France, but in early September, FDR announced the transfer of fifty old destroyers to England in exchange for rights to build air and naval bases on eight British possessions in the Western Hemisphere. Giving warships to a belligerent nation was clearly a breach of neutrality, but Roosevelt stressed the importance of guarding the Atlantic approaches, calling the destroyers-for-bases deal "the most important action in the reinforcement of our national defense that has been taken since the Louisiana Purchase."

Charles Lindbergh, Radio Address (1941)

Isolationists cried out against this departure from neutrality. A bold headline in the *St. Louis Post-Dispatch* read, "Dictator Roosevelt Commits Act of War." A group of Roosevelt's opponents in the Midwest formed the America First Committee to protest the drift toward war. Such diverse individuals as aviator-hero Charles Lindbergh, conservative Senator Robert A. Taft of Ohio, socialist leader Norman Thomas, and liberal educator Robert M. Hutchins condemned FDR for involving the United States in a foreign conflict. Voicing belief in a "Fortress America," they denied that Hitler threatened American security and claimed that the nation had the strength to defend itself regardless of what happened in Europe.

To support the administration's policies, opponents of the isolationists organized the Committee to Defend America by Aiding the Allies. Eastern Anglophiles, moderate New Dealers, and liberal Republicans made up the bulk of the membership, with Kansas newspaper editor William Allen White serving as chairman. The White Committee, as it became known, advocated unlimited assistance to England short of war, although some of its members privately favored entry into the conflict. Above all, the interventionists challenged the isolationist premise that events in Europe did not affect American security. "The future of western civilization is being decided upon the battlefield of Europe," White declared.

In the ensuing debate, the American people gradually came to agree with the interventionists. The Battle of Britain—Germany's bombing campaign against England—helped. "Every time Hitler bombed London, we got a couple of votes," noted one interventionist. Frightened by the events in Europe, Congress approved

THE ELECTION OF 1940			
Candidate	Party	Popular Vote	Electoral Vote
Roosevelt	Democratic	27,244,160	449
Willkie	Republican	22,305,198	82

large sums for preparedness, increasing the defense budget from $2 billion to $10 billion during 1940. Roosevelt courageously asked for a peacetime draft, the first in American history, to build up the army; in September, Congress agreed.

The sense of crisis affected domestic politics. Roosevelt ran for an unprecedented third term in 1940 because of the European war; the Republicans nominated Wendell Willkie, a former Democratic businessman who shared FDR's commitment to aid for England. Both candidates made appeals to peace sentiment during the campaign, but Roosevelt's decisive victory made it clear that the nation supported his increasing departure from neutrality.

After the election, FDR took his boldest step. Responding to British Prime Minister Winston Churchill's warning that England was running out of money, the president asked Congress to approve a new program to lend and lease goods and weapons to countries fighting against aggressors. Roosevelt's call for America to become "the great arsenal of democracy" seemed straightforward enough, but he acted somewhat deviously by naming the program **Lend-Lease** and by comparing it to loaning a neighbor a garden hose to put out a fire.

Isolationists angrily denounced Lend-Lease as both unnecessary and untruthful. "Lending war equipment is a good deal like lending chewing gum," commented Senator Taft. "You don't want it back." In March 1941, however, Congress voted by substantial margins to authorize the president to "sell, transfer title to, exchange, lease, lend, or otherwise dispose of" war supplies to "any country the President deems vital to the defense of the United States." The accompanying $7 billion appropriation ended the "cash" part of cash-and-carry and ensured Britain full access to American war supplies.

The "carry" problem still remained. German submarines were sinking more than 500,000 tons of shipping a month. England desperately needed the help of the American navy in escorting convoys across the U-boat–infested waters of the North Atlantic. Roosevelt, fearful of isolationist reaction, responded with naval patrols in the western half of the ocean. Hitler placed his submarine commanders under strict restraints to avoid drawing America into the European war. Nevertheless, incidents were bound to occur. In September 1941, after a U-boat narrowly missed torpedoing an American destroyer tracking it, Roosevelt denounced the German submarines as the "rattlesnakes of the Atlantic" and issued orders for the navy to convey British ships halfway across the ocean.

Undeclared naval war quickly followed. On October 17, 1941, a German submarine damaged the U.S. destroyer *Kearney;* ten days later, another U-boat sank the *Reuben James,* killing more than one hundred American sailors. FDR issued orders for the destroyers to shoot U-boats on sight. He also asked Congress to repeal the "carry" section of the neutrality laws and permit American ships to deliver supplies to England. In mid-November, Congress approved these moves by slim margins. Now American merchant ships as well as destroyers would become targets for German attacks. By December, it seemed only a matter of weeks—or

DOCUMENT

Franklin D. Roosevelt, "The Four Freedoms" (1941)

Lend-Lease

Arguing that aiding Britain would help America's own self-defense, President Roosevelt in 1941 asked Congress for the $7 billion Lend-Lease plan. This would allow the president to sell, lend, lease, or transfer war materials to any country whose defense he declared as vital to that of the United States.

Kneeling at the Capitol Plaza in Washington, members of the "Mothers' Crusade" conduct a pray-in to protest the passage of the Lend-Lease Act.

Why were they upset?

months at most—until repeated sinkings would lead to a formal declaration of war against Germany.

In leading the nation to the brink of war in Europe, Roosevelt opened himself to criticism from both sides in the domestic debate. Interventionists believed he had been too cautious in dealing with the danger to the nation from Nazi Germany. Isolationists were equally critical of the president, claiming he had misled the American people by professing peace while plotting for war. Roosevelt was certainly less than candid, relying on executive discretion to engage in highly provocative acts in the North Atlantic. He agreed with the interventionists that in the long run a German victory in Europe would threaten American security. But he also was aware that a poll taken in September 1941 showed nearly 80 percent of the American people wanted to stay out of World War II. Realizing that leading a divided nation into war would be disastrous, FDR played for time, inching the country toward war while waiting for the Axis nations to make the ultimate move. Japan finally obliged at Pearl Harbor.

QUICK CHECK ✓

How did FDR overcome the opposition to war?

Showdown in the Pacific

Japan had taken advantage of the war in Europe to expand farther in Asia. Although successful after 1937 in conquering the populous coastal areas of China, the Japanese had been unable to defeat Chiang Kai-shek, whose forces retreated into the vast interior of the country. The German defeat of France and the Netherlands in 1940, however, left their colonial possessions in the East Indies and Indochina vulnerable and defenseless. Japan now set out to incorporate these territories—rich in oil, tin, and rubber—into a Greater East Asia Co-Prosperity Sphere.

The Roosevelt administration countered with economic pressure. Japan depended heavily on the United States for petroleum and scrap metal. In July 1940, President Roosevelt signed an order setting up a licensing and quota system for the export of these crucial materials to Japan and banned the sale of aviation gasoline altogether. With Britain fighting for survival and France and the Netherlands occupied by Germany, the United States was now employing economic sanctions to defend Southeast Asia against Japanese expansion.

Tokyo appeared to be unimpressed. In early September, Japanese troops occupied strategic bases in the northern part of French Indochina. Later in the month, Japan signed the Tripartite Pact with Germany and Italy, a defensive treaty that confronted the United States with a possible two-ocean war. The new Axis alignment confirmed American suspicions that Japan was part of a worldwide totalitarian threat. Roosevelt and his advisers, however, saw Germany as the primary danger; thus they pursued a policy of all-out aid to England while hoping that economic measures alone would deter Japan.

The embargo on aviation gasoline, extended to include scrap iron and steel in late September 1940, was a burden Japan could bear, but a possible ban on all oil shipments was a different matter. Japan lacked petroleum reserves of its own and was entirely dependent on imports from the United States and the Dutch East Indies. In an attempt to ease the economic pressure through negotiation, Japan sent a new envoy to Washington in the spring of 1941. But the talks quickly broke down. Tokyo wanted nothing less than a free hand in China and an end to American sanctions, while the United States insisted on an eventual Japanese evacuation of all China.

In July 1941, Japan invaded southern Indochina, beginning the chain of events that led to war. Washington knew of this aggression before it occurred. Naval intelligence experts had broken the Japanese diplomatic code and were intercepting and reading all messages between Tokyo and the Japanese embassy in Washington. President Roosevelt responded on July 25, 1941, with an order freezing all Japanese assets in the United States. This step, initially intended only as a temporary warning to Japan, soon became a permanent embargo due to positive public reaction and State Department zeal. Trade with Japan, including the vital oil shipments, came to a complete halt. When the Dutch government in exile took similar action, Japan faced a dilemma: In order to have oil shipments resumed, Tokyo would have to end its aggression; the alternative would be to seize the needed petroleum supplies in the Dutch East Indies, an action that would mean war.

After one final diplomatic effort failed, General Hideki Tojo, an army militant, became the new premier of Japan. To mask its war preparations, Tokyo sent yet another envoy to Washington with new peace proposals. Code breaking enabled American diplomats to learn that the Japanese terms were unacceptable even before they were formally presented. Army and navy leaders urged President Roosevelt to seek at least a temporary settlement with Japan to give them time to prepare American defenses in the Pacific. Secretary of State Cordell Hull, however, refused to allow any concession; on November 26, he sent a stiff ten-point reply to Tokyo that included a demand for Japanese withdrawal from China.

The Japanese response came two weeks later. On the evening of December 6, 1941, the first thirteen parts of the reply to Hull's note arrived in Washington, with the fourteenth part to follow the next morning. Naval intelligence actually

American ships were destroyed in the surprise attack on Pearl Harbor, December 7, 1941. Caught completely off guard, U.S. forces still managed to shoot down twenty-nine enemy planes.

What effect did the attack have on American attitudes?

Pearl Harbor

On December 7, 1941, Japanese warplanes attacked U.S. naval forces at Pearl Harbor, Hawaii, sinking several ships and killing more than 2400 American sailors. The event marked America's entrance into World War II.

 QUICK CHECK

What led Japan to attack Pearl Harbor?

decoded the message faster than the Japanese embassy clerks. A messenger delivered the text to President Roosevelt late that night; after glancing at it, he commented, "This means war." The next day, December 7, the fourteenth part arrived, revealing that Japan totally rejected the American position.

Officials in Washington immediately sent warning messages to American bases in the Pacific, but they failed to arrive in time. At 7:55 in the morning, just before 1 P.M. in Washington, squadrons of Japanese carrier-based planes caught the American fleet at Pearl Harbor totally by surprise. In little more than an hour, they crippled the American Pacific fleet and its major base, sinking or damaging eight battleships and killing more than twenty-four hundred American sailors.

In Washington, the Japanese envoys had requested a meeting with Secretary Hull at 1 P.M. Just before the meeting, news arrived of the attack on **Pearl Harbor**. An irate Cordell Hull read the note the Japanese handed him and then, unable to restrain himself any longer, burst out, "In all my fifty years of public service, I have never seen a document that was more crowded with infamous falsehoods and distortions—on a scale so huge that I never imagined until today that any government was capable of uttering them."

Speaking before Congress the next day, President Roosevelt termed December 7 "a date which will live in infamy" and asked for a declaration of war on Japan. With only one dissenting vote, both branches passed the measure. On December 11, Germany and Italy declared war against the United States; the nation was now fully involved in World War II.

Turning the Tide Against the Axis

In the first few months after the United States entered the war, the outlook for victory was bleak. In Europe, Hitler's armies controlled virtually the entire continent, from Norway in the north to Greece in the south. Despite the nonaggression pact, German armies had penetrated deep into Russia after an initial invasion in June 1941. Although they had failed to capture either Moscow or Leningrad, the Nazi forces had conquered the Ukraine and by the spring of 1942 were threatening to sweep across the Volga River and seize vital oil fields in the Caucasus. In North Africa, General Erwin Rommel's Afrika Korps had pushed the British back into Egypt and threatened the Suez Canal (see the map on p. 748).

The situation was no better in Asia. The Pearl Harbor attack had enabled the Japanese to move unopposed across Southeast Asia. Within three months, they had conquered Malaya and the Dutch East Indies, with its valuable oil fields, and were pressing the British back both in Burma and New Guinea. American forces under General Douglas MacArthur had tried vainly to block the Japanese conquest of the Philippines. MacArthur finally escaped by torpedo boat to Australia; the American garrison at Corregidor surrendered after a long siege, the survivors then enduring the cruel death march across the Bataan peninsula. With the American navy still recovering from the devastation at Pearl Harbor, Japan controlled the western half of the Pacific (see the map on p. 741).

Over the next two years, the United States and its allies would finally halt the German and Japanese offensives in Europe and Asia. But then they faced the difficult process of driving back the enemy, freeing the vast conquered areas, and finally defeating the Axis powers on their home territory. It would be a difficult and costly struggle that would require great sacrifice and heavy losses; World War II would test American will and resourcefulness to the utmost.

HOW did America and its allies halt the advances of Germany and Japan?

Wartime Partnerships

The greatest single advantage that the United States and its partners possessed was their willingness to form a genuine coalition to bring about the defeat of the Axis powers. Although there were many strains within the wartime alliance, it did permit a high degree of coordination. In striking contrast was the behavior of Germany and Japan, each fighting a separate war without any attempt at cooperation.

The United States and Britain achieved a complete wartime partnership. Prewar military talks led to the formation of a Combined Chiefs of Staff, headquartered in Washington, which directed Anglo-American military operations. The close cooperation between President Roosevelt and Prime Minister Churchill ensured a common strategy. The leaders decided at the outset that a German victory posed the greater danger and thus gave priority to the European theater in the conduct of the war. In a series of meetings in December 1941, Roosevelt and Churchill signed a Declaration of the United Nations, eventually subscribed to by twenty-six countries, that pledged them to fight together until the Axis powers were defeated.

Relations with the other members of the United Nations coalition in World War II were not quite so harmonious. The decision to defeat Germany first displeased the Chinese, who had been at war with Japan since 1937. Roosevelt tried to appease Chiang Kai-shek with a trickle of supplies, flown in at great risk by

At their meeting at Casablanca, Morocco, in January 1943, President Roosevelt and British Prime Minister Winston Churchill announced that the unconditional surrender of the Axis powers would be the only acceptable basis for ending the war.

How did the personal relationship between Roosevelt and Churchill shape the war effort?

American airmen over the Himalayas from India. France posed a more delicate problem. FDR virtually ignored the Free French government in exile under General Charles de Gaulle. Roosevelt preferred to deal with the Vichy regime, despite its collaboration with Germany, because it still controlled the French fleet and retained France's overseas territories.

The greatest strain of all within the wartime coalition was with the Soviet Union. Although Roosevelt had ended the long period of nonrecognition in 1933, close ties had failed to develop. The Russian refusal to pay prerevolutionary debts, together with continued Soviet support of domestic communist activity in the United States in the 1930s, intensified American distaste for Stalin's regime. The great Russian purge trials and the temporary Nazi-Soviet alliance from 1939 to 1941, along with deep-seated cultural and ideological differences, made wartime cooperation difficult.

Ever the pragmatist, Roosevelt tried hard to break down the old hostility and establish a more cordial relationship with Russia during the war. Even before Pearl Harbor, he extended Lend-Lease aid to Russia, and after American entry into the war, this economic assistance grew rapidly, limited only by the difficulty of delivering the supplies. Eager to keep Russia in the war, the president promised a visiting

Russian diplomat in May 1942 that the United States would create a second front in Europe by the end of that year—a pledge he could not fulfill. In January 1943, Roosevelt and Churchill met in Casablanca, Morocco, where they declared a policy of unconditional surrender, vowing that the Allies would fight until the Axis nations were completely defeated.

Despite these promises, the Soviet Union bore the brunt of battle against Hitler in the early years of the war, fighting alone against more than two hundred German divisions. The United States and England, grateful for the respite to build up their forces, could do little more than offer promises of future help and send Lend-Lease supplies. The result was a rift that never fully healed—one that did not prevent the defeat of Germany but did ensure future tensions and uncertainties between the Soviet Union and the Western nations.

QUICK CHECK ✔

What countries were America's principal allies during the war?

Halting the German Blitz

From the outset, the United States favored an invasion across the English Channel. Army planners, led by Chief of Staff George C. Marshall and his protégé, Dwight D. Eisenhower, were convinced such a frontal assault would be the quickest way to win the war. Roosevelt concurred, in part because it fulfilled his second-front commitment to the Soviets.

The initial plan, drawn up by Eisenhower, called for a full-scale invasion of Europe in the spring of 1943, with provision for a temporary beachhead in France in the fall of 1942 if necessary to keep Russia in the war. Marshall surprised everyone by placing Eisenhower, until then a relatively junior general, in charge of implementing the plan.

But the British, remembering the heavy casualties of trench warfare in World War I, and hoping to protect the route to India, their most important colony, preferred a perimeter approach. Air and naval attacks around the edge of the continent, especially in the Mediterranean, would be a prelude to a final invasion of Germany. British strategists assented to the basic plan but strongly urged a preliminary invasion of North Africa in the fall of 1942. Roosevelt, too, wanted American troops engaged in combat against Germany before the end of 1942 to offset growing pressure at home to concentrate on the Pacific; hence, after he overruled objections from his military advisers, American and British troops landed on the Atlantic and Mediterranean coasts of Morocco and Algeria in November 1942.

MAP

World War II in Europe and North Africa

The British launched an attack against Rommel at El Alamein in Egypt and soon forced the Afrika Korps to retreat across Libya to Tunisia. Eisenhower, delayed by poor roads and bad weather, was slow in bringing up his forces, and in their first encounter with Rommel at the Kasserine Pass in the desert south of Tunis, inexperienced American troops suffered a humiliating defeat. General George Patton quickly rallied the demoralized soldiers, and by May 1943, Germany had been driven from Africa, leaving behind nearly 300,000 troops.

During these same months, the Soviet Union's Red Army had broken the back of German military power in the battle of Stalingrad. Turned back at the critical bend in the Volga, Hitler had poured in division after division in what was ultimately a losing cause; never again would Germany be able to take the offensive in Europe.

At Churchill's insistence, FDR agreed to follow up the North African victory with the invasion first of Sicily and then Italy in the summer of 1943. Italy dropped out of the war when Mussolini fled to Germany, but the Italian campaign proved to be a strategic dead end. Germany sent in enough divisions to establish a strong defensive line in the mountains south of Rome; American and British troops were forced to fight their way slowly up the peninsula, suffering heavy casualties.

More important, these Mediterranean operations delayed the second front, postponing it eventually to the spring of 1944. Meanwhile, the Soviets began to push the Germans out of Russia and looked forward to the liberation of Poland, Hungary, and Romania, where they could establish "friendly" communist regimes. Having borne the brunt of the fighting against Nazi Germany, Russia was ready to claim its reward—the postwar domination of eastern Europe.

QUICK CHECK ✓

Where did the Allies achieve early victories over Germany?

Checking Japan in the Pacific

Both the decision to defeat Germany first and the vast expanses of the Pacific dictated the nature of the war against Japan. The United States conducted amphibious island-hopping campaigns rather than attempting to reconquer the Dutch East Indies, Southeast Asia, and China. There would be two separate American operations. One, led by Douglas MacArthur based in Australia, would move from New Guinea back to the Philippines, while the other, commanded by Admiral Chester Nimitz from Hawaii, was directed at key Japanese islands in the Central Pacific. The original plan called for the two offensives to come together for the final invasion of the Japanese home islands.

MAP

World War II in the Pacific

Success in the Pacific depended above all else on control of the sea. The devastation at Pearl Harbor gave Japan the initial edge, but fortunately, the United States had not lost any of its four aircraft carriers. In the battle of the Coral Sea in May 1942, American naval forces blocked a Japanese thrust to outflank Australia. The turning point came one month later at Midway. A powerful Japanese task force threatened to seize this remote American outpost more than a thousand miles west of Pearl Harbor; Japan's real objective was the destruction of what remained of the American Pacific fleet. Superior American airpower enabled Nimitz's forces to engage the enemy at long range. Japanese fighters shot down thirty-five of forty-one attacking torpedo bombers, but a second wave of dive-bombers scored hits on three Japanese carriers. The battle of Midway ended with the loss of four Japanese aircraft carriers compared to just one American carrier. It was the first defeat the modern Japanese navy had ever suffered, and it left the United States in control of the Central Pacific.

Encouraged by the victory, American forces launched their first Pacific offensive in the Solomon Islands, east of New Guinea, in August 1942. Both sides suffered heavy losses, but six months later the last Japanese were driven from the key island of Guadalcanal. At the same time, MacArthur began the long, slow, and bloody job of driving the Japanese back along the north coast of New Guinea.

By early 1943, the defensive phase of the war with Japan was over. The enemy surge had been halted in both the central and the southwestern Pacific, and the United States was preparing to penetrate the Gilbert, Marshall, and Caroline Islands and recapture the Philippines. Just as Russia had broken German power in Europe, so the United States, fighting alone except for Australia and New Zealand, had halted the Japanese. And, like the USSR with its plans for eastern Europe, America expected to reap the rewards of victory by dominating the Pacific in the future.

QUICK CHECK ✓

How did the United States break Japan's momentum in the Pacific?

The Home Front

World War II had a greater impact than the Great Depression on American life. While American soldiers and sailors fought abroad, the nation underwent sweeping social and economic changes at home. American industry worked to capacity to meet the need for war materials. Increased production in both industry and agriculture benefited workers and farmers alike. The expansion of war-related industries encouraged many people to move to where new jobs had sprung up. Women moved out of the home into the paid workforce; rural dwellers relocated to urban areas; and northerners and easterners sought new opportunities and new homes in the South and West. Another beneficiary of the return to prosperity

WHAT changes occurred in American domestic life during World War II?

WORLD WAR II IN THE PACIFIC   The tide of battle turned in the Pacific the same year as in Europe. The balance of sea power shifted back to the United States from Japan after the naval victories of 1942.

What were the most important of those victories?

brought on by the war was FDR, who had seen the nation through the dark days of the depression. The nation's economic recovery helped him win re-election to the presidency for a fourth term in 1944.

The Arsenal of Democracy

American industry made the nation's single most important contribution to victory. Even though more than fifteen million Americans served in the armed forces, it was the nearly sixty million who worked on farms and factories who achieved the miracle of production that ensured the defeat of Germany and Japan. The manufacturing plants that had run at half capacity through the 1930s now hummed with activity. In Detroit, automobile assembly lines were converted to produce tanks and airplanes; Henry Ford built the giant Willow Run factory, covering 67 acres, where forty-two thousand workers turned out a B-24 bomber every hour. Henry J. Kaiser, a California industrialist who constructed huge West Coast shipyards to meet the demand for cargo vessels and landing craft, operated on an equally large scale. His plant in Richmond, California, reduced the time to build a

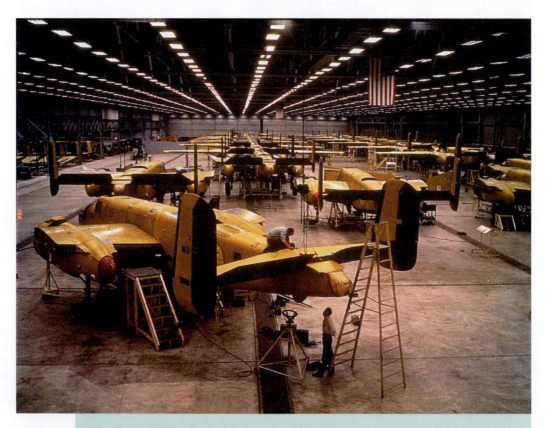

To keep up with the demand for war matériel, shipyards and factories operated around the clock, such as this North American aviation factory in Kansas City, where workers are shown assembling B-25 bombers.

How important were such factories to the ultimate Allied victory?

merchant ship from 105 to 14 days. In part, America won the battle of the Atlantic by building ships faster than German U-boats could sink them.

This vast industrial expansion, however, created many problems. In 1942, President Roosevelt appointed Donald Nelson, a Sears, Roebuck executive, to head a War Production Board (WPB). A jovial, easygoing man, Nelson soon was out-maneuvered by the army and the navy, which preferred to negotiate directly with large corporations. The WPB allowed business to claim rapid depreciation, and thus huge tax credits, for new plants and awarded lucrative cost-plus contracts for urgently needed goods. Shortages of critical materials such as steel, aluminum, and copper led to an allocation system based on military priorities. Rubber, cut off by the Japanese conquest of Southeast Asia, was particularly scarce; the administration finally began gasoline rationing in 1943 to curb pleasure driving and pro-long tire life. The government itself built fifty-one synthetic-rubber plants, which by 1944 were producing nearly one million tons a year for the tires of American airplanes and military vehicles. All in all, the nation's factories turned out twice as many goods as did German and Japanese industry combined.

Roosevelt revealed the same tendency toward compromise in directing the economic mobilization as he did in shaping the New Deal. When the Office of Price Administration—which tried to curb inflation by controlling prices and rationing scarce goods such as sugar, canned food, and shoes—clashed with the WPB, FDR appointed James Byrnes to head an Office of Economic Stabilization. Byrnes, a for-mer South Carolina senator and Supreme Court justice, used political judgment to settle disputes between agencies and keep all groups happy. The president was also forced to compromise with Congress, which pared down the administration's requests for large tax increases. Half the cost of the war was financed by borrowing; the other half came from revenues. A $7 billion revenue increase in 1942 included so many first-time taxpayers that in the following year the Treasury Department instituted a new practice—withholding income taxes from workers' wages.

"When You Ride Alone You Ride With Hitler" Poster

"Get in the Scrap" Poster

QUICK CHECK ✓

How was industry reorganized during the war?

A Nation on the Move

The war led to a vast migration of the American population. Young men left their homes for training camps and then for service overseas. Defense workers and their families, some nine million people in all, moved to work in the new booming shipyards, munitions factories, and aircraft plants. Norfolk, Virginia; San Diego, California; Mobile, Alabama; and other centers of defense production grew by more than 50 percent in just a year or two. Rural areas lost population while coastal regions, especially along the Pacific and the Gulf of Mexico, drew millions of people. The location of army camps in the South and West created boom con-ditions in the future Sunbelt, as did the concentration of aircraft factories and shipyards in this region. California had the greatest gains, adding nearly two million to its population in less than five years.

This movement of people caused severe social problems. Housing was in short supply. Migrating workers crowded into house trailers and boardinghouses, bring-ing unexpected windfalls to landlords. In one boomtown, a reporter described an old Victorian house that had five bedrooms on the second floor. "Three of them," he wrote, "held two cots apiece, the two others held three cots." But the owner revealed that "the third floor is where we pick up the velvet…. We rent to workers in different shifts… three shifts a day… seven bucks a week apiece."

Family life suffered under these crowded living conditions. An increase in the number of marriages, as young people searched for something to hang on to in the midst of wartime turmoil, was offset by a rising divorce rate. The baby boom that would peak in the 1950s began during the war and brought its own set of problems. Only a few publicly funded daycare centers were available, and working mothers worried about their "latchkey children." Schools in the boom areas were unable to cope with the influx of new students; a teacher shortage, intensified by the lure of higher wages in war industries, compounded the education crisis.

Despite these problems, women found the war a time of economic opportunity. The demand for workers led to a dramatic rise in women's employment, from fourteen million working women in 1940 to nineteen million by 1945. Most of the new women workers were married and many were middle-aged, thus broadening the composition of the female workforce, which in the past had been composed primarily of young single women. Women entered industries once viewed as exclusively male; by the end of the war, they worked alongside men tending blast furnaces in steel mills and welding hulls in shipyards. Few challenged the traditional view of gender roles, yet the wartime experience helped temporarily undermine the concept that woman's only proper place was in the home. Women enjoyed the hefty weekly paychecks, which rose by 50 percent from 1941 to 1943, and they took pride in their contributions to the war effort. "To hell with the life I have had," commented a former fashion designer. "This war is too damn serious, and it is too damn important to win it."

African Americans shared in the wartime migration, but racial prejudice limited their social and economic gains. Nearly one million served in the armed forces, but relatively few saw combat. The army placed black soldiers in segregated units, usually led by white officers, and used them for service and construction tasks. The navy was even worse, relegating them to menial jobs until late in the war. African Americans were denied the chance to become petty officers, Secretary of the Navy Frank Knox explained, because experience had shown that "men of the colored race… cannot maintain discipline among men of the white race."

African American civilians fared a little better. In 1941, black labor leader A. Philip Randolph threatened a massive

Rosie the Riveter

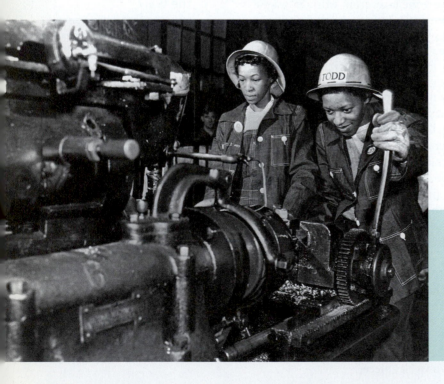

As men left for military service in World War II and U.S. industry expanded to keep up with the defense needs, millions of women joined the paid labor force. The women shown here are operating a bolt cutting machine at a factory in Erie, Pennsylvania.

Did women hold such jobs before the war?

march on Washington to force President Roosevelt to end racial discrimination in defense industries and government employment and to integrate the armed forces. FDR compromised, persuading Randolph to call off the march and drop his integration demand in return for an executive order creating a Fair Employment Practices Committee (FEPC) to ban racial discrimination in war industries. As a result, African American employment by the federal government rose from 60,000 in 1941 to 200,000 by the end of the war. The FEPC proved less successful in the private sector. Weak in funding and staff, the FEPC was able to act on only one-third of the eight thousand complaints it received. The nationwide shortage of labor was more influential than the FEPC in accounting for the rise in black employment during wartime. African Americans moved from the rural South to northern and western cities, finding jobs in the automobile, aircraft, and shipbuilding industries.

A. Philip Randolph, "Why Should We March" (1942)

The movement of an estimated 700,000 people helped transform black-white relations from a regional issue into a national concern that could no longer be ignored. The limited housing and recreational facilities for both black and white war workers created tensions that led to urban race riots. On a hot Sunday evening in June 1943, blacks and whites began exchanging insults and then blows near Belle Isle recreation park in Detroit. The next day, a full-scale riot broke out in which twenty-three blacks and nine whites died. The fighting raged for twenty-four hours until national guard troops were brought in to restore order. Later that summer, only personal intervention by New York Mayor Fiorello LaGuardia quelled a Harlem riot that took the lives of six blacks.

Sterling A. Brown, "Out of Their Mouths" (1942)

These outbursts of racial violence fueled the resentments that would grow into the postwar civil rights movement. For most African Americans, despite economic gains, World War II was a reminder of the inequality of American life. "Just carve on my tombstone," remarked one black soldier in the Pacific, "'Here lies a black man killed fighting a yellow man for the protection of a white man.'"

One-third of a million Mexican Americans served in the armed forces and shared some of the same experiences as African Americans. Although they were not as completely segregated, many served in the 88th Division, made up largely of Mexican American officers and troops, which earned the nickname "Blue Devils" in the Italian campaign. At home, Spanish-speaking people left the rural areas of Texas, New Mexico, and California for jobs in the cities, especially in aircraft plants and petroleum refineries. Despite low wages and union resistance, they improved their economic position substantially. But they still faced discrimination based both on skin color and language, most notably in the Los Angeles "zoot suit" riots in 1943 when white sailors attacked Mexican American youths dressed in their distinctive outfits—long jackets worn with pants tightly pegged at the ankles. The racial prejudice heightened feelings of ethnic identity and led returning Mexican American veterans to form organizations such as the American G.I. Forum to press for equal rights in the future.

A tragic counterpoint to the voluntary movement of American workers in search of jobs was the forced relocation of 120,000 Japanese Americans from the West Coast. Responding to racial fears in California after Pearl Harbor, President Roosevelt approved an army order in February 1942 to move all Japanese Americans on the West Coast to concentration camps in the interior. More than two-thirds of those detained were *Nisei*, native-born Americans whose only crime was their Japanese ancestry. Forced to sell their farms and businesses at distress prices, the Japanese Americans lost not only their liberty but also most of their worldly goods. Herded into ten hastily built detention centers in seven western

A Young Nisei and Her Family's Belongings

and southern states, they lived as prisoners in tar-papered barracks behind barbed wire, guarded by armed troops.

Appeals to the Supreme Court proved fruitless; in 1944, six justices upheld relocation on grounds of national security in wartime. Beginning in 1943, individual Nisei could win release by pledging their loyalty and finding a job away from the West Coast. Some thirty-five thousand left the camps during the next two years, including more than thirteen thousand who joined the armed forces. The all-Nisei 442nd Combat Team served gallantly in the European theater, losing more than five hundred men in battle and winning more than a thousand citations for bravery. One World War II veteran remembers that when his unit was in trouble, the commander would issue a familiar appeal: "Call in the Japs."

For other Nisei, the experience was bitter. More than five thousand renounced their American citizenship and chose to live in Japan at the war's end. The government did not close down the last detention center until March 1946. Japanese Americans never experienced the torture and mass death of the German concentration camps, but their treatment was a disgrace to a nation fighting for freedom and democracy. Finally, in 1988, Congress voted an indemnity of $1.2 billion for the estimated sixty thousand surviving Japanese Americans detained during World War II. Susumi Emori, who had been moved with his wife and four children from his farm in Stockton, California, to a camp in Arkansas, felt vindicated. "It was terrible," he said, with tears in his eyes, "but it was a time of war. Anything can happen. I didn't blame the United States for that."

QUICK CHECK ✔

How did the war affect women and minorities?

Victory

HOW ❓

did the war end, and what were its consequences?

World War II ended with surprising swiftness. By 1943, the Axis tide had been turned in Europe and Asia, and it did not take long for Russia, the United States, and England to mount the offensives that drove Germany and Japan back across the vast areas they had conquered and set the stage for their final defeat.

The long-awaited second front finally came on June 6, 1944. For two years, the United States and England concentrated on building up an invasion force of nearly three million troops and a vast armada of ships and landing craft to carry them across the English Channel. Hoping to catch Hitler by surprise, Eisenhower chose the Normandy peninsula, where the absence of good harbors had led to lighter German fortifications. Allied aircraft bombed northern France for six weeks preceding the assault in order to block the movement of German reinforcements once the invasion began.

D-Day

D-Day (June 6, 1944) was the day Allied troops crossed the English Channel and opened a second front in western Europe during World War II. The "D" stands for "disembarkation": to leave a ship and go ashore.

D-Day, when the invasion would begin, was originally set for June 5, but bad weather forced a delay. Relying on a forecasted break in the storm, Eisenhower gambled on going ahead on June 6. During the night, three divisions parachuted down behind the German defenses; at dawn, the British and American troops fought their way ashore at five points along a sixty-mile stretch of beach, encountering stiff German resistance at several points. By the end of the day, however, Eisenhower had won his beachhead; a week later, more than one-third of a million men were slowly pushing back the German forces through the hedgerows of Normandy. The breakthrough came on July 25 when General Omar Bradley decimated the enemy with a massive artillery and aerial bombardment at Saint-Lô, opening a gap for General George Patton's Third Army. American tanks raced across the French countryside, trapping thousands of Germans and liberating Paris by August 25. Allied troops reached the Rhine River by September, but a shortage of supplies, especially gasoline, forced a three-month halt.

Hitler took advantage of this breathing spell to deliver a daring counterattack. In mid-December, the remaining German armored divisions burst through a weak point in the Allied lines in the Ardennes Forest, planning a breakout to the coast that would have cut off nearly one-third of Eisenhower's forces. A combination of tactical surprise and bad weather, which prevented Allied air support, led to a huge bulge in the American lines. But an airborne division dug in at the key crossroads of Bastogne, in Belgium, and held off a much larger German force. Allied reinforcements and clearing weather then combined to end the attack. By committing nearly all his reserves to the Battle of the Bulge, Hitler had delayed Eisenhower's advance into Germany, but he also had fatally weakened German resistance in the west.

The end came quickly. A massive Russian offensive began in mid-January and swept across the Oder River toward Berlin. General Bradley's troops, finding a bridge left virtually intact by the retreating Germans, crossed the Rhine on March 7. Eisenhower overruled the British, who favored one concentrated drive on Berlin. Instead the Allied forces advanced on a broad front, capturing the industrial Ruhr basin and breaking the Nazi death grip on prisoner populations, including the tragically pitiful remnant of the **Nazi Holocaust,** the slaughter of six million Jews and other persons despised by Hitler's regime. The Americans and British met the Russians at the Elbe in late April. With the Red Army already in the suburbs of Berlin, Adolf Hitler committed suicide on April 30. A week later, on May 7, 1945, Eisenhower accepted the unconditional surrender of all German forces. Just eleven months and a day after the landings in Normandy, the Allied forces had brought the war in Europe to a successful conclusion.

War Aims and Wartime Diplomacy

The American contribution to Hitler's defeat was relatively minor compared to the damage inflicted by the Soviet Union. At the height of the German invasion of Russia, more than 300 Soviet divisions had been locked in battle with 250 German ones, a striking contrast to the 58 divisions the United States and Britain used in the Normandy invasion. As his armies overran Poland and the Balkan countries, Joseph Stalin was determined to retain control over this region, which had been the historic pathway for Western invasion into Russia. Delay in opening the second front and an innate distrust of the West convinced the Soviets that they should maximize their territorial gains by imposing communist regimes on eastern Europe.

American postwar goals were quite different. Now believing the failure to join the League of Nations in 1919 had led to the coming of World War II, the American people and their leaders vowed to put their faith in a new attempt at collective security. At Moscow in 1943, Secretary of State Cordell Hull had won Russian agreement to participate in a future world organization at the war's end. The first wartime Big Three conference brought together Roosevelt, Churchill, and Stalin at Teheran, Iran, in late 1943. Stalin reaffirmed this commitment and also indicated to President Roosevelt that Russia would enter the war against Japan once Germany was defeated.

By the time the Big Three met again in February 1945 at the **Yalta Conference,** the military situation favored the Russians. While British and American forces

IMAGE

Eisenhower and Paratroopers in World War II

Nazi Holocaust
The slaughter of six million Jews and other persons despised by Hitler's regime.

Yalta Conference
Yalta, a city in the Russian Crimea, hosted this wartime conference of the Allies in February 1945 in which the Allies agreed to final plans for the defeat of Germany and the terms of its occupation. The Soviets agreed to allow free elections in Poland, but the elections were never held.

Axis Powers before World War II

Extent of Axis control, early Nov. 1942

Allies

Neutral nations

Allied troop movements

Major battles

WORLD WAR II IN EUROPE AND NORTH AFRICA The tide of battle shifted in this theater during the winter of 1942–1943. The massive German assault on the eastern front was turned back by the Russians at Stalingrad, and the Allied forces recaptured North Africa.

Where did the Allies attack next?

WATCH

The Big Three—Yalta Conference

were still recovering from the Battle of the Bulge, the Red Army was advancing to within fifty miles of Berlin. Stalin drove a series of hard bargains. He refused to give up his plans for communist domination of Poland and the Balkans, although he did agree to Roosevelt's request for a Declaration of Liberated Europe, which called for free elections without providing for any method of enforcement or supervision. More important for the United States, Stalin promised to enter the Pacific war three months after Germany surrendered. In return, Roosevelt offered extensive concessions in Asia, including Russian control over Manchuria. While neither a sellout nor a betrayal, as some critics have charged, Yalta was a significant diplomatic victory for the Soviets—one that reflected Russia's major contribution to a victory in Europe.

For the president, the long journey to Yalta proved to be too much. His health continued to fail after his return to Washington. In early April, FDR left the capital for Warm Springs, Georgia, where he had always been able to relax. He was sitting for his portrait at midday on April 12, 1945, when he suddenly complained of a "terrific headache," then slumped forward and died.

The nation mourned a man who had gallantly met the challenge of depression and global war. Unfortunately, FDR had taken no steps to prepare his successor for the difficult problems that lay ahead. The defeat of Nazi Germany dissolved the one strong bond between the United States and the Soviet Union. With very different histories, cultures, and ideologies, the two nations were bound to drift apart. It was now up to the inexperienced Harry Truman to manage the growing rivalry that was destined to develop into the future Cold War.

> **QUICK CHECK** ✓
>
> How did the objectives of the United States and the Soviet Union conflict?

Triumph and Tragedy in the Pacific

The total defeat of Germany in May 1945 turned all eyes toward Japan. Although the combined chiefs of staff had originally estimated it would take eighteen months after Germany's surrender to conquer Japan, American forces moved with surprising speed. Admiral Nimitz swept through the Gilbert, Caroline, and Marshall Islands in 1944, securing bases for further advances and building air-fields for American B-29s to begin a deadly bombardment of the Japanese home islands. General MacArthur cleared New Guinea of the last Japanese defender in early 1944 and began planning his long-heralded return to the Philippines. American troops landed on the island of Leyte on October 20, 1944, and Manila fell in early February 1945. The Japanese navy, in a Pacific version of the Battle of the Bulge, launched a daring three-pronged attack on the American invasion fleet in Leyte Gulf. The U.S. Navy rallied to blunt all three Japanese thrusts, sinking four carriers and ending any further Japanese naval threat.

The defeat of Japan was now only a matter of time. The United States had three possible ways to proceed. The military favored a full-scale invasion, beginning on the southernmost island of Kyushu in November 1945 and culminating with an assault on Honshu (the main island of Japan) and a climactic battle for Tokyo in 1946; casualties were expected to run into the hundreds of thousands. Diplomats suggested a negotiated peace, urging the United States to modify the unconditional surrender formula to permit Japan to retain the institution of the emperor.

The third possibility involved the **Manhattan Project,** the top-secret program that developed the atom bomb. Scientists, many of them refugees from Europe, had worked since 1939 to perfect this deadly new weapon at the University of Chicago; Oak Ridge, Tennessee; Hanford, Washington; and a remote laboratory in Los Alamos, New Mexico. In the New Mexico desert on July 16, 1945, they successfully tested the first atomic bomb, creating a fireball brighter than several suns and a telltale mushroom cloud that rose some 40,000 feet above an enormous crater in the desert floor.

Truman had been unaware of the existence of the Manhattan Project before he became president on April 12. Now he simply followed the recommendation of a committee headed by Secretary of War Henry L. Stimson to drop the bomb on a Japanese city. The committee discussed but rejected the possibility of inviting the Japanese to observe a demonstration shot at a remote Pacific site and even ruled

Manhattan Project
The top-secret World War II program that produced the first atomic weapons.

Albert Einstein, Letter to President Roosevelt (1939)

The nation's grief at FDR's death is mirrored in the face of this serviceman as the president's funeral cortege passes.

Why was the death such an emotional blow?

Truman on the End of World War II

out the idea of giving advance notice of the bomb's destructive power. Neither Truman nor Stimson had any qualms about the decision to drop the bomb without warning. They viewed it as a legitimate wartime measure, one designed to save the lives of hundreds of thousands of Americans—and Japanese—that would be lost in a full-scale invasion.

Weather conditions on the morning of August 6 dictated the choice of Hiroshima as the bomb's target. The explosion incinerated 4 square miles of the city, killing more than sixty thousand. Two days later, Russia entered the war against

The atomic bomb dropped on Nagasaki, a provincial capital and naval base in southern Japan, on August 9, 1945, virtually obliterated the city and killed more than 60,000 people. Only buildings made with reinforced concrete remained standing after the blast.

What was so controversial about the use of the bomb?

Japan, and the next day, August 9, the United States dropped a second bomb on Nagasaki. There were no more atomic bombs available, but no more were needed. The emperor personally broke a deadlock in the Japanese cabinet and persuaded his ministers to surrender unconditionally on August 14, 1945. Three weeks later, Japan signed a formal capitulation agreement on the decks of the battleship *Missouri* in Tokyo Bay to bring World War II to its official close.

Many years later, scholars charged that Truman had more in mind than defeating Japan when he decided to use the atomic bomb. Citing air force and naval officers who claimed Japan could be defeated by a blockade or by conventional air attacks, these revisionists suggested the real reason for dropping the bomb was to impress the Soviet Union with the fact that the United States had exclusive possession of the ultimate weapon. The available evidence indicates that while Truman and his associates were aware of the possible effect on the Soviet Union, their primary motive was to end World War II as quickly and effortlessly as possible. The saving of American lives, along with a desire for revenge for Pearl Harbor, were uppermost in the decision to bomb Hiroshima and Nagasaki. Yet in using the atomic bomb to defeat Japan, the United States virtually guaranteed a postwar arms race with the Soviet Union.

Nagasaki Atomic Bomb Attack, 1945

QUICK CHECK

What was the role of the atomic bomb in ending the war against Japan?

Conclusion: The Transforming Power of War

The second great war of the twentieth century had a lasting impact on American life. For the first time, the nation's military potential had been reached. In 1945, the United States was unquestionably the strongest country on the earth, with twelve million men and women in uniform; a vast array of shipyards, aircraft plants, and munitions factories in full production; and a monopoly over the atomic bomb. For better or worse, the nation was now launched on a global career. In the future, the United States would be involved in all parts of the world, from western Europe to remote jungles in Asia, from the nearby Caribbean to the distant Persian Gulf. And despite its enormous strength in 1945, the nation's new world role would encompass failure and frustration as well as power and dominion.

The legacy of war was equally strong at home. Four years of fighting brought about industrial recovery and unparalleled prosperity. The old pattern of unregulated free enterprise was as much a victim of the war as of the New Deal; big government and huge deficits had now become the norm as economic control passed from New York and Wall Street to Washington and Pennsylvania Avenue. The war led to far-reaching changes in American society that would become apparent only decades later. Such distinctive patterns of recent American life as the baby boom and the growth of the Sunbelt can be traced back to wartime origins. World War II was a watershed in twentieth-century America, ushering in a new age of global concerns and domestic upheaval.

For a list of additional titles related to this chapter's topics, please see www.pearsonamericanhistory.com.

MyHistoryLab

STUDY RESOURCES

KEY TERMS

Kellogg-Briand Pact, p. 725
Axis Powers, p. 728
neutrality acts, p. 729

Lend-Lease, p. 733
Pearl Harbor, p. 736
D-Day, p. 746

Nazi Holocaust, p. 747
Yalta Conference, p. 747
Manhattan Project, p. 749

CHAPTER REVIEW

WHAT was isolationism, and why was it so appealing to Americans in the 1920s and 1930s?

American disillusionment with the outcome of World War I led to a policy of isolationism, by which Americans hoped to avoid responsibility for the peace of Europe and Asia, and to spare themselves the agony of war if peace failed. Isolationism had traditionally served Americans well, and many Americans expected that it would continue to do so. *(p. 727)*

HOW did the United States go from neutrality in the 1930s to war in 1941?

Franklin Roosevelt gradually led the United States from neutrality in the 1930s to war in 1941, responding to the aggression of Germany and Japan with a series of carefully chosen political and diplomatic steps, including aid to Britain, an undeclared naval war against Germany, and economic pressure on Japan, which lashed out by attacking Pearl Harbor. *(p. 731)*

HOW did America and its allies halt the advances of Germany and Japan?

The United States formed an alliance with Britain and the Soviet Union against Germany and Japan. American and British forces fought the Germans in North Africa and Italy, while Soviet forces beat back the Germans in Russia. American ships and planes defeated Japanese forces at the battles of Midway and the Coral Sea. *(p. 737)*

WHAT changes occurred in American domestic life during World War II?

During the war American industry mobilized as never before, churning out arms and other equipment at a rate unimagined before 1941. The war effort provided jobs that allowed women and minorities to enter the workforce in record numbers. The war also led to discrimination against Japanese Americans, of whom 120,000 were forced into concentration camps. *(p. 741)*

HOW did the war end, and what were its consequences?

The war in Europe ended after the D-Day invasion of Normandy by American and British troops, and the invasion of Germany by American, British, French, and Soviet troops. The collapse of German resistance resulted in the partition of Germany among the victors. The war in the Pacific ended after the atomic bombing of Hiroshima and Nagasaki, and left the United States in undisputed control of Japan. *(p. 746)*

MAKING CONNECTIONS

1. How did the memory of World War I affect the American approach to World War II?
2. How did Franklin Roosevelt aid Britain prior to American entry into World War II? Why did he have to be so careful in doing so?
3. What were some causes of tension within the American alliance during the war?
4. What happened to the civil rights movement during the war?
5. Was the atom bomb necessary to end the war? Why or why not?

PRACTICE QUIZ

1. The _____ Powers consisted of Germany, Italy, and Japan.
   a. Axis
   b. Allied
   c. Neutral
   d. None of the above answers are accurate.

2. The invasion of _____ by Germany in 1939 began World War II in Europe.
   a. Czechoslovakia   b. Hungary
   c. Poland   d. China

3. The attack on _____ brought the United States quickly into World War II.
   a. Pearl Harbor
   b. The World Trade Center
   c. The White House
   d. The Pentagon

4. What country invaded southern Indochina in 1941?
   a. China   b. Australia
   c. Japan   d. The United States

5. During World War II, the federal government incarcerated 120,000
   a. Chinese Americans
   b. Mexican Americans
   c. Native Americans
   d. Japanese Americans

6. The D-Day attack of June 1944 took place in what country?
   a. Japan   b. France
   c. England   d. China

7. All of the following statements explain how the U.S. *finally* defeated Japan *except*
   a. The United States no longer had to fight a two-front war with Germany *and* Japan.
   b. Admiral Nimitz rapidly secured island bases for further United States advance.

   c. The United States launched a one-million-man land invasion that captured Tokyo.
   d. American bombers pounded Japanese cities to rubble.

8. Which of the following does *not* accurately relate the atomic bombing of Hiroshima?
   a. Several bombs fell on the city.
   b. Weather conditions influenced the choice to bomb Hiroshima.
   c. Sixty thousand people immediately perished.
   d. The explosion incinerated 4 square miles of the city.

9. Which of the following reflects the experiences of Mexican American soldiers during the war?
   a. They shared none of the experiences of African American soldiers.
   b. Over three million Mexican Americans served in the conflict.
   c. No Mexican American men became officers.
   d. The United States partially segregated Mexican American troops.

10. Which of the following describes the postwar goals of the Soviet Union?
   a. The Soviets wanted to leave Poland and the Balkans.
   b. The Soviets wanted a buffer zone of communist states in Eastern Europe.
   c. The Soviets preferred a collective approach to postwar security.
   d. The Soviets trusted their ally, the United States.

Find more practice at
www.myhistorylab.com

SAMPLE ESSAY QUESTIONS

1. Compare the major similarities and differences between the European and Pacific theaters of World War II.

2. Evaluate how World War II influenced the American domestic scene.

The Onset
of the Cold War
1945–1960

The explosion of a U.S. test bomb over an uninhabited island in the Pacific on November 1, 1952, demonstrated to the world the fearsome power of the hydrogen bomb. This early H-bomb was capable of destroying a city the size of Washington, D.C.

How did the nuclear arms race shape American foreign policy?

The Potsdam Summit

"I am getting ready to go see Stalin and Churchill," President Truman wrote to his mother in July 1945, "and it is a chore." On board the cruiser *Augusta*, the new president continued to complain about the upcoming Potsdam Conference in his diary. "How I hate this trip!" he confided. "But I have to make it win, lose, or draw and we must win. I am giving nothing away except to save starving people and even then I hope we can only help them to help themselves."

Halfway around the world, Joseph Stalin left Moscow a day late because of a slight heart attack. The Russian leader hated to fly, so he traveled by rail. Moreover, he ordered the heavily guarded train to detour around Poland for fear of an ambush, further delaying his arrival. When he made his entrance into Potsdam, a suburb of Berlin miraculously spared the total destruction that his forces had created in the German capital, he was ready to claim the spoils of war.

These two men, one the veteran revolutionary who had been in power for two decades, the other an untested leader in office for barely three months, symbolized the enormous differences that now separated the wartime allies. Stalin was above all a realist. Brutal in securing total control at home, he was more flexible in his foreign policy, bent on exploiting Russia's victory in World War II rather than aiming at world domination. Cunning and caution were the hallmarks of his diplomatic style. Small in stature, ungainly in build, he radiated a catlike quality as he waited behind his unassuming facade, ready to dazzle an opponent with his "brilliant, terrifying

KEY EVENTS

1945   Truman meets Stalin at Potsdam Conference (July), *p. 755*

1946   Winston Churchill gives "Iron Curtain" speech, *p. 757*

1947   Truman Doctrine announced to Congress (March), *p. 761* ■ Truman orders loyalty program for government employees (March), *p. 773* ■ George Marshall outlines Marshall Plan (June), *p. 762*

1948   Soviets begin blockade of Berlin (June), *p. 763* ■ Truman scores upset victory in presidential election, *p. 772*

1949   NATO treaty signed in Washington (April), *p. 763* ■ Soviet Union tests its first atomic bomb (August), *p. 766*

1950   Truman authorizes building of hydrogen bomb (January), *p. 766* ■ Senator Joseph McCarthy claims communists in government (February), *p. 773* ■ North Korea invades South Korea (June), *p. 768*

1951   Truman recalls MacArthur from Korea, *p. 769*

1952   Dwight D. Eisenhower elected president, *p. 776*

tactical mastery." Truman, in contrast, personified traditional Wilsonian idealism. Lacking Roosevelt's guile, the new president placed his faith in international cooperation. Like many Americans, he believed implicitly in his country's innate goodness. Self-assured to the point of cockiness, he came to Potsdam clothed in the armor of self-righteousness.

Truman and Stalin met for the first time on July 17, 1945. "I told Stalin that I am no diplomat," the president recorded in his diary, "but usually said yes and no to questions after hearing all the argument." The Russian dictator's reaction to Truman remains a mystery, but Truman believed the first encounter went well. "I can deal with Stalin," he wrote. "He is honest—but smart as hell."

Together with Winston Churchill and his replacement, Clement Attlee, whose Labour party had just triumphed in British elections, Truman and Stalin clashed for the next ten days over such difficult issues as reparations, the Polish border, and the fate of eastern Europe. Truman presented the ideas and proposals formulated by his advisers; he saw his task as essentially procedural, and when he presided, he moved the agenda along in brisk fashion. After he had "banged through" three items one day, he commented, "I am not going to stay around this terrible place all summer, just to listen to speeches. I'll go home to the Senate for that." In an indirect, roundabout way, he informed Stalin of the existence of the atomic bomb, tested successfully in the New Mexico desert just before the conference began. Truman offered no details, and the impassive Stalin asked for none, commenting only that he hoped the United States would make "good use of it against the Japanese."

Reparations proved to be the crucial issue at Potsdam. The Russians wanted to rebuild their war-ravaged economy with German industry; the United States

Churchill, Truman, and Stalin during the Potsdam Conference in July 1945.

How did this conference reveal the tensions that would produce the Cold War?

feared it would be saddled with the entire cost of caring for the defeated Germans. A compromise was finally reached. Each side would take reparations primarily from its own occupation zone, a solution that foreshadowed the future division of Germany. "Because they could not agree on how to govern Europe," wrote historian Daniel Yergin, "Truman and Stalin began to divide it." The other issues were referred to the newly created Council of Foreign Ministers, which would meet in the fall in London.

The Potsdam Conference thus ended on an apparent note of harmony; beneath the surface, however, the bitter antagonism of the Cold War was festering. A dozen years later, Truman reminisced to an old associate about Potsdam. "What a show that was!" Describing himself as "an innocent idealist" surrounded by wolves, he claimed that all the agreements reached there were "broken as soon as the unconscionable Russian Dictator returned to Moscow!" He added ruefully, "And I liked the little son of a bitch."

Potsdam marked the end of the wartime alliance. America and Russia, each distrustful of the other, began to engage in a long and bitter confrontation. For the next decade, the two superpowers would vie for control of postwar Europe, and later clash over the spread of communism to Asia. By the time Truman's and Stalin's successors met for the next summit conference, at Geneva in 1955, the Cold War was at its height.

Potsdam Conference

The final wartime meeting of the leaders of the United States, Great Britain, and the Soviet Union was held at Potsdam, outside Berlin, in July 1945. Truman, Churchill, and Stalin discussed the future of Europe but their failure to reach meaningful agreements soon led to the onset of the Cold War.

The Cold War Begins

The conflict between the United States and the Soviet Union began gradually. For two years, the nations tried to adjust their differences over the division of Europe and the atomic bomb through discussion and negotiation. The Council of Foreign Ministers provided the forum. Beginning in London during the fall of 1945 and meeting with their Russian counterparts in Paris, New York, and Moscow, American diplomats searched for a way to live in peace with a suspicious Soviet Union.

HOW did the Cold War begin?

The Division of Europe

The fundamental disagreement was over who would control postwar Europe. In the east, the Red Army had swept over Poland and the Balkans, laying the basis for Soviet domination there. American and British forces had liberated western Europe from Scandinavia to Italy. The Russians, mindful of past invasions from the west across the plains of Poland, were intent on imposing communist governments loyal to Moscow in the Soviet sphere. The United States, on the other hand, upheld the principle of national self-determination, insisting the people in each country should freely choose their postwar rulers. The Soviets saw the demand for free elections as subversive, since they knew that popularly chosen regimes would be unfriendly to Russia. Suspecting American duplicity, Stalin brought down an **Iron Curtain** (Churchill's phrase for the suppression of individual rights in Eastern Europe) and created a series of satellite governments.

Iron Curtain

British Prime Minister Winston Churchill coined the phrase "Iron Curtain" to refer to the boundary in Europe that divided Soviet-dominated eastern and central Europe from western Europe, which was free from Soviet control.

EUROPE AFTER WORLD WAR II The heavy red line splitting Germany shows in graphic form the division of Europe between the Western and Soviet spheres of influence. "From Stettin in the Baltic to Trieste in the Adriatic," said Winston Churchill in a speech at Fulton, Missouri, in 1946, "an iron curtain has descended across the Continent."

How did the "Iron Curtain" image shape American thinking about the Cold War?

Churchill's "Iron Curtain" Speech (March 5, 1946)

Germany was the key. The temporary zones of occupation gradually hardened into permanent lines of division. Ignoring the Potsdam Conference agreement that the country be treated as an economic unit, the United States and Great Britain were by 1946 refusing to permit the Russians to take reparations from the industrial western zones. The initial harsh occupation policy gave way to more humane treatment of the German people and a slow but steady economic recovery. The United States and Britain merged their zones and championed the idea of the unification of all Germany. Russia, fearing a resurgence of German military power, responded by intensifying the communization of its zone, which included the jointly occupied city of Berlin. By 1947, Britain, France, and the United States were laying plans to transfer their authority to an independent West Germany.

The Soviet Union consolidated its grip on eastern Europe in 1946 and 1947. One by one, communist regimes replaced coalition governments in Poland, Hungary, Romania, and Bulgaria. Moving cautiously to avoid provoking the West, Stalin used communism as a means to dominate half of Europe, both to protect the security of the Soviet state and to advance its international power. The climax came in March 1948 when a coup in Czechoslovakia overthrew a democratic government and gave the Soviets a strategic foothold in central Europe.

The division of Europe was an inevitable aftereffect of World War II. Both sides were intent on imposing their values in the areas liberated by their troops. The Russians were no more likely to withdraw from eastern Europe than the United States and Britain were from Germany, France, and Italy. A frank recognition of competing spheres of influence might have avoided further escalation of tension. But the Western nations, remembering Hitler's aggression in the 1930s, began to see Stalin as an equally dangerous threat to their well-being. Instead of accepting him as a cautious leader bent on protecting Russian security, they perceived him as an aggressive dictator leading a communist drive for world domination.

QUICK CHECK ✓

What caused the division of Europe after World War II?

The Atomic Dilemma

Overshadowing all else was the atomic bomb. Used by the United States with deadly success at Hiroshima and Nagasaki, the new weapon raised problems that would have been difficult for even friendly nations to resolve. Given the uneasy state of Soviet-American relations, the effect was disastrous.

The wartime policy followed by Roosevelt and Churchill ensured a postwar nuclear arms race. Instead of informing their major ally of the developing atomic bomb, they kept it a closely guarded secret. Stalin learned of the Manhattan Project through espionage and responded by starting a Soviet atomic program in 1943. By the time Truman informed Stalin of the weapon's existence at Potsdam, the Russians, aided by a steady stream of information from spies in the United States, were well on the way to making their own bomb.

After the war, the United States developed a disarmament plan that would turn control of fissionable material, then the processing plants, and ultimately the American stockpile of bombs over to an international agency. When President Truman appointed financier Bernard Baruch to present this proposal to the United Nations, Baruch insisted on changing it in several important ways, adding sanctions against violators and exempting the international agency from the UN veto. Ignoring scientists who pleaded for a more cooperative position, Baruch followed instead the advice of Army Chief of Staff Dwight D. Eisenhower, who cited the rapid demobilization of the American armed forces (from nearly twelve million personnel in 1945 to fewer than two million in 1947) to argue that "we cannot at this time limit our capability to produce or use this weapon." In effect, the **Baruch Plan,** with its multiple stages and emphasis on inspection, would preserve the American atomic monopoly for the indefinite future.

The Soviets responded predictably. Diplomat Andrei Gromyko presented a simple plan calling for a total ban on the production and use of the new weapon as well as the destruction of all existing bombs. The Russian proposal was founded on the same perception of national self-interest as the Baruch Plan. Although Russia had also demobilized rapidly, it still had nearly three million men under arms in 1947 and wanted to maximize its conventional strength by outlawing the atomic bomb.

No agreement was possible. Neither the United States nor the Soviet Union could abandon its position without surrendering a vital national interest. Wanting to preserve its monopoly, America stressed inspection and control; hoping to

Atomic Age Begins

Kenneth MacFarland, "The Unfinished Work" (1946)

Baruch Plan

In 1946, Bernard Baruch presented an American plan to control and eventually outlaw nuclear weapons. The plan called for United Nations control of nuclear weapons in three stages before the United States gave up its stockpile. Soviet insistence on immediate nuclear disarmament without inspection doomed the Baruch Plan and led to a nuclear arms race between the United States and the Soviet Union.

QUICK CHECK ✓

How did the atomic bomb influence international relations?

neutralize the U.S. advantage, Russia advocated immediate disarmament. The nuclear dilemma, inherent in the Soviet-American rivalry, blocked any negotiated settlement. Instead, the two superpowers agreed to disagree. Trusting neither each other nor any form of international cooperation, each concentrated on taking maximum advantage of its wartime gains. Thus the Russians exploited the territory they had conquered in Europe while the United States retained its economic and strategic advantages over the Soviet Union. The result was the Cold War.

Containment

WHAT
was containment,
and why was it
adopted?

George F. Kennan, "The Long Telegram" (1946)

A major departure in American foreign policy occurred in January 1947, when General George C. Marshall, the wartime army chief of staff, became secretary of state. Calm, mature, and orderly of mind, Marshall had the capability—honed in World War II—to think in broad strategic terms. An extraordinarily good judge of ability, he relied on gifted subordinates to handle the day-to-day implementation of his policies. In the months after taking office, he came to rely on two men in particular: Dean Acheson and George Kennan.

Acheson, an experienced Washington lawyer and bureaucrat, was appointed undersecretary of state and given free rein by Marshall to conduct American diplomacy. In appearance, he seemed more British than American, with his impeccable Ivy League clothes and bushy mustache. A man of keen intelligence, he had a carefully cultivated reputation for arrogance and a low tolerance for mediocrity. As an ardent Anglophile, he wanted to see the United States take over a faltering Britain's role as the supreme arbiter of world affairs. Recalling the lesson of Munich, he opposed appeasement and advocated a policy of negotiating only from strength.

George Kennan, Marshall's other mainstay, headed the newly created Policy Planning Staff. A career foreign service officer, Kennan had become a Soviet expert, mastering Russian history and culture as well as speaking the language fluently. He served in Moscow after U.S. recognition in 1933 and again during World War II, developing there a profound distrust for the Soviet regime. In a crucial telegram in 1946, he warned that the Kremlin believed "that there can be no compromise with rival power" and advocated a policy of containment, arguing that only strong and sustained resistance could halt the outward flow of Russian power. As self-assured as Acheson, Kennan believed that neither Congress nor public opinion should interfere with the conduct of foreign policy by the experts.

In the spring of 1947, a sense of crisis impelled Marshall, Acheson, and Kennan to set out on a new course in American diplomacy. Dubbed **containment,** after an article by Kennan in *Foreign Affairs*, the new policy both consolidated the evolving postwar anticommunism and established guidelines that would shape America's role in the world for more than two decades. What Kennan proposed was "a long-term, patient but firm, and vigilant containment of Russian expansive tendencies." Such a policy of halting Soviet aggression would not lead to any immediate victory, Kennan warned. In the long run, however, he believed that the United States could force the Soviet Union to adopt more reasonable policies and live in peace with the West.

containment

First proposed by George Kennan in 1947, containment became the basic strategy of the United States throughout the Cold War. Kennan argued that firm American resistance to Soviet expansion would eventually compel Moscow to adopt more peaceful policies.

The Truman Doctrine

The initial step toward containment came in response to an urgent British request. Since March 1946, England had been supporting the Greek government in a bitter civil war against communist guerrillas. On February 21, 1947, the British informed the United States that they could no longer afford to aid Greece or Turkey, the latter under heavy pressure from the Soviets for access to the Mediterranean. Believing the Russians responsible for the strife in Greece (in fact, they were not), Marshall, Acheson, and Kennan quickly decided the United States would have to assume Britain's role in the eastern Mediterranean.

Worried about congressional support, especially since the Republicans had gained control of Congress in 1946, Marshall called a meeting with the legislative leadership in late February. He outlined the problem; then Acheson took over to warn that "a highly possible Soviet breakthrough might open three continents to Soviet penetration." Comparing the situation in Greece to one rotten apple spoiling an entire barrel, Acheson warned that "the corruption of Greece would infect Iran and all to the east. It would also carry infection to Africa through Asia Minor and Egypt, and to Europe through Italy and France." Claiming that the Soviets were "playing one of the greatest gambles in history," Acheson concluded that "we and we alone were in a position to break up the play."

The bipartisan group of congressional leaders was deeply impressed. Finally, Republican Senator Arthur M. Vandenberg spoke up, saying he would support the president, but adding that to ensure public backing, Truman would have to "scare hell" out of the American people.

The president followed the senator's advice. On March 12, 1947, he asked Congress for $400 million for military and economic assistance to Greece and Turkey. In stating what would become known as the **Truman Doctrine,** he made clear that more was involved than just these two countries—the stakes in fact were far higher. "It must be the policy of the United States," Truman told the Congress, "to support free peoples who are resisting attempted subjugation by armed minorities or by outside pressure." After a brief debate, both the House and the Senate approved the program by margins of better than three to one.

The Truman Doctrine marked an informal declaration of cold war against the Soviet Union. Truman used the crisis in Greece to secure congressional approval and build a national consensus for the policy of containment. In less than two years, the civil war in Greece ended, but the American commitment to oppose communist expansion, whether by internal subversion or external aggression, placed the United States on a collision course with the Soviet Union around the globe.

President Truman and the Threat of Communism

Truman Doctrine

In 1947, President Truman asked Congress for money to aid the Greek and Turkish governments that were then threatened by communist rebels. Arguing for the appropriations, Truman asserted his doctrine that the United States was committed to support free people everywhere who were resisting subjugation by communist attack or rebellion.

QUICK CHECK

What was the significance of the Truman Doctrine?

The Marshall Plan

Despite American interest in controlling Soviet expansion into Greece, western Europe was far more vital to U.S. interests than was the eastern Mediterranean. Yet by 1947, many Americans believed that western Europe was open to Soviet penetration. The problem was economic in nature. Despite $9 billion in piecemeal American loans, England, France, Italy, and the other European countries had great difficulty in recovering from World War II. Food was scarce, with millions existing on less than fifteen hundred calories a day; industrial machinery was broken down and obsolete;

George Marshall, The Marshall Plan (1947)

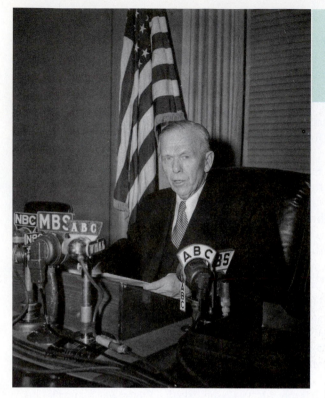

Secretary of State George Marshall broadcasts to the nation a report on foreign relations. In 1947, Marshall proposed a plan for economic aid to assist European recovery after World War II.

How well did the Marshall Plan work?

and workers were demoralized by years of depression and war. The cruel winter of 1947, the worst in fifty years, compounded the problem. Resentment and discontent led to growing communist voting strength, especially in Italy and France. If the United States could not reverse the process, it seemed as though all Europe might drift into the communist orbit.

In the weeks following proclamation of the Truman Doctrine, American officials dealt with this problem. Secretary of State Marshall, returning from a frustrating Council of Foreign Ministers meeting in Moscow, warned that "the patient is sinking while the doctors deliberate." Acheson believed that it was time to extend American "economic power" in Europe, both "to call an effective halt to the Soviet Union's expansionism" and "to create a basis for political stability and economic well-being." The experts drew up a plan for the massive infusion of American capital to finance the economic recovery of Europe. Speaking at a Harvard commencement on June 5, 1947, Marshall presented the broad outline. He offered extensive economic aid to all the nations of Europe if they could reach agreement on ways to achieve "the revival of a working economy in the world so as to permit the emergence of political and social conditions in which free institutions can exist."

Marshall Plan

In 1947, Secretary of State George Marshall proposed a massive economic aid program to rebuild the war-torn economies of western European nations. The plan was motivated by both humanitarian concern for the conditions of those nations' economies and fear that economic dislocation would promote communism in western Europe.

The fate of the **Marshall Plan,** as the aid program was called, depended on the reaction of the Soviet Union and the U.S. Congress. Marshall had taken, in the words of one American diplomat, "a hell of a gamble" by including Russia in his offer of aid. At a meeting of the European nations in Paris in July 1947, the Soviet foreign minister ended the suspense by abruptly withdrawing. Neither the Soviet Union nor its satellites would take part, apparently because Moscow saw the Marshall Plan as an American attempt to weaken Soviet control over eastern Europe. The other European countries then made a formal request for $17 billion in assistance over the next four years.

Congress responded cautiously to the proposal, appointing a special joint committee to investigate. The administration lobbied vigorously, pointing out that the Marshall Plan would help the United States by stimulating trade with Europe as well as checking Soviet expansion. It was the latter argument, however, that proved decisive. When the Czech coup touched off a war scare in March 1948, Congress quickly approved the Marshall Plan by heavy majorities. Over the next four years, the huge American investment paid rich dividends, generating a broad industrial revival in western Europe that became self-sustaining by the 1950s. The threat of communist domination faded, and a prosperous Europe proved to be a bonanza for American farmers, miners, and manufacturers.

QUICK CHECK ✓

What was the purpose of the Marshall Plan?

The Western Military Alliance

The third and final phase of containment came in 1949 with the establishment of the **North Atlantic Treaty Organization (NATO).** NATO grew out of European fears of Russian military aggression.

Recalling Hitler's tactics in the 1930s, the people of western Europe wanted assurance that the United States would protect them from attack as they began to achieve economic recovery. American diplomats were sympathetic. "People could not go ahead and make investments for the future," commented Averell Harriman, "without some sense of security."

England, France, and the Low Countries (Belgium, the Netherlands, and Luxembourg) began the process in March 1948 when they signed the Brussels Treaty, providing for collective self-defense. In January 1949, President Truman called for a broader defense pact including the United States; ten European nations, from Norway in the north to Italy in the south, joined the United States and Canada in signing the North Atlantic Treaty in Washington on April 4, 1949. This historic departure from the traditional policy of isolation—the United States had not signed such a treaty since the French alliance in the eighteenth century— caused extensive debate, but the Senate ratified it in July by a vote of 82 to 13.

There were two main features of NATO. First, the United States committed itself to the defense of Europe in the key clause, which stated that "an armed attack against one or more shall be considered an attack against them all." In effect, the United States was extending its atomic shield over Europe. The second feature was designed to reassure worried Europeans that the United States would honor this commitment. In late 1950, President Truman appointed General Dwight D. Eisenhower to the post of NATO supreme commander and authorized the stationing of four American divisions in Europe to serve as the nucleus of the NATO army. It was believed the threat of American troop involvement in any Russian assault would deter the Soviet Union from making such an attack.

The Western military alliance escalated the developing Cold War. Whatever its advantage in building a sense of security among worried Europeans, it represented an overreaction to the Soviet danger. Americans and Europeans alike were attempting to apply the lesson of Munich—that appeasement of aggressors led to more aggression—to the Cold War. But Stalin was not Hitler, and the Soviets were not the Nazis. There was no evidence of any Russian plan to invade western Europe, and in the face of the American atomic bomb, none was likely. NATO only intensified Russian fears of the West and thus increased the level of international tension.

North Atlantic Treaty Organization (NATO)
In 1949, the United States, Canada, and ten European nations formed this military mutual-defense pact. In 1955, the Soviet Union countered NATO with the formation of the Warsaw Pact, a military alliance among those nations within its own sphere of influence.

MAP

Cold War in Europe, 1950

QUICK CHECK

What were the important features of NATO?

The Berlin Blockade

The main Russian response to containment came in 1948 at the West's most vulnerable point. American, British, French, and Soviet troops each occupied a sector of Berlin, but the city was located more than a hundred miles within the Russian zone of Germany (see the map of postwar Europe on p. 758). Stalin decided to test his opponents' resolve by cutting off all rail and highway traffic to Berlin on June 20, 1948.

The timing was very awkward for Harry Truman. He had his hands full resisting efforts to force him off the Democratic ticket, and he faced a difficult re-election effort against a strong Republican candidate, Governor Thomas E. Dewey

The Berlin airlift of 1948–1949 broke the Soviet blockade. Called Operation Vittles, it provided food and fuel for West Berliners. Here, children atop a pile of rubble wave to an American cargo plane flying overhead.

How did the Berlin crisis mark a turning point in the Cold War?

of New York. Immersed in election-year politics, Truman was caught unprepared by the Berlin blockade. The alternatives were not very appealing. The United States could withdraw its forces and lose not just a city but the confidence of all Europe; it could try to send in reinforcements and fight for Berlin; or it could sit tight and attempt to find a diplomatic solution. Truman made the basic decision in characteristic fashion, telling the military that there would be no thought of pulling out. "We were going to stay, period," an aide reported Truman as saying.

In the next few weeks, the president and his advisers developed ways to implement the decision. Rejecting proposals for provoking a showdown by sending an armored column down the main highway, the administration adopted a two-phase policy. The first part was a massive airlift of food, fuel, and supplies for the ten thousand troops and the two million civilians in Berlin. A fleet of fifty-two C-54s and eighty C-47s began making two daily round-trip flights to Berlin, carrying 2500 tons every twenty-four hours. Then, to guard against Soviet interruption of the **Berlin airlift,** Truman transferred sixty American B-29s, planes capable of delivering atomic bombs, to bases in England. The president was bluffing; the B-29s were not equipped with atomic bombs, but the threat was effective.

For a few weeks, the world teetered on the edge of war. Stalin did not attempt to disrupt the flights to Berlin, but he rejected all American diplomatic initiatives. Although at any time the Russians could have halted it by jamming radar or shooting down the defenseless cargo planes, the airlift gradually increased to more than 4000 tons a day. Governor Dewey patriotically supported the president's policy,

Berlin airlift

In 1948, in response to a Soviet land blockade of Berlin, the United States carried out a massive effort to supply the two million Berlin citizens with food, fuel, and other goods by air for more than six months. The airlift forced the Soviets to end the blockade in 1949.

thus removing foreign policy from the presidential campaign. Yet for Truman, the tension was fierce. In early September, he asked his advisers to brief him "on bases, bombs, Moscow, Leningrad, etc." "I have a terrible feeling afterward that we are very close to war," he confided in his diary. "I hope not."

Slowly, the tension eased. The Russians did not shoot down any planes, and the daily airlift climbed to nearly 7000 tons. Truman, a decided underdog, won a surprising second term in November over a complacent Dewey, in part because the Berlin crisis had rallied the nation behind his leadership. In early 1949, the Soviets gave in, ending the blockade in return for another meeting of the Council of Foreign Ministers on Germany—a conclave that proved as unproductive as all the earlier ones.

The Berlin crisis marked the end of the initial phase of the Cold War. The airlift had given the United States a striking political victory, showing the world the triumph of American ingenuity over Russian stubbornness. Yet it could not disguise the fact that the Cold War had cut Europe in two. Behind the Iron Curtain, the Russians had consolidated control over the areas won by their troops in the war, while the United States had used the Marshall Plan to revitalize western Europe. But a divided continent was a far cry from the wartime hopes for a peaceful world. And the rivalry that began in Europe would soon spread into a worldwide contest between the superpowers.

QUICK CHECK ✓

How did the United States respond to the Berlin blockade?

The Cold War Expands

The rivalry between the United States and the Soviet Union grew in the late 1940s and early 1950s. Both sides began to rebuild their military forces with new methods and new weapons. Equally significant, the diplomatic competition spread from Europe to Asia as each of the superpowers sought to enhance its influence in East Asia. By the time Truman left office in early 1953, the Cold War had taken on global proportions.

HOW did the Cold War expand from Europe to Asia?

The Military Dimension

After World War II, American leaders were intent on reforming the nation's military system in light of their wartime experience. Two goals were uppermost. First, nearly everyone agreed in the aftermath of Pearl Harbor that the U.S. armed services should be unified into an integrated military system. The developing Cold War reinforced this decision. Without unification, declared George Marshall in 1945, "there can be little hope that we will be able to maintain through the years a military posture that will secure for us a lasting peace." Equally important, planners realized, was the need for new institutions to coordinate military and diplomatic strategy so the nation could cope effectively with threats to its security.

In 1947, Congress passed the **National Security Act**. It established a Department of Defense, headed by a civilian secretary of cabinet rank presiding over three separate services—the army, the navy, and the new air force. In addition, the act created the Central Intelligence Agency (CIA) to coordinate the intelligence-gathering

National Security Act
Congress passed the National Security Act in 1947 in response to perceived threats from the Soviet Union after World War II. It established the Department of Defense and created the Central Intelligence Agency (CIA) and National Security Council.

activities of various government agencies. Finally, the act provided for a National Security Council (NSC)—composed of the service secretaries, the secretary of defense, and the secretary of state—to advise the president on all matters regarding the nation's security.

Despite the appearance of equality among the services, the air force quickly emerged as the dominant power in the atomic age, based on its capability both to deter an enemy from attacking and to wage war if deterrence failed. President Truman, intent on cutting back defense expenditures, favored the air force in his 1949 military budget, allotting this branch more than one-half the total sum. After the Czech coup and the resulting war scare, Congress granted an additional $3 billion to the military. The appropriation included funds for a new B-36 to replace the B-29 as the nation's primary strategic bomber.

American military planners received even greater support in the fall of 1949 after the Soviet Union exploded its first atomic bomb. President Truman appointed a high-level committee to explore mounting an all-out effort to build a hydrogen bomb to maintain American nuclear supremacy.

Some scientists had technical objections to the H-bomb, which was still far from being perfected, while others opposed the new weapon on moral grounds, claiming that its enormous destructive power (intended to be one thousand times greater than the atomic bomb) made it unthinkable. George Kennan suggested a new effort at international arms control with the Soviets, but Dean Acheson—who succeeded Marshall as secretary of state in early 1949—believed it was imperative that the United States develop the hydrogen bomb before the Soviet Union. When Acheson presented the committee's favorable report to the president in January 1950, Truman took only seven minutes to decide to go ahead with the awesome new weapon.

At the same time, Acheson ordered the Policy Planning Staff (headed by Paul Nitze after Kennan resigned in protest) to draw up a new statement of national defense policy. **NSC-68,** as the document eventually became known, was based on the premise that the Soviet Union sought "to impose its absolute authority over the rest of the world" and thus "mortally challenged" the United States. Rejecting options such as appeasement or a return to isolation, Nitze advocated a massive expansion of American military power so the United States could halt and overcome the Soviet threat. Contending the nation could afford to spend "upward of 50 percent of its gross national product" for security, NSC-68 proposed increasing defense spending from $13 to $45 billion annually. Approved in principle by the National Security Council in April 1950, NSC-68 stood as a symbol of the Truman administration's determination to win the Cold War regardless of cost.

DOCUMENT

National Security Council Memorandum Number 68 (1950)

NSC-68

National Security Council planning paper No. 68 redefined America's national defense policy. Adopted in 1950, it committed the United States to a massive military buildup to meet the challenge posed by the Soviet Union.

QUICK CHECK ✓

What changes did the Cold War prompt in American military institutions and policies?

The Cold War in Asia

The Soviet-American conflict developed more slowly in Asia. At Yalta, the two superpowers had agreed to a Far Eastern balance of power, with the Russians dominating Northeast Asia and the Americans in control of the Pacific, including both Japan and its former island empire.

The United States moved quickly to consolidate its sphere of influence. General Douglas MacArthur, in charge of Japanese occupation, denied the Soviet Union any role in the reconstruction of Japan. Instead, he supervised the transition of the Japanese government into a constitutional democracy, shaped along Western lines, in which communists were barred from all government posts. The Japanese willingly renounced war in their new constitution, relying instead on American forces to protect their security. American policy was equally nationalistic in the Pacific. A trusteeship arrangement with the United Nations merely disguised the fact that the United States held full control over the Marshall, Mariana, and Caroline Islands. American scientists conducted atomic bomb tests at Bikini atoll in 1946, and by 1949, MacArthur was declaring that the entire Pacific "had become an Anglo-Saxon lake and our line of defense runs through the chain of islands fringing the coast of Asia."

As defined at Yalta, China lay between the Soviet and American spheres. When World War II ended, the country was torn between Chiang Kai-shek's Nationalists in the South and Mao Zedong's communists in the North. Chiang had many advantages, including American political and economic backing and official Soviet recognition. But corruption was widespread among the Nationalist leaders, and a raging inflation that soon reached 100 percent a year devastated the Chinese middle classes and thus eroded Chiang's base of power. Mao used tight discipline and patriotic appeals to strengthen his hold on the peasantry and extend his influence. When the Soviets abruptly vacated Manchuria in 1946, after stripping it of virtually all the industrial machinery Japan had installed, Mao inherited control of this rich northern province. Ignoring American advice, Chiang rushed north to occupy Manchurian cities, overextending his supply lines and exposing his forces to communist counterattack.

American policy sought to prevent a Chinese civil war. Before he became secretary of state, George Marshall undertook the difficult task of forming a coalition government between Chiang and Mao. For a few months in early 1946, Marshall appeared to have succeeded, but Chiang's attempts to gain control of Manchuria doomed the agreement. In reality, there was no basis for compromise. Chiang insisted he "was going to liquidate communists," while Mao was trying to play the United States against Russia in his bid for power. By 1947, as China plunged into full-scale civil war, the Truman administration had given up any meaningful effort to influence the outcome. Political mediation had failed, military intervention was out of the question so soon after World War II, and a policy of continued American economic aid served only to appease domestic supporters of Chiang Kai-shek; 80 percent of the military supplies ended up in communist hands.

The Chinese conflict climaxed at the end of the decade. Mao's forces drove the Nationalists out of Manchuria in late 1948 and advanced across the Yangtze by mid-1949. Acheson released a lengthy report justifying American policy in China on the grounds that the civil war there "was beyond the control of the government of the United States." An American military adviser concurred, telling Congress that the Nationalist defeat was due to "the world's worst leadership" and "a complete loss of will to fight." Republican senators, however, disagreed, blaming American diplomats for sabotaging the Nationalists and terming Acheson's report "a 1054-page white-wash of a wishful, do-nothing policy." While the domestic debate raged over responsibility for the loss of China, Chiang's forces fled the mainland for sanctuary on Formosa (Taiwan) in December 1949. Two months later, Mao and Stalin signed a Sino-Soviet treaty of mutual assistance that clearly placed China in the Russian orbit.

The American response to the communist triumph in China was twofold. First, the State Department refused to recognize the legitimacy of the new regime in Beijing, maintaining instead formal diplomatic relations with the Nationalists on Formosa. Citing the Sino-Soviet alliance, Assistant Secretary of State Dean Rusk called the Beijing regime "a colonial Russian government" and declared, "It is not the Government of China. It does not pass the first test. It is not Chinese." Then, to compensate for the loss of China, the United States focused on Japan as its main ally in Asia. The State Department encouraged the buildup of Japanese industry, and the Pentagon expanded American bases on the Japanese home islands and Okinawa. A Japanese-American security pact led to the end of American occupation by 1952. The Cold War had now split east Asia in two.

> **QUICK CHECK** ✔
>
> What was the role of the United States in China's civil war?

The Korean War

The showdown between the United States and the Soviet Union in Asia came in Korea. Traditionally the cockpit of international rivalry in Northeast Asia, Korea had been divided at the 38th parallel in 1945. The Russians occupied the industrial North, installing a communist government under the leadership of Kim II-Sung. In the agrarian South, Syngman Rhee, a conservative nationalist, emerged as the American-sponsored ruler. Neither regime heeded a UN call for elections to unify the country. The two superpowers pulled out most of their occupation forces by 1949. The Russians, however, helped train a well-equipped army in the North, while the United States—fearful Rhee would seek unification through armed conquest—gave much more limited military assistance to South Korea.

On June 25, 1950, the North Korean army suddenly crossed the 38th parallel in great strength. Stalin had approved this act of aggression in advance. In January 1950, the Soviet leader had told Mao Zedong that he was ready to overthrow the Yalta settlement in the Far East ("and to hell with it," he exclaimed to Mao). In April, when Kim II-Sung came to Moscow to gain approval for the assault on South Korea, Stalin gave it willingly, apparently in the belief that the United States was ready to abandon Syngman Rhee. But the ever-cautious Stalin warned Kim not to count on Soviet assistance, saying, "If you should get kicked in the teeth, I shall not lift a finger. You have to ask Mao for all the help." In May, despite expressing some reservations, Mao also approved the planned North Korean aggression.

Both Stalin and Mao had badly miscalculated the American response. President Truman saw the invasion as a clear-cut case of Soviet aggression reminiscent of the 1930s. "Communism was acting in Korea just as Hitler, Mussolini, and the Japanese had acted ten, fifteen, and twenty years earlier," he commented in his memoirs. Following Acheson's advice, the president convened the UN Security Council and, taking advantage of a temporary Soviet boycott, secured a resolution condemning North Korea as an aggressor and calling on the member nations to engage in a collective security action. Within a few days, American troops from Japan were in combat in South Korea. The conflict, which would last for more than three years, was technically a police action fought under UN auspices; in reality, the United States was at war with a Soviet satellite in Asia.

In the beginning, the fighting went badly as the North Koreans continued to drive down the peninsula. But by August, American forces had halted the communist advance near Pusan. In September, General MacArthur changed the whole complexion of the war by carrying out a brilliant amphibious assault at Inchon,

MAP

The Korean War, 1950–1953

on the waist of Korea, cutting off and destroying most of the North Korean army in the South. Encouraged by this victory, Truman began to shift from his original goal of restoring the 38th parallel to a new one: the unification of Korea by military force.

The administration ignored Beijing's repeated warnings not to invade North Korea. "I should think it would be sheer madness for the Chinese to intervene," commented Acheson. Despite CIA reports of a massive Chinese force assembling in Manchuria, President Truman and his advisers continued to believe that the Soviet Union, not ready for all-out war, would hold China in check. General MacArthur was equally certain that China would not attack his troops in Korea. "We are no longer fearful of their intervention," he told Truman in October, adding that if they crossed the Yalu into Korea, "there would be the greatest slaughter."

Rarely has an American president received worse advice. China was not a Soviet puppet. When UN forces crossed the 38th parallel and moved confidently toward the Yalu, the Chinese launched a devastating counterattack in late November, which caught MacArthur by surprise and drove his armies out of North Korea by the end of the year. MacArthur finally stabilized the fighting near the 38th parallel, but when Truman decided to give up his attempt to unify Korea, the general protested to Congress, calling for a renewed offensive and proclaiming, "There is no substitute for victory."

Truman courageously relieved the popular hero of the Pacific of his command on April 11, 1951. At first, MacArthur seemed likely to force the president to back down. Huge crowds came forward to welcome him home and hear him call for victory over the communists in Asia. At a special congressional hearing, the administration struck back effectively by warning that MacArthur's strategy would expose all Europe to Soviet attack. General Omar Bradley, Truman's chief military adviser, succinctly pointed out that a "showdown" with communism in Asia would be "the wrong war, at the wrong place, at the wrong time, and with the wrong enemy."

Congress and the American people came to accept MacArthur's recall. The Korean War settled into a stalemate near the 38th parallel as truce talks with the communists bogged down. The president had achieved his primary goal, defense of South Korea and the principle of collective security. Yet by taking the gamble to unify Korea by force, he had

THE KOREAN WAR, 1950–1953   After a year of rapid movement up and down the Korean peninsula, the fighting stalled just north of the 38th parallel.

What was the outcome of the Korean War?

confused the American people and humiliated the United States in the eyes of the world.

In the last analysis, the most significant result of the Korean conflict was the massive American rearmament it brought about. The war led to the implementation of NSC-68—the army expanded to 3.5 million troops, the defense budget increased to $50 billion a year by 1952, and the United States acquired distant military bases from Saudi Arabia to Morocco. America was now committed to waging a global contest against the Soviet Union with arms as well as words.

QUICK CHECK ✓

How did the Korean War begin? How did it end?

The Cold War at Home

HOW

did the Cold War affect life in America?

The Cold War cast a long shadow over American life in the late 1940s and early 1950s. Truman tried to carry on the New Deal reform tradition he had inherited from FDR, but the American people were more concerned about events abroad. The Republican party used both growing dissatisfaction with postwar economic adjustment and fears of communist penetration of the United States to revive its sagging fortunes and regain control of the White House in 1952 for the first time in twenty years.

Truman's Troubles

Matching his foreign policy successes with equal achievements at home was not easy for Harry S. Truman. As a loyal supporter of Franklin D. Roosevelt's New Deal programs during his Senate career, Truman had earned a reputation for being a hardworking, reliable, and intensely partisan legislator. But he was relatively unknown to the general public, and his background as a Missouri county official associated with Kansas City machine politics did little to inspire confidence in his ability to lead the nation. Surprisingly well-read—especially in history and biography—Truman possessed sound judgment, the ability to reach decisions quickly, and a fierce and uncompromising sense of right and wrong.

Two weaknesses marred his performance in the White House. One was a fondness for old friends, which resulted in the appointment of many Missouri and Senate cronies to high office. Men such as Attorney General Tom Clark, Secretary of the Treasury Charles Snyder, and White House military aide Harry Vaughn brought little credit to the Truman administration, while the loss of such effective public servants as Secretary of the Interior Harold Ickes and Labor Secretary Frances Perkins hurt it. The president's other serious limitation was his lack of political vision. Failing to pursue a coherent legislative program of his own, he tried to perpetuate FDR's New Deal and, as a result, engaged in a running battle with Congress.

The postwar mood was not conducive to an extension of New Deal reforms. Americans were weary of shortages and sacrifices; they wanted the chance to buy the consumer goods denied them under wartime conditions. But in the rush to convert industry from producing planes and tanks to cars and appliances, problems soon emerged. Prices and wages rose quickly as Congress voted to end wartime controls. With prices going up 25 percent in two years, workers demanded higher wages to offset the loss of overtime pay. A wave of labor unrest swept over the country in the spring of 1946, culminating in two critical strikes: a walkout by coal miners that threatened to close down much of American industry and a paralyzing strike by railroad workers.

President Truman was caught in the middle. Sensitive to union demands, he permitted businesses to negotiate large pay increases for their workers and then pass on the cost to consumers in the form of higher prices. He criticized Congress for weakening wartime price controls, but he failed to offer anything else to curb inflation. Homemakers blamed him for the rising price of food, while organized labor condemned Truman as the country's "No. 1 Strikebreaker" when he asked Congress for power to draft striking railway workers into the army.

In the face of this rising discontent, Truman's efforts to extend the New Deal met with little success. Congress ignored his September 1945 call for measures to ensure economic security and enacted only the Employment Act of 1946. This legislation created the Council of Economic Advisers to assist the president and asserted the principle that the government was responsible for the state of the economy, but it failed to address Truman's original goal of mandatory federal planning to achieve full employment.

The Republicans took advantage of increasing public dissatisfaction with postwar economic woes to attack the Democrats. "To err is Truman," the GOP proclaimed and then adopted a very effective two-word slogan for the 1946 congressional elections: "Had enough?" The American people, weary of inflation and labor unrest, responded by electing Republican majorities in both the House and Senate for the first time since 1930.

QUICK CHECK ✓

What troubles did the country encounter on converting from war to peace?

Truman Vindicated

The president's relations with Congress became even stormier after the 1946 elections. Truman successfully vetoed two GOP measures to give large tax cuts to the wealthy, but Congress overrode his veto of the **Taft-Hartley Act** in 1947. Designed to correct the imbalance in labor-management relations created by the Wagner Act, the Taft-Hartley Act outlawed specific labor union activities—including the closed shop and secondary boycotts—and it permitted the president to invoke an eighty-day cooling-off period to delay strikes that might endanger national health or safety. Despite Truman's claim that it was a "slave-labor" bill, unions were able to survive its provisions.

President Truman's political fortunes reached their lowest ebb in early 1948. Former vice president Henry A. Wallace, claiming to represent the New Deal, announced his third-party (Progressive) candidacy in the presidential contest that year. Worried Democratic party leaders sought to persuade Truman to step aside and allow General Dwight D. Eisenhower to become the Democratic candidate. When Eisenhower turned down bids from both parties, the Democrats reluctantly nominated Truman. His prospects for victory in the fall, however, looked very dim—especially after disgruntled Southerners bolted the Democratic party in protest over a progressive civil rights platform. The Dixiecrats, as they became known, nominated Strom Thurmond, the governor of South Carolina, on a States' Rights party ticket.

Taft-Hartley Act
This 1947 antiunion legislation outlawed the closed shop and secondary boycotts. It also authorized the president to seek injunctions to prevent strikes that posed a threat to national security.

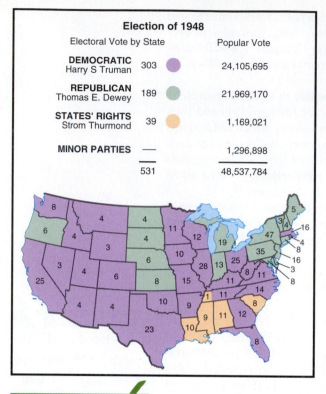

Election of 1948

Electoral Vote by State		Popular Vote
DEMOCRATIC Harry S Truman	303	24,105,695
REPUBLICAN Thomas E. Dewey	189	21,969,170
STATES' RIGHTS Strom Thurmond	39	1,169,021
MINOR PARTIES	—	1,296,898
	531	48,537,784

QUICK CHECK ✓

What were the key issues in the 1948 presidential election?

The defection of the Dixiecrats in the South and Wallace's liberal followers in the North led political experts to predict an almost certain Republican victory. Governor Thomas E. Dewey of New York, the GOP candidate, was so sure of winning that he waged a cautious and bland campaign designed to give him a free hand once he was in the White House. With nothing to lose, Truman barnstormed around the country denouncing the "do-nothing" Republican Eightieth Congress. The president's "give-'em hell" tactics reminded voters of how much they owed the Democrats for helping them survive the Great Depression. To the amazement of the pollsters, Truman won a narrow but decisive victory in November. The old Roosevelt coalition—farmers, organized labor, urban ethnic groups, and blacks—had held together, enabling Truman to remain in the White House and the Democrats to regain control of Congress.

There was one more reason for Truman's win in 1948. During this election, held at the height of the Berlin crisis, the GOP failed to challenge Truman's conduct of the Cold War. Locked in a tense rivalry with the Soviet Union, the American people saw no reason to reject a president who had countered aggression overseas with the Truman Doctrine and the Marshall Plan. The Republicans, committed to support the bipartisan policy of containment, had allowed the Democrats to preempt the foreign policy issue. Until they found a way to challenge Truman's Cold War policies, GOP leaders had little chance to regain the White House.

The Loyalty Issue

Despite Truman's surprising victory in 1948, there was one area in which the Democrats were vulnerable. The fear of communism abroad that had led to the bipartisan containment policy could be used against them at home by politicians who were more willing to exploit the public's deep-seated anxiety.

Fear of radicalism had been a recurrent feature of American life since the early days of the republic. Federalists had tried to suppress dissent with the Alien and Sedition Acts in the 1790s; the Know-Nothings had campaigned against foreigners and Catholics in the 1850s; and the Red Scare after World War I had been directed against both aliens and radicals. The Cold War heightened the traditional belief that subversion from abroad endangered the republic. Bold rhetoric from members of the Truman administration, portraying the men in the Kremlin as inspired revolutionaries bent on world conquest, frightened the American people. They viewed the Soviet Union as a successor to Nazi Germany—a totalitarian police state that threatened the basic liberties of a free people.

A series of revelations of communist espionage activities reinforced these fears, sparking a second Red Scare. Canadian officials uncovered a Soviet spy ring in 1946, and the House Un-American Activities Committee (HUAC) held hearings indicating that communist agents had flourished in the Agriculture and Treasury Departments in the 1930s.

Although Truman tried to dismiss the loyalty issue as a "red herring," he felt compelled to take protective measures, thus lending substance to the charges of subversion. In March 1947, he had initiated a loyalty program, ordering security checks of government employees in order to root out communists. Originally intended to remove subversives for whom "reasonable grounds exist for belief that the person involved is disloyal," within four years the Loyalty Review Board was dismissing workers as security risks if there was "reasonable doubt" of their loyalty. Thousands of government workers lost their jobs, charged with guilt by association with radicals or with membership in left-wing organizations. Often those who were charged had no chance to face their accusers.

The most famous disclosure came in August 1948, when Whittaker Chambers, a repentant communist, accused Alger Hiss of having been a Soviet spy in the 1930s. When Hiss, who had been a prominent State Department official, denied the charges, Chambers led investigators to a hollowed-out pumpkin on his Maryland farm. Inside the pumpkin were microfilms of confidential government documents. Chambers claimed that Hiss had passed the State Department materials to him in the late 1930s. Although the statute of limitations prevented a charge of treason against Hiss, he was convicted of perjury in January 1950 and sentenced to a five-year prison term.

In 1948, the Justice Department further heightened fears of subversion. It charged eleven officials of the Communist party with advocating the violent overthrow of the government. After a long trial, the jury found them guilty, and the party officials received prison sentences and heavy fines; in 1951, the Supreme Court upheld the convictions as constitutional.

Such repressive measures failed, however, to reassure the nation. Events abroad intensified the sense of danger. The communist triumph in China in the fall of 1949 came as a shock; soon there were charges that "fellow travelers" in the State Department were responsible for "the loss of China." In September 1949, when the Truman administration announced that the Russians had detonated their first atomic bomb, the end of America's nuclear monopoly was blamed on Soviet espionage. In early 1950, Klaus Fuchs—a British scientist who had worked on the wartime Manhattan Project—admitted giving the Russians vital information about the A-bomb.

A few months later, the government charged American communists Ethel and Julius Rosenberg with conspiracy to transmit atomic secrets to the Soviet Union. In 1951, a jury found the Rosenbergs guilty of treason, and Judge Irving Kaufman sentenced them to die for what he termed their "loathsome offense." Despite their insistent claims of innocence and worldwide appeals on their behalf, the Rosenbergs were electrocuted on June 19, 1953. Thus by the early 1950s, nearly all the ingredients were at hand for a new outburst of hysteria—fear of Russia, evidence of espionage, and a belief in a vast unseen conspiracy. The only element missing was a leader to release the new outburst of intolerance.

Ronald Reagan, Testimony before HUAC (1947)

QUICK CHECK ✓

How did the fear of communism permeate American domestic life?

McCarthyism in Action

On February 12, 1950, Senator Joseph R. McCarthy of Wisconsin delivered a routine Lincoln's Birthday speech in Wheeling, West Virginia. This little known Republican suddenly attracted national attention when he declared, "I have here

McCarthyism

In 1950, Senator Joseph R. McCarthy began a sensational campaign against communists in government that led to more than four years of charges and countercharges, ending when the Senate censured him in 1954. McCarthyism became the contemporary name for the Red Scare of the 1950s.

in my hand a list of 205—a list of names that were made known to the secretary of state as being members of the Communist party and who nevertheless are still working and shaping policy in the State Department." The charge that there were communists in the State Department—repeated on different occasions with the number changed to 57, then 81—was never substantiated. But McCarthy's Wheeling speech triggered a four-and-a-half-year crusade to hunt down alleged communists in government. The stridency and sensationalism of the senator's accusations soon won the name **McCarthyism**.

McCarthy's basic technique was the multiple untruth. He leveled a series of charges of treasonable activities in government. While officials were refuting his initial accusations, he brought forth a steady stream of new ones, so the corrections never caught up with the latest blast. He failed to unearth a single confirmed communist in government, but he kept the Truman administration in turmoil. Drawing on an army of informers, primarily disgruntled federal workers with grievances against their colleagues and superiors, McCarthy charged government agencies with harboring and protecting communist agents and accused the State Department of deliberately losing the Cold War. His briefcase bulged with documents, but he did very little actual research, relying instead on reports (often outdated) from earlier congressional investigations. He exploited the press with great skill, combining current accusations with promises of future disclosures to guarantee headlines.

The secret of McCarthy's power was the fear he engendered among his Senate colleagues. In 1950, Maryland Senator Millard Tydings, who headed a committee critical of McCarthy's activities, failed to win re-election when McCarthy opposed him; after that, other senators ran scared. McCarthy delighted in making sweeping, startling charges of communist sympathies against prominent public figures. A favorite target was patrician Secretary of State Dean Acheson, whom McCarthy ridiculed as the "Red Dean," with his "cane, spats and tea-sipping little finger"; he even went after General George Marshall, claiming that the wartime army chief of staff was an agent of the communist conspiracy. Nor were fellow Republicans immune. One GOP senator was described as "a living miracle in that he is without question the only man who has lived so long with neither brains nor guts."

The attacks on the wealthy, famous, and privileged won McCarthy a devoted national following,

Senator Joseph McCarthy maintained a steady stream of unsubstantiated charges, always ready to make new accusations of communist infiltration before the preceding ones could be proven untrue.

How did McCarthy's allegations affect the careers of those he targeted?

though at the height of his influence in early 1954, he gained the approval of only 50 percent of the respondents in a Gallup poll. McCarthy drew a disproportionate backing from working-class Catholics and ethnic groups, especially the Irish, Poles, and Italians, who normally voted Democratic. He offered a simple solution to the complicated Cold War: Defeat the enemy at home rather than continue to engage in costly foreign aid programs and entangling alliances abroad. Above all, McCarthy appealed to conservative Republicans in the Midwest who shared his right-wing views and felt cheated by Truman's upset victory in 1948. Even GOP leaders who viewed McCarthy's tactics with distaste, such as Robert A. Taft of Ohio, quietly encouraged him to attack the vulnerable Democrats.

QUICK CHECK ✓

What was McCarthyism?

The Republicans in Power

In 1952, the GOP capitalized on a growing sense of national frustration to capture the presidency. The stalemate in Korea and the second Red Scare created a desire for political change; revelations of scandals by several individuals close to Truman intensified the feeling that someone needed to clean up "the mess in Washington." In Dwight D. Eisenhower, the Republican party found the perfect candidate to explore what one senator called K_1C_2—Korea, communism, and corruption.

Immensely popular because of his amiable manner, winning smile, and heroic stature, Eisenhower alone appeared to have the ability to unite a divided nation. In

DOCUMENT

Joseph R. McCarthy, Wheeling, West Virginia Speech (1950)

DOCUMENT

McCarthy Telegram and Truman Draft Response (1950)

Eisenhower's landslide victories in the presidential elections of 1952 and 1956 seemed to prove his slogan that Americans did, indeed, "like Ike," as expressed on this campaign pennant.

What did the voters like about Ike?

THE ELECTION OF 1952			
Candidate	Party	Popular Vote	Electoral Vote
Eisenhower	Republican	33,778,963	442
Stevenson	Democratic	27,314,992	89

WATCH

Ike for President: Campaign Ad, 1952

the 1952 campaign, Ike displayed hidden gifts as a politician in running against Adlai Stevenson, the eloquent Illinois governor whose appeal was limited to diehard Democrats and liberal intellectuals. Eisenhower allowed his young running mate, Senator Richard M. Nixon of California, to hammer away at the Democrats on the communist and corruption issues, but he himself delivered the most telling blow of all on the Korean War. Speaking in Detroit in late October, just after the fighting had intensified again in Korea, Ike promised if elected he would go personally to the battlefield in an attempt "to bring the Korean War to an early and honorable end."

"That does it—Ike is in," several reporters exclaimed after they heard this pledge. The hero of World War II had clinched his election by committing himself to end an unpopular war. Ten days later, he won the presidency handily, carrying thirty-nine states, including four in the formerly solid Democratic South. The Republican party, however, did not fare as well in Congress; it gained just a slight edge in the House and controlled the Senate by only one seat.

Once elected, Eisenhower moved quickly to fulfill his campaign pledge. He spent three days in early December touring the battlefront in Korea, quickly ruling out the new offensive the military favored. "Small attacks on small hills," he later wrote, "would not end the war." Instead he turned to diplomacy, relying on subtle hints to China on the possible use of nuclear weapons to break the stalemated peace talks. These tactics, together with the death of Joseph Stalin in early March, finally led to the signing of an armistice on July 27, 1953, which ended the fighting but left Korea divided—as it had been before the war—near the 38th parallel.

The new president was less effective in dealing with the problem raised by Senator McCarthy's continuing witch-hunt. Instead of toning down his anticommunist crusade after the Republican victory in 1952, McCarthy used his new position as chairman of the Senate Committee on Government Operations as a base for ferreting out communists on the federal payroll. He made a series of charges against the foreign affairs agencies and demanded that certain books be purged from American information libraries overseas. Eisenhower's advisers urged the president to use his own great prestige to stop McCarthy. But Ike refused such a confrontation, saying, "I will not get into a pissing contest with a skunk." Eisenhower preferred to play for time, hoping the American people would eventually come to their senses.

The Wisconsin senator finally overreached himself. In early 1954, he uncovered an army dentist suspected of disloyalty and proceeded to attack the upper echelons of the U.S. Army, telling one much decorated general that he was "not fit to wear the uniform." The controversy culminated in the televised Army-McCarthy hearings. For six weeks, the senator revealed his crude, bullying behavior to the American people. Viewers were repelled by his frequent outbursts that began with the insistent cry, "Point of order, Mr. Chairman, point of order," and by his attempt to slur the reputation of a young lawyer associated with army counsel Joseph Welch. This last maneuver led Welch to condemn McCarthy for his "reckless cruelty" and ask rhetorically, as millions watched on television, "Have you no sense of decency, sir?"

Courageous Republicans, led by Senators Ralph Flanders of Vermont and Margaret Chase Smith of Maine, joined with Democrats to bring about the Senate's censure of McCarthy in December 1954, by a vote of 67 to 22. Once rebuked, McCarthy fell quickly from prominence. He died three years later virtually unnoticed and unmourned.

Yet his influence was profound. Not only did he paralyze national life with what a Senate subcommittee described as "the most nefarious campaign of half-truth and untruth in the history of the Republic," but he also helped impose a political and cultural conformity that froze dissent for the rest of the 1950s. Long after McCarthy's passing, the nation tolerated loyalty oaths for teachers, the banning of left-wing books in public libraries, and the blacklisting of entertainers in radio, television, and films. Freedom of expression was inhibited, and the opportunity to try out new ideas and approaches was lost as the United States settled into a sterile Cold War consensus.

While Dwight Eisenhower could claim that his policy of giving McCarthy enough rope to hang himself had worked, it is possible that a bolder and more forthright presidential attack on the senator might have spared the nation some of the excesses of the second Red Scare.

QUICK CHECK

What foreign and domestic issues influenced the election of Eisenhower in 1952?

Conclusion: The Continuing Cold War

Eisenhower's election calmed things at home but didn't end the Cold War abroad. During Ike's presidency the United States extended its policy of containment, and greatly expanded its nuclear arsenal. Eisenhower himself sometimes wondered where it all would lead. In his final years in office he tried to defuse tensions with the Soviet Union, and he warned about the danger of massive military spending in his farewell address to the American people. "In the councils of government, we must guard against the acquisition of unwarranted influence, whether sought or unsought, by the military-industrial complex," he declared. "The potential for the disastrous rise of misplaced power exists and will persist."

Rarely has an American president been more prophetic. In the next few years, the level of defense spending would skyrocket as the Cold War escalated. Eisenhower had succeeded in keeping the peace, but he had failed to halt the momentum of the Cold War he had inherited from Harry Truman.

For a list of additional titles related to this chapter's topics, please see www.pearsonamericanhistory.com.

MyHistoryLab

STUDY RESOURCES

KEY TERMS

Potsdam Conference, p. 755
Iron Curtain, p. 757
Baruch Plan, p. 759
containment, p. 760
Truman Doctrine, p. 761

Marshall Plan, p. 762
North Atlantic Treaty
    Organization (NATO), p. 763
Berlin airlift, p. 764

National Security Act, p. 765
NSC-68, p. 766
Taft-Hartley Act, p. 771
McCarthyism, p. 774

CHAPTER REVIEW

HOW did the Cold War begin?

The Cold War began as the United States and the Soviet Union discovered that their interests in Europe conflicted. Each feared the other, and each, acting on its fears, took steps that heightened the other's fears. Atomic weapons made the mistakes of miscalculation far greater than in the past and made everyone more fearful. *(p. 757)*

WHAT was containment, and why was it adopted?

Containment was the American policy of preventing the expansion of Soviet power and influence. It was adopted as a way of preserving American interests without excessively risking war. *(p. 760)*

HOW did the Cold War expand from Europe to Asia?

The Cold War expanded from Europe to Asia when the United States and the Soviet Union took opposite sides in the Chinese civil war. Shortly after the communist victory in China, the Cold War spilled into Korea, where communist North Korea battled anti-communist South Korea, with the United States siding with South Korea, and the Soviet Union and Communist China backing North Korea. *(p. 765)*

HOW did the Cold War affect life in America?

The Cold War spawned widespread fears of communist subversion in the United States. It led to a campaign to ensure loyalty on the part of government workers, and fostered the broader phenomenon of McCarthyism, an exaggerated effort to find communists in nearly every corner of American life. Although McCarthyism eventually burned itself out, it contributed to the election of Eisenhower in 1952, which ended twenty years of Democratic control of the White House. *(p. 770)*

MAKING CONNECTIONS

1. Why was the Soviet Union suspicious of the United States?
2. In what ways did the Marshall Plan demonstrate American generosity? In what ways did it reflect American self-interest?
3. How was the Cold War in Asia similar to the Cold War in Europe? How was it different?
4. To what extent was McCarthyism justified?

PRACTICE QUIZ

1. The phrase_____ was coined by British Prime Minister Winston Church regarding the Soviet Union's control over Eastern Europe.
   a. *Red Wall*
   b. *Russian Barrier*
   c. *Iron Curtain*
   d. *Stalinist Fence*

2. The_____ Doctrine reflected President Harry Truman's plan to contain communism abroad.
   a. Monroe
   b. Truman
   c. NATO
   d. Roosevelt

3. The_____ Plan became a U.S. attempt to rebuild Europe after the war.
   a. Eisenhower
   b. Baruch
   c. Marshall
   d. Kennedy

4. The_____ airlift became a point of tension between the Soviets and the United States in 1948.
   a. Paris
   b. Prague
   c. Dresden
   d. Berlin

5. The_____ Act, which established the Department of Defense, passed in Congress in 1947.
   a. Homeland Security
   b. Department of Justice
   c. National Security
   d. Security Cooperation

6. The showdown between the United States and the Soviet Union in Asia in 1950 came in
   a. Korea
   b. Vietnam
   c. China
   d. Japan

7. The Dixiecrats were
   a. Disgruntled Southerners who left the Democratic Party over civil rights.
   b. Disgruntled Westerners who rejected federal control of water rights.
   c. Disgruntled Northerners who resented southern power in Congress.
   d. Disgruntled Southerners who left the Republican Party because of Eisenhower.

8. All of the following accurately relate the Alger Hiss spy case *except*
   a. He formerly worked as a State Department official.
   b. He was accused of being a Soviet spy.
   c. He admitted to the charges.
   d. The government convicted him of perjury in 1950 and sentenced him to five years in prison.

9. Which of the following does *not* accurately describe the operations of Senator Joseph McCarthy?
   a. His basic technique was to provide a barrage of multiple untruths.
   b. He failed to uncover a single confirmed communist in government.
   c. He relied upon a wide range of disgruntled informers.
   d. He conducted a large amount of research in his quest for communists.

10. The 1952 presidential campaign included all of the following issues *except*
    a. Stalemate in Korea
    b. The Second Red Scare
    c. The Bay of Pigs fiasco
    d. Scandals close to President Truman

Find more practice at
www.myhistorylab.com

SAMPLE ESSAY QUESTIONS

1. Explain why American presidents pursued a policy of containing communism following World War II.

2. Summarize the Cold War influence on U.S. culture and politics.

Answers to Practice Quiz 1. c, p. 757 2. b, p. 761 3. c, p. 762 4. d, p. 764 5. c, p. 765 6. a, p. 768 7. a, p. 771 8. c, p. 773 9. d, p. 774 10. c, p. 775

Affluence and Anxiety

1945–1960

The houses of Levittown spread over 1200 acres of former potato fields on Long Island, New York.

What does this image say about suburban life?

Levittown: The Flight to the Suburbs

On May 7, 1947, William Levitt announced plans to build two thousand rental houses in a former potato field on Long Island, thirty miles from Midtown Manhattan. Using mass production techniques he had learned while erecting navy housing during the war, Levitt quickly built four thousand homes and rented them to young veterans eager to leave crowded city apartments or their parents' homes to begin raising families. A change in government financing regulations led him to begin offering his houses for sale in 1948 for a small amount down and a low monthly payment. Young couples, many of them the original renters, quickly bought the first four thousand; by the time **Levittown**—as he called the new community—was completed in 1951, it contained more than seventeen thousand homes. So many babies were born in Levittown that it soon became known as "Fertility Valley" and "the Rabbit Hutch."

Levitt eventually built two more Levittowns, one in Pennsylvania and one in New Jersey; each contained the same curving streets, neighborhood parks and playgrounds, and community swimming pools characteristic of the first development. The secret of Levittown's appeal was the basic house, a 720-square-foot Cape Cod design built on a concrete slab. It had a kitchen, two bedrooms

KEY EVENTS

1947   William Levitt announces first Levittown, *p. 781*

1948   Truman orders end to segregation in armed forces, *p. 789*

1949   Minimum wage raised from 40 to 75 cents an hour, *p. 784*

1954   Supreme Court orders schools desegregated in *Brown* v. *Board of Education of Topeka, p. 790*

1955   African Americans begin boycott of Montgomery, Alabama, bus company (December), *p. 792*

1957   Congress passes first Civil Rights Act since Reconstruction, *p. 791*

and bath, a living room complete with a fireplace and 16-foot picture window, and an expansion attic with room for two more bedrooms. Levitt built only one interior, but there were four different facades to break the monotony. The original house sold for $6990 in 1948; even the improved model, a ranch-style house, sold for less than $10,000 in 1951.

Levitt's houses were ideal for young people just starting out in life. They were cheap, comfortable, and efficient, and each home came with a refrigerator, cooking range, and washing machine. Despite the conformity of the houses, the three Levittowns were surprisingly diverse communities; residents had a wide variety of religious, ethnic, and occupational backgrounds. African Americans, however, were rigidly excluded. In time, as the more successful families moved on to larger homes in more expensive neighborhoods, the Levittowns became enclaves for lower-middle-class families.

Levittown

In 1947, William Levitt used mass production techniques to build inexpensive homes in suburban New York to help relieve the postwar housing shortage. Levittown became a symbol of the movement to the suburbs in the years after World War II.

baby boom

Post–World War II Americans idealized the family. The booming birth rate after the war led children born to this generation to be commonly referred to as "baby boomers."

Levittown symbolized the most significant social trend of the postwar era in the United States—the flight to the suburbs. The residential areas surrounding cities such as New York and Chicago nearly doubled in the 1950s. While central cities remained relatively stagnant during the decade, suburbs grew by 46 percent; by 1960, some sixty million people, one-third of the nation, lived in suburban rings around the cities. This massive shift in population from the central city was accompanied by a **baby boom** that started during World War II. Young married couples began to have three, four, or even five children (compared with only one or two children in American families during the 1930s). These larger families led to a 19 percent growth in the nation's population between 1950 and 1960, the highest growth rate since 1910.

The economy boomed as residential construction soared. By 1960, one-fourth of all existing homes were less than ten years old, and factories were turning out large quantities of appliances and television sets for the new households. A multitude of new consumer products—ranging from frozen foods to filter cigarettes, from high-fidelity phonographs to cars equipped with automatic transmissions and tubeless tires—appeared in stores and showrooms. In the suburbs, the corner grocery gave way to the supermarket carrying a vast array of items that enabled homemakers to provide their families with a more varied diet.

A new affluence replaced the poverty and hunger of the Great Depression for most Americans, but many had haunting memories of the 1930s. The obsession with material goods took on an almost desperate quality, as if a profusion of houses, cars, and home appliances could guarantee that the nightmare of depression would never return. Critics were quick to disparage the quality of life in suburban society. They condemned the conformity, charging the newly affluent with forsaking traditional American individualism to live in identical houses, drive look-alike cars, and accumulate the same material possessions.

Events abroad added to the feeling of anxiety in the postwar years. Nuclear war became a frighteningly real possibility. The rivalry with the Soviet Union had led to

A floor plan and elevation for a Levittown house. The Levittown builders applied the principles of mass production used in auto manufacturing to house construction. Construction was broken down into twenty-seven separate tasks, and a house could be assembled in fifteen minutes.

How did this make houses cheaper?

the second Red Scare, with charges of treason and disloyalty being leveled at loyal Americans. Many Americans joined Senator Joseph McCarthy in searching for the communist enemy at home rather than abroad. Loyalty oaths and book burning revealed how insecure Americans had become in the era of the Cold War. The 1950s also witnessed a growing demand by African Americans for equal opportunity in an age of abundance. The civil rights movement, along with strident criticism of the consumer culture, revealed that beneath the bland surface of suburban affluence forces for change were at work.

The Postwar Boom

For fifteen years following World War II, the nation witnessed a period of unparalleled economic growth. A pent-up demand for consumer goods fueled a steady industrial expansion. Heavy government spending during the Cold War added an extra stimulus to the economy, offsetting brief recessions in 1949 and 1953 and moderating a steeper one in 1957–1958. By the end of the 1950s, the American people had achieved an affluence that finally erased the lingering fears of the Great Depression.

HOW did the American economy evolve in the years after World War II?

Postwar Prosperity

The economy began its upward surge as the result of two long-term factors. First, American consumers—after being held in check by depression and then by wartime scarcities—finally had a chance to indulge their suppressed appetites for material goods. At the war's end, personal savings in the United States stood at more than $37 billion, providing a powerful stimulus to consumption. Initially, American factories could not turn out enough automobiles and appliances to satisfy the horde of buyers. By 1950, however, production lines had finally caught up with the demand. In that year, Americans bought more than six million cars, and the gross national product (GNP) reached $318 billion (50 percent higher than in 1940).

The Cold War provided the additional stimulus the economy needed when postwar expansion slowed. The Marshall Plan and other foreign aid programs financed a heavy export trade. The Korean War helped overturn a brief recession and ensured continued prosperity as the government spent massive amounts on guns, planes,

BIRTHRATE, 1940–1970

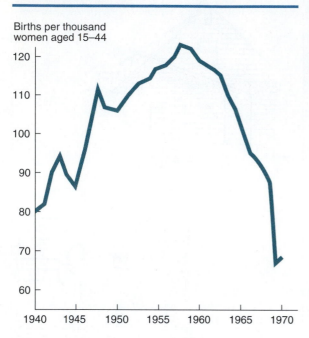

Births per thousand women aged 15–44

Source: Compiled from U.S. Bureau of the Census, *Historical Statistics of the United States, Colonial Times to 1970,* Bicentennial Edition, Washington, D.C., 1975.

MAP

Population Shifts, 1940–1950

QUICK CHECK ✓

What drove the prosperity of the postwar decades?

and munitions. In 1952, the nation spent $44 billion, two-thirds of the federal budget, on national defense. Although Eisenhower managed to bring about some modest reductions, defense spending continued at a level of $40 billion throughout the decade.

The nation achieved an affluence in the 1950s that made the persisting fear of another Great Depression seem irrational. The baby boom and the spectacular growth of suburbia served as great stimulants to the consumer goods industries. Manufacturers turned out an ever increasing number of refrigerators, washing machines, and dishwashers to equip the kitchens of Levittown and its many imitators across the country. The automobile industry thrived with suburban expansion as two-car families became more and more common. In 1955, in an era when oil was abundant and gasoline sold for less than 30 cents a gallon, Detroit sold a record eight million cars. The electronics industry boomed. Consumers were eager to acquire the latest marvel of home entertainment—the television set.

Commercial enterprises snapped up office machines and the first generation of computers; industry installed electronic sensors and processors as it underwent extensive automation; and the military displayed an insatiable appetite for electronic devices for its planes and ships. As a result, American industry averaged more than $10 billion a year in capital investment, and the number of persons employed rose above the long-sought goal of sixty million nationwide.

Yet the economic abundance of the 1950s was not without its problems. While some sections of the nation (notably the emerging Sunbelt areas of the South and West) benefited enormously from the growth of the aircraft and electronics industries, older manufacturing regions, such as New England, did not fare as well. The steel industry increased its capacity during the decade, but it began to fall behind the rate of national growth. Agriculture continued to experience bumper crops and low prices, so rural regions, like the vast areas of the Plains states, failed to share in the general affluence. Unemployment persisted despite the boom, rising to more than 7 percent in a sharp recession that hit the country in the fall of 1957 and lasted through the summer of 1958. The rate of economic growth slowed in the second half of the decade, causing concern about the continuing vitality of the American economy.

None of these flaws, however, could disguise the fact that the nation was prospering to an extent no one dreamed possible in the 1930s. The GNP grew to $440 billion by 1960, more than double the 1940 level. More important, workers now labored fewer than forty hours a week; they rarely worked on Saturdays, and nearly all enjoyed a two-week paid vacation each year. By the mid-1950s, the average American family had twice as much real income to spend as its counterpart had possessed in the boom years of the 1920s. From 1945 to 1960, per capita disposable income rose by $500—to $1845—for every man, woman, and child in the country. The American people, in one generation, had moved from poverty and depression to the highest standard of living the world had ever known.

Life in the Suburbs

Sociologists had difficulty describing the nature of suburban society in the 1950s. Some saw it as classless, while others noted the absence of both the very rich and the very poor and consequently labeled it "middle class." Rather than forming a homogeneous social group, though, the suburbs contained a surprising variety of people, whether classified as "upper lower," "lower middle," and "upper middle" or simply as blue collar, white collar, and professional. Doctors and lawyers often lived in the same developments as salesclerks and master plumbers. The traditional distinctions of ancestry, education, and size of residence no longer differentiated people as easily as they had in the past.

Yet suburbs could vary widely, from working-class communities clustered near factories built in the countryside to old, elitist areas such as Scarsdale, New York, and Shaker Heights, Ohio. Most were almost exclusively white and Christian, but suburbs such as Great Neck on Long Island and Richmond Heights outside Miami enabled Jews and blacks to take part in the flight from the inner city.

Life in all the suburban communities depended on the automobile. Highways and expressways allowed fathers to commute to jobs in the cities, often an hour or more away. Children might ride buses to and from school, but mothers had to drive them to piano lessons and Little League ballgames. Two cars became a necessity for almost every suburban family, thus helping spur the boom in automobile production. In 1948, only 59 percent of American families owned a car; just a few years later, nearly every suburban family had at least one vehicle, and many had several.

In the new drive-in culture, people shopped at the stores that grew up first in "miracle miles" along the highways and later at the shopping centers that spread across the countryside in the 1950s. There were only eight shopping centers in the entire country in 1946; hundreds appeared over the next fifteen years, including Poplar Plaza in Memphis, with one large department store, thirty retail shops, and parking for more than five hundred cars. In 1956, the first enclosed air-conditioned mall, the Southdale Shopping Center, opened outside Minneapolis.

Despite the increased mobility provided by the car, the home became the focus for activities and aspirations. The postwar shortage of housing that often forced young couples to live with their parents or in-laws created an intense demand for new homes in the suburbs. When questioned, prospective buyers expressed a desire for "more space," for "comfort and roominess," and for "privacy and freedom of action" in their new residences. Men and women who moved to the suburbs prized the new kitchens with their built-in dishwashers, electric ovens, and gleaming counters; the extra bedrooms that ensured privacy from and for the children; the large garages that could be converted into recreation rooms; and the small, neat lawns that gave them an area for outdoor activities as well as a new way to compete with their neighbors. "Togetherness" became the code word of the 1950s. Families did things together, whether gathering around the TV sets that dominated living rooms, attending community activities, or taking vacations in the huge station wagons of the era.

But there were some less attractive consequences of the new suburban lifestyle. The extended family, in which several generations had lived in close proximity, was a casualty of the boom in small detached homes. As historian Kenneth Jackson noted, suburban life "ordained that most children would grow up in intimate contact only with their parents and siblings." For many families, grandparents, aunts and uncles, cousins, and more distant relatives would become remote figures, seen only on special occasions.

Ladies Home Journal, "Young Mother" (1956)

QUICK CHECK ✔

How did the growth of suburbs change the way Americans lived?

The nuclear family, typical of the suburb, did little to encourage the development of feminism. The end of the war saw many women who had entered the workforce return to the home, where the role of wife and mother continued to be viewed as the ideal for women in the 1950s. Trends toward getting married earlier and having larger families reinforced the pattern of women devoting all their efforts to housework and child raising rather than acquiring professional skills and pursuing careers outside the home. Adlai Stevenson, extolling "the humble role of housewife," told Smith College graduates that there was much they could do "in the living room with a baby in your lap or in the kitchen with a can opener in your hand." Dr. Benjamin Spock's 1946 best-seller, *Baby and Child Care,* became a fixture in millions of homes, while the traditional women's magazines such as *McCall's* and *Good Housekeeping* thrived by featuring articles on natural childbirth and inspirational pieces such as "Homemaking Is My Vocation."

Nonetheless, the number of working wives doubled between 1940 and 1960. By the end of the 1950s, 40 percent of American women, and nearly one-third of all married women, had jobs outside the home. The heavy expenses involved in rearing and educating children led wives and mothers to seek ways to augment the family income, inadvertently preparing the way for a new demand for equality in the 1960s.

The Good Life?

WHAT changes marked American culture after the war?

Consumerism became the dominant social theme of the 1950s. Yet even with an abundance of creature comforts and added hours of leisure time, the quality of life left many Americans anxious and dissatisfied.

Areas of Greatest Growth

Organized religion flourished in the climate of the 1950s. Ministers, priests, and rabbis all commented on the rise in church and synagogue attendance in the new communities. Will Herberg claimed that religious affiliation had become the primary identifying feature of modern American life, dividing the nation into three separate segments—Protestant, Catholic, and Jewish.

Some observers condemned the bland, secular nature of suburban churches, which seemed to be an integral part of the consumer society. "On weekdays one shops for food," wrote one critic, "on Saturdays one shops for recreation, and on Sundays one shops for the Holy Ghost." But the popularity of religious writer Norman Vincent Peale, with his positive gospel that urged people to "start thinking faith, enthusiasm and joy," suggested that the new churches filled a genuine if shallow human need. At the same time, the emergence of neo-orthodoxy in Protestant seminaries (notably through the ideas of Reinhold Niebuhr) and the rapid spread of radical forms of fundamentalism (such as the Assemblies of God) indicated that millions of Americans still were searching for a more personal religious faith.

Schools provided an immediate problem for the growing new suburban communities. The increase in the number of school-age children, from twenty to thirty million in the first eight grades, overwhelmed the resources of many local districts,

One of the most popular television programs of the 1950s was *I Love Lucy,* a situation comedy featuring the real-life husband-and-wife team of Lucille Ball and Desi Arnaz portraying the fictional couple Lucy and Ricky Ricardo.

How did television shape American life in the postwar decades?

leading to demands for federal aid. Congress granted limited help for areas affected by defense plants and military bases, but Eisenhower's reluctance to unbalance the budget—along with traditional adherence to state control over public education—blocked further federal assistance prior to 1957, when the government reacted to *Sputnik,* the Soviet satellite that ushered in the space age, by sharply increasing federal support for science education.

Equally important, a controversy arose over the nature of education in the 1950s. Critics of "progressive" education called for sweeping educational reforms and a new stress on traditional academic subjects. Suburban communities often had bitter fights; affluent parents demanded kindergarten enrichment programs and grade school foreign language instruction while working-class people resisted such costly innovations. The one thing all seemed to agree on was the desirability of a college education. The number of young people attending colleges increased from 1.5 million in 1940 to 3.6 million in 1960.

The largest advances were made in the exciting new medium of television. From a shaky start just after the war, TV boomed in the 1950s, pushing radio aside and undermining many of the nation's magazines. By 1957, three networks controlled the airwaves, reaching forty million sets over nearly five hundred stations. Advertisers soon took charge of the new medium, using techniques first pioneered in radio—including taped commercials, quiz shows, and soap operas.

At first, the insatiable demand for programs encouraged a burst of creativity. Playwrights such as Reginald Rose, Rod Serling, and Paddy Chayefsky wrote a series of notable dramas for *Playhouse 90, Studio One,* and the *Goodyear Television Playhouse.* Broadcast live from cramped studios, these productions thrived on tight dramatic structures, movable scenery, and frequent close-ups of the actors.

Advertisers, however, quickly became disillusioned with the live dramatic programs, which usually dealt with controversial subjects or focused on ordinary people and events. In contrast, sponsors wanted shows that stressed excitement, glamour, and instant success. Aware that audiences were fascinated by contestants with unusual expertise (a shoemaker answering tough questions on operas, a grandmother stumping experts on baseball), producers began giving away huge cash prizes on *The $64,000 Question* and *Twenty-one.* In 1959, the nation was shocked when Charles Van Doren, a Columbia University professor, confessed he had been given the answers in advance to win $129,000 on *Twenty-one.* The three networks quickly dropped all the big-prize quiz programs, replacing them with comedy, action, and adventure shows such as *The Untouchables* and *Bonanza.* Despite its early promise of artistic innovation, television had become a technologically sophisticated but safe conveyor of the consumer culture.

QUICK CHECK

What was the effect of television on American life?

Critics of the Consumer Society

One striking feature of the 1950s was the disenchantment expressed by many authors and artists. This disenchantment reached its most eloquent expression with the beats, literary groups that rebelled against the materialistic society of the era. Jack Kerouac's novel *On the Road,* published in 1957, set the tone for the new movement. The name came from the quest for beatitude, a state of inner grace sought in Zen Buddhism. Flouting the respectability of suburbia, the "beatniks"— as middle America termed them—were easily identified by their long hair and bizarre clothing; they also had a penchant for sexual promiscuity and drug experimentation. They were conspicuous dropouts from a society they found senseless. Poet Lawrence Ferlinghetti, who held forth in the City Lights Bookshop in San Francisco (a favorite resort of the beats), summed it up this way: "I was a wind-up toy someone had dropped wound up into a world already running down."

The social protest inherent in the books and poems of the beats found its artistic counterpart in the rise of abstract expressionism. Abstract expressionists worked in styles that emphasized individuality and freedom from the constraints of representational, realistic art. Painters Jackson Pollock and Mark Rothko, among others, challenged mainstream America's notions about the form and function of art. For Pollock, the act of creating a painting was as important as the painting itself. Rothko pioneered a style known as color field painting; his works in this style are monumental pieces in which enormous areas of color lacking any distinct structure or central focus are used to create a mood.

Despite the disapproval they evoked from mainstream Americans, the beat generation had some compassion for their detractors. "We love everything," Kerouac proclaimed, "Billy Graham, the Big Ten, Rock and Roll, Zen, apple pie, Eisenhower—we dig it all." Yet, as highly visible nonconformists in an era of stifling conformity, the beats demonstrated a style of social protest that would flower into the counterculture of the 1960s.

QUICK CHECK

What did critics find lacking in American postwar culture?

The Struggle over Civil Rights

The questioning of American life was nowhere more evident than in the area of race relations, where the white majority continued to deny basic rights to the nation's black minority. In the midst of the Cold War, the contradiction between the denunciation of the Soviet Union for its human rights violations and the second-class status of African Americans began to arouse the national conscience. Fighting for freedom against communist tyranny abroad, Americans had to face the reality of the continued denial of freedom to a submerged minority at home.

African Americans had benefited economically from World War II, but they were still a seriously disadvantaged group. Those who had left the South for better opportunities in northern and western cities were concentrated in blighted and segregated neighborhoods, working at low-paying jobs, suffering economic and social discrimination, and failing to share fully in the postwar prosperity. The rising expectations of African Americans in the postwar years led them to challenge the older patterns of racial segregation and inequality.

In the South, conditions were much worse. State laws forced blacks to live almost totally segregated from white society. Not only did African Americans attend separate (and almost always inferior) schools, but they also were rigidly segregated in all public facilities. They were forced to use separate waiting rooms in train stations, separate seats on all forms of transportation, separate drinking fountains, and even separate telephone booths. "Segregation was enforced at all places of public entertainment, including libraries, auditoriums, and circuses," Chief Justice Earl Warren noted. "There was segregation in the hospitals, prisons, mental institutions, and nursing homes. Even ambulance service was segregated."

HOW did the civil rights movement develop in the 1940s and 1950s?

Civil Rights as a Political Issue

Truman was the first president to attempt to alter the historic pattern of racial discrimination in the United States. In 1946, he appointed a presidential commission on civil rights. A year later, in a sweeping report titled "To Secure These Rights," the commission recommended the reinstatement of the wartime Fair Employment Practices Committee (FEPC), the establishment of a permanent civil rights commission, and the denial of federal aid to any state that condoned segregation in schools and public facilities. The president's ten-point legislative program proposed in 1948 included some of these measures, notably the establishment of a permanent FEPC and a civil rights commission. But southern resistance had blocked any action by Congress, and the inclusion of a strong civil rights plank in the 1948 Democratic platform had led to the walkout of some southern delegations and a separate States' Rights (Dixiecrat) ticket in several states of the South that fall.

African American voters in the North overwhelmingly backed Truman over Dewey in the 1948 election. The African American vote in key cities—Los Angeles, Cleveland, and Chicago—ensured the Democratic victory in California, Ohio, and Illinois. Truman responded by including civil rights legislation in his Fair Deal program in 1949. Once again, however, determined southern opposition blocked congressional action on both a permanent FEPC and an anti-lynching measure.

DOCUMENT

Executive
Order 9981
(1948)

Even though President Truman was unable to secure any significant legislation, he did succeed in adding civil rights to the liberal agenda. From this time forward, it would be an integral part of the Democratic reform program. Also, Truman used his executive power to assist African Americans. He strengthened the civil rights division of the Justice Department, which aided black groups in their efforts to challenge school segregation and restrictive housing covenants in the courts. Most important, in 1948 Truman issued an order calling for the desegregation of the armed forces. The navy and the air force quickly complied, but the army resisted until the personnel needs of the Korean War finally overcame the military's objections. By the end of the 1950s, the armed forces had become far more integrated than American society at large.

QUICK CHECK ✓

How did civil rights shape the politics of the postwar years?

Desegregating the Schools

The nation's schools soon became the primary target of civil rights advocates. The NAACP concentrated first on universities, successfully waging an intensive legal battle to win admission for qualified African Americans to graduate and professional schools. Led by Thurgood Marshall, NAACP lawyers then took on the broader issue of segregation in the country's public schools. Challenging the 1896 Supreme Court decision that upheld the constitutionality of separate but equal public facilities, Marshall argued that even substantially equal but separate schools did profound psychological damage to African American children and thus violated the Fourteenth Amendment.

The Supreme Court was unanimous in its 1954 decision in the case of **Brown v. Board of Education of Topeka.** Chief Justice Earl Warren, recently appointed by President Eisenhower, wrote the landmark opinion flatly declaring that "separate educational facilities are inherently unequal." To divide grade school children "solely because of their race," Warren argued, "generates a feeling of inferiority as to their status in the community that may affect their hearts and minds in a way unlikely ever to be undone." Despite this sweeping language, Warren realized it would be difficult to change historic patterns of segregation quickly. Accordingly, in 1955 the Court ruled that desegregation of the schools should proceed "with all deliberate speed" and left the details to the lower federal courts.

"All deliberate speed" proved to be agonizingly slow. Officials in the border states quickly complied with the Court's ruling, but states deeper in the South responded with a policy of massive resistance. Local white citizens' councils organized to fight for retention of racial separation; 101 representatives and senators signed a Southern Manifesto in 1956 that denounced the *Brown* decision as "a clear abuse of judicial power." School boards, encouraged by this show of defiance, found a variety of ways to evade the Court's ruling. The most successful was the passage of pupil placement laws. These laws enabled local officials to assign individual students to schools on the basis of scholastic aptitude, ability to adjust, and "morals, conduct, health and personal standards." These stalling tactics led to long disputes in the federal courts; by the end of the decade, fewer than 1 percent of the black children in the Deep South attended school with whites.

A conspicuous lack of presidential support further weakened the desegregation effort. Dwight Eisenhower believed that people's attitudes could not be altered by "cold lawmaking"—only "by appealing to reason, by prayer, and by constantly working at it through our own efforts" could change be enacted. Quietly and unobtrusively, he worked to achieve desegregation in federal facilities, particularly

Brown v. Board of Education of Topeka

In 1954, the Supreme Court reversed the *Plessy v. Ferguson* decision (1896) that established the "separate but equal" doctrine. The *Brown* decision found segregation in schools inherently unequal and initiated a long and difficult effort to integrate the nation's public schools.

Brown v. Board of Education of Topeka, Kansas (1954)

The Southern Manifesto (1956)

Cooper v. Aaron, 358 U.S.C. 1 (1958)

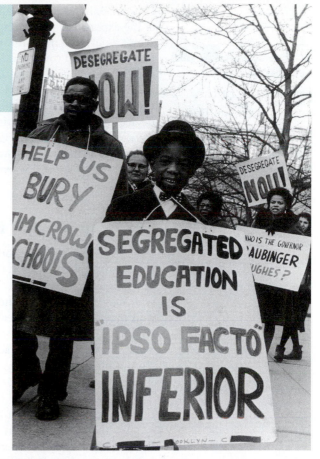

Demonstrators bearing signs in support of the Supreme Court's 1954 *Brown* v. *Board of Education* ruling to desegregate the nation's schools. The ruling also sparked protests, many of them violent and destructive, from opponents of integration.

Why did a school case get people so upset?

in veterans' hospitals, navy yards, and the District of Columbia school system. Yet he refrained from endorsing the Brown decision, which he told an aide he believed had "set back progress in the South at least fifteen years."

Southern leaders mistook Ike's silence for tacit support of segregation. In 1957, Governor Orval Faubus of Arkansas called out the National Guard to prevent the integration of Little Rock's Central High School on grounds of a threat to public order. After 270 armed troops turned back 9 young African American students, a federal judge ordered the guardsmen removed; but when the black students entered the school, a mob of 500 jeering whites surrounded the building. Eisenhower, who had told Faubus that "the Federal Constitution will be upheld by me by every legal means at my command," sent in 1000 paratroopers to ensure the rights of the Little Rock Nine to attend Central High. The students finished the school year under armed guard. Then Little Rock authorities closed Central High School for the next two years; when it reopened, there were only three African Americans in attendance.

Despite the snail's pace of school desegregation, the *Brown* decision led to other advances. In 1957, the Eisenhower administration proposed the first general civil rights legislation since Reconstruction. Senate Majority Leader

Nine African American students who enrolled at Little Rock's Central High School in 1957 are shown at the end of a school day with paratrooper guards. The Arkansas National Guard, acting on orders from the state's governor Orval Faubus, had refused the students entry into the school.

How do you think the students felt about all this?

Lyndon B. Johnson overcame strong southern resistance to avoid a filibuster, but at the expense of weakening the measure considerably. The final act, however, did create a permanent Commission for Civil Rights, one of Truman's original goals. It also provided for federal efforts aimed at "securing and protecting the right to vote." A second civil rights act in 1960 slightly strengthened the voting rights section.

Like the desegregation effort, the attempt to ensure African American voting rights in the South was still largely symbolic. Southern registrars used a variety of devices, ranging from intimidation to unfair tests, to deny African Americans suffrage. Yet the actions of Congress and the Supreme Court marked a vital turning point in national policy toward racial justice.

QUICK CHECK ✔

What was the importance of the case of *Brown v. Board of Education of Topeka?*

MAP

Civil Rights Movement

The Beginnings of Black Activism

The most dynamic force for change came from African Americans themselves. The shift from legal struggles in the courts to protest in the streets began with an incident in Montgomery, Alabama. On December 1, 1955, Rosa Parks—a black seamstress who had been active in the local NAACP chapter—violated a city ordinance by refusing to give up her seat to a white person on a local bus. Her action, often viewed as spontaneous, grew out of a long tradition of black protest against the rigid segregation of the races in the South. Rosa Parks herself had been ejected from a bus a decade earlier for refusing to obey the driver's command, "Niggers move back." In 1953, black church leaders in Baton Rouge, Louisiana, had mounted a weeklong boycott of that city's bus system and succeeded in modifying the traditional segregated seating rules.

In Montgomery, Rosa Parks's arrest sparked a massive protest movement. Black women played a particularly important role in the protest, printing and handing out 50,000 leaflets to rally the African American community behind Parks. The movement also led to the emergence of Martin Luther King, Jr., as an eloquent new spokesman for African Americans.

King agreed to lead the subsequent bus boycott. The son of a famous Atlanta preacher, he had recently taken his first church in Montgomery after years of studying theology while earning a Ph.D. at Boston University. Now he would be able to combine his wide learning with his charismatic appeal in behalf of a practical goal—fair treatment for the African Americans who made up the bulk of the riders on the city's buses.

Montgomery bus boycott

In late 1955, African Americans led by Martin Luther King, Jr., boycotted the buses in Montgomery, Alabama, after seamstress Rosa Parks was arrested for refusing to move to the back of a bus. The boycott, which ended when the Supreme Court ruled in favor of the protesters, marked the beginning of a new, activist phase of the civil rights movement.

The **Montgomery bus boycott** started out with a modest goal. Instead of challenging the legality of segregated seating, King simply asked that seats be taken on a first-come, first-served basis, with African Americans being seated from the back and the whites from the front of each bus. As the protest continued, however, and as they endured both legal harassment and sporadic acts of violence, the protesters began to be more assertive. An effective system of car pools enabled them to avoid using the city buses. Soon they were insisting on a complete end to segregated seating as they sang their new song of protest:

Ain't gonna ride them buses no more
Ain't gonna ride no more
Why in the hell don't the white folk know
That I ain't gonna ride no more.

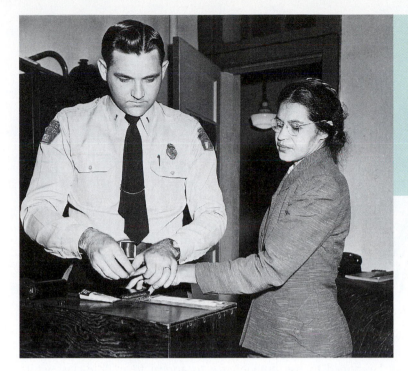

Rosa Parks's refusal to surrender her seat to a white man on a Montgomery, Alabama, bus led to a citywide bus boycott that brought Rev. Martin Luther King, Jr., to prominence as a leader of the civil rights movement. Parks remained active in the movement as well; she is shown here being fingerprinted in February 1956 after her arrest for violating an antiboycott law.

What role did women in general play in the civil rights movement?

The boycott ended in victory a year later when the Supreme Court ruled the Alabama segregated seating law unconstitutional. The protest movement had triumphed, not only in denting the wall of southern segregation, but in featuring the leadership of Martin Luther King, Jr. He had emerged as the charismatic leader of a new civil rights movement—a man who won acclaim not only at home but around the world. A year after the successful bus boycott, King founded the **Southern Christian Leadership Conference (SCLC)** to direct the crusade against segregation. He visited Third World leaders in Africa and Asia and paid homage to India's Mahatma Gandhi, who had influenced his reliance on civil disobedience. He led a triumphant Prayer Pilgrimage to Washington in 1957 on the third anniversary of the *Brown* decision, stirring the crowd of thirty thousand with his ringing demand for the right to vote. His cry "Give us the ballot" boomed in salvos that civil rights historian Taylor Branch likened to "cannon bursts in a diplomatic salute." His remarkable voice became familiar to the entire nation. Unlike many African American preachers, he never shouted, yet he captured his audience by presenting his ideas with both passion and a compelling cadence. "Though still a boy to many of his older listeners," Branch noted, "he had the commanding air of a burning sage."

Even more important, he had a strategy and message that fitted perfectly with the plight of his followers. Drawing on sources as diverse as Gandhi and Henry David Thoreau, King came out of the bus boycott with the concept of passive resistance. "If cursed," he had told protesters in Montgomery, "do not curse back. If struck, do not strike back, but evidence love and goodwill at all times."

Southern Christian Leadership Conference (SCLC)

An organization founded by Martin Luther King, Jr., to direct the crusade against segregation. Its weapon was passive resistance that stressed nonviolence and love, and its tactic was direct, though peaceful, confrontation.

In February 1960, black students from North Carolina A&T College staged a sit-in at a "whites only" Woolworth's lunch counter in Greensboro, North Carolina. Their act of nonviolent protest spurred similar demonstrations in public spaces across the South.

How important was it that the protests were nonviolent?

Student Nonviolent Coordinating Committee, Statement

Student Nonviolent Coordinating Committee (SNCC)

A radical group advocating black power. SNCC's leaders, scornful of integration and interracial cooperation, broke with Martin Luther King, Jr., to advocate greater militancy and acts of violence.

QUICK CHECK ✔

By what means did African American individuals and groups challenge segregation?

The essence of his strategy was to use the apparent weakness of southern blacks—their lack of power—and turn it into a conquering weapon. His message to southern whites was clear and unmistakable: "We will match your capacity to inflict suffering with our capacity to endure suffering. We will meet your physical force with soul force. We will not hate you, but we will not obey your evil laws. We will soon wear you down by pure capacity to suffer."

His ultimate goal was to unite the broken community through bonds of Christian love. He hoped to use nonviolence to appeal to middle-class white America, "to the conscience of the great decent majority who through blindness, fear, pride or irrationality have allowed their consciences to sleep." The result, King prophesied, would be to enable future historians to say of the effort, "There lived a great people—a black people—who injected new meaning and dignity into the veins of civilization."

King was not alone in championing the cause of civil rights. JoAnn Robinson helped pave the way in Montgomery with the Women's Political Caucus, and leaders as diverse as Bayard Rustin and Ella Baker were advancing the cause at the grassroots level.

In February 1960, another spontaneous event sparked a further advance for passive resistance. Four African American students from North Carolina Agricultural and Technical College sat down at a dime-store lunch counter in Greensboro, North Carolina, and refused to move after being denied service. Other students, both whites and blacks, joined in similar "sit-ins" across the South, as well as "kneel-ins" at churches and "wade-ins" at swimming pools. By the end of the year, some fifty thousand young people had succeeded in desegregating public facilities in more than a hundred southern cities. Several thousand of the demonstrators were arrested and put in jail, but the movement gained strength, leading to the formation of the **Student Nonviolent Coordinating Committee (SNCC)** in April 1960. From this time on, the SCLC and SNCC, with their tactic of direct, though peaceful, confrontation, would replace the NAACP and its reliance on court action in the forefront of the civil rights movement. The change would eventually lead to dramatic success for the movement, but it also ushered in a period of heightened tension and social turmoil in the 1960s.

Conclusion: Restoring National Confidence

In 1959 President Eisenhower appointed a Commission on National Goals "to develop a broad outline of national objectives for the next decade and longer." Ten prominent citizens from all walks of life, led by Henry W. Wriston of Brown University, issued a report that called for increased military spending abroad, greater economic growth at home, broader educational opportunities, and more government support for both scientific research and the advancement of the arts. The consensus seemed to be that rather than a change of direction, all the United States needed was a renewed commitment to the pursuit of excellence.

The 1950s ended with the national mood less troubled than when the decade began amid the turmoil of the second Red Scare and the Korean War, yet hardly as tranquil or confident as Eisenhower had hoped it would be. The American people felt reassured about the state of the economy, no longer fearing a return to the grim years of the Great Depression. At the same time, however, they were aware that abundance alone did not guarantee the quality of everyday life and realized that there was still a huge gap between American ideals and the reality of race relations, in the North as well as the South.

For a list of additional titles related to this chapter's topics, please see
www.pearsonamericanhistory.com.   MyHistoryLab

STUDY RESOURCES

KEY TERMS

Levittown, p. 781
baby boom, p. 782
Brown v. Board of Education of Topeka, p. 790

Montgomery bus boycott, p. 792
Southern Christian Leadership Conference (SCLC), p. 793

Student Nonviolent Coordinating Committee (SNCC), p. 794

CHAPTER REVIEW

HOW did the American economy evolve in the years after World War II?

The American economy boomed after World War II, as the nation recovered from the Great Depression and the war. The GNP doubled between 1940 and 1960, with individuals spending heavily on housing, automobiles, and other consumer goods, and the government spending heavily on defense. New communities emerged in the suburbs of old cities and in the Sunbelt states of the West and South. *(p. 783)*

WHAT changes marked American culture after the war?

American culture reflected both the promise of material prosperity and the failure of material goods to yield true happiness. More people went to church than ever; more young people went to college. Television provided endless information and entertainment. But suburban life exhibited a shallow sameness that prompted critics to wonder if it all was worthwhile. *(p. 786)*

HOW did the civil rights movement develop in the 1940s and 1950s?

Civil rights became a major issue in the period after World War II. Truman desegregated the military, and federal courts ordered the desegregation of schools. Black activists such as Rosa Parks and Martin Luther King, Jr., led protests against segregation on buses and in other areas of public life. Students organized sit-ins at lunch counters and parks. *(p. 789)*

MAKING CONNECTIONS

1. What are some advantages of suburban life? What are some disadvantages?
2. Did television bring Americans together, or drive them apart?
3. Were the civil rights marchers justified in breaking Jim Crow laws?

PRACTICE QUIZ

1. The _____ started at the end of World War II and lasted until the early 1960s.
   a. Baby boom
   b. Cold War
   c. Evangelical movement
   d. Civil Rights movement

2. The _____ rebelled against the materialistic society of the 1950s.
   a. Hippies
   b. Yuppies
   c. Progressives
   d. Beats

3. In the 1954 case of _____, the Supreme Court ruled that segregated schools were unconstitutional.
   a. *Plessy v. Ferguson*
   b. *Brown v. Board of Education of Topeka*
   c. *Roe v. Wade*
   d. *McCullough v. Maryland*

4. The _____ evolved into the first successful event of the modern civil rights movement.
   a. Selma March
   b. Freedom Rides
   c. Montgomery Bus Boycott
   d. Little Rock High School integration

5. The _____ formed in 1960 and was composed of young people dedicated to overcoming racism and segregation in the South.
   a. Southern Christian Leadership Conference
   b. Ku Klux Klan
   c. Student Nonviolent Coordinating Committee
   d. Black Panthers

6. The automobile and suburb intersected in all of the following ways *except*
   a. The car enabled suburban dads to remain at home longer during the day.
   b. Highways near suburbs meant many children had to ride the bus to school.
   c. Two cars became a necessity because multiple children needed transportation to a bevy of after-school activities.
   d. Suburban communities *depended* on cars.

7. All of the following describe the history of the television industry during the decade *except*
   a. TV boomed in the 1950s after a shaky start during the late 1940s.
   b. TV pushed radio aside and undermined many magazines.
   c. Advertisers soon took charge of the new medium.
   d. Shows stressed *artistic* creativity.

8. Which of the following *does not* accurately describe the development of religion in the United States during the 1950s?
   a. Organized religion flourished during the decade.
   b. Radical forms of fundamentalism did not spread rapidly.
   c. Church and synagogue membership rose.
   d. Observers claimed that religious affiliation was now the primary identifying feature of modern American life.

9. Which of the following became an important publication for women during the era?
   a. Dr. Benjamin Spock's *Baby and Child Care*
   b. *McCall's* magazine
   c. *Good Housekeeping* magazine
   d. All of the above answers are accurate.

10. Which of the following does *not* accurately explain the participation of women in the workforce during the decade?
    a. The number of working wives doubled between 1940 and 1960.
    b. By 1960, forty percent of American women had jobs outside the home.
    c. Less than one-fourth of all married women worked outside the home by 1960.
    d. Women worked outside of the home to augment family income.

Find more practice at
www.myhistorylab.com

SAMPLE ESSAY QUESTIONS

1. Describe how Levittown symbolized important historical trends of the 1950s.

2. Discuss the gains made by African Americans in the early civil rights movement.

Answers to Practice Quiz 1. a, *p. 782* 2. d, *p. 788* 3. b, *p. 790* 4. c, *p. 792* 5. c, *p. 794* 6. a, *p. 785* 7. d, *p. 787* 8. b, *p. 786* 9. d, *p. 786* 10. c, *p. 786*

Study Resources **797**

The Turbulent Sixties
1960–1968

Robert Rauschenberg memorialized some of the events of the 1960s in this screen print (*Signs, 1970*). (*Source: Robert Rauschenberg, Signs, 1970. © Robert Rauschenberg/Licensed by VAGA, New York, NY.*)

How does the image reveal the confusion of the time?

Kennedy versus Nixon: The First Televised Presidential Candidate Debate

On Monday evening, September 26, 1960, John F. Kennedy and Richard M. Nixon faced each other in the nation's first televised debate between two presidential candidates. Kennedy, the relatively unknown Democratic challenger, had proposed the debates; Nixon, confident of his mastery of television, had accepted even though, as Eisenhower's vice president and the early front-runner in the election, he had more to lose and less to gain.

Richard Nixon arrived an hour early at the CBS studio in Chicago, looking tired and ill at ease. He was still recovering from a knee injury that had slowed his campaign and left him pale and weak as

KEY EVENTS

Kennedy-
Nixon
Debate

New Frontier

The New Frontier was the campaign program advocated by John F. Kennedy in the 1960 election. He promised to revitalize the stagnant economy and enact reform legislation in education, health care, and civil rights.

he pursued a hectic catch-up schedule. Makeup experts offered to hide Nixon's heavy beard and soften his prominent jowls, but the GOP candidate declined, preferring to let an aide apply a light coat of Max Factor's "Lazy Shave," a pancake cosmetic. John Kennedy, tanned from open-air campaigning in California and rested by a day spent nearly free of distracting activity, wore very light makeup. He also changed from a gray to a dark blue suit better adapted to the intense television lighting.

At 8:30 P.M. central time, moderator Howard K. Smith welcomed a viewing audience estimated at seventy-seven million. Kennedy led off, echoing Abraham Lincoln by saying that the nation faced the question of "whether the world will exist half-slave and half-free." Although the ground rules limited the first debate to domestic issues, Kennedy argued that foreign and domestic policy were inseparable. He accused the Republicans of letting the country drift at home and abroad. "I think it's time America started moving again," he concluded. Nixon, caught off guard, seemed to agree with Kennedy's assessment of the nation's problems, but he contended that he had better solutions. "Our disagreement," the vice president pointed out, "is not about the goals for America but only about the means to reach those goals."

For the rest of the hour, the two candidates answered questions from a panel of journalists. Radiating confidence and self-assurance, Kennedy used a flow of statistics and details to create the image of a man deeply knowledgeable about all aspects of government. Nixon fought back with a defense of the Eisenhower record, but he seemed nervous and unsure of himself. The reaction shots of each candidate listening to the other's remarks showed Kennedy calm and serene, Nixon tense and uncomfortable.

Polls taken during the following few weeks revealed a sharp swing to Kennedy. Many Democrats and independents who had thought him too young or too inexperienced were impressed by his performance. Nixon suffered more from his unattractive image than from what he said; those who heard the debate on radio thought the Republican candidate more than held his own. In the three additional debates held during the campaign, Nixon improved his performance notably, wearing makeup to soften his appearance and taking the offensive from Kennedy on the issues. But the damage had been done. A postelection poll revealed that of four million voters who were influenced by the debates, three million voted for Kennedy.

The televised debates were only one of many factors influencing the outcome of the 1960 election. In essence, Kennedy won because he took full advantage of all his opportunities. Lightly regarded by Democratic leaders, he won the nomination by appealing to the rank and file in the primaries, but then he astutely chose Lyndon Johnson of Texas as his running mate to blunt Nixon's southern strategy.

During the fall campaign, Kennedy exploited the national mood of frustration that had followed *Sputnik.* At home, he promised to stimulate the lagging economy and carry forward long-overdue reforms in education, health care, and civil rights under the banner of the **New Frontier.** Abroad, he pledged a renewed commitment to the

Cold War, vowing he would lead the nation to victory over the Soviet Union. He met the issue of his Catholicism head on, telling a group of Protestant ministers in Houston that as president he would always place country above religion. In the shrewdest move of all, he won over African American voters by helping to secure the release of Martin Luther King, Jr., from a Georgia jail where the civil rights leader was being held on a trumped-up charge.

The Democratic victory in 1960 was paper-thin. Kennedy's edge in the popular vote was only two-tenths of 1 percent, and his wide margin in the electoral college (303 to 219) was tainted by voting irregularities in several states—notably Illinois and Texas—which went Democratic by very slender majorities. Yet even though he had no mandate, Kennedy's triumph did mark a sharp political shift. In contrast to the aging Eisenhower, Kennedy symbolized youth, energy, and ambition. His mastery of the new medium of television reflected his sensitivity to the changes taking place in American life in the 1960s. He came to office promising reform at home and advances abroad. Over the next eight years, he and Lyndon Johnson achieved many of their goals. Yet the nation also became engulfed in angry protests, violent demonstrations, and sweeping social change in one of the stormiest decades in American history.

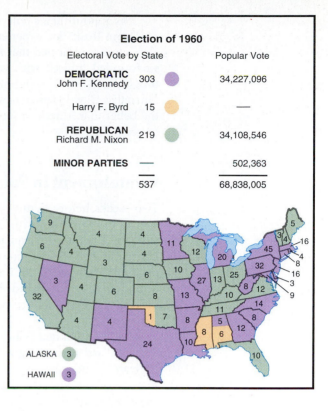

Kennedy Intensifies the Cold War

John F. Kennedy was determined to succeed where he believed Eisenhower had failed. Critical of his predecessor for holding down defense spending and apparently allowing the Soviet Union to open up a dangerous lead in nuclear missiles, Kennedy sought to warn the nation of its peril and lead it to victory in the Cold War.

In his inaugural address, the young president sounded the alarm. Ignoring the domestic issues aired during the campaign, he dealt primarily with the world. "Let every nation know, whether it wishes us well or ill, that we shall pay any price, bear any burden, meet any hardship, support any friend, oppose any foe," Kennedy declared, "to assure the survival and success of liberty. We will do all this and more."

From the day he took office, John F. Kennedy gave foreign policy top priority. In part, the decision reflected the perilous world situation, the immediate dangers ranging from troubles over Berlin to the emergence of Fidel Castro as a Soviet ally in Cuba. But it also corresponded to Kennedy's personal priorities. As a congressman and senator, he had been an intense cold warrior. Bored by committee work and legislative details, he had focused on foreign policy in the Senate, gaining a seat on the Foreign Relations Committee and publishing a book of speeches, *The Strategy of Peace*, in early 1960.

HOW

did the Cold War intensify under Kennedy?

John F. Kennedy, Inaugural Address (1961)

His appointments reflected his determination to win the Cold War. His choice of Dean Rusk, an experienced but unassertive diplomat, to head the State Department indicated that Kennedy planned to be his own secretary of state. He surrounded himself with young pragmatic advisers who prided themselves on toughness. These New Frontiersmen, later dubbed "the best and the brightest" by journalist David Halberstam, all shared a hard-line view of the Soviet Union and the belief that American security depended on superior force and the willingness to use it.

Containment in Southeast Asia

Two weeks before Kennedy's inauguration, Soviet Premier Khrushchev gave a speech in Moscow in which he declared Soviet support for "wars of national liberation." The Russian leader's words were actually aimed more at China than the United States; the two powerful communist nations were now rivals for influence in the Third World. But the new American president, ignoring the growing Sino-Soviet split, concluded the United States and Russia were locked in a struggle for the hearts and minds of the uncommitted in Asia, Africa, and Latin America.

Calling for a new policy of nation building, Kennedy advocated financial and technical assistance designed to help Third World nations achieve economic modernization and stable pro-Western governments. Measures ranging from the formation of the idealistic Peace Corps to the ambitious Alliance for Progress—a massive economic aid program for Latin America—were part of this effort. Unfortunately, Kennedy relied even more on counterinsurgency and the Green Berets to beat back the communist challenge in the Third World.

Southeast Asia offered the gravest test. After Vietnam gained independence from France in the mid-1950s, an anti-communist government emerged in the southern part of the country, under Ngo Dinh Diem. A communist regime, headed by Ho Chi Minh, controlled the north. The United States supported Diem and South Vietnam, and opposed Ho and North Vietnam.

When Kennedy entered the White House, North Vietnam was directing the efforts of Vietcong rebels in the South. As the guerrilla war intensified in the fall of 1961, the president sent two trusted advisers, Walt Rostow and General Maxwell Taylor, to South Vietnam. They returned favoring the dispatch of eight thousand American combat troops. "As an area for the operation of U.S. troops," reported General Taylor, "SVN [South Vietnam] is not an excessively difficult or unpleasant place to operate.... The risks of backing into a major Asian war by way of SVN are present but are not impressive."

The president decided against sending in combat troops in 1961, but he authorized substantial increases in economic aid to Diem and in the size of the military mission in Saigon. The number of American advisers in Vietnam grew from fewer than one thousand in 1961 to more than sixteen thousand by late 1963. The flow of supplies and the creation of "strategic hamlets," fortified villages designed to protect the peasantry from the Vietcong, slowed the communist momentum. American helicopters gave government forces mobility against the Vietcong, but by 1963, the situation had again become critical. Diem had failed to win the support of his own people; Buddhist monks set themselves aflame in public protests against him; and even Diem's own generals plotted his overthrow.

Flames engulf a Buddhist monk, the Reverend Quang Duc, who set himself afire at an intersection in Saigon, Vietnam, to protest persecution of Buddhists by Vietnam president Ngo Dinh Diem and his government.

What was the political effect of this protest?

President Kennedy was in a quandary. He realized that the fate of South Vietnam would be determined not by America but by the Vietnamese. "In the final analysis," he said in September 1963, "it is their war. They are the ones who have to win it or lose it." But at the same time, Kennedy was not prepared to accept the possible loss of all Southeast Asia. Saying it would be "a great mistake" to withdraw from South Vietnam, he told reporters, "Strongly on our mind is what happened in the case of China at the end of World War II, where China was lost. We don't want that." Although aides later claimed he planned to pull out after the 1964 election, Kennedy raised the stakes by tacitly approving a coup that led to Diem's overthrow and death on November 1, 1963. The resulting power vacuum in Saigon made further American involvement in Vietnam almost certain.

QUICK CHECK
What was Kennedy's dilemma in Vietnam?

Containing Castro: The Bay of Pigs Fiasco

Kennedy's determination to check global communist expansion reached a peak of intensity in Cuba. In the 1960 campaign, pointing to the growing ties between the Soviet Union and Fidel Castro's regime, he had accused the Republicans of permitting a "communist satellite" to arise on "our very doorstep." Kennedy had even issued a statement backing "anti-Castro forces in exile," calling them "fighters for freedom" who held out hope for "overthrowing Castro."

In reality, the Eisenhower administration had been training a group of Cuban exiles in Guatemala since March 1960 as part of a CIA plan to topple the Castro regime. Eisenhower had employed the CIA before, to oust the unfriendly regimes in Iran in 1953 and in Guatemala in 1954. The success of those operations caused Eisenhower and then Kennedy to dismiss skeptics who thought Castro would be harder to overthrow, and who contended that, in any case, covert operations damaged

America's reputation. Senator J. William Fulbright of Arkansas, Chairman of the Foreign Relations Committee, was especially critical. "The Castro regime is a thorn in the flesh," Fulbright argued, "but it is not a dagger in the heart." Kennedy, however, committed by his own campaign rhetoric and assured of success by the military, decided to proceed.

On April 17, 1961, fourteen hundred Cuban exiles moved ashore at the Bay of Pigs on the southern coast of Cuba. Even though the United States had master-minded the entire operation, Kennedy insisted on covert action, even canceling at the last minute a planned American air strike on the beachhead. With air superi-ority, Castro's well-trained forces had no difficulty in quashing the invasion. They killed nearly five hundred exiles and forced the rest to surrender within forty-eight hours, in what became known as the Bay of Pigs.

Aghast at the swiftness of the defeat, President Kennedy took personal responsibility for the **Bay of Pigs.** In his address to the American people, however, he showed no remorse for arranging the violation of a neighboring country's sovereignty, only regret at the outcome. Above all, he expressed renewed defiance, warning the Soviets that "our restraint is not inexhaustible." He went on to assert that the United States would resist "communist penetration" in the Western Hemisphere, terming it part of the "primary obligations… to the security of our nation." For the remainder of his presidency, Kennedy continued to harass the Castro regime, imposing an economic blockade on Cuba, supporting a continuing series of raids by exile groups operating out of Florida, and failing to stop the CIA from experimenting with bizarre plots to assassinate Fidel Castro.

Bay of Pigs

In April 1961, a group of Cuban exiles organized and supported by the U.S. Central Intelligence Agency (CIA) landed on the southern coast of Cuba in an effort to overthrow Fidel Castro. When the invasion ended in disaster, President Kennedy took full responsibility for the failure.

QUICK CHECK ✔

What was the Bay of Pigs affair?

Containing Castro: The Cuban Missile Crisis

The climax of Kennedy's crusade came in October 1962 with the **Cuban missile crisis.** Throughout the summer and early fall, the Soviets engaged in a massive arms buildup in Cuba, ostensibly to protect Castro from an American invasion. In the United States, Republican candidates in the 1962 congressional elections called for a firm American response; Kennedy contented himself with a stern warning against the introduction of any offensive weapons, believing their presence would directly threaten American security. Khrushchev publicly denied any such intent, but secretly he took a daring gamble, building sites for twenty-four medium-range (1000-mile) and eighteen intermediate-range (2000-mile) missiles in Cuba. Later he claimed his purpose was purely defensive, but most likely he was responding to the pressures from his own military to close the enormous strategic gap in nuclear striking power that Kennedy had opened.

Cuban missile crisis

In October 1962, the United States and the Soviet Union came close to nuclear war when President Kennedy insisted that Nikita Khrushchev remove the 42 missiles he had secretly deployed in Cuba. The Soviets eventually did so, nuclear war was averted, and the crisis ended.

Executive Discussions on the Cuban Missile Crisis (1962)

Unfortunately, the Kennedy administration had stopped overflights of Cuba by U-2 spy planes in August. Fearful that recently installed Soviet surface-to-air missiles could bring down the American spy plane and create an international incident, the White House, over the objections of CIA Director John McCone, limited U-2 flights to the air space bordering the island. McCone finally prevailed on the president to resume direct overflights, and on October 14 the first such mission brought back indisputable photographic evidence of the missile sites, which were nearing completion.

As soon as President Kennedy was informed of this development, he decided to keep it secret while he consulted with a hand-picked group of advisers to consider how to respond. In the ExComm, as this group became known, the initial preference for an immediate air strike gradually gave way to discussion of either a full-scale invasion of Cuba or a naval blockade of the island. The president and his advisers ruled out diplomacy, rejecting a proposal to offer the withdrawal of obsolete American Jupiter missiles from Turkey in return for a similar Russian pullout in Cuba. Kennedy finally agreed to a two-step procedure. He would proclaim a quarantine of Cuba to prevent the arrival of new missiles and threaten a nuclear confrontation to force the removal of those already there. If the Russians did not cooperate, then the United States would invade Cuba and dismantle the missiles by force.

On the evening of October 22, the president informed the nation of the existence of the Soviet missiles and his plans to remove them. He blamed Khrushchev for "this clandestine, reckless, and provocative threat to world peace," and he made it clear that any missile attack from Cuba would lead to "a full retaliatory response upon the Soviet Union."

For the next six days, the world hovered on the brink of nuclear catastrophe. Khrushchev replied defiantly, accusing Kennedy of pushing mankind "to the abyss of a world nuclear-missile war." In the Atlantic, some sixteen Soviet ships continued on course toward Cuba, while the American navy was deployed to intercept them five hundred miles from the island. In Florida, nearly a quarter million men were being concentrated in the largest invasion force ever assembled in the continental United States.

John F. Kennedy, Cuban Missile Crisis Address

The first break came at midweek when the Soviet ships suddenly halted to avert a confrontation at sea. "We're eyeball to eyeball," commented Secretary of State Dean Rusk, "and I think the other fellow just blinked." On Friday, Khrushchev sent Kennedy a long, rambling letter offering a face-saving way out: Russia would remove the missiles in return for an American promise never to invade Cuba. The president was ready to accept when a second Russian message raised the stakes by insisting that American Jupiter missiles be withdrawn from Turkey. Heeding the advice of his brother, attorney general Robert Kennedy, the president refused to bargain; Khrushchev had endangered world peace by putting the missiles in Cuba secretly, and he must take them out immediately. Nevertheless, while the military went ahead with plans for the invasion of Cuba, the president, heeding his brother's advice, decided to make one last appeal for peace. Ignoring the second Russian message, he sent a cable to Khrushchev accepting his original offer.

On Saturday night, October 27, Robert Kennedy met with Soviet ambassador Anatoly Dobrynin to make clear it was the last chance to avert nuclear confrontation. "We had to have a commitment by tomorrow that those bases would be removed," Robert Kennedy recalled telling him. "He should understand that if they did not remove those bases, we would remove them." Then the president's brother calmly remarked that if Khrushchev did not back down, "there would be not only dead Americans but dead Russians as well."

In reality, John F. Kennedy was not quite so ready to risk nuclear war. He instructed his brother to assure Dobrynin that the Jupiter missiles would soon be removed from Turkey. The president preferred that the missile swap be done privately, but twenty-five years later, Secretary of State Dean Rusk revealed that JFK had instructed him to arrange a deal through the United Nations involving "the removal of both the Jupiters and the missiles in Cuba." In recently released transcripts of his meetings with his advisers, the president reaffirmed his intention of making a missile trade with Khrushchev publicly as a last resort to avoid nuclear war. "We can't very well invade Cuba with all its toil," he commented, "when we could have gotten them out by making a deal on the same missiles in Turkey."

Aerial photographs taken by a U-2 reconnaissance plane flying over Cuba revealed the presence of Russian missile sites under construction on the island. Recently released information about the type and number of Soviet nuclear warheads in Cuba reveals just how imminent was the threat of nuclear war had not the Soviets capitulated to U.S. demands for removal of the missiles.

Did Kennedy do the right thing in issuing his ultimatum?

President Kennedy never had to make this final concession. At nine the next morning, Khrushchev agreed to remove the missiles in return only for Kennedy's promise not to invade Cuba. The crisis was over.

The world, however, had come perilously close to a nuclear conflict. We now know the Soviets had nuclear warheads in Cuba, not only for twenty of the medium-range missiles, but also for short-range tactical launchers designed to be used against an American invading force. If Kennedy had approved the military's recommendations for an invasion of Cuba, the consequences might have been disastrous.

The peaceful resolution of the Cuban missile crisis became a personal and political triumph for Kennedy. His party successfully overcame the Republican challenge in the November elections, and his own popularity reached new heights. The American people, on the defensive since *Sputnik*, suddenly felt that they had proved their superiority over the Russians. Arthur Schlesinger, Jr., Kennedy's confidant and later his biographer, claimed that the Cuban crisis showed the "whole world… the ripening of an American leadership unsurpassed in the responsible management of power…. It was this combination of toughness and restraint, of will, nerve and wisdom, so brilliantly controlled, so matchlessly calibrated, that dazzled the world."

The Cuban missile crisis had more substantial results as well. Shaken by their close call, Kennedy and Khrushchev agreed to install a "hot line" to speed direct communication between Washington and Moscow in an emergency. Long-stalled negotiations over the reduction of nuclear testing suddenly resumed, leading to the limited test ban treaty of 1963, which outlawed tests in the atmosphere while still permitting them underground. Above all, Kennedy displayed a new maturity as a result of the crisis. In a speech at American University in June 1963, he shifted from the rhetoric of confrontation to that of conciliation. Speaking of the

Russians, he said, "Our most basic common link is the fact that we all inhabit this planet. We all breathe the same air. We all cherish our children's future. And we are all mortal."

Despite these hopeful words, the missile crisis also had an unfortunate consequence. Those who believed that the Russians understood only the language of force were confirmed in their penchant for a hard line. Hawks who had backed Kennedy's military buildup believed events had justified a policy of nuclear superiority. The Russian leaders drew similar conclusions. Aware the United States had a four-to-one advantage in nuclear striking power during the Cuban crisis, one Soviet official told his American counterpart, "Never will we be caught like this again." After 1962, the Soviets embarked on a crash program to build up their navy and to overtake the American lead in nuclear missiles. Within five years, they had the nucleus of a modern navy and had surpassed the United States in ICBMs. Kennedy's fleeting moment of triumph thus ensured the escalation of the arms race. His legacy was a bittersweet one of short-term success and long-term anxiety.

QUICK CHECK

What were the causes and consequences of the Cuban missile crisis?

The New Frontier at Home

Kennedy hoped to change the course of history at home as well as abroad. His election marked the arrival of a new generation of leadership. For the first time, people born in the twentieth century who had entered political life after World War II were in charge of national affairs. Kennedy's inaugural call to get the nation moving again was particularly attractive to young people, who had shunned political involvement during the Eisenhower years.

The new administration reflected Kennedy's aura of youth and energy. Major cabinet appointments went to activists—notably Connecticut governor Abraham Ribicoff as secretary of Health, Education, and Welfare; labor lawyer Arthur J. Goldberg as secretary of Labor; and Arizona congressman Stuart Udall as secretary of the Interior. The most controversial choice was Robert Kennedy, the president's brother, as attorney general. Critics scoffed at his lack of legal experience, leading JFK to note jokingly he wanted to give Bobby "a little experience before he goes out to practice law." In fact, the president prized his brother's loyalty and shrewd political advice.

Equally important were the members of the White House staff who handled domestic affairs. Like their counterparts in foreign policy, these New Frontiersmen—Kenneth O'Donnell, Theodore Sorensen, Richard Goodwin, and Walter Heller—prided themselves on being tough-minded and pragmatic. In contrast to Eisenhower, Kennedy relied heavily on academics and intellectuals to help him infuse the nation with energy and a new sense of direction.

Kennedy's greatest asset was his own personality. A cool, attractive, and intelligent man, he possessed a sense of style that endeared him to the American public. Encouraged by his wife, Jacqueline, the president invited artists and musicians as well as corporate executives to White House functions, and he sprinkled his speeches with references to Emerson and Shakespeare. He seemed to be a new Lancelot, bent on calling forth the best in national life; admirers likened

WHAT

?
was the "New Frontier," and what did it accomplish?

his inner circle to King Arthur's court at Camelot. Reporters loved him, both for his fact-filled and candid press conferences and for his witty comments. After an embarrassing foreign policy failure, when his standing in the polls actually went up, he remarked, "It's just like Eisenhower. The worse I do, the more popular I get."

Moving Slowly on Civil Rights

Kennedy faced a genuine dilemma over the issue of civil rights. Despite his own lack of a strong record while in the Senate, he had portrayed himself during the 1960 campaign as a crusader for African American rights. He had promised to launch an attack on segregation in the Deep South, but his fear of alienating the large bloc of southern Democrats forced him to downplay civil rights legislation.

The president's solution was to defer congressional action in favor of executive leadership in this area. He directed his brother, Attorney General Robert Kennedy, to continue and expand the Eisenhower administration's efforts to achieve voting rights for southern blacks. To register previously disfranchised citizens, the Justice Department worked with the civil rights movement—notably the Student Nonviolent Coordinating Committee (SNCC)—in the Deep South. In two years, the Kennedy administration increased the number of voting rights suits fivefold. Yet the attorney general could not force the FBI to provide protection for the civil rights volunteers who risked their lives by encouraging African Americans to register. "SNCC's only contact with federal authority," noted one observer,

Charles Sherrod, SNCC Memorandum (1961)

The attempts of African Americans to end discrimination and secure their civil rights met with violent resistance in Birmingham, Alabama, where police used snarling dogs, fire hoses, clubs, and electric cattle prods to turn back the unarmed demonstrators.

How did other Americans react to the harsh police tactics?

"consisted of the FBI agents who stood by taking notes while local policemen beat up SNCC members."

Other efforts had equally mixed results. Vice President Lyndon Johnson headed a presidential Commission on Equal Employment Opportunities that worked with defense industries and other government contractors to increase the number of jobs for African Americans. But a limited budget and a reliance on voluntary cooperation prevented any dramatic gains; African American employment improved only in direct proportion to economic growth in the early 1960s.

Kennedy did succeed in appointing a number of African Americans to high government positions: Robert Weaver became chief of the federal housing agency, and Thurgood Marshall, who pleaded the *Brown* v. *Topeka* school desegregation case before the Supreme Court, was named to the U.S. Circuit Court. On the other hand, among his judicial appointments, Kennedy included one Mississippi jurist who referred to African Americans in court as "niggers" and once compared them to "a bunch of chimpanzees."

The civil rights movement refused to accept Kennedy's indirect approach. In May 1961, the Congress of Racial Equality (CORE) sponsored a **freedom ride** in which a biracial group attempted to test a 1960 Supreme Court decision outlawing segregation in all bus and train stations used in interstate commerce. When they arrived in Birmingham, Alabama, the freedom riders were attacked by a mob of angry whites. The attorney general quickly dispatched several hundred federal marshals to protect the freedom riders, but the president was more upset at the distraction the protesters created. Kennedy directed one of his aides to get in touch with the leaders of CORE. "Tell them to call it off," he demanded. "Stop them."

In September, after the attorney general finally convinced the Interstate Commerce Commission to issue an order banning segregation in interstate terminals and buses, the freedom rides ended. The Kennedy administration then sought to prevent further confrontations by involving civil rights activists in its voting drive.

A pattern of belated reaction to southern racism marked the basic approach of the Kennedys. When James Meredith courageously sought admission to the all-white University of Mississippi in 1962, the president and the attorney general worked closely with Mississippi governor Ross Barnett to avoid violence. Despite Barnett's promise of cooperation, the night before Meredith enrolled at the University of Mississippi, a mob attacked the federal marshals and National Guard troops sent to protect him. The violence left 2 dead and 375 injured, including 166 marshals and 12 guardsmen, but Meredith attended the university and eventually graduated.

In 1963, Kennedy sent the deputy attorney general to face down Governor George C. Wallace, an avowed segregationist who had promised "to stand in the schoolhouse door" to prevent the integration of the University of Alabama. After a brief confrontation, Wallace yielded to federal authority, and two African American students peacefully desegregated the state university.

freedom ride
Bus trips taken by both black and white civil rights advocates in the 1960s. Sponsored by the Congress of Racial Equality (CORE), freedom rides in the South were designed to test the enforcement of federal regulations that prohibited segregation in interstate public transportation.

QUICK CHECK ✓
What was Kennedy's response to the civil rights movement?

"I Have a Dream"

Martin Luther King, Jr., finally forced Kennedy to abandon his cautious tactics and come out openly in behalf of racial justice. In the spring of 1963, King began a massive protest in Birmingham, one of the South's most segregated cities. Public

Civil Rights
March on
Washington

Reverend Martin Luther King, Jr., addresses the crowd at the March on Washington in August 1963. In his speech, King recounted the difficulties of blacks' struggle for freedom, then stirred the crowd with the description of his dream for America: "I have a dream that one day this nation will rise up and live out the true meaning of its creed—we hold these truths to be self-evident, that all men are created equal."

How did the march and speech reflect the spirit and determination of the civil rights movement?

marches and demonstrations aimed at integrating public facilities and opening up jobs for African Americans quickly led to police harassment and many arrests, including that of King himself. Police Commissioner Eugene "Bull" Connor was determined to crush the civil rights movement; King was equally determined to prevail. Writing from his cell in Birmingham, he vowed an active campaign to bring the issue of racial injustice to national attention.

Bull Connor played directly into King's hands. On May 3, as six thousand children marched in place of the jailed protesters, authorities broke up a demonstration with clubs, snarling police dogs, and high-pressure water hoses strong enough to take the bark off a tree. With a horrified nation watching scene after scene of this brutality on television, the Kennedy administration quickly intervened to arrange a settlement with the Birmingham civic leaders that ended the violence and granted the protesters most of their demands.

More important, Kennedy finally ended his long hesitation and sounded the call for action. "We are confronted primarily with a moral issue," he told the nation on June 11. "It is as old as the Scriptures and is as clear as the American Constitution." Eight days later, the administration sponsored civil rights legislation providing equal access to all public accommodations as well as an extension of voting rights for African Americans.

Despite pleas from the government for an end to demonstrations and protests, civil rights leaders kept pressure on the administration. They scheduled a massive **March on Washington** for August 1963. On August 28, more than 200,000 marchers gathered for a daylong rally in front of the Lincoln Memorial where they listened to hymns, speeches, and prayers for racial justice. The climax of the event was Martin Luther King, Jr.'s eloquent description of his dream for America. It concluded:

When we let freedom ring, when we let it ring from every village and every hamlet, from every state and every city, we will be able to speed up that day when all God's children, black men and white men, Jews and Gentiles, Protestants and Catholics, will be able to join hands and sing, in the words of that old Negro spiritual, "Free at last! Free at last! Thank God almighty, we are free at last!"

March on Washington

In August 1963, civil rights leaders organized a massive rally in Washington to urge passage of President Kennedy's civil rights bill. The high point came when Martin Luther King, Jr., gave his "I Have a Dream" speech to more than 200,000 marchers in front of the Lincoln Memorial.

QUICK CHECK ✔

How did King's role evolve during the Kennedy years?

LBJ's Great Society

The New Frontier came to a sudden and violent end on November 22, 1963, when Lee Harvey Oswald assassinated Kennedy as the president rode in a motorcade in downtown Dallas. The shock of losing the young president, who had become a symbol of hope and promise for a whole generation, stunned the entire world. The American people were bewildered by the rapid sequence of events: the brutal killing of their young president; the televised slaying of Oswald by Jack Ruby in the basement of the Dallas police station; the composure and dignity of Kennedy's widow, Jacqueline, at the ensuing state funeral; and the hurried Warren Commission report, which identified Oswald as the lone assassin. Afterward, critics would charge that Oswald had been part of a vast conspiracy, but at the time, the prevailing national reaction was a numbing sense of loss.

Vice President Johnson moved quickly to fill the vacuum left by Kennedy's death. Sworn in on board Air Force One as he returned to Washington, Johnson soon met with a stream of world leaders to reassure them of American political stability. Five days after the tragedy in Dallas, Johnson spoke eloquently to a special joint session of Congress. Recalling JFK's inaugural summons, "Let us begin," the new president declared, "Today in the moment of new resolve, I would say to all my fellow Americans, 'Let us continue.'" Asking Congress to enact Kennedy's tax and civil rights bills as a tribute to the fallen leader, LBJ concluded, "Let us here highly resolve that John Fitzgerald Kennedy did not live or die in vain."

were Johnson's domestic priorities, and what were his achievements?

President Johnson Responds to the Death of JFK

Johnson in Action

Lyndon Johnson suffered from the inevitable comparison with his young and stylish predecessor. LBJ was acutely aware of his own lack of polish; he sought to surround himself with Kennedy advisers and insiders, hoping their sophistication would rub off on him. Johnson's assets were very real—he possessed an intimate knowledge of Congress, an incredible energy and determination to succeed, and a fierce ego. When a young marine officer tried to direct him to the proper helicopter, saying, "This one is yours," Johnson replied, "Son, they are *all* my helicopters."

LBJ's height and intensity gave him a powerful presence; he dominated any room he entered, and he delighted in using his physical power of persuasion. One Texas politician explained why he had given in to Johnson: "Lyndon got me by the lapels and put his face on top of mine and he talked and talked and talked. I figured it was either getting drowned or joining."

Yet LBJ found it impossible to project his intelligence and vitality to large audiences. Unlike Kennedy, he wilted before the camera, turning his televised speeches into stilted and awkward performances. Trying to belie his reputation as a riverboat gambler, he came across like a foxy grandpa, clever, calculating, and not to be trusted. He lacked Kennedy's wit and charm, and reporters delighted in describing the way he berated his aides or shocked the nation by baring his belly to show the scar from a recent operation.

Whatever his shortcomings in style, however, Johnson possessed far greater ability than Kennedy in dealing with Congress. He entered the White House with more than thirty years of experience in Washington as a legislative aide, congressman,

President Johnson applies the "Johnson treatment" to Senator Theodore Francis Green of Rhode Island. A shrewd politician and master of the legislative process, Johnson always knew which votes he could count on, those he couldn't, and where and how to apply pressure to swing votes his way.

Is the "treatment" working here?

and senator. His encyclopedic knowledge of the legislative process and his shrewd manipulation of individual senators had enabled him to become the most influential Senate majority leader in history. Famed for "the Johnson treatment," a legendary ability to use personal persuasion to reach his goals, Johnson in fact relied more on his close ties with the Senate's power brokers—or "whales," as he called them—than on his exploitation of the "minnows."

Above all, Johnson sought consensus. Indifferent to ideology, he had moved easily from New Deal liberalism to oil-and-gas conservatism as his career advanced. He had carefully cultivated Richard Russell of Georgia, leader of the Dixie bloc, but he also had taken Hubert Humphrey, a Minnesota liberal, under his wing. He had performed a balancing act on civil rights, working with the Eisenhower administration on behalf of the 1957 Voting Rights Act, yet carefully weakening it to avoid alienating southern Democrats. When Kennedy dashed Johnson's own intense presidential ambitions in 1960, LBJ had gracefully agreed to be his running mate and had endured the disappointment of the vice presidency loyally and silently. Suddenly thrust into power, Johnson used his gifts wisely. Citing his favorite scriptural passage from Isaiah, "Come now, and let us reason together, saith the Lord," he concentrated on securing passage of Kennedy's tax and civil rights bills in 1964.

The tax cut came first. Aware of the power wielded by Senate Finance Committee Chairman Harry Byrd, a Virginia conservative, Johnson astutely lowered Kennedy's projected $101.5 billion budget for 1965 to $97.9 billion. Although Byrd voted against the tax cut, he let the measure out of his committee, telling Johnson, "I'll be working for you behind the scenes." In February, Congress reduced personal income taxes by more than $10 billion, touching off a sustained economic boom. Consumer spending increased by an impressive $43 billion during the next eighteen months, and new jobs opened up at the rate of one million a year.

Johnson was even more influential in passing the Kennedy civil rights measure. Staying in the background, he encouraged liberal amendments that strengthened the bill in the House. With Hubert Humphrey leading the floor fight in the Senate, Johnson refused all efforts at compromise, counting on growing public pressure to force northern Republicans to abandon their traditional alliance with southern Democrats. Everett M. Dirksen of Illinois, the GOP leader in the Senate, met repeatedly with Johnson at the White House. When LBJ refused to yield, Dirksen finally led a Republican vote to end a 57-day filibuster.

The 1964 Civil Rights Act, signed on July 2, made illegal the segregation of African Americans in public facilities, established an Equal Employment Opportunity Commission to lessen racial discrimination in employment, and protected the voting rights of African Americans. An amendment sponsored by segregationists in an effort to weaken the bill added gender to the prohibition of discrimination in Title VII of the act; in the future, women's groups would use the clause to secure government support for greater equality in employment and education.

DOCUMENT

The Civil Rights Act of 1964

QUICK CHECK ✓

How did Johnson's personality influence his politics?

The Election of 1964

Passage of two key Kennedy measures within six months did not satisfy Johnson, who wanted now to win the presidency in his own right. Eager to surpass Kennedy's narrow victory in 1960, he hoped to win by a great landslide.

Searching for a cause of his own, LBJ found one in the issue of poverty. Beginning in the late 1950s, economists had warned that the prevailing affluence disguised a persistent and deep-seated problem of poverty. Johnson quickly took over proposals that Kennedy had been developing and made them his own. In his January 1964 State of the Union address, LBJ announced, "This administration, today, here and now, declares unconditional war on poverty in America." During the next eight months, Johnson fashioned a comprehensive poverty program under the direction of R. Sargent Shriver, Kennedy's brother-in-law. The president added $500 million to existing programs to come up with a $1 billion effort that Congress passed in August 1964.

DOCUMENT

Lyndon Johnson, "The War on Poverty" (1964)

The new Office of Economic Opportunity (OEO) set up a wide variety of programs, ranging from Head Start for preschoolers to the Job Corps for high

THE ELECTION OF 1964			
Candidate	**Party**	**Popular Vote**	**Electoral Vote**
Johnson	Democratic	43,126,506	486
Goldwater	Republican	27,176,799	52

school dropouts in need of vocational training. The emphasis was on self-help, with the government providing money and know-how so the poor could reap the benefits of neighborhood day care centers, consumer education classes, legal aid services, and adult remedial reading programs. The level of funding was never high enough to meet the OEO's ambitious goals, and a controversial attempt to include representatives of the poor in the Community Action Program led to bitter political feuding with city and state officials. Nonetheless, the **war on poverty**, along with the economic growth provided by the tax cut, helped reduce the ranks of the poor by nearly ten million between 1964 and 1967.

The new program established Johnson's reputation as a reformer in an election year, but he still faced two challenges to his authority. The first was Robert Kennedy, the late president's brother, who continued as attorney general but who wanted to become vice president and Johnson's eventual successor in the White House. Desperate to prove his ability to succeed without Kennedy help, LBJ commented, "I don't need that little runt to win" and chose Hubert Humphrey as his running mate.

The second challenge was the Republican candidate, Senator Barry Goldwater, an outspoken conservative from Arizona. An attractive and articulate man, Goldwater advocated a rejection of the welfare state and a return to unregulated free enterprise. To Johnson's delight, Goldwater chose to place ideology ahead of political expediency. The senator spoke out boldly against the Tennessee Valley Authority, denounced Social Security, and advocated a hawkish foreign policy. "In Your Heart, You Know He's Right," read the Republican slogan, leading the Democrats to reply, "Yes, Far Right," and in reference to a careless Goldwater comment about using nuclear weapons, Johnson backers punned, "In Your Heart, You Know He Might."

Johnson stuck carefully to the middle of the road, embracing the liberal reform program—which he now called the **Great Society**—while stressing his concern for balanced budgets and fiscal orthodoxy. The more Goldwater sagged in the polls, the harder Johnson campaigned, determined to achieve his treasured landslide. On election day, LBJ received 61.1 percent of the popular vote and an overwhelming majority in the electoral college; Goldwater carried only Arizona and five states of the Deep South. Equally important, the Democrats achieved huge gains in Congress, controlling the House by a margin of 295 to 140 and the Senate by 68 to 32. Kennedy's legacy and Goldwater's candor had enabled Johnson to break the conservative grip on Congress for the first time in a quarter century.

war on poverty

Lyndon Johnson declared war on poverty in his 1964 State of the Union address. A new Office of Economic Opportunity (OEO) oversaw a variety of programs to help the poor, including the Job Corps and Head Start.

Great Society

President Johnson called his version of the Democratic reform program the Great Society. In 1965, Congress passed many Great Society measures, including Medicare, civil rights legislation, and federal aid to education.

QUICK CHECK ✔

What were the key issues in the election of 1964?

The Triumph of Reform

LBJ moved quickly to secure his legislative goals. Despite solid majorities in both Houses, including seventy first-term Democrats who had ridden into office on his coattails, Johnson knew he would have to enact the Great Society as swiftly as possible. "You've got to give it all you can, that first year," he told an aide. "Doesn't matter what kind of majority you come in with. You've got just one year when they treat you right, and before they start worrying about themselves."

Johnson gave two traditional Democratic reforms—health care and education—top priority. Aware of strong opposition to a comprehensive medical program, LBJ settled for **Medicare,** which mandated health insurance under the Social Security program for Americans over age 65, and a supplementary Medicaid program for the poor. To symbolize the end of a long struggle, Johnson flew to

Medicare

The 1965 Medicare Act provided Social Security funding for hospitalization insurance for people over age 65 and a voluntary plan to cover doctor bills paid in part by the federal government.

Independence, Missouri, so Truman could witness the ceremonial signing of the Medicare law, which had its origins in Truman's 1949 health insurance proposal.

LBJ overcame the religious hurdle on education by supporting a child-benefit approach, allocating federal money to advance the education of students in parochial as well as public schools. The Elementary and Secondary Education Act of 1965 provided more than $1 billion in federal aid, the largest share going to school districts with the highest percentage of impoverished pupils.

Civil rights proved to be the most difficult test of Johnson's leadership. Martin Luther King, Jr., concerned that three million southern blacks were still denied the right to vote, in early 1965 chose Selma, Alabama, as the site for a test case. The white authorities in Selma, led by Sheriff James Clark, used cattle prods and bullwhips to break up the demonstrations. More than two thousand African Americans were jailed. Johnson intervened in March, after TV cameras showed Sheriff Clark's deputies brutally halting a march from Selma to Montgomery. The president ordered the Alabama National Guard to federal duty to protect the demonstrators, had the Justice Department draw up a new voting rights bill, and personally addressed the Congress on civil rights. "I speak tonight for the dignity of man and the destiny of democracy," he began. Calling the denial of the right to vote "deadly wrong," LBJ issued a compelling call to action. "Their cause must be our cause, too. Because it is not just Negroes, but really it is all of us who must overcome the crippling legacy of bigotry and injustice."

Five months later, Congress passed the **Voting Rights Act of 1965**. Once again Johnson had worked with Senate Republican leader Dirksen to break a southern filibuster and assure passage of a measure. The act banned literacy tests in states and counties in which less than half the population had voted in 1964 and provided for federal registrars in these areas to assure African Americans the franchise.

The results were dramatic. In less than a year, 166,000 African Americans were added to the voting rolls in Alabama; African American registration went up 400 percent in Mississippi. By the end of the decade, the percentage of eligible African American voters who had registered had risen from 40 to 65 percent. For the first time since Reconstruction, African Americans had become active participants in southern politics.

Before the 89th Congress ended its first session in the fall of 1965, it had passed eighty-nine bills. These included measures to create two new cabinet departments (Transportation and Housing and Urban Affairs); acts to provide for highway safety and to ensure clean air and water; large appropriations for higher education, public housing, and the continuing war on poverty; and sweeping immigration reform legislation. In nine months, Johnson had enacted the entire Democratic reform agenda.

The man responsible for this great leap forward, however, had failed to win the public adulation he so deeply desired. His legislative skills had made the most of the opportunities offered by the 1964 Democratic landslide, but the people did not respond to Johnson's leadership with the warmth and praise they had showered on Kennedy. Reporters continued to portray him as a crude wheeler-dealer; as a maniac who drove around Texas back roads at 90 miles an hour, one hand on the wheel and the other holding a can of beer; or as a bully who picked up his dog by the ears. No one was more aware of this lack of affection than LBJ himself. His public support, he told an aide, is "like a Western river, broad but not deep."

Johnson's realization of the fleeting nature of his popularity was all too accurate. The dilemmas of the Cold War began to divert his attention from domestic concerns and eventually, in the case of Vietnam, would overwhelm him. Yet his

Voting Rights Act of 1965

The 1965 Voting Rights Act effectively banned literacy tests for voting rights and provided for federal registrars to assure the franchise of minority voters. Within a few years, a majority of African Americans had become registered voters in the southern states.

Voting Literacy Test (1965)

Impact of the Voting Rights Act of 1965

legislative achievements were still remarkable. In one brief outburst of reform, he had accomplished more than any president since FDR.

Difficulties abroad would dim the luster of the Johnson presidency, but they could not diminish the lasting impact of the Great Society on American life. Federal aid to education, the enactment of Medicare and Medicaid, and, above all, the civil rights acts of 1964 and 1965 changed the nation irrevocably. The aged and the poor now were guaranteed access to medical care; communities saw an infusion of federal funds to improve local education; and African Americans could now begin to attend integrated schools, enjoy public facilities, and gain political power by exercising the right to vote. But even at this moment of triumph for liberal reform, new currents of dissent and rebellion were brewing.

QUICK CHECK ✓

What were the major reforms of Johnson's Great Society?

Johnson Escalates the Vietnam War

HOW did Johnson's Vietnam policy evolve?

Lyndon Johnson stressed continuity in foreign policy just as he had in enacting Kennedy's domestic reforms. He not only inherited the policy of containment from his fallen predecessor, but he shared the same Cold War assumptions and convictions. And, feeling less confident about dealing with international issues, he tended to rely heavily on Kennedy's advisers—notably Secretary of State Rusk, Secretary of Defense McNamara, and McGeorge Bundy (the national security adviser until he was replaced in 1966 by the even more hawkish Walt Rostow).

Johnson had broad exposure to national security affairs. He had served on the Naval Affairs Committee in the House before and during World War II, and as Senate majority leader he had been briefed and consulted regularly on the crises of the 1950s. A confirmed cold warrior, he had also seen in the 1940s the devastating political impact on the Democratic party of the communist triumph in China. "I am not going to lose Vietnam," he told the American ambassador to Saigon just after taking office in 1963. "I am not going to be the president who saw Southeast Asia go the way China went."

Aware of the problem Castro had caused John Kennedy, LBJ moved firmly to contain communism in the Western Hemisphere. When a military junta overthrew a leftist regime in Brazil, Johnson offered covert aid and open encouragement. He was equally forceful in compelling Panama to restrain rioting aimed at the continued American presence in the Canal Zone.

In 1965, to block the possible emergence of a Castro-type government, LBJ sent twenty thousand American troops to the Dominican Republic. Johnson's flimsy justifications—ranging from the need to protect American tourists to a dubious list of suspected communists among the rebel leaders—served only to alienate liberal critics in the United States, particularly Senate Foreign Relations Committee Chairman J. William Fulbright, a former Johnson favorite. The intervention ended in 1966 with the election of a conservative government. Senator Fulbright, however, continued his criticism of Johnson's foreign policy by publishing *The Arrogance of Power*, a biting analysis of the fallacies of containment. Fulbright's defection symbolized a growing gap between the president and liberal intellectuals; the more LBJ struggled to uphold the Cold War policies he had inherited from Kennedy, the more he found himself under attack from Congress, the media, and the universities.

The Vietnam Dilemma

It was Vietnam rather than Latin America that became Lyndon Johnson's obsession and led ultimately to his political downfall. Inheriting an American commitment that dated back to Eisenhower to support an independent South Vietnam, the new president believed he had little choice but to continue Kennedy's policy in Vietnam. The crisis created by Diem's overthrow only three weeks before Kennedy's assassination led to a vacuum of power in Saigon that prevented Johnson from conducting a thorough review and reassessment of the strategic alternatives in Southeast Asia. In 1964, seven different governments ruled South Vietnam; power changed hands three times within one month. According to an American officer, the atmosphere in Saigon "fairly smelled of discontent," with "workers on strike, students demonstrating, [and] the local press pursuing a persistent campaign of criticism of the new government."

Resisting pressure from the Joint Chiefs of Staff for direct American military involvement, LBJ continued Kennedy's policy of economic and technical assistance. He sent in seven thousand more military advisers and an additional $50 million in aid. While he insisted it was still up to the Vietnamese themselves to win the war, he expanded American support for covert operations, including amphibious raids on the North.

These undercover activities led directly to the Gulf of Tonkin affair. On August 2, 1964, North Vietnamese torpedo boats attacked the *Maddox*, an American destroyer engaged in electronic intelligence gathering in the Gulf of Tonkin. The attack was prompted by the belief the American ship had been involved in a South Vietnamese raid nearby. The *Maddox* escaped unscathed, but to show American resolve, the navy sent in another destroyer, the *C. Turner Joy*. On the evening of August 4, the two destroyers, responding to sonar and radar contacts, opened fire on North Vietnamese gunboats in the area. Johnson ordered retaliatory air strikes on North Vietnamese naval bases. Later investigation indicated that the North Vietnamese gunboats had not launched a second attack on the American ships.

The next day, the president asked Congress to pass a resolution authorizing him to take "all necessary measures to repel any armed attack against the forces

SOUTHEAST ASIA AND THE VIETNAM WAR
American combat forces in South Vietnam rose from sixteen thousand in 1963 to a half million in 1968, but a successful conclusion to the conflict was no closer.

What were some major events of the war?

of the United States and to prevent further aggression." He did not in fact need this authority; he had already ordered the retaliatory air strike without it. Later, critics charged that LBJ wanted a blank check from Congress to carry out the future escalation of the Vietnam War, but such a motive is unlikely. He had already rejected immediate military intervention. In part, he wanted the **Gulf of Tonkin Resolution** to demonstrate to North Vietnam the American determination to defend South Vietnam at any cost. "The challenge we face in Southeast Asia today," he told Congress, "is the same challenge that we have faced with courage and that we have met with strength in Greece and Turkey, in Berlin and Korea." He also wanted to preempt the Vietnam issue from his Republican opponent, Barry Goldwater, who had been advocating a tougher policy. By taking a firm stand on the Gulf of Tonkin incident, Johnson could both impress the North Vietnamese and outmaneuver a political rival at home.

Congress responded with alacrity. The House acted unanimously, while only two senators voted against the Gulf of Tonkin Resolution. Johnson appeared to have won a spectacular victory. His standing in the Gallup poll shot up from 42 to 72 percent, and he had effectively blocked Goldwater from exploiting Vietnam as a campaign issue.

In the long run, however, this easy victory proved costly. Having used force once against North Vietnam, LBJ was more likely to do so in the future. And although he apparently had no intention of widening the conflict in August 1964, the congressional resolution was phrased broadly enough to enable him to use whatever level of force he wanted—including unlimited military intervention. Above all, when he did wage war in Vietnam, he left himself open to the charge of deliberately misleading Congress. Presidential credibility proved ultimately to be Johnson's Achilles' heel; his political downfall began with the Gulf of Tonkin Resolution.

Gulf of Tonkin Resolution

After a North Vietnamese attack on an American destroyer in the Gulf of Tonkin in 1964, President Johnson persuaded Congress to pass a resolution giving him the authority to use armed force in Vietnam.

QUICK CHECK ✔

What happened in the Gulf of Tonkin, and how did it reflect Johnson's Vietnam problem?

Escalation

Full-scale American involvement in Vietnam began in 1965 in a series of steps designed primarily to prevent a North Vietnamese victory. With the political situation in Saigon growing more hopeless every day, the president's advisers urged the bombing of the North. American air attacks would serve several purposes: They would block North Vietnamese infiltration routes, make Hanoi pay a heavy price for its role, and lift the sagging morale of the South Vietnamese. But most important, as McGeorge Bundy reported after a visit to Pleiku (site of a Vietcong attack on an American base that took nine lives), "Without new U.S. action defeat appears inevitable—probably not in a matter of weeks or perhaps even months, but within the next year or so." In February 1965, Johnson cited the Pleiku attack in ordering a long-planned aerial bombardment of selected North Vietnamese targets.

The air strikes, aimed at impeding the communist supply line and damaging Hanoi's economy, proved ineffective. In April, Johnson authorized the use of American combat troops in South Vietnam, restricting them to defensive operations intended to protect American air bases. The Joint Chiefs then pressed the president for both unlimited bombing of the North and the aggressive use of American ground forces in the South. In mid-July, Secretary of Defense McNamara recommended sending a hundred thousand combat troops to Vietnam, more than doubling the American forces there. He believed this escalation would lead to a "favorable outcome," but he also told the president that an

Lyndon Johnson, The Tonkin Gulf Resolution Message

MAP

Vietnam War

additional hundred thousand soldiers might be needed in 1966 and that American battle deaths could rise as high as five hundred a month (by early 1968, they hit a peak of more than five hundred a week).

At the same time, other advisers, most notably Undersecretary of State George Ball, spoke out against military escalation in favor of a political settlement. Warning that the United States was likely to suffer "national humiliation," Ball told the president that he had "serious doubt that an army of westerners can successfully fight Orientals in an Asian jungle."

Johnson was genuinely torn, asking his advisers at one point, "Are we starting something that in two to three years we simply can't finish?" But he finally decided he had no choice but to persevere in Vietnam. Although he insisted on paring down McNamara's troop request, LBJ settled on a steady military escalation designed to compel Hanoi to accept a diplomatic solution. In late July, the president permitted a gradual increase in the bombing of North Vietnam and allowed American ground commanders to conduct offensive operations in the South. Most ominously, he approved the immediate dispatch of fifty thousand troops to Vietnam and the future commitment of fifty thousand more.

These July decisions formed "an open-ended commitment to employ American military forces as the situation demanded," wrote historian George Herring, and they were "the closest thing to a formal decision for war in Vietnam." Convinced that withdrawal would destroy American credibility before the world and that an invasion of the North would lead to World War III, Johnson opted for large-scale but limited military intervention. Moreover, LBJ feared the domestic consequences of either extreme. A pullout could cause a massive political backlash at home, as conservatives condemned him for betraying South Vietnam to communism. All-out war, however, would mean the end of his social programs. Once Congress focused on the conflict, he explained to biographer Doris Kearns Goodwin, "that bitch of a war" would destroy "the woman I really loved—the Great Society." So he settled for a limited war, committing a half million American troops to battle in Southeast Asia, all the while pretending it was a minor engagement and refusing to ask the American people for the support and sacrifice required for victory.

Lyndon Johnson was not solely responsible for the Vietnam War. He inherited both a policy that assumed Vietnam was a vital national interest and a deteriorating situation in Saigon that demanded a more active American role. Truman, Eisenhower, and Kennedy had taken the United States deep into the Vietnam maze; it was Johnson's fate to have to find a way out. But LBJ bears full responsibility for the way he tried to resolve his dilemma. The failure to confront the people with the stark choices the nation faced in Vietnam, the insistence on secrecy and deceit, the refusal to acknowledge that he had committed the United States to a dangerous military involvement—these were Johnson's sins in Vietnam. His lack of self-confidence in foreign policy and fear of domestic reaction led directly to his undoing.

QUICK CHECK ✔

How and why did Johnson escalate American involvement in Vietnam?

Stalemate

For the next three years, Americans waged an intensive war in Vietnam and succeeded only in preventing a communist victory. American bombing of the North proved ineffective. The rural, undeveloped nature of the North Vietnamese economy

U.S. troops wade through marshland during an operation on South Vietnam's Mekong Delta. Although the United States conducted thousands of air strikes over North Vietnam and committed a half million troops to the South, it failed to win the advantage.

Why?

meant there were few industrial targets; a political refusal to bomb the main port of Haiphong allowed Soviet and Chinese arms to flow freely into the country. Nor were the efforts to destroy supply lines any more successful. American planes pounded the Ho Chi Minh Trail that ran down through Laos and Cambodia, but the North Vietnamese used the jungle canopy effectively to hide their shipments and their massive efforts to repair damaged roads and bridges. In fact, the American air attacks, with their inadvertent civilian casualties, gave North Vietnam a powerful propaganda weapon, which it used to sway world opinion against the United States.

The war in the South went no better. Despite the steady increase in American ground forces, from 184,000 in late 1965 to more than 500,000 by early 1968, the Vietcong still controlled much of the countryside. The search-and-destroy tactics employed by the American commander, General William Westmoreland, proved ill-suited to the situation. The Vietcong, aided by North Vietnamese regulars, were waging a war of insurgency, avoiding fixed positions and striking from ambush. In a vain effort to destroy the enemy, Westmoreland used superior American firepower wantonly, devastating the countryside, causing many civilian casualties, and driving the peasantry into the arms of the guerrillas. Inevitably, these tactics led to the slaughter of innocent civilians, most notably at the hamlet of My Lai. In March 1968, an American company led by Lieutenant William Calley, Jr., killed more than two hundred unarmed villagers.

The main premise of Westmoreland's strategy was to wage a war of attrition that would finally reach a "crossover point" when communist losses each month would be greater than the number of new troops they could recruit. He hoped to lure the Vietcong and the North Vietnamese regulars into pitched battles in which American firepower would inflict heavy casualties. But soon it was the communists who were deciding where and when the fighting would take place, provoking American attacks in remote areas of South Vietnam that favored the defenders and made Westmoreland pay heavily in American lives for the communist losses. By the end of 1967, the nearly half million American troops Johnson had sent to Vietnam had failed to defeat the enemy. At best, LBJ had only achieved a bloody stalemate that gradually turned the American people against a war they had once eagerly embraced.

QUICK CHECK ✓
What was the result of the escalation?

Years of Turmoil

The Vietnam War became the focal point for a growing movement of youthful protest that made the 1960s the most turbulent decade of the twentieth century. Disenchantment with conventional middle-class values, a rapid increase in college enrollments as a result of the post–World War II baby boom, a reaction against the crass materialism of the affluent society—with its endless suburbs and shopping malls—all led American youth to embrace an alternative lifestyle based on the belief that people are "sensitive, searching, poetic, and capable of love." They were ready to create a counterculture.

WHAT were the protests of the 1960s about?

The agitation of the 1960s was at its height between 1965 and 1968, the years that marked the escalation of the Vietnam War. Disturbances on college campuses reflected growing discontent in other parts of society, from the urban ghettos to the lettuce fields of the Southwest. All who felt disadvantaged and dissatisfied—students, African Americans, Hispanics, Native Americans, women, hippies—took to the streets to give vent to their feelings.

Protesting the Vietnam War

The most dramatic aspect of the youthful rebellion came in opposing the Vietnam War. The first student "teach-ins"—organized but informal discussions and debates—began at the University of Michigan in March 1965; soon they spread to campuses across the nation. More than twenty thousand protesters, under the auspices of the **Students for a Democratic Society (SDS)**, a radical student organization, gathered in Washington in April to listen to entertainers Joan Baez and Judy Collins sing antiwar songs. "End the War in Vietnam Now, Stop the Killing" read the signs.

One of the great ironies of the Vietnam War was the system of student draft deferments, which enabled most of those enrolled in college to avoid military service. As a result, the children of the well-to-do, who were more likely to attend college, were able to escape the draft. One survey revealed that men from disadvantaged families, including a disproportionately large number of African and Hispanic Americans, were twice as likely to be drafted and engage in combat in Vietnam as those from more privileged backgrounds. Consequently, a sense of

Students for a Democratic Society (SDS)
Founded in 1962, the SDS was a popular college student organization that protested shortcomings in American life, notably racial injustice and the Vietnam War. It led thousands of campus protests before it split apart at the end of the 1960s.

U.S. troops use their rifles in an encounter with antiwar demonstrators outside the Pentagon in Washington, D.C. on October 21, 1967. Leaders of the march on the Pentagon announced that the demonstration marked the end of peaceful protest against the war and the beginning of a new stage of "active resistance." Borrowing techniques from the civil rights movement, some of the demonstrators staged a sit-down in the Pentagon parking lot.

Were the antiwar protests effective?

Protests Against the Vietnam War

guilt led many college activists who were safe from Vietnam because of their student status to take the lead in denouncing an unjust war.

As the fighting in Southeast Asia intensified in 1966 and 1967, the protests grew larger and the slogans more extreme. "Hey, hey, LBJ, how many kids did you kill today?" chanted students as they proclaimed, "Hell, no, we won't go!" At the Pentagon in October 1967, more than a hundred thousand demonstrators—mainly male students but housewives, teachers, and young professionals as well—confronted a cordon of military policemen guarding the heart of the nation's war machine.

The climax came in the spring of 1968. Driven by both opposition to the war and concern for social justice, the SDS and African American radicals at Columbia University joined forces in April. They seized five buildings, effectively paralyzing one of the country's leading colleges. After eight days of tension, the New York City police regained control. The brutal repression quickened the pace of protest elsewhere. Students held sit-ins and marches at more than one hundred colleges, from Cheyney State in Pennsylvania to Northwestern in Illinois.

The students failed to stop the war, but they did succeed in gaining a voice in their education. University administrations allowed undergraduates to sit on faculty curriculum-planning committees and gave up their once rigid control of dormitory and social life. But the students' greatest impact lay outside politics and the campus. They spawned a cultural uprising that transformed the manners and morals of America.

QUICK CHECK ✓

What forms did opposition to the war in Vietnam take?

The Cultural Revolution

In contrast to the elitist political revolt of the SDS, the cultural rebellion by youth in the 1960s was pervasive. Led by college students, young people challenged the prevailing adult values in clothing, hairstyles, sexual conduct, work habits, and music. Blue jeans and love beads took the place of business suits and wristwatches; long hair and unkempt beards for men, bare feet and bralessness for women became a new uniform of protest. Communes emerged for the "flower children" of the 1960s.

Music became the touchstone of the new departure. Folksingers such as Joan Baez and Bob Dylan, popular for their songs of social protest in the mid-1960s, gave way first to rock groups such as the Beatles, whose lyrics were often suggestive of drug use, and then to "acid rock" as symbolized by the Grateful Dead. The climactic event of the decade came at the Woodstock concert at Bethel in upstate New York when 400,000 young people indulged in a three-day festival of rock music, drug experimentation, and public sexual activity.

Former Harvard psychology professor Timothy Leary encouraged youth to join him in trying out the drug scene. Millions accepted his invitation to "tune in, turn on, drop out" literally, as they experimented with marijuana and with LSD, a new and dangerous chemical hallucinogen. The ultimate expression of insurgency was the Yippie movement, led by Jerry Rubin and Abbie Hoffman. Shrewd buffoons who mocked the consumer culture, they delighted in capitalizing on the mood of social protest to win attention. Once, when testifying before a congressional committee investigating internal subversion, Rubin dressed as a Revolutionary War soldier; Hoffman appeared in the gallery of the New York Stock Exchange in 1967, raining money down on the cheering brokers below.

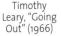

Timothy Leary, "Going Out" (1966)

QUICK CHECK

How did young people challenge adult culture during the 1960s?

"Black Power"

The civil rights movement, which had spawned the mood of protest in the 1960s, fell on hard times later in the decade. The legislative triumphs of 1964 and 1965 were relatively easy victories over southern bigotry; now the movement faced the far more complex problem of achieving economic equality in the cities of the North, where more than half of the nation's African Americans lived in poverty. The civil rights movement had raised the expectations of urban African Americans for improvement; frustration mounted as they failed to experience any significant economic gain.

The first sign of trouble came in the summer of 1964, when African American teenagers in Harlem and Rochester, New York, rioted. The next summer, a massive outburst of rage and destruction swept over the Watts area of Los Angeles as the inhabitants burned buildings and looted stores. Riots in the summer of 1966 were less destructive, but in 1967 the worst ones yet took place in Newark and in Detroit, where forty-three were killed and thousands were injured. The mobs attacked the shops and stores, expressing a burning grievance against a consumer society from which they were excluded by their poverty.

The civil rights coalition fell apart, a victim of both its legislative success and economic failure. Black militants took over the leadership of the Student Nonviolent Coordinating Committee (SNCC); they disdained white help and

Reports from the Commission on the Watts Riots

Stokely Carmichael and Charles V. Hamilton, from *Black Power*

even reversed Martin Luther King's insistence on nonviolence. The SNCC's new leader, Stokely Carmichael, told blacks they should seize power in those parts of the South where they outnumbered whites. "I am not going to beg the white man for anything I deserve," he said, "I'm going to take it." Soon his calls for "black power" became a rallying cry for more militant blacks who advocated the need for African Americans to form "our own institutions, credit unions, co-ops, political parties" and even write "our own history."

Others went further than calls for ethnic separation. H. Rap Brown, who replaced Carmichael as the leader of the SNCC in 1967, told an African American crowd in Cambridge, Maryland, to "get your guns" and "burn this town down"; Huey Newton, one of the founders of the militant Black Panther party, proclaimed, "We make the statement, quoting from Chairman Mao, that Political Power comes through the Barrel of a Gun."

King suffered the most from this extremism. His denunciation of the Vietnam War cost him the support of the Johnson administration and alienated him from the more conservative civil rights groups such as the NAACP and the Urban League. He finally seized on poverty as the proper enemy for attack, but before he could lead his Poor People's March on Washington in 1968, he was assassinated in Memphis in early April.

Both blacks and whites realized the nation had lost its most eloquent voice for racial harmony. His tragic death elevated King to the status of a martyr, but it also led to one last outbreak of urban violence. African Americans exploded in angry riots in 125 cities across the nation; the worst rioting took place in Washington, D.C., where buildings were set on fire within a few blocks of the White House. "It was as if the city were being abandoned to an invading army," wrote a British journalist. "Clouds of smoke hung over the Potomac, evoking memories of the London blitz."

Yet there was a positive side to the emotions engendered by black nationalism. Leaders urged African Americans to take pride in their ethnic heritage, to embrace their blackness as a positive value. African Americans began to wear Afro hairstyles and dress in dashikis, stressing their African roots. Students began to demand new black studies programs in the colleges; the word *Negro*—identified with white supremacy of the past—virtually disappeared from usage overnight, replaced by the favored *Afro-American* or *black*. Singer James Brown best expressed the sense of racial identity: "Say It Loud—I'm Black and I'm Proud."

QUICK CHECK ✓

What was "Black Power," and what did it represent?

Ethnic Nationalism

Other groups quickly emulated the African American phenomenon. Native Americans decried the callous use of their identity as football mascots; in response, universities such as Stanford changed their symbols. Puerto Ricans demanded their history be included in school and college texts. Polish, Italian, and Czech groups insisted on respect for their nationalities. Congress acknowledged these demands with passage of the Ethnic Heritage Studies Act of 1972. Instead of trying to melt all groups down into a standard American type, Congress now gave what one sponsor of the measure called "official recognition to ethnicity as a positive constructive force in our society today."

Mexican Americans were in the forefront of the ethnic groups that became active in the 1970s. The primary impulse came from the efforts of César Chávez to organize the poorly paid grape pickers and lettuce workers in California into the National

In March 1966, César Chávez, shown here talking with workers, led striking grape pickers on a 250-mile march from Delano, California, to the state capital at Sacramento to dramatize the plight of the migrant farmworkers.

How successful were Chávez's efforts?

Farm Workers Association (NFWA). Chávez appealed to ethnic nationalism in mobilizing Mexican American field hands to strike against grape growers in the San Joaquin Valley in 1965. A national boycott of grapes by Mexican Americans and their sympathizers among the young people of the counterculture led to a series of hard-fought victories over the growers. The five-year struggle resulted in a union victory in 1970, but at an enormous cost—95 percent of the farmworkers involved had lost their homes and their cars. Nevertheless, Chávez succeeded in raising the hourly wage of farmworkers in California to $3.53 by 1977 (it had been $1.20 in 1965).

Chávez's efforts helped spark an outburst of ethnic consciousness among Mexican Americans that swept through the urban barrios of the Southwest. Mexican American leaders campaigned for bilingual programs and improved educational opportunities. Young activists began to call themselves Chicanos, which had previously been a derogatory term, and to take pride in their cultural heritage; in 1968, they succeeded in establishing the first Mexican American studies program at California State College at Los Angeles. Campus leaders called for reform, urging high school students to insist on improvements. Heeding such appeals, nearly ten thousand students at East Los Angeles high schools walked out of class in March 1968. These walkouts sparked similar movements in San Antonio, Texas, and Phoenix, Arizona, and led to the introduction of bilingual programs in grade schools and the hiring of more Chicano teachers at all levels.

QUICK CHECK

What did César Chávez want, and what did he get?

Women's Liberation

Active as they were in the civil rights and antiwar movements, women soon learned that the male leaders of these causes were little different from corporate executives—they expected women to fix the food and type the communiqués while the men made the decisions. Understandably, women soon realized that they could only achieve respect and equality by mounting their own protest.

In some ways, the position of women in American society was worse in the 1960s than it had been in the 1920s. After forty years, a lower percentage of women were enrolled in the nation's colleges and professional schools. Women were still relegated to stereotyped occupations such as nursing and teaching; there were few female lawyers and even fewer women doctors. And gender roles, as portrayed on television commercials, continued to call for the husband to be the breadwinner and the wife to be the homemaker.

Betty Friedan poses with a copy of her groundbreaking book, *The Feminine Mystique*. In the work, Friedan castigated advertisers, educators, and others for promoting what she labeled the feminine mystique—the idea that women could find fulfillment only in their roles as wives and mothers.

How did other women respond to Friedan's ideas?

National Organization for Women, Statement of Purpose (1966)

Shirley Chisholm, Equal Rights for Women (May 21, 1969)

National Organization for Women (NOW)

Founded in 1966, the National Organization for Women (NOW) called for equal employment opportunity and equal pay for women. NOW also championed the legalization of abortion and passage of an Equal Rights Amendment to the Constitution.

QUICK CHECK ✓

What were the aims of the women's rights movement?

Betty Friedan was one of the first to seize on the sense of grievance and discrimination that developed among white middle-class women in the 1960s. The beginning of the effort to raise women's consciousness was her 1963 book, *The Feminine Mystique*. Calling the American home "a comfortable concentration camp," she attacked the prevailing view that women were completely contented with their housekeeping and child-rearing tasks, claiming that housewives had no self-esteem and no sense of identity. "I'm a server of food and putter on of pants and a bedmaker," a mother of four told Friedan, "somebody who can be called on when you want something. But who am I?"

The 1964 Civil Rights Act helped women attack economic inequality head-on by making it illegal to discriminate in employment on the basis of gender. Women filed suit for equal wages, demanded that companies provide day care for their infants and preschool children, and entered politics to lobby against laws that—in the guise of protection of a weaker gender—were unfair to women. As the women's liberation movement grew, its advocates began to attack laws banning abortion and waged a campaign to toughen the enforcement of rape laws.

The women's movement met with many of the same obstacles as other protest groups in the 1960s. The moderate leadership of the **National Organization for Women (NOW),** founded by Betty Friedan in 1966, soon was challenged by those with more extreme views. Ti-Grace Atkinson and Susan Brownmiller attacked revered institutions—the family and the home—and denounced sexual intercourse with men, calling it a method of male domination. Many women were repelled by the harsh rhetoric of the extremists and expressed satisfaction with their lives. But despite these disagreements, most women supported the effort to achieve equal status with men, and in 1972, Congress responded by voting to send the Equal Rights Amendment to the state legislatures for ratification.

The Return of Richard Nixon

The turmoil of the 1960s reached a crescendo in 1968 as the American people responded to the two dominant events of the decade—the war in Vietnam and the cultural insurgency at home. In an election marked by a series of bizarre events, including riots and an assassination, Richard Nixon staged a remarkable comeback to win the post denied him in 1960.

HOW did the Vietnam War influence American politics?

Vietnam Undermines Lyndon Johnson

A controversial Vietcong offensive in early 1968 proved to be the decisive event in breaking the stalemate in Vietnam and driving Lyndon Johnson from office. Using deceptive tactics, the North Vietnamese began a prolonged siege of an American marine base at Khe Sanh, deep in the northern interior. Fearing another Dien Bien Phu, Westmoreland rushed in reinforcements, sending more than 40 percent of all American infantry and armor battalions into the two northernmost provinces of South Vietnam.

The Vietcong then used the traditional lull in the fighting at Tet, the lunar New Year, to launch a surprise attack in the heavily populated cities. Beginning on January 30, 1968, the Vietcong struck at thirty-six of the forty-four provincial capitals. The most daring raid came at the American embassy compound in Saigon. Although the guerrillas were unable to penetrate the embassy proper, for six hours television cameras caught the dramatic battle that ensued in the courtyard before military police finally overcame the attackers.

Although caught off guard, American and South Vietnamese forces succeeded in repulsing the **Tet offensive** quickly everywhere except in Hue, the old imperial capital, which was retaken only after three weeks of heavy fighting that left this beautiful city, in the words of one observer, "a shattered, stinking hulk, its streets choked with rubble and rotting bodies."

Tet proved to be the turning point of the Vietnam War. Although the communists failed to win control of the cities and suffered heavy losses, they still held on to most of the rural areas and had scored an impressive political victory. For months, President Johnson had been telling the American people the war was almost over and victory was in sight; suddenly it appeared to be nearly lost. CBS-TV newscaster Walter Cronkite took a quick trip to Saigon to find out what had happened. Horrified at what he saw, he exclaimed to his guides, "What the hell is going on? I thought we were winning the war." He returned home to tell the American people, "It seems now more certain than ever that the bloody experience of Vietnam is to end in a stalemate."

President Johnson reluctantly came to the same conclusion after the Joint Chiefs of Staff requested an additional 205,000 troops to achieve victory in Vietnam following the Tet offensive. He began to listen to his new secretary of defense, Clark Clifford, who had replaced Robert McNamara in January 1968. In mid-March, after receiving advice from the "wise men," a group of experienced cold warriors that included such illustrious figures as Dean Acheson and Omar Bradley, the president decided to limit the bombing of North Vietnam in an effort to open up peace negotiations with Hanoi. In a speech to the nation on Sunday evening, March 31, 1968, Johnson outlined his plans for a new effort at ending the war peacefully and then concluded by saying, as proof of his sincerity, "I shall not seek, and I will not accept, the nomination of my party for another term as your president."

Tet offensive
Beginning in January 1968, the Vietcong launched a major offensive in the cities of South Vietnam. Although caught by surprise, American and South Vietnam forces successfully repelled this attack, yet the Tet offensive was a blow to American public opinion and led President Johnson to end the escalation of the war and seek a negotiated peace.

DOCUMENT

Lyndon Johnson, Address to the Nation (1968)

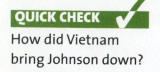

QUICK CHECK ✓

How did Vietnam bring Johnson down?

Three years of inconclusive fighting and a steadily mounting loss of American lives had disillusioned the American people and finally cost Lyndon Johnson the presidency. And the full price the nation would have to pay for its folly in Southeast Asia was still unknown—the Vietnam experience would continue to cast a shadow over American life for years to come.

The Republican Resurgence

The primary beneficiary of Johnson's Vietnam troubles was Richard Nixon. Written off as politically dead after his unsuccessful race for governor of California in 1962, Nixon had slowly rebuilt his place within the party by working loyally for Barry Goldwater in 1964 and for GOP congressional candidates two years later. Positioning himself squarely in the middle, he quickly became the front-runner for the Republican nomination. At the GOP convention in Miami Beach, Nixon won an easy first-ballot nomination and chose Maryland governor Spiro Agnew as his running mate. Agnew, little known on the national scene, had won the support of conservatives by taking a strong stand against African American rioters.

Richard Nixon Presidential Campaign Ad

In the fall campaign, Nixon opened up a wide lead by avoiding controversy and reaping the benefit of discontent with the Vietnam War. He played the peace issue shrewdly, appearing to advocate an end to the conflict without ever taking a definite stand. The United States should "end the war and win the peace," he declared, hinting he had a secret formula for peace but never revealing what it was. Above all, he chose the role of reconciler for a nation torn by emotion, a leader who promised to bring a divided country together again.

Humphrey, in contrast, found himself hounded by antiwar demonstrators who heckled him constantly. He walked a tightwire, desperate for the continued support of President Johnson but handicapped by LBJ's stubborn refusal to end all bombing of North Vietnam. Only when he broke with Johnson in late September by announcing that if elected he would "stop the bombing of North Vietnam as an acceptable risk for peace" did his campaign begin to gain momentum.

Unfortunately for Humphrey, a third-party candidate cut deeply into the normal Democratic majority. George C. Wallace had first gained national attention as the racist governor of Alabama whose motto was "Segregation now... segregation tomorrow... segregation forever." In 1964, he had shown surprising strength in Democratic primaries in northern states. By attacking both black leaders and their liberal white allies, Wallace appealed to the sense of powerlessness among the urban working classes. "Liberals, intellectuals, and longhairs have run the country for too long," Wallace told his followers. "When I get to Washington," he promised, "I'll throw all these phonies and their briefcases into the Potomac."

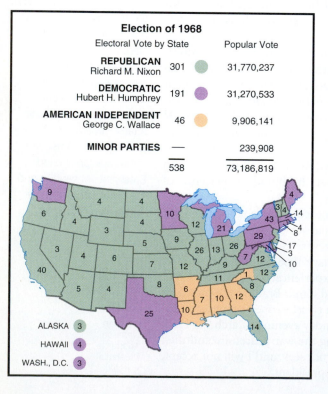

Election of 1968

Electoral Vote by State   Popular Vote

REPUBLICAN Richard M. Nixon	301	31,770,237
DEMOCRATIC Hubert H. Humphrey	191	31,270,533
AMERICAN INDEPENDENT George C. Wallace	46	9,906,141
MINOR PARTIES	—	239,908
	538	73,186,819

ALASKA 3
HAWAII 4
WASH., D.C. 3

Running on the ticket of the American Independent Party, Wallace was a close third in the September polls, gaining support from more than 20 percent of the electorate. But as the election neared, his following declined. Humphrey continued to gain, especially after Johnson agreed in late October to end all bombing of North Vietnam. By the first week in November, the outcome was too close for the experts to call.

Nixon won the election with the smallest share of the popular vote of any winning candidate since 1916. But he swept a broad band of states from Virginia and the Carolinas through the Midwest to the Pacific for a clear-cut victory in the electoral college. Humphrey held on to the urban Northeast; Wallace took just five states in the Deep South, but his heavy inroads into blue-collar districts in the North shattered the New Deal coalition.

QUICK CHECK ✓

How did Nixon capitalize on Johnson's troubles?

Conclusion: The End of an Era

The election of 1968 was a repudiation of the politics of protest and the cultural insurgency of the mid-1960s. The combined popular vote for Nixon and Wallace, 56.5 percent of the electorate, signified there was a silent majority that was fed up with violence and confrontation. A growing concern over psychedelic drugs, rock music, long hair, and sexual permissiveness had offset the usual Democratic advantage on economic issues and led to the election of a Republican president.

Richard Nixon's victory marked the end of an era with the passing of two concepts that had guided American life since the 1930s. First, the liberal reform impulse, which reached its zenith with the Great Society legislation in 1965, had clearly run its course. Civil rights, Medicare, and federal aid to education would continue in place, but Nixon's election signaled a strong reaction against the growth of federal power. At the same time, the Vietnam fiasco spelled the end of an activist foreign policy that had begun with American entry into World War II. Containment, so successful in protecting western Europe against the Soviet threat, had proved a disastrous failure when applied on a global scale. The last three decades of the twentieth century would witness a struggle to replace outmoded liberal internationalism with new policies at home and abroad.

For a list of additional titles related to this chapter's topics, please see www.pearsonamericanhistory.com.

MyHistoryLab

STUDY RESOURCES

KEY TERMS

New Frontier, p. 800
Bay of Pigs, p. 804
Cuban missile crisis, p. 804
freedom ride, p. 809
March on Washington, p. 810
war on poverty, p. 814

Great Society, p. 814
Medicare, p. 814
Voting Rights Act of 1965, p. 815
Gulf of Tonkin Resolution, p. 818

Students for a Democratic Society (SDS), p. 821
National Organization for Women (NOW), p. 826
Tet offensive, p. 827

CHAPTER REVIEW

HOW did the Cold War intensify under Kennedy?

Kennedy intensified the Cold War by increasing American support to South Vietnam and by pressuring the Cuban government of Fidel Castro. Kennedy raised troop levels in Vietnam and authorized the overthrow of Diem. He ordered a covert operation against Castro at the Bay of Pigs (which failed) and delivered an ultimatum to the Soviets to pull their missiles out of Cuba (which succeeded). *(p. 801)*

WHAT was the "New Frontier," and what did it accomplish?

The "New Frontier" was Kennedy's domestic program, and on its most important issue, civil rights, it achieved mixed results. Kennedy supported civil rights, but only hesitantly and not very effectively. Black activists, especially King, pushed the cause of racial equality farther than Kennedy was prepared to take it. *(p. 807)*

WHAT were Johnson's domestic priorities, and what were his achievements?

Johnson's "Great Society" included civil rights reform, notably the 1964 Civil Rights Act and the 1965 Voting Rights Act; Medicare, which provided health insurance for the elderly; and federal aid to education, which focused on children disadvantaged by poverty. *(p. 811)*

HOW did Johnson's Vietnam policy evolve?

Johnson seized upon an ambiguous incident in the Gulf of Tonkin to persuade Congress to grant him authority to escalate American involvement in Vietnam. He initiated a major troop buildup and air attacks against North Vietnam. The escalation failed to achieve Johnson's goal of a secure South Vietnam, producing only a bloody stalemate. *(p. 816)*

WHAT were the protests of the 1960s about?

During the 1960s, students protested the war in Vietnam, condemning its destruction of both American and Vietnamese life. Many young people rebelled against the values of their parents, experimenting with new kinds of music, styles of clothing, and types of drugs. Black militants demanded faster progress toward racial equality, and sometimes employed violence to achieve it. Chávez led a campaign to improve the lot of Mexican American farmworkers. Feminists sought greater equality for women. *(p. 821)*

HOW did the Vietnam War influence American politics?

Johnson's failure in Vietnam discredited his administration and produced more desire for change. He abandoned plans to run for re-election in 1968, thereby opening the door to Nixon. *(p. 827)*

MAKING CONNECTIONS

1. How did American foreign policy in the 1960s reflect the personalities of Kennedy and Johnson?
2. Why did MLK, Jr., command such respect?
3. How did the War on Poverty influence Johnson's handling of the Vietnam War?
4. Why did Americans turn to Nixon in 1968?

PRACTICE QUIZ

1. The _____ was an attempt by the Kennedy administration to remove Fidel Castro.
   a. Cuban Missile Crisis
   b. Bay of Pigs
   c. Guatemalan bombing
   d. Gulf of Tonkin Resolution

2. Robert _____ became Attorney General under President Kennedy in 1960.
   a. Frost
   b. La Follette
   c. Kennedy
   d. Eisenhower

3. All of the following explain the development of the freedom rides in 1961 *except*
   a. The Congress of Racial Equality sponsored the ride.
   b. The riders consisted of a multi-racial group who tested a 1960 Supreme Court desegregation ruling.
   c. Klansmen attacked the riders with pipes and bottles in Birmingham.
   d. The U.S. attorney general failed to dispatch marshals to the scene.

4. The _____ on Washington took place in August of 1963.
   a. Ride
   b. March
   c. Flood
   d. Strike

5. The _____ became President Johnson's greatest achievement in office.
   a. War on Poverty
   b. War on Vietnam
   c. War on Communists
   d. War on Religion

6. In 1965 Congress passed civil rights legislation known as
   a. The Voting Rights Act
   b. The Equal Rights Amendment
   c. The Affirmative Action Act
   d. The Roe Act

7. President Lyndon Johnson's style in the White House can be described by all *except*
   a. He dealt effectively with Congress due to his previous experience as a Senator.
   b. He lacked a strong ego to make subordinates follow his orders.
   c. He utilized television ineffectively.
   d. He lacked the wit of his predecessor, JFK.

8. All of the following reflect President Johnson's actions in Latin America *except*
   a. He attempted to contain communism from spreading beyond Cuba.
   b. He offered covert aid to a junta that overthrew a leftist regime in Brazil.
   c. He sent ten thousand American troops to Cuba.
   d. He sent twenty thousand American troops to the Dominican Republic.

9. President Johnson wanted to use the Gulf of Tonkin Resolution specifically to
   a. Show to North Vietnam that the United States remained determined to defend South Vietnam.
   b. Show to North Korea that the United States remained determined to defend South Korea.
   c. Show to China that the United States was willing to defend Taiwan.
   d. Show to Russia that the United States was willing to defend Japan.

10. What were the accomplishments of Chávez?
    a. He mobilized Mexican American fieldworkers to strike for better conditions through the National Farm Workers Association.
    b. He organized a national boycott of grapes to call attention to worker abuse.
    c. He helped the National Farm Workers Association win the strike in 1970.
    d. All of the above answers are accurate.

Find more practice at www.myhistorylab.com

SAMPLE ESSAY QUESTIONS

1. Explain the ways in which President John F. Kennedy intensified the Cold War.

2. Discuss how President Lyndon B. Johnson escalated the Vietnam War.

Answers to Practice Quiz **1.** b, p. 804 **2.** c, p. 805 **3.** d, p. 809 **4.** b, p. 810 **5.** a, p. 814 **6.** a, p. 815 **7.** b, p. 811 **8.** c, p. 816 **9.** a, p. 818 **10.** d, p. 825

The Arab oil embargo of 1973 and increasing tensions in the Middle East through the end of the 1970s threatened American's love affair with the automobile. As gas prices rose and supplies dwindled, service stations cut their hours and restricted the amount of gasoline customers could buy.

What were the indirect effects of the gas crisis?

Reagan and America's Shift to the Right

In October 1964, the Republican National Committee sponsored a televised address by Hollywood actor Ronald Reagan on behalf of Barry Goldwater's presidential candidacy. Reagan's speech had originally been aired on a Los Angeles station; the resulting outpouring of praise and campaign contributions led to its national rebroadcast.

In contrast to Goldwater's strident rhetoric, Reagan used relaxed, confident, and persuasive terms to put forth the case for a return to individual freedom. Instead of the usual choice between increased government activity and less government involvement, often couched in terms of the left and the right, Reagan presented the options of either going up or down—"up to the maximum of human freedom consistent with law and order, or down to the ant heap of totalitarianism." Then, borrowing a phrase from FDR, he told his audience: "You and I have a rendezvous with destiny. We can preserve for our children this the last best hope of man on earth, or we can sentence them to take the first step into a thousand years of darkness."

Although the speech did not rescue Goldwater's unpopular candidacy, it marked the beginning of Ronald Reagan's remarkable political career. A popular actor whose movie career had begun to fade in the 1950s, Reagan had become an effective television performer as host of *The General Electric Theater*. His political views, once liberal, moved steadily to the right as he became a spokesperson for a major American corporation. In 1965, a group of wealthy friends persuaded him, largely on the basis of the success of "the speech," to run for the California governorship.

Reagan proved to be an attractive candidate. His approachable manner and his mastery of television enabled him to present his strongly conservative message without appearing to be a rigid ideologue of the right. He won handily by appealing effectively to rising middle-class suburban resentment over high taxes, expanding welfare programs, and bureaucratic regulation.

In two terms as governor, Reagan displayed natural ability as a political leader. Instead of insisting on implementing all of his conservative beliefs, he proved surprisingly flexible. Faced with a Democratic legislature, he yielded on raising taxes and increasing state spending while managing to trim the welfare rolls. Symbolic victories were his specialty; in one example he managed to confront campus radicals and fire Clark Kerr, chancellor of the University of California, while at the same time generously funding higher education.

By the time Reagan left the governor's office in 1974, many signs pointed to a growing conservative mood across the nation. In a popular rebellion against escalating property taxes in 1978, California's voters passed Proposition 13, which slashed property taxes in half and resulted in a gradual reduction in social services. Religious leaders were especially outraged over the 1962 Supreme Court ruling in *Engel v. Vitale* outlawing school prayer on the grounds that it was "no part of the business of government to compose official prayers." In the South, where daily prayers were the customary way of beginning the school day, the reaction was intense. One Alabama congressman denounced the Supreme Court justices, proclaiming,

"They put the Negroes in the schools and now they're driving God out."

Concern over school prayer, along with rising abortion and divorce rates, impelled religious groups to engage in political activity to defend what they viewed as traditional family values. Jerry Falwell, a successful Virginia radio and television evangelist, founded the **Moral Majority,** a fundamentalist group dedicated to preserving the "American way of life."

The population shift of the 1970s, especially the rapid growth of the Sunbelt region in the South and West (see pp. 870–871), added momentum to the conservative upsurge. Those moving to the Sunbelt tended to be white, middle- and upper-class suburbanites—mainly skilled workers, young professionals, and business executives who were attracted both by economic opportunity and by a political climate stressing low taxes, less government regulation, and more reliance on the marketplace. The political impact of population shifts from East to West and North to South during the 1970s was reflected in the congressional gains (seventeen seats) by Sunbelt and Far West states after the 1980 census.

Conservatives also succeeded, for the first time since World War II, in making their cause intellectually respectable. Scholars and academics on the right flourished in new "think tanks"; writer William Buckley and economist Milton Friedman proved to be effective advocates of conservative causes in print and on television. **Neoconservatism,** led by Norman Podhoretz's magazine *Commentary*, became fashionable among many intellectuals who were former liberal stalwarts. They denounced liberals for being too soft on the communist threat abroad and too willing to compromise high standards at home in the face of demands for equality from African Americans, women, and the disadvantaged. Neoconservatives called for a reaffirmation of capitalism and a new emphasis on what was right about America rather than an obsessive concern with social ills.

Ronald Reagan and his wife Nancy wave to the crowd during the 1980 Republican convention in Detroit.

What did voters find appealing about Reagan?

By the end of the 1970s, a decade marked by military defeat in Vietnam, political scandal that destroyed the administration of Richard Nixon, economic ills that vexed the country under Gerald Ford and Jimmy Carter, and unprecedented social strains on families and traditional institutions, millions of Americans had come to believe that Cold War liberalism had run its course. Ronald Reagan, as the acknowledged leader of the conservative resurgence, was ideally placed to capitalize on this discontent. His personal charm softened the hard edges of his right-wing call to arms, and his conviction that America could regain its traditional self-confidence by reaffirming basic ideals had a broad appeal to a nation facing new challenges at home and abroad. In 1976, Reagan had barely lost to President Ford at the Republican convention; four years later, he overcame an early upset by George Bush in Iowa to win the GOP presidential nomination handily.

Moral Majority

In 1979, the Reverend Jerry Falwell founded the Moral Majority to combat "amoral liberals," drug abuse, "coddling" of criminals, homosexuality, communism, and abortion. The Moral Majority represented the rise of political activism among organized religion's radical right wing.

neoconservatism

Former liberals who advocated a strong stand against communism abroad and free market capitalism at home became known as neoconservatives. The intellectuals stressed the positive values of American society in contrast to liberals who emphasized social ills.

In his acceptance speech at the Republican convention in Detroit, Reagan set forth the themes that endeared him to conservatives: less government, a balanced budget, family values, and peace through greater military spending. Unlike Barry Goldwater, who frightened people with his rigid ideology, Reagan offered reassurance and hope for the future. He spoke of restoring to the federal government "the capacity to do the people's work without dominating their lives." As historian Robert Dallek pointed out, Reagan "assured his listeners that he was no radical idealist courting defeat, but a sensible, thoroughly likable American with a surefire formula for success that would please everyone." In Ronald Reagan, the Republicans had found the perfect figure to lead Americans into a new conservative era.

The Tempting of Richard Nixon

WHAT were the major accomplishments and failures of the Nixon presidency?

Following the divisive campaign of 1968, Richard Nixon's presidency proved to be one of the most controversial in American history. Though his diplomacy broke new ground in relations with China and the Soviet Union and ended American fighting in Vietnam, he was forced to resign the presidency under the dark cloud of the Watergate scandal.

Détente

détente

President Nixon and Henry Kissinger pursued a policy of détente, a French word meaning a relaxation of tension, with the Soviet Union as a way to lessen the possibility of nuclear war in the 1970s.

Foreign policy was Nixon's pride and joy. Nixon had thought long about the state of the world, and he was determined to improve it. To assist him in this endeavor, he appointed Henry Kissinger to be national security adviser. A refugee from Nazi Germany, Kissinger had become a professor of government at Harvard, the author of several influential books, and an acknowledged authority on international affairs. Nixon and Kissinger approached foreign policy from a practical, realistic perspective. Instead of viewing the Cold War as an ideological struggle for survival with communism, they saw it as a traditional great-power rivalry, one to be managed and controlled rather than to be won.

Nixon and Kissinger had a grand design. Realizing that recent events, especially the Vietnam War and the rapid Soviet arms buildup of the 1960s, had eroded America's position of primacy in the world, they planned a strategic retreat. Russia had great military strength, but its economy was weak and it had a dangerous rival in China. Nixon planned to use American trade—notably grain and high technology—to induce Soviet cooperation, while at the same time improving U.S. relations with China.

Nixon and Kissinger shrewdly played the China card as their first step toward achieving **détente**—a relaxation of tension—with the Soviet Union. In February 1972, accompanied by a planeload of reporters and television camera crews, Nixon visited China, meeting with the communist leaders and ending more than two decades of Sino-American hostility. Nixon agreed to establish an American liaison mission in Beijing as a first step toward diplomatic recognition.

The Soviets, who viewed China as a dangerous adversary, responded by agreeing to an arms control pact with the United States. The **Strategic Arms Limitation Talks (SALT)** had been under way since 1969. During a visit to Moscow in May 1972,

Strategic Arms Limitation Talks (SALT)

In 1972, the United States and the Soviet Union culminated four years of Strategic Arms Limitation Talks (SALT) by signing a treaty limiting the deployment of antiballistic missiles (ABMs) and an agreement to freeze the number of offensive missiles for five years.

Kissinger's search for détente began with a calculated decision to improve relations with China. In a highly publicized state visit, Nixon and Chinese leaders were photographed sharing banquets and touring the Great Wall of China.

What was the purpose of the trip?

Nixon signed two vital documents with Soviet leader Leonid Brezhnev. The first limited the two superpowers to two hundred antiballistic missiles (ABMs) apiece; the second froze the number of offensive ballistic missiles for a five-year period. These SALT 1 agreements recognized the existing Soviet lead in missiles, but the American deployment of multiple independently targeted reentry vehicles (MIRVs) ensured a continuing strategic advantage for the United States.

The SALT 1 agreements were most important as a symbolic first step toward control of the nuclear arms race. They signified that the United States and the Soviet Union were trying to achieve a settlement of their differences by peaceful means.

QUICK CHECK ✓

What was détente, and why did it appeal to Nixon?

Ending the Vietnam War

Vietnam remained the one foreign policy challenge that Nixon could not overcome. He had a three-part plan to end the conflict—gradual withdrawal of American troops, accompanied by training of South Vietnamese forces to take over the combat role; renewed bombing; and a hard line in negotiations with Hanoi. The number of American soldiers in Vietnam fell from 540,000 in early 1969 to less than 30,000 by 1972; domestic opposition to the war declined sharply with the accompanying drop in casualties and reductions in the draft call.

Renewed bombing proved the most controversial part of the plan. As early as the spring of 1969, Nixon secretly ordered raids on communist supply lines in neutral Cambodia. Then in April 1970, he ordered both air and ground strikes into Cambodia, causing a massive outburst of antiwar protests at home. Students demonstrated against the invasion of Cambodia on campuses across the nation. Tragedy struck at Kent State University in Ohio in early May. After rioters had firebombed an ROTC building, the governor sent in National Guard troops who were taunted and harassed by irate students. The guardsmen then opened fire, killing four students and wounding eleven more. The victims were innocent bystanders; two were young women caught in the fusillade on their way between classes. A week later, two African American student demonstrators were killed at Jackson State

The renewed bombing of North Vietnam and invasion of Cambodia ordered by Nixon in hopes of ending the conflict precipitated student protests at many campuses. At Kent State University in Ohio, demonstrators and bystanders were shot by national guardsmen.

Why did the guardsmen use such violence?

College in Mississippi; soon riots and protests raged on more than four hundred campuses across the country.

Nixon had little sympathy for the demonstrators, calling the students "bums" who were intent on "blowing up the campuses." The "silent majority" to whom he appealed seemed to agree; one poll showed that most Americans blamed the students, not the National Guard, for the deaths at Kent State. An "Honor America Day" program, held in Washington, D.C., on July 4, attracted 250,000 people who heard Billy Graham and Bob Hope endorse the president's policies. Nixon's Cambodian invasion did little to shorten the Vietnam War, but the public reaction reinforced the president's resolve not to surrender.

The third tactic, negotiation with Hanoi, finally proved successful. Beginning in the summer of 1969, Kissinger held a series of secret meetings with North Vietnam's foreign minister, Le Duc Tho. In the summer and fall of 1972, the two sides neared agreement, but South Vietnamese objections blocked a settlement before the 1972 election. When the North Vietnamese tried to make last-minute changes, Nixon ordered a series of heavy B-52 raids on Hanoi that finally led to the signing of a truce on January 27, 1973. In return for the release of all American prisoners of war, the United States agreed to remove its troops from South Vietnam within sixty days. The political clauses allowed the North Vietnamese to keep their troops in the South, thus virtually guaranteeing future control of all Vietnam by the communists.

For two years after the accords the communists waited, weighing, among other things, the willingness of Americans to continue to support South Vietnam.

As Nixon became enmeshed in the Watergate scandal (see below), his grip on foreign policy weakened, and by the time he was forced from office in August 1974, most Americans simply wanted to forget Vietnam. The following spring the communists mounted a major offensive and in just weeks completed their takeover of Vietnam. Ten years after the American escalation of the war, and after the loss of sixty thousand American lives, the American effort to preserve South Vietnam from communism had proved a tragic failure.

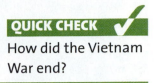

QUICK CHECK

How did the Vietnam War end?

The Watergate Scandal

Nixon's Vietnam problems and especially his formulation of détente made him sensitive to the unauthorized release of information about American foreign policy. He had good reason for fearing leaks, since they might tip the administration's hand in sensitive negotiations with the communists. When leaks did occur, Nixon grew outraged and demanded that they be stopped. The White House established an informal office of covert surveillance—the "plumbers," its operatives were called—which began by investigating the national security breaches but, during the presidential campaign of 1972, branched out into spying on Nixon's Democratic opponents and engaging in political dirty tricks.

Five of the "plumbers" were arrested in June 1972 during a break-in at the headquarters of the Democratic National Committee at the Watergate office complex in Washington. The Nixon White House took pains to conceal its connection to what its spokesman dismissed as a "third-rate burglary attempt." Nixon personally ordered the cover-up. "I want you to stonewall it, let them plead the Fifth Amendment, cover-up, or anything else," Nixon told John Mitchell, his former attorney general and then campaign director.

The cover-up succeeded long enough to ensure Nixon's landslide re-election victory over Democrat George S. McGovern of South Dakota, but in the months after the election the cover-up began to unravel. James McCord, one of the Watergate burglars, was the first to break the silence. Sentenced to a long jail term by Judge John Sirica, McCord asked for leniency, informing Sirica he had received money from the White House and had been promised a presidential pardon in return for his silence. By April 1973, Nixon was compelled to fire aide John Dean, who had directed the cover-up but who now refused to become a scapegoat. Two other aides, H. R. Haldeman and John Ehrlichman, were forced to resign.

The Senate then appointed a special committee to investigate the unfolding **Watergate scandal**. In a week of dramatic testimony, Dean revealed the president's personal involvement in the cover-up. Still, it was basically a matter of whose word was to be believed—the president's or a discredited aide's—and Nixon hoped to weather the storm.

Watergate scandal

A break-in at the Democratic National Committee offices in the Watergate complex in Washington was carried out under the direction of White House staff members. Disclosure of the White House involvement in the break-in and subsequent cover-up forced President Richard Nixon to resign in 1974 to avoid impeachment.

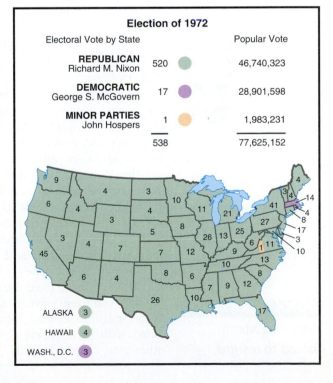

Election of 1972

	Electoral Vote by State		Popular Vote
REPUBLICAN Richard M. Nixon	520	🟢	46,740,323
DEMOCRATIC George S. McGovern	17	🟣	28,901,598
MINOR PARTIES John Hospers	1	🟠	1,983,231
	538		77,625,152

ALASKA 3
HAWAII 4
WASH., D.C. 3

In an April 29, 1974, television address, Nixon announced that he would release Watergate tape transcripts, shown stacked in the background, to the House Judiciary Committee's impeachment probe. The transcripts were edited versions of taped conversations in the Oval Office.

How did the release of the transcripts, and later of the tapes, lead to Nixon's resignation?

Watergate Special Prosecution Force Memo (August 9, 1974)

Richard Nixon, "I am not a crook"

The committee's discovery of the existence of tape recordings of conversations in the Oval Office, made regularly since 1970, proved the beginning of the end for Nixon. At first, the president tried to invoke executive privilege to withhold the tapes. When Archibald Cox, appointed as Watergate special prosecutor, demanded the release of the tapes, Nixon fired him. Yet the new Watergate prosecutor, Leon Jaworski, continued to press for the tapes. Nixon tried to release only a few of the less damaging ones, but the Supreme Court ruled unanimously in June 1974 that the tapes had to be turned over to Judge Sirica.

By this time, the House Judiciary Committee, acting on evidence compiled by the staff of the Senate committee, had voted three articles of impeachment, charging Nixon with obstruction of justice, abuse of power, and contempt of Congress. Faced with the release of tapes that directly implicated him in the cover-up, the president chose to resign on August 9, 1974.

Nixon's resignation proved to be the culmination of the Watergate scandal. The entire episode revealed both the weaknesses and strengths of the American political system. Most regrettable was the abuse of presidential authority—a reflection both of the growing power of the modern presidency and of fatal flaws in Richard Nixon's character. Unlike previous executive branch scandals such as the Whiskey Ring and Teapot Dome, Watergate involved a lust for power rather than for money. Having achieved his ambition of becoming president, Nixon did everything possible to retain his hold on his office. He used the plumbers to maintain executive secrecy and he directed the Internal Revenue Service and the Justice Department to punish his enemies and reward his friends.

But Watergate also demonstrated the vitality of a democratic society. The press showed how investigative reporting could unlock even the most closely guarded executive secrets. Judge Sirica proved that an independent judiciary was still the best bulwark for individual freedom. And Congress rose to the occasion, both by carrying out a successful investigation of executive misconduct and by following a scrupulous and nonpartisan impeachment process that left Nixon with no chance to escape his fate.

The nation survived the shock of Watergate with its institutions intact. John Mitchell and twenty-five presidential aides were sentenced to jail terms. Congress, in decline since Lyndon Johnson's exercise of executive dominance, was rejuvenated, with its members now intent on extending congressional authority into other areas of American life.

QUICK CHECK ✓

Why was Nixon forced to resign?

Oil and Inflation

In the midst of Watergate, the outbreak of war in the Middle East threatened a vital national interest: the unimpeded and inexpensive flow of oil to the United States. The resulting energy crisis helped spark a raging price inflation that had a profound impact on the national economy and on American society at large.

War and Oil

On October 6, 1973, Egypt and Syria launched a surprise attack on Israel. The fighting followed decades of tension between Israel and its Arab neighbors, which had grown only worse upon the stunning Israeli victory in the Six Day War of 1967. In that conflict, the Israelis routed the Arabs, seizing the Golan Heights from Syria, the Sinai Peninsula from Egypt, and Jerusalem and the West Bank from Jordan. The Arabs ached for revenge, and in 1973 the Egyptians and Syrians attacked. Catching Israel off guard, they won early battles but eventually lost the initiative and were forced to give up the ground they had recovered. The Israelis would have delivered another devastating defeat to the Arabs if not for the diplomatic intervention of Nixon and Kissinger, who, despite America's previous strong support for Israel, believed a decisive Israeli victory would destabilize the Middle East even more.

The American diplomatic triumph, however, was offset by an unforeseen consequence of the October War (also called the Yom Kippur War, as it started on the Jewish holy day). On October 17, the Arab members of the **Organization of Petroleum Exporting Countries (OPEC)** announced a 5 percent cut in oil production, and vowed additional cuts of 5 percent each month until Israel surrendered the lands it had taken in 1967. Three days later, following Nixon's announcement of an emergency aid package for Israel, Saudi Arabia cut off oil shipments to the United States.

The Arab oil embargo had a disastrous impact on the American economy. With Arab producers cutting production by 25 percent from the September 1973 level, world supplies fell by 10 percent. For the United States, which imported one-third of its daily consumption, this meant a loss of nearly 2 million barrels a day. Long lines formed at gas stations as motorists who feared running out of fuel kept filling their tanks.

A dramatic increase in oil prices proved to be a far more significant result of the embargo. After the Arab embargo began, OPEC, led by the shah of Iran, raised crude oil prices fourfold. In the United States, gasoline prices at the pumps nearly doubled in a few weeks' time, while the cost of home heating fuel rose even more.

Nixon responded with a series of temporary measures, including pleas to Americans to turn down their thermostats in homes and offices and avoid driving simply for pleasure. When the Arab oil embargo ended in March, after Kissinger negotiated an Israeli pullback in the Sinai, the American public relaxed. Gasoline once again became plentiful, thermostats were raised, and people resumed their love affair with the automobile.

The energy crisis, however, did not end with the lifting of the embargo. The Arab action marked the beginning of a new era in American history. The United States, with only 6 percent of the world's population, had been responsible for nearly 40 percent of the world's energy consumption. In 1970, domestic oil

HOW were oil and inflation linked during the 1970s?

Organization of Petroleum Exporting Countries (OPEC)
A cartel of oil-exporting nations. In late 1973, OPEC took advantage of the October War and an oil embargo by its Arab members to quadruple the price of oil. This huge increase had a devastating impact on the American economy.

THE OIL SHOCKS: PRICE INCREASES OF CRUDE OIL AND GASOLINE, 1973–1985

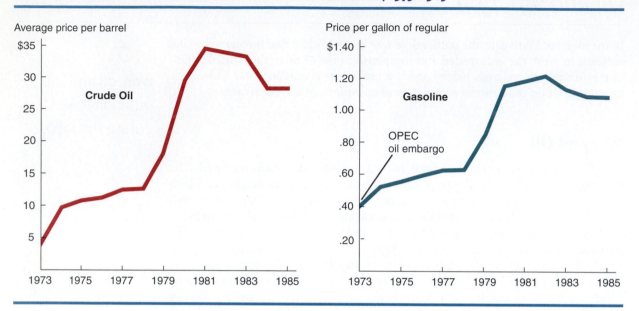

Average price per barrel

Price per gallon of regular

<table>
<tr><td>**QUICK CHECK** ✓</td></tr>
</table>

Why did oil prices quadruple in the 1970s?

production began to decline; the embargo served only to highlight the fact that the nation was now dependent on other countries, notably those in the Persian Gulf, for its economic well-being. A nation that based its way of life on abundance and expansion suddenly was faced with the reality of limited resources and economic stagnation.

The Great Inflation

The price spike from the October War was merely the first of the "oil shocks" of the 1970s. Cheap energy had been a primary contributor to the relentless growth of the American economy after World War II. The GNP had more than doubled between 1950 and 1973; the American people had come to base their standard of living on oil prices that yielded gas at about 35 cents a gallon. Large cars, sprawling suburbs, detached houses heated by fuel oil and natural gas and cooled by central air-conditioning produced a dependence on inexpensive energy that Americans took for granted.

The quadrupling of oil prices in 1973–1974 suddenly put all this at risk. Because oil or its equivalent in energy is required for the production and transportation of manufactured goods, the rising oil prices caused the prices of nearly everything else to increase as well. Most services require energy; they went up as well.

Other factors added to the trend of rising prices. The Vietnam War created federal budget deficits that grew from $63 billion for the entire decade of the 1960s to a total of $420 billion in the 1970s. A worldwide shortage of food, resulting from both rapid population increases and poor harvests around the globe in the mid-1970s, triggered a 20 percent rise in American food prices in 1973 alone. But above all else, the primary source of the great inflation of the 1970s was the historic increase in petroleum prices.

The impact on consumers was staggering. The price of an automobile jumped 72 percent between 1973 and 1978. During the decade, the price of a hamburger doubled, milk went from 28 to 59 cents a quart, and a loaf of bread—the proverbial staff of life—rose from 24 to 89 cents. Corresponding wage increases failed to keep pace with inflation; in 1980, the real income of the average American family fell by 5.5 percent.

Often inflation signals economic exuberance, and rising prices indicate a rapid rate of growth. Not so with the inflation of the 1970s, which reflected economic weakness. The great inflation contributed to the worst recession in the United States since World War II. American GNP dropped by 6 percent in 1974, and unemployment rose to more than 9 percent, the highest level since the Great Depression of the 1930s.

President Gerald R. Ford, who followed Richard Nixon into the White House (see p. 849), responded belatedly to the economic crisis by proposing a tax cut to stimulate consumer spending. Congress passed a $23 billion reduction in taxes in early 1975, which led to a gradual recovery by 1976. The resulting budget deficits, however, helped keep inflation above 5 percent and prevented a return to full economic health.

Jimmy Carter of Georgia, who succeeded Ford (see pp. 850–852), had little more success in reviving the economy. Continued federal deficits and relatively high interest rates kept the economy sluggish throughout 1977 and 1978. Then in 1979, the outbreak of the Iranian Revolution and the overthrow of the shah touched off another oil shock. The members of the OPEC cartel took advantage of the situation to double prices over the next eighteen months. A barrel of crude oil now cost more than $30. Gasoline prices climbed to more than $1 a gallon at American service stations, leading to an even greater wave of inflation than in 1973.

Finally, in late 1979, the Federal Reserve Board, led by Carter appointee Paul Volcker, began a sustained effort to halt inflation by mandating increased bank reserves to curtail the supply of money in circulation. The new tight-money policy served only to heighten inflation in the short run by driving interest rates up to record levels. By the spring of 1980, the prime interest rate reached 20 percent.

QUICK CHECK ✓

How did rising oil prices help trigger the inflation of the 1970s?

Private Lives, Public Issues

Sweeping changes in the private lives of the American people began in the 1970s and continued for the rest of the century. The traditional American family, with the husband as wage earner and the wife as homemaker, gave way to much more diverse living arrangements. The number of working women, including wives and mothers, increased sharply; the wage gap between the sexes narrowed, but women still lagged noticeably behind men in earnings. Then, in the years following 1970, came the emergence of an active gay rights movement as more and more gay, lesbian, and bisexual Americans began to disclose their sexual identities and demand an end to discrimination.

WHAT

? changes occurred in private life during this period?

The Changing American Family

Family life underwent a number of significant shifts after 1970. The most notable was a decline in the number of families with two parents and one or more children under 18. By the end of the 1980s, in only one two-parent family out of five was the mother solely engaged in child rearing. A few fathers stayed at home with the children, but in the great majority of these families, both parents worked outside the home.

The traditional nuclear family of the 1950s no longer prevailed in America by the end of the twentieth century. The number of married couple households with children dropped from 30 percent in the 1970s to 23 percent by 2000. The number of unmarried couples doubled in the 1990s, while adults living alone surpassed the number of married couples with children for the first time in American history. "Being married is great," commented demographer William H. Frey, "but being married with kids is tougher in today's society with spouses in different jobs and expensive day care and schools."

The divorce rate, which doubled between the mid-1960s and the late 1970s, leveled off for the rest of the century. Nevertheless, half of all first marriages still ended in divorce. After a sharp fall in the 1970s, the birthrate climbed again as the baby boom generation began to mature. There was a marked increase in the number of births to women over age 30, as well as a very high proportion of children born to single mothers, who composed 7 percent of all households by 2000, a 25 percent increase since 1990. Conservatives, alarmed by the decline of the nuclear family, called for change. "We need to discourage people from living together outside of marriage," observed Bridget Maher of the Family Research Council, "and encourage them to have children within marriage."

For better or worse, the American family structure changed significantly in the last three decades of the twentieth century, with a large number of people either never marrying or postponing marriage until late in the childbearing period. The traditional family unit, with the working father and the mother rearing the children at home, rapidly declined. Most mothers worked outside the home, and many were the sole support for their children. The proportion of children living with only one parent doubled in twenty years. Women without partners headed more than one-third of all impoverished families, and children made up 40 percent of the nation's poor. Although politicians, especially Republicans, would refer to family values during campaigns, those values underwent great stress due to social changes in the last third of the twentieth century, and children suffered disproportionately.

QUICK CHECK ✓

How did American family life change during the 1970s?

Gains and Setbacks for Women

American women experienced significant changes in their way of life and their place in society in the last quarter of the twentieth century. The prevailing theme concerned the increasing percentage of working women. There was a rapid movement of women into the labor force in the 1970s; six million more married women held jobs by the end of the decade as two incomes became increasingly necessary to keep up with inflation. The trend continued through the 1980s. Fully 61 percent of the nearly nineteen million new jobs created during the decade were filled by women; many of these new jobs, however, were entry-level or low-paying service positions.

Women scored some impressive breakthroughs. They began to enter corporation boardrooms, became presidents of major universities, and were admitted to the nation's military academies. Women entered blue-collar, professional, and small-business fields traditionally dominated by men. Ronald Reagan's appointment of Sandra Day O'Connor to the Supreme Court in 1981 marked a historic first;

Bill Clinton doubled the number of women on the Court with his selection of Ruth Bader Ginsburg.

Yet at the same time, women encountered a great deal of resistance. Most women continued to work in female-dominated fields—as nurses, secretaries, teachers, and waitresses. Those who entered such "male" areas as management and administration soon encountered the so-called glass ceiling, which kept them from advancing beyond mid-level executive status. In 1990, only 4.3 percent of corporate officers were women. Most in business worked at the middle and lower rungs of management with staff jobs in personnel and public relations, not key operational positions in sales and marketing that would lead to the boardroom; women held fewer than 3 percent of the top jobs in Fortune 500 companies. The economic boom of the 1990s, however, led to a steady increase in the number of women executives; in 1998, there was an increase of 514,000.

Even with these gains, however, by 2004 women's wages still averaged only 76.5 percent of men's earnings. A college education helped close the gap, but a woman with a degree made only $600 a year more on the average than a man with a high school diploma. Younger women did best; those between 16 and 24 earned almost 90 cents for every dollar paid to a male in the same age group. Older women, who often had no other source of support, fared poorly; those over the age of 50 earned only 64 percent as much as men their age. Feminists had once hoped to close the gender gap by the year 2000, but experts predicted women would not reach pay equity with men until 2018.

The most encouraging development for women came in business ownership. Often blocked by the glass ceiling and seeking flexible schedules, more and more women went into business for themselves. The number of female business owners increased 40 percent between 1987 and 1992, twice the national rate of business growth. A women's trade group estimated that in 1996 women owned almost eight million businesses, employing more than eighteen million workers—one out of four American workers. A speaker at the first National Women's Economic Summit in 1996 exaggerated only slightly in crediting her group with restoring prosperity, claiming that "the American economy has been revitalized in good measure because of the participation of and contributions of women business owners."

Beyond economic opportunity, the women's movement had two goals. The first was ratification of the **Equal Rights Amendment (ERA)**. Approved by Congress in 1972, the ERA stated simply, "Equality of rights under the law shall not be denied or abridged by the United States or any state on account of sex." Within a year, twenty-two states had approved the amendment, but the efforts gradually faltered just three states short of ratification. The opposition came in part from working-class women who feared, as one union leader explained, that those employed as "maids, laundry workers, hospital cleaners, or dishwashers" would lose the protection of state laws that regulated wages and hours of work for women. Right-wing activist Phyllis

During the 1970s and 1980s employment opportunities expanded for women, including jobs in fields traditionally dominated by men. This photograph from 1980 shows a woman working as a union electrician in Harlem.

How did the new opportunities affect women's average income?

Equal Rights Amendment (ERA)

In 1972, Congress approved the Equal Rights Amendment (ERA) to the Constitution, a measure designed to guarantee women equal treatment under the law. Despite a three-year extension in the time allowed for ratification, ERA supporters fell three states short of winning adoption.

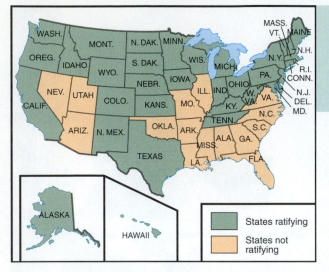

WASH. MONT. N. DAK. MINN.
OREG. IDAHO WYO. S. DAK. WIS. MICH. MASS. VT. MAINE N.H. N.Y.
NEV. UTAH COLO. NEBR. IOWA ILL. IND. OHIO PA. R.I. CONN. N.J. DEL. MD.
CALIF. ARIZ. N. MEX. KANS. MO. KY. W. VA. VA. N.C.
OKLA. ARK. TENN. S.C.
TEXAS MISS. ALA. GA.
LA. FLA.

ALASKA

HAWAII

■ States ratifying
■ States not ratifying

VOTING ON THE EQUAL RIGHTS AMENDMENT By the end of 1974, thirty-four states had ratified the ERA; Indiana finally approved the amendment in 1977, but the remaining fifteen states held out, leaving ratification three states short of the required three-fourths majority.

Why did the holdouts refuse to ratify?

Schlafly led an organized effort to defeat the ERA, claiming the amendment would lead to unisex toilets, homosexual marriages, and the drafting of women. The National Organization of Women (NOW) fought back, persuading Congress to extend the time for ratification by three years and waging intense campaigns for approval in Florida and Illinois. But the deadline for ratification finally passed on June 30, 1982, with the ERA forces still three states short. NOW leader Eleanor Smeal vowed a continuing struggle: "The crusade is not over. We know that we are the wave of the future."

The women's movement focused even more of its energies in protecting a major victory it had won in *Roe v. Wade,* the 1973 Supreme Court case that guaranteed women's right to abortion. Right-to-life groups, consisting mainly of orthodox Catholics, fundamentalist Protestants, and conservatives, fought back. In 1978, with strong support from President Carter, Congress passed the Hyde amendment, which denied the use of federal funds to pay for abortions for poor women. Nevertheless, prochoice groups organized privately funded family planning agencies and abortion clinics to give more women a chance to exercise their constitutional right to abortion.

As Presidents Reagan and Bush appointed more conservative judges to the Court, however, prochoice groups began to fear the future overturn of *Roe v. Wade.* The Court avoided a direct challenge, contenting itself with lesser actions that upheld the rights of states to regulate abortion clinics, impose a 24-hour waiting period, and require the approval of one parent or a judge before a minor could have an abortion. Abortion became an issue in presidential contests, with the Republicans upholding a prolife position and the Democrats taking a prochoice stand. Bill Clinton's election and appointment of Ruth Bader Ginsburg to the Court appeared to end the challenge to *Roe v. Wade,* but in 2000 the Court margin in rejecting a Nebraska law forbidding certain late-term abortions fell to a bare majority, 5–4. And even the exercise of the right to abortion proved difficult and sometimes dangerous in view of the often violent protests of prolife groups outside abortion clinics. For many women, abortion was a hard-won right they still had to struggle to protect.

Roe v. Wade

In 1973, the Supreme Court ruled in *Roe v. Wade* that women had a constitutional right to abortion during the early stages of pregnancy. The decision provoked a vigorous right-to-life movement that opposed abortion.

QUICK CHECK ✔

What new challenges and opportunities faced women during the decade?

The Gay Liberation Movement

On the night of June 27, 1969, a squad of New York policemen raided the Stonewall Inn, a Greenwich Village bar frequented by "drag queens" and lesbians. As the patrons were being herded into vans, a crowd of gay onlookers began to jeer and taunt the police. A riot quickly broke out. "Beer cans and bottles were heaved at the windows and a rain of coins descended on the cops," reported the *Village Voice.* "Almost by signal the crowd erupted into cobblestone and bottle heaving." The next

IMAGE
Jimmy Carter Signs House Resolution for ERA, 1978

DOCUMENT
Roe v. Wade (January 22, 1973)

night, more than four hundred police officers battled two thousand gay demonstrators through the streets of Greenwich Village. The two-day Stonewall Riots marked the beginning of the modern gay liberation movement. Refusing to play the role of victims any longer, gays and lesbians decided to affirm their sexual orientation and demand an end to discrimination against homosexuals.

Within a few days, two new organizations were formed in New York, the Gay Liberation Front and the Gay Activist Alliance, with branches and offshoots quickly appearing in cities across the country. The basic theme of gay liberation was to urge all homosexuals to "come out of the closet" and affirm with pride their sexual identity; instead of shame, they would find freedom and self-respect in the very act of coming out. "Come out for freedom! Come out now!" proclaimed the Gay Liberation Front's newspaper. "Come out of the closet before the door is nailed shut!"

Sign at a Gay
Pride March

In the course of the 1970s, hundreds of thousands of gays and lesbians responded to this call. They formed more than a thousand local clubs and organizations and won a series of notable victories. In 1974, the American Psychiatric Association stopped classifying homosexuality as a mental disorder, and by the end of the decade, half the states had repealed their sodomy statutes. Gays fought hard in cities and states for laws forbidding discrimination against homosexuals in housing and employment, and in 1980, they finally succeeded in getting a gay rights plank in the Democratic National Platform.

In the 1980s, the AIDS epidemic put the gay liberation movement on the defensive. A disease caused by the HIV virus, AIDS initially was almost always fatal. And because it was first observed among male homosexuals, the gay community faced new condemnation at a time when its members were trying desperately to care for the growing number of victims of the disease within their ranks. The gay organizations formed in the 1970s to win new rights now were channeling their energies into caring for the ill, promoting safe sex practices, and fighting for more public funding to help conquer AIDS. In 1986, ACT UP (AIDS Coalition to Unleash Power) began a series of violent demonstrations in an effort to shock the nation into doing more about AIDS. ACT UP members disrupted public meetings, chained themselves to a New York Stock Exchange balcony, and spray-painted outlines of corpses on the streets of San Francisco to call attention to those who had died of AIDS.

The movement also continued to stimulate gay consciousness in the 1980s. In 1987, an estimated 600,000 gays and lesbians took part in a march on Washington on behalf of gay rights. Every year afterward, gay groups held a National Coming Out Day in October to encourage homosexuals to proclaim proudly their sexual identity. In a more controversial move, some gay leaders encouraged "outing"—releasing the names of prominent homosexuals, primarily politicians and movie stars—in an effort to make the nation aware of how many Americans were gay or lesbian. Gay leaders claimed there were more than twenty million gays and lesbians in the nation, basing this estimate on a Kinsey report which had stated in the late 1940s that one in ten American males had engaged in homosexual behavior. A sociological survey released in the spring of 1993 contradicted those numbers, finding only 1.1 percent of American males exclusively homosexual. Whatever the actual number, it was clear by the 1990s that gays and lesbians formed a significant minority that had succeeded in forcing the nation, however grudgingly, to respect its rights.

There was one battle, however, in which victory eluded the gay liberation movement. In the 1992 election, gays and lesbians strongly backed Democratic candidate Bill Clinton, who promised, if elected, to end the ban on homosexuals in the military. In his first days in office, however, President Clinton stirred up great resistance in the Pentagon and Congress when he tried to issue an executive

Backtracking on his campaign promise to end the ban on homosexuals in the military, President Clinton disappointed many by agreeing to the compromise "Don't ask, don't tell" policy that permitted gays to serve in the military as long as they did not reveal their sexual orientation. (*Source: The New Yorker Collection 2000. Christopher Weyant from cartoonbank.com. All Rights Reserved.*)

What does the caroonist think of the policy?

"This one's for not asking, and this one's for not telling."

order forbidding such discrimination. The Joint Chiefs of Staff and many Democrats, led by Georgia Senator Sam Nunn, warned that acceptance of gays and lesbians would destroy morale and seriously weaken the armed forces. Clinton finally settled for the Pentagon's compromise "Don't ask, don't tell" policy that would permit homosexuals to continue serving in the military as they had in the past as long as they did not reveal their sexual preference and refrained from homosexual conduct. However disappointed gays and lesbians were in Clinton's retreat, their leaders understood that the real problem was the resistance of mainstream America to full acceptance of homosexuality.

Public attitudes toward gays and lesbians seemed to be changing in the 1990s, but the growing tolerance had definite limits. In a 1996 poll, 85 percent of those questioned believed that gays should be treated equally in the workplace, up from 76 percent in 1992. Violence against gays, however, continued, most notably in the 1998 fatal beating of Matthew Shepard, a 21-year-old gay college student, in Wyoming. The brutal attack spurred calls for hate-crime legislation and the judge in the case, banning a so-called gay-panic defense, sentenced Shepard's assailant to two consecutive terms of life imprisonment.

The issue of same-sex marriage came to a head at the end of the century. In 1996, President Clinton signed the Defense of Marriage Act, which decreed that states did not have to recognize same-sex marriages performed elsewhere. But in 2000, following a state supreme court ruling, the Vermont legislature legalized civil unions between individuals of the same sex, enabling gays and lesbians to receive all the legal benefits available to married couples. Whether sanctioned by law or not, the number of gay and lesbian households steadily increased; the 2000 census revealed that there were nearly 600,000 homes in America headed by same-sex couples. While nearly one-quarter were in California and New York, there was at least one gay or lesbian couple living in 99 percent of the nation's counties.

QUICK CHECK

What was "gay liberation," and how did the movement develop?

Politics and Diplomacy after Watergate

The economic and social disruptions of the era contributed to problems of governance left over from Watergate. Even as many Americans worried about shrinking paychecks and disintegrating families, Congress increasingly challenged the prerogatives of the presidency. This made life in the White House difficult for Richard Nixon's immediate successors—and it made solving America's pressing problems nearly impossible.

WHY did the presidencies of Ford and Carter largely fail?

The Ford Administration

Gerald R. Ford had the distinction of being the first president who had not been elected to national office. Richard Nixon had appointed him to the vice presidency to succeed Spiro Agnew, who had been forced to resign in order to avoid prosecution for accepting bribes while he was governor of Maryland. Ford, an amiable and unpretentious Michigan congressman who had risen to the post of House minority leader, seemed ready to restore public confidence in the presidency when he replaced Nixon in August 1974.

Ford's honeymoon lasted only a month. On September 8, 1974, he shocked the nation by announcing he had granted Richard Nixon a full and unconditional pardon for all federal crimes he may have committed. Some critics charged darkly that Nixon and Ford had made a secret bargain; others pointed out how unfair it was for Nixon's aides to serve their prison terms while the chief criminal went free. Ford apparently acted in an effort to end the bitterness over Watergate, but his attempt backfired, eroding public confidence in his leadership and linking him indelibly with the scandal.

Gerald Ford

Ford soon found himself fighting an equally difficult battle on behalf of the beleaguered CIA. The Watergate scandal and the Vietnam fiasco had eroded public confidence in the government and lent credibility to a startling series of disclosures about past covert actions. The president allowed the CIA to confirm some of the charges, and then he made things worse by blurting out to the press the juiciest item of all: The CIA had been involved in plots to assassinate foreign leaders.

Senate and House select committees appointed to investigate the CIA now focused on the assassination issue, eventually charging that the agency had been involved in no less than eight separate attempts to kill Fidel Castro. The chairman of the Senate committee, Frank Church of Idaho, worried that the revelations would damage the reputations of Democratic Presidents Kennedy and Johnson; he tried to put all the blame on the CIA, likening it to "a rogue elephant on the rampage."

In late 1975, President Ford finally moved to limit the damage to the CIA. He appointed George H. W. Bush, then a respected former Republican congressman, as the agency's new director and gave him the authority both to reform the CIA and to strengthen its role in shaping national security policy. Most notably, Ford issued an executive order outlawing assassination as an instrument of American foreign policy. To prevent future abuses, Congress created permanent House and Senate intelligence committees to exercise general oversight for covert CIA operations.

Ford proved less successful in his dealings with Congress on other issues. Although he prided himself on his good relations with members of both houses, he opposed Democratic measures such as federal aid to education and control over strip mining. In a little more than a year, he vetoed thirty-nine separate bills. In fact, Ford, who as a congressman had opposed virtually every Great Society measure, proved far more conservative than Nixon in the White House.

QUICK CHECK What ended Ford's honeymoon with the American people?

THE ELECTION OF 1976			
Candidate	**Party**	**Popular Vote**	**Electoral Vote**
Jimmy Carter	Democratic	40,828,587	297
Gerald Ford	Republican	39,147,613	241

Carter and American Malaise

Gerald Ford Presidential Campaign Ad

Ford's lackluster record and the legacy of Watergate made the Democratic nomination a prize worth fighting for in 1976. A large field of candidates entered the contest, but a virtual unknown, former Georgia governor James Earl Carter, quickly became the front-runner. Aware of the voters' disgust with politicians of both parties, Jimmy Carter ran as an outsider, portraying himself as a southerner who had no experience in Washington and one who could thus give the nation fresh and untainted leadership. On television, the basic Carter commercial showed him at his Georgia peanut farm, dressed in blue jeans, looking directly into the camera and saying, "I'll never tell a lie."

Voters took Carter at his word, and elected him over Ford in a close contest. Unfortunately, Carter's outsider status, while attractive in a campaign, made governing as president difficult. He had no discernible political philosophy, no clear sense of direction. He called himself a populist, but that label meant little more than an appeal to the common man, a somewhat ironic appeal, given Carter's personal wealth. "The idea of a millionaire populist has always amused me," commented his attorney general, fellow Georgian Griffin Bell.

Lacking both a clear set of priorities and a coherent political philosophy, the Carter administration had little chance to succeed. The president strove hard for a balanced budget but was forced to accept mounting deficits. Federal agencies fought to save the environment and help consumers but served only to anger industry.

Jimmy Carter, The "Crisis of Confidence" Speech (1979)

In the crucial area of social services, Joseph Califano, secretary of Health, Education, and Welfare (HEW), failed repeatedly in efforts to carry out long-overdue reforms. His attempts to overhaul the nation's welfare program, which had become a $30 billion annual operation serving some thirty million Americans, won little support from the White House. Carter's unwillingness to take the political risks involved in revamping the overburdened Social Security system by reducing benefits and raising the retirement age blocked Califano's efforts. And the HEW secretary finally gave up his attempt to draw up a workable national health insurance plan.

Informed by his pollsters in 1979 that he was losing the nation's confidence, Carter sought desperately to redeem himself. After a series of meetings at Camp David with a wide variety of advisers, he gave a speech in which he seemed to blame his failure on the American people, accusing them of creating "a crisis of confidence… that strikes at the very heart and soul and spirit of our national will." Then, a week after what his critics termed the "national malaise" speech, he requested the resignation of Califano and the secretary of the treasury. But neither the attempt to pin responsibility on the American people nor the firing of cabinet members could hide the fact that Carter, despite his good intentions and hard work, had failed to provide the bold leadership the nation needed.

QUICK CHECK ✓

What mood did Carter detect in American society?

Troubles Abroad

In the aftermath of the Vietnam War, most Americans wanted to have little to do with the world. Military intervention had failed in Southeast Asia, and with the American economy in trouble, the country's economic leverage appeared minimal. Moreover, the point of détente was to diminish the need for American intervention abroad by directing the superpower contest with the Soviet Union into political channels.

Yet various groups in the Third World didn't get the message of détente. Central America, for example, witnessed numerous uprisings against entrenched authoritarian regimes. In mid-1979, dictator Anastasio Somoza capitulated to the Sandinista forces in Nicaragua. Despite American attempts to moderate the Sandinista revolution, the new regime moved steadily to the left, developing close ties with Castro's Cuba. In neighboring El Salvador, a growing leftist insurgency against a repressive regime put the United States in an awkward position. Unable to find a workable alternative between the extremes of reactionary dictatorship and radical revolution in Central America, Carter tried to use American economic aid to encourage the military junta in El Salvador to carry out democratic reforms. But after the guerrillas launched a major offensive in January 1981, he authorized large-scale military assistance to the government for its war against the insurgents, setting a precedent for the future.

Carter initially had better luck in the Middle East. In 1978, he invited Egyptian president Anwar Sadat and Israeli prime minister Menachem Begin to negotiate a peace treaty under his guidance at Camp David. For thirteen days, Carter met with Sadat and Begin, finally emerging with the **Camp David accords.**

Camp David accords
In 1978, President Carter mediated a peace agreement between the leaders of Egypt and Israel at Camp David, a presidential retreat near Washington, D.C. The next year, Israel and Egypt signed a peace treaty based on the Camp David accords.

Blindfolded American hostages stand among their Iranian captors after Iranian militants captured the American embassy in Tehran on November 4, 1979. The Iranians' capture of fifty-three Americans as hostages and their violent attacks on the embassy shocked U.S. citizens.

What effect did the hostage crisis have on Carter's presidency?

Iranian hostage crisis
In 1979, Iranian fundamentalists seized the American embassy in Tehran and held fifty-three American diplomats hostage for over a year. The Iranian hostage crisis weakened the Carter presidency; the hostages were finally released on January 20, 1981, the day Ronald Reagan became president.

QUICK CHECK ✔

What happened at Camp David, and why were Americans taken hostage in Iran?

A framework for negotiations rather than an actual peace settlement, the Camp David accords nonetheless paved the way for a 1979 treaty between these principal antagonists in the Arab-Israeli conflict. The treaty provided for the gradual return of the Sinai to Egypt but left the fate of the Palestinians, the Arab inhabitants of the West Bank and the Gaza Strip, unsettled.

Any sense of progress in the Middle East was quickly offset in 1979 by the outbreak of the Iranian Revolution. Under Nixon and Kissinger, the United States had come to depend heavily on the shah for defense of the vital Persian Gulf. Carter continued the close relationship with the shah, despite growing signs of domestic discontent with his leadership. By 1978, Iran was in chaos as the exiled Ayatollah Ruholla Khomeini led a fundamentalist Muslim revolt against the shah, who was forced to flee the country.

In October 1979, Carter permitted the shah to enter the United States for medical treatment. Irate mobs in Iran denounced the United States, and on November 4, militants seized the U.S. embassy in Tehran and took fifty-three Americans prisoner. The prolonged **Iranian hostage crisis** revealed the extent to which American power had declined in the 1970s. Carter relied first on diplomacy and economic reprisals in a vain attempt to free the hostages. In April 1980, the president authorized a desperate rescue mission that ended in failure when several helicopters broke down in the Iranian desert and an accident cost the lives of eight crewmen. The hostage crisis dragged on through the summer and fall of 1980, a symbol of American weakness that proved to be a powerful political handicap to Carter in the upcoming presidential election.

The Reagan Revolution

WHAT was the "Reagan revolution"?

After the turmoil of the 1960s, the economic and political troubles of the 1970s made Americans' turn to conservatism almost inevitable. The Watergate scandal won the Democrats a brief reprieve, but when the Republicans discovered an attractive candidate in Ronald Reagan, a decisive Republican victory was essentially assured.

The Election of 1980

In 1980, Jimmy Carter, who had used the Watergate trauma to win the presidency, found himself in serious trouble. Inflation, touched off by the second oil shock of the 1970s, reached double-digit figures. The Federal Reserve Board's effort to tighten the money supply had led to a recession, with unemployment climbing to nearly 8 percent by July 1980. What Ronald Reagan dubbed the "misery index," the combined rate of inflation and unemployment, hit 28 percent early in 1980 and stayed above 20 percent throughout the year.

Foreign policy proved almost as damaging to Carter. The Soviet invasion of Afghanistan had exploded hopes for continued détente and made Carter appear naive. The continuing hostage crisis in Iran underlined the administration's helplessness.

Ronald Reagan and his running mate, George H. W. Bush, hammered away at the state of the economy and the world. Reagan scored heavily among tradition-ally Democratic blue-collar groups by blaming Carter for inflation, which robbed workers of any gain in real wages. Reagan also accused Carter of allowing the

Soviets to outstrip the United States militarily and promised a massive buildup of American forces if he was elected. Carter's position was further hurt by the independent candidacy of liberal Republican John Anderson of Illinois, who appealed to voters disenchanted with Carter but not yet ready to embrace Reagan.

The president fought back by claiming that Reagan was too reckless to conduct American foreign policy in the nuclear age. Charging that the election would decide "whether we have peace or war," Carter tried to portray his Republican challenger as a warmonger. Reagan deflected the charge and summarized the case against the administration by putting a simple question to voters: "Are you better off now than you were four years ago?"

Voters answered with a resounding "no." Reagan carried forty-four states and gained 51 percent of the popular vote. Carter won only six states and 41 percent of the popular vote, while John Anderson received the remaining 8 percent but failed to carry a single state. Reagan clearly benefited from the growing political power of the Sunbelt; he carried every state west of the Mississippi except Minnesota, the home state of Carter's running mate, Walter

Election of 1980

	Electoral Vote by State		Popular Vote
REPUBLICAN Ronald Reagan	489	(green)	43,901,812
DEMOCRATIC Jimmy Carter	49	(purple)	35,483,820
INDEPENDENT John B. Anderson	—		5,719,437
MINOR PARTIES	—		921,188
	538		86,026,257

ALASKA 3
HAWAII 4
WASH., D.C. 3

Mondale. In the South, Reagan lost only Georgia, Carter's home state. Even more impressive were Reagan's inroads into the old New Deal coalition. He received 50.5 percent of the blue-collar vote and 46 percent of the Jewish vote, the best showing by a Republican since 1928. Only one group remained loyal to Carter: African American voters gave him 85 percent of their ballots.

Republican gains in Congress were even more surprising. For the first time since 1954, the GOP gained control of the Senate, 53 to 46, and the party picked up 33 seats in the House to narrow the Democratic margin from 114 to 50.

Though the full implications of the 1980 election remained to be seen, the outcome suggested that the Democratic coalition that had dominated American politics since the days of Franklin Roosevelt was falling apart. In the eight presidential elections from 1952 to 1980, Republican candidates received 52.3 percent of the popular vote, compared with 47.7 percent for the Democrats. Reagan's victory in 1980 thus marked the culmination of a Republican presidential realignment that ended a half-century of Democratic dominance.

WATCH

Jimmy Carter Presidential Campaign Ad

QUICK CHECK ✓

Why did Americans find Reagan so attractive?

Cutting Taxes and Spending

When Ronald Reagan took office in January 1981, the ravages of inflation had devastated the economy. Interest rates hovered near 20 percent, while the value of the dollar, compared to 1960, had dropped to just 36 cents. The new president blamed what he termed "the worst economic mess since the Great Depression" on high federal spending and excessive taxation. "Government is not the solution to our problems," Reagan announced in his inaugural address. "Government is the problem."

DOCUMENT

Ronald Reagan, First Inaugural Address (1981)

supply-side economics
Advocates of supply-side economics claimed that tax cuts would stimulate the economy by giving individuals a greater incentive to earn more money, which would lead to greater investments and eventually larger tax revenues at a lower rate. Critics replied that supply-side economics would only burden the economy with larger government deficits.

Paul Craig Roberts, *The Supply-Side Revolution* (1984)

Ronald Reagan on the Wisdom of the Tax Cut

QUICK CHECK ✔

What was Reagan's philosophy on taxes?

The president embraced the concept of **supply-side economics** as the remedy for the nation's economic ills. Supply-side economists believed that the private sector, if encouraged by tax cuts, would shift its resources from tax shelters to productive investment, leading to an economic boom that would provide enough new income to offset the lost revenue. Although many economists worried that the 30 percent cut in income taxes that Reagan favored would lead to large deficits, the president was confident that his program would both stimulate the economy and reduce the role of government.

The president made federal spending his first target. Quickly deciding not to attack such popular middle-class entitlement programs as Social Security and Medicare, and sparing critical social services for the "truly deserving needy," the so-called safety net, the Republicans concentrated on slashing $41 billion from the budget by cutting heavily into other social services such as food stamps and by reducing public service jobs, student loans, and support for urban mass transit. Reagan used his charm and powers of persuasion to woo conservative Democrats from the West and South. Appearing before a joint session of Congress only weeks after an attempt on his life, Reagan won a commanding 253 to 176 margin of victory for his budget in the House, and an even more lopsided vote of 78 to 20 in the Senate in May. A jubilant Reagan told a Los Angeles audience that he had achieved "the greatest reduction in government spending that has ever been attempted."

The president proved equally successful in trimming taxes. He initially advocated annual cuts of 10 percent in personal income taxes for three consecutive years. When the Democrats countered with a two-year plan that would reduce taxes by only 15 percent, Reagan compromised with a proposal to cut taxes by 5 percent the first year but insisted on the full 10 percent reduction for the second and third years. In July, both houses passed the tax cut by impressive margins.

In securing reductions in spending and lowering taxes, Reagan demonstrated beyond doubt his ability to wield presidential power effectively. As *Time* magazine commented, no president since FDR had "done so much of such magnitude so quickly to change the economic direction of the country."

Reagan and the World

HOW ? did Reagan reshape American foreign relations?

Reagan was determined to reverse the course of American policy abroad no less than at home. He believed that under Carter, American prestige and standing in the world had dropped to an all-time low. Intent on restoring traditional American pride and influence, Reagan devoted himself to strengthening America's defenses and recapturing world supremacy from the Soviet Union.

Challenging the "Evil Empire"

The president scored his first foreign policy victory on the day he took office, thanks to diplomatic efforts begun under Carter. On January 20, 1981, Iran released the fifty-three Americans held hostage and thus enabled Reagan to begin his presidency on a positive note.

Defense spending during the Reagan administration focused on weapons such as this F-117, the first operational aircraft to use "stealth" technology that made it difficult to detect in flight.

What prompted the Reagan defense buildup?

He built upon this accomplishment by embarking on a major military expansion. Here again he continued efforts begun by Carter, who after the Soviet invasion of Afghanistan had persuaded Congress to fund a 5 percent increase in defense spending. The Reagan expansion went far beyond Carter's. Secretary of Defense Caspar Weinberger proposed a plan that would more than double defense spending. The emphasis was on new weapons, ranging from the B-1 bomber and the controversial MX nuclear missile to the expansion of the navy from 456 to 600 ships. Despite some opposition in Congress, Reagan and Weinberger got most of what they wanted, and by 1985 the defense budget grew to more than $300 billion.

The justification for all the new weapons was Reagan's belief that the Soviet Union was a deadly enemy that threatened the well-being and security of the United States. Reagan saw the Russians as bent on world revolution, ready "to commit any crime, to lie, to cheat" to advance their cause. Citing what he called a "record of tyranny," Reagan denounced the Russians before the UN in 1982, claiming, "Soviet-sponsored guerrillas and terrorists are at work in Central and South America, in Africa, the Middle East, in the Caribbean and in Europe, violating human rights and unnerving the world with violence."

Given this view of Russia as "the focus of evil in the modern world," it is not surprising that the new president continued the hard line that Carter had adopted after the invasion of Afghanistan. Abandoning détente, Reagan proceeded to implement a 1979 decision to place 572 Pershing II and cruise missiles in western Europe within range of Moscow and other Russian population centers to match Soviet deployment of medium-range missiles aimed at NATO countries. Despite strong protests from the Soviet Union, as well as growing uneasiness in Europe and an increasingly vocal nuclear freeze movement at home, the United States began putting the weapons in bases in Great Britain and Germany in November 1983. The Soviets, claming the move gave them only ten minutes of warning time in case of an American attack, responded by breaking off disarmament negotiations in Geneva.

The nuclear arms race had now reached a more dangerous level than ever before. The United States stepped up research and development of the **Strategic Defense Initiative (SDI),** an antimissile system based on the use of lasers and particle beams to destroy incoming missiles in outer space. SDI was quickly dubbed "star wars" by the media. Critics doubted that SDI could be perfected, but they warned that even if it were, the result would be to escalate the arms race by forcing the

DOCUMENT

Ronald Reagan, Speech to the House of Commons (1982)

Strategic Defense Initiative (SDI)

Popularly known as "star wars," President Ronald Reagan's Strategic Defense Initiative (SDI) proposed the construction of an elaborate computer-controlled, antimissile defense system capable of destroying enemy missiles in outer space. Critics claimed that SDI could never be perfected.

QUICK CHECK ✓

Why did Reagan think the Soviet Union was evil, and what did he intend to do about it?

Russians to build more offensive missiles in order to overcome the American defense system. The Reagan administration, however, defended SDI as a legitimate attempt to free the United States from the deadly trap of deterrence, with its reliance on the threat of nuclear retaliation to keep the peace. Meanwhile, the Soviet Union kept deploying larger and more accurate land-based ICBMs. Although both sides continued to observe the unratified SALT II agreements, the fact remained that between them the two superpowers had nearly fifty thousand warheads in their nuclear arsenals.

Confrontation in Central America

MAP

Conflict in Central America, 1970–1998

Reagan perceived the Soviet challenge as extending across the globe. In Central America, an area marked by great extremes of wealth, with a small landowning elite and masses of peasants mired in poverty, the United States had traditionally looked for moderate middle-class regimes to support. But these were hard to find, and Washington often ended up backing repressive right-wing dictatorships rather than the leftist groups that raised the radical issues of land reform and redistribution of wealth. Yet it was often oppression by U.S.-supported regimes that drove those seeking political change to embrace revolutionary tactics.

Guatemala. Military coup against President Cerezo fails, May 1989; free elections held, 1993.

Haiti. Duvalier forced out of office, Feb. 1986; military coup against elected government, 1991.

Jamaica. Former socialist Michael Manley elected prime minister, Feb. 1989.

Nicaragua. Sandinista rebels come to power, 1979; Sandinista government defeated by opposition candidate Violetta Barrios de Chamorro, Feb. 1990.

Grenada. U.S. and regional forces land after military coup, Oct. 1983; elections held, Dec. 1984.

Panama Canal. Canal Zone comes under Panamanian control, 1979; Canal comes under Panamanian control in 2000.

El Salvador. Civil war, 1980–1990; opposing sides hold peace talks, 1990; peace treaty signed, 1992.

Panama. U.S. forces invade and capture drug trafficker General Manuel Noriega, Dec. 1989; Noriega is flown to federal prison in United States, Jan. 1990.

TROUBLE SPOTS IN CENTRAL AMERICA AND THE CARIBBEAN   U.S. involvement in Central American trouble spots intensified in the 1980s and early 1990s.

Which spots were the most controversial?

This was precisely what happened in Nicaragua, where the leftist Sandinista coalition finally succeeded in overthrowing the authoritarian Somoza regime in 1979. In an effort to strengthen the many middle-class elements in the original Sandinista government and to avoid forcing Nicaragua into the Cuban and Soviet orbit, Carter extended American economic aid.

The Reagan administration quickly reversed this policy. Secretary of State Alexander Haig cut off aid to Nicaragua in the spring of 1981, accusing the Sandinistas of driving out the moderates, welcoming Cuban advisers and Soviet military assistance, and serving as a supply base for leftist guerrillas in nearby El Salvador. The criticism became a self-fulfilling prophecy as Nicaragua grew even more dependent on Cuba and the Soviet Union.

The United States and Nicaragua were soon on a collision course. In April 1983, declaring that "the national security of all the Americas is at stake in Central America," Reagan asked Congress for the money and authority to oust the Sandinistas. When Congress, fearful of repeating the Vietnam fiasco, refused, Reagan opted for covert action. The CIA began supplying the Contras, exiles fighting against the Sandinistas from bases in Honduras and Costa Rica. The U.S.-backed rebels tried to disrupt the Nicaraguan economy, raiding villages, blowing up oil tanks, and even mining harbors. Then, in 1984, Congress passed the Boland Amendment prohibiting any U.S. agency from spending money in Central America. The withdrawal of U.S. financial backing left the Contras in a precarious position.

Ronald Reagan, Support for the Contras (1984)

QUICK CHECK ✓

How did Reagan deal with leftists in Central America?

Trading Arms for Hostages

Reagan was re-elected easily in 1984. Voters gave him credit for curbing inflation, reviving the economy, and challenging communism. Democratic candidate Walter Mondale, formerly Jimmy Carter's vice president, provided a jolt to the campaign by choosing Representative Geraldine Ferraro of New York as his running mate. But even the presence of the first woman on the national ticket of a major American party couldn't dent Reagan's enormous popularity. He swept to victory with 59 percent of the popular vote and carried every state but Mondale's home, Minnesota.

Yet the troubles abroad persisted. Not long after Reagan's second inauguration, his administration's policies in the Middle East and Central America converged in the **Iran-Contra affair.** In mid-1985, Robert McFarlane, who had become national security adviser a year earlier, began a new initiative designed to restore American influence in the troubled Middle East. Concerned over the fate of six Americans held hostage in Lebanon by groups thought to be loyal to Iran's Ayatollah Khomeini, McFarlane proposed trading American antitank missiles to Iran in return for the hostages' release. The Iranians, desperate for weapons in the war they had been waging against Iraq since 1980, seemed willing to comply.

Ronald Reagan Presidential Campaign Ad

The Middle East in the 1980s and 1990s

Iran-Contra affair
The Iran-Contra affair involved officials high in the Reagan administration secretly selling arms to Iran and using the proceeds to finance the Contra rebels in Nicaragua. This illegal transaction usurped the power of Congress.

THE ELECTION OF 1984			
Candidate	**Party**	**Popular Vote**	**Electoral Vote**
Reagan	Republican	54,455,075	525
Mondale	Democratic	37,577,185	13

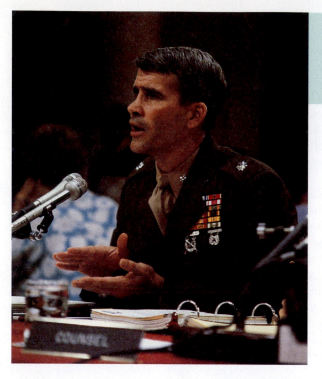

Despite Oliver North's questionable conduct, the public elevated him to near hero status during the televised Iran-Contra hearings. The bemedaled marine testified that he believed his deeds were justified as a defense of democracy.

Do you agree?

McFarlane soon found himself in over his head. He relied heavily on a young marine lieutenant colonel assigned to the National Security Council (NSC), Oliver North, and North in turn sought the assistance of CIA director William Casey, who interpreted the Iran initiative as an opportunity to use the NSC to mount the kind of covert operation denied the CIA under the post-1975 congressional oversight policy. By early 1986, when John Poindexter, a naval officer with little political experience, replaced a burned-out McFarlane as national security adviser, Casey was able to persuade the president to go ahead with shipments of TOW antitank missiles and HAWK anti-aircraft missiles to Iran.

The arms deal with Iran was bad policy, but what came next was criminal. Ever since the Boland Amendment in late 1984 had cut off congressional funding, the Reagan administration had been searching for ways to supply the Contras in Nicaragua. Oliver North was put in charge of soliciting donations from wealthy right-wing Americans. In early 1986, North had what he later described as a "neat idea" (apparently shared by Casey as well)—he could use profits from the sale of weapons to Iran (charging as much as $10,000 for a TOW that cost the United States only $3500) to finance the Contras. North's ploy was clearly not only illegal but unconstitutional, since it meant usurping the congressional power of the purse.

Ultimately the secret got out. Administration officials tried to shield Reagan from blame, and even after a congressional investigation it was unclear whether the president had approved the Contra diversion. Reagan's reputation survived the scandal, albeit tarnished. Several of his subordinates, including North and Poindexter, were prosecuted. William Casey might have joined them in the dock but died suddenly of a brain tumor.

Oliver North
Hearing

Ronald
Reagan, Iran
Contra
Address
(March 4,
1987)

QUICK CHECK

What was the Iran-Contra affair?

Reagan the Peacemaker

Americans' tolerance of Reagan's mistakes in the Iran-Contra affair resulted in part from the progress he was making on the larger issue of U.S.-Soviet relations. Elected as an anticommunist hardliner, Reagan softened during his second term to become an advocate of cooperation with Moscow.

A momentous change in leadership in the Soviet Union had much to do with the change in Reagan's approach. The illness and death of Leonid Brezhnev in 1982, followed in rapid succession by the deaths of his aged successors, Yuri Andropov and Konstantin Chernenko, led finally to the selection of Mikhail Gorbachev, a younger and more dynamic Soviet leader. Gorbachev was intent on

Reagan and Gorbachev in Red Square. During the summits between the two leaders, the American public grew to admire the Soviet premier for his policies of *perestroika* (restructuring) and *glasnost* (openness).

How important is the personal element in diplomacy?

improving relations with the United States as part of his new policy of *perestroika* (restructuring the Soviet economy) and *glasnost* (political openness). Soviet economic performance had been deteriorating steadily and the war in Afghanistan had become a major liability. Gorbachev needed a breathing spell in the arms race and a reduction in Cold War tensions in order to carry out his sweeping changes at home.

A series of summit meetings between Reagan and Gorbachev broke the chill in superpower relations and led in December 1987 to an **Intermediate Nuclear Forces Treaty (INF),** by which Reagan and Gorbachev agreed to remove and destroy all intermediate-range missiles in Europe. The most important arms-control agreement since SALT 1 of 1972, the INF treaty raised hopes that an end to the Cold War was finally in sight.

During the president's last year in office, the Soviets cooperated with the United States in pressuring Iran and Iraq to end their long war. Most significant of all, Gorbachev moved to end the war in Afghanistan. The first Soviet units pulled out in April 1988, with the final evacuation due to be completed early the next year. By the time Reagan left office in January 1989, he had scored a series of foreign policy triumphs that offset the Iran-Contra fiasco and thus helped redeem his presidency.

QUICK CHECK ✓

What did the INF treaty do?

Intermediate Nuclear Forces Treaty (INF)
Signed by President Reagan and Soviet President Gorbachev in Washington in late 1987, this agreement provided for the destruction of all intermediate-range nuclear missiles and permitted onsite inspection for the first time during the Cold War.

Conclusion: Challenging the New Deal

Though trouble dogged the final years of his presidency, the overall effect of Reagan's two terms was to reshape the landscape of American politics. The Democratic coalition forged by Franklin Roosevelt during the New Deal finally broke down as the Republicans captured the South and made deep inroads into organized labor.

More significantly, Reagan challenged the liberal premises of the New Deal by asserting that the private sector, rather than the federal government, ought to be the source of remedies to most of America's ills. Reagan prudently left intact the centerpieces of the welfare state—Social Security and Medicare—but he trimmed other programs and made any comparable expansion of federal authority nearly impossible. By the time he left office, small-government conservatism seemed the undeniable wave of the American future.

For a list of additional titles related to this chapter's topics, please see
www.pearsonamericanhistory.com.

MyHistoryLab

STUDY RESOURCES

KEY TERMS

Moral Majority, p. 835

neoconservatism, p. 835

détente, p. 836

Strategic Arms Limitation Talks (SALT), p. 836

Watergate scandal, p. 839

Organization of Petroleum Exporting Countries (OPEC), p. 841

Equal Rights Amendment (ERA), p. 845

Roe. v. Wade, p. 846

Camp David accords, p. 851

Iranian hostage crisis, p. 852

supply-side economics, p. 854

Strategic Defense Initiative (SDI), p. 855

Iran-Contra affair, p. 857

Intermediate Nuclear Forces Treaty (INF), p. 859

CHAPTER REVIEW

WHAT were the major accomplishments and failures of the Nixon presidency?

Nixon opened diplomatic relations with China and initiated détente with the Soviet Union. He withdrew American troops from Vietnam, terminating a quarter-century of American involvement in that unhappy country. But his role in the Watergate scandal led to a constitutional crisis that didn't end until Nixon had been forced from office in disgrace. *(p. 836)*

HOW were oil and inflation linked during the 1970s?

Oil prices jumped dramatically in the 1970s, as a result of growing demand for oil and of turmoil in the oil-producing regions of the Middle East. The rising oil prices contributed to a sharp increase in the overall price level, leading to the worst inflation in modern American history. *(p. 841)*

WHAT changes occurred in private life during this period?

The private lives of Americans underwent substantial changes during the 1970s. The divorce rate rose significantly, and the number of married couples with children declined. Women entered the professions in greater numbers, and *Roe v. Wade* guaranteed their right to abortion. Gay men and lesbian women achieved greater freedom than before, though they still lacked certain rights accorded to heterosexuals. *(p. 843)*

WHY did the presidencies of Ford and Carter largely fail?

Ford and Carter had to deal with the aftermath of Vietnam and Watergate, as well as the economic disruptions that followed the oil price rises of the 1970s. Ford alienated many Americans by pardoning Nixon, and Carter fumbled the hostage crisis in Iran. *(p. 849)*

WHAT was the "Reagan revolution"?

The Reagan revolution was the return to conservatism in American politics and diplomacy upon Reagan's 1980 election as president. Reagan pledged to reduce the role of government in American life, and to restore American honor and confidence abroad. *(p. 852)*

HOW did Reagan reshape American foreign relations?

Reagan rejected the policy of détente and challenged the Soviet Union more directly than any American president in decades. He called for the creation of the SDI missile system, and he waged covert war against leftists in Central America. The Iran-Contra affair, in which Reagan traded arms for hostages, tarnished his reputation, but he recovered sufficiently to negotiate the INF treaty with the Soviet Union. *(p. 854)*

MAKING CONNECTIONS

1. If Nixon hadn't resigned, would he have been impeached? Would that have been a good thing or a bad thing?
2. What did feminism and gay liberation have to do with each other?
3. Should Ford have pardoned Nixon? Why or why not?
4. Which was more scandalous: Iran-Contra or Watergate? Why?

PRACTICE QUIZ

1. The late _____ founded the Moral Majority, a Christian fundamentalist group.
   a. Nathan Bedford Forrest
   b. Jerry Falwell
   c. Jim Jones
   d. Charles Manson

2. The ideology of _____ became fashionable during the 1970s and 1980s among many former liberal intellectuals.
   a. Feminism
   b. Racism
   c. Neoconservatism
   d. Populism

3. The _____ scandal helped to bring down the Nixon administration in 1974.
   a. Travelgate
   b. Teapot Dome
   c. Watergate
   d. Iran-Contra

4. In 1973 the _____ announced a 5 percent cut in oil production.
   a. United States
   b. French government
   c. British government
   d. Organization of Petroleum Exporting Countries (OPEC)

5. The modern _____ movement began with a riot at the Stonewall Inn in New York City.
   a. Feminist
   b. Civil rights
   c. Gay liberation
   d. American Indian

6. President Ford shocked the nation when he announced in 1974 that he had pardoned
   a. Richard Nixon
   b. Ronald Reagan
   c. Daniel Ellsberg
   d. Leonard Peltier

7. Which of the following problems did *not* beset the Carter administration?
   a. Sex scandals
   b. The energy and oil crisis
   c. The Iranian hostage crisis
   d. Inflation

8. All of the following describe the Iranian hostage crisis in Tehran *except*
   a. Militants seized more than fifty hostages from the U.S. embassy.
   b. Many of the hostages were executed.
   c. The crisis revealed the decline of American power in recent years.
   d. Carter authorized a rescue mission that failed miserably.

9. Ronald Reagan pulled off victory in the 1980 election through these techniques *except*
   a. He hammered away at the state of the economy.
   b. He accused Carter of allowing the Soviets to beat the United States militarily.
   c. He criticized Carter for making tax cuts.
   d. He blamed Carter for the Iranian hostage crisis.

10. Reagan's Central American foreign policy initiatives were characterized by
    a. The use of covert aid and action in Nicaragua, Costa Rica, and Honduras.
    b. The cutting off of aid to leftist regimes.
    c. Supporting right wing dictatorships to fulfill American economic interests.
    d. All of the above answers are accurate.

Find more practice at
www.myhistorylab.com

SAMPLE ESSAY QUESTIONS

1. Trace the events leading to the resignation of President Nixon in 1974.

2. Explain why historians label Reagan's years in the White House a "revolution"?

To the Twenty-first Century
1989–2008

"This Will Not Stand": Foreign Policy in the Post–Cold War Era

Raymond Saunders, *Joseph Fitzpatrick Was Our Teacher, 1991.* This powerful mixed media piece on canvas by African American artist Raymond Saunders includes layered visual references to contemporary political and social issues, popular culture, advertising, and artistic predecessors.

Can you identify some of those issues?

On the evening of August 1, 1990, George H. W. Bush sat in a T-shirt in the medical office in the basement of the White House. Bush was an avid golfer, but his duties as president kept him from playing as much as he would have liked, and when he did find time to squeeze in a round or some practice, he tended to overdo things. This summer day he had strained a shoulder muscle hitting practice balls, and now he rested on the exam table while a therapist applied deep heat. He planned a quiet evening and hoped the soreness would be gone by morning.

Two unexpected visitors altered his plans. Brent Scowcroft, Bush's national security adviser, and Richard Haass, the Middle East expert of the National Security Council, appeared at the door of the exam room. Bush had known Scowcroft for years, and the look on his face told him something was seriously amiss. Scowcroft's words confirmed the impression. "Mr. President, it looks very bad," Scowcroft said. "Iraq may be about to invade Kuwait."

For months the Bush administration had been monitoring a territorial and financial dispute between Iraq and Kuwait. Iraqi dictator Saddam Hussein was rattling the saber against the much smaller Kuwait, but Saddam had rattled sabers before without actually using them. The previous week Saddam had spoken with the American

KEY EVENTS

ambassador in Iraq, April Glaspie, who came away from the meeting with the belief that his bellicose talk was chiefly for political effect. The United States had indicated its displeasure with Saddam's threats, and Glaspie judged that he had gotten the message. "He does not want to further antagonize us," she wrote to Washington.

For this reason, Saddam's decision to invade Kuwait at the beginning of August caught the Bush administration by surprise. American intelligence agencies detected Iraq's mobilization; this was what brought Scowcroft and Haass to the White House on the evening of August 1. Haass suggested that the president call Saddam and warn him not to go through with the attack. But even as Bush considered this suggestion, Scowcroft received a message from the State Department that the American embassy in Kuwait had reported shooting in downtown Kuwait City. "So much for calling Saddam," Bush said. Within hours the Iraqi forces crushed all resistance in Kuwait.

Bush, Scowcroft, and other American officials recognized that the Iraqi takeover of Kuwait constituted the first crisis of the post–Cold War era. As Lawrence Eagleburger, the deputy secretary of state, asserted in an emergency meeting of the National Security Council, "This is the first test of the postwar system. As the bipolar world is relaxed, it permits this, giving people more flexibility because they are not worried about the involvement of the superpowers." During the Cold War, a de facto division of labor had developed, with the United States and the Soviet Union each generally keeping its clients and allies in line, typically by threatening to withhold weapons or other assistance. Had the Soviet Union still been a superpower, Saddam, a longtime recipient of Soviet aid, likely would have heeded Moscow's warnings to settle his dispute with Kuwait peacefully. But in 1990 the Soviet system was disintegrating, and the Kremlin's clients were on their own. "Saddam Hussein now has greater flexibility because the Soviets are tangled up in domestic issues," Eagleburger explained. The world was watching. "If he succeeds, others may try the same thing."

It was this belief that shaped the Bush administration's response to the crisis. The president and his advisers understood that they were entering uncharted territory after the Cold War. As the sole remaining superpower, the United States had the opportunity to employ its military and economic resources more freely than at any time in history.

President George Bush confers with National Security Council adviser Brent Scowcroft (left), White House Chief of Staff John Sununu (center), and Vice President Dan Quayle (right), at the Oval Office on August 1, 1990, following the Iraqi invasion of Kuwait.

What was Bush's response?

But with that freedom came unprecedented responsibility. During the Cold War the United States could cite the threat of Soviet retaliation as reason to avoid intervening in the affairs of other countries; with that threat gone, American leaders would have to weigh each prospective intervention on its own merits. If one country attacked another, should the United States defend the victim? If the government of a country oppressed its own people, should the United States move to stop the oppression? These questions—and the answers American presidents gave to them—would define American foreign policy in the era after the Cold War.

Bush sensed the importance of the United States's responses, and he responded accordingly. He convened his principal deputies for a series of White House meetings. The particular stakes with Iraq and in the surrounding Persian Gulf were discussed at length. "The rest of the world badly needs oil," Defense Secretary Dick Cheney observed, restating the obvious. Saddam's seizure of Kuwait gave him control of a large part of the world's oil supply, but the real prize was Saudi Arabia. "Saudi Arabia and others will cut and run if we are weak," Cheney predicted.

Bush consulted America's oldest allies. Britain's Margaret Thatcher urged the president to oppose Saddam most vigorously. "If Iraq wins, no small state is safe," the prime minister declared. She offered to help. "We must win this.… We cannot give in to dictators."

Bush asked his generals what his military options were. "Iraq is not ten feet tall, but it is formidable," Norman Schwarzkopf, the U.S. commander for the Middle East, replied. American air power could punish Saddam and perhaps soften him up, but ground forces—in large numbers—would be required to guarantee victory.

By August 5, Bush had made up his mind. As he exited the helicopter that brought him back from Camp David to the White House from another high-level meeting, reporters crowded the South Lawn. What was he planning to do? they asked.

"I'm not going to discuss what we're doing in terms of moving forces, anything of that nature," Bush answered. "But I view it very seriously, not just that but any threat to any other countries." Bush was no orator, and these remarks were unscripted. But one sentence summarized the policy that soon began to unfold: "This will not stand, this aggression against Kuwait."

The First President Bush

WHAT
were the important issues in George H. W. Bush's presidency, and how were they handled?

George Bush Presidential Campaign Act

Elected on the strength of his association with Ronald Reagan, George H. W. Bush appeared poised to confirm the ascendancy of the conservative values Reagan forced to the center stage of American life. But events, especially abroad, distracted Bush, whose principal contribution proved to be in the area of foreign affairs. Bush brought the Cold War to a peaceful and triumphant conclusion, and he launched America toward the twenty-first century, an era when the United States faced new opportunities and new challenges.

Republicans at Home

Democrats approached the 1988 presidential election with high hopes, having regained control of the Senate in 1986 and not having to face the popular Reagan. But Vice President George H. W. Bush proved a stronger candidate than almost anyone had expected, and in a contest that confirmed the Republicans' hold on the Sunbelt, he defeated Massachusetts governor Michael Dukakis.

Many people expected the policies of the Bush administration to reflect the reputation of the new president—bland and cautious, lacking in vision but safely predictable. At home, he lived up (or down) to his reputation, sponsoring few initiatives in education, health care, or environmental protection while continuing the Reagan theme of limiting federal interference in the everyday lives of American citizens. He vetoed family leave legislation, declined to endorse meaningful health care reform, and watered down civil rights proposals in Congress. The one exception was the **Americans with Disabilities Act (ADA),** passed by Congress in 1990, which prohibited discrimination against the disabled in hiring, transportation, and public accommodations. Beginning in July 1992, ADA called for all public buildings, restaurants, and stores to be made accessible to those with physical handicaps and required that businesses with twenty-five or more workers hire new employees without regard to disability.

Much of Bush's time on domestic affairs was taken up with the soaring federal budget deficit. The deficits Bush inherited from Reagan topped $150 billion per year, and conventional financial wisdom dictated that something be done to bring them down. In campaigning for president, Bush had promised "no new taxes," but in the fall of 1990 he broke the pledge. In a package deal negotiated with the leaders of Congress, he agreed to a budget that included new taxes along with substantial spending cuts, especially on the military. The resulting agreement projected a savings of $500 billion over five years, half from reduced spending and half from new revenue generated mainly by increasing the top tax rate from 28 percent to 31 percent and raising the gasoline tax by 5.1 cents a gallon.

Americans with Disabilities Act (ADA)

Passed by Congress in 1991, this act banned discrimination against the disabled in employment and mandated easy access to all public and commercial buildings.

THE ELECTION OF 1988			
Candidate	**Party**	**Popular Vote**	**Electoral Vote**
Bush	Republican	48,886,097	426
Dukakis	Democratic	41,809,074	111

Advocates for the disabled and a sign language interpreter look on as President Bush signs the Americans with Disabilities Act.

What were some effects of the act?

Unfortunately for the president, the budget deal coincided with the beginning of a slow but painful recession that ended the Republican prosperity of the 1980s. Not only did Bush face recriminations from voters for breaking a campaign pledge not to raise taxes, but the economic decline led to greatly reduced government revenues. As a result, the deficit continued to soar, rising from $150 billion in fiscal year 1989 to just under $300 billion in 1992. Despite the 1990 budget agreement, the national debt increased by more than $1 trillion during Bush's presidency.

QUICK CHECK ✓

What were the principal domestic accomplishments of the Bush administration?

Ending the Cold War

Bush might have accomplished more in domestic affairs had not the international developments begun during the Reagan years accelerated dramatically. Bush had been in office only months when the communist system of the Cold War began falling apart. In country after country, communism gave way to democracy as the old order collapsed more quickly than anyone had expected.

An early attempt at anticommunist liberation proved tragically abortive. In May 1989, students in China began a month-long demonstration for democracy in Beijing's Tiananmen Square that attracted worldwide attention. Watching American television coverage of Gorbachev's visit to China in mid-May, Americans were fascinated to see the Chinese students call for democracy with a hunger strike and a handcrafted replica of the Statue of Liberty. But on the evening of June 4, the Chinese leaders sent tanks and troops to Tiananmen Square to crush the student demonstration. By the next day, full-scale repression swept over China; several hundred protesters were killed, and thousands were injured. Chinese leaders imposed martial law to quell the dissent and shatter American hopes for a democratic China.

Bush responded cautiously. He wanted to preserve American influence with the Chinese government. Hence, despite official statements denouncing the crackdown, Bush sent National Security Adviser Brent Scowcroft on a secret mission to Beijing to maintain a working relationship with the Chinese leaders.

A far more promising trend toward freedom began in Europe in mid-1989. In June, Lech Walesa and his Solidarity movement came to power in free elections in Poland. Soon the winds of change were sweeping over the former Iron Curtain countries. A new regime in Hungary opened its borders to the West in September, allowing thousands of East German tourists in Hungary to flee to freedom. One by one, the repressive governments of East Germany, Czechoslovakia, Bulgaria, and Romania fell. The most heartening scene of all took place in East Germany in early November when the new communist leaders suddenly announced the opening of the Berlin Wall. Workers quickly demolished a 12-foot-high section of this despised physical symbol of the Cold War, joyously singing a German version of "For He's a Jolly Good Fellow."

The Berlin Wall

Most people realized it was Mikhail Gorbachev who was responsible for the liberation of eastern Europe. In late 1988, the Soviet leader signaled the spread of his reforms to the Soviet satellites by announcing that the Brezhnev doctrine, which called for Soviet control of eastern Europe, was now replaced with "the Sinatra doctrine," which meant that the people of this region could now do things "their way." It was Gorbachev's refusal to use armed force to keep repressive regimes in power that permitted the long-delayed liberation of the captive peoples of central and eastern Europe.

Yet by the end of 1991, both Gorbachev and the Soviet Union had become victims of the demise of communism. On August 19, 1991, right-wing plotters placed Gorbachev under arrest. Boris Yeltsin, the newly elected president of the Russian Republic, broke up the coup by mounting a tank in Moscow and demanding Gorbachev's release. The Red Army rallied to Yeltsin's side. The coup failed and Gorbachev was released, only to resign in December 1991 after the fifteen republics dissolved the Soviet Union. Russia, by far the largest and most powerful of the former Soviet republics, took the lead in joining with ten others to form a loose alignment called the Commonwealth of Independent States (CIS). Yeltsin then disbanded the Communist party and continued the reforms begun by Gorbachev to establish democracy and a free market system in Russia.

The Bush administration, although criticized for its cautious approach, welcomed the demise of communism. Bush facilitated the reunification of Germany and offered economic assistance to Russia and the other members of the new CIS. On the critical issue of nuclear weapons, Bush and Gorbachev in 1991 signed START I, agreeing to reduce nuclear warheads to less than ten thousand apiece. In late 1992, Bush and Yeltsin agreed on the terms of START II, which would eliminate land missiles with multiple warheads and reduce the number of nuclear weapons on each side to just over three thousand, a level not seen since the mid-1960s.

QUICK CHECK

How did Bush help end the Cold War?

The Gulf War

Amid the disintegration of the Soviet system, Iraq in August 1990 invaded Kuwait. Although Bush quickly concluded that Saddam Hussein's aggression must be reversed, actually removing Iraq from Kuwait took time and great effort. The president started by persuading Saudi Arabia to accept a huge American troop buildup, dubbed Desert Shield. This American presence would prevent Saddam from advancing beyond Kuwait into Saudi Arabia; it would also allow the United States to launch a ground attack against Iraqi forces if and when the president determined such an attack was necessary.

While the American buildup took place, Bush arranged an international coalition to condemn the Iraqi invasion and endorse economic sanctions against Iraq. Not every member of the coalition subscribed to the "new world order" that Bush said the liberation of Kuwait would help establish, but all concurred in the general principle of deterring international aggression. Essential to the success of Bush's diplomatic offensive was the support of the Soviet Union, which during the Cold War had regularly blocked American initiatives in the United Nations. Soviet leaders may have been sincere in wishing to see Saddam punished, but they also hoped to receive American aid in restructuring their economy.

Congress required somewhat more convincing. Many Democrats supported economic sanctions against Iraq but opposed the use of force. Yet as the troop buildup in the Persian Gulf proceeded—as Operation Desert Shield evolved into what would be called Operation **Desert Storm**—and as the sanctions failed to dislodge Iraq from Kuwait, some of the skeptics gradually came around. After securing UN support for military action, Bush persuaded Congress (with just five votes to spare in the Senate) to approve the use of force to liberate Kuwait.

On January 17, 1991, the president unleashed a devastating aerial assault on Iraq. After knocking out the Iraqi air defense network in a few hours, F-117A stealth fighters and Tomahawk cruise missiles hit key targets in Baghdad. The air attack, virtually unchallenged by the Iraqis, wiped out command and control centers and enabled the bombers of the United States and its coalition partners (chiefly Britain) to demoralize the beleaguered enemy troops.

After five weeks of this, Bush gave the order for the ground assault. Led by General Schwarzkopf, American and allied armored units swept across the desert in a great flanking operation while a combined force of U.S. marines and Saudi troops drove directly into Kuwait City. In just one hundred hours,

George H. W. Bush, Gulf War Address (1990)

George Bush, Address to the Nation on Persian Gulf (1991)

Desert Storm

Desert Storm was the code name used by the United States and its coalition partners in waging war against Iraq in early 1991 to liberate Kuwait.

Anti-aircraft fire lights up the sky over Baghdad, Iraq, during the Persian Gulf War. A month of strikes on Iraqi targets was followed by a ground offensive that lasted only one hundred hours before Iraqi troops began to surrender and President Bush ordered a ceasefire.

Why was this order criticized?

the American-led offensive liberated Kuwait and sent Saddam Hussein's vaunted Republican Guard fleeing back into Iraq.

In a controversial decision, President Bush, acting on the advice of General Colin Powell, chairman of the Joint Chiefs, halted the advance and agreed to an armistice with Iraq. Critics claimed that with just a few more days of fighting, perhaps even just a few more hours, American forces could have encircled the Republican Guard and ended Saddam's cruel regime. But the president, fearful of disrupting the allied coalition and of having American troops mired down in a guerrilla war, stopped when he had achieved his announced goal of liberating Kuwait. Moreover, he hoped that a chastened Saddam would help balance the threat of Iran in the volatile Persian Gulf region.

QUICK CHECK ✓

What provoked the Gulf War of 1991, and how did it turn out?

The Changing Faces of America

HOW did the American population shift and grow during the 1990s and after?

From the *Mayflower* to the covered wagon, movement has always characterized the American people. The final years of the twentieth century and the early years of the twenty-first witnessed two significant shifts in the American population: continued movement internally to the Sunbelt region of the South and West, and a remarkable influx of immigrants from developing nations. These changes led to increased urbanization, greater ethnic diversity, and growing social unrest.

A People on the Move

Sunbelt

This region consists of a broad band of states running across the South from Florida to Texas and north to include California and the Pacific Northwest. Beginning in the 1970s, this area experienced rapid economic growth and major gains in population.

By the 1990s, a majority of Americans lived in the **Sunbelt** of the South and West. Best defined as a broad band running across the country below the 37th parallel from the Carolinas to Southern California, the Sunbelt had begun to flourish with the buildup of military bases and defense plants during World War II. Rapid population growth continued with the stimulus of heavy Cold War defense spending and accelerated in the 1970s when both new high-technology firms and more established industries were attracted by lower labor costs and the favorable climate of the Sunbelt states. Florida, Texas, and California led the way, each gaining more than two million new residents in the 1970s.

The flow continued at a slightly lower rate over the next two decades. The Northeast and the Middle West continued losing people to the South and West, and in 1994 Texas surpassed New York as the nation's second most populous state. The 2000 census revealed that while all regions had gained population in the 1990s, the South and West had expanded by nearly 20 percent, compared to around 6 percent for the Northeast and Middle West. Phoenix was typical of the phenomenal growth of Sunbelt cities, adding a million residents in the 1990s to grow at a 45 percent rate. "Phoenix is flat and it's easy," explained a geographer who saw no end in sight. "You stick a shovel in the ground and pour a slab and you have a house."

The increasing urbanization of America had positive and negative aspects. People living in the large metropolitan areas were both more affluent and better educated than their rural counterparts. Family income among people living in the bigger cities and their suburbs ran $9000 a year more, and three-fourths of the urban population had graduated from high school, compared to two-thirds of other Americans. A metropolitan American was twice as likely to be a college graduate as a rural resident. Yet these advantages were offset by higher urban crime rates, longer commuting time in heavy traffic, and higher living costs. Nevertheless, the big cities and their suburbs continued to thrive, accounting for 80 percent of all Americans by 2000.

Another striking population trend was the nationwide rise in the number of the elderly. At the beginning of the twentieth century, only 4.1 percent of the population was aged 65 or older; by 2000, those over 65 made up more than 12 percent of the population, with the nearly four million over 85 the fastest growing group of all. Census Bureau projections suggest that by the year 2030, one out of every five Americans will be over age 65.

QUICK CHECK

Why did Americans migrate to the Sunbelt?

The Revival of Immigration

The flow of immigrants into the United States grew dramatically during the last decade of the twentieth century and the first decade of the twenty-first. By 2005, a record high of 35 million foreign-born persons lived in the United States, constituting 12 percent of the total population.

The new wave of immigrants came mainly from Latin America and Asia. By 2005, over half the foreign-born population of the United States came from Latin

DOCUMENT

Illegal Immigration Reform and Immigrant Responsibility Act of 1996

Newly sworn-in citizens of the United States wave U.S. flags during a naturalization ceremony in Miami on April 28, 2006. Days later, more than one million immigrants participated in a nationwide boycott called "A Day Without Immigrants" to protest the proposed tightening of U.S. immigration laws.

What did they dislike about the proposals?

America, about one-quarter from Asia, and about one out of seven from Europe. The new immigrants tended to settle in urban areas in six states—California, Texas, New York, Florida, Illinois, and New Jersey. In California, the influx of immigrants from Asia and Mexico created growing pressure on public services, especially during the recessions of the early 1990s and the early 2000s.

The arrival of so many immigrants was bound to lead to controversy over whether immigrants were a benefit or a liability to American society. A study by the National Academy of Sciences in 1997 reported that while government services used by immigrants—schools, welfare, health clinics—cost more initially than was collected from them in taxes, in the long run, immigrants and their families more than paid their way. In regard to employment, immigrants tended to help consumers and employers by working for relatively low wages in restaurants, the textile industry, and farming, but they hurt low-skilled U.S. workers, notably high school dropouts and many African Americans, by keeping wages low. Economist George J. Borjas, a refugee from Cuba, claimed that immigrants from developing countries lacked the education and job skills needed to achieve the level of prosperity attained by newcomers in the past; instead of entering the mainstream of American life, they were likely to remain a permanent underclass.

 QUICK CHECK

What prompted the renewed growth in immigration?

Emerging Hispanics

People of Hispanic origin became the nation's largest ethnic group in 2002, surpassing African Americans for the first time. The rapidly growing Hispanic population climbed to over 41 million by 2005, accounting for 14 percent of the nation's population. "It doesn't surprise me," commented the leader of the League of Latin American Citizens. "Anybody that travels around... can see Latinos everywhere, working everywhere, trying to reach the American dream."

The Census Bureau identified four major Hispanic groups: Mexican Americans, Puerto Ricans, Cuban Americans, and other Hispanics, including many from Central America. Even though most of the Hispanic population was concentrated in cities such as New York, Los Angeles, San Antonio, and Miami, the 2000 census showed a surprising geographical spread. Hispanics made up 20 percent of the population in individual counties in states such as Georgia, Iowa, and Minnesota. "The Latinization of the country is not just happening in New York, Miami, or L.A.," observed a Puerto Rican leader. "Its greatest impact is in the heartland in places like Reading, Pennsylvania; Lorain, Ohio; and Lowell, Massachusetts."

The Hispanic groups had several features in common. All were relatively youthful, with a median age of 22 and a high fertility rate. They tended to be relatively poor, with one-fourth falling below the poverty line, and to be employed in low-paying positions as manual laborers, domestic servants, and migrant workers. Although the position of Hispanics had improved considerably in the boom years of the 1980s and 1990s, they still lagged behind mainstream America. The poverty rate among Hispanics was twice the national average, and family median income in 2005 was $34,000, or roughly two-thirds the level for whites.

Lack of education was a key factor in preventing economic progress for Hispanics. Fewer Hispanics graduated from high school than other minorities and their school dropout rate was the nation's highest at more than 50 percent. Hispanic leaders warned that these figures boded ill not just for their own group, but for society as a whole. "You either educate us," claimed a San Antonio activist, "or you pay for building more jails or for more welfare."

The entry of several million illegal immigrants from Mexico, once derisively called "wetbacks" and now known as **undocumented aliens,** created a substantial social problem for the nation and especially for the Southwest. Critics charged that the flagrant violation of the nation's border with Mexico had led to a subculture beyond the boundaries of law and ordinary custom. They argued that the aliens took jobs from U.S. citizens, kept wages artificially low, and received extensive welfare and medical benefits that strained budgets in states such as Texas and California.

Defenders of the undocumented aliens contended that the nation gained from the abundant supply of workers who were willing to work in fields and factories at backbreaking jobs shunned by most Americans. Moreover, defenders stated, illegal entrants usually paid sales and withholding taxes but rarely used government services for fear of being deported. Whichever view was correct, an exploited class of illegal aliens was living on the edge of poverty. The *Wall Street Journal* summed it up best by observing, "The people who benefit the most from this situation are certainly the employers, who have access to an underground market of cheap, productive labor, unencumbered by minimum wage laws, union restrictions, or pension requirements."

Concern over economic competition from Mexican "illegals" had led Congress to pass legislation in 1986 that penalized employers who hired undocumented workers. Congress permitted those aliens who could show that they were living in the United States before 1982 to become legal residents; nearly three million accepted this offer of amnesty to become legal residents. The reform effort, however, failed to stem the continued flow of undocumented workers northward from Mexico in the 1990s and early 2000s—more than 500,000 in some years. While experts debated the exact number, the most widely accepted estimates indicated that more than 10 million foreigners, mainly from Mexico and Central America, were living illegally in the United States in 2005.

Despite stepped-up border enforcement efforts after the September 11, 2001, terrorist attacks, illegal immigrants continued to move northward from Mexico and Central America. The trip could be dangerous, even lethal. Human-rights advocates estimated that more than 3000 migrants lost their lives attempting to enter the United States illegally between 1997 and 2006. Nineteen Mexican and Central American workers died from suffocation in south Texas in May 2003—nearly one hundred illegal aliens had been jammed into a truck trailer without access to water or fresh air. Yet the movement continued. As one rural Mexican official commented, "There are great problems in the countryside. And that famous American dream keeps calling."

undocumented aliens
Once derisively called "wetbacks," undocumented aliens are illegal immigrants, mainly from Mexico and Central America.

QUICK CHECK

Why was immigration from Mexico so controversial?

Advance and Retreat for African Americans

African Americans formed the second largest of the nation's ethnic minorities. In 2004, there were just over 39 million blacks in the United States, 13.4 percent of the population. Although the heaviest concentration of African Americans was in northern cities, notably New York and Chicago, there was a significant movement back to the South. This shift, which began in the 1970s and accelerated during the 1990s, meant that by 2000 nearly 54 percent of those identifying themselves as black for the census lived in the sixteen states of the Sunbelt. Family ties and a search for ancestral roots explained much of this movement, but it also reflected the same economic incentives that drew so many Americans to the Sunbelt in the last three decades of the twentieth century.

African Americans made substantial gains in certain areas of life. In 2004, some 81 percent of blacks aged 25 and older had earned a high school diploma, an increase of 8 percent during the previous decade. Eighteen percent of African Americans possessed a college degree, 5 percent more than a decade earlier. The number of black-owned businesses topped 1.2 million, up more than 45 percent since 1997.

Yet in other respects African Americans did less well. The black poverty rate was nearly 25 percent, and the median income for black families was less than two-thirds of that for whites. Blacks remained clustered in entry-level jobs, where they faced increasing competition from immigrants. The African American incarceration rate was much higher than the national average; in 2002, more than 10 percent of black males aged 25 to 29 were in prison, and more than one out of four black men could expect to spend time in a state or federal prison during their lives. Blacks were also more likely to be victims of crime, especially violent crime. Homicide was the leading cause of death among black males between the ages of 15 and 34.

Two events, one from 1991 and the other from 2005, summarized much of the frustration African Americans felt. In March 1991, a bystander videotaped four Los Angeles policemen brutally beating Rodney King, an African American who had been stopped for a traffic violation. The pictures of the rain of blows on King shocked the nation. Nearly a year later, when an all-white jury acquitted the four officers of charges of police brutality, rioting erupted in South Central Los Angeles that for a time threatened the entire city when the police failed to respond promptly. In the aftermath of the riot, which took fifty-three lives (compared to thirty-four deaths in the 1965 riot in the nearby Watts area) and did more than

In August 2005, the catastrophic Hurricane Katrina devastated much of the Louisiana and Mississippi Gulf Coast. In the wake of the storm, the levee system of New Orleans failed and flooded nearly 80 percent of the city. Particularly hard hit were low-lying areas such as the Lower Ninth Ward, where police rescue boats are shown here rescuing residents.

Why was the government response widely criticized?

$1 billion in damage, government and state agencies promised new efforts to help the inner-city dwellers. But the efforts produced little effect, and life for many urban blacks remained difficult and dangerous.

A tragedy of a different sort occurred fourteen years later. In August 2005, Hurricane Katrina ravaged the Gulf Coast and broke levees in New Orleans. The high winds and water killed more than a thousand persons, destroyed hundreds of thousands of homes, and forced the evacuation of millions of men, women, and children. Television cameras captured the plight of the several thousand who took refuge in the New Orleans Superdome, only to be stranded when state and federal relief efforts failed. Most conspicuous in the footage was the fact that the vast majority of those suffering the worst in New Orleans were black. Their neighborhoods were the lowest-lying in the city, and hence the worst flooded. Many lacked the cars necessary to flee the city in advance of the hurricane; others lacked the means to pay for hotels or apartments had they been able to get out. Though the relief efforts were largely color-blind (despite early allegations to the contrary), the entire experience demonstrated that poverty in America most certainly was not.

QUICK CHECK

How did Hurricane Katrina reveal problems of African American life?

Americans from Asia and the Middle East

Asian Americans were the fasting-growing minority group at the beginning of the twenty-first century. According to the 2000 census, there were more than 12 million Americans of Asian or Pacific Island descent. Although they represented only 4 percent of the total population, they were increasing at seven times the national rate, and future projections indicated that by 2050 one in ten Americans would be of Asian ancestry.

The Chinese formed the largest single group of Asian Americans, followed by Filipinos, Japanese, Indians, Koreans, and Vietnamese. Immigration was the primary reason for the rapid growth of all these groups except the Japanese; during the 1980s, Asia had provided nearly half of all immigrants to the United States. Though the influx subsequently slowed, the children of the immigrants added to the Asian numbers.

Compared to other minorities, Asian Americans were well educated and affluent. Three out of four Asian youths graduated from high school, compared to less than one out of two for blacks and Hispanics. Asian Americans also had the highest percentage of college graduates and recipients of doctoral degrees of any minority group; in fact, they were better represented in colleges and universities than the white majority. Many Asians entered professional fields, and in part as a result, the median income for Asian American families in 2004 was nearly 20 percent higher than the national average.

Not all Asian Americans fared so well, however. Refugees from Southeast Asia experienced both economic hardship and persecution. The median family income for Vietnamese Americans fell substantially below the national average. Nearly half the Laotian refugees living in Minnesota were unemployed because they had great difficulty learning to read and write English. Vietnamese fishermen who settled on the Gulf Coast of Texas and Louisiana experienced repeated attacks on their livelihood and their homes. In the Los Angeles riots in 1992, Korean stores and shops became a main target for looting and firebombing.

But the overall experience of Asian Americans was a positive one. They came to America seeking economic opportunity, or as many put it, "to climb the mountain of gold." "People are looking for a better life," a Chinese spokeswoman explained. "It's as simple as that, and we will continue to come here, especially if the situations over there [in Asia] stay tight, or get worse."

The number of Americans from the Middle East grew almost as fast as the number of those from Asia in the 1990s. The 2000 census counted 1.5 million Americans of Middle Eastern ancestry, up from 200,000 thirty years earlier. Most came from Arab countries, as well as Israel and Iran. Concentrated in California, New York, and Michigan, Middle Eastern Americans were well educated, with nearly half having college degrees. Many Arab Americans felt nervous after the terrorist attacks of September 11, 2001, committed by Arab extremists; some experienced actual violence at the hands of persons who wanted to blame anyone of Arab descent for the shocking mass murders. Yet most Arab Americans carried on as before, pursuing their interpretation of the American dream.

> **QUICK CHECK** ✓
>
> How did the new immigration from Asia and the Middle East differ from earlier phases of immigration?

The New Democrats

> **WHAT** were the accomplishments and failures of the Clinton administration?

The Democrats, political victims of the runaway inflation of the 1970s, became the beneficiaries of the lingering recession of the early 1990s. Moving away from its traditional liberal reliance on big government, the party regained strength by choosing moderate candidates and tailoring its programs to appeal to the hard-pressed middle class. These tactics enabled the Democrats to regain the White House in 1992 and retain it in 1996, despite a Republican sweep of Congress in 1994. The key figure in this political shift was Bill Clinton, who overcame some early setbacks to reap the rewards of a sustained economic boom.

Clinton and Congress

DOCUMENT

President Clinton's First Inaugural Address (1993)

A recession that began in 1990 soured voters on George Bush, allowing Clinton to defeat the incumbent in a three-way race that included eccentric Texas billionaire H. Ross Perot. In the White House, Clinton proved to be the most adept politician since Franklin Roosevelt. Born in Hope, Arkansas, in 1946, Clinton weathered a difficult childhood with an alcoholic stepfather by developing skills at dealing with people and using personal charm to achieve his goals. Intelligent and ambitious, he completed his undergraduate work at Georgetown University, studied law at Yale, and spent two years as a Rhodes scholar at Oxford University in England. Entering politics after teaching law briefly at the University of Arkansas, he won election first as Arkansas attorney general and then as governor. Defeated after his first term in 1980, Clinton won the nickname "Comeback Kid" by regaining the governor's office in 1982. He was elected three more times, earning a reputation as one of the nation's most successful young political leaders.

In keeping with the theme of his campaign, Clinton concentrated at first on the economy. The federal budget he proposed to Congress in February 1993 called for tax increases and spending cuts to achieve a balanced budget. Congress was skeptical of such unpopular measures, but Clinton cajoled, shamed, and threatened

Anti-NAFTA demonstrators broadcast their views at a rally in Austin, Texas, in 1993.

What were the protesters afraid of?

sufficient members to win approval of $241 billion in new taxes and $255 billion in spending cuts, for a total deficit reduction of $496 billion over four years. This major achievement earned Clinton the confidence of financial markets and helped fuel the economic boom of the 1990s.

Clinton scored another victory when Congress approved the **North American Free Trade Agreement (NAFTA)** in the fall of 1993. NAFTA, initiated and nearly completed by Bush, was a free trade plan that united the United States, Mexico, and Canada into a common market without tariff barriers. Clinton endorsed the treaty as a way of securing American prosperity and spreading American values. Critics complained that free trade would cost American workers their jobs as American companies moved production overseas; Ross Perot, the defeated 1992 third-party candidate, predicted a "giant sucking sound" as American jobs went south to Mexico. But Clinton carried the day, winning a bruising fight in the House and an easier contest in the Senate.

Although Clinton's NAFTA coalition included many congressional Republicans, on other issues the GOP staunchly opposed the president. Republicans decried his budget as entailing "the biggest tax increase in the history of the world," and they scuttled an ambitious attempt to revamp the nation's health care system. Leading the opposition was a young congressman from Georgia, Newton Leroy "Newt" Gingrich, who asked all GOP candidates in the 1994 congressional races to sign a ten-point **Contract with America.** The contract consisted of familiar conservative goals, including a balanced budget amendment to the Constitution, term limits for members of Congress, a line-item veto for the president, and a middle-class

North American Free Trade Agreement (NAFTA)

A free trade plan initiated in the Bush administration and enacted by a narrow vote in Congress in the early months of the Clinton administration. It established a common market without tariff barriers among the United States, Canada, and Mexico.

Contract with America

In the 1994 congressional elections, Congressman Newt Gingrich had Republican candidates sign a document in which they pledged their support for such things as a balanced budget amendment, term limits for members of Congress, and a middle-class tax cut.

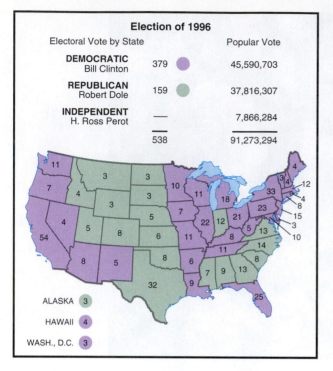

Election of 1996

	Electoral Vote by State		Popular Vote
DEMOCRATIC Bill Clinton	379		45,590,703
REPUBLICAN Robert Dole	159		37,816,307
INDEPENDENT H. Ross Perot	—		7,866,284
	538		91,273,294

ALASKA 3

HAWAII 4

WASH., D.C. 3

DOCUMENT

Statements on the Clinton Health Care Plan (1993)

QUICK CHECK ✔

What victories did Clinton score in domestic affairs?

tax cut. For the first time in recent political history, a party sought to win Congress on ideological issues rather than relying on individual personalities.

A series of embarrassing disclosures involving Bill Clinton's character made this tactic particularly effective in 1994. During the 1992 campaign, the *New York Times* had raised questions about a bankrupt Arkansas land development called Whitewater in which the Clintons had lost a modest investment. Additional scandals cropped up over activities that had taken place after Clinton was elected president. Travelgate was the name given to the firing, apparently at the urging of First Lady Hillary Clinton, of several White House employees who arranged travel for the press covering the president. Then in early 1994, Paula Jones, a former Arkansas state employee, filed a sexual harassment suit against Clinton, charging that in 1991 then-Governor Clinton had made sexual advances to her.

The outcome of the November 1994 vote stunned political observers. The Republicans gained 9 seats in the Senate and an astonishing 53 in the House to take control of both houses. Newt Gingrich, who had worked so hard to ensure the change in leadership in the Congress, became speaker of the House. The GOP also captured 32 governorships, including those of New York, California, and Texas, where George W. Bush, the son of the man Clinton beat in 1992, won handily.

The Republicans claimed a mandate to resume the Reagan Revolution: to cut taxes, diminish the scope of government, and empower the private sector. Clinton and the Democrats managed to keep the Republicans in check on matters of substance, but the Republicans in turn contrived to hobble Clinton. The administration and the Republicans collaborated on welfare reform and a modest increase in the minimum wage, but otherwise deadlock descended on Washington.

Clinton turned the deadlock to his benefit in 1996 after the Republicans, having failed to force him to accept cuts in Medicare, college loans, and other social services, refused to pass a budget bill, and thereby shut down the federal government. Clinton proved more deft at finger-pointing than Gingrich and the Republicans did, and he succeeded in persuading voters that they were to blame. He carried this theme into his 1996 re-election campaign. The Republican nominee, Robert Dole of Kansas, lacked Clinton's charisma and failed to shake the impression that the Republicans were flint-hearts who wanted to cut the pet programs of the American people. Clinton won decisively, holding the presidency for the Democrats even while the Republicans continued to control Congress.

Scandal in the White House

Despite Clinton's re-election, rumors of wrongdoing still clung to his presidency. The special prosecutor appointed to probe the Whitewater transactions, Kenneth Starr, turned over stone after stone in search of evidence of malfeasance, until he came across rumors that Clinton had conducted a clandestine affair with a White House intern, Monica Lewinsky.

Clinton initially denied the affair. "I did not have sexual relations with that woman, Miss Lewinsky," he said in January 1998. But Starr subpoenaed Lewinsky, who eventually gave a detailed account of her sexual encounters with the president and provided crucial physical evidence implicating Clinton.

Realizing that he could no longer deny the affair, the president sought to limit the damage. On August 17, 1998, he appeared before Starr's grand jury and admitted to having "inappropriate intimate contact" with Lewinsky. That evening Clinton spoke briefly to the nation. Claiming that he had given the grand jury "legally accurate" answers, the president for the first time admitted to a relationship with Lewinsky that was "not appropriate" and "wrong." He said he regretted misleading the people and especially his wife, but he refused to apologize for his behavior or his false denials.

Clinton's fate hung in the balance. For the first time, some Democrats began to speak out, most notably Senator Joseph Lieberman of Connecticut, who called the president's behavior "disgraceful" and "immoral." But just when Clinton seemed most vulnerable, the special prosecutor inadvertently rescued him. In early September, Starr sent a 452-page report to Congress outlining eleven possible impeachment charges against Clinton. The key one was perjury, and Starr provided painstakingly graphic detail on all of the sexual encounters between Clinton and Lewinsky to prove that the president had lied when he denied engaging in sexual relations with the intern.

Many Americans responded by condemning Starr rather than the president. Shocked by the sordid details, they blamed the prosecutor for exposing families to distasteful sexual practices on the evening news. When Hillary Clinton stood staunchly by her husband, a majority of the public seemed to conclude that however bad the president's conduct, it was a private matter, one to be settled between a husband and a wife, not in the public arena.

Republican leaders ignored the public sentiment and pressed ahead with impeachment proceedings. In December, the House (where the 1998 midterm elections had narrowed the GOP advantage to six) voted on four articles of impeachment, rejecting two, but approving two others—perjury and obstruction of justice—by small margins in nearly straight party-line votes.

DOCUMENT

Exhibition of Articles of Impeachment (1999)

DOCUMENT

Bill Clinton, Answers to the Articles of Impeachment

Members of the House Judiciary Committee listen to Clinton's testimony during the hearings on the president's impeachment in December 1998. The Committee sent four articles of impeachment to the full House, and the House adopted two—one count of perjury and one of obstruction of justice.

What was the outcome of the impeachment effort?

The final showdown in the Senate was anticlimactic. With a two-thirds vote required to find the president guilty and remove him from office, there was no chance of conviction in the highly charged partisan mood that prevailed. On February 12, 1999, the GOP was unable to muster even a majority on the perjury charge, with 45 in favor and 55 opposed. After a second, closer vote, 50 to 50, on obstruction of justice, the presiding officer, Chief Justice William Rehnquist, declared, "Acquitted of the charges."

Clinton had survived the Monica Lewinsky affair, but he emerged from the ordeal with his presidency badly damaged. His final two years in office would be devoted to a concerted effort to restore his damaged reputation. Desperate for a legacy to mark his White House years, Clinton failed to realize that he had already created an enduring one—he would always be remembered as the president who dishonored his office by his affair with a young intern.

QUICK CHECK ✔

Why was Clinton impeached?

Republicans Triumphant

HOW did George W. Bush become president, and what did he do in the White House?

Clinton's eight years in the White House gave Democrats hope that the conservative gains of the 1980s had been only temporary. They pointed to the booming economy of the 1990s and the absence of any serious threat to American security as reasons for voters to leave the presidency in Democratic hands. The election of 2000 proved a bitter disappointment—all the more bitter by reason of the way in which it made Republican George W. Bush president.

The Disputed Election of 2000

If history had been the guide, the prosperity of the 1990s should have guaranteed victory to Clinton's protégé, Vice President Al Gore. The state of the economy generally determines the outcome of presidential elections, and entering 2000 the American economy had never appeared stronger. The stock market soared, spreading wealth among tens of millions of Americans; the federal deficit of the Reagan years had given way to large and growing surpluses.

But Clinton's personal problems muddled the issue. Clinton had survived his impeachment trial, yet the experience tainted his record and left many voters unwilling to reward the Democrats by promoting his vice president.

Certain other domestic problems unnerved voters, as well. The 1995 bombing of a federal building in Oklahoma City by two domestic terrorists killed 168 people and suggested that irrational violence threatened the daily lives of ordinary Americans. This feeling was reinforced by a 1999 shooting rampage at Columbine High School near Denver, which left twelve students and a teacher dead, besides the two shooters, who killed themselves. The apparent conflict between material abundance and eroding personal values resulted in the closest election in more than a century.

The two candidates, Vice President Gore of Tennessee and Governor Bush of Texas, had little in common beyond being the sons of successful political fathers. Gore had spent eighteen years in Washington as a congressman, senator, and vice president. Somewhat stiff and aloof in manner, he had mastered the intricacies of

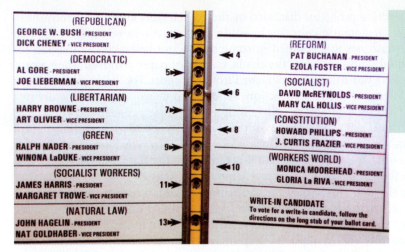

In the contested 2000 presidential election, voters in Palm Beach County, Florida, used this confusing "butterfly" ballot, which resulted in thousands of accidentally mismarked ballots.

How was the election controversy resolved?

all the major policy issues and had the experience and knowledge to lead the nation. Bush, by contrast, had pursued a business career before winning the governorship of Texas in 1994. Personable and outgoing, Bush had the temperament for leadership but lacked not only experience but a full grasp of national issues. Journalists were quick to seize on the weaknesses of both men, accusing Gore of frequent and misleading exaggeration and Bush of mangling words and speaking only in generalities.

The candidacy of consumer advocate Ralph Nader, who ran on the Green party ticket, complicated the political reckoning. Nader never seemed likely to win more than a small percentage of the votes, but in a close election a few points could make all the difference. Nader's mere presence pushed Gore to the left, leaving room for Bush among independent-minded swing voters.

The race appeared close until election day, and even closer on election night. Gore seemed the likely winner when the major television networks predicted a Democratic victory in Florida. They reconsidered as Bush swept the South, including the Clinton-Gore home states of Arkansas and Tennessee. After midnight, the networks again called Florida, but this time for Bush, and the vice president telephoned the governor to concede, only to recant an hour later when it became clear that the Bush margin in Florida was paper thin.

There things stuck, and for the next month all eyes were on Florida. Gore had 500,000 more popular votes nationwide than Bush, and 267 electoral votes to Bush's 246. Yet with Florida's 25 electoral votes, Bush could win the presidency. Both sides sent teams of lawyers to Florida. Bush's team, working with Florida's Republican secretary of state, sought to certify the results that showed the GOP candidate with a lead of 930 votes out of nearly 6 million cast.

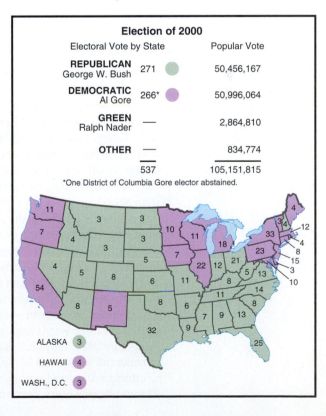

Election of 2000

	Electoral Vote by State	Popular Vote
REPUBLICAN George W. Bush	271	50,456,167
DEMOCRATIC Al Gore	266*	50,996,064
GREEN Ralph Nader	—	2,864,810
OTHER	—	834,774
	537	105,151,815

*One District of Columbia Gore elector abstained.

ALASKA 3
HAWAII 4
WASH., D.C. 3

Citing many voting problems disclosed by the media, Gore asked for a recount in three heavily Democratic counties in south Florida. All three used antiquated punch card machines that resulted in some ballots not being clearly marked for any presidential candidate when the chads, the bits of paper removed when a card is punched, were not completely detached from the cards. For weeks the results in Florida, and hence of the entire election, appeared to depend on how one divined the intent of a voter based on hanging, dimpled, or bulging chads.

The decision finally came in the courts. Democrats appealed the initial attempt to certify Bush as the victor to the Florida Supreme Court. The Florida court twice ordered recounts, the second time for all counties in the state, but Bush's lawyers appealed to the United States Supreme Court. On December 12, five weeks after the election, the Court overruled the state court's call for a recount, in a 5 to 4 decision that reflected a long-standing ideological divide among the nine justices. The next day, Gore gracefully conceded, and Bush finally became president-elect.

Bush's narrow victory revealed deep divisions in American life at the beginning of the twenty-first century. The rural West and South went for Bush, along with a few key Midwest and border states, while Gore won the urban states along both coasts. There was an equally strong divide along economic lines, with the poor voting for Gore, the rich for Bush, and the middle class dividing evenly between the two candidates. Gore benefited from the gender gap, winning 54 percent of the women's vote, and he won an even larger share of the black vote, 90 percent, than Clinton in 1996. Bush did manage to narrow the Democratic margin among Hispanic voters, taking 35 percent, compared to only 28 percent for Dole four years earlier. The two candidates split the suburban vote evenly, while Bush reclaimed the Catholic vote for Republicans.

QUICK CHECK ✓

What was controversial about the 2000 election?

George W. Bush at Home

Bush's first order of business was a large tax cut, which required intense lobbying from the White House. The president had to win over enough conservative southern Democrats to compensate for losing Republican moderates who insisted on reducing the federal debt before cutting taxes. Bush managed the feat, and in June 2001 Congress passed legislation that slashed taxes by a staggering $1.35 trillion over a ten-year period. Many of the cuts would take effect only in future years, but Congress offered an immediate stimulus to the economy by authorizing rebate payments to taxpayers: $600 for couples and $300 for individuals earning more than $6000 a year. While critics saw this measure as a betrayal of the long effort to balance the budget, Bush contended that future budget surpluses would more than offset the loss of tax revenue.

A slowdown in the American economy, triggered by the bursting of the 1990s high-tech bubble, soon turned the projected budget surplus into annual deficits. But it failed to halt the Bush administration's tax cut momentum. In 2003, arguing that a further reduction in taxes would stimulate the stalled economy, Bush prevailed upon Congress to adopt another $350 billion in cuts. Like the 2001 cuts, the new reductions were temporary in order to preserve the possibility of a balanced budget by 2010. Opponents charged that if a future Congress made these tax cuts permanent, as seemed likely, the total cost would rise to nearly $1 trillion. While Clinton had favored a policy of eliminating the deficit, Bush made tax reduction the centerpiece of his economic policy.

Although it took a bit longer, the president also succeeded in persuading Congress to enact a program of education reform. Borrowing the label, "No Child Left Behind," from liberal Democrats, the administration pushed hard for a new policy requiring states to give annual performance tests to all elementary school students. Democrats countered with demands for increased federal funding of public education to assist states and local school boards in raising their standards. Bush shrewdly cultivated the support of Senator Edward Kennedy, a leading liberal Democrat, to forge a bipartisan consensus. The final measure increased federal aid to education by $4 billion, to a total of $22 billion annually, and mandated state tests in reading and math for all students in grades three through eight, and at least once during grades ten to twelve.

By this time the economic slowdown had become a full-blown recession, the first in ten years. A glut of unsold goods forced manufacturers to curtail production and lay off workers. Unemployment rose, eventually to 6 percent, despite the efforts of the Federal Reserve to stem the economic decline by cutting interest rates. The tax rebates authorized by Congress had boosted the economy slightly during the summer of 2001, but then the September 11 terrorist attacks on New York and the Pentagon led to a further decline. In 2002, the economy once again began to recover, only to relapse late in the year amid concern over the threat of war with Iraq.

One of the most troubling aspects of the economic downturn was the implosion of several major corporations and the subsequent revelation of shocking financial practices. WorldCom, Inc., a major telecommunications company, became the largest corporation in American history to declare bankruptcy, while a New York grand jury charged executives of Tyco International, a large electronics company, with stealing more than $600 million from shareholders through stock fraud, false expense reports, and unauthorized bonuses.

These scandals, however, paled before the misdeeds of Enron, a Houston energy company that failed in late 2001 as the result of astonishingly corrupt business practices, including fraudulent accounting and private partnerships designed to inflate profits and hide losses. When investors began to sell their overvalued Enron stock, shares that were once worth nearly $100 fell to less than $1. Enron declared bankruptcy and the remaining shareholders lost over $50 billion, while rank-and-file employees lost not only their jobs but much of their retirement savings, invested largely in now worthless Enron stock.

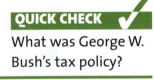

QUICK CHECK
What was George W. Bush's tax policy?

The War on Terrorism

On the morning of September 11, 2001, nineteen Islamic militant terrorists hijacked four U.S. airliners and turned them to attack targets in New York City and Washington, D.C. The hijackers took over two planes flying out of Boston's Logan Airport en route to California, and flew them into the World Trade Center (WTC) in New York. One plane slammed into the north tower just before 9 A.M. and the second hit the south tower only 20 minutes later. Within two hours, both towers had collapsed, taking the lives of nearly 3000 victims trapped in the buildings or crushed by the debris and more than 300 firefighters and other rescue workers who had attempted to save them.

In Washington, an American Airlines flight that left Dulles Airport bound for Los Angeles met a similar fate. Taken over by five terrorists, the Boeing 757 plowed

As rescue efforts continued in the rubble of the World Trade Center, President Bush toured the site on September 14, 2001. In CNN's televised coverage of the visit, Bush is shown here addressing rescue workers through a bullhorn. Firefighter Bob Beckwith stands beside him.

How did Americans respond to the 9/11 attacks?

AMERICA'S NEW WAR
PRES. BUSH VISITS RESCUE
WORKERS IN NEW YORK
OSAMA BIN LADEN POWELL TELLS TALIBAN YOU NEED

George W. Bush, Address to Congress (September 20, 2001)

into the Pentagon, destroying one wing of the building and killing 189 military personnel and civilian workers. The terrorists had seized a fourth plane, United Airlines flight 93, scheduled to fly from Newark, New Jersey, to San Francisco. Over Pennsylvania, as the hijackers attempted to turn the plane toward the nation's capital, the passengers fought to regain control of the plane. They failed to do so, but prevented the plane from hitting another target in Washington—perhaps the White House or the Capitol building. Flight 93 crashed in southern Pennsylvania, killing all forty-four passengers and crew as well as the hijackers.

"None of us will forget this day," President Bush told the American people in a televised speech that evening. Bush vowed to find and punish those responsible for the attacks, as well as any who assisted them. "We will make no distinction between those who planned these acts and those who harbor them."

Bush didn't have to look long to discover the mastermind behind the September 11 attacks. Osama bin Laden, a wealthy Saudi, released videotapes claiming responsibility on behalf of his terrorist organization, al Qaeda ("the Base" in Arabic). Bin Laden had originally been part of the international Muslim resistance to the Soviet invasion of Afghanistan that had received support and weapons from the CIA in the 1980s. He turned against the United States at the time of the Persian Gulf War, outraged by the presence of large numbers of American troops in his native Saudi Arabia. Evidence linked bin Laden and al Qaeda to the bombing of two American embassies in East Africa in 1998 and an attack on the American destroyer USS *Cole* in Yemen in 2000.

The United States had been trying to neutralize al Qaeda for a decade without success. Ordered out of Saudi Arabia in 1991, bin Laden had sought refuge in Sudan and later in Afghanistan after the Taliban, another extremist Muslim group, took over that country. In Afghanistan, bin Laden set up camps to train hundreds of would-be terrorists, mainly from Arab countries but including recruits from the Philippines, Indonesia, and Central Asia. After the 1998 embassy bombings, President Clinton ordered cruise missile attacks on several of these camps in the hope of killing bin Laden. The al Qaeda leader survived, though, leaving one of the targets only a few hours before the strike.

Bush's determination to go after those harboring terrorists made Afghanistan the prime target for the American counterattack. The president ordered the Pentagon and the CIA, which already had agents on the scene, to launch an invasion of Afghanistan to destroy the Taliban, wipe out al Qaeda, and capture or kill Osama bin Laden.

In early October 2001, the CIA and Army Special Forces began the operation, relying on the Northern Alliance, an Afghan political coalition resisting the Taliban. Using a variety of methods, ranging from bribes of local warlords to air strikes, American forces quickly routed the Taliban and by December had installed a U.S.-friendly regime in Kabul. Most of Afghanistan, however, remained in chaos, and despite extensive efforts and several near misses, bin Laden avoided capture.

While waging the **war on terror** abroad, the Bush administration also focused on the problem of securing the United States from any further terrorist assaults. At the president's urging, Congress approved a new Department of Homeland Security, combining the Customs Bureau, the Coast Guard, the Immigration and Naturalization Service (INS), and other government bureaus.

A primary focus of homeland security was on ensuring the safety of airline travel in the wake of the September 11 hijackings. In November 2001, Bush signed legislation replacing private companies with government employees at all airport screening stations. The airlines were required to replace cockpit doors with secure barriers and to permit armed air marshals to ride among the passengers. The understandable public fear of flying after September 11 nevertheless had a devastating effect on the airline industry, forcing the cancellation of many flights and the laying off of thousands of pilots and other workers. Despite a $15 billion government bailout approved in late September 2001, the airlines continued to experience heavy losses. Several, including United Airlines, filed for bankruptcy. Although air travel began to revive slowly in 2002, the industry, along with other forms of tourism, continued to be a drag on an already sluggish economy.

The war on terror raised an even more fundamental question than economic stagnation. Attorney General John Ashcroft, using new powers granted by Congress under the Patriot Act, conducted a broad crackdown on possible terrorists, detaining many Muslim Americans on flimsy evidence and insisting that concern for national security outweighed traditional civil liberties. Opponents quickly challenged Ashcroft, arguing that the terrorists would win their greatest victory if the United States violated its own historic principles of individual freedom in the name of fighting terrorism. It was a debate that troubled many Americans who had difficulty reconciling the need for security with respect for civil liberties.

war on terror
Initiated by President George W. Bush after the attacks of September 11, 2001, the broadly defined war on terror aimed to weed out terrorist operatives and their supporters throughout the world.

What prompted America's war on terrorism?

A New American Empire?

The terrorist attacks on the United States were the catalyst for a major change in direction for American foreign policy. Not only did the Bush administration wage an intensive effort to avenge the September 11 attacks and prevent further assaults, it initiated a new global policy of American preeminence. For the first time since the end of the Cold War, the United States had a clear, if controversial, blueprint for international affairs.

The new administration rejected traditional forms of international cooperation. President Bush ended U.S. participation in the Kyoto Protocol to control global warming and announced plans to terminate the 1972 Antiballistic Missile (ABM) treaty with Russia. And he was outspoken in refusing to expose American military personnel to the jurisdiction of the International Criminal Court for possible crimes committed in worldwide peacekeeping efforts.

The new direction of American foreign policy became clear on January 29, 2002, when Bush delivered his second State of the Union address to Congress and the nation. He repeated his vow to punish all nations sponsoring terrorism, and he specified three countries in particular. Iraq, Iran, and North Korea, he declared in a memorable phrase, constituted an "axis of evil." Nine months later, in September 2002, the Bush administration released a fully developed statement of its new world policy, "National Security Strategy (NSS) of the United States." The goal of American policy, Bush's NSS declared, was to "extend the peace by encouraging free and open societies on every continent."

unilateralism
A national policy of acting alone without consulting others.

There were two main components of the new strategy, which critics quickly called **unilateralism.** The first was to accept fully the role the nation had been playing since the end of the Cold War: global policeman. The United States would not shrink from defending freedom anywhere in the world—with allies if possible, by itself if necessary. To implement this policy, the NSS asserted that the Bush administration would maintain "military strength beyond challenge." "Our forces," the NSS declared, "will be strong enough to dissuade potential adversaries from pursuing a military buildup in hopes of surpassing, or equaling, the power of the United States."

In playing the role of world cop, Bush and his advisers asserted the right to the preventive use of force. Reacting to September 11, the NSS continued, "We cannot let our enemies strike first." Although promising to seek the support of the international community before using force, the NSS stated, "we will not hesitate to act alone, if necessary, to exercise our right of self-defense." In other words, the Bush administration, aware that the United States was far stronger militarily and economically than any other nation, asserted America's role as final arbiter of all international disputes.

weapons of mass destruction (WMD)
Biological, chemical, and nuclear weapons capable of widespread destruction.

Iraq quickly became the test case for this new shift in American foreign policy. After his "axis of evil" speech in January, President Bush focused on what he and his Pentagon advisers called **weapons of mass destruction (WMD)** that they claimed Saddam Hussein had been secretly amassing in large quantities. The United States demanded that Iraq permit UN inspectors (forced out of the country in 1998) to search for such weapons. Meanwhile, the Bush administration perfected plans for a unilateral American military solution to the Iraq question.

Slowly, but inevitably, the United States moved toward war with Iraq in late 2002 and early 2003. Congress approved a resolution in October authorizing the president to use force against Saddam Hussein's regime. A month later, the UN Security Council voted unanimously to send its team of inspectors back into Iraq, warning Saddam of "severe consequences" if he failed to comply. Despite the failure of the international inspectors to find any evidence of chemical, biological, or nuclear weapons in Iraq, the Bush administration kept pressing for a Security Council resolution authorizing the use of force to compel Saddam to disarm. When France and Russia vowed to veto any such measure, Bush and his advisers decided to ignore the world body and proceed on their own. Preventive war would have its first real test.

The ensuing conflict with Iraq surprised both the backers and the critics of unilateralism. In March 2003, three columns of American troops, a total of

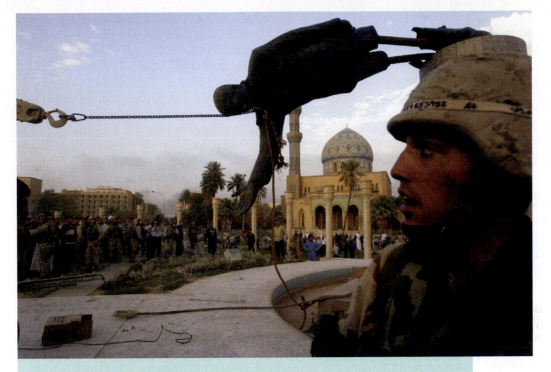

In a memorable image from the war in Iraq, Iraqi civilians and U.S. soldiers pull down a statue of Saddam Hussein in Baghdad on April 9, 2003.

What happened to Saddam himself?

65,000, began to execute a two-pronged invasion of Iraq from bases in Kuwait. Britain, the only major power to join the United States in the fighting, helped by besieging the city of Basra and taking control of southern Iraq. Within two weeks, the U.S. army had captured the Baghdad international airport, and on April 8, just three weeks after the fighting had begun, marines marched virtually unopposed into the heart of the city. The American people watched the televised scene of joyous Iraqis toppling a statue of Saddam in Fardos Square. An Iraqi major summed up the magnitude of his country's defeat: "Losing a war is one thing, but losing Baghdad is another," he explained. "It was like losing the dearest thing in life."

The rapid success of the anti-Saddam offensive seemed to confirm the wisdom of Bush's decision for war. But the subsequent failure to find any weapons of mass destruction led critics to question the validity of the war. In response, the president's defenders stressed the importance of deposing Saddam by pointing to his brutal prisons and to the killing fields south of Baghdad where thousands of Shi'ite rebels had been slaughtered in 1991.

The problems of restoring order and rebuilding the shattered Iraqi economy quickly overshadowed the debate over the war's legitimacy. Daily attacks on American troops in the Sunni triangle north of Baghdad began in the summer of 2003 and increased in intensity during the fall, killing an average of three American soldiers each week. By October, more troops had died from these attacks than had been killed during the combat phase in March and April. Widespread looting, sabotage of oil pipelines, and difficulties in repairing and operating outdated power plants and oil facilities made economic recovery very slow and halting. U.S. efforts to involve occupation forces from other UN members yielded only a few troops.

The December 2003 arrest of Saddam, who had eluded capture until then despite determined efforts to find him, revived American optimism. Yet the overall situation remained troubling. Despite slow but steady progress in restoring public services such as electric power and the gradual recovery of the Iraq oil industry, the armed insurrection continued. Mortar attacks on Baghdad hotels, roadside bombs aimed at American armored convoys, and handheld missile attacks on American helicopters made Iraq a very dangerous place. Equally disturbing, conflicts of interest between Shi'ite and Sunni Muslims, as well as the Kurdish demand for autonomy, threatened the American goal of creating a stable Iraqi government.

QUICK CHECK ✔

Why did Bush order the invasion of Iraq?

Bush Re-elected

Not surprisingly, the war in Iraq became the central issue in the 2004 presidential race. Bush cast himself as the resolute commander in the war on terror; he and his supporters contended that it would be reckless to change commanders in mid-conflict. Democrats initially favored former Vermont governor Howard Dean, who had opposed the invasion of Iraq and still strongly criticized Bush's conduct of the war. But the nomination ultimately went to Senator John Kerry of Massachusetts, a decorated Vietnam War veteran who voted for the war but later criticized Bush for misleading the country regarding the causes of the conflict, and who contended that the war in Iraq, rather than contributing to the war on terror, actually distracted from it.

The campaign was the most vitriolic in years. Democrats accused Bush of having stolen the election of 2000 (with the help of the Supreme Court) and of lying about Saddam's weapons. Republicans called Kerry's belated opposition to the war in Vietnam an insult to those Americans who had died there, and they cited certain of his votes in the Senate as evidence of a fatal inconsistency. Both sides (following the example of Howard Dean in the primaries) employed the Internet to rally the faithful, raise money, and spread rumors.

The strong emotions produced a record turnout: 12 million more than in 2000. Bush won the popular vote by 2.5 percent, becoming the first victor since his father in 1988 to gain an absolute popular majority. The electoral race was comparably close, with 286 for Bush and 252 for Kerry.

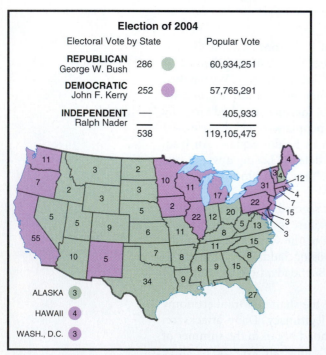

Election of 2004

	Electoral Vote by State	Popular Vote
REPUBLICAN George W. Bush	286 ●	60,934,251
DEMOCRATIC John F. Kerry	252 ●	57,765,291
INDEPENDENT Ralph Nader	—	405,933
	538	119,105,475

Taken together with the congressional elections, which increased the Republican majorities in both the Senate and the House of Representatives, the 2004 race confirmed a "red state/blue state" split in America, with the Republicans dominating the South, the Plains, and the Rockies, while the Democrats carried the Northeast, the Great Lakes, and the West Coast.

Despite his modest margin of victory, Bush claimed a mandate. He proposed to privatize part of the Social Security system and promised to stay the course in Iraq. His Social Security plan went nowhere, but the situation in Iraq briefly seemed to improve. Elections in January 2005 took place more calmly than many observers expected and appeared to place Iraq well on the road to self-government.

Yet an escalation of the insurgency during 2006 and 2007 pushed American deaths in Iraq beyond 3,600, and the violence grew more clearly sectarian. As the country slipped into civil war, the American public grew more disillusioned than ever. An opinion poll in July 2007 revealed that 66 percent of Americans thought U.S. troop levels in Iraq should be reduced, with 40 percent calling for complete withdrawal.

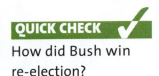

QUICK CHECK

How did Bush win re-election?

Challenges of the New Century

The war in Iraq was merely one example of the challenges facing Americans in the new century. Americans remained as divided as ever over cultural issues. A revival of the American economy after its recession masked a growing inequality between rich and poor and increasing insecurity even among those comparatively well off. The nation's health care and retirement systems sagged under the increasing demands placed upon them. Environmental worries rose along with rising global temperatures.

WHAT challenges faced the American people during the first decade of the twenty-first century?

The Culture Wars Continue

The war in Iraq and the broader concerns about terrorism sometimes overshadowed but didn't erase the divisions among Americans on social and cultural issues. The race question remained alive and contentious, as **affirmative action** policies—policies designed to ensure greater participation by minorities—came under increasing scrutiny. The *Bakke* v. *Regents of the University of California* decision of 1978 had allowed the use of race as one factor in determining admission to colleges and universities, so long as rigid racial quotas weren't employed. This dissatisfied many conservatives, who during the 1980s and 1990s attacked affirmative action politically and in the courts. In 1992, Cheryl Hopwood, an unsuccessful white applicant to the University of Texas Law School, challenged her rejection, contending that the school had admitted less-qualified African American applicants. In 1996, the Fifth Circuit Court of Appeals decided in her favor, and the *Hopwood* decision raised the hopes of anti-affirmative action groups that the

affirmative action
The use of laws or regulations to achieve racial, ethnic, gender, or other diversity, as in hiring or school admissions. Such efforts are often aimed at improving employment or educational opportunities for women and minorities.

Marriage ceremony of Hillary, left, and Julie Goodridge in Boston on May 17, 2004, the first day of state-sanctioned same-sex marriage in the United States. The couple were the lead plaintiffs in the lawsuit in which the Massachusetts supreme court struck down a state law barring same-sex marriages.

How did other states respond to Massachusetts' example?

Supreme Court would overturn *Bakke*. But in a 2003 case involving the University of Michigan, the Supreme Court ruled that "student body diversity is a compelling state interest that can justify the use of race in university admissions." In other words, affirmative action in higher education could continue. But the 5–4 vote indicated that the court remained split, and it suggested that affirmative action would continue to spark controversy.

Even more controversial was abortion. The issue had roiled American politics for years, but it did so particularly after the death of Chief Justice William Rehnquist in September 2005 and the concurrent retirement of Associate Justice Sandra Day O'Connor allowed George W. Bush to nominate their replacements. Rehnquist had been a reliable conservative, but O'Connor was a swing vote, and liberals feared that a more conservative successor would tip the balance against abortion rights, among other contentious issues. Yet John Roberts, Bush's nominee for chief justice, and Samuel Alito, the nominee for associate justice, dodged Democrats' questions in hearings, and though the Democrats briefly threatened to filibuster Alito, both nominations succeeded. Almost immediately, South Dakota passed a law essentially banning abortion, and the law, which directly challenged the abortion rights guaranteed by the 1973 *Roe* decision, appeared bound for the newly reconfigured court.

Gay rights provoked fresh controversy as gay advocates pushed for equal marital rights. After the Massachusetts supreme court in 2004 struck down a state law barring same-sex marriages, gay advocates celebrated, but conservatives in dozens of states pressed for laws and constitutional amendments reaffirming traditional views on the subject and defining marriage as the union of one man and one woman. Nearly all the efforts were successful, suggesting that, on this front at least, the advances gay men and women had achieved since the 1960s had hit a wall.

Science and religion continued to battle in America's classrooms. Opponents of evolution revised their challenge to Darwin, replacing creationism with "intelligent design" and demanding that this version of their beliefs be aired in biology classes. School board elections hinged on the issue; Ohio embraced intelligent design only to reject it following an adverse 2005 court decision in a case from the Dover school district. For the moment the evolutionists held their own, but given that public-opinion polls consistently showed a majority of Americans rejecting evolution in favor of divine creation—the margin was 3 to 1 in a CBS News poll in early 2006—the fight was sure to continue.

QUICK CHECK ✔

What were the principal issues in the culture wars of the early twenty-first century?

Prosperity—for Whom?

After the recession of George W. Bush's first term, the economy gradually recovered. The economy as a whole grew steadily, and the jobless rate fell to less than 5 percent, not far from the level of the booming 1990s. Corporate profits soared, registering double-digit increases for three years running.

But the good news disguised some unsettling trends. The median family income declined slightly, and although corporate executives commanded seven- and eight-digit pay packages, ordinary workers watched their compensation diminish. Wages were flat, while medical and retirement benefits fell. The poverty rate increased; in 2004, some 37 million Americans, or 12.7 percent of the population, lived below the poverty line. Nearly 46 million Americans lacked health insurance, which, besides jeopardizing their health, often meant that personal bankruptcy was a broken arm or ruptured appendix away.

Uncertainty came in other forms as well. The globalization of the economy placed continued pressure on American jobs. The automobile industry, long a mainstay of the American economy, suffered grievously. General Motors lost billions and was forced to slash tens of thousands of jobs. In early 2006, Ford announced the closing of fourteen plants in the United States and Canada. Even workers in industries formerly thought exempt from the export of jobs found themselves facing direct foreign competition. Telephone call centers moved from the American Midwest to Ireland and India; computer and other high-tech companies relocated research facilities to India and China. What Silicon Valley in California had been to the birth of the personal computer industry in the 1970s, Bangalore in India promised—or threatened—to be to the industry's maturation in the 2010s.

Rising oil prices—triggered by the turmoil in the Middle East but also by rising demand from China—threatened the status quo in other ways. The rise this time took place more gradually than during the 1970s—the price required a year, rather than weeks, to double, to more than $60 a barrel in early 2006—and though nothing quite like the oil shocks of that earlier decade occurred, the higher price of oil did contribute to higher prices for a wide array of other goods, and it rekindled fears of inflation. At the gas pump, prices leaped to more than $3 a gallon. As was often the case, persons at the lower end of the income scale were hit harder than those higher up, as transportation took a larger share of their income. In the long term, the higher prices would prompt the purchase of more efficient cars; in the meantime, drivers simply had to grin and bear $40 fill-ups as best they could.

QUICK CHECK ✓

What economic problems faced American society?

Doubting the Future

During most of American history, every generation had been better off materially than the generation before. Events of the early twenty-first century called this implicit guarantee into question. To an unprecedented extent, the American economy was at the mercy of developments beyond American shores. The pressure on American jobs would continue and probably intensify; no less alarming, as a result of America's large and growing trade deficit, foreign investors held huge quantities of America's public debt. Should these investors lose confidence in America's economic future, or for whatever other reason decide to divest themselves of their dollar holdings, interest rates in the United States would probably balloon, touching off a major recession. Already some of the foreign investors were diversifying from Treasury bonds into ownership of American capital assets, making the American economy—and even American physical safety—further subject to foreign influence. When, in early 2006, a firm from the United Arab Emirates applied to purchase the concession to operate six American port facilities, a public outcry arose that American security was in danger.

Internal problems appeared hardly more tractable. As the baby boom generation neared retirement, the load on the Social Security system increased. Everyone realized something would have to be done to keep the pension program afloat, but after the rejection of George W. Bush's privatization scheme, no one could figure out how to make the necessary changes politically palatable. Middle-aged Americans faced the prospect of delayed retirement, smaller pensions, or both. Not surprisingly, they resisted. Younger Americans resisted the tax increases that could have spared the elders such sacrifice.

The trend in health care costs was even more alarming. For years, medical costs had grown rapidly, and as the population aged, they appeared certain to claim an ever larger share of the nation's income. Combined with the growth in the number of Americans without medical insurance, the health care system seemed to require a major overhaul. But, again, the status quo stubbornly resisted changing, and the situation only grew worse.

Immigration became more controversial than at any time since the 1920s. The number of persons entering the country illegally soared, but efforts to rectify the situation—as by tighter enforcement at the border, by sanctions on employers hiring undocumented aliens, by temporary visas for guest workers—stalled on the opposition of immigrant advocates, of businesses, and of assorted other groups.

Environmental problems demanded attention, which they got, and solutions, which they didn't. A consensus emerged among the scientific community that global warming had to be addressed, but the proposed solutions—higher mileage standards for automobiles, a "carbon tax" on emissions of greenhouse gases, greater reliance on nuclear energy, among others—were costly, intrusive, unproven, or environmentally problematic in their own ways. As on other issues, there was broad agreement that current trends were unsustainable, but little agreement on what should replace them.

QUICK CHECK

What questions clouded America's future?

Conclusion: The Paradox of Power

Events of the early twenty-first century highlighted a paradox of contemporary American life. Never in their history had Americans been more powerful relative to the rest of the world, yet rarely in their history had they felt more at risk. Their superpower status couldn't preserve them from the terrorist attacks of September 11, 2001, nor could it guarantee victory over the insurgents in Iraq. Had the United States been less powerful, it might not have become the target of al Qaeda's hijackers; had it been less powerful, it probably wouldn't have been tempted to invade Iraq. Power excited envy; it invited hubris. America might be the only remaining superpower, but it wasn't omnipotent, and it wasn't invulnerable.

Nor were Americans invulnerable to the challenges that crowded domestic life as the new century took shape. The American economy was still far and away the most powerful and dynamic in the world, but it was increasingly subject to unsettling foreign influences, and it failed distressingly often to deliver on the promise of equality to the most vulnerable in society. Conservatives and liberals fought over the values that ought to guide the country; different racial and ethnic groups proposed competing models of American pluralism.

The fundamental challenge for Americans of the twenty-first century was to balance their power against their vulnerabilities. This wasn't new; it has been the challenge for Americans of every generation. At times they have met the challenge brilliantly; at other times they've done less well. How they would fare this time was for the present generation to determine—guided, ideally, by the lessons of the past.

For a list of additional titles related to this chapter's topics, please see www.pearsonamericanhistory.com. MyHistoryLab

STUDY RESOURCES

KEY TERMS

Americans with Disabilities Act (ADA), p. 866

Desert Storm, p. 869

Sunbelt, p. 870

undocumented aliens, p. 873

North American Free Trade Agreement (NAFTA), p. 877

Contract with America, p. 877

war on terror, p. 885

unilateralism, p. 886

weapons of mass destruction (WMD), p. 886

affirmative action, p. 889

CHAPTER REVIEW

WHAT were the important issues in George H. W. Bush's presidency, and how were they handled?

In domestic affairs, the first President Bush focused on fixing the savings and loan industry and balancing the budget. In foreign affairs, he managed the end the Cold War peacefully and successfully. The Gulf War of 1991 liberated Kuwait and weakened the Iraqi regime of Saddam Hussein, but didn't remove Saddam from power in Baghdad. (*p. 866*)

HOW did the American population shift and grow during the 1990s and after?

Americans continued to migrate to the Sunbelt in the 1990s and early 2000s, and immigration continued to grow. Hispanics formed the largest segment of the immigrant population and included several million illegal immigrants. African Americans gained ground economically but in many communities still suffered from poverty, as Hurricane Katrina demonstrated. (*p. 870*)

WHAT were the accomplishments and failures of the Clinton administration?

Clinton balanced the federal budget and helped revive the economy, which boomed during the 1990s. The North American Free Trade Agreement eliminated tariff barriers among the United States, Canada, and Mexico. But personal scandals led to Clinton's impeachment trial in the Senate, which he survived, although not without serious damage to his own reputation and that of the Democrats. (*p. 876*)

HOW did George W. Bush become president, and what did he do in the White House?

George W. Bush became president in an election that turned on a ballot dispute in Florida, which was resolved only by the intervention of the Supreme Court. As president, Bush persuaded Congress to cut taxes and, after the terrorist attacks of September 11, 2001, to authorize invasions of Afghanistan and Iraq. The war in Iraq started well but bogged down amid an insurgency against the American-supported government in Baghdad. (*p. 880*)

WHAT challenges faced the American people during the first decade of the twenty-first century?

The culture wars between conservatives and liberals continued into the twenty-first century, with abortion, affirmative action, gay rights, and evolution provoking particular controversy. Economic inequality grew, and Americans wondered how they would deal with problems of health care, retirement, illegal immigration, and the environment. (*p. 889*)

MAKING CONNECTIONS

1. Was the first Bush lucky or skillful in ending the Cold War so successfully?
2. What do the internal migration to the Sunbelt and the immigration to America from other countries have in common?
3. Do you think Clinton should have been convicted on his impeachment charges?
4. Many people thought the outcome of the 2000 election was a violation of democracy. Do you?
5. Are you optimistic about America's future, or pessimistic? Why?

PRACTICE QUIZ

1. The _____ massacre of 1989 in China sent shock waves around the world.
   a. Great Wall
   b. Tiananmen Square
   c. Boston Square
   d. Yellow River

2. Operation _____ in 1991 was the name of the first U.S. invasion of Iraq.
   a. Desert Shield
   b. Desert Victory
   c. Desert Storm
   d. Desert Wall

3. The _____ region of the South and West contained the majority of Americans by the early 1990s.
   a. Mountain
   b. Valley
   c. Sunbelt
   d. Shoreline

4. The _____ Agreement approved by Congress in 1993 became a major victory for President Clinton.
   a. North American Free Trade
   b. Kyoto
   c. SALT I
   d. NATO

5. The _____ issue most significantly marred President Clinton's historical legacy.
   a. Balkans
   b. Gays in the military
   c. Impeachment
   d. Northern Ireland

6. In 1995, a bombing took place at a federal building in
   a. Virginia City
   b. Oklahoma City
   c. Atlantic City
   d. Panama City

7. After the attack on September 11, 2001, President George Bush announced a war on
   a. Islam
   b. The Middle East
   c. Civilians
   d. Terror

8. The Bush administration claimed that the United States needed to invade Iraq because Saddam Hussein possessed
   a. Weapons of mass destruction
   b. The Republican Guard
   c. Oil reserves
   d. A strategic geopolitical location in the Middle East

9. President George W. Bush's long-term historical legacy will be shaped by all of the following *except*
   a. Invading Afghanistan
   b. Appointing two new justices to the Supreme Court
   c. A sex scandal
   d. Tax cuts

10. Which of the following are considered long-term problems of the twenty-first century?
    a. Immigration
    b. Environmental pollution
    c. Rising health care costs
    d. All of the above answers are accurate.

QUIZ

Find more practice at
www.myhistorylab.com

SAMPLE ESSAY QUESTIONS

1. Compare the administrations of Bush I and Bush II regarding domestic and foreign policy.

2. Trace the rise of Bill Clinton from Arkansas boyhood to the White House.

Answers to Practice Quiz 1. b, p. 867 2. c, p. 869 3. c, p. 870 4. a, p. 877 5. c, p. 879 6. b, p. 880 7. d, p. 885 8. a, p. 886 9. c, p. 882, 885, 890 10. d, p. 889

APPENDIX

The Declaration of Independence

The Articles of Confederation

The Constitution of the United States of America

Amendments to the Constitution

Presidential Elections

Presidents and Vice Presidents

For additional reference material, go to
www.pearsonamericanhistory.com
The on-line appendix includes the following:

The Declaration of Independence

In Congress, July 4, 1776

The Unanimous Declaration of the Thirteen United States of America,

When, in the course of human events, it becomes necessary for one people to dissolve the political bonds which have connected them with another, and to assume, among the powers of the earth, the separate and equal station to which the laws of nature and of nature's God entitle them, a decent respect to the opinions of mankind requires that they should declare the causes which impel them to the separation.

We hold these truths to be self-evident: That all men are created equal; that they are endowed by their Creator with certain unalienable rights; that among these are life, liberty, and the pursuit of happiness; that, to secure these rights, governments are instituted among men, deriving their just powers from the consent of the governed; that whenever any form of government becomes destructive of these ends, it is the right of the people to alter or to abolish it, and to institute new government, laying its foundation on such principles, and organizing its powers in such form, as to them shall seem most likely to effect their safety and happiness. Prudence, indeed, will dictate that governments long established should not be changed for light and transient causes; and accordingly all experience hath shown that mankind are more disposed to suffer, while evils are sufferable, than to right themselves by abolishing the forms to which they are accustomed. But when a long train of abuses and usurpations, pursuing invariably the same object, evinces a design to reduce them under absolute despotism, it is their right, it is their duty, to throw off such government, and to provide new guards for their future security. Such has been the patient sufferance of these colonies; and such is now the necessity which constrains them to alter their former systems of government. The history of the present King of Great Britain is a history of repeated injuries and usurpations, all having in direct object the establishment of an absolute tyranny over these states. To prove this, let facts be submitted to a candid world.

He has refused his assent to laws, the most wholesome and necessary for the public good.

He has forbidden his governors to pass laws of immediate and pressing importance, unless suspended in their operation till his assent should be obtained; and, when so suspended, he has utterly neglected to attend to them.

He has refused to pass other laws for the accommodation of large districts of people, unless those people would relinquish the right of representation in the legislature, a right inestimable to them, and formidable to tyrants only.

He has called together legislative bodies at places unusual, uncomfortable, and distant from the depository of their public records, for the sole purpose of fatiguing them into compliance with his measures.

He has dissolved representative houses repeatedly, for opposing, with manly firmness, his invasions on the rights of the people.

He has refused for a long time, after such dissolutions, to cause others to be elected; whereby the legislative powers, incapable of annihilation, have returned to the people at large for their exercise; the state remaining, in the mean time, exposed to all the dangers of invasions from without and convulsions within.

He has endeavored to prevent the population of these states; for that purpose obstructing the laws for naturalization of foreigners; refusing to pass others to encourage their migration hither, and raising the conditions of new appropriations of lands.

He has obstructed the administration of justice, by refusing his assent to laws for establishing judiciary powers.

He has made judges dependent on his will alone, for the tenure of their offices, and the amount and payment of their salaries.

He has erected a multitude of new offices, and sent hither swarms of officers to harass our people and eat out their substance.

He has kept among us, in times of peace, standing armies, without the consent of our legislatures.

He has affected to render the military independent of, and superior to, the civil power.

He has combined with others to subject us to a jurisdiction foreign to our constitution, and unacknowledged by our laws, giving his assent to their acts of pretended legislation:

For quartering large bodies of armed troops among us;

For protecting them, by a mock trial, from punishment for any murder which they should commit on the inhabitants of these states;

For cutting off our trade with all parts of the world;

For imposing taxes on us without our consent;

For depriving us, in many cases, of the benefits of trial by jury;

For transporting us beyond seas, to be tried for pretended offenses;

For abolishing the free system of English laws in a neighboring province, establishing therein an arbitrary government, and enlarging its boundaries, so as to render it at once an example and fit instrument for introducing the same absolute rule into these colonies;

For taking away our charters, abolishing our most valuable laws, and altering fundamentally the forms of our governments;

For suspending our own legislatures, and declaring themselves invested with power to legislate for us in all cases whatsoever.

He has abdicated government here, by declaring us out of his protection and waging war against us.

He has plundered our seas, ravaged our coasts, burned our towns, and destroyed the lives of our people.

He is at this time transporting large armies of foreign mercenaries to complete the works of death, desolation, and tyranny already begun with circumstances of cruelty and perfidy scarcely paralleled in the most barbarous ages, and totally unworthy the head of a civilized nation.

He has constrained our fellow-citizens, taken captive on the high seas, to bear arms against their country, to become the executioners of their friends and brethren, or to fall themselves by their hands.

He has excited domestic insurrection among us, and has endeavored to bring on the inhabitants of our frontiers the merciless Indian savages, whose known rule of warfare is an undistinguished destruction of all ages, sexes, and conditions.

In every stage of these oppressions we have petitioned for redress in the most humble terms; our repeated petitions have been answered only by repeated injury. A prince, whose character is thus marked by every act which may define a tyrant, is unfit to be the ruler of a free people.

Nor have we been wanting in our attentions to our British brethren. We have warned them, from time to time, of attempts by their legislature to extend an unwarrantable jurisdiction over us. We have reminded them of the circumstances of our emigration and settlement here. We have appealed to their native justice and magnanimity; and we have conjured them, by the ties of our common kindred, to disavow these usurpations, which would inevitably interrupt our connections and correspondence. They, too, have been deaf to the voice of justice and of consanguinity. We must, therefore, acquiesce in the necessity which denounces our separation, and hold them, as we hold the rest of mankind, enemies in war, in peace friends.

We, therefore, the representatives of the United States of America, in General Congress assembled, appealing to the Supreme Judge of the world for the rectitude of our intentions, do, in the name and by the authority of the good people of these colonies, solemnly publish and declare, that these United Colonies are, and of right ought to be, FREE AND INDEPENDENT STATES; that they are absolved from all allegiance to the British crown, and that all political connection between them and the state of Great Britain is, and ought to be, totally dissolved; and that, as free and independent states, they have full power to levy war, conclude peace, contract alliances, establish commerce, and do all other acts and things which independent states may of right do. And for the support of this declaration, with a firm reliance on the protection of Divine Providence, we mutually pledge to each other our lives, our fortunes, and our sacred honor.

John Hancock

Button Gwinnett	Francis Lightfoot Lee	Jno. Witherspoon
Lyman Hall	Carter Braxton	Fras. Hopkinson
Geo. Walton	Robt. Morris	John Hart
Wm. Hooper	Benjamin Rush	Abra. Clark
Joseph Hewes	Benja. Franklin	Josiah Bartlett
John Penn	John Morton	Wm. Whipple
Edward Rutledge	Geo. Clymer	Saml. Adams
Thos. Heyward, Junr.	Jas. Smith	John Adams
Thomas Lynch, Junr.	Geo. Taylor	Robt. Treat Paine
Arthur Middleton	James Wilson	Elbridge Gerry
Samuel Chase	Geo. Ross	Step. Hopkins
Wm. Paca	Caesar Rodney	William Ellery
Thos. Stone	Geo. Read	Roger Sherman
Charles Carroll of Carrollton	Tho. M'kean	Sam'el Huntington
George Wythe	Wm. Floyd	Wm. Williams
Richard Henry Lee	Phil. Livingston	Oliver Wolcott
Th. Jefferson	Frans. Lewis	Matthew Thornton
Benj. Harrison	Lewis Morris	
Thos. Nelson, Jr.	Richd. Stockton	

The Articles of Confederation

Between the States of New Hampshire, Massachusetts Bay, Rhode Island and Providence Plantations, Connecticut, New York, New Jersey, Pennsylvania, Delaware, Maryland, Virginia, North Carolina, South Carolina, Georgia

ARTICLE 1

The stile of this confederacy shall be "The United States of America."

ARTICLE 2

Each State retains its sovereignty, freedom and independence, and every power, jurisdiction, and right, which is not by this confederation expressly delegated to the United States, in Congress assembled.

ARTICLE 3

The said states hereby severally enter into a firm league of friendship with each other for their common defence, the security of their liberties and their mutual and general welfare; binding themselves to assist each other against all force offered to, or attacks made upon them, or any of them, on account of religion, sovereignty, trade, or any other pretence whatever.

ARTICLE 4

The better to secure and perpetuate mutual friendship and intercourse among the people of the different states in this union, the free inhabitants of each of these states, paupers, vagabonds, and fugitives from justice excepted, shall be entitled to all privileges and immunities of free citizens in the several states; and the people of each State shall have free ingress and regress to and from any other State, and shall enjoy therein all the privileges of trade and commerce, subject to the same duties, impositions, and restrictions, as the inhabitants thereof respectively; provided, that such restrictions shall not extend so far as to prevent the removal of property, imported into any State, to any other State of which the owner is an inhabitant; provided also, that no imposition, duties, or restriction, shall be laid by any State on the property of the United States, or either of them.

If any person guilty of, or charged with treason, felony, or other high misdemeanor in any State, shall flee from justice and be found in any of the United States, he shall, upon demand of the governor or executive power of the State from which he fled, be delivered up and removed to the State having jurisdiction of his offence.

Full faith and credit shall be given in each of these states to the records, acts, and judicial proceedings of the courts and magistrates of every other State.

ARTICLE 5

For the more convenient management of the general interests of the United States, delegates shall be annually appointed, in such manner as the legislature of each State shall direct, to meet in Congress, on the 1st Monday in November in every year, with a power reserved to each State to recall its delegates, or any of them, at any time within the year, and to send others in their stead for the remainder of the year.

No State shall be represented in Congress by less than two, nor by more than seven members; and no person shall be capable of being a delegate for more than three years in any term of six years; nor shall any person, being a delegate, be capable of holding any office under the United States, for which he, or any other for his benefit, receives any salary, fees, or emolument of any kind.

Each State shall maintain its own delegates in a meeting of the states, and while they act as members of the committee of the states.

In determining questions in the United States, in Congress assembled, each State shall have one vote.

Freedom of speech and debate in Congress shall not be impeached or questioned in any court or place out of Congress: and the members of Congress shall be protected in their persons from arrests and imprisonments, during the time of their going to and from, and attendance on Congress, except for treason, felony, or breach of the peace.

ARTICLE 6

No State, without the consent of the United States, in Congress assembled, shall send any embassy to, or receive any embassy from, or enter into any conference, agreement, alliance, or treaty with any king, prince, or state; nor shall any person, holding any office of profit or trust under the United States, or any of them, accept of any present, emolument, office or title, of any kind whatever, from any king, prince, or foreign state; nor shall the United States, in Congress assembled, or any of them, grant any title of nobility.

No two or more states shall enter into any treaty, confederation, or alliance, whatever, between them, without the consent of the United States, in Congress assembled, specifying accurately the purposes for which the same is to be entered into, and how long it shall continue.

No State shall lay any imposts or duties which may interfere with any stipulations in treaties entered into by the United States, in Congress assembled, with any king, prince, or state, in pursuance of any treaties already proposed by Congress to the courts of France and Spain.

No vessels of war shall be kept up in time of peace by any State, except such number only as shall be deemed necessary by the United States, in Congress assembled, for the defence of such State or its trade; nor shall any body of forces be kept up by any State, in time of peace, except such number only as, in the judgment of the United States, in Congress assembled, shall be deemed requisite to garrison the forts necessary for the defence of such State; but every State shall always keep up a well regulated and disciplined militia, sufficiently armed and accoutred, and shall provide, and constantly have ready for use, in public stores, a due number, of field pieces and tents, and a proper quantity of arms, ammunition and camp equipage.

No State shall engage in any war without the consent of the United States, in Congress assembled, unless such State be actually invaded by enemies, or shall have received certain advice of a resolution being formed by some nation of Indians to invade such State, and the danger is so imminent as not to admit of a delay till the United States, in Congress assembled, can be consulted; nor shall any State grant commissions to any ships or vessels of war, nor letters of marque or reprisal, except it be after a declaration of war by the United States, in Congress assembled, and then only against the kingdom or state, and the subjects thereof, against which war has been so declared, and under such regulations as shall be established by the United States, in Congress assembled, unless such States be infested by pirates, in which case vessels of war may be fitted out for that occasion, and kept so long as the danger shall continue, or until the United States, in Congress assembled, shall determine otherwise.

ARTICLE 7

When land forces are raised by any State for the common defence, all officers of or under the rank of colonel, shall be appointed by the legislature of each State respectively, by whom such forces shall be raised, or in such manner as such State shall direct; and all vacancies shall be filled up by the State which first made the appointment.

ARTICLE 8

All charges of war and all other expences, that shall be incurred for the common defence or general welfare, and allowed by the United States, in Congress assembled, shall be defrayed out of a common treasury, which shall be supplied by the several states, in proportion to the value of all land within each State, granted to or surveyed for any person, as such land and the buildings and improvements thereon shall be estimated according to such mode as the United States, in Congress assembled, shall, from time to time, direct and appoint.

The taxes for paying that proportion shall be laid and levied by the authority and direction of the legislatures of the several states, within the time agreed upon by the United States, in Congress assembled.

ARTICLE 9

The United States, in Congress assembled, shall have the sole and exclusive right and power of determining on peace and war, except in the cases mentioned in the 6th article; of sending and receiving ambassadors; entering into treaties and alliances, provided that no treaty of commerce shall be made, whereby the legislative power of the respective states shall be restrained from imposing such imposts and duties on foreigners as their own people are subjected to, or from prohibiting the exportation or importation of any species of goods or commodities whatsoever; of establishing rules for deciding, in all cases, what captures on land or water shall be legal, and in what manner prizes, taken by land or naval forces in the service of the United States, shall be divided or appropriated; of granting letters of marque and reprisal in times of peace; appointing courts for the trial of piracies and felonies committed on the high seas, and establishing courts for receiving and determining, finally, appeals in all cases of captures; provided, that no member of Congress shall be appointed a judge of any of the said courts.

The United States, in Congress assembled, shall also be the last resort on appeal in all disputes and differences now subsisting, or that hereafter may arise between two or more states concerning boundary, jurisdiction or any other cause whatever; which authority shall always be exercised in the manner following: whenever the legislative or executive authority, or lawful agent of any State, in controversy with another, shall present a petition to Congress, stating the matter in question, and praying for a hearing, notice thereof shall be given, by order of Congress, to the legislative or executive authority of the other State in controversy, and a day assigned for the appearance of the parties by their lawful agents, who shall then be directed to appoint, by joint consent, commissioners or judges to constitute a court for hearing and determining the matter in question; but, if they cannot agree, Congress shall name three persons out of each of the United States, and from the list of such persons each party shall alternately strike out one, in the petitioners beginning, until the number shall be reduced to thirteen; and from that number not less than seven, nor more than nine names, as Congress shall direct, shall, in the presence of Congress, be drawn out by lot; and the persons whose names shall be drawn, or any five of them, shall be commissioners or judges to hear and finally determine the controversy, so always as a major part of the judges who shall hear the cause shall agree in the determination; and if either party shall neglect to attend at the day appointed, without shewing reasons which Congress shall judge sufficient, or, being present, shall refuse to strike, the Congress shall proceed to nominate three persons out of each State, and the secretary of Congress shall strike in behalf of such party absent or refusing; and the judgment and sentence of the court to be appointed, in the manner before prescribed, shall be final and conclusive;

and if any of the parties shall refuse to submit to the authority of such court, or to appear or defend their claim or cause, the court shall nevertheless proceed to pronounce sentence or judgment, which shall, in like manner, be final and decisive, the judgment or sentence and other proceedings being, in either case, transmitted to Congress, and lodged among the acts of Congress for the security of the parties concerned: provided, that every commissioner, before he sits in judgment, shall take an oath, to be administered by one of the judges of the supreme or superior court of the State where the cause shall be tried, "well and truly to hear and determine the matter in question, according to the best of his judgment, without favor, affection, or hope of reward": provided, also, that no State shall be deprived of territory for the benefit of the United States.

All controversies concerning the private right of soil, claimed under different grants of two or more states, whose jurisdictions, as they may respect such lands and the states which passed such grants, are adjusted, the said grants, or either of them, being at the same time claimed to have originated antecedent to such settlement of jurisdiction, shall, on the petition of either party to the Congress of the United States, be finally determined, as near as may be, in the same manner as is before prescribed for deciding disputes respecting territorial jurisdiction between different states.

The United States, in Congress assembled, shall also have the sole and exclusive right and power of regulating the alloy and value of coin struck by their own authority, or by that of the respective states; fixing the standard of weights and measures throughout the United States; regulating the trade and managing all affairs with the Indians not members of any of the states; provided that the legislative right of any State within its own limits be not infringed or violated; establishing and regulating post offices from one State to another throughout all the United States, and exacting such postage on the papers passing through the same as may be requisite to defray the expences of the said office; appointing all officers of the land forces in the service of the United States, excepting regimental officers; appointing all the officers of the naval forces, and commissioning all officers whatever in the service of the United States; making rules for the government and regulation of the said land and naval forces, and directing their operations.

The United States, in Congress assembled, shall have authority to appoint a committee to sit in the recess of Congress, to be denominated "a Committee of the States," and to consist of one delegate from each State, and to appoint such other committees and civil officers as may be necessary for managing the general affairs of the United States, under their direction; to appoint one of their number to preside; provided that no person be allowed to serve in the office of president more than one year in any term of three years; to ascertain the necessary sums of money to be raised for the service of the United States, and to appropriate and apply the same for defraying the public expences; to

borrow money or emit bills on the credit of the United States, transmitting, every half year, to the respective states, an account of the sums of money so borrowed or emitted; to build and equip a navy; to agree upon the number of land forces, and to make requisitions from each State for its quota, in proportion to the number of white inhabitants in such State; which requisitions shall be binding; and, thereupon, the legislature of each State shall appoint the regimental officers, raise the men, and cloathe, arm, and equip them in a soldier-like manner, at the expence of the United States; and the officers and men so cloathed, armed, and equipped, shall march to the place appointed and within the time agreed on by the United States, in Congress assembled; but if the United States, in Congress assembled, shall, on consideration of circumstances, judge proper that any State should not raise men, or should raise a smaller number than its quota, and that any other State should raise a greater number of men than the quota thereof, such extra number shall be raised, officered, cloathed, armed, and equipped in the same manner as the quota of such State, unless the legislature of such State shall judge that such extra number cannot be safely spared out of the same, in which case they shall raise, officer, cloathe, arm, and equip as many of such extra number as they judge can be safely spared. And the officers and men so cloathed, armed, and equipped, shall march to the place appointed and within the time agreed on by the United States, in Congress assembled.

The United States, in Congress assembled, shall never engage in a war, nor grant letters of marque and reprisal in time of peace, nor enter into any treaties or alliances, nor coin money, nor regulate the value thereof, nor ascertain the sums and expences necessary for the defence and welfare of the United States, or any of them: nor emit bills, nor borrow money on the credit of the United States, nor appropriate money, nor agree upon the number of vessels of war to be built or purchased, or the number of land or sea forces to be raised, nor appoint a commander in chief of the army or navy, unless nine states assent to the same; nor shall a question on any other point, except for adjourning from day to day, be determined, unless by the votes of a majority of the United States, in Congress assembled.

The Congress of the United States shall have power to adjourn to any time within the year, and to any place within the United States, so that no period of adjournment be for a longer duration than the space of six months, and shall publish the journal of their proceedings monthly, except such parts thereof, relating to treaties, alliances or military operations, as, in their judgment, require secrecy; and the yeas and nays of the delegates of each State on any question shall be entered on the journal, when it is desired by any delegate; and the delegates of a State, or any of them, at his, or their request, shall be furnished with a transcript of the said journal, except such parts as are above excepted, to lay before the legislatures of the several states.

ARTICLE 10

The committee of the states, or any nine of them, shall be authorized to execute, in the recess of Congress, such of the powers of Congress as the United States, in Congress assembled, by the consent of nine states, shall, from time to time, think expedient to vest them with; provided, that no power be delegated to the said committee for the exercise of which by the articles of confederation, the voice of nine states, in the Congress of the United States assembled, is requisite.

ARTICLE 11

Canada acceding to this confederation, and joining in the measures of the United States, shall be admitted into and entitled to all the advantages of this union; but no other colony shall be admitted into the same, unless such admission be agreed to by nine states.

ARTICLE 12

All bills of credit emitted, monies borrowed and debts contracted by, or under the authority of Congress before the assembling of the United States, in pursuance of the present confederation, shall be deemed and considered as a charge against the United States, for payment and satisfaction whereof the said United States and the public faith are hereby solemnly pledged.

ARTICLE 13

Every State shall abide by the determinations of the United States, in Congress assembled, on all questions which, by this confederation, are submitted to them. And the articles of this confederation shall be inviolably observed by every State, and the union shall be perpetual; nor shall any alteration at any time hereafter be made in any of them, unless such alteration be agreed to in a Congress of the United States, and be afterwards confirmed by the legislatures of every State.

These articles shall be proposed to the legislatures of all the United States, to be considered, and if approved of by them, they are advised to authorize their delegates to ratify the same in the Congress of the United States; which being done, the same shall become conclusive.

The Constitution of the United States of America

PREAMBLE

We the People of the United States, in Order to form a more perfect Union, establish Justice, insure domestic Tranquility, provide for the common defence, promote the general Welfare, and secure the Blessings of Liberty to ourselves and our Posterity, do ordain and establish this Constitution for the United States of America.

ARTICLE 1

Section 1

All legislative Powers herein granted shall be vested in a Congress of the United States, which shall consist of a Senate and House of Representatives.

Section 2

The House of Representatives shall be composed of Members chosen every second Year by the People of the several States, and the Electors in each State shall have the Qualifications requisite for Electors of the most numerous Branch of the State Legislature.

No Person shall be a Representative who shall not have attained to the Age of twenty five Years, and been seven Years a Citizen of the United States, and who shall not, when elected, be an inhabitant of that State in which he shall be chosen.

Representatives and direct Taxes shall be apportioned among the several States which may be included within this Union, according to their respective Numbers, *which shall be determined by adding to the whole Number of free Persons, including those bound to Service for a Term of Years, and excluding Indians not taxed, three fifths of all other Persons.** The actual Enumeration shall be made within three Years after the first Meeting of the Congress of the United States, and within every subsequent Term of ten Years, in such Manner as they shall by Law direct. The Number of Representatives shall not exceed one for every thirty Thousand, but each State shall have at Least one Representative; *and until such enumeration shall be made, the State of New Hampshire shall be entitled to chuse three, Massachusetts eight, Rhode-Island and Providence Plantations one, Connecticut five, New York six, New Jersey four, Pennsylvania eight, Delaware one, Maryland six, Virginia ten, North Carolina five, South Carolina five, and Georgia three.*

When vacancies happen in the Representation from any State, the Executive Authority thereof shall issue Writs of Election to fill such Vacancies.

The House of Representatives shall chuse their Speaker and other Officers; and shall have the sole Power of Impeachment.

Section 3

The Senate of the United States shall be composed of two Senators from each State, *chosen by the Legislature thereof,* for six Years; and each Senator shall have one Vote.

Immediately after they shall be assembled in Consequence of the first Election, they shall be divided as equally as may be into three Classes. The Seats of the Senators of the first Class shall be vacated at the Expiration of the second Year, of the second Class at the Expiration of the fourth Year, and of the third Class at the Expiration of the sixth Year so that one third may be chosen every second Year; and if Vacancies happen by Resignation, or otherwise, during the Recess of the Legislature of any state, the Executive thereof may make temporary Appointments until the next Meeting of the Legislature, which shall then fill such Vacancies.

No Person shall be a Senator who shall not have attained to the Age of thirty Years, and been nine Years a Citizen of the United States, and who shall not, when elected, be an Inhabitant of that State for which he shall be chosen.

The Vice President of the United States shall be President of the Senate, but shall have no Vote, unless they be equally divided.

The Senate shall chuse their other Officers, and also a President *pro tempore,* in the Absence of the Vice President, or when he shall exercise the Office of President of the United States.

The Senate shall have the sole Power to try all Impeachments. When sitting for that Purpose, they shall be on Oath or Affirmation. When the President of the United States is tried the Chief Justice shall preside: And no Person shall be convicted without the Concurrence of two thirds of the Members present.

Judgment in Cases of Impeachment shall not extend further than to removal from Office, and disqualification to hold and enjoy any Office of honor, Trust or Profit under the United States: but the Party convicted shall nevertheless be liable and subject to Indictment, Trial, Judgment and Punishment, according to Law.

Section 4

The Times, Places and Manner of holding Elections for Senators and Representatives, shall be prescribed in each State by the Legislature thereof; but the Congress may at any time by Law make or alter such Regulations, except as to the Places of chusing Senators.

The Congress shall assemble at least once in every Year, *and such Meeting shall be on the first Monday in December, unless they shall by Law appoint a different Day.*

---

*Passages no longer in effect are printed in italic type.

Section 5

Each House shall be the Judge of the Elections, Returns and Qualifications of its own Members, and a Majority of each shall constitute a Quorum to do Business; but a smaller Number may adjourn from day to day, and may be authorized to compel the Attendance of absent Members, in such Manner, and under such Penalties as each House may provide.

Each House may determine the Rules of its Proceedings, punish its Members for disorderly Behaviour, and, with the Concurrence of two thirds, expel a Member.

Each House shall keep a Journal of its Proceedings, and from time to time publish the same, excepting such Parts as may in their Judgment require Secrecy; and the Yeas and Nays of the Members of either House on any question shall, at the Desire of one fifth of those Present, be entered on the Journal.

Neither House, during the Session of Congress, shall, without the Consent of the other, adjourn for more than three days, nor to any other Place than that in which the two Houses shall be sitting.

Section 6

The Senators and Representatives shall receive a Compensation for their Services, to be ascertained by Law, and paid out of the Treasury of the United States. They shall in all Cases, except Treason, Felony and Breach of the Peace, be privileged from Arrest during their Attendance at the Session of their respective Houses, and in going to and returning from the same; and for any Speech or Debate in either House, they shall not be questioned in any other Place.

No Senator or Representative shall, during the Time for which he was elected, be appointed to any civil Office under the Authority of the United States, which shall have been created, or the Emoluments whereof shall have been encreased during such time, and no Person holding any Office under the United States, shall be a Member of either House during his Continuance in Office.

Section 7

All Bills for raising Revenue shall orginate in the House of Representatives; but the Senate may propose or concur with Amendments as on other Bills.

Every Bill which shall have passed the House of Representatives and the Senate, shall, before it become a Law, be presented to the President of the United States; If he approve he shall sign it, but if not he shall return it, with his Objections to the House in which it shall have originated, who shall enter the Objections at large on their Journal, and proceed to reconsider it. If after such Reconsideration two thirds of that House shall agree to pass the Bill, it shall be sent, together with the Objections, to the other House, by which it shall likewise be reconsidered, and if approved by two thirds of that House, it shall become a Law. But in all such Cases the Votes of both Houses shall be determined by yeas and Nays, and the Names of the Persons voting for and against the Bill shall be entered on the Journal of each House respectively. If any Bill shall not be returned by the President within ten Days (Sundays excepted) after it shall have been presented to him, the Same shall be a Law, in like Manner as if he had signed it, unless the Congress by their Adjournment prevent its Return, in which Case it shall not be a Law.

Every Order, Resolution, or Vote to which the Concurrence of the Senate and House of Representatives may be necessary (except on a question of Adjournment) shall be presented to the President of the United States; and before the Same shall take Effect, shall be approved by him, or being disapproved by him, shall be repassed by two thirds of the Senate and House of Representatives, according to the Rules and Limitations prescribed in the Case of a Bill.

Section 8

The Congress shall have Power To lay and collect Taxes, Duties, Imposts and Excises, to pay the Debts and provide for the common Defence and general Welfare of the United States; but all Duties, Imposts and Excises shall be uniform throughout the United States;

To borrow Money on the credit of the United States;

To regulate Commerce with foreign Nations, and among the several States, and with the Indian Tribes;

To establish an uniform Rule of Naturalization, and uniform Laws on the subject of Bankruptcies throughout the United States;

To coin Money, regulate the Value thereof, and of foreign Coin, and fix the Standard of Weights and Measures;

To provide for the Punishment of counterfeiting the Securities and current Coin of the United States;

To establish Post Offices and post Roads;

To promote the Progress of Science and useful Arts, by securing for limited Times to Authors and Inventors the exclusive Right to their respective Writings and Discoveries;

To constitute Tribunals inferior to the supreme Court;

To define and punish Piracies and Felonies committed on the high Seas, and Offences against the Law of Nations;

To declare War, grant Letters of Marque and Reprisal, and make Rules concerning Captures on Land and Water;

To raise and support Armies, but no Appropriation of Money to that Use shall be for a longer Term than two Years;

To provide and maintain a Navy;

To make Rules for the Government and Regulation of the land and naval Forces;

To provide for calling forth the Militia to execute the Laws of the Union, suppress Insurrections and repel Invasions;

To provide for organizing, arming, and disciplining, the Militia, and for governing such Part of them as may be employed in the Service of the United States, reserving to the States respectively, the Appointment of the Officers, and the Authority of training the Militia according to the discipline prescribed by Congress;

To exercise exclusive Legislation in all Cases whatsoever, over such District (not exceeding ten Miles square) as may, by Cession of particular States, and the Acceptance of Congress, become the Seat of the Government of the United States, and to exercise like Authority over all Places purchased by the Consent of the Legislature of the State in which the Same shall be, for the Erection of Forts, Magazines, Arsenals, dock-Yards, and other needful Buildings;—And

To make all Laws which shall be necessary and proper for carrying into Execution the foregoing Powers, and all other Powers vested by this Constitution in the Government of the United States, or in any Department of Officer thereof.

Section 9

The Migration or Importation of such Persons as any of the States now existing shall think proper to admit, shall not be prohibited by the Congress prior to the Year one thousand eight hundred and eight, but a Tax or duty may be imposed on such Importation, not exceeding ten dollars for each Person.

The Privilege of the Writ of Habeas Corpus shall not be suspended, unless when in Cases of Rebellion or Invasion the public Safety may require it.

No Bill of Attainder or ex post facto Law shall be passed.

No Capitation, or other direct, Tax shall be laid, unless in Proportion to the Census or Enumeration herein before directed to be taken.

No Tax or Duty shall be laid on Articles exported from any State.

No Preference shall be given by any Regulation of Commerce or Revenue to the Ports of one State over those of another: nor shall Vessels bound to, or from, one State, be obliged to enter, clear, or pay Duties in another.

No Money shall be drawn from the Treasury, but in Consequence of Appropriations made by Law; and a regular Statement and Account of the Receipts and Expenditures of all public Money shall be published from time to time.

No Title of Nobility shall be granted by the United States: And no Person holding any Office of Profit or Trust under them, shall, without the Consent of the Congress, accept of any present, Emolument, Office, or Title, of any kind whatever, from any King, Prince, or foreign State.

Section 10

No State shall enter into any Treaty, Alliance, or Confederation; grant Letters of Marque and Reprisal; coin Money; emit Bills of Credit; make any Thing but gold and silver Coin a Tender in Payment of Debts; pass any Bill of Attainder, ex post facto Law, or Law impairing the obligation of Contracts, or grant any Title of Nobility.

No State shall, without the Consent of the Congress, lay any Imposts or Duties on Imports or Exports, except what may be absolutely necessary for executing its inspection Laws: and the net Produce of all Duties and Imposts, laid by any State on Imports or Exports, shall be for the Use of the Treasury of the United States; and all such Laws shall be subject to the Revision and Controul of the Congress.

No State shall, without the Consent of Congress, lay any Duty of Tonnage, keep Troops, or Ships of War in time of Peace, enter into any Agreement or Compact with another State, or with a foreign Power, or engage in War, unless actually invaded, or in such imminent Danger as will not admit of delay.

ARTICLE II

Section 1

The executive Power shall be vested in a President of the United States of America. He shall hold his Office during the Term of four Years, and, together with the Vice President, chosen for the same Term, be elected, as follows:

Each State shall appoint, in such Manner as the Legislature thereof may direct, a Number of Electors, equal to the whole Number of Senators and Representatives to which the State may be entitled in the Congress: but no Senator or Representative, or Person holding an Office of Trust or Profit under the United States, shall be appointed an Elector.

The Electors shall meet in their respective States, and vote by Ballot for two Persons, of whom one at least shall not be an Inhabitant of the same State with themselves. And they shall make a List of all the Persons voted for, and of the Number of Votes for each; which List they shall sign and certify, and transmit sealed to the Seat of the Government of the United States, directed to the President of the Senate. The President of the Senate shall, in the Presence of the Senate and House of Representatives, open all the Certificates, and the Votes shall then be counted. The Person having the greatest Number of Votes shall be the President, if such Number be a Majority of the whole number of Electors appointed; and if there be more than one who have such Majority, and have an equal Number of Votes, then the House of Representatives shall immediately chuse by Ballot one of them for President; and if no Person have a Majority, then from the five highest on the List the said House shall in like Manner chuse the President. But in chusing the President, the Votes shall be taken by States, the Representation from each State having one Vote; A quorum for this Purpose shall consist of a Member or Members from two thirds of the States, and a Majority of all the States shall be necessary to a Choice. In every Case, after the Choice of the President, the Person having the greatest Number of Votes of the Electors shall be the Vice President. But if there should remain two or more who have equal Votes, the Senate shall chuse from them by Ballot the Vice President.

The Congress may determine the time of chusing the Electors, and the Day on which they shall give their Votes; which Day shall be the same throughout the United States.

No person except a natural born Citizen, *or a Citizen of the United States, at the time of the Adoption of this Constitution,* shall be eligible to the Office of President; neither shall any Person be eligible to that Office who shall not have attained to the Age of thirty five Years, and been fourteen Years a Resident within the United States.

In Case of the Removal of the President from Office, or of his Death, Resignation, or Inability to discharge the Powers and Duties of the said Office, the Same shall devolve on the Vice President, and the Congress may by Law provide for the Case of Removal, Death, Resignation or Inability, both of the President and Vice President, declaring what Officer shall then act as President, and such Officer shall act accordingly, until the Disability be removed, or a President shall be elected.

The President shall, at stated Times, receive for his Services, a Compensation, which shall neither be encreased nor diminished during the Period for which he shall have been elected, and he shall not receive within that period any other Emolument from the United States, or any of them.

Before he enter on the Execution of his Office, he shall take the following Oath or Affirmation:—"I do solemnly swear (or affirm) that I will faithfully execute the Office of President of the United States, and will to the best of my Ability, preserve, protect and defend the Constitution of the United States."

Section 2

The President shall be Commander in Chief of the Army and Navy of the United States, and of the Militia of the several States, when called into the actual Service of the United States; he may require the Opinion, in writing, of the principal Officer in each of the executive Departments, upon any Subject relating to the Duties of their respective Offices, and he shall have Power to grant Reprieves and Pardons for Offences against the United States, except in Cases of Impeachment.

He shall have Power, by and with the Advice and Consent of the Senate, to make Treaties, provided two thirds of the Senators present concur; and he shall nominate, and by and with the Advice and Consent of the Senate, shall appoint Ambassadors, other public Ministers and Consuls, Judges of the supreme Court, and all other Officers of the United States, whose Appointments are not herein otherwise provided for, and which shall be established by Law: but the Congress may by Law vest the Appointment of such inferior Officers, as they think proper in the President alone, in the Courts of Law, or in the Heads of Departments.

The President shall have Power to fill up all Vacancies that may happen during the Recess of the Senate, by granting Commissions which shall expire at the End of their next Session.

Section 3

He shall from time to time give to the Congress Information of the State of the Union, and recommend to their Consideration such Measures as he shall judge necessary and expedient; he may, on extraordinary Occasions, convene both Houses, or either of them, and in Case of disagreement between them, with Respect to the Time of Adjournment, he may adjourn them to such Time as he shall think proper; he shall receive Ambassadors and other public Ministers; he shall take Care that the Laws be faithfully executed, and shall Commission all the officers of the United States.

Section 4

The President, Vice President and all civil Officers of the United States, shall be removed from Office on Impeachment for, and Conviction of, Treason, Bribery or other high Crimes and Misdemeanors.

ARTICLE III

Section 1

The judicial Power of the United States, shall be vested in one supreme Court, and in such inferior Courts as the Congress may from time to time ordain and establish. The Judges, both of the supreme and inferior Courts, shall hold their offices during good Behaviour, and shall, at stated Times, receive for their Services, a Compensation, which shall not be diminished during their Continuance in Office.

Section 2

The judicial Power shall extend to all Cases, in Law and Equity, arising under this Constitution, the Laws of the United States, and Treaties made, or which shall be made, under their Authority;—to all Cases affecting Ambassadors, other public Ministers and Consuls;—to all Cases of admiralty and maritime Jurisdiction;—to Controversies to which the United States shall be a Party;—to Controversies between two or more States;—*between a State and Citizens of another State;*—between Citizens of different States;—between Citizens of the same State claiming Lands under Grants of different States, and between a State, or the Citizens thereof, and foreign States, Citizens or Subjects.

In all Cases affecting Ambassadors, other public Ministers and Consuls, and those in which a State shall be Party, the supreme Court shall have original Jurisdiction. In all the other Cases before mentioned, the supreme Court shall have appellate Jurisdiction, both as to Law and Fact, with such Exceptions, and under such Regulations as the Congress shall make.

The Trial of all Crimes, except in Cases of Impeachment, shall be by Jury; and such Trial shall be held in the State where the said Crimes shall have been committed, but when not committed within any State, the Trial shall be at such Place or Places as the Congress may by Law have directed.

Section 3

Treason against the United States, shall consist only in levying War against them, or in adhering to their Enemies, giving them Aid and Comfort. No person shall be convicted of Treason unless on the Testimony of two Witnesses to the same overt Act, or on Confession in open Court.

The Congress shall have Power to declare the Punishment of Treason, but no Attainder of Treason shall work Corruption of Blood, or Forfeiture except during the Life of the Person attainted.

ARTICLE IV

Section 1

Full Faith and Credit shall be given in each State to the public Acts, Records, and judicial Proceedings of every other State. And the Congress may by general Laws prescribe the Manner in which such Acts, Records and Proceedings shall be proved, and the Effect thereof.

Section 2

The Citizens of each State shall be entitled to all Privileges and Immunities of Citizens in the several States.

A Person charged in any State with Treason, Felony, or other Crime, who shall flee from Justice, and be found in another State, shall on Demand of the executive Authority of the State from which he fled, be delivered up, to be removed to the State having Jurisdiction of the Crime.

No Person held to Service or Labour in one State, under the Laws thereof, escaping into another, shall, in Consequence of any Law or Regulation therein, be discharged from such Service or Labour, but shall be delivered up on Claim of the Party to whom such Service or Labour may be due.

Section 3

New States may be admitted by the Congress into this Union; but no new State shall be formed or erected within the Jurisdiction of any other State; nor any State be formed by the Junction of two or more States, or Parts of States, without the Consent of the Legislatures of the States concerned as well as of the Congress.

The Congress shall have Power to dispose of and make all needful Rules and Regulations respecting the Territory or other Property belonging to the United States; and nothing in this Constitution shall be so construed as to Prejudice any Claims of the United States, or of any particular States.

Section 4

The United States shall guarantee to every State in this Union a Republican Form of Government, and shall protect each of them against Invasion; and on Application of the Legislature, or of the Executive (when the Legislature cannot be convened) against domestic violence.

ARTICLE V

The Congress, whenever two thirds of both Houses shall deem it necessary, shall propose Amendments to this Constitution, or, on the Application of the Legislatures of two thirds of the several States, shall call a Convention for proposing Amendments, which, in either Case, shall be valid to all Intents and Purposes, as Part of this Constitution, when ratified by the Legislatures of three fourths of the several States, or by Conventions in three fourths thereof, as the one or the other Mode of Ratification may be proposed by the Congress; Provided *that no Amendment which may be made prior to the Year One thousand eight hundred eight shall in any Manner affect the first and fourth Clauses in the Ninth Section of the first Article;* and that no State, without its Consent, shall be deprived of its equal Suffrage in the Senate.

ARTICLE VI

All Debts contracted and Engagements entered into, before the Adoption of this Constitution, shall be as valid against the United States under this Constitution, as under the Confederation.

This Constitution, and Laws of the United States which shall be made in Pursuance thereof; and all Treaties made, or which shall be made, under the Authority of the United States, shall be the supreme Law of the Land; and the Judges in every State shall be bound thereby, any Thing in the Constitution or Laws of any State to the Contrary notwithstanding.

The Senators and Representatives before mentioned, and the Members of the several State Legislatures, and all executive and Judicial Officers, both of the United States and of the several States, shall be bound by Oath or Affirmation, to support this Constitution; but no religious Test shall ever be required as a Qualification to any Office of public Trust under the United States.

ARTICLE VII

The Ratification of the Conventions of nine States, shall be sufficient for the Establishment of this Constitution between the States so ratifying the Same.

Done in Convention by the Unanimous Consent of the States present the Seventeenth Day of September in the Year of our Lord one thousand seven hundred and Eighty seven and of the Independence of the United States of America the Twelfth* IN WITNESS whereof We have hereunto subscribed our Names,

---

*The Constitution was submitted on September 17, 1787, by the Constitutional Convention, was ratified by the Convention of several states at various dates up to May 29, 1790, and became effective on March 4, 1789.

George Washington
President and Deputy from Virginia

Delaware
George Read
Gunning Bedford, Jr.
John Dickinson
Richard Bassett
Jacob Broom

Maryland
James McHenry
Daniel of St. Thomas Jenifer
Daniel Carroll

Virginia
John Blair
James Madison, Jr

North Carolina
William Blount
Richard Dobbs Spraight
Hugh Williamson

South Carolina
John Rutledge
Charles Cotesworth Pinckney
Charles Pinckney
Pierce Butler

Georgia
William Few
Abraham Baldwin

New Hampshire
John Langdon
Nicholas Gilman

Massachusetts
Nathaniel Gorham
Rufus King

Connecticut
William Samuel Johnson

Roger Sherman

New York
Alexander Hamilton

New Jersey
William Livingston
David Brearley
William Paterson
Jonathan Dayton

Pennsylvania
Benjamin Franklin
Thomas Mifflin
Robert Morris
George Clymer
Thomas FitzSimons
Jared Ingersoll
James Wilson
Gouverneur Morris

Amendments to the Constitution

AMENDMENT I

Congress shall make no law respecting an establishment of religion, or prohibiting the free exercise thereof; or abridging the freedom of speech, or of the press; or the right of the people peaceably to assemble, and to petition the Government for a redress of grievances.

AMENDMENT II

A well regulated Militia being necessary to the security of a free State, the right of the people to keep and bear Arms, shall not be infringed.

AMENDMENT III

No Soldier shall, in time of peace be quartered in any house, without the consent of the Owner, nor in time of war, but in a manner to be prescribed by law.

AMENDMENT IV

The right of the people to be secure in their persons, houses, papers, and effects, against unreasonable searches and seizures, shall not be violated, and no Warrants shall issue, but upon probable cause, supported by Oath or affirmation, and particularly describing the place to be searched, and the persons or things to be seized.

AMENDMENT V

No person shall be held to answer for a capital, or otherwise infamous crime, unless on a presentment or indictment of a Grand Jury, except in cases arising in the land or naval forces, or in the Militia, when in actual service in time of War or public danger; nor shall any person be subject for the same offense to be twice put in jeopardy of life or limb; nor shall be compelled in any criminal case to be a witness against himself, nor be deprived of life, liberty, or property, without due process of law; nor shall private property be taken for public use, without just compensation.

AMENDMENT VI

In all criminal prosecutions, the accused shall enjoy the right to a speedy and public trial, by an impartial jury of the State and district wherein the crime shall have been committed, which district shall have been previously ascertained by law, and to be informed of the nature and cause of the accusation; to be confronted with the witnesses against him; to have compulsory process for obtaining witnesses in his favor, and to have the Assistance of Counsel for his defence.

AMENDMENT VII

In Suits at common law, where the value in controversy shall exceed twenty dollars, the right of trial by jury shall be preserved, and no fact tried by a jury, shall be otherwise reexamined in any Court of the United States, than according to the rules of the common law.

AMENDMENT VIII

Excessive bail shall not be required, nor excessive fines imposed, nor cruel and unusual punishments inflicted.

AMENDMENT IX

The enumeration in the Constitution, of certain rights, shall not be construed to deny or disparage others retained by the people.

AMENDMENT X*

The powers not delegated to the United States by the Constitution, nor prohibited by it to the States, are reserved to the States respectively, or to the people.

AMENDMENT XI

[ADOPTED 1798]

The Judicial power of the United States shall not be construed to extend to any suit in law or equity, commenced or prosecuted against one of the United States by Citizens of another State, or by Citizens or Subjects of any Foreign State.

AMENDMENT XII

[ADOPTED 1804]

The Electors shall meet in their respective states, and vote by ballot for President and Vice President, one of whom, at least, shall not be an inhabitant of the same state with themselves; they shall name in their ballots the person voted for as President, and in distinct ballots the person voted for as Vice President, and they shall make distinct lists of all persons voted for as President, and of all persons voted for as Vice President, and of the number of votes for each, which lists they shall sign and certify, and transmit sealed to the seat of the government of the United States, directed to the President of the Senate;—The President of the Senate shall, in the presence of the Senate and House of Representatives, open all the certificates and the votes shall then be counted;—The person having the greatest number of votes for President, shall be the President, if such number be a majority of the whole number of Electors appointed; and if no person have such majority, then from the persons

---

*The first ten amendments (the Bill of Rights) were ratified and their adoption was certified on December 15, 1791.

having the highest numbers not exceeding three on the list of those voted for as President, the House of Representatives shall choose immediately, by ballot, the President. But in choosing the President, the votes shall be taken by states, the representation from each state having one vote; a quorum for this purpose shall consist of a member or members from two-thirds of the states, and a majority of all the states shall be necessary to a choice. And if the House of Representatives shall not choose a President whenever the right of choice shall devolve upon them, before *the fourth day of March* next following, then the Vice President shall act as President, as in the case of the death or other constitutional disability of the President.—The person having the greatest number of votes as Vice President, shall be the Vice President, if such number be a majority of the whole number of Electors appointed, and if no person have a majority, then from the two highest numbers on the list, the Senate shall choose the Vice President; a quorum for the purpose shall consist of two-thirds of the whole number of Senators, and a majority of the whole number shall be necessary to a choice. But no person constitutionally ineligible to the office of President shall be eligible to that of Vice President of the United States.

AMENDMENT XIII
[ADOPTED 1865]

Section 1

Neither slavery nor involuntary servitude, except as a punishment for crime whereof the party shall have been duly convicted, shall exist within the United States, or any place subject to their jurisdiction.

Section 2

Congress shall have power to enforce this article by appropriate legislation.

AMENDMENT XIV
[ADOPTED 1868]

Section 1

All persons born or naturalized in the United States, and subject to the jurisdiction thereof, are citizens of the United States and of the State wherein they reside. No State shall make or enforce any law which shall abridge the privileges or immunities of citizens of the United States; nor shall any State deprive any person of life, liberty, or property, without due process of law; nor deny to any person within its jurisdiction the equal protection of the laws.

Section 2

Representatives shall be apportioned among the several States according to their respective numbers, counting the whole number of persons in each State, excluding Indians not taxed. But when the right to vote at any election for the choice of electors for President and Vice President of the United States, Representatives in Congress, the Executive and Judicial officers of a State, or the members of the Legislature thereof, is denied to any of the male inhabitants of such State, being twenty-one years of age, and citizens of the United States, or in any way abridged, except for participation in rebellion, or other crime, the basis of representation therein shall be reduced in the proportion which the number of such male citizens shall bear to the whole number of male citizens twenty-one years of age in such State.

Section 3

No person shall be a Senator or Representative in Congress, or elector of President and Vice President, or hold any office, civil or military, under the United States, or under any State, who, having previously taken an oath, as a member of Congress, or as an officer of the United States, or as a member of any State legislature, or as an executive or judicial officer of any State, to support the Constitution of the United States, shall have engaged in insurrection or rebellion against the same, or given aid or comfort to the enemies thereof. But Congress may by a vote of two-thirds of each House, remove such disability.

Section 4

The validity of the public debt of the United States, authorized by law, including debts incurred for payment of pensions and bounties for services in suppressing insurrection or rebellion, shall not be questioned. But neither the United States nor any State shall assume or pay any debt or obligation incurred in aid of insurrection or rebellion against the United States, or any claim for the loss or emancipation of any slave; but all such debts, obligations and claims shall be held illegal and void.

Section 5

The Congress shall have power to enforce, by appropriate legislation, the provisions of this article.

AMENDMENT XV
[ADOPTED 1870]

Section 1

The right of citizens of the United States to vote shall not be denied or abridged by the United States or by any State on account of race, color, or previous condition of servitude.

Section 2

The Congress shall have power to enforce this article by appropriate legislation.

AMENDMENT XVI
[ADOPTED 1913]

The Congress shall have power to lay and collect taxes on incomes, from whatever source derived, without apportionment among the several States, and without regard to any census or enumeration.

AMENDMENT XVII
[ADOPTED 1913]

The Senate of the United States shall be composed of two Senators from each State, elected by the people thereof, for six years; and each Senator shall have one vote. The electors in each State shall have the qualifications requisite for electors of the most numerous branch of the State legislatures.

When vacancies happen in the representation of any State in the Senate, the executive authority of such State shall issue writs of election to fill such vacancies: *Provided,* That the legislature of any State may empower the executive thereof to make temporary appointments until the people fill the vacancies by election as the legislature may direct.

This amendment shall not be so construed as to affect the election or term of any Senator chosen before it becomes valid as part of the Constitution.

AMENDMENT XVIII
[ADOPTED 1919, REPEALED 1933]

Section 1
After one year from the ratification of this article the manufacture, sale, or transportation of intoxicating liquors within, the importation thereof into, or the exportation thereof from the United States and all territory subject to the jurisdiction thereof for beverage purposes is hereby prohibited.

Section 2
The Congress and the several States shall have concurrent power to enforce this article by appropriate legislation.

Section 3
This article shall be inoperative unless it shall have been ratified as an amendment to the Constitution by the legislatures of the several States, as provided in the Constitution, within seven years from the date of the submission hereof to the States by the Congress.

AMENDMENT XIX
[ADOPTED 1920]

The right of citizens of the United States to vote shall not be denied or abridged by the United States or by any State on account of sex.

Congress shall have power to enforce this article by appropriate legislation.

AMENDMENT XX
[ADOPTED 1933]

Section 1
The terms of the President and Vice President shall end at noon on the 20th day of January, and the terms of Senators and Representatives at noon on the 3d day of January, of the years in which such terms would have ended if this article had not been ratified and the terms of their successors shall then begin.

Section 2
The Congress shall assemble at least once in every year, and such meeting shall begin at noon on the 3d day of January, unless they shall by law appoint a different day.

Section 3
If, at the time fixed for the beginning of the term of the President, the President elect shall have died, the Vice President elect shall become President. If a President shall not have been chosen before the time fixed for the beginning of his term, or if the President elect shall have failed to qualify, then the Vice President elect shall act as President until a President shall have qualified; and the Congress may by law provide for the case wherein neither a President elect nor a Vice President elect shall have qualified, declaring who shall then act as President, or the manner in which one who is to act shall be selected, and such person shall act accordingly until a President or Vice President shall have qualified.

Section 4
The Congress may by law provide for the case of the death of any of the persons from whom the House of Representatives may choose a President whenever the right of choice shall have devolved upon them, and for the case of the death of any of the persons from whom the Senate may choose a Vice President whenever the right of choice shall have devolved upon them.

Section 5
Sections 1 and 2 shall take effect on the 15th day of October following the ratification of this article.

Section 6
This article shall be inoperative unless it shall have been ratified as an amendment to the Constitution by the legislatures of three fourths of the several States within seven years from the date of its submission.

AMENDMENT XXI
[ADOPTED 1933]

Section 1
The eighteenth article of amendment to the Constitution of the United States is hereby repealed.

Section 2
The transportation or importation into any State, Territory, or possession of the United States for delivery or use therein of intoxicating liquors in violation of the laws thereof, is hereby prohibited.

Section 3
This article shall be inoperative unless it shall have been ratified as an amendment to the Constitution by conventions in the several States, as provided in the Constitution,

within seven years from the date of the submission hereof to the States by the Congress.

AMENDMENT XXII

[ADOPTED 1951]

Section 1

No person shall be elected to the office of the President more than twice, and no person who has held the office of President, or acted as President, for more than two years of a term to which some other person was elected President shall be elected to the office of the President more than once. But this Article shall not apply to any person holding the office of President when this Article was proposed by the Congress, and shall not prevent any person who may be holding the office of President, or acting as President, during the term within which this Article becomes operative from holding the office of President or acting as President during the remainder of such term.

Section 2

This article shall be inoperative unless it shall have been ratified as an amendment to the Constitution by the legislatures of three-fourths of the several States within seven years from the date of its submission to the States by the Congress.

AMENDMENT XXIII

[ADOPTED 1961]

Section 1

The District constituting the seat of Government of the United States shall appoint in such manner as the Congress shall direct:

A number of electors of President and Vice President equal to the whole number of Senators and Representatives in Congress to which the District would be entitled if it were a State, but in no event more than the least populous State; they shall be in addition to those appointed by the States, but they shall be considered, for the purposes of the election of President and Vice President, to be electors appointed by a State; and they shall meet in the District and perform such duties as provided by the twelfth article of amendment.

Section 2

The Congress shall have power to enforce this article by appropriate legislation.

AMENDMENT XXIV

[ADOPTED 1964]

Section 1

The right of citizens of the United States to vote in any primary or other election for President or Vice President, for electors for President or Vice President, or for Senator or Representative in Congress, shall not be denied or abridged by the United States or any state by reason of failure to pay any poll tax or other tax.

Section 2

The Congress shall have the power to enforce this article by appropriate legislation.

AMENDMENT XXV

[ADOPTED 1967]

Section 1

In case of the removal of the President from office or his death or resignation, the Vice President shall become President.

Section 2

Whenever there is a vacancy in the office of the Vice President, the President shall nominate a Vice President who shall take the office upon confirmation by a majority vote of both houses of Congress.

Section 3

Whenever the President transmits to the President pro tempore of the Senate and the Speaker of the House of Representatives his written declaration that he is unable to discharge the powers and duties of his office, and until he transmits to them a written declaration to the contrary, such powers and duties shall be discharged by the Vice President as Acting President.

Section 4

Whenever the Vice President and a majority of either the principal officers of the executive departments or of such other body as Congress may by law provide, transmit to the President pro tempore of the Senate and the Speaker of the House of Representatives their written declaration that the President is unable to discharge the powers and duties of his office, the Vice President shall immediately assume the powers and duties of the office as Acting President.

Thereafter, when the President transmits to the President pro tempore of the Senate and the Speaker of the House of Representatives his written declaration that no inability exists, he shall resume the powers and duties of his office unless the Vice President and a majority of either the principal officers of the executive department or of such other body as Congress may by law provide, transmit within four days to the President pro tempore of the Senate and the Speaker of the House of Representatives their written declaration that the President is unable to discharge the powers and duties of his office. Thereupon Congress shall decide the issue, assembling within 48 hours for that purpose if not in session. If the Congress, within 21 days after receipt of the latter written declaration, or, if Congress is not in session, within 21 days after Congress is required to assemble, determines by two-thirds vote of both houses that the President is unable to discharge the powers and duties of his office, the Vice President shall continue to discharge the same as Acting President; otherwise, the President shall resume the powers and duties of his office.

AMENDMENT XXVI
[ADOPTED 1971]

Section 1

The right of citizens of the United States, who are 18 years of age or older, to vote shall not be denied or abridged by the United States or any state on account of age.

Section 2

The Congress shall have the power to enforce this article by appropriate legislation.

AMENDMENT XXVII
[ADOPTED 1992]

No law, varying the compensation for the services of the Senators and Representatives shall take effect, until an election of Representatives shall have intervened.

Presidential Elections

Year	Candidates	Parties	Popular Vote	Electoral Vote	Voter Participation
1789	George Washington		*	69	
	John Adams			34	
	Others			35	
1792	George Washington		*	132	
	John Adams			77	
	George Clinton			50	
	Others			5	
1796	John Adams	Federalist	*	71	
	Thomas Jefferson	Democratic-Republican		68	
	Thomas Pinckney	Federalist		59	
	Aaron Burr	Dem.-Rep.		30	
	Others			48	
1800	Thomas Jefferson	Dem.-Rep.	*	73	
	Aaron Burr	Dem.-Rep.		73	
	John Adams	Federalist		65	
	C. C. Pinckney	Federalist		64	
	John Jay	Federalist		1	
1804	Thomas Jefferson	Dem.-Rep.	*	162	
	C. C. Pinckney	Federalist		14	
1808	James Madison	Dem.-Rep.	*	122	
	C. C. Pinckney	Federalist		47	
	George Clinton	Dem.-Rep.		6	
1812	James Madison	Dem.-Rep.	*	128	
	De Witt Clinton	Federalist		89	
1816	James Monroe	Dem.-Rep.	*	183	
	Rufus King	Federalist		34	

Year	Candidates	Parties	Popular Vote	Electoral Vote	Voter Participation
1820	**James Monroe**	Dem.-Rep.	*	231	
	John Quincy Adams	Dem.-Rep.		1	
1824	**John Quincy Adams**	Dem.-Rep.	108,740 (30.5%)	84	26.9%
	Andrew Jackson	Dem.-Rep.	153,544 (43.1%)	99	
	William H. Crawford	Dem.-Rep.	46,618 (13.1%)	41	
	Henry Clay	Dem.-Rep.	47,136 (13.2%)	37	
1828	**Andrew Jackson**	Democratic	647,286 (56.0%)	178	57.6%
	John Quincy Adams	National Republican	508,064 (44.0%)	83	
1832	**Andrew Jackson**	Democratic	688,242 (54.2%)	219	55.4%
	Henry Clay	National Republican	473,462 (37.4%)	49	
	John Floyd	Independent		11	
	William Wirt	Anti-Mason	101,051 (7.8%)	7	
1836	**Martin Van Buren**	Democratic	762,198 (50.8%)	170	57.8%
	William Henry Harrison	Whig	549,508 (36.6%)	73	
	Hugh L. White	Whig	145,342 (9.7%)	26	
	Daniel Webster	Whig	41,287 (2.7%)	14	
	W. P. Magnum	Independent		11	
1840	**William Henry Harrison**	Whig	1,274,624 (53.1%)	234	80.2%
	Martin Van Buren	Democratic	1,127,781 (46.9%)	60	
	J. G. Birney	Liberty	7069	—	
1844	**James K. Polk**	Democratic	1,338,464 (49.6%)	170	78.9%
	Henry Clay	Whig	1,300,097 (48.1%)	105	
	J. G. Birney	Liberty	62,300 (2.3%)	—	
1848	**Zachary Taylor**	Whig	1,360,967 (47.4%)	163	72.7%
	Lewis Cass	Democratic	1,222,342 (42.5%)	127	
	Martin Van Buren	Free-Soil	291,263 (10.1%)	—	
1852	**Franklin Pierce**	Democratic	1,601,117 (50.9%)	254	69.6%
	Winfield Scott	Whig	1,385,453 (44.1%)	42	
	John P. Hale	Free-Soil	155,825 (5.0%)	—	
1856	**James Buchanan**	Democratic	1,832,955 (45.3%)	174	78.9%
	John C. Frémont	Republican	1,339,932 (33.1%)	114	
	Millard Fillmore	American	871,731 (21.6%)	8	
1860	**Abraham Lincoln**	Republican	1,865,593 (39.8%)	180	81.2%
	Stephen A. Douglas	Democratic	1,382,713 (29.5%)	12	
	John C. Breckinridge	Democratic	848,356 (18.1%)	72	
	John Bell	Union	592,906 (12.6%)	39	
1864	**Abraham Lincoln**	Republican	2,213,655 (55.0%)	212[†]	73.8%
	George B. McClellan	Democratic	1,805,237 (45.0%)	21	

Year	Candidates	Parties	Popular Vote	Electoral Vote	Voter Participation
1868	**Ulysses S. Grant**	**Republican**	**3,012,833 (52.7%)**	214	78.1%
	Horatio Seymour	Democratic	2,703,249 (47.3%)	80	
1872	**Ulysses S. Grant**	**Republican**	**3,597,132 (55.6%)**	286	71.3%
	Horace Greeley	Dem.; Liberal Republican	2,834,125 (43.9%)	66[‡]	
1876	**Rutherford B. Hayes**[§]	**Republican**	**4,036,298 (48.0%)**	185	81.8%
	Samuel J. Tilden	Democratic	4,300,590 (51.0%)	184	
1880	**James A. Garfield**	**Republican**	**4,454,416 (48.5%)**	214	79.4%
	Winfield S. Hancock	Democratic	4,444,952 (48.1%)	155	
1884	**Grover Cleveland**	**Democratic**	**4,874,986 (48.5%)**	219	77.5%
	James G. Blaine	Republican	4,851,981 (48.2%)	182	
1888	**Benjamin Harrison**	**Republican**	**5,439,853 (47.9%)**	233	79.3%
	Grover Cleveland	Democratic	5,540,309 (48.6%)	168	
1892	**Grover Cleveland**	**Democratic**	**5,556,918 (46.1%)**	277	74.7%
	Benjamin Harrison	Republican	5,176,108 (43.0%)	145	
	James B. Weaver	People's	1,029,329 (8.5%)	22	
1896	**William McKinley**	**Republican**	**7,104,779 (51.1%)**	271	79.3%
	William Jennings Bryan	Democratic People's	6,502,925 (47.7%)	176	
1900	**William McKinley**	**Republican**	**7,207,923 (51.7%)**	292	73.2%
	William Jennings Bryan	Dem.-Populist	6,358,133 (45.5%)	155	
1904	**Theodore Roosevelt**	**Republican**	**7,623,486 (57.9%)**	336	65.2%
	Alton B. Parker	Democratic	5,077,911 (37.6%)	140	
	Eugene V. Debs	Socialist	402,400 (3.0%)	—	
1908	**William H. Taft**	**Republican**	**7,678,908 (51.6%)**	321	65.4%
	William Jennings Bryan	Democratic	6,409,104 (43.1%)	162	
	Eugene V. Debs	Socialist	402,820 (2.8%)	—	
1912	**Woodrow Wilson**	**Democratic**	**6,293,454 (41.9%)**	435	58.8%
	Theodore Roosevelt	Progressive	4,119,538 (27.4%)	88	
	William H. Taft	Republican	3,484,980 (23.2%)	8	
	Eugene V. Debs	Socialist	900,672 (6.0%)	—	
1916	**Woodrow Wilson**	**Democratic**	**9,129,606 (49.4%)**	277	61.6%
	Charles E. Hughes	Republican	8,538,221 (46.2%)	254	
	A. L. Benson	Socialist	585,113 (3.2%)	—	
1920	**Warren G. Harding**	**Republican**	**16,152,200 (60.4%)**	404	49.2%
	James M. Cox	Democratic	9,147,353 (34.2%)	127	
	Eugene V. Debs	Socialist	917,799 (3.4%)	—	
1924	**Calvin Coolidge**	**Republican**	**15,725,016 (54.0%)**	382	48.9%
	John W. Davis	Democratic	8,386,503 (28.8%)	136	
	Robert M. La Follette	Progressive	4,822,856 (16.6%)	13	

Year	Candidates	Parties	Popular Vote	Electoral Vote	Voter Participation
1928	**Herbert Hoover**	**Republican**	**21,391,381 (58.2%)**	444	56.9%
	Alfred E. Smith	Democratic	15,016,443 (40.9%)	87	
	Norman Thomas	Socialist	267,835 (0.7%)	—	
1932	**Franklin D. Roosevelt**	**Democratic**	**22,821,857 (57.4%)**	472	56.9%
	Herbert Hoover	Republican	15,761,841 (39.7%)	59	
	Norman Thomas	Socialist	884,781 (2.2%)	—	
1936	**Franklin D. Roosevelt**	**Democratic**	**27,751,597 (60.8%)**	523	61.0%
	Alfred M. Landon	Republican	16,679,583 (36.5%)	8	
	William Lemke	Union	882,479 (1.9%)	—	
1940	**Franklin D. Roosevelt**	**Democratic**	**27,244,160 (54.8%)**	449	62.5%
	Wendell L. Willkie	Republican	22,305,198 (44.8%)	82	
1944	**Franklin D. Roosevelt**	**Democratic**	**25,602,504 (53.5%)**	432	55.9%
	Thomas E. Dewey	Republican	22,006,285 (46.0%)	99	
1948	**Harry S Truman**	**Democratic**	**24,105,695 (49.5%)**	304	53.0%
	Thomas E. Dewey	Republican	21,969,170 (45.1%)	189	
	J. Strom Thurmond	State-Rights Democratic	1,169,021 (2.4%)	38	
	Henry A. Wallace	Progressive	1,157,326 (2.4%)	—	
1952	**Dwight D. Eisenhower**	**Republican**	**33,778,963 (55.1%)**	442	63.3%
	Adlai E. Stevenson	Democratic	27,314,992 (44.4%)	89	
1956	**Dwight D. Eisenhower**	**Republican**	**35,575,420 (57.6%)**	457	60.6%
	Adlai E. Stevenson	Democratic	26,033,066 (42.1%)	73	
	Other	—	—	1	
1960	**John F. Kennedy**	**Democratic**	**34,227,096 (49.9%)**	303	62.8%
	Richard M. Nixon	Republican	34,108,546 (49.6%)	219	
	Other	—	—	15	
1964	**Lyndon B. Johnson**	**Democratic**	**43,126,506 (61.1%)**	486	61.7%
	Barry M. Goldwater	Republican	27,176,799 (38.5%)	52	
1968	**Richard M. Nixon**	**Republican**	**31,770,237 (43.4%)**	301	60.6%
	Hubert H. Humphrey	Democratic	31,270,533 (42.7%)	191	
	George Wallace	American Indep.	9,906,141 (13.5%)	46	
1972	**Richard M. Nixon**	**Republican**	**46,740,323 (60.7%)**	520	55.2%
	George S. McGovern	Democratic	28,901,598 (37.5%)	17	
	Other	—	—	1	
1976	**Jimmy Carter**	**Democratic**	**40,828,587 (50.0%)**	297	53.5%
	Gerald R. Ford	Republican	39,147,613 (47.9%)	241	
	Other	—	1,575,459 (2.1%)	—	
1980	**Ronald Reagan**	**Republican**	**43,901,812 (50.7%)**	489	52.6%
	Jimmy Carter	Democratic	35,483,820 (41.0%)	49	
	John B. Anderson	Independent	5,719,437 (6.6%)	—	
	Ed Clark	Libertarian	921,188 (1.1%)	—	

Year	Candidates	Parties	Popular Vote	Electoral Vote	Voter Participation
1984	**Ronald Reagan**	**Republican**	**54,455,075 (59.0%)**	525	53.3%
	Walter Mondale	Democratic	37,577,185 (41.0%)	13	
1988	**George H. W. Bush**	**Republican**	**48,886,097 (53.4%)**	426	57.4%
	Michael S. Dukakis	Democratic	41,809,074 (45.6%)	111	
1992	**William J. Clinton**	**Democratic**	**44,908,254 (43%)**	370	55.0%
	George H. W. Bush	Republican	39,102,343 (37.5%)	168	
	H. Ross Perot	Independent	19,741,065 (18.9%)	—	
1996	**William J. Clinton**	**Democratic**	**45,590,703 (50%)**	379	48.8%
	Robert Dole	Republican	37,816,307 (41%)	159	
	Ross Perot	Reform	7,866,284	—	
2000	**George W. Bush**	**Republican**	**50,456,167 (47.88%)**	271	51.2%
	Al Gore	Democratic	50,996,064 (48.39%)	266[‖]	
	Ralph Nader	Green	2,864,810 (2.72%)	—	
	Other		834,774 (less than 1%)	—	
2004	**George W. Bush**	**Republican**	**60,934,251 (51.0%)**	286	50.0%
	John F. Kerry	Democratic	57,765,291 (48.0%)	252	
	Ralph Nader	Independent	405,933 (less than 1%)	—	

*Electors selected by state legislatures.
[†]Eleven secessionist states did not participate.
[‡]Greeley died before the electoral college met. His electoral votes were divided among the four minor candidates.
[§]Contested result settled by special election.
[‖]One District of Columbia Gore elector abstained.

Presidents and Vice Presidents

	President	Vice President	Term
1.	George Washington	John Adams	1789–1793
	George Washington	John Adams	1793–1797
2.	John Adams	Thomas Jefferson	1797–1801
3.	Thomas Jefferson	Aaron Burr	1801–1805
	Thomas Jefferson	George Clinton	1805–1809
4.	James Madison	George Clinton (d. 1812)	1809–1813
	James Madison	Elbridge Gerry (d. 1814)	1813–1817
5.	James Monroe	Daniel Tompkins	1817–1821
	James Monroe	Daniel Tompkins	1821–1825
6.	John Quincy Adams	John C. Calhoun	1825–1829
7.	Andrew Jackson	John C. Calhoun	1829–1833
	Andrew Jackson	Martin Van Buren	1833–1837
8.	Martin Van Buren	Richard M. Johnson	1837–1841
9.	William H. Harrison (d. 1841)	John Tyler	1841
10.	John Tyler	—	1841–1845
11.	James K. Polk	George M. Dallas	1845–1849
12.	Zachary Taylor (d. 1850)	Millard Fillmore	1849–1850
13.	Millard Fillmore	—	1850–1853
14.	Franklin Pierce	William R. King (d. 1853)	1853–1857
15.	James Buchanan	John C. Breckinridge	1857–1861
16.	Abraham Lincoln	Hannibal Hamlin	1861–1865
	Abraham Lincoln (d. 1865)	Andrew Johnson	1865
17.	Andrew Johnson	—	1865–1869
18.	Ulysses S. Grant	Schuyler Colfax	1869–1873
	Ulysses S. Grant	Henry Wilson (d. 1875)	1873–1877
19.	Rutherford B. Hayes	William A. Wheeler	1877–1881
20.	James A. Garfield (d. 1881)	Chester A. Arthur	1881
21.	Chester A. Arthur	—	1881–1885
22.	Grover Cleveland	Thomas A. Hendricks (d. 1885)	1885–1889
23.	Benjamin Harrison	Levi P. Morton	1889–1893
24.	Grover Cleveland	Adlai E. Stevenson	1893–1897
25.	William McKinley	Garret A. Hobart (d. 1899)	1897–1901
	William McKinley (d. 1901)	Theodore Roosevelt	1901
26.	Theodore Roosevelt	—	1901–1905
	Theodore Roosevelt	Charles Fairbanks	1905–1909
27.	William H. Taft	James S. Sherman (d. 1912)	1909–1913

	President	Vice President	Term
28.	**Woodrow Wilson**	Thomas R. Marshall	1913–1917
	Woodrow Wilson	Thomas R. Marshall	1917–1921
29.	**Warren G. Harding (d. 1923)**	Calvin Coolidge	1921–1923
30.	**Calvin Coolidge**	—	1923–1925
	Calvin Coolidge	Charles G. Dawes	1925–1929
31.	**Herbert Hoover**	Charles Curtis	1929–1933
32.	**Franklin D. Roosevelt**	John N. Garner	1933–1937
	Franklin D. Roosevelt	John N. Garner	1937–1941
	Franklin D. Roosevelt	Henry A. Wallace	1941–1945
	Franklin D. Roosevelt (d. 1945)	Harry S Truman	1945
33.	**Harry S Truman**	—	1945–1949
	Harry S Truman	Alben W. Barkley	1949–1953
34.	**Dwight D. Eisenhower**	Richard M. Nixon	1953–1957
	Dwight D. Eisenhower	Richard M. Nixon	1957–1961
35.	**John F. Kennedy (d. 1963)**	Lyndon B. Johnson	1961–1963
36.	**Lyndon B. Johnson**	—	1963–1965
	Lyndon B. Johnson	Hubert H. Humphrey	1965–1969
37.	**Richard M. Nixon**	Spiro T. Agnew	1969–1973
	Richard M. Nixon (resigned 1974)	Gerald R. Ford	1973–1974
38.	**Gerald R. Ford**	Nelson A. Rockefeller	1974–1977
39.	**Jimmy Carter**	Walter F. Mondale	1977–1981
40.	**Ronald Reagan**	George H. W. Bush	1981–1985
	Ronald Reagan	George H. W. Bush	1985–1989
41.	**George H. W. Bush**	J. Danforth Quayle	1989–1993
42.	**William J. Clinton**	Albert Gore, Jr.	1993–1997
	William J. Clinton	Albert Gore, Jr.	1997–2001
43.	**George W. Bush**	Richard Cheney	2001–2005
	George W. Bush	Richard Cheney	2005–

Adams-Onís Treaty (p. 241) Signed by Secretary of State John Quincy Adams and Spanish minister Luis de Onís in 1819, this treaty allowed for U.S. annexation of Florida.

affirmative action (p. 889) The use of laws or regulations to achieve racial, ethnic, gender, or other diversity, as in hiring or school admissions. Such efforts are often aimed at improving employment or educational opportunities for women and minorities.

African Methodist Episcopal (AME) Church (p. 158) Richard Allen founded the African Methodist Episcopal Church in 1816 as the first independent black-run Protestant church in the United States. The AME Church was active in the promotion of abolition and the founding of educational institutions for free blacks.

Agricultural Adjustment Administration (AAA) (p. 711) Created by Congress in 1933 as part of the New Deal, this agency attempted to restrict agricultural production by paying farmers subsidies to take land out of production. The object was to raise farm prices, and it did, but the act did nothing for tenant farmers and sharecroppers. The Supreme Court declared it unconstitutional in 1936.

Agricultural Revolution (p. 7) The gradual shift from hunting and gathering to cultivating basic food crops that occurred worldwide from 7000 to 9000 years ago.

Alamo (p. 345) In 1835, Americans living in the Mexican state of Texas fomented a revolution. Mexico lost the conflict, but not before its troops defeated and killed a group of American rebels at the Alamo, a fort in San Antonio.

Albany Plan (p. 110) Plan of intercolonial cooperation proposed by prominent colonists including Benjamin Franklin at a conference in Albany, New York, in 1754. The plan envisioned the formation of a Grand Council of elected delegates from the colonies that would have powers to tax and provide for the common defense. It was rejected by the colonial and British governments, but was a prototype for colonial union.

Alien and Sedition Acts (p. 202) Collective name given to four laws passed in 1798 designed to suppress criticism of the federal government and to curb liberties of foreigners living in the United States.

American Colonization Society (p. 307) Founded in 1817, this abolitionist organization hoped to provide a mechanism by which slavery could gradually be eliminated. The society advocated the relocation of free blacks (followed by freed slaves) to the African colony of Monrovia, present day Liberia.

American Federation of Labor (AFL) (p. 497) Founded by Samuel Gompers in 1886, the AFL was a loose alliance of national craft unions that organized skilled workers by craft and worked for specific practical objectives such as higher wages, shorter hours, and better working conditions. The AFL avoided politics, and while it did not expressly forbid black and women workers from joining, it used exclusionary practices to keep them out.

Americans with Disabilities Act (ADA) (p. 866) Passed by Congress in 1991, this act banned discrimination against the disabled in employment and mandated easy access to all public and commercial buildings.

Antifederalist (p. 175) Critic of the Constitution who expressed concern that it seemed to possess no specific provision for the protection of natural and civil rights.

Anti-Imperialist League (p. 580) This organization was formed in November 1898 to fight against the **Treaty of Paris** ending the Spanish-American War. Members opposed the acquisition of overseas colonies by the United States, believing it would subvert American ideals and institutions. Membership centered in New England; the cause was less popular in the South and West.

Antinomianism (p. 47) Religious belief rejecting traditional moral law as unnecessary for Christians who possess saving grace and affirming that an individual could experience divine revelation and salvation without the assistance of formally trained clergy.

Articles of Confederation (p. 163) Ratified in 1781, this document was the United States' first constitution, providing a framework for national government. The articles sharply limited central authority by denying the national government any taxation or coercive power.

Ashcan School (p. 610) This school of early twentieth-century realist painters took as their subjects the slums and streets of the nation's cities and the lives of ordinary urban dwellers. They often celebrated life in the city but also advocated political and social reform.

Axis Powers (p. 726) During World War II, the alliance between Italy, Germany, and Japan was known as the "Rome-Berlin-Tokyo axis," and the three members were called the Axis Powers. They fought against the Allied Powers, led by the United States, Britain, and the Soviet Union.

baby boom (p. 782) Post–World War II Americans idealized the family. The booming birth rate after the war led children born to this generation to be commonly referred to as "baby boomers."

backcountry (p. 90) In the eighteenth century, the edge of settlement extending from western Pennsylvania to Georgia. This region formed the second frontier as settlers moved westward from the Atlantic coast into the nation's interior.

Bacon's Rebellion (p. 79) An armed rebellion in Virginia (1675–1676) led by Nathaniel Bacon against the colony's royal governor Sir William Berkeley. Although some of his followers called for an end of special privilege in government, Bacon was chiefly interested in gaining a larger share of the lucrative Indian trade.

Bank of the United States (p. 189) National bank proposed by Secretary of the Treasury Alexander Hamilton and established in 1791. It served as a central depository for the U.S. government and had the authority to issue currency.

Bank War (p. 280) Between 1832–1836, Andrew Jackson used his presidential power to fight and ultimately destroy the second Bank of the United States.

Baruch Plan (p. 759) In 1946, Bernard Baruch presented an American plan to control and eventually outlaw nuclear weapons. The plan called for United Nations control of nuclear weapons in three stages before the United States gave up its stockpile. Soviet insistence on immediate nuclear disarmament without inspection doomed the Baruch Plan and led to a nuclear arms race between the United States and the Soviet Union.

Battle of New Orleans (p. 232) Battle that occurred at the end of the War of 1812 when U.S. forces defeated the British army's attempt to seize New Orleans, the key to the trade of the Mississippi River Valley. Even though diplomats from both sides were coming to a peace agreement, the news had not yet reached the combatants.

Bay of Pigs (p. 804) In April 1961, a group of Cuban exiles organized and supported by the U.S. Central Intelligence Agency (CIA) landed on the southern coast of Cuba in an effort to overthrow Fidel Castro. When the invasion ended in disaster, President Kennedy took full responsibility for the failure.

Beringia (p. 5) Land bridge connecting Asia and North America that is now submerged beneath the Bering Sea.

Berlin airlift (p. 764) In 1948, in response to a Soviet land blockade of Berlin, the United States carried out a massive effort to supply the two million Berlin citizens with food, fuel, and other goods by air for more than six months. The airlift forced the Soviets to end the blockade in 1949.

Bill of Rights (p. 178) The first ten amendments to the U.S. Constitution, adopted in 1791 to preserve the rights and liberties of individuals.

birds of passage (p. 603) Temporary migrants who came to the United States to work and save money and then returned home to their native countries during the slack season. World War I interrupted the practice, trapping thousands of migrant workers in the United States.

Black Codes (p. 455) Laws passed by southern states immediately after the Civil War in an effort to maintain the pre-war social order. The codes attempted to tie freedmen to field work and prevent them from becoming equal to white Southerners.

Bland-Allison Silver Purchase Act (p. 537) This act, a compromise between groups favoring the coinage of silver and those opposed to it, called for the partial coinage of silver. Those favoring silver coinage argued that it would add to the currency and help farmers and workers; those who opposed it pointed out that few other major countries accepted silver coinage. President Rutherford B. Hayes vetoed the Bland-Allison bill in 1878, but Congress overrode his veto.

Bonus Army (p. 707) In June 1932, a group of twenty thousand World War I veterans marched on Washington, D.C., to demand im-

mediate payment of their "adjusted compensation" bonuses voted by Congress in 1924. Congress rejected their demands, and President Hoover, fearing that their ranks were infested with criminals and radicals, had the Bonus Army forcibly removed from their encampment. It was a public relations disaster for Hoover.

Boston Massacre (p. 132) A violent confrontation between British troops and a Boston mob on March 5, 1770. Five citizens were killed when the troops fired into the crowd. The incident inflamed anti-British sentiment in Massachusetts.

Boston Tea Party (p. 135) Foray on British ships in which Patriots disguised as Mohawk Indians threw hundreds of chests of tea into Boston Harbor as a means of protesting British taxes and the involvement of the East India Company.

***Brown v. Board of Education of Topeka* (p. 790)** In 1954, the Supreme Court reversed the *Plessy* v. *Ferguson* decision (1896) that established the "separate but equal" doctrine. The *Brown* decision found segregation in schools inherently unequal and initiated a long and difficult effort to integrate the nation's public schools.

Camp David accords (p. 851) In 1978, President Carter mediated a peace agreement between the leaders of Egypt and Israel at Camp David, a presidential retreat near Washington, D.C. The next year, Israel and Egypt signed a peace treaty based on the Camp David accords.

Chinese Exclusion Act (p. 467) Legislation passed in 1882 that excluded Chinese immigrant workers for ten years and denied U.S. citizenship to Chinese nationals living in the United States. It was the first U.S. exclusionary law that was aimed at a specific racial group.

Civilian Conservation Corps (CCC) (p. 709) One of the most popular **New Deal** programs, the CCC was created by Congress to provide young men between ages 18 and 25 with government jobs in reforestation and other conservation projects. It eventually employed over 300,000.

***Civil Rights Cases* (p. 520)** A group of cases in 1883 in which the Supreme Court ruled that the **Fourteenth Amendment** barred state governments from discriminating on the basis of race but did not prevent private individuals or organizations from doing so. The ruling dealt a major blow to the Republican party's earlier efforts to provide protection for African Americans.

Clayton Antitrust Act (p. 641) An attempt to improve the **Sherman Antitrust Act** of 1890, this law outlawed interlocking directorates (companies in which the same people served as directors), forbade policies that created monopolies, and made corporate officers responsible for antitrust violations. Benefiting labor, it declared that unions were not conspiracies in restraint of trade and outlawed the use of injunctions in labor disputes unless they were necessary to protect property.

Coercive Acts of 1774 (p. 135) Also known as the Intolerable Acts, the four pieces of legislation passed by Parliament in 1774 in response to the Boston Tea Party that were meant to punish the colonies.

Columbian Exchange (p. 12) The exchange of plants, animals, culture, and diseases between Europe and the Americas from first contact throughout the era of exploration.

committee of correspondence (p. 133) Vast communication network formed in Massachusetts and other colonies to communicate grievances and provide colonists with evidence of British oppression.

Committee on Public Information (CPI) (p. 665) Created in 1917 by President Wilson and headed by progressive journalist George Creel, this organization rallied support for American involvement in World War I through art, advertising, and film. Creel worked out a system of voluntary censorship with the press and distributed colorful posters and pamphlets. The CPI's Division of Industrial Relations rallied labor to help the war effort.

Common Sense **(p. 138)** Revolutionary tract written by Thomas Paine in January 1776. It called for independence and the establishment of a republican government in America.

Compromise of 1850 (p. 369) This series of five congressional statutes temporarily calmed the sectional crisis. Among other things, the compromise made California a free state, ended the slave trade in the District of Columbia, and strengthened the Fugitive Slave Law.

Compromise of 1877 (p. 472) Compromise struck during the contested Presidential election of 1876, in which Democrats accepted the election of Rutherford B. Hayes (Republican) in exchange for the withdrawal of federal troops from the South and the ending of Reconstruction.

Comstock Lode (p. 466) Discovered in 1859 near Virginia City, Nevada, this ore deposit was the richest discovery in the history of mining. Named after T. P. Comstock, a drifter who talked his way into partnership in the claim, between 1859 and 1879 the deposit produced silver and gold worth more than $306 million.

conquistadores (p. 16) Sixteenth-century Spanish adventurers, often of noble birth, who subdued the Native Americans and created the Spanish empire in the New World.

conservation (p. 633) As President, Theodore Roosevelt made this principle one of his administration's top goals. Conservation in his view aimed at protecting the nation's natural resources, but called for the wise use of them rather than locking them away. Roosevelt's policies were opposed by those who favored preservation of the wilderness over its development.

consumer revolution (p. 99) Period between 1740 and 1770 when English exports to the American colonies increased by 360 percent due to Americans' increased buying behavior.

containment (p. 760) First proposed by George Kennan in 1947, containment became the basic strategy of the United States throughout the Cold War. Kennan argued that firm American resistance to Soviet expansion would eventually compel Moscow to adopt more peaceful policies.

Contract with America (p. 877) In the 1994 congressional elections, Congressman Newt Gingrich had Republican candidates sign a document in which they pledged their support for such things as a balanced budget amendment, term limits for members of Congress, and a middle-class tax cut.

cooperationists (p. 392) In late 1860, southern secessionists debated two strategies: unilateral secession by each state or "cooperative" secession by the South as a whole. The cooperationists lost the debate.

Copperheads (p. 406) Northern Democrats suspected of being indifferent or hostile to the Union cause in the Civil War.

cotton gin (p. 312) Invented by Eli Whitney in 1793, this device for separating the seeds from the fibers of short-staple cotton enabled a slave to clean fifty times more cotton as by hand, which reduced production costs and gave new life to slavery in the South.

coureurs de bois **(p. 22)** Forest runners.

"court-packing" scheme (p. 719) Concerned that the conservative Supreme Court might declare all his New Deal programs unconstitutional, President Franklin Delano Roosevelt asked Congress to allow him to appoint additional justices to the Court. Both Congress and the public rejected this "court-packing" scheme and it was defeated.

Crittenden compromise (p. 394) Faced with the specter of secession and war, Congress tried and failed to resolve the sectional crisis in the months between Lincoln's election and inauguration. The leading proposal, introduced by Kentucky Senator John Crittenden, would have extended the **Missouri Compromise** line west to the Pacific.

Cuban missile crisis (p. 804) In October 1962, the United States and the Soviet Union came close to nuclear war when President Kennedy insisted that Nikita Khrushchev remove the 42 missiles he had secretly deployed in Cuba. The Soviets eventually did so, nuclear war was averted, and the crisis ended.

Cult of Domesticity (p. 324) Term used by historians to characterize the dominant gender role for white women in the antebellum period. The ideology of domesticity stressed the virtue of women as guardians of the home, which was considered their proper sphere.

Dartmouth College **v.** *Woodward* **(p. 256)** In this 1819 case, the Supreme Court ruled that the Constitution protected charters given to corporations by states.

Dawes Severalty Act (p. 458) Legislation passed by Congress in 1887 that aimed at breaking up traditional Indian life by promoting individual land ownership. It divided tribal lands into small plots that were distributed among members of each tribe. Provisions were made for Indian education and eventual citizenship. The law led to corruption, exploitation, and the weakening of Native American tribal culture.

D-Day (p. 746) D-Day (June 6, 1944) was the day Allied troops crossed the English Channel and opened a second front in western Europe during World War II. The "D" stands for "disembarkation": to leave a ship and go ashore.

Desert Storm (p. 869) Desert Storm was the code name used by the United States and its coalition partners in waging war against Iraq in early 1991 to liberate Kuwait.

détente (p. 836) President Nixon and Henry Kissinger pursued a policy of détente, a French word meaning a relaxation of tension, with the Soviet Union as a way to lessen the possibility of nuclear war in the 1970s.

"dollar diplomacy" (p. 654) This policy, adopted by President William Howard Taft and Secretary of State Philander C. Knox, sought to promote U.S. financial and business interests abroad. It aimed to replace military alliances with economic ties, with the idea of increasing American influence and securing lasting peace. Under this policy, Taft worked in Latin America to replace European loans with American ones, assumed the debts of countries such as Honduras to fend off foreign bondholders, and helped Nicaragua secure a large loan in exchange for U.S. control of its national bank.

Dominion of New England (p. 80) Incorporation of Massachusetts, Connecticut, Rhode Island, Plymouth, New York, New Jersey, and

New Hampshire under a single appointed royal governor that lasted from 1686–1689.

Eastern Woodland Cultures (p. 8) Term given to Indians from the Northeast region who lived on the Atlantic coast and supplemented farming with seasonal hunting and gathering.

Emancipation Proclamation (p. 437) On January 1, 1863, President Lincoln proclaimed that the slaves of the Confederacy were free. Since the South had not yet been defeated, the proclamation did not immediately free anyone, but it made emancipation an explicit war aim of the North.

Embargo Act (p. 228) In response to a British attack on an American warship off the coast of Virginia, this 1807 law prohibited foreign commerce.

encomienda **system (p. 19)** An exploitative labor system designed by Spanish rulers to reward **conquistadores** in the New World by granting them local villages and control over native labor.

Enlightenment (p. 96) Philosophical and intellectual movement that began in Europe during the eighteenth century. It stressed the application of reason to solve social and scientific problems.

enumerated goods (p. 76) Certain essential raw materials produced in the North American colonies, such as tobacco, sugar, and rice specified in the **Navigation Acts**, which stipulated that these goods could be shipped only to England or its colonies.

Equal Rights Amendment (ERA) (p. 845) In 1972, Congress approved the Equal Rights Amendment (ERA) to the Constitution, a measure designed to guarantee women equal treatment under the law. Despite a three-year extension in the time allowed for ratification, ERA supporters fell three states short of winning adoption.

Era of Good Feeling (p. 253) A descriptive term for the era of President James Monroe, who served two terms from 1817–1823. During Monroe's administration, partisan conflict abated and bold federal initiatives suggested increased nationalism.

Espionage Act (p. 668) This law, passed after the United States entered **World War I**, imposed sentences of up to twenty years on anyone found guilty of aiding the enemy, obstructing recruitment of soldiers, or encouraging disloyalty. It allowed the postmaster general to remove from the mail any materials that incited treason or insurrection.

Exodusters (p. 470) A group of about six thousand African Americans who left their homes in Louisiana, Mississippi, and Texas in 1879, seeking freer lives in Kansas, where they worked as farmers or laborers.

Farewell Address (p. 198) In this 1796 speech, President George Washington announced his intention not to seek a third term in office. He also stressed federalist interests and warned the American people to avoid political factions and foreign entanglements that could sacrifice U.S. security.

Federal Reserve Act (p. 640) One of the most important laws in the history of the country, this act created a central banking system, consisting of twelve regional banks governed by the Federal Reserve Board. It was an attempt to provide the United States with a sound yet flexible currency. The Board it created still plays a vital role in the American economy today.

Federalist (p. 175) Supporter of the Constitution who advocated its ratification.

Fifteenth Amendment (p. 436) Ratified in 1870, this amendment prohibited the denial or abridgment of the right to vote by the federal government or state governments on the basis of race, color, or prior condition as a slave. It was intended to guarantee African Americans the right to vote in the South.

fireside chats (p. 708) A series of radio addresses by Franklin D. Roosevelt from 1933 to 1944, in which the president spoke to the American people about such issues as the banking crisis, social security, and World War II. The fireside chats were broadly credited with enhancing Roosevelt's popularity among ordinary Americans.

First Continental Congress (p. 136) A meeting of delegates from twelve colonies in Philadelphia in 1774, the Congress denied Parliament's authority to legislate for the colonies, condemned British actions toward the colonies, created the Continental Association, and endorsed a call to take up arms.

Food Administration (p. 670) A wartime government agency that encouraged Americans to save food in order to supply the armies overseas. It fixed prices to boost production, asked people to observe "meatless" and "wheatless" days to conserve food, and promoted the planting of "victory gardens" behind homes, schools, and churches.

Force acts (p. 438) Congress attacked the Ku Klux Klan with three Enforcement or "Force" acts in 1870–1871. Designed to protect black voters in the South, these laws placed state elections under federal jurisdiction and imposed fines and imprisonment on those guilty of interfering with any citizen exercising his right to vote.

Fourteen Points (p. 671) In January 1918, President Wilson presented these terms for a far-reaching, nonpunitive settlement of World War I. He called, among other things, for removal of barriers to trade, open peace accords, reduction of armaments, and the establishment of a League of Nations. While generous and optimistic, the Points did not satisfy wartime hunger for revenge, and thus were largely rejected by European nations.

Fourteenth Amendment (p. 424) Ratified in 1868, this amendment provided citizenship to ex-slaves after the Civil War and constitutionally protected equal rights under the law for all citizens. Its provisions were used by Radical Republicans to enact a congressionally controlled Reconstruction policy of the former Confederate states.

Freedmen's Bureau (p. 423) Agency established by Congress in March 1865 to provide freedmen with shelter, food, and medical aid and to help them establish schools and find employment. The Bureau was dissolved in 1872.

freedom ride (p. 809) Bus trips taken by both black and white civil rights advocates in the 1960s. Sponsored by the Congress of Racial Equality (CORE), freedom rides in the South were designed to test the enforcement of federal regulations that prohibited segregation in interstate public transportation.

French Revolution (p. 193) A social and political revolution in France (1789–1799) that toppled the monarchy.

Fugitive Slave Law (p. 370) Passed in 1850, this federal law made it easier for slaveowners to recapture runaway slaves; it also made it easier for kidnappers to take free blacks. The law became an object of hatred in the North.

Ghost Dances (p. 456) A religious movement that arose in the late nineteenth century under the prophet Wavoka, a Paiute Indian. It involved a set of dances and rites that its followers believed would cause white men to disappear and restore lands to the Native Americans. The Ghost Dance religion was outlawed by the U.S. government, and army intervention to stop it led to the **Wounded Knee Massacre.**

Gibbons **v.** *Ogden* (**p. 257**) In this 1824 case, the Supreme Court affirmed and expanded the power of the federal government to regulate interstate commerce.

Glorious Revolution (p. 80) Replacement of James II by William and Mary as English monarchs in 1688, marking the beginning of constitutional monarchy in Britain. American colonists celebrated this moment as a victory for the rule of law over despotism.

Gold Rush of 1849 (p. 460) Individual prospectors made the first gold strikes along the Sierra Nevada Mountains in 1849, touching off a mining boom that helped shape the development of the West and set the pattern for subsequent strikes in other regions.

Gold Standard Act (p. 555) Passed by Congress in 1900, this law declared gold the nation's standard of currency, meaning that all currency in circulation had to be redeemable in gold. The United States remained on the gold standard until 1933.

Great Awakening (p. 101) Widespread evangelical religious revival movement of the mid-1700s. The movement divided congregations and weakened the authority of established churches in the colonies.

Great Migration (p. 44) Migration of 16,000 Puritan men and women from England to the Massachusetts Bay Colony during the 1630s.

Great Society (p. 814) President Johnson called his version of the Democratic reform program the Great Society. In 1965, Congress passed many Great Society measures, including **Medicare,** civil rights legislation, and federal aid to education.

greenbacks (p. 399) Paper currency issued by the Union beginning in 1862.

Gulf of Tonkin Resolution (p. 818) After a North Vietnamese attack on an American destroyer in the Gulf of Tonkin in 1964, President Johnson persuaded Congress to pass a resolution giving him the authority to use armed force in Vietnam.

Harlem Renaissance (p. 686) An African American cultural, literary, and artistic movement centered in Harlem, an area in New York City, in the 1920s. Harlem, the largest black community in the world outside of Africa, was considered the cultural capital of African Americans.

Hartford Convention (p. 233) An assembly of New England Federalists who met in Hartford, Connecticut, in December 1814 to protest Madison's foreign policy in the War of 1812, which had undermined commercial interests in the North. They proposed amending the Constitution to prevent future presidents from declaring war without a two-thirds majority in Congress.

Hay-Bunau-Varilla Treaty (p. 651) This 1903 treaty granted the United States control over a canal zone ten miles wide across the Isthmus of Panama. In return, the United States guaranteed the independence of Panama and agreed to pay Colombia a onetime fee of $10 million and an annual rental of $250,000.

headright (p. 38) System of land distribution in which settlers were granted a fifty-acre plot of land from the colonial government for each servant or dependent they transported to the New World. The system encouraged the recruitment of a large servile labor force.

Hepburn Act (p. 631) A law that strengthened the rate-making power of the **Interstate Commerce Commission**, again reflecting the era's desire to control the power of the railroads. It increased the ICC's membership from five to seven, empowered it to fix reasonable railroad rates, and broadened its jurisdiction. It also made ICC rulings binding pending court appeals.

Homestead Act of 1862 (p. 462) Legislation granting 160 acres of land to anyone who paid a $10 fee and pledged to live on and cultivate the land for five years. Although there was a good deal of fraud, the act encouraged a large migration to the West. Between 1862 and 1900, nearly 600,000 families claimed homesteads under its provisions.

Homestead Strike (p. 500) In July 1892, wage-cutting at Andrew Carnegie's Homestead Steel Plant in Pittsburgh provoked a violent strike in which three company-hired detectives and ten workers died. Using ruthless force and strikebreakers, company officials effectively broke the strike and destroyed the union.

House of Burgesses (p. 37) An elective representative assembly in colonial Virginia. It was the first example of representative government in the English colonies.

imperialism (p. 564) The policy of extending a nation's power through military conquest, economic domination, or annexation.

implied powers (p. 190) Powers which the Constitution did not explicitly grant the federal government, but which it could be interpreted to grant.

indentured servants (pp. 38, 68) Individuals who agreed to serve a master for a set number of years in exchange for the cost of boat transport to America. Indentured servitude was the dominant form of labor in the Chesapeake colonies before slavery.

Industrial Workers of the World (IWW) (p. 605) Founded in 1905, this radical union, also known as the Wobblies, aimed to unite the American working class into one union to promote labor's interests. It worked to organize unskilled and foreign-born laborers, advocated social revolution, and led several major strikes. Stressing solidarity, the IWW took as its slogan, "An injury to one is an injury to all."

Intermediate Nuclear Forces Treaty (p. 859) Signed by President Reagan and Soviet President Gorbachev in Washington in late 1987, this agreement provided for the destruction of all intermediate-range nuclear missiles and permitted on-site inspection for the first time during the Cold War.

Iran-Contra affair (p. 867) The Iran-Contra affair involved officials high in the Reagan administration secretly selling arms to Iran and using the proceeds to finance the Contra rebels in Nicaragua. This illegal transaction usurped the congressional power of the purse.

Iranian hostage crisis (p. 852) In 1979, Iranian fundamentalists seized the American embassy in Tehran and held fifty-three American diplomats hostage for over a year. The Iranian hostage crisis weakened the Carter presidency; the hostages were finally released on January 20, 1981, the day Ronald Reagan became president.

Iron Curtain (p. 757) British Prime Minister Winston Churchill coined the phrase "Iron Curtain" to refer to the boundary in Europe that divided Soviet-dominated eastern and central Europe from western Europe, which was free from Soviet control.

isolationism (p. 564) A belief that the United States should stay out of entanglements with other nations. Isolationism was widespread after the Spanish-American War in the late 1890s and influenced later U.S. foreign policy.

itinerant preachers (p. 103) Traveling revivalist ministers of the **Great Awakening** movement. These charismatic preachers spread revivalism throughout America.

Jay's Treaty (p. 194) Controversial treaty with Britain negotiated by Chief Justice John Jay in 1794 to settle American grievances and avert war. Though the British agreed to surrender forts on U.S. territory, the treaty failed to realize key diplomatic goals and provoked a storm of protest in America.

Jim Crow laws (p. 441) Laws enacted by states to segregate the population. They became widespread in the South after Reconstruction.

joint-stock company (p. 34) Business enterprise that enabled investors to pool money for commercial trading activity and funding for sustaining colonies.

judicial review (p. 224) The authority of the Supreme Court to determine the constitutionality of federal statutes.

Kansas-Nebraska Act (p. 373) This 1854 act repealed the Missouri Compromise, split the Louisiana Purchase into two territories, and allowed its settlers to accept or reject slavery by popular sovereignty. This act enflamed the slavery issue and led opponents to form the Republican party.

Kellogg-Briand Pact (p. 726) Also called the Pact of Paris, this 1928 agreement was the brainchild of U.S. Secretary of State Frank B. Kellogg and French premier Aristide Briand. It pledged its signatories, eventually including nearly all nations, to shun war as an instrument of policy. Derided as an "international kiss," it had little effect on the actual conduct of world affairs.

Kentucky and Virginia Resolutions (p. 204) Statements penned by Thomas Jefferson and James Madison to mobilize opposition to the Alien and Sedition Acts, which they argued were unconstitutional. Jefferson's statement (the Kentucky Resolution) suggested that states should have the right to declare null and void congressional acts they deemed unconstitutional. Madison produced a more temperate resolution, but most Americans rejected such an extreme defense of states' rights.

Knights of Labor (p. 496) Also known as the Noble and Holy Order of the Knights of Labor. Founded in 1869, this labor organization pursued broad-gauged reforms as much as practical issues such as wages and hours. Unlike the **American Federation of Labor**, the Knights of Labor welcomed all laborers regardless of race, gender, or skill.

Ku Klux Klan (p. 437) A secret terrorist society first organized in Tennessee in 1866. The original Klan's goals were to disfranchise African Americans, stop Reconstruction, and restore the prewar social order of the South. The Ku Klux Klan re-formed after World War II to promote white supremacy in the wake of the "Second Reconstruction."

Lend-Lease (p. 733) Arguing that aiding Britain would help America's own self-defense, President Roosevelt in 1941 asked Congress for a $7 billion Lend-Lease plan. This would allow the president to sell, lend, lease, or transfer war materials to any country whose defense he declared as vital to that of the United States.

Levittown (p. 782) In 1947, William Levitt used mass production techniques to build inexpensive homes in suburban New York to help relieve the postwar housing shortage. Levittown became a symbol of the movement to the suburbs in the years after World War II.

Lewis and Clark Expedition (p. 222) Overland expedition to the Pacific coast (1804–1806) led by Meriwether Lewis and William Clark. Commissioned by President Thomas Jefferson, the exploration of the Far West brought back a wealth of scientific data about the country and its resources.

Louisiana Purchase (p. 220) U.S. acquisition of the Louisiana Territory from France in 1803 for $15 million. The purchase secured American control of the Mississippi River and doubled the size of the nation.

Loyalists (p. 125) Throughout the conflict with Great Britain, many colonists sided with the king and Parliament. Also called Tories, these people feared that American liberty might promote social anarchy.

Manhattan Project (p. 747) The top-secret World War II program that produced the first atomic weapons.

Manifest Destiny (p. 344) Coined in 1845, this term referred to a doctrine in support of territorial expansion based on the beliefs that population growth demanded territorial expansion, that God supported American expansion, and that national expansion equaled the expansion of freedom.

Marbury v. Madison (p. 224) In this 1803 landmark decision, the Supreme Court first asserted the power of judicial review by declaring an act of Congress, the Judiciary Act of 1789, unconstitutional.

March on Washington (p. 810) In August 1963, civil rights leaders organized a massive rally in Washington to urge passage of President Kennedy's civil rights bill. The high point came when Martin Luther King, Jr., gave his "I Have a Dream" speech to more than 200,000 marchers in front of the Lincoln Memorial.

Marshall Plan (p. 762) In 1947, Secretary of State George Marshall proposed a massive economic aid program to rebuild the war-torn economies of western European nations. The plan was motivated by both humanitarian concern for the conditions of those nations' economies and fear that economic dislocation would promote communism in western Europe.

Mayflower Compact (p. 43) Agreement among the Pilgrims aboard the Mayflower in 1620 to create a civil government at Plymouth Colony.

McCarthyism (p. 774) In 1950, Senator Joseph R. McCarthy began a sensational campaign against communists in government that led to more than four years of charges and countercharges, ending when the Senate censured him in 1954. McCarthyism became the contemporary name for the red scare of the 1950s.

McCulloch v. Maryland (p. 257) Ruling on this banking case in 1819, the Supreme Court propped up the idea of "implied powers" meaning the Constitution could be broadly interpreted. This pivotal ruling also asserted the supremacy of federal power over state power.

Medicare (p. 814) The 1965 Medicare Act provided Social Security funding for hospitalization insurance for people over age 65 and a voluntary plan to cover doctor bills paid in part by the federal government.

mercantilism (p. 75) An economic theory that shaped imperial policy throughout the colonial period, mercantilism was built on the assumption that the world's wealth was a fixed supply. In order to increase its wealth, a nation needed to export more goods than it imported. Favorable trade and protective economic policies, as well as new colonial possessions rich in raw materials, were important in achieving this balance.

Metacomet (p. 79) Wampanoag chief, also known as King Philip, who declared war against the colonies in 1675.

Mexican-American War (p. 349) Conflict (1846–1848) between the United States and Mexico after the U.S. annexation of Texas, which Mexico still considered its own. As victor, the United States acquired vast new territories from Mexico according to the terms of the Treaty of Guadalupe Hidalgo.

middle ground (p. 92) A geographical area where two distinct cultures met and merged with neither bolding a clear upper hand.

Missouri Compromise (p. 254) A sectional compromise in Congress in 1820 that admitted Missouri to the Union as a slave state and Maine as a free state. It also banned slavery in the remainder of the Louisiana Purchase territory above the latitude of 36°30'.

Monroe Doctrine (p. 259) A key foreign policy made by President James Monroe in 1823, it declared the western hemisphere off limits to new European colonization; in return, the United States promised not to meddle in European affairs.

Montgomery bus boycott (p. 792) In late 1955, African Americans led by Martin Luther King, Jr., boycotted the buses in Montgomery, Alabama, after seamstress Rosa Parks was arrested for refusing to move to the back of a bus. The boycott, which ended when the Supreme Court ruled in favor of the protesters, marked the beginning of a new, activist phase of the civil rights movement.

moral diplomacy (p. 654) Policy adopted by President Woodrow Wilson that rejected the approach of "**dollar diplomacy.**" Rather than focusing mainly on economic ties with other nations, Wilson's policy was designed to bring right principles to the world, preserve peace, and extend to other peoples the blessings of democracy. Wilson, however, often ended up pursuing policies much like those followed by Roosevelt and Taft.

Moral Majority (p. 835) In 1979, the Reverend Jerry Falwell founded the Moral Majority to combat "amoral liberals," drug abuse, "coddling" of criminals, homosexuality, communism, and abortion. The Moral Majority represented the rise of political activism among organized religion's radical right wing.

muckrakers (p. 592) Unflattering term coined by Theodore Roosevelt to describe the writers who made a practice of exposing the wrongdoings of public figures. Muckraking flourished from 1903 to 1909 in magazines such as *McClure's* and *Collier's*, exposing social and political problems and sparking reform.

Mugwumps (p. 515) Drawing their members mainly from among the educated and upper class, these reformers crusaded for lower tariffs, limited federal government, and civil service reform to end political corruption. They were best known for their role in helping to elect Grover Cleveland to the presidency in 1884.

National American Woman Suffrage Association (p. 519, 622) Founded by Susan B. Anthony in 1890, this organization worked to secure women the right to vote. While some suffragists urged militant action, it stressed careful organization and peaceful lobbying. By 1920 it had nearly two million members.

National Association for the Advancement of Colored People (NAACP) (p. 602) Created in 1909, this organization quickly became one of the most important civil rights organizations in the country. The NAACP pressured employers, labor unions, and the government on behalf of African Americans.

National Farmers' Alliance and Industrial Union (p. 540) One of the largest reform movements in American history, the Farmer's Alliance sought to organize farmers in the South and West to fight for reforms that would improve their lot, including measures to overcome low crop prices, burdensome mortgages, and high railroad rates. The Alliance ultimately organized a political party, the **People's (Populist) party**.

National Grange of the Patrons of Husbandry (p. 471) Founded by Oliver H. Kelly in 1867, the Grange sought to relieve the drabness of farm life by providing a social, educational, and cultural outlet for its members. It also set up grain elevators, cooperative stores, warehouses, insurance companies, and farm machinery factories. Although its constitution banned political involvement, the Grange often supported railroad regulation and other measures.

National Organization for Women (NOW) (p. 826) Founded in 1966, the National Organization for Women (NOW) called for equal employment opportunity and equal pay for women. NOW also championed the legalization of abortion and passage of an equal rights amendment to the Constitution.

National Origins Quota Act (p. 692) This 1924 law established a quota system to regulate the influx of immigrants to America. The system restricted the new immigrants from southern and eastern Europe and Asia. It also reduced the annual total of immigrants.

National Reclamation Act (Newlands Act) (p. 463) Passed in 1902, this legislation set aside the majority of the proceeds from the sale of public land in sixteen Western states to fund irrigation projects in the arid states.

National Recovery Administration (NRA) (p. 710) A keystone of the early New Deal, this federal agency was created in 1933 to promote economic recovery and revive industry during the Great Depression. It permitted manufacturers to establish industrywide codes of "fair business practices" setting prices and production levels. It also provided for minimum wages and maximum working hours for labor and guaranteed labor the right to organize and bargain collectively (Section 7a). The Supreme Court declared it unconstitutional in 1935.

National Security Act (p. 765) Congress passed the National Security Act in 1947 in response to perceived threats from the Soviet Union after World War II. It established the Department of Defense and created the Central Intelligence Agency (CIA) and National Security Council.

nativism (p. 692) Hostility to things foreign.

natural rights (p. 162) Fundamental rights over which the government could exercise no control. An uncompromising belief in such rights energized the popular demand for a formal bill of rights in 1791.

Navigation Acts (p. 76) A series of commercial restrictions passed by Parliament intended to regulate colonial commerce in such a way as to favor England's accumulation of wealth.

Nazi Holocaust (p. 747) The slaughter of 6 million Jews and other persons despised by Hitler's regime.

neoconservatism (p. 836) Former liberals who advocated a strong stand against communism abroad and free market capitalism at home became known as neoconservatives. These intellectuals stressed the positive values of American society in contrast to liberals who emphasized social ills.

neutrality acts (p. 729) Reacting to their disillusionment with World War I and absorbed in the domestic crisis of the Great Depression, Americans backed Congress's three neutrality acts in the 1930s. The 1935 and 1936 acts forbade selling munitions or lending money to belligerents in a war. The 1937 act required that all remaining trade be conducted on a cash-and-carry basis.

New Deal (p. 703) In accepting the nomination of the Democratic Party in 1932, Franklin Delano Roosevelt promised a "new deal" for the American people. After his election, the label was applied to his program of legislation passed to combat the Great Depression. The New Deal included measures aimed at relief, reform, and recovery. They achieved some relief and considerable reform but little recovery.

New Freedom (p. 638) Woodrow Wilson's program in his campaign for the presidency in 1912, the New Freedom emphasized business competition and small government. It sought to rein in federal authority, release individual energy, and restore competition. It echoed many of the progressive social-justice objectives while pushing for a free economy rather than a planned one.

New Frontier (p. 800) The New Frontier was the campaign program advocated by John F. Kennedy in the 1960 election. He promised to revitalize the stagnant economy and enact reform legislation in education, health care, and civil rights.

new immigrants (p. 510) Starting in the 1880s, immigration into the United States began to shift from northern and western Europe, its source for most of the nation's history, to southern and eastern Europe. These new immigrants tended to be poor, non-Protestant, and unskilled; they tended to stay in close-knit communities and retain their language, customs, and religions. Between 1880 and 1910, approximately 8.4 million of these so-called new immigrants came to the United States.

New Nationalism (p. 638) Theodore Roosevelt's program in his campaign for the presidency in 1912, the New Nationalism called for a national approach to the country's affairs and a strong president to deal with them. It also called for efficiency in government and society; it urged protection of children, women, and workers; accepted "good" trusts; and exalted the expert and the executive. Additionally, it encouraged large concentrations of capital and labor.

Niagara Movement (p. 600) A movement, led by W. E. B. Du Bois, that focused on equal rights and the education of African American youth. Rejecting the gradualist approach of Booker T. Washington, members kept alive a program of militant action and claimed for African Americans all the rights afforded to other Americans. It spawned later civil rights movements.

North American Free Trade Agreement (NAFTA) (p. 877) A free trade plan initiated in the Bush administration and enacted by a narrow vote in Congress in the early months of the Clinton administration. It established a common market without tariff barriers between the United States, Canada, and Mexico.

North Atlantic Treaty Organization (NATO) (p. 763) In 1949, the United States, Canada, and ten European nations formed this military mutual-defense pact. In 1955, the Soviet Union countered NATO with the formation of the Warsaw Pact, a military alliance among those nations within its own sphere of influence.

Northwest Ordinance (p. 165) Legislation that formulated plans for governments in America's northwestern territories, defined a procedure for the territories' admission to the Union as states, and prohibited slavery north of the Ohio River.

NSC-68 (p. 766) National Security Council planning paper No. 68 redefined America's national defense policy. Adopted in 1950, it committed the United States to a massive military buildup to meet the challenge posed by the Soviet Union.

nullification (p. 278) The supposed right of any state to declare a federal law inoperative within its boundaries. In 1832, South Carolina created a firestorm when it attempted to nullify the federal tariff.

Ocala Demands (p. 542) Adopted by the Farmers' Alliance at an 1890 meeting in Ocala, Florida, these demands became the organization's main platform. They called for the creation of a sub-treasury system to allow farmers to store their crops until they could get the best price, the free coinage of silver, an end to protective tariffs and national banks, a federal income tax, the direct election of senators by voters, and tighter regulation of railroads.

Open Door policy (p. 584) Established in a series of notes by Secretary of State John Hay in 1900, this policy established free trade between the United States and China and attempted to enlist major European and Asian nations in recognizing the territorial integrity of China. It marked a departure from the American tradition of **isolationism** and signaled the country's growing involvement in the world.

Organization of Petroleum Exporting Countries (OPEC) (p. 841) A cartel of oil-exporting nations. In late 1973, OPEC took advantage of the October War and an oil embargo by its Arab members to quadruple the price of oil. This huge increase had a devastating impact on the American economy.

Ostend Manifesto (p. 374) Written by American officials in 1854, this secret memo—later dubbed a "manifesto"—urged the acquisition of Cuba by any means necessary. When it became public, Northerners claimed it was a plot to extend slavery and the manifesto was disavowed.

Overland Trail (p. 460) The route taken by thousands of travelers from the Mississippi Valley to the Pacific Coast in the last half of the nineteenth century. It was extremely difficult, often taking six months or more to complete.

Panic of 1837 (p. 284) A financial depression that lasted until the 1840s.

parliamentary sovereignty (p. 123) Principle that emphasized the power of Parliament to govern colonial affairs as the preeminent authority.

Peace of Paris of 1763 (p. 113) Treaty ending the French and Indian War, which marked the beginning of Great Britain's expansion of its empire outside of Europe.

Pearl Harbor (p. 736) On December 7, 1941, Japanese warplanes attacked U.S. naval forces at Pearl Harbor, Hawaii, sinking several ships and killing more than 2400 American sailors. The event marked America's entrance into World War II.

Pendleton Act (p. 537) Passed by Congress in 1883 with the backing of President Chester A. Arthur, this act sought to lessen the involvement of politicians in the running of the government. It created a bipartisan Civil Service Commission to administer competitive exams to candidates for civil service jobs and to appoint officeholders based on merit. It also outlawed forcing political contributions from appointed officials. The measure served as the basis for later expansion of a professional civil service.

People's (or Populist) party (p. 543) This political party was organized in 1892 by farm, labor, and reform leaders, mainly from the Farmers' Alliance. It offered a broad-based reform platform reflecting the **Ocala Demands**. It nominated James B. Weaver of Iowa for president in 1892 and William Jennings Bryan of Nebraska in 1896. After 1896, it became identified as a one-issue party focused on free silver and gradually died away.

Philippine-American War (p. 581) A war fought from 1899 to 1903 to quell Filipino resistance to U.S. control of the Philippine Islands. Although often forgotten, it lasted longer than the Spanish-American War and resulted in more casualties. Filipino guerilla soldiers finally gave up when their leader, Emilio Aguinaldo, was captured.

placer mining (p. 465) A form of mining that required little technology or skill, placer mining techniques included using a shovel and a washing pan to separate gold from the ore in streams and riverbeds. An early phase of the mining industry, placer mining could be performed by miners working as individuals or in small groups.

Plessy* v. *Ferguson* (p. 521)** A Supreme Court case in 1896 that established the doctrine of "separate but equal" and upheld a Louisiana law requiring that blacks and whites occupy separate rail cars. The Court applied it to schools in *Cumming* v. *County Board of Education* (1899). The doctrine was finally overturned in 1954, in ***Brown* v. *Board of Education of Topeka.

popular sovereignty (p. 368) The concept that the settlers of a newly organized territory have the right to decide (through voting) whether or not to accept slavery. Promoted as a solution to the slavery question, popular sovereignty became a fiasco in Kansas during the 1850s.

Potsdam Conference (p. 757) The final wartime meeting of the leaders of the United States, Great Britain, and the Soviet Union was held at Potsdam, outside Berlin, in July, 1945. Truman, Churchill, and Stalin discussed the future of Europe but their failure to reach meaningful agreements soon led to the onset of the Cold War.

pragmatism (p. 624) A doctrine that emerged in the early twentieth century, built largely on the ideas of Harvard psychologist and philosopher William James. Pragmatists were impatient with theories that held truth to be abstract; they believed that truth should work for the individual. They also believed that people were not only shaped by their environment but also helped to shape it. Ideas that worked, according to pragmatists, became truth.

preemption (p. 243) The right of first purchase of public land. Settlers enjoyed this right even if they squatted on the land in advance of government surveyors.

Progressive (or "Bull Moose") party (p. 617) This political party was formed by Theodore Roosevelt in an attempt to advance progressive ideas and unseat President William Howard Taft in the election of 1912. After Taft won the Republican party's nomination, Roosevelt ran on the Progressive party ticket.

progressivism (p. 630) Movement for social change between the late 1890s and World War I. Its orgins lay in a fear of big business and corrupt government and a desire to improve the lives of countless Americans. Progressives set out to cure the social ills brought about by industrialization and urbanization, social disorder, and political corruption.

prohibition (p. 690) The ban of the manufacture, sale, and transportation of alcoholic beverages in the United States. The Eighteenth Amendment, adopted in 1919, established prohibition. It was repealed by the Twenty-first Amendment in 1933. While prohibition was in effect, it reduced national consumption of alcohol, but it was inconsistently enforced and was often evaded, especially in the cities.

Protestant Reformation (p. 23) Sixteenth-century religious movement to reform and challenge the spiritual authority of the Roman Catholic Church, associated with figures such as Martin Luther and John Calvin.

Pullman Strike (p. 545) Beginning in May 1894, this strike of employees at the Pullman Palace Car Company near Chicago was one of the largest strikes in American history. Workers struck to protest wage cuts, high rents for company housing, and layoffs; the American Railway Union, led by Eugene V. Debs, joined the strike in June. Extending into twenty-seven states and territories, it effectively paralyzed the western half of the nation. President Grover Cleveland secured an injunction to break the strike on the grounds that it obstructed the mail and sent federal troops to enforce it. The Supreme Court upheld the use of the injunction in *In re Debs* (1895).

Puritans (p. 43) Members of a reformed Protestant sect in Europe and America that insisted on removing all vestiges of Catholicism from popular religious practice.

Quakers (p. 51) Members of a radical religious group, formally known as the Society of Friends, that rejected formal theology and stressed each person's "inner light," a spiritual guide to righteousness.

quasi-war (p. 200) Undeclared war between the United States and France in which French privateers began seizing U.S. ships in 1797.

Radical Reconstruction (p. 425) The Reconstruction Acts of 1867 divided the South into five military districts. They required the states to guarantee black male suffrage and to ratify the **Fourteenth Amendment** as a condition of their readmission to the Union.

Radical Republicans (p. 420) The Radical Republicans in Congress, headed by Thaddeus Stevens and Charles Sumner, insisted on black suffrage and federal protection of civil rights of African Americans.

Red Scare (p. 687) A wave of anticommunist, antiforeign, and antilabor hysteria that swept over America at the end of World War I. It resulted in the deportation of many alien residents and the violation of the civil liberties of many of its victims.

Redeemers (p. 440) A loose coalition of prewar Democrats, Confederate Army veterans, and southern Whigs who took over southern state governments in the 1870s, supposedly "redeeming" them from the corruption of Reconstruction. They shared a commitment to white supremacy and laissez-faire economics.

republicanism (p. 155) Concept that ultimate political authority is vested in the citizens of the nation. The character of republican government was dependent on the civic virtue of its citizens to preserve the nation from corruption and moral decay.

Roe v. *Wade* (p. 846) In 1973, the Supreme Court ruled in *Roe* v. *Wade* that women had a constitutional right to abortion during the early stages of pregnancy. The decision provoked a vigorous right-to-life movement that opposed abortion.

Roosevelt Corollary (p. 650) A corollary to the Monroe Doctrine, which asserted that the United States would intervene in Latin American affairs if the countries themselves could not keep their affairs in order.

Royal African Company (p. 72) Slaving company created to meet colonial planters' demands for black laborers.

Sanitary Commission (p. 413) An association chartered by the Union government during the Civil War to promote health in the northern army's camps though attention to cleanliness, nutrition, and medical care.

Scopes trial (p. 693) Also called the "monkey trial," the 1924 Scopes trial was a contest between modern liberalism and religious fundamentalism. John T. Scopes was on trial for teaching Darwinian evolution in defiance of a Tennessee state law. He was found guilty and fined $100. On appeal, Scopes's conviction was later set aside on a technicality.

Second Continental Congress (p. 137) This meeting took place in Philadelphia in May 1775, in the midst of rapidly unfolding military events. It organized the Continental Army and commissioned George Washington to lead it, then began requisitioning men and supplies for the war effort.

Second Great Awakening (p. 319) A series of evangelical Protestant revivals that swept over America in the early nineteenth century.

second-party system (p. 285) A historian's term for the national two-party rivalry between Democrats and **Whigs**. The second party system began in the 1830s and ended in the 1850s with the demise of the Whig party and the rise of the Republican party.

Sedition Act (p. 669) A wartime law that imposed harsh penalties on anyone using "disloyal, profane, scurrilous, or abusive language" about the U.S. government, flag, or armed forces.

Selective Service Act (p. 663) This 1917 law provided for the registration of all American men between the ages of 21 and 30 for a military draft. By the end of World War I, 24.2 million men had registered; 2.8 million had been inducted into the army. The age limits were later changed to 18 and 45.

settlement houses (p. 526) Located in poor districts of major cities, these were community centers that tried to soften the impact of urban life for immigrant and other families. Often run by young, educated women, they provided social services and a political voice for their neighborhoods. Chicago's Hull House, founded by Jane Addams in 1889, became the most famous of the settlement houses.

Seven Years' War (p. 112) Worldwide conflict (1756–1763) that pitted Britain against France for control of North America. With help from the American colonists, the British won the war and eliminated France as a power on the North American continent. Also known in America as the French and Indian War.

sharecropping (p. 431) After the Civil War, the southern states adopted a sharecropping system as a compromise between former slaves, who wanted land of their own and former slave owners who

needed labor. The landowners provided land, tools, and seed to a farming family, who in turn provided labor. The resulting crop was divided between them, with the farmers receiving a "share" of one-third to one-half of the crop.

Shays's Rebellion (p. 169) Armed insurrection of farmers in western Massachusetts led by Daniel Shays, a veteran of the Continental Army. Intended to prevent state courts from foreclosing on debtors unable to pay their taxes, the rebellion was put down by the state militia. Nationalists used the event to justify the calling of a constitutional convention to strengthen the national government.

Sherman Antitrust Act (p. 538) Passed by Congress in 1890, this act was the first major U.S. attempt to deal legislatively with the problem of the increasing size of business. It declared illegal "every contract, combination in the form of trust or otherwise, or conspiracy, in restraint of trade or commerce." Penalties for violations were strict, ranging from fines to imprisonment and even the dissolution of guilty trusts. The law was weakened when the Supreme Court, in *United States* v. *E. C. Knight and Co.* (1895), drew a sharp distinction between manufacturing and commerce and ruled that manufacturing was excluded from its coverage. Nonetheless, the law shaped all future antitrust legislation.

Sherman Silver Purchase Act (p. 539) An act that attempted to resolve the controversy over silver coinage. Under it, the U.S. Treasury would purchase 4.5 million ounces of silver each month and issue legal tender (in the form of Treasury notes) for it. The act pleased opponents of silver because it did not call for free coinage; it pleased proponents of silver because it bought up most of the nation's silver production.

social Darwinism (p. 524) Adapted by English social philosopher Herbert Spencer from Charles Darwin's theory of evolution, this theory held that the "laws" of evolution applied to human life, that change or reform therefore took centuries, and that the "fittest" would succeed in business and social relationships. It promoted the ideas of competition and individualism, saw as futile any intervention of government into human affairs, and was used by influential members of the economic and social elite to oppose reform.

Social Gospel (p. 526) Preached by a number of urban Protestant ministers, the Social Gospel focused as much on improving the conditions of life on earth as on saving souls for the hereafter. Its adherents worked for child-labor laws and measures to alleviate poverty.

Social Security Act (p. 714) The 1935 Social Security Act established a system of old age, unemployment, and survivors' insurance funded by wage and payroll taxes. It did not include health insurance and did not originally cover many of the most needy groups and individuals.

social-justice movement (p. 620) During the 1890s and after, this important movement attracted followers who sought to free people from the often devastating impact of urban life. It focused on the need for tenement house laws, more stringent child labor regulations, and better working conditions for women. Social-justice reformers also brought pressure on municipal agencies for better community services and facilities.

Southern Christian Leadership Conference (SCLC) (p. 793) An organization founded by Martin Luther King, Jr., to direct the crusade against segregation. Its weapon was passive resistance that stressed nonviolence and love, and its tactic direct, though peaceful, confrontation.

spectral evidence (p. 82) In the Salem witch trials, the court allowed reports of dreams and visions in which the accused appeared as the devil's agent to be introduced as testimony. The accused had no defense against this kind of "evidence." When the judges later disallowed this testimony, the executions for witchcraft ended.

Stamp Act Congress (p. 129) Meeting of colonial delegates in New York City in October 1765 to protest the Stamp Act, a law passed by Parliament to raise revenue in America. The delegates drafted petitions denouncing the Stamp Act and other taxes imposed on Americans without colonial consent.

Stamp Act of 1765 (p. 128) Placed a tax on newspapers and printed matter produced in the colonies, causing a mass political movement among colonists.

Strategic Arms Limitations Talks (SALT) (p. 836) In 1972, the United States and the Soviet Union culminated four years of Strategic Arms Limitation Talks (SALT) by signing a treaty limiting the deployment of antiballistic missiles (ABM) and an agreement to freeze the number of offensive missiles for five years.

Strategic Defense Initiative (SDI) (p. 855) Popularly known as "Star Wars," President Ronald Reagan's Strategic Defense Initiative (SDI) proposed the construction of an elaborate computer-controlled, antimissile defense system capable of destroying enemy missiles in outer space. Critics claimed that SDI could never be perfected.

Student Nonviolent Coordinating Committee (SNCC) (p. 794) A radical group advocating black power. SNCC's leaders, scornful of integration and interracial cooperation, broke with Martin Luther King, Jr., to advocate greater militancy and acts of violence.

Students for a Democratic Society (SDS) (p. 821) Founded in 1962, the SDS was a popular college student organization that protested shortcomings in American life, notably racial injustice and the Vietnam War. It led thousands of campus protests before it split apart at the end of the 1960s.

Sunbelt (p. 870) This region consists of a broad band of states running across the South from Florida to Texas, extending west and north to include California and the Pacific Northwest. Beginning in the 1970s, this area experienced rapid economic growth and major gains in population.

supply-side economics (p. 854) Advocates of supply-side economics claimed that tax cuts would stimulate the economy by giving individuals a greater incentive to earn more money, which would lead to greater investment and eventually larger tax revenues at a lower rate. Critics replied that supply-side economics would only burden the economy with larger government deficits.

Taft-Hartley Act (p. 771) This 1947 anti-union legislation outlawed the closed shop and secondary boycotts. It also authorized the president to seek injunctions to prevent strikes that posed a threat to national security.

tariff of abominations (p. 273) An 1828 protective tariff, or tax on imports, motivated by special interest groups. It resulted in a substantial increase in duties that angered many southern free traders.

Teapot Dome scandal (p. 694) A 1924 scandal in which Secretary of the Interior Albert Fall was convicted of accepting bribes in exchange for leasing government-owned oil lands in Wyoming (Teapot Dome) and California (Elks Hill) to private oil businessmen.

Tecumseh (p. 216) Shawnee leader who organized a union of native peoples, along with the help of his brother Tenskwatawa, to resist white encroachment of Native American lands.

Teller Amendment (p. 572) In this amendment, sponsored by Senator Henry M. Teller of Colorado, the United States pledged that it did not intend to annex Cuba and that it would recognize Cuban independence from Spain after the Spanish-American War.

temperance movement (p. 322) Temperance—moderation or abstention in the use of alcoholic beverages—attracted many advocates in the early nineteenth century. Their crusade against alcohol, which grew out of the Second Great Awakening, became a powerful social and political force.

Ten Percent Plan (p. 420) Reconstruction plan proposed by President Abraham Lincoln as a quick way to readmit the former Confederate States. It called for full pardon of all Southerners except Confederate leaders, and readmission to the Union for any state after 10 percent of its voters in the 1860 election signed a loyalty oath and the state abolished slavery.

Tennessee Valley Authority (TVA) (p. 708) A **New Deal** effort at regional planning created by Congress in 1933, this agency built dams and power plants on the Tennessee River. Its programs for flood control, soil conservation, and reforestation helped raise the standard of living for millions in the Tennessee River valley.

Tet offensive (p. 827) In February 1968, the Viet Cong launched a major offensive in the cities of South Vietnam. Although caught by surprise, American and South Vietnam forces successfully quashed this attack, yet the Tet offensive was a blow to American public opinion and led President Johnson to end the escalation of the war and seek a negotiated peace.

The Spanish Armada (p. 26) Fleet of hundreds of Spanish vessels sent by Philip II of Spain to invade England in 1588.

Thirteenth Amendment (p. 422) Ratified in 1865, this amendment to the U.S. Constitution prohibited slavery and involuntary servitude.

three-fifths rule (p. 172) Decision among committee members that, for the purpose of determining representation in the lower house, for every five slaves a Congressional district would receive credit for three free voters.

Trail of Tears (p. 276) In the winter of 1838–1839, the Cherokee were forced to evacuate their lands in Georgia and travel under military guard to present-day Oklahoma. Due to exposure and disease, roughly one-quarter of the 16,000 forced migrants died en route.

Treaty of Guadalupe Hidalgo (p. 351) Signed in 1848, this treaty ended the Mexican-American War. Mexico relinquished its claims to Texas and ceded an additional 500,000 square miles to the United States for $15 million.

Treaty of Paris of 1783 (p. 148) Agreement signed between American delegates and Great Britain that ended the American Revolution and also transferred territory east of the Mississippi River, except for Spanish Florida, to the new republic.

Treaty of Paris (p. 579) Signed by the United States and Spain in December 1898, this treaty ended the Spanish-American War. Under its terms, Spain recognized Cuba's independence and assumed the Cuban debt; it also ceded Puerto Rico and Guam to the United States. At the insistence of the U.S. representatives, Spain also ceded the Philippines. The Senate ratified the treaty on February 6, 1899.

Treaty of Tordesillas (p. 18) Treaty negotiated by the pope in 1494 to resolve competing land claims of Spain and Portugal in the New World. It divided the world along a north-south line in the middle of the Atlantic Ocean, granting to Spain all lands west of the line and to Portugal lands east of the line.

Truman Doctrine (p. 761) In 1947, President Truman asked Congress for money to aid the Greek and Turkish governments that were then threatened by communist rebels. Arguing for the appropriations, Truman asserted his doctrine that the United States was committed to support free people everywhere who were resisting subjugation by communist attack or rebellion.

trunk lines (p. 483) Four major railroad networks that emerged after the Civil War to connect the eastern seaports to the Great Lakes and western rivers. They reflected the growing integration of transportation across the country that helped spur large-scale industrialization.

trust (p. 489) A business-management device designed to centralize and make more efficient the management of diverse and far-flung business operations. It allowed stockholders to exchange their stock certificates for trust certificates, on which dividends were paid. John D. Rockefeller organized the first major trust, the Standard Oil Trust, in 1882.

Turner's thesis (p. 473) Put forth by historian Frederick Jackson Turner in his 1893 paper, "The Significance of the Frontier in American History," this thesis asserted that the existence of a frontier and its settlement had shaped American character; given rise to individualism, independence, and self-confidence; and fostered the American spirit of invention and adaptation. Later historians, especially a group of "new Western historians," modified the thesis by pointing out the environmental and other consequences of frontier settlement, the role of the federal government in peopling the arid West, and the clash of races and cultures that took place on the frontier.

Underground Railroad (p. 297) A network of safe houses organized by abolitionists (usually free blacks) to aid slaves in their attempts to escape slavery in the North or Canada.

Underwood Tariff Act (p. 640) An early accomplishment of the Wilson administration, this law reduced the tariff rates of the Payne-Aldrich law of 1909 by about 15 percent. It also levied a graduated income tax to make up for the lost revenue.

undocumented aliens (p. 873) Once derisively called "wetbacks," undocumented aliens are illegal immigrants, mainly from Mexico and Central America.

unilateralism (p. 886) A national policy of acting alone without consulting others.

Vesey conspiracy (p. 297) A plot to burn Charleston, South Carolina, and thereby initiate a general slave revolt, led by a free African American, Denmark Vesey, in 1822. The conspirators were betrayed before the plan was carried out, and Vesey and thirty-four others were hanged.

Virgin of Guadalupe (p. 21) Religious figure who served as a powerful symbol of Mexican nationalism in wars for independence against Spain.

Virginia Plan (p. 171) Offered by James Madison and the Virginia delegation at the Constitutional Convention, this proposal called for a new government with a strong executive office and two houses of Congress, each with representation proportional to a state's population.

Voting Rights Act of 1965 (p. 815) The 1965 Voting Rights Act effectively banned literacy tests for voting rights and provided for federal registrars to assure the franchise to minority voters. Within a few years, a majority of African Americans had become registered voters in the southern states.

Wade-Davis Bill (p. 420) In 1864, Congress passed the Wade-Davis bill to counter Lincoln's **Ten Percent Plan** for Reconstruction. The bill required that a majority of a former Confederate state's white male population take a loyalty oath and guarantee equality for African Americans. President Lincoln pocket-vetoed the bill.

Wagner Act (p. 716) The 1935 Wagner Act, formally known as the National Labor Relations Act, created the National Labor Relations Board to supervise union elections and designate winning unions as official bargaining agents. The board could also issue cease-and-desist orders to employers who dealt unfairly with their workers.

War Hawks (p. 230) Congressional leaders who, in 1811 and 1812, called for war against Britain to defend the national honor and force Britain to respect America's maritime rights.

War Industries Board (WIB) (p. 670) An example of the many boards and commissions created during World War I, this government agency oversaw the production of all American factories. It determined priorities, allocated raw materials, and fixed prices; it told manufacturers what they could and could not produce.

War of 1812 (p. 231) War between Britain and the United States. U.S. justifications for war included British violations of American maritime rights, impressment of seamen, provocation of the Indians, and defense of national honor.

war on poverty (p. 814) Lyndon Johnson declared war on poverty in his 1964 State of the Union address. A new Office of Economic Opportunity (OEO) oversaw a variety of programs to help the poor, including the Job Corps and Head Start.

war on terror (p. 885) Initiated by President George W. Bush after the attacks of September 11, 2001, the broadly defined war on terror aimed to weed out terrorist operatives and their supporters throughout the world.

Watergate scandal (p. 839) A break-in at the Democratic National Committee offices in the Watergate complex in Washington was carried out under the direction of White House employees. Disclosure of the White House involvement in the break-in and subsequent coverup forced President Richard Nixon to resign in 1974 to avoid impeachment.

weapons of mass destruction (WMD) (p. 886) Biological, chemical, and nuclear weapons capable of widespread destruction.

Whigs (p. 122) In mid-eighteenth century Britain, the Whigs were a political faction that dominated Parliament. Generally they were opposed to royal influence in government and wanted to increase the control and influence of Parliament. In America, a Whig party—named for the British Whigs who opposed the king in the late seventeenth century—coalesced in the 1830s around opposition to Andrew Jackson. In general, the American Whigs supported federal power and internal improvements but not territorial expansion. The Whig party collapsed in the 1850s.

Whiskey Rebellion (p. 197) Protests in 1794 by western Pennsylvania farmers resisting payment of a federal tax on whiskey. The uprising was forcibly suppressed when President George Washington called an army of 15,000 troops to the area, where they encountered almost no resistance.

Wilmot Proviso (p. 368) In 1846, shortly after outbreak of the **Mexican-American War,** Congressman David Wilmot of Pennsylvania introduced this controversial amendment stating that any lands won from Mexico would be closed to slavery.

Women's Christian Temperance Union (WCTU) (p. 517) Founded by Frances E. Willard, this organization campaigned to end drunkenness and the social ills that accompanied it. The largest women's organization in the country, by 1898 it had 10,000 branches and 500,000 members. The WCTU illustrated the large role women played in politics and reform long before they won the right to vote.

Women's Trade Union League (WTUL) (p. 605) Founded in 1903, this group worked to organize women into trade unions. It also lobbied for laws to safeguard female workers and backed several successful strikes, especially in the garment industry. It accepted all women who worked, regardless of skill, and while it never attracted many members, its leaders were influential enough to give the union considerable power.

Works Progress Administration (WPA) (p. 709) New Deal agency created to provide work relief for the unemployed.

Wounded Knee Massacre (p. 454) In December 1890, troopers of the Seventh Cavalry, under orders to stop the **Ghost Dance** religion among the Sioux, took Chief Big Foot and his followers to a camp on Wounded Knee Creek in South Dakota. It is uncertain who fired the first shot, but violence ensued and approximately two hundred Native American men, women, and children were killed.

XYZ Affair (p. 201) A diplomatic incident in which American peace commissioners sent to France by President John Adams in 1797 were insulted with bribe demands from their French counterparts, dubbed X, Y, and Z, in American newspapers. The incident heightened war fever against France.

Yalta Conference (p. 747) Yalta, a city in the Russian Crimea, hosted this wartime conference of the Allies in February 1945 in which the Allies agreed to final plans for the defeat of Germany and the terms of its occupation. The Soviets agreed to allow free elections in Poland, but the elections were never held.

yellow journalism (p. 571) In order to sell newspapers to the public before and during the Spanish-American War, publishers William Randolph Hearst and Joseph Pulitzer engaged in blatant sensationalization of the news, which became known as "yellow journalism." Although it did not cause the war with Spain, it helped turn U.S. public opinion against Spain's actions in Cuba.

yeomen (pp. 66, 305) Southern small landholders who owned no slaves, and who lived primarily in the foothills of the Appalachian and Ozark mountains. These farmers were self-reliant and grew mixed crops, although they usually did not produce a substantial amount to be sold on the market.

Yorktown (p. 147) Tobacco market located on a peninsula bounded by the York and James rivers, where Cornwallis based operations.

Young America (p. 361) In the 1840s and early 1850s, many public figures—especially younger members of the Democratic party—used this term to describe a movement that advocated territorial expansion and industrial growth in the name of patriotism.

CREDITS

CHAPTER 16

416 The Granger Collection, New York **419** Library of Congress **422** The Chicago Historical Society **427** Stock Montage, Inc./Historical Pictures Collection **430** Collection of the New-York Historical Society [negative number 50475] **434** Courtesy of the Sixth Mount Zion Baptist Church of Richmond, Virginia **435** Valentine Museum/Richmond History Center **437** Rutherford B. Hayes Presidential Center **441** Culver Pictures, Inc. **443** ©Historical Picture Archive/CORBIS **445** Yale Joel / Life Magazine © Time Inc. / Getty Images

CHAPTER 17

448 1961.86 Charles M. Russell, "Cowboy Camp During the Roundup," oil on canvas, ca. 1885–1887, 23 $\frac{1}{2}$ × 47 $\frac{1}{4}$ inches / Amon Carter Museum, Fort Worth, Texas **453** Neg./Transparency no. 1540–2. Courtesy Dept. of Library Services, American Museum of Natural History **457** From "A Pictographic History of the Oglala Sioux," by Amos Bad Heart Bull, text by Helen Blish / University of Nebraska Press **458L & 458R** Courtesy of the Arizona Historical Society, Tuscon, Arizona **459** Thomas Gilcrease Institute of American History & Art **464** Louis Theodore Jean Gentilz (1819–1906), "El Convite (Invitation to the Dance)", oil on canvas, 9 × 12 in (23 × 30.7 cm). Yanaguana Society, gift in memory of Frederick C. Chabot. Courtesy of the Daughters of the Republic of Texas Library **465** Collection of The New-York Historical Society, negative number 16212

CHAPTER 18

476 "The Corliss Engine," The Metropolitan Museum of Art, New York, NY, U.S.A. Image copyright © The Metropolitan Museum of Art / Art Resource, NY **482** Culver Pictures, Inc. **485** Courtesy of the Union Pacific Railroad Museum Collection **488** Library of Congress **493** Courtesy of the Chicago Historical Society **494** © Bettmann/CORBIS All Rights Reserved **498** Carnegie Library of Pittsburgh **500** © Bettmann/CORBIS All Rights Reserved

CHAPTER 19

504 Courtesy of Christopher Cardozo, Inc. **508** Library of Congress **509** © The Museum of the City of New York, The Byron Collection **512** The New York Public Library/Art Resource, NY **515** The Advertising Archives **516** Courtesy of the Library of Congress **520** Brown Brothers **522** J. Jefferson / University of Michigan Medical School records, Bentley Historical Library, University of Michigan **523** Library of Congress **527L** Wallace Kirkland/Time Life Pictures/ Getty Images/Time Life Pictures **527R** Jane Addams Memorial Collection, Special Collections, University Library, University of Illinois at Chicago

CHAPTER 20

532 Courtesy of Janice L. and David Frent **536** Library of Congress **539** © Bettmann/CORBIS All Rights Reserved **541** Wisconsin Historical Society, WHi-704 **542** The Kansas State Historical Society, Topeka, Kansas **544** © Minnesota Historical Society / CORBIS All Rights Reserved **548L** © Bettman/CORBIS All Rights Reserved **548R** Valentine Museum/Richmond History Center **549** University of Virginia Library, Special Collections Department **550** © Bettman/ CORBIS All Rights Reserved **553** Culver Pictures, Inc. **556** Courtesy of the Library of Congress

CHAPTER 21

560 "Return of the Conquerors," by Edward Moran / Courtesy of the U.S. Naval Academy Museum, The Beverley Robinson Collection **561** Courtesy of the U.S. Naval Academy Museum, The Beverley Robinson Collection **567** Courtesy of the Hawaiian Historical Society **569** Puck Magazine/Library of Congress **575T** Courtesy of the Chicago Historical Society **575B** © CORBIS All Rights Reserved **583** Culver Pictures, Inc.

CHAPTER 22

588 George Benjamin Luks, American, 1867-1933. "Hester Street" 1905. Oil on canvas. 66.3 × 91.8 (26 $\frac{1}{8}$ × 36 $\frac{1}{8}$). Brooklyn Museum of Art. Dick S. Ramsay Fund. 40.339 **591** The Granger Collection, New York **592** © Bettman/CORBIS All Rights Reserved **594** Art Resource/The New York Public Library **596L & 596R** Brown Brothers **599L** Courtesy of the Library of Congress **599R** George Eastman House **600** Corbis/Bettmann **603** Courtesy of the California Historical Society, FN-18240 **606** Wayne P. Reuther Library, Wayne State University **610** George Bellows, "Cliff Dwellers". Oil on canvas, 40 $\frac{3}{16}$" × 42 $\frac{1}{16}$" (102.07 × 106.82 cm). Los Angeles County Museum of Art. Los Angeles County Fund. Photograph © 2007 Museum

CHAPTER 23

614 The Granger Collection, New York **617** Culver Pictures, Inc. **621** Chicago Historical Museum **623** Culver Pictures, Inc. **627** State Historical Society of Wisconsin, WHi-2394 **629** The Granger Collection, New York **632** Courtesy of the Lilly Library, Indiana University, Bloomington, Indiana **634** Library of Congress **638** Museum of American Political Life, University of Hartford **640** Culver Pictures, Inc.

CHAPTER 24

646 National Archives and Records Administration **649** Courtesy of the Library of Congress **652** Courtesy of the Library of Congress